DICTIONARY OF LIBERAL THOUGHT

DICTIONARY
OF
LIBERAL THOUGHT

Collected and edited by
Duncan Brack
Ed Randall

with
Detmar Doering
Richard S. Grayson
Graham Lippiatt
Tony Little
John Meadowcroft
Jaime Reynolds
Iain Sharpe

Liberal Democrat History Group

POLITICO'S

First published in Great Britain in 2007 by
Politico's Publishing, an imprint of Methuen Publishing Limited
11–12 Buckingham Gate
London SW1E 6LB
www.politicospublishing.co.uk

10 9 8 7 6 5 4 3 2 1

A CIP catalogue record for this book is available from the British Library.

ISBN10:   1 84275 167 0
ISBN13:   978 1 84275 167 1

Printed and bound in Great Britain by Cromwell Press, Trowbridge, Wiltshire.
Cover design by Jonathan Wadman.
Designed and typeset in Bembo by Duncan Brack.

CONTENTS

INDEX TO IDEAS

CONTENTS

INDEX TO ORGANISATIONS

INDEX TO THINKERS

CONTENTS

FOREWORD
by
Paddy Ashdown

Politics must rest on beliefs. Political parties that operate without a philosophical framework stand for little more than personality and populism. But equally, beliefs must rest on thought – they must be continually defined, tested and debated rather than simply inherited unquestioningly.

Despite the immense challenges that face us in today's world, British politics today still focuses too much on superficialities and personalities. Even we Liberal Democrats, although we pride ourselves on our liberal inheritance, still spend most of our time discussing specific policies – and campaigning techniques! – rather than the ideology that underlies them.

Which is why I particularly welcome this *Dictionary of Liberal Thought*. Within these pages you will find an immense range of individual thinkers and organisations and schools of thought that have contributed to the development of liberalism in all its many variations – not just in Britain but throughout the world – together with analyses of the key concepts that form the core of liberals' beliefs.

You will be able to read here how liberals, in different countries and at different times, have grappled with the great issues of their times – freedom, democracy, the rule of law, the need for open and tolerant societies, peace and prosperity, the balance between state and market. And you will be able to read about the beliefs of some people you may not think of as liberals, but who have nevertheless contributed important insights to liberal thought.

No other such collection of liberal thought has ever been published – so this *Dictionary* will prove an immensely valuable reference source. But I hope it will be much more than that. If you think you are a liberal, I hope that this book will act as a stimulus to you to explore and test and redefine your own beliefs.

Isaac Newton's quote – 'if I have seen further, it is by standing on the shoulders of giants' – applies just as much to political thought as it does to science. The contents of this book enable us all to look further and to think deeper in the ceaseless evolution of liberalism.

Lord Ashdown of Norton-sub-Hamdon

ACKNOWLEDGEMENTS

The *Dictionary of Liberal Thought* is the fourth in the series of books produced by the Liberal Democrat History Group and published by Politico's Publishing. The *Dictionary of Liberal Biography* was the first, in 1998, followed by the *Dictionary of Liberal Quotations* in 1999 and *Great Liberal Speeches* in 2001. As with each of those books, the support and encouragement of the History Group's executive and members was vital to the successful completion of this volume, and we place on record our thanks to them.

Its production would not have been possible, of course, without the effort and hard work of a very wide range of people. The editorial team – Detmar Doering, Richard Grayson, Graham Lippiatt, Tony Little, John Meadowcroft, Jaime Reynolds and Iain Sharpe – drew up lists of potential contents, identified contributors, processed their entries and tolerated our ever-increasing demands with efficiency and good humour over a period of almost three years. Special thanks are due to Jaime Reynolds, for coming up with the idea in the first place, and steering us through the first year or so of the project before departing for a job overseas.

Our team of reviewers – Robert Falkner, Robert Ingham, Ian Machin, Mark Pack, Ian Packer and John Powell – provided careful comments on all the draft entries as they came in. Sean Magee and then Jonathan Wadman, of Politico's Publishing, were always supportive and understanding. And we thank Paddy Ashdown for his foreword.

Most of all, though, the contributors – almost a hundred of them, drawn from politics and academia – made everything possible. They are listed at the back of the *Dictionary*, and our warmest thanks go to them all.

Duncan Brack
Ed Randall
January 2007

GUIDE TO THE *DICTIONARY*

The *Dictionary of Liberal Thought* provides in one volume an accessible guide to the key thinkers, groups and concepts associated with liberalism. No such reference book has ever been published before.

The entries are published alphabetically but are listed (on pages vi–xii) under three headings. The entries on *ideas* provide concise summaries of key liberal concepts, such as freedom, or environmentalism, or community politics, together with schools of thought or ideologies, such as classical liberalism, the New Liberalism, or utilitarianism. The entries on *organisations* summarise the history of bodies relevant to the development of liberal thought, such as the Anti-Corn Law League, Liberal International, or the Unservile State Group. And the entries on *thinkers* provide brief biographies of individuals important in the development of liberalism, together with summaries of their ideas.

The main criterion for the inclusion of an entry was its relevance to the development of liberalism in Britain. We have not, however, allowed that focus to restrict our choice of entries only to British liberals, or even to people who called themselves liberals, but to concepts, organisations and thinkers which *influenced* British liberalism. You will therefore find a wide range of entries included, many of which cover European and American liberals, and several of which are relevant also to political ideologies other than liberalism.

Since the entries have been written by different authors, inevitably they vary somewhat in style and language, but they follow a similar structure. Each entry opens with an introductory summary paragraph. The entries on ideas and organisations then follow, where appropriate, a roughly chronological structure. The entries on thinkers summarise the individual's key ideas, provide a brief biographical sketch, and then explore their ideas at more length. All three groups of entries end with lists of key works and suggestions for further reading for those stimulated to explore further. (Note that references to *Dictionary of Liberal Biography* and *Dictionary of National Biography* entries are not included, as almost every thinker entry could have had one or both.)

Individual thinkers are listed according to the name by which they were most commonly known: thus, Jo Grimond, L. T. Hobhouse, Lord Acton. Titles are not generally included in the entry title, but are always noted in the biography. Many entries cross-refer to each other; we have used the standard 'q.v.' (*quod vide*, 'which see') for the *first* occurrence of a cross-reference in each entry. We have also adopted a number of conventions, including using 'Liberal' only where the reference is clearly to the political party, and 'liberal' and 'liberalism' for all other references.

The final choice of entries was a very difficult one; we could easily have produced a book twice the size, although whether any publisher would have printed it or any reader picked it up would have been open to doubt. Undoubtedly readers will notice omissions; let us know who or what they are, and we'll try and include them in a second edition!

We hope you enjoy this collection, that it adds to your knowledge and understanding of the philosophy of liberalism, and that it encourages you to explore further the enormous depth and range of liberal thought.

Duncan Brack
Ed Randall
January 2007

INTRODUCTION
by
Ed Randall

The purpose of the *Dictionary of Liberal Thought* is to give readers a sense of the range, depth and diversity of liberal political thought. It represents an invitation to all those who are interested in political ideas, and in particular in liberalism, to explore a tradition of political thought which not only possesses an immensely rich history but underlies many of the political and economic institutions of the modern world.

Liberalism is conventionally traced back some 300 years to the European Enlightenment and to English political thinkers, most notably John Locke, leading members of the Scottish Enlightenment, including David Hume and Adam Smith, and French thinkers and writers such as the arch-polemicist and dramatist Voltaire. Of course, liberalism has a deeper ancestry than this, and its cultural roots can be found in the aspirations and actions of countless human beings who have fought for individual freedom, the rule of law, the open exchange of opinions, accountable government, the dispersion of political power and unfettered economic exchange.

The invention of the printing press and the breakdown of the feudal order in Europe led in the seventeenth and eighteenth centuries to an extraordinary growth in the willingness and ability of individuals to communicate political ideas. Ever since then, liberalism has been represented by a vast number of political actors, thinkers and writers who have attached importance to the articulation of their ideas for social and economic reform, the creation and development of political institutions, the expansion of human opportunities, the general improvement of society, and – above all – the promotion and defence of human freedom.

Liberalism permeates the modern world. Liberal ideas are fundamental to established and aspiring democracies. They are embedded in modern constitutions, legal systems, markets and the political cultures that underpin and help to sustain civil society in liberal and democratic states throughout the world. Whether or not you are a liberal, there are many good reasons to investigate this liberal tradition – even if to take issue with it – because it contains so much of the intellectual core of the ideas that have shaped, and continue to shape, the world we live in.

Indeed, it will quickly become apparent to readers who set out on their own personal exploration of the history and content of liberal thought that the works of the greatest liberal thinkers have been relied upon not only by liberals but also by liberalism's political opponents. Conservatives have shown little propensity, or capacity, to develop a political philosophy of their own; indeed, conservatism's most important thinker, Edmund Burke, was a parliamentarian and writer whose liberal origins were never in doubt. Similarly, socialism can be seen as the badly behaved child of liberal political thought; liberalism's intellectual energy, challenge to the old order and belief in the role of human reason in fostering social improvement were common bequests from Enlightenment thinkers.

Although historians of freedom, such as Lord Acton, have identified the origins of liberal thought in the classical world, liberalism and liberal political parties sprang mainly from the ideas and social changes that transformed seventeenth- and eighteenth-century Europe. Adam Smith, writing at the end of this period, described his thoughts as offering a 'liberal plan of equality, liberty and justice'. The use of the term 'liberal' as a description for a particular kind of political belief is generally associated with the establishment of a party of Spanish radicals, the *Liberales*, in 1812. The year of the Great Reform Act, 1832, was taken by Disraeli to mark the advent of liberalism in Britain. At this stage, 'liberal' was a word that signalled a generous and open-minded outlook; indeed, the term 'liberalism' has continued to stand for an intellectual attitude and set of beliefs that embrace the use of reason in human affairs every bit as much as the adoption of a particular political programme.

The unfolding and development of liberal thought over more than three centuries has reflected a deepening and broadening of liberal interest in the relationship between the citizen, markets and the state. The discussion of liberal ideas and the work of liberal thinkers and organisations that follows reflect an intellectual journey, from Locke and Paine to Kymlicka and Nozick, from the Manchester School to Liberal International, from Nonconformity to community politics, that has no fixed or certain end. It constantly renews shared concerns with core liberal ideas, including liberty and opportunity, the rule of law and equality before the law, political equality and open markets, fairness and fundamental human rights.

All liberals possess a concern for individual liberty, but different groups of liberals have emphasised different aspects of the 'constitution of liberty' at different times and in different countries. In the seventeenth century, Locke was determined to assert the rights of the individual against the state and secure, for citizens, the right to bear arms against a tyrannous government. In the eighteenth century Adam Smith made a compelling case for free markets and a society built upon individual conscience – what he called 'moral sentiments'. In the nineteenth century Jeremy Bentham urged a vital role for the state in improving the human condition, and John Stuart Mill, the greatest liberal thinker of the century, sought to reconcile liberalism and democracy. Amongst Mill's successors were Hobson and Hobhouse, who, at the beginning of the twentieth century, made the case for a much more active and interventionist state than hitherto. Throughout the last century thinkers such as Berlin, Hayek and Rawls continued to interpret and apply the idea of human liberty in fresh and different ways.

At the core of liberal political thought lies belief in individual liberty and faith in the role of reason in human affairs. Starting from this core, liberals in different countries and at different times have favoured a very wide variety of policies and measures to promote and defend freedom – but all have been engaged in a great project to extend individual opportunity while defending individual liberty.

Liberalism enjoys a particularly strong association with the idea of progress. Liberal faith in reason and human progress had its roots in what liberals perceived as the necessity of dissolving the old order and replacing it with something better. In the midst of the extraordinary upheavals experienced by European societies emerging from feudalism, liberals articulated a belief in social systems based upon respect for common humanity and individual achievement, rather than on inherited social status. The French and American revolutions confirmed the liberal belief that it was not only undesirable but impossible to dam up the ambitions of individual human beings, even if the results of the social changes subsequently unleashed often left much to be desired. Intellectual insight and leadership were necessary in order to achieve beneficial social change, and they had to be constantly replenished in order to create and sustain the institutions and the economic arrangements that opened the way to a society where constant improvement became possible. Most of the classical liberal thinkers represented in this dictionary, including Locke, Smith, Condorcet, Hamilton, Madison and Constant, advocated a new order while at the same time insisting that it should be considered a work in progress, endlessly capable of and open to improvement.

If the greatest American, French and British liberal thinkers differed with each another over the details of jurisprudence, constitutional government and economic organisation they were, almost without exception, keen believers in the possibility of improving the human condition and reforming political institutions. They conceived of a world in which human potential, the creative energy of many different individuals, would be released, and where individuals would be able to assert themselves, within the law, against groups that might have been able to insist on conformity in earlier times. Human dignity would be treated as a birthright and every adult would enjoy political equality. Shared humanity would override appeals to sectional interests and the idea of a marriage between individual (self-) improvement and general betterment would be accepted as the foundation of political community.

A strong belief in individualism, political equality before the law, recognition of common humanity and the idea of progress are therefore found throughout the liberal tradition, even if the precise mixture of liberal ideals varies from place to place and time to time. In refining, validating and applying the liberal mix, the imprint of different national traditions on liberal thought will be readily apparent throughout this *Dictionary*. French liberalism has been less taken with empiricism than the British variety, and German liberalism has wrestled, in its own way, with idealist philosophy and the need to accommodate national identity. American liberalism has incorporated a great deal from both the French and British traditions, but has gone on to develop a distinctive character of its own.

In using the *Dictionary* readers should bear in mind that liberal moral and political arguments have been refracted not only through the changing spirit of their times but also by philosophical theories that have grown up alongside or as part of liberalism – including idealism, utilitarianism, human-rights and social-contract theory; these are all touched on in their own entries or many of the entries for individual thinkers. It is clear, however, that they reflect common concerns. While John Rawls and Robert Nozick, for example, disagreed about the starting point for a liberal theory of justice, Rawls, in revitalising the social-contract tradition, and Nozick, in building upon the liberal tradition of rights-based political philosophy, were unapologetic exponents of the power and relevance of specifically liberal political argument in the modern world. Though John Locke and Immanuel Kant represent strikingly different national traditions of political and philosophical thought, both were remarkably influential liberal exponents of the power of reason in human affairs. While John Stuart Mill and Herbert Spencer had decidedly different ideas about the motors of human progress and social development they shared a liberal concern over the limits of state action. Even though John Maynard Keynes and Friedrich von Hayek found themselves on different sides of one of the most important debates in twentieth-century economics, over the balance between state and market, they shared a common liberal concern with ensuring that economic thought was subservient to liberal politics.

While it is increasingly common for commentators to distinguish between social liberals and economic liberals, readers of this *Dictionary* should quickly become aware that the labels can be highly misleading. It is undeniable that liberals have varied a good deal in how much enthusiasm they have shown for markets and for government intervention in economic and social life, reflecting sincere liberal differences over how best to maximise liberty – as can be seen in the entries on the New Liberalism and the Institute of Economic Affairs, among many others. In turn these different viewpoints have been connected with the evolution of liberal ideas on the role of the state in protecting and promoting personal liberty.

Liberal societies aim to govern themselves in ways that enable individual citizens to pursue their own plans of life. Government is called upon to play the most constructive and yet least inhibiting role possible in aiding this pursuit. It is this goal, of fashioning a state that is as helpful and at the same time as limited as possible, that has been the principal focus of liberal political argument, particularly in the course of the last hundred years – and which continues to stimulate liberal political debate. The fact that this debate has taken place against a background of huge economic and social change helps to explain many of the distinctions between different schools of liberalism.

The classical liberals never had to wrestle with the implications of competing to satisfy a mass electorate. Their goals, of establishing equality before the law, liberating citizens from aristocratic and religious constraints, and allowing the free exchange of goods across national boundaries, called for no great extension of the powers of government. The New Liberals, in contrast, had to face the realities of an industrialised society, in which the old structures of feudal obligation, extended families and close-knit rural communities had given way, and in which the relief of poverty, ignorance and disease necessary to realise the extension of liberty appeared to need much greater state intervention. Today, the growth of global economic interdependence and the growing evidence of human impact on the environment faces liberals with yet further challenges.

However, the differences between classical and modern liberalism stem from more than simply the growth of industrial societies and democratic institutions. They were also driven by a process of reassessment within the liberal tradition. John Stuart Mill broke away from the moorings of classical liberalism and qualified, though did not abandon, the utilitarian liberalism with which he had grown up. British liberal idealists, led by T. H. Green, writing in the closing decades of the nineteenth century, were determined to ensure that liberal political theory placed much greater emphasis on the role of the state in fostering the conditions for individual development and a fuller and more socially aware citizenship. Between them they paved the way for the New Liberals, Hobson, Hobhouse and others, convinced that a modern liberal conception of social and economic progress needed to reflect an organic, rather than an individualist, conception of the community, and had to accept a leading role for government.

What Hobson and Hobhouse insisted was necessary, a much more interventionist liberalism, has been described by John Gray as 'a new and hubristic rationalism'; he compares it with the more circumscribed faith of British classical liberals and French liberals, such as Constant and Tocqueville, in human reason. Others have urged the adoption of a Humean liberal perspective, modest and realistic about what human reason can achieve, calling upon liberals not to be too ambitious in the change they seek.

The classical liberals envisaged a narrow domain in which government would be able to operate. They had little or no conception of just how far organised politics would advance and how important party competition would become. Max Weber, the German sociologist and liberal, whose *Dictionary* entry exemplifies twentieth-century liberal concerns with the growth of bureaucratic government, was deeply depressed by the growth of party. Eighteenth- and early nineteenth-century liberals had little reason to imagine the scale of modern government and mostly doubted the ability of even the most intelligent and enlightened of humans to manage economic and social systems as a whole. This was the outlook that Hayek, with his re-emergent belief in the values of markets, also shared.

Here, then, we have a great watershed in the development of liberal thought. Classical liberals, responsible for a liberal tradition that nurtured great hopes for a free society of competing and cooperating individuals, anticipated a world in which individuals would seize the opportunity to make better lives for themselves and others. Only a modest state was required to support the institutions and apply the laws that this required. By way of contrast, New Liberals, strongly influenced by utilitarian liberalism and British idealist liberalism and appalled by the social and economic inequalities that persisted in the world's most advanced industrial society at the end of the nineteenth and the beginning of the twentieth century, favoured *positive liberty* and a more active state, over *negative liberty* and an umpire state, long before Isaiah Berlin coined the terms.

The confidence of the New Liberals, however, was shaken by war and global economic depression, as the old belief in free trade appeared to weaken. From that economic failure Keynes, Beveridge and others, including the authors of the New Deal in America, held out the prospect of a sophisticated modern liberalism capable of reconciling, in a mixed economy with large public and private sectors, the interests of a multiplicity of different social groups and the liberal commitment to personal freedom. In turn, however, Hayek warned, in *The Road to Serfdom*, that the interventionist welfare-providing state thus created would grow too powerful and would endanger personal freedom. Milton Friedman declared that Keynesianism was incapable of delivering all that had been promised.

These arguments continue to rage. Despite them, however, liberal democracies have been remarkably successful, judged by any reasonable historical standard, in promoting prosperity, safeguarding individual liberties and building institutions effective enough to manage international relations in a rational way. And liberal political and economic recipes and arguments – from Keynes and Rawls as well as from Hayek and Friedman – have been extraordinarily influential. Liberals, rather than conservatives or socialists, can claim to have set the terms of political debate for most of the second half of the twentieth century.

Now we have entered a new age, readers of this *Dictionary* may want to consider how the history of liberal thought can inform political argument and party competition in the twenty-first century. This is an age in which political theory needs to address great ecological challenges that appear to threaten the very survival of liberal democracies and the capitalist societies with which they have been twinned.

Liberals join the environmental debate with some advantages: a good number of liberal thinkers have been interested in the relationship between human society, economic prosperity and trade, and the condition of the environment we all share. Liberal thinkers such as John Stuart Mill, who envisaged forms of economic and social growth that had little or no impact on the natural environment, J. K. Galbraith, who contrasted public squalor with private wealth, Henry Thoreau, who wrote about the vital role of nature in human well-being, and E. F. Schumacher, the author of *Small Is Beautiful*, all have important things to tell us.

Liberals, at the start of the twenty-first century, need to consider how far it is possible to integrate liberal principles of citizenship with civic republicanism, balancing self-interest with the common good, and political ecology, the study of how political, economic, and social factors affect environmental issues. If liberal citizenship is concerned primarily with political, civic and social rights, how can liberals develop political approaches to the protection of the natural environment so that it can be passed on in a good condition to future generations? What does this imply for the future management of international affairs and the global economy?

The work of liberals is never done. It never can be; liberals reject the idea that there is an end to history. There is no final destination, no ideal state for any particular human society, let alone all human societies. Instead there is a continuous process of experimentation and evolution – which helps to explain the rich diversity and wide range of liberal thought.

And so the liberal tradition makes it clear that liberals need to be doers as well as thinkers. Whether liberals or not, we can all begin by clambering up on to the shoulders of the giants of liberal political thought – Locke, Bentham, Mill, Hobhouse, Keynes, Hayek, Rawls, and all the others – not to look back but in order to see further and better ahead. The need to develop and adapt liberalism, given the unparalleled challenges of our age, should surely impress everyone who thinks of themselves as a liberal – and many others besides.

Further reading

- Isaiah Berlin (ed. Henry Hardy and Roger Hausheer), *The Proper Study of Mankind* (Chatto & Windus, 1997)
- E. K. Bramstead and K. J. Melhuish, *Western Liberalism: A History in Documents from Lock to Groce* (Longman, 1978)
- Andrew Dobson, *Citizenship and Environment* (Oxford University Press, 2003)
- John Gray, *Liberalism* (Open University Press, 1st edn., 1986, 2nd edn., 1995)
- See also entries throughout the *Dictionary* for the ideas, organisations and thinkers mentioned in this Introduction.

Ed Randall

THE DICTIONARY OF LIBERAL THOUGHT

Sir Richard Acland   1906–90

Radical liberal who developed the theory, principles and programme for a libertarian, ethical form of socialism. During the Second World War, he became the leader of Common Wealth, a political movement providing an important focus for the growing public interest in progressive ideas.

Key ideas

- Building a new society based on Christian values, with the means of production held in common ownership.
- The community should meet the material needs of all citizens and enable people to lead fulfilled, altruistic lives.
- Development of a democratic economic plan to determine how the nation's resources should be used; elected works councils to run individual enterprises.
- Progress towards world governance.

Biography

Richard Thomas Dyke Acland was born at Broadclyst, Devon on 26 November 1906 into a privileged background: his father was a Liberal MP who held office under Asquith, while his mother was an anti-war campaigner. Educated at Rugby and Balliol College, Oxford, he practiced as a barrister-at-law of the Inner Temple (1930–34). He succeeded to the baronetcy in 1939.

Acland was elected Liberal MP for Barnstaple in 1935. However, he became disillusioned with liberalism and published a series of booklets and pamphlets advocating a form of Christian socialism. In 1942, he left the Liberal Party and became the leader, main advocate and prophet of Common Wealth, which demanded the urgent implementation of a libertarian socialist programme. The following year, he donated his family estates to the National Trust.

A skilled propagandist and tireless campaigner, Acland provided through Common Wealth a focus for the new progressive mood of the wartime electorate, contesting by-elections to provide an alternative to 'reactionary' government candidates. By the end of the war Common Wealth had four MPs, but the 1945 election saw it reduced to irrelevance and Acland heavily defeated at Putney. Two years later, he returned to Parliament as Labour member for Gravesend. He resigned from the Commons in 1955, however, in protest at Labour's support for developing the hydrogen bomb and later co-founded the Campaign for Nuclear Disarmament.

Acland stood unsuccessfully as an independent candidate in Gravesend in 1955. He was senior lecturer at St Luke's College of Education, Exeter, from 1959 to 1974, and died on 24 November 1990.

Ideas

Acland's main political text, *Unser Kampf* ('Our Struggle') (1940) called for a new society based on Christian principles, with the means of production held in common ownership. In *Forward March* (1941), he developed the case for what he called the 'new service community for humanity in peace'. *What It Will Be Like in the New Britain* (1942) and *How It Can Be Done* (1943) described in more detail his proposals for economic and workforce planning, banking, finance and world trade.

Acland argued that the existing economic system was morally indefensible because it was based on individuals and companies acting in pursuit of their own personal interests. He deplored the fact that profits created through the combined efforts of workers were enjoyed by a small minority rather than being shared out amongst the community, and believed capitalism was incapable of delivering the new investment that would be needed after the war. Common ownership of the means of production was to be the essential foundation for a new society in which people would work together for the benefit of the community as a whole. In this New Britain, the community would meet the material needs of all its citizens and enable them to lead happy, rewarding lives. Acland was convinced that people could only be genuinely fulfilled if they worked to help others and were part of a cause that was greater than themselves. Such was the reasoning behind his repudiation of liberalism, which he saw as predicated on the narrow belief that individuals should be encouraged to fulfil their own aspirations.

Acland called for an economic plan, to be developed democratically under the aegis of the House of Commons, to determine how the nation's resources would be used. Individual industries would be responsible for its detailed execution, with specialist government agencies established to 'find each man a job he can do', own and run essential services and provide funding for new technologies and processes.

Acland's brand of socialism was democratic and libertarian, rather than bureaucratic; ethical and Christian, rather than doctrinaire. Factory workers would manage their enterprises through representative works councils, which would be responsible for achieving the aims and objectives of the national economic plan. In this way, common ownership and political democracy would reinforce one another. He was adamant that political liberties should be preserved, and believed that neither the capitalist system nor one founded on public ownership could adequately protect them. He was prepared to promote a wide distribution of economic power, giving people the choice to own or work in small-scale, privately owned enterprises, which he saw

as both economically valuable and socially desirable.

Acland wanted everyone to have the greatest possible opportunity to have a complete sense of personal fulfilment. His later writings proposed that after the war, government should guarantee every citizen a good home, an adequate diet and a high-quality education, as well as access to sports fields, amusement centres, holidays, cinemas, theatres and dance halls. God would provide the higher moral authority for the new society which would need organised, established churches. To avoid future world depressions, he proposed a system of international organisations to maintain stable currencies, provide finance to rebuild cities devastated by the war, reduce tariffs, help to stabilise production and advise nation-states on engaging in world trade. These would all be kept free of the influences of private enterprise since that would subvert their principles and objectives. To ensure peace, Acland called for an international defence force to replace national armies. These measures would, over the long term, lead to the development of an elected world government, with the powers of national governments greatly reduced.

Many of Acland's proposals, most notably the abolition of private ownership, lay well outside the boundaries of liberal thinking, and his faith in human nature, and his proposals that the state should plan the economy and guarantee all citizens a high standard of living, now seem quaint, if not naïve. Nevertheless, he represented a strand of thought in the Liberal Party that was left-wing but did not follow established socialist prescriptions. Like him, many of its proponents drifted to Labour.

Acland's attempts to synthesise libertarian and egalitarian ideals would surely strike a chord with modern liberals, and the Liberal Party and Liberal Democrats have, at various times, adopted many of his key policies, including economic planning, European federation and works councils. His championing of a politics that looked beyond economic considerations and sought to provide people with a sense of personal well-being has many echoes in the political debates of the early twenty-first century.

Key works
- *Unser Kampf* (1940)
- *Forward March* (1941)
- *What It Will Be Like in the New Britain* (1942)
- *How It Can Be Done* (1943)

Neil Stockley

Lord Acton   1834–1902

One of the great historical thinkers of the Victorian age, Acton was also a Liberal MP, and was later raised to the peerage by W. E. Gladstone, to whom he remained close as friend and adviser. Through his personality, journalism and writings, Acton played an important role in liberal Catholic thought. From the papacy's own history, however, Acton learned that 'all power tends to corrupt, and absolute power corrupts absolutely', a realisation in which he also anticipated the coming totalitarian age.

Key ideas
- The test of liberty and democracy is the amount of protection afforded to minorities.
- The role of the state must be limited but must include ensuring the liberty of the individual.
- The importance of reason reigning over will, and right above might.
- The tendency of power to corrupt and the near-certainty that a great

concentration of power will completely corrupt those who hold it.
- The duty of each human being to pursue their conception of the good.
- The importance of independent thought and intellectual integrity in the writing of history.

Biography

John Emerich Edward Dalberg-Acton was born on 10 January 1834 at Naples, where his English grandfather had been first minister to King Ferdinand VII. As Shropshire baronets, knighted for supporting the Stuart cause, the Actons had, in the eighteenth century, returned to the Catholic faith of their ancestors. This impeded their professional advancement in England and they sought their fortune abroad.

Acton's father died early, and the young Acton-Dalberg widow soon remarried, to the second Earl Granville, of the old family of English Whigs. The Conservative Actons thus turned Liberal, the young Acton following the political career of his Anglican stepfather. His devout mother insisted, however, on a Catholic upbringing. Aged sixteen, Acton went to Munich to study under the eminent church historian Dr Ignaz von Döllinger (1799–1890), a scholar of conservative views but friendly with the leading liberal Catholics, who became his friend and mentor.

On coming of age, Acton returned to England to take over Aldenham, his paternal Shropshire estate, and seek a professional opening, becoming Liberal MP for Carlow, an Irish constituency (1859–65). In 1865 he married a distant Bavarian cousin, Marie Anna von Valley. He was raised to the peerage in 1869.

Acton found his real métier as a Catholic journalist and editor of the *Rambler*, later renamed as *Home and Foreign Review*. Its circulation never exceeded a thousand copies, but it enjoyed widespread renown, mainly among convert Anglican readers. Acton particularly argued against the dogma of papal infallibility and played an important role in the first Vatican Council, supporting the hundred or so bishops who unsuccessfully opposed the dogma. His articles were denounced in Rome and he felt he had no choice but voluntarily to suspend publication of his *Review* rather than risk its ban. The opponents of infallibility had to toe the line; Döllinger was excommunicated. Acton evaded a similar fate, remaining loyal to the Catholic church. But the shock he received was expressed in his new sympathy for his friend, the novelist George Eliot, who defied the conventions of her time by living openly with a married man. Although an atheist, she constructed for herself a set of moral beliefs which Acton regarded as superior to some religious ones.

On the occasion of his appointment to the Cambridge Regius Chair of Modern History, widely regarded as an honour for Britain's Catholic minority, Acton was publicly reconciled to his church by Cardinal Vaughan. Surprisingly, Acton's nomination was due not to Gladstone (q.v.) but to his successor, Lord Rosebery, while Gladstone and Queen Victoria voiced anxieties over possible anti-Catholic reactions. Late in his life Acton became estranged from Döllinger, due to the importance he increasingly attached to moral judgments in history, which the aged Döllinger rejected. Cambridge's power did not corrupt Acton, but the university undoubtedly played its part in shortening his life by overburdening him with tasks such as editing the heavy tomes of the *Cambridge Modern History* which became a failed monument to Acton's ideal of a 'universal modern history'. He died of the effects of a stroke on 19 June 1902 at Tegernsee, in Bavaria, where he is buried at the lakeside cemetery.

Ideas

For Acton, liberty was the foundation of the good society and the standard against which society and government were to be judged. The measure of a free society was the level of security it provided for minorities; everyone had the right to be protected against both state power and the tyranny of the majority. For this reason Acton believed that the power of the state must be limited and individual responsibility enhanced. While people cannot be made good by the state, they can be made bad, because morality depends on liberty, which it is the role of the state to guarantee.

Acton believed that absolute democracy and socialism were inimical to liberty – as was political atheism and the doctrine that the end justifies the means, which Acton thought one of the most widespread of all the opinions hostile to liberty. He felt that liberalism should distance itself from the Whig tradition of pragmatism and compromise and be instead a principled philosophy promoting a reign of ideas. He was attached to the primacy of reason – both in politics, believing that people (particularly the newly enfranchised and less well-educated voters) were easily deceived by appeals to prejudice and passion, and in religion, where he rejected the primacy of dogma over morality and the support of authority through evil methods, such as the Spanish Inquisition. To counter these trends politically he supported liberal notions of self-help and the defeat of ignorance, and in religion championed ethics over dogma.

In the personal sphere, Acton placed a high value on the role of the individual in seeking a moral way, whether through an established church or not. However, as a liberal, he also possessed a distrust of state or religious government of a single ruler, a select few, or a single class, and understood the corrupting nature of power on holders of high office in state or church. To avoid this, he conceived of government as a moral obligation and opposed the doctrine of papal infallibility.

Key works
- Joseph L. Altholz, Damian McElrath and James C. Holland (eds.), *The Correspondence of Lord Acton and Richard Simpson* (three vols., Cambridge University Press, 1971–75)
- J. Rufus Fears (ed.), *Writings of Lord Acton* (three vols., Liberty Classics, 1984–88)

Further reading
- Roland Hill, *Lord Acton* (Yale University Press, 2000)
- Gertrude Himmelfarb, *Lord Acton, A Study in Politics and Conscience* (University of Chicago Press, 1962)

Roland Hill and Graham Lippiatt

Anarchism

Anarchism is a political philosophy which holds that direct democracy should replace the authority of the state. It stands in a complex relationship with liberalism.

Individualist anarchists, such as Max Stirner (1806–56), hold that there is no authority other than the individual's will. The individual should be completely in control of their own will and should not surrender it to anyone or anything else. Alternatively, more communally minded anarchists, such as Mikhail Bakunin (1814–76) or Peter Kropotkin (1842–1921), prefer to distinguish between society and state. They regard people as naturally social beings who habitually live in communities: society is natural, while the state is not. Rather, the state is an oppressive entity which is set up over society and which usurps functions that properly belong to autonomous communities and individuals. People should be free to flourish according to their own idea of the good, developing their own ways of fulfilling needs and meeting challenges. The state prevents this free development: it is coercive and holds a monopoly over law and government, punishing the non-compliant and encouraging passive obedience. Hence, anarchists want to replace the state with autonomous, small-scale, non-hierarchical communities which empower and liberate citizens, allowing their cooperative and creative faculties to flourish.

One can identify both clear resemblances and strong differences between anarchism and liberalism. In their intellectual structures, these two political philosophies share much. Both are children of the Enlightenment: at their origins, both share a common faith in progress, rationality (q.v.), toleration and humanitarian values. Anarchist political philosophers have on occasion been quite explicit in recognising this common debt: Rudolf Rocker (1873–1958) and Noam Chomsky (1928–) both stress the similarities between liberalism and anarchism. Moreover, one can also cite a number of political philosophers with a foot in both camps; whether one considers the high-minded idealism of William Godwin (1756–1836) or the rugged, anti-state individualism of Herbert Spencer (q.v.), there is a nineteenth-century intellectual tradition which blurs the distinctions between the philosophies. The key common themes are a faith in self-reliant individual reason, often contrasted with the inhuman qualities of the state or the irrational passions of the crowd, plus a demanding sense of individual responsibility.

Another important similarity is the tradition in liberal thought which jealously protects the freedom of the individual and is suspicious that the state might encroach upon individual liberty. Hence Locke's (q.v.) preference for a 'night-watchman' state, which protects the rights of individual citizens to life, liberty and property. In a similar vein, Robert Nozick (q.v.) argues that anything beyond a minimal state would violate individuals' rights and freedoms. This tradition places a strong emphasis on negative liberty: the state exists to protect citizens and enforce contracts. Beyond this, people should be left free to pursue their own vision of what is good. Some individualist anarchists find certain elements in this tradition sympathetic. Yet while anarchists want to see people empowered so that they can take control over their own destiny, they may be suspicious of liberal traditions which promote positive liberty for fear that the state will impose its own view of the good.

The relationship between human beings and the environment is another area of common concern. Many liberals worry about the environmental impact of big business and globalisation. Anarchists share this concern, and have organised a number of colourful protests against proposed airports, roads and at international summit meetings. The relationship between people, technology and the environment is the subject of keen debate within contemporary anarchism. Some post-scarcity anarchists embrace certain advances in technology as a potentially liberating force which could free individuals from the drudgery of production. Others fear that advanced technology may end up controlling people's lives, so must be resisted.

The differences between the two traditions are clearer when one considers their respective social bases. Particularly in the nineteenth century, liberalism rarely became a genuinely popular movement: instead, its social base was among reform-minded elites, seeking to guide modernisation. Such liberals might see the state as a neutral arbiter between conflicting interest groups in society; many also considered that a reformist state was the best instrument through which to implement their ideas. Anarchism, on the other hand, appealed to an eclectic mixture of social groups: dissident artists and writers, such as Camille Pissarro (1830–1903), Octave Mirbeau (1848–1917), Oscar Wilde (1854–1900) and Ursula le Guin (1929–); artisans, such as the Swiss carpenters who formed the backbone of Bakuninist support for the First International in the 1860s; peasants, such as the impoverished rural labourers of Andalusia in the late nineteenth and early twentieth century; and industrial workers, such as those of early twentieth-century Catalonia and northern Italy. In many cases, prominent anarchist thinkers such as Bakunin or Georges Sorel (1847–1922) stressed working-class action to the point that their thinking appeared close to that of the Marxist tradition. More commonly, anarchism was genuinely populist, attempting to create a counter-community capable not just of overthrowing the old system, but of creating new structures of organisation and direction. To such eager revolutionaries, the caution of the liberal reformers was frustrating and unwelcome.

More importantly, there was often a real class division between anarchists and liberals: whatever their individual social origins, anarchists looked to the people, while increasingly liberals sided with the bosses and the rulers. Important aspects of their developing political cultures demonstrated these differences: liberals remained attached to the utopian eighteenth-century attitude to private property, seeing it as an instrument by which the honest individual could liberate him- or herself from a corrupt state, while anarchists shared much of the Marxist critique of private property, believing that market capitalism possessed an internal dynamic which inevitably led the successful small workshop to grow into the big, exploitative factory that could buck the market.

Despite these significant political and social divisions, there remained important areas on which anarchists and liberals could both agree and work together. For example, both could share a common anti-clericalism, and the aggressive attacks on the entrenched, political power of the church could draw support from both movements. More significantly, perhaps, educational reform was something on which the two movements shared values: it is noteworthy that the main audience for the free schools of Francisco Ferrer (1859–1909), which operated in early twentieth-century Barcelona, was among the city's liberal elite. In France, Ferdinand Buisson (1841–1932) worked as an official for the Ministry of Public Instruction, and was to pioneer the French equivalent of comprehensive schooling in the mid-twentieth century, but he also retained friends and allies among the anarchists, and defended experiments in libertarian education at the very margins of the state's programme. In Britain, A. S. Neill's Summerhill could be cited as an approximate equivalent of such initiatives.

Key works
- William Godwin, *An Enquiry into Political Justice* (1797)
- Max Stirner, *The Ego and His Own* (1844)
- Mikhail Bakunin, *God and the State* (1870)
- Oscar Wilde, *The Soul of Man under Socialism* (1897)
- Peter Kropotkin, *Mutual Aid* (1902)

- Rudolf Rocker, *Nationalism and Culture* (1937)
- Ursula le Guin, *The Dispossessed* (1975)
- Murray Bookchin, *The Ecology of Freedom* (1982)
- Noam Chomsky, *Rogue States* (2000)

Further reading
- Peter Marshall, *Demanding the Impossible: A History of Anarchism* (Fontana, 1992)
- Jon Purkis and James Bowen (eds.), *Twenty-First Century Anarchism* (Cassell, 1997)
- *Anarchist Studies* (six-monthly academic journal, 1994–)

Sharif Gemie and Patricia Clark

Norman Angell   1872–1967

A leading anti-war activist, Angell became famous in 1910 for his work *The Great Illusion*. Never formally a Liberal, though openly respected by many Liberal politicians, he was one of a number of progressive radicals who joined Labour after the First World War. He consistently expounded the thesis that global economic interdependence made recourse to war financially detrimental to all participants.

Key ideas
- War is economically unsound, resulting in disaster for the victor as well as the vanquished.
- Rational thought can transcend patriotism and nationalism and recognise common interests across national borders.
- Imposing draconian reparations on a defeated Germany would bankrupt the country and provoke an extreme reaction.
- International bodies, with the Great Powers committed to their aims and purposes, are essential to the maintenance of world peace.

Biography

Ralph Norman Angell Lane was born on 26 December 1872 into a comfortably-off Lincolnshire merchant family. He was a precocious child and absorbed John Stuart Mill's (q.v.) *Essay on Liberty*, a work that he acknowledged to be a major influence on his subsequent thinking, at the age of twelve. Frustrated by what he saw as the constraints of his private middle-class education, first in Paris and then in Geneva, and the prospect of a conventional career thereafter, he went to the US, where he worked as a migrant farm worker, cowboy and prospector. Only when that life became too difficult and he began earning a living as a journalist did he realise what his real profession could be. Whilst in America he shortened his name to Norman Angell, ratifying this change by deed poll in March 1920.

In 1909 he paid for the printing and distribution of a pamphlet, *Europe's Optical Illusion*. It elicited no response until Hugh Massingham devoted two pages in the influential radical weekly *The Nation* to this 'new and brilliant writer' and his pamphlet. The following year Angell produced an expanded version, *The Great Illusion*, which over the following three years sold two million copies and was translated into twenty languages.

When it became increasingly clear in 1914 that there would be war in mainland Europe, Angell launched the short-lived Neutrality League with the aim of keeping Britain out of the conflict, in the role of peacemaker. When war began, he became a founder member of the Union of Democratic Control; never a pacifist, 'stop the war', movement, it was severely critical of the way Britain was conducting the war.

Angell increasingly found his involvement in the political hothouse distasteful, and he departed for the US. Within a year, however, the introduction of conscription disturbed him enough to draw him back to Britain. After the war he attended the Paris Peace Conference as an observer and found its deliberations and conclusions highly distressing. At this point he decided that, despite his personal discomfort in the political arena, it was the duty of like-minded radicals to join the Labour movement and to seek election to Parliament, so in 1920, along with a number of radical Liberal friends he joined the Independent Labour Party (ILP). After standing unsuccessfully in 1922 and 1923, he was elected for Bradford North in 1929. His short experience of the Commons confirmed his distaste for the parliamentary rough and tumble and this, along with his view that Macdonald's National Government was economically justified but politically disloyal, meant that he did not seek re-election in 1931. Macdonald generously recommended him for a knighthood in 1931 and – rather curiously timed – he was awarded the Nobel Peace Prize in 1933. He fought the London University seat unsuccessfully in 1935, nominally as the Labour candidate but more as a protagonist for the League of Nations.

Angell's anti-war stance never rested on pacifist foundations, even though until 1935 he happily worked alongside pacifists. His anti-war efforts in the 1920s and early 1930s were largely based on the crucial role of the League of Nations as a vital step towards a meaningful international order. Its evident weakness disillusioned him and by 1938 he had aligned himself with the anti-appeasers in support of Churchill. Soon after the Second World War broke out he again went to the US, where he remained until after the publication of his memoirs in 1951. He promoted internationalism into great old age, carrying out a lecture tour of America at the age of ninety.

Angell never married. He died on 7 October 1967.

Ideas

The core of Angell's philosophy fitted comfortably into classical liberalism (q.v.). His affiliation to the ILP was more a pragmatic decision than a commitment to socialism. A number of liberals of the First World War era, including Charles Trevelyan, Noel Buxton, Arthur Ponsonby and J. A. Hobson (q.v.), were provoked by the weakness of the post-war Liberal Party to align themselves with Labour as the more effective vehicle for the promotion of their views. They coexisted with Labour's socialist left, alongside many hitherto unaligned individuals like Angell.

The theme of Angell's definitive work, *The Great Illusion*, was rooted in liberalism, rejecting equally the Marxist obscurantism that war was the product of capitalism and the Tory jingoism that banged the patriotic drum for the nation-state. The illusion in question was that war could be economically advantageous.

Angell accepted that defective human nature could espouse irrational motivations such as a desire for *lebensraum*, or for the pursuit of a narrow patriotism or other codes of honour, and that this could – and manifestly did – transcend the rationality he propounded. He believed it was possible to abandon economic rivalry as a *casus belli*, citing the abandonment of barbaric practices such as duelling, judicial torture and the burning of heretics as examples of the progress of rational human society. His eventual perception that Nazi Germany was putting civilised progress into reverse led him to advocate rearmament, believing that a united stance by Britain, France and the US would be powerful enough to deter German aggression. For the same reason he was passionately in favour of the League of Nations as the key international vehicle for joint action against nationalist expansionism.

His attendance at the Paris Peace Conference and the clarity of his perception that the attempts to impose impossible reparations on Germany would have disastrous consequences led him to publish his own analysis of the resulting likelihood of a coming European crisis, even before John Maynard Keynes's (q.v.) more famous work on the same topic.

His 'pure' internationalism was inhibited after 1945 by his view that the Soviet Union had replaced Germany as the world's most dangerous potential aggressor and that therefore a strong Anglo-American alliance, plus Western unity, were integral to a strong United Nations and the maintenance of world peace. He remains the most cogent exponent of a political rationalism which has the potential to underpin international relations in the interests of peace.

Key works

- *The Great Illusion* (1910; revised and expanded in 1933)
- *The Foundations of International Polity* (1914)
- *The Economic Chaos and the Peace Treaty* (1919)
- *Must it be War?* (1939)

Further reading

- Norman Angell, *After All* (Hamish Hamilton, 1951)
- J. D. B. Miller, *Norman Angell and the Futility of War* (Macmillan, 1986)
- H. Weinroth, 'Norman Angell and The Great Illusion – an Episode in Pre-1914 Pacifism', *Historical Journal* 17:3 (1974)

Michael Meadowcroft

Anti-Corn Law League

The Anti-Corn Law League was created during the economic depression of the late 1830s to campaign for repeal of the Corn Laws, a raft of protective duties on imported foodstuffs introduced after the fall of Napoleon in response to collapsing agricultural prices. The passage of a Bill to repeal the Corn Laws in 1846 helped to establish free trade as British economic orthodoxy until the 1930s, and led to the League being perceived as the most effective extra-parliamentary organisation of its day.

The Anti-Corn Law League developed in 1839 from the Manchester Anti-Corn Law Association, itself founded in September 1838. Its most well-known leaders were Richard Cobden (q.v.), de facto leader of the League and acknowledged mainspring of the movement, and John Bright (1811–89), powerful orator and Cobden's most trusted lieutenant. The Manchester radical John Benjamin Smith (1794–1879) was the League's first president, while Charles Pelham Villiers (1802–98), though never officially a member, was its parliamentary champion before Cobden's election to Parliament in 1841, moving an annual resolution for the total and immediate abolition of the Corn Laws every year between 1838 and 1846.

The League deployed several arguments in its campaign:

- The Corn Laws had been enacted in the interests of the British aristocracy and were the keystone of aristocratic power; repeal would therefore hand power to the rising industrial and commercial middle classes.
- By excluding foreign corn, the Corn Laws were effectively a tax on bread; repeal would cheapen food prices and expand overseas markets for British manufactures in grain-exporting countries.
- Repeal would lead to the collapse of protection and Britain's example would be followed abroad, again expanding the market for British manufactures.
- The free market was divinely ordained and so essentially benign; it was therefore the most effective way of supplying the needs of all.
- Free trade (q.v.) would bring universal peace by binding nations together through ties of commerce and friendship.

Initially the League's activities were limited to petitions and lecture tours, and its early years were a continual struggle. It faced Chartist disruption, money shortages and competition from other reform organisations. However, under the guidance of George Wilson (1808–70), its chairman from 1841, it became a supremely efficient propaganda machine (after its demise, Wilson remained a key figure in Lancashire politics). By 1843, the League had eclipsed its rivals and grown into a truly national movement, with a headquarters in London and a strong regional structure. Its activities now included a huge propaganda effort, with millions of free-trade tracts being distributed via the new penny post, and a campaign for the wholesale revision of the electoral registers in key county constituencies.

The repeal of the Corn Laws in 1846 gave rise to what McCord has called the 'legend of the League': the idea that this was achieved primarily through League pressure, and in particular the threat of the next general election being fought on a register revised by the League's agents. More important, however, was Sir Robert Peel's 1845 conversion to free trade in corn after earlier experimentation with the tariff, particularly in his 1842 budget. Peel's ostensible reason for supporting repeal was not the power of the League but the emerging potato famine in Ireland, although in truth the famine only influenced the timing of Peel's volte-face. In reality, the influence of the League was more diffuse. It had kept the Corn Laws in the public eye since 1839, and its rhetoric may have persuaded Peel that repeal had more public support than proved to be the case. On the other hand, its existence persuaded him that temporary suspension of the Corn Laws was impossible without risking widespread disturbances on their reimposition.

The impact of repeal is debatable. It did not lead to dramatic reductions in food prices, and the predicted influx of grain from the United States did not begin until the 1880s. The aristocracy retained their political influence until the early twentieth century, while the middle classes were content with their gains and continued to lend allegiance to the traditional parties. Despite relaxation of the US tariff between 1846 and 1861, and a network of commercial treaties in the 1860s, the expected emulation of Britain by other nations did not materialise. Instead, the League's vision of benign, peaceful globalisation gave way to the reality of mutually antagonistic imperial expansion and the forcible opening of markets by European gunboats.

However, the legend of the League helped to maintain free trade as British economic orthodoxy until the return to protection in 1932. The League also became a model for other campaigns, while the apparatus it created for electoral registration and canvassing, and its active promotion of the personalities of its leaders, became a blueprint for political organisation in the era of mass democracy. Finally, it pioneered the involvement of women in political campaigning, and many supporters of women's suffrage served their apprenticeship in the League.

Further reading
- Norman McCord, *The Anti-Corn Law League, 1838–1846* (George Allen & Unwin, 1958)
- Archibald Prentice, *The History of the Anti-Corn Law League* (2 vols., 1853; reprint, Routledge, 1968)
- Paul Pickering and Alex Tyrrell, *The People's Bread: A History of the Anti-Corn Law League* (Leicester University Press, 2000)

Simon J. Morgan

Association of Liberal (Democrat) Councillors

The Association of Liberal Democrat Councillors – the successor body to the Association of Liberal Councillors – is the strongest of the Liberal Democrats' internal organisations, described by the party's website as the 'premier campaigning organisation ... a source of campaigning ideas, advice and information' for campaigners and councillors. In its earlier incarnation, it played an important role as the voice of the party's grassroots activists.

A 1965 conference organised by Michael Meadowcroft (q.v.) saw David Evans installed as Chair of the new Association of Liberal Councillors (ALC). The early ALC was able to call upon some of the most tireless and charismatic Liberal activists, and by 1969 it had become established as a recognised body of the party. As the authors of the 1970 Assembly resolution on community politics (q.v.) became involved in the Association, the template was in place for the organisation of today.

Early *ALC Bulletins* resonated with the names of Trevor Jones, Michael Meadowcroft, Bernard Greaves, Gordon Lishman, Richard Wainwright and other champions of grassroots Liberalism.

However, it was Tony (now Lord) Greaves, ALC's organising secretary from 1977 until 1985, who, more than any other, provided the Association its lifeblood and distinct Pennine flavour. In 1975 he began editing the *ALC Bulletin* and moved its printing operation to the north-west of England. Resources were still very scarce and ALC led a hand-to-mouth existence until December 1976, when Trevor Jones received an offer of accommodation for the purpose of 'supporting regional groups of councillors' from the Joseph Rowntree Social Services Trust (now the Joseph Rowntree Reform Trust Ltd., q.v.). ALC moved into the Birchcliffe Centre in Hebden Bridge, West Yorkshire, where, as the Association of Liberal Democrat Councillors (ALDC) it remains to this day.

The party's growth in local government in the 1970s typified the application of community politics to Liberal campaigning and the surge of support for the Alliance in the 1980s was facilitated by local success. ALC was able to play a crucial role in consolidating new power bases, from South Somerset to North East Fife, and training councillors to deal with the possibility of holding or sharing office throughout the country.

The merger between the Liberals and the SDP necessitated a new Association, ALDC – taken from the ALC and its sister organisation, the Association of Social Democratic Councillors. This might have proved a difficult operation, but key individuals such as Paul Burstow from the SDP and Andrew Stunell from the Liberals eased the path. (Both men were elected to Parliament as Liberal Democrat MPs in 1997, as was another ALC staff member, Jackie Ballard.) Stunell was political secretary from 1989 until 1996 and remains president of the ALDC Management Committee.

After the initial difficulties faced by the merged party, local government advances

resumed in 1991. ALDC's organisational and campaigning strength was key to electoral success against both Conservative and Labour, and the growth of the party's council base became synonymous with the growth of ALDC. By 1995 the party controlled fifty-four councils, and it subsequently made inroads into Labour's local government heartlands in Liverpool, Stockport, Sheffield, Islington, Newcastle and Leeds. Local success often provided the springboard for national breakthrough – between 1992 and 2005 the parliamentary party tripled in size and ALDC campaigning tactics were increasingly copied by other parties trying to replicate their success. In 2006 the party had over 4,700 councillors and was in majority control of thirty-four local authorities; ALDC boasted over 2,700 members.

As well as the development of campaigning techniques, ALC also made a significant contribution to the political debate within the Liberal Party, particularly during the Greaves era. Its voice was unashamedly radical, and Hebden Bridge became the source of policy papers on a broad range of topics. The organisation has often viewed itself, and has been seen as, the legitimate voice of the grassroots activist party membership. Ian Bradley, writing in *The Strange Rebirth of Liberal Britain*, noted the 'frosty relationship' between ALC and the Liberal leadership and described the ALC of the early 1980s in the following terms:

> The atmosphere at the group's headquarters, a converted Baptist Chapel high in the Pennines, where the bearded Greaves and his earnest colleagues sit submerged under piles of *Focus* newsletters breathing provincial defiance and northern fervour, does in some ways seem rather closer to the spirit and traditions of British Liberalism than the metropolitan smoothness, and media-oriented style, which sometimes

seems to characterise the Liberal Party's dealings at national level.

ALC was not afraid to express unease at the direction of the Liberal–SDP Alliance, and during the 2006 Liberal Democrat leadership crisis ALDC again portrayed itself as the voice of the rank and file, against the parliamentary party. But since the early 1990s, there have been important shifts in ALDC's role. It has gradually ceased to play much of a direct role in policy formulation; it is many years since it submitted a policy motion to party conference, for example. (This is partly due to the formation of the Local Government Association in 1997; to a certain extent this role has been taken on by the Liberal Democrat group there.) The expansion of the Liberal Democrat parliamentary parties (in Westminster, the European Parliament, Scottish Parliament and National Assembly for Wales) and the mushrooming of staff numbers therein has also tipped the party's fulcrum away from ALDC.

The organisation remains, however, the key grassroots campaigning body in the party; but while Liberal Democrat MPs have proved amazingly resilient electorally, the retention record of local councillors is less impressive, particularly once the party has taken control of a council. This may reflect a key flaw in relying on the techniques of community politics to win elections. Contemporary local campaigning has developed a kind of shorthand – the model (but mythical) ALDC campaign where local voters are beaten into submission by *Focus* leaflets and local petitions about the failure of the local council to deliver decent services. Although undoubtedly effective at winning elections from opposition, this approach is not well suited to defending the actions of Liberal Democrats in power. One of the contemporary challenges for

the party in general, and ALDC in particular, is to revisit the contemporary notion of community politics as a campaigning tactic and re-engage with the broader original concept.

Notwithstanding this, the continuing importance of local government to Liberal Democrat activists, who by their nature are decentralist and generally suspicious of strong central leadership, gives ALDC the chance to play a continuing role as a link between the party in Cowley Street, at Westminster, in Brussels, in Edinburgh or in Cardiff, and grassroots activists and voter networks.

Further reading
- ALDC, *Community Politics Today* (2006)
- Colin Copus, 'Liberal Democrat Councillors: Community politics, local campaigning and the role of the political party' (paper for British Liberal Political Studies Group Annual Conference, Gregynog, Wales, January 2006)
- Phoebe Winch, *Action with the ALC; Ten Years at the Birchcliffe Centre* (Association of Liberal Councillors, 1987)

Andrew Russell

Austrian School

The Austrian School is a principally economic school of thought that offers an alternative methodology to mainstream neo-classical economics. The methodological assumptions of Austrian economics tend to produce economically liberal and libertarian policy conclusions.

The key principles of the Austrian School are:
- Methodological individualism.
- Radical subjectivism and radical ignorance.

- An emphasis on the communicative function of prices.

A distinct Austrian School of economics emerged in late nineteenth-century Vienna. Carl Menger (1840–1921), usually described as the founder of the school, was one of three people who independently developed the theory of marginal utility around 1870 (the others being William S. Jevons and Leon Walras) and also showed that many economic institutions – notably money – emerge spontaneously wherever advanced exchanges take place, rather than being created by the state. Menger's initial insights into the subjective nature of value were developed by Friedrich von Weiser (1851–1926) and Eugen von Böhm-Bawerk (1851–1914), but it was the contributions of Ludwig von Mises (1881–1973) and Friedrich von Hayek (q.v.) that established the distinct approach of the modern Austrian School. While the initial Austrians were Austrian by nationality – hence the name – today the school is international.

The first principle of Austrian economics is methodological individualism; that is, it is concerned with the study of individuals, rather than societies or collectives. Austrians do not accept that individuals respond to external stimuli in the manner of automatons, so that, for example, a rise in interest rates must always produce an entirely predictable decrease in borrowing. There are, Austrians would point out, many examples of people responding to economic and social changes in wholly unexpected and unpredictable ways. Many Austrians reject macro-economics outright as a fallacious framework of analysis that conceals the fact that an economy is ultimately the sum of the actions of many individual men and women and not the product of mysterious societal forces.

The methodological individualism of the Austrian school logically leads to its belief in radical subjectivism and radical ignorance. Because the economy is driven by the subjective perceptions, and hence subjective choices, of individuals the future must always be unknowable because we do not know how individuals will interpret and respond to present and future economic conditions. For this reason, many of the assumptions of neo-classical economics, such as the existence of perfect information and perfect competition, are rejected as inherently unrealistic. Similarly, formal economic models that seek to predict the future on the basis of past behaviour (or other variables) are also rejected.

In common with mainstream classical economics, Austrians emphasise the importance of prices as a means of communicating information about the scarcity and relative value of different goods, services and factors of production. Only market prices can communicate the information necessary to ensure that the value of goods and services produced exceeds the value of the resources and factors used in their production. Without market prices simple economic calculation – and hence wealth creation – is deemed impossible.

The assumptions and methodology of the Austrian School have led its followers to be highly suspicious of government intervention. The rejection of macro-economics and the emphasis on the subjective perceptions of individuals leads to strong scepticism as to attempts to engineer particular macro-economic outcomes; given that the future must be essentially unknowable and unpredictable, attempts to deliberately plan economic outcomes are destined to fail. The public provision of goods and services without the benefit of market prices is judged to be inherently inefficient as those charged with the management of such services have no way of knowing the relative values, and hence the most efficient allocation, of the resources at their disposal. Rather, the Austrian School has tended to emphasis the self-ordering and self-regulating nature of markets free from attempts to direct them to attain pre-ordained outcomes.

The influence of the Austrian School has increased dramatically in recent decades. Whereas in the 1950s and 1960s its ideas were largely neglected, the apparent failure of attempts to macro-manage advanced economies in the 1970s and 1980s fuelled a revival in Austrian ideas. Although neo-classical economics remains the dominant approach in academic economics and economic policy-making, today most mainstream economists are familiar with Austrian ideas and would be comfortable employing them in specific contexts, such as consideration of imperfect information and ignorance of future market conditions.

Further reading

- P. J. Boettke, *The Elgar Companion to Austrian Economics* (Edward Elgar, 1994)
- F. A. Hayek, *Individualism and Economic Order* (University of Chicago Press, 1948)
- L. von Mises, *Human Action* (Liberty Fund, 2006; first edn. 1949)

John Meadowcroft

Walter Bagehot   1826–77

A political commentator, economist and journalist of the mid-nineteenth century, who edited *The Economist* and wrote a classic analysis of the nineteenth-century liberal constitution, in which he discussed the superiority of parliamentary democracy as a form of government. He also emphasised the importance of government by discussion.

Key ideas

- The distinction between the 'dignified' and 'efficient' parts of the constitution.
- The superiority of parliamentary government.
- The importance of government by discussion.

Biography

Walter Bagehot was born on 3 February 1826 in Langport, Somerset. He was the son of Thomas Watson Bagehot, the vice-chairman of Stuckey's Bank, a major bank in the west of England, and his mother was a niece of the founder of the bank. Bagehot was educated at Langport Grammar School and Bristol College. At the age of sixteen, he went to University College, London, where he graduated in 1846 with a first-class honours degree in classics. Two years later, he was awarded a master's degree from the same university, and its gold medal for moral and intellectual philosophy. After university, Bagehot read law and was called to the bar in 1852, although he did not practice. Instead, he joined the family bank, went on to manage the London branch and later succeeded his father as vice-chairman.

A career in banking gave Bagehot the freedom to write literary essays. In 1855, he co-founded the *National Review*, and was its joint editor for nine years. In 1858, he married Eliza, the eldest daughter of the Rt Hon James Wilson, a Liberal MP, Financial Secretary to the Treasury, and the founder and owner of *The Economist*. Bagehot's friendship with Wilson provided him with important contacts with the Westminster and Whitehall establishment, including W. E. Gladstone (q.v.). He became a director of *The Economist* and was its editor from 1861 until his death sixteen years later.

Bagehot was a prolific writer, combining his position as editor of *The Economist*, in which he discussed political and economic issues in his weekly essays, with writing articles in other leading periodicals. He was consulted on financial and banking matters by government ministers and senior civil servants, and invented the Treasury bill; he was described by Gladstone as 'a kind of spare Chancellor of the Exchequer'. Bagehot's argument, in his book *Lombard Street*, that the Bank of England should act as a lender of last resort, was highly influential in the development of modern central banking.

Bagehot was a Liberal, unsuccessfully fighting Bridgwater at a by-election in 1866. His connections with the Liberal Party were strengthened by his lengthy editorship of *The Economist*, a journal that had been associated with the free trade movement (q.v.) and the Manchester School (q.v.).

Bagehot suffered from poor health in his later years and died of pneumonia in Langport on 24 March 1877.

Ideas

Despite his close links with the Liberal Party, it is difficult to put a label on Bagehot's political views; he has been described as a reforming Liberal, as a Whig, and as a Conservative. Bagehot himself declared that he was a conservative Liberal, and that he was 'between size in politics'. Above all, however, Bagehot was a perceptive observer of the Victorian political scene, who explored beneath the surface of the governmental system and attempted to distinguish the myths of British politics from the reality.

Bagehot's most famous and enduring political work was *The English Constitution*, written as a series of essays for the liberal journal the *Fortnightly Review*, between 1865 and 1867, and published in book form in 1867. It examined the workings of the liberal constitution that had developed in the period following the Reform Act of 1832 – a so-called 'golden age', when the House of Commons was at the heart of the governing system, and when governments could be dismissed and ministers forced to resign by MPs. Bagehot's analysis went beyond the 'paper description' of the constitution and attempted to describe its 'living reality', famously distinguishing between what he described as the 'dignified' and the 'efficient' parts of Britain's constitutional arrangements. He argued that the dignified parts of the governmental system – the monarchy and the House of Lords – had no real power in the governing process, but played a valuable role in generating respect for the system. Real power was exercised through the Cabinet and the House of Commons – the efficient parts of the constitution.

Bagehot was a great admirer of the parliamentary form of government that he described in *The English Constitution*, contrasting it unfavourably with the presidential form of government, based on the separation of powers, found in the United States. He argued that in a parliamentary system of government, the Cabinet – famously described as 'a combining committee, a *hyphen* which joins, a *buckle* which fastens' the executive to the legislature – was chosen, and could be dismissed, by the House of Commons. Importantly, the Cabinet was collectively responsible to the Commons. Parliamentary government also provided genuine debate. For Bagehot, the distinguishing quality of parliamentary government was that it was government by discussion – 'in each stage of a public transaction there is a discussion'.

Bagehot's views on the importance of discussion and debate in the governmental process were developed in his other major political work, *Physics and Politics*, published in 1872. This book applied the ideas of evolution to the analysis of political society, arguing that the evolution of societies into advanced nations involved passing through a 'preliminary age' to an age of nation-building, culminating with a third stage called the 'age of discussion'. For Bagehot, discussion was the hallmark of a civilised society, a view that he shared with his contemporary, John Stuart Mill (q.v.). Government by discussion, Bagehot argued, had been 'a principal organ for improving mankind' and the root of progress.

Key works
- *The English Constitution* (1867)
- *Physics and Politics* (1872)
- *Lombard Street: A Description of the Money Market* (1873)
- *Literary Studies* (1879)
- *Economic Studies* (1880)
- *The Works of Walter Bagehot* (1889)

Further reading
- A. Buchan, *The Spare Chancellor: the Life of Walter Bagehot* (Chatto & Windus, 1959)
- R. H. S. Crossman, 'Introduction' to Bagehot, *The English Constitution* (Fontana, 1963)
- P. Smith (ed.), Bagehot: *The English Constitution* (Cambridge University Press, 2001)
- N. St John-Stevas, *The Collected Works of Walter Bagehot* (15 vols., *The Economist*, 1965–86).
- G. M. Young, 'The greatest Victorian', in *Today and Yesterday: Collected Essays and Addresses* (Hart-Davis, 1948).

Tony Butcher

Ernest Barker   1874–1960

English liberal political theorist and historian of political thought, he wrote two seminal books on Greek political theory. He was the first holder of the Chair of Political Science at Cambridge University.

Key ideas
- The state as moral community but rooted in the 'organising' idea of law and order.
- The sanctity of the individual as the irreducible basis of society.
- The limits of pluralism in the 'eruption of groups' in inter-war Europe.
- The importance of the established church to English nationhood.
- 'Civility' as a strength of European, particularly English life.

Biography
Ernest Barker was born in Woodley, Cheshire, on 23 September 1874. His father was a miner turned farm labourer. He won scholarships to Manchester Grammar School and to Balliol College, Oxford, where he gained firsts in classical moderations, *Literae Humaniores* and modern history. He taught classics and modern history at Oxford until 1920, when he became the principal of King's College, London. He held the Chair of Political Science at Cambridge from 1927 until his retirement in 1939. Always conscious of his northern working-class roots and how they limited certain avenues of professional advancement, he declined to become a candidate for the wardenship of New College, Oxford, in 1924. However, he bore no resentment; indeed, he was grateful for the ladder of ascent he had enjoyed, regarding the existence of such ladders as one of many sources of legitimate national pride.

Barker remained active in the cause of liberalism throughout his life. His ancestral allegiance was to the Liberal Party, which had enfranchised his father in 1884. He was an ardent follower of Asquith, particularly over home rule, before 1914, but was unsympathetic to the increasing progressivism of the Liberal Party, and supported Chamberlain's policy of appeasement in 1938–39. Nevertheless, he sat on the Liberal Council as well as the executive of the Free Trade Union (q.v.) in the 1940s.

Barker was a prolific contributor to national and local newspapers and journals. His concern to spread the fruits of scholarship and academic reflection widely was inspired by a strong sense of public duty and service. He worked for voluntary organisations such as the National Council for Social Service as well as national government. In the First World War he worked for the Ministry of Labour, and in the Second World War he wrote pamphlets for the Ministry of Information and the British Council and was active in army education. He was knighted in 1944.

Much of the inspiration behind his work was a deep love of country, not just of England but of the wider United Kingdom; and his staunch Christian commitment, which shifted from Congregationalism to Anglicanism. He died on 17 February 1960.

Ideas

Barker's political thought developed from his studies of Plato and Aristotle, approached through the political philosophy of T. H. Green (q.v.). He derived from Green his conception of the state as a moral community, bound by ties of mutual obligation and expressed in the idea of common citizenship. However, influenced by the concept of the rule of law (q.v.) exemplified by thinkers such as A. V. Dicey (q.v.), Barker qualified his enthusiasm for Plato's political thought, particularly his conception of the sovereignty of reason unlimited by law and detached from the will of the 'whole community'. This was despite the roots of Plato's idea of the sovereignty of reason in

a conception of justice in the individual soul as the source of all moral excellence, which Barker endorsed emphatically. His concern for individual liberty comes across clearly in his championship of Aristotle's more flexible view of the state as merely the 'supreme association and the dominant end'; in contrast, Plato in *The Republic* had been consumed by a zeal for the state which left individuals and other communities out of the count.

The pluralism of F. W. Maitland and J. N. Figgis was influential on Barker's early thought. He celebrated the wealth of group life in England, which rivalled that of Germany. Germany was the home of pluralist political theory through the writings of the legal scholar Otto von Gierke, part of which Maitland translated. According to Maitland, the peculiarly English concept of the 'trust' held the key to the vitality of associations in Britain, neutralising the invidious effects of the 'concession' theory of group personality that plagued much of the Continent. However, Barker drew back from the concept of the 'real personality' of groups that informed Figgis's pluralism, in particular taking refuge in the notion of groups as founded on 'organising ideas', a concept he borrowed from the idealist thinker Bernard Bosanquet (q.v.). His doubts about the pluralist elevation of groups increased in the inter-war period as he witnessed what he termed the 'eruption of the group' in European politics that seemed to underlie fascism and communism. He was one of the first political theorists to note the significance of Carl Schmitt's 'friend–foe' analysis of politics as a threat to the liberal state, particularly its contrast with the easy-going nature of political life in Britain, permeated as it was with the spirit of compromise. England, he argued, in characteristic Whiggish (q.v.) style, had recovered from the totalitarianism to which it had been brought in the sixteenth century thanks to the ascendancy of this temper.

Barker's sense of Englishness came out strongly in his later work. Historically, the English had counted their blessings and cut their losses, eschewing the indulgence in sentimentality and despair that prevailed elsewhere, and readily adapting to new circumstances. His Christianity also intensified in later years. He had defended the Anglican establishment in the fall-out from Parliament's rejection of the new prayer book in 1928, particularly as an expert witness for the Archbishops' Commission on the Relations between Church and State in 1935. But his mind was not moved by narrow nationalism; on the contrary, in emphasising the importance of religion to politics, he was drawing on a wider conception of the legacy of Plato as the informing spirit of the Middle Ages, and the deepened sense of self in the early Christian centuries.

Barker's conception of the irreducible nature of individual personality was integral to his liberalism. He was an eclectic thinker, but one who ensured that the themes of late-Victorian liberalism were securely hitched to the classical and Christian heritage, with due appreciation of the role that England/Britain had played in its maintenance.

Key works

- *The Political Thought of Plato and Aristotle* (1906)
- *Political Thought in England from Herbert Spencer to the Present Day* (1915)
- *Greek Political Theory: Plato and His Predecessors* (1918)
- *Reflections on Government* (1942)
- *Essays on Government* (1945)
- *The Principles of Social and Political Theory* (1951)

Further reading

- Arthur Aughey, *The Politics of Englishness* (Manchester University Press, 2007)
- Andrzej Olechnowicz, 'Liberal Anti-Fascism in the 1930s: The Case of Ernest Barker', *Albion*, 36:4 (2004)
- *Polis*, 23:2 (2006), Ernest Barker, *The Political Thought of Plato and Aristotle (1906): A Centenary Tribute*, ed. Julia Stapleton.
- Julia Stapleton, *Englishness and the Study of Politics: The Social and Political Thought of Ernest Barker* (Cambridge University Press, 1994)
- Julia Stapleton, 'Third-Generation Idealism: Religion and Nationality in the Political Thought of Ernest Barker', in Tim Battin (ed.), *A Passion for Politics: Essays in Honour of Graham Maddox* (Pearson Education, Australia, 2005)

Julia Stapleton

Claude Bastiat   1801–50

The leading proponent of the doctrine of universal free trade in nineteenth-century France. An economist and a talented satirical publicist, Bastiat was responsible for the popularisation of the British Manchester School in France. He also radicalised many of the ideas of Richard Cobden and his influence on public opinion in continental Europe can hardly be over-estimated.

Key ideas

- Free trade and free markets are the best way towards wealth for all people.
- Free exchange creates a harmonious society because it can only exist if all parties engaged benefit from it.
- Free trade promotes peace among nations.
- Freedom is a natural right unless others are harmed by its exercise.

Biography

Claude Frédéric Bastiat was born in Bayonne, in the south-west of France. He became an orphan at the age of nine and was brought up by his grandfather. At the age of seventeen he joined his grandfather's business. His early interest in economics and his admiration for Richard Cobden (q.v.) led him to champion free trade (q.v.).

In 1845 Bastiat travelled to England to acquire first-hand information about the struggle for free trade there. There he met his hero Cobden, who also became his close friend. Impressed by what he had seen, Bastiat published a book titled *Cobden and the League*, a vivid description of the Anti-Corn Law League's (q.v.) campaign. Inspired by Cobden he founded the Association for Free Trade in 1846, thus uniting the various local free trade associations on the national level. However, it is not Bastiat's reputation as a political organiser of the French free trade movement that has survived him, but that of an economic writer.

Bastiat started his career as a writer at a time of heated political debate. The revolution of 1848 had brought an end to the monarchy of Louis Philippe. Bastiat had always remained sceptical about the old regime; after all, it was the economic pseudo-liberalism of Louis Philippe's monarchy which had served the vested interests of industrialists (who were mostly staunch protectionists) rather than the cause of universal freedom (q.v.) that had made Bastiat take up his pen.

The revolution of 1848, however, soon took a non-liberal turn: in February the Right to Work was proclaimed, followed by the limitation of working hours to ten a day, which ran counter to Bastiat's laissez-faire (q.v.) principles. Still optimistic, he ran as a candidate for the National Assembly, and was elected in April 1848; he found himself confronted with a vast coalition of anti-liberal interest groups and mostly voted with the minority. He not only had to face the protectionism of the old elites, but also a new political force which had transformed protectionist interventionism into the economic creed of the 'progressives'. Socialism became the fashion of the day, and although Bastiat resisted the call of many conservatives for repressive measures to be taken against the socialists, he saw socialism as the enemy of the future.

Along with economic issues, Bastiat dedicated himself to the causes of pacifism (q.v.), anti-colonialism and disarmament. He vigorously campaigned against French colonialism in Algeria and, together with Victor Hugo, organised the First International Peace Congress in August 1848 and remained associated with the international peace movement thereafter.

Amidst the revolutionary chaos of 1848, partly caused by socialist uprisings, Napoleon's nephew Louis Napoleon Bonaparte entered the political arena. Bastiat foresaw disaster and campaigned against him during the presidential election, but in vain; in October Louis Napoleon was elected with an overwhelming majority. His grab for dictatorship in 1851, which destroyed all liberal dreams, however, came only after Bastiat's demise. In 1850 he contracted tuberculosis, which shattered all his plans. In September he travelled to Italy, where the climate was better suited for his ill-health but it was too late, and he died on 24 December 1850, in Rome.

Ideas

Long after his death, Bastiat's writings were still huge best sellers; although largely forgotten today, he was perhaps the most popular economist of his time, partly due to the literary quality of his writings. In 1954, Josef Schumpeter claimed that Bastiat was 'the most brilliant economic journalist who ever lived'.

Bastiat's satirical pieces, many of which can be found in *Economic Sophisms* (1846), became true classics. The most famous of these is the *Petition of the Candle-makers*, where a fictitious group of candle-makers asks the minister in charge for protection against the 'unfair competition' from the sun. His predilection for amusing parables can also be seen in his essay *What Is Seen and What Is Not Seen* (1850), in which he explains the difference between a good and a bad economist. According to Bastiat, a bad economist, who is mostly on the interventionist and protectionist side, only sees the visible dimension of an economic problem. In his essay *The State*, Bastiat demolished all theories that represent the state as the standard-bearer of the common good. He came up with his own definition: the state is a great fiction, where everyone tries to live at the expense of everyone else.

However, Bastiat was not just a talented publicist; he was also a serious economist, as his greatest work, *Economic Harmonies* (1850), demonstrated. Under the influence of David Ricardo (q.v.), who in his *Principles of Political Economy and Taxation* (1817) maintained that the wages of labourers could never be raised above the level of mere subsistence, classical English economics had absorbed some distinctly pessimistic undertones, which did not fit well with its liberal reformist approach. The refutation of the Ricardian iron law of wages is perhaps Bastiat's greatest achievement as an economist. Hence, it does not come as a surprise that Bastiat, a Frenchman, became the economist who was most associated with the Manchester School's (q.v.) reform agenda.

Bastiat began his argument with the share of labour and capital in total production. He maintained that if capital increases, interest rates would fall. If total production then grows, the share of capital would increase in absolute numbers, but its relative share would fall. As a consequence, the relative share of labour would increase. Although this theory did not allow for quantitative predictions about linear growth rates, it did show that wealth for all was not out of reach. Further economic development in Europe proved Bastiat, and not Ricardo, right.

Key works
- *Cobden and the League* (1845)
- *Economic Sophisms* (1846)
- *What Is Seen and What Is Not Seen* (1850)
- *The Law* (1850)
- *The State* (1850)
- *Economic Harmonies* (1850)

Further reading
- Louis Baudin, *Frédéric Bastiat* (Dalloz, 1962)
- George Roche, *Free Markets, Free Men: Frederic Bastiat 1801–1850* (Hillsdale College Press, 1993)
- Dean Russell, *Frederic Bastiat: Ideas and Influence* (Foundation for Economic Education, 1969)

Detmar Doering

Hilaire Belloc   1870–1953

Poet, novelist, historian and social critic, Belloc's main contributions to political thought were fiercely anti-political and written after his period as a Liberal MP. His bitter anti-modernist and pro-Roman Catholic polemics won him few friends in the Liberal Party after his controversial and stormy departure from it; yet, as the main creator of the movement that became known as distributism, he did, paradoxically, became an important influence on liberal thinking after the Second World War, as liberals searched for a coherent critique of the prevailing Fabianism.

Key ideas

- Both socialism and capitalism tend towards slavery.
- The growth of centralised government and monopolistic business is a threat to human freedom, fulfilment and spirituality.
- Small-scale property, small enterprises and agricultural smallholdings are the only sustainable basis for dignity, independence and liberty.
- European perspective based on a resurgence of Roman Catholic culture.

Biography

Joseph Hilaire Pierre Belloc was born outside Paris on 27 July 1870, the son of a French father who died when he was two, and an English Catholic mother. His maternal grandfather had been a friend of John Stuart Mill (q.v.). He was Liberal MP for South Salford from 1906–11.

Belloc was educated at the Oratory School in Birmingham, and served briefly in the French artillery before returning to England and to Balliol College, Oxford, where he took the university by storm as an eloquent conversationalist, speaker and debater in the generation of liberals which included John Simon and J. L. Hammond (q.v.).

The leading figures of English Catholicism were critical influences on him, but particularly Cardinal Henry Manning (1807–92), through whom he was exposed to the developing tenets of Catholic social doctrine, including the idea of 'subsidiarity' enshrined in Pope Leo XIII's encyclical *Rerum Novarum* (1891). The agrarian radicalism of William Cobbett was also an important influence. In later life, his friendship with G. K. Chesterton (1874–1936) was the partnership that forged the economic doctrine known as distributism (q.v.).

It was as a writer, historian and man of letters that Belloc made his way in the world after the disappointment of failing to be elected as a fellow of All Souls; his first literary success came with *Verses and Sonnets* (1896), and he is best remembered for *Cautionary Tales for Children* (1907).

He was also, however, involved in Liberal politics from an early age, and was one of the six prominent young authors of *Essays in Liberalism* (1897). He failed to win the Liberal nomination for Dover in 1903, because (he believed) of his Catholicism, but was nominated the following year for South Salford, which he won in 1906 by 852 votes. He held the seat in 1910 with a reduced majority but was by then disillusioned with Parliament and with the Liberal Party, which had rejected his campaign for the public auditing of secret party political funds. His satirical novel *Mr Clutterbuck's Election* (1908) did nothing to endear himself to party colleagues, and his enthusiasm for beer alienated the party's teetotal wing. His book *The Party System* (1911) was as critical of Liberals as everyone else. His involvement in formal politics ended when he stepped down from Parliament in 1911 because of his increasing disillusionment with what he saw as the failures and corruption of parliamentary politics. The rift between the Liberal Party and Belloc and Chesterton and their associates was sealed with their vigorous campaigning against leading party figures in the Marconi scandal of 1912, which ended in a celebrated libel case brought against their newspaper *Eye-Witness*, then edited by Chesterton's anti-Semitic brother Cecil (1879–1918). The same publication continued after Cecil Chesterton's death in various guises, occasionally under Belloc's editorship, emerging finally under G. K. Chesterton's wing as *GK's Weekly*. It became the central organ of distributist campaigning.

Belloc later flirted with French monarchism, as well as with anti-communists like Mussolini and Franco. His views about Europe's Jewish heritage were complicated enough for him to be accused of anti-Semitism, though he was among the first to warn about the danger to Europe from Adolf Hitler and Nazism. He died in Guildford on 16 July 1953.

Ideas

'The choice lies between property on the one hand and slavery, public or private, on the other. There is no third issue,' wrote Belloc in his *Essay on the Restoration of Property* (1936), and this is the essence of what became his credo. The critical importance of small-scale property which is at the heart of distributism was also, in many ways, the guarantee that this movement would remain at the margins of mainstream radicalism, whether it was Fabianism or New Liberalism (q.v.), which were increasingly suspicious of private property.

The idea of distributing small-scale property was Belloc's solution to the threat of what he dubbed the 'Servile State', set out in his book of the same name (1912). Both capitalism and socialism, he said, tended towards slavery, but could not do so if people had the basic independence that their own home, business or smallholding gave them.

Belloc and the distributists were anti-industrial, anti-finance, anti-corporation, anti-bureaucrat, and most of all anti–giantism, either in big bureaucracy or in big business – which he described as the 'Big Rot'. He regarded the original sin perpetrated in English history as the Reformation and its effective privatisation of monasteries and other institutions that he believed were the bastions of independence for ordinary

people. He consistently urged a renewed European vision based on Roman Catholic radicalism. He was also profoundly critical of the financial system, commercialism and banking.

Distributism petered out after Chesterton's death in 1936 but some of Belloc's ideas about small-scale ownership found their way into the Liberal Party's policy document *Ownership for All* (1937). His thinking was also echoed in the establishment of the Unservile State (q.v.) ginger group of Liberal policy reformers in 1953, and in the interest in new forms of industrial ownership under Jo Grimond (q.v.) in the 1950s.

Key works

- *The Party System* (1911)
- *The Servile State* (1912)
- *An Essay on the Restoration of Property* (1936)

Further reading

- Joseph Pearce, *Old Thunder: A Life of Hilaire Belloc* (HarperCollins, 2002).
- Robert Speaight, *The Life of Hilaire Belloc* (Hollis & Carter, 1957)
- A. N. Wilson, *Hilaire Belloc* (Hamilton, 1984)

David Boyle

Jeremy Bentham   1748–1832

One of the greatest English thinkers of the Enlightenment, most noted for his formulation of utilitarian doctrine. He wrote extensively on legal and constitutional matters, on which reformers from many countries sought his advice.

Key ideas

- Rejection of tradition as a justification of institutions and behaviour.

- Advocacy of rational analysis of all institutions.
- The importance of the idea of happiness as the aim of life.
- Coined the slogan 'the greatest happiness of the greatest number' and believed that pleasure and pain could be measured according to a 'felicific calculus'.

Biography

Jeremy Bentham was born in London on 15 February 1748. He began his intellectual work at a young age, studying Latin when he was only three. Already at Westminster School he was known as 'the philosopher', a sobriquet that the remainder of his life amply merited. He entered Oxford at twelve and graduated when he was fifteen.

Bentham was the son and grandson of lawyers and was trained for the legal profession, which he rejected; he was called to the bar in 1769 but never practised. His father died in 1792, leaving him with an income of nearly £600 a year, so satisfactory a sum at that time that he did not need to earn a living. In others this might have led to a life of leisure; not so with Bentham, who remained a prodigious worker for reform. He was one of a number of foreign radicals made an honorary citizen of revolutionary France in 1792, even though he was no advocate of violence and by then was already becoming disillusioned with the revolution.

Bentham had the ambition to legislate for many countries. He not only volunteered to provide a complete penal law for Russia and for the United States of America, but additionally made a 'Codification Proposal ... to All Nations Professing Liberal Opinions'. He also made up new words. Some, such as 'social science' and 'internationalism' (q.v.), have remained in use; others have not: no one, for example, now refers to 'anteprandial circumnavigation'

when referring to a walk round the garden before dinner.

Bentham died in 1832 and, in accordance with his will, now sits in a glass box at University College, London (where he looks remarkably well for a man of his age. This is not so difficult as he has been given a wax head, the real one being kept in a fridge). Nearby a pub has been named in his honour, the 'Jeremy Bentham'; it is dedicated to 'the greatest happiness of the greatest number'.

Ideas

Many of Bentham's writings relate to the reform of the law and the pursuit of rational constitutionalism. As a student at Oxford, he had attended the lectures of Sir William Blackstone (q.v.), later published as *Commentaries on the Laws of England* (1765–69). Bentham's *A Fragment on Government*, published anonymously in 1776, was the first major work of English utilitarianism (q.v.). Its basic purpose was to attack Blackstone's *Commentaries* for their 'antipathy to reformation'. Bentham believed that every law and institution should be judged according to its utility and swept away if it failed the test. In his opinion there was nothing to worry about in the free censure of institutions: 'a system that is never to be censured, will never be improved'.

Bentham denounced obsolete and effete institutions. He derided the mysticism and corruption of the House of Lords as a sectional interest opposed to that of society as a whole, and believed that privilege was only justified if it made itself useful. He also rejected monarchy and religion. He complained that undue religious influence was exerted on children at school. Bentham opposed the Church of England because of its powerful social role and coupled his hatred of priests with that of lawyers, but saw both as only tools of the monarchy.

These were all what he called 'sinister interests', which gave their selfish concerns priority over the general good.

Whereas Blackstone had defended precedent, Bentham was generally indifferent to history. He was uninterested in how governments had originated; the important point was how well they operated. Consequently, obedience to government should not be based upon a supposed contract in the past, upon consent that *had* been granted, but solely upon current utility and self-interest.

Bentham was more concerned with reform of the law and administration than of society as a whole. He complained that lawyers' fees deprived ninety per cent of the population of any hope of justice. He wanted the judiciary reorganised so as to make it more intelligible to ordinary people. He also wanted the state to provide a system of public instruction, believing that ignorance was one of the major causes of crime.

Bentham's *An Introduction to the Principles of Morals and Legislation* was published in 1789. Its famous first sentence declares that 'nature has placed mankind under the governance of two sovereign masters, *pain* and *pleasure*'. We seek one and despise the other. The pursuit of happiness is Bentham's first principle. Individuals decide for themselves exactly what brings them happiness or pleasure. For Bentham, happiness was the core concept of moral philosophy and he hoped to produce a science of morality. For this the component parts had to be measurable. He had a passion for quantification and produced his 'felicific calculus' for the measurement of happiness. It was given seven dimensions: intensity, duration, certainty or uncertainty, nearness or remoteness, fecundity, purity, and extent. People should add up the pleasures on one side and pains on the other to ascertain whether any

particular action would be beneficial. In a strict sense this is an unattainable objective, but the point for Bentham was that rational behaviour is calculated behaviour; he objected to impulsive or habitual behaviour, to all actions not subjected to the test of whether they would maximise happiness. Bentham did not really expect that people would continuously act in this calculated way, but thought that the arithmetical balance could 'always be kept in view'. What was important was that governments should apply the utilitarian arithmetic, for their decisions were the most consequential. Bentham saw government as a kind of 'super-accountant'. It had the function of teaching people how to maximise happiness by imposing sanctions on actions that increased pain.

One consequence of Bentham's legal training was that he thought a lot about punishment. He designed a 'panopticon', a model prison in which prisoners would be productive and could all be seen from a central point. Bentham thought this would both solve a social problem and make a profit. He spent a lot of time and money on this scheme, which was never fully put into operation, although Wandsworth prison was built in 1851 (nineteen years after his death) to his design.

Bentham took it as an aspect of human nature that individuals primarily pursue their own happiness. So, whatever people might think, whatever the nature of their self-consciousness, they are utilitarians. What, then, was the point of telling them to act in a way they already do? Bentham's answer was that the utilitarian endeavour was one of what is now called 'consciousness-raising'. If people were made aware of their true motives, then they would be able to pursue them more effectively. As a scientist Bentham tells people what they are like, but there was more to it than that.

Utilitarianism is presented as both a science and an ethic: what people are like is what they should be like. They both do and should pursue their own happiness.

Seeing that both then and now there have been people unconvinced by this doctrine, what can Bentham say to them? It seems that he regarded them as reasoning falsely. To those who reject utilitarianism and declare duty as a basic motive, Bentham retorts that clearly it is duty that makes you happy, so his theory is confirmed rather than refuted. He believed you could not consistently reject utilitarianism as it could only be opposed in Utilitarian terms. Bentham decided that opponents of his theory were of two types. The first were supporters of the principle of asceticism; as examples, Bentham mentioned 'the Spartan regimen ... and the societies of the Quakers, Dumplers, Moravians'. Such people believe that avoiding pleasure is the best thing to do. Bentham peremptorily dismissed them as having made a false deduction from actions in the world. The second group of opponents were supporters of the principle of sympathy and antipathy. These people punish as they hate. Their approach is based on mood rather than rationality (q.v.); it is subjective rather than scientific.

Like Robert Owen (q.v.), at about the same time, Bentham originally hoped that the intrinsic rationality of his ideas would produce immediate support from Parliament. Both men were to be disappointed. Having originally favoured 'enlightened despotism', Bentham eventually realised that corrupt governments would not reform themselves. Partially under the influence of James Mill (q.v.) he became more of a democrat. In his *Plan of Parliamentary Reform* (1817), he advocated the secret ballot, annual parliaments and universal male suffrage – challenging suggestions for the time. One year later similar proposals were turned down in Parliament by 108 votes to nil. It might seem that at the age of sixty-nine, Bentham had reached his most radical position; but he, however, thought that he had been radical all along.

In the late 1770s, Solicitor-General Alexander Wedderburn said of utilitarianism: 'This principle is a dangerous one.' Bentham accepted the charge and launched a counter-attack: 'Dangerous it unquestionably is, to every government which has for its *actual* end or object, the greatest happiness of a certain *one*.' He then turned to the wider legal profession: 'Dangerous it therefore really was, to the interest – the sinister interest – of all those functionaries, himself included, whose interest it was, to maximise delay, vexation, and expense, in judicial and other modes of procedure, for the sake of the profit, extractable out of the expense.'

In the period of the Napoleonic Wars and for some years thereafter British radicalism (q.v.) was continually under suspicion of kinship with Jacobinism. Bentham, however, was no advocate of 'the rights of man'; he famously attacked natural rights as 'nonsense on stilts'. He propounded an alternative liberalism to the one that had caused such havoc in France, a factor that fortuitously became favourable to its acceptance in England. Bentham's greatest influence was on such nineteenth-century politicians and reformers as Edwin Chadwick, Francis Place, Lord Brougham and Sir Robert Peel. Also, partially through the influence of his friend James Mill and of John Stuart Mill (q.v.), he had a significant effect on British policy in India. Bentham also drew up the charter for a British colony in south Australia. From various other countries Bentham's advice was sought, especially from South America when, following independence from Spain, new constitutions were being written in Argentina,

Chile, Colombia and Mexico. Bentham's influence on practical men is countered by scathing derision from writers as various as Carlyle, Marx, Nietzsche and Dostoevsky.

In a celebrated account of nineteenth-century thought, A. V. Dicey (q.v.) described Benthamism as 'fundamentally a middle-class creed', which had been at the height of its influence between 1825 and 1870, when the middle class was dominant in Parliament. Since then its appeal had extended in a way that Bentham never intended. There were, said Dicey, unintended consequences of the greatest happiness principle. The greatest number in the society were the working class, so the theory provided a justification for rule which favoured them rather than the middle class to which most Benthamites belonged. 'Benthamism', Dicey complained, 'had forged the arms most needed by socialists.'

Key works

- *A Fragment on Government* (1776)
- *The Principles of Morals and Legislation* (1789)
- *The Theory of Legislation* (1802)
- *Plan of Parliamentary Reform* (1817)

Further reading

- A. V. Dicey, *Law and Public Opinion in England during the Nineteenth Century* (Macmillan, 1963; first published 1905)
- E. Halévy, *The Growth of Philosophic Radicalism* (Faber & Faber, 1952)
- R. Harrison, *Bentham* (Routledge & Kegan Paul, 1983)
- F. Rosen, *Jeremy Bentham and Representative Democracy* (Oxford University Press, 1983)
- E. Stokes, *The English Utilitarians and India* (Oxford University Press, 1959)

Michael Levin

Sir Isaiah Berlin   1909–97

One of the most influential liberal thinkers of the twentieth century; a political philosopher and historian of ideas, he is best known for his defence of 'negative' liberty and critique of 'positive' liberty, and for his idea of 'value pluralism'. He also made important contributions in several other fields, including nineteenth-century Russian thought, 'Counter-Enlightenment' writers such as Vico and Herder, the nature of historical explanation, and the resilience of nationalism.

Key ideas

- Negative liberty is less dangerous, politically, than positive liberty.
- Fundamental human values are irreducibly plural, often conflicting, and sometimes incommensurable.
- This plurality of values gives rise to hard choices, rules out the possibility of a single, perfect form of society, and suggests a commitment to liberalism.
- Understanding human conduct is not possible from a wholly scientific, 'external' point of view, but requires an 'inside view' from the perspective of the actor.
- The search for belonging, especially national belonging, is an important element of human nature.

Biography

Berlin came from a middle-class Russian-Jewish background. He was born on 6 June 1909 in Riga, in what is now Latvia but was then part of the Russian Empire; his father was a successful timber merchant. After moving to Petrograd, the Berlins were caught up in the revolutions of 1917. Isaiah was seven when he saw a Tsarist policeman being dragged away by a crowd, apparently to his death – an image that remained with him for the rest of his life, crystallising his abiding fear of revolutionary violence and of political extremism in general.

The family left Russia, settling in England in 1921. Berlin was educated at St Paul's School in London, before winning a scholarship to Oxford in 1928. As a philosopher, he was initially drawn to the vigorous empiricism of the logical positivists, led by A. J. Ayer, but became frustrated by their abstract and ahistorical approach to philosophy, and increasingly attracted to the historically and socially richer fields of the history of ideas and political theory. Researching his first book, *Karl Marx* (first edition 1939), he began to read the eighteenth- and nineteenth-century thinkers who preoccupied him later.

During the Second World War Berlin served as a British official, first at the Ministry of Information in New York, and then at the embassy in Washington. In 1945 he was briefly transferred to the Soviet Union, where he came into contact with dissident Russian writers, most notably Boris Pasternak and Anna Akhmatova. These meetings brought home to him the plight of the creative individual under Soviet communism, and sharpened his sense of his own Russian heritage.

After the war Berlin returned to Oxford, but soon acquired a more public profile as a leading commentator on the intellectual dimensions of the developing Cold War. Throughout the early 1950s, he produced a steady stream of essays, lectures and radio broadcasts developing his central theme of the modern betrayal of freedom (q.v.). In 1957 he was knighted and appointed Chichele Professor of Social and Political Theory at Oxford, a post he held until 1967. His inaugural lecture in 1958 was the famous 'Two Concepts of Liberty', which remains his most influential piece and must be one of the most frequently cited works of twentieth-century political philosophy. By the time he retired he had become one of Britain's most prominent public intellectuals

and a figure of international significance. He died in Oxford on 5 November 1997.

Ideas

Berlin's work covers a great range, but its dominant focus is a defence of liberal values against those currents of thought that had resulted in twentieth-century totalitarianism. His characteristic method is not the conventional analytical technique of constructing arguments and counter-arguments, but a historical approach that traces ideas to their origins in the work of key thinkers, whose personalities are shown to be as important as their logic. Berlin's speciality is to step into the mental world of the thinker he is examining and present that world for readers to make their own judgement. This 'inside view' is in keeping with his general approach to the explanation of human conduct, which opposes coolly objective, impersonal methods based on the natural sciences (as championed, for example, by the logical positivists) in favour of an emphasis on the purposes, values and worldviews of the actors themselves.

In this way, Berlin finds the roots of modern totalitarianism at three principal levels in the history of Western ideas. The first is what he calls 'the betrayal of freedom'. This is the idea not of a simple rejection of liberty but of a systematic distortion of what freedom truly is. According to Berlin, the fundamental sense of liberty is 'negative': the absence of coercive interference. This he contrasts with 'positive' liberty, the freedom of self-mastery, where a person is ruled not by arbitrary desires but by the 'true' or authentic self. While both negative and positive ideas represent genuine and important aspects of liberty, the positive idea leaves open the possibility that a person's authentic wishes may be identified with the commands of some external authority – for example, the state or the party. Freedom can then be defined as obedience, and in effect twisted into its opposite. Berlin associates this kind of thinking with writers such as Rousseau, Fichte, Hegel (q.v.) and Marx. He does not reject positive liberty entirely, but sees negative liberty as the safer option politically.

At a second level, totalitarianism is traced by Berlin to the complex relationship between the Enlightenment on one side and the 'Counter-Enlightenment' and romanticism on the other. Romanticism, with its stress on uniqueness and the will (both individual and collective), is the matrix of modern nationalism and of the irrationalism with which it combined in twentieth-century fascism. On the other hand, romanticism and nationalism express more fully than the Enlightenment the desire for cultural belonging that is, Berlin stresses, an essential component of human nature – in this respect his identity as a member of the Jewish diaspora is especially significant. Berlin's acceptance of the resilience, indeed the value, of nationalism sets him apart somewhat from the more cosmopolitan stream of liberal thought, and makes him an important influence on the school of 'liberal nationalism'. Further, he sees Counter-Enlightenment thinkers like Vico, Herder and Hamann as rightly emphasising the cultural and historical aspects of social explanation – the inside view – against the impersonal scientism that he takes to be characteristic of the Enlightenment.

Indeed, the legacy of the Enlightenment is as mixed, according to Berlin, as that of the Counter-Enlightenment. As a liberal, he defends the faith of the French *philosophes* and their supporters in reason, personal liberty and toleration. But he also argues that certain strains of Enlightenment thought take the claims of reason and science to utopian extremes, playing a significant part in the genesis of the totalitarianism of the left, which is Berlin's principal target. Berlin disagrees with those who would attribute Stalinism simply to the personality of the dictator or to the political extremism of the nineteenth-century Russian intelligentsia – Herzen and Turgenev, he points out, were progressive thinkers but also strong critics of revolutionary ruthlessness. Rather, Soviet communism can be traced back, through Marx, to the hyper-optimistic scientism of well-meaning eighteenth-century philosophers like Helvétius, Holbach and Condorcet (q.v.).

The third level of Berlin's analysis, the opposition between monist and pluralist conceptions of morality, is his deepest. The scientist, utopian side of the Enlightenment is really a modern instance of a more deep-seated tendency in Western thought as a whole, which is to suppose that all genuine moral values must somehow fit together into a single formula capable of yielding a correct answer to any moral problem. This is moral 'monism'. Its political implication is utopian: that the true moral system, once known, will make possible a perfect society in which there will be universal agreement on a single way of life. Such a view, Berlin protests, is dangerous. To suppose that moral and political perfection is possible is to invite its realisation by any means at whatever cost.

Moreover, moral monism is false to human experience, which teaches that we are frequently faced with choices among competing goods, choices to which no clear answers are forthcoming from simple rules. The truer and safer view of the deep nature of morality is 'value pluralism'. There are many human values, we can know objectively what these are, and some of them are universal – such as liberty and equality (q.v.). But values are sometimes 'incommensurable': they are so distinct that each has its own character and force, untranslatable into the terms of any other. When they come into conflict, the choices between them will be difficult, in part because in choosing one good we necessarily forgo another, and also because we will not be able to apply any simple rule that reduces the rival goods to a common denominator or that arranges them in a single hierarchy that applies in all cases.

Berlin finds hints of value pluralism in many sources – Machiavelli, Montesquieu (q.v.), Vico, Herder, Hamann, Herzen, Turgenev, for example – but his explicit formulation of the idea as a central theme of a whole political outlook is highly original. The political system that fits best with pluralism, according to Berlin, is liberalism. The inescapability of choice in human experience, he maintains, implies an argument for freedom of choice. Also, the anti-utopian aspect of pluralism suggests a case for liberalism as a realistic, humane form of politics that seeks to contain and manage conflict rather than to transcend it.

In recent years this liberal reading of value pluralism has been disputed by writers like John Gray (q.v.), who argue that if pluralism is true then liberalism itself is no more than one political option among others with no valid claim to universal superiority. But Berlin's link between pluralism and liberal universalism also has its defenders, and they have restated, revised and added to his arguments.

Key works
- *Karl Marx: His Life and Environment* (1939; 4th edn., 1978)
- *Russian Thinkers*, ed. Henry Hardy and Aileen Kelly (Hogarth, 1978)
- *Against the Current: Essays in the History of Ideas*, ed. Henry Hardy (Hogarth, 1979)

- *The Crooked Timber of Humanity: Chapters in the History of Ideas*, ed. Henry Hardy (John Murray, 1990)
- *The Power of Ideas*, ed. Henry Hardy (Chatto & Windus, 2000)
- *Three Critics of the Enlightenment: Vico, Hamann, Herder*, ed. Henry Hardy (Pimlico, 2000) [supersedes *Vico and Herder* (1976) and *The Magus of the North* (1993)]
- *Freedom and its Betrayal: Six Enemies of Human Liberty*, ed. Henry Hardy (Chatto & Windus, 2002)
- *Liberty*, ed. Henry Hardy (Oxford University Press, 2002) [supersedes *Four Essays on Liberty* (1969)]

Further reading
- Joshua Cherniss and Henry Hardy, 'Berlin, Isaiah', *Stanford Encyclopedia of Philosophy*
- George Crowder, *Isaiah Berlin: Liberty and Pluralism* (Polity, 2004)
- John Gray, *Isaiah Berlin* (HarperCollins, 1995)
- Michael Ignatieff, *Isaiah Berlin: A Life* (Chatto & Windus, 1998)

George Crowder

William Beveridge   1879–1963

Journalist, senior civil servant and academic, best known for writing the war-time report on Social Insurance and Allied Services (the Beveridge Report). He was also, very briefly, a Liberal MP (1944–45) and in 1946 entered the House of Lords as a Liberal peer.

Key ideas
- Social problems should be studied with the same rigour as natural phenomena.
- Voluntary action should be encouraged and supported, as it plays a vital role in a free society.

- Government has the responsibility and the means to achieve and maintain full employment.
- Modern governments have the ability to defeat the greatest social evils: want, disease, ignorance, squalor and idleness.
- A shared commitment to social welfare can be reconciled with personal freedom and the operation of a market economy.
- Intelligent and well-informed public officials – aided by experts – can be of great service to society.

Biography

William Henry Beveridge was born in Bengal, India on 5 March 1879; his father was a judge in the Indian civil service. He was sent to school in England, aged five, an experience said to have scarred him psychologically. He studied at Charterhouse and Balliol College, Oxford.

His family expected him to pursue a career in the law but he became deeply interested in social reform. Although his involvement in the university settlement movement was described as 'sentimental philanthropy' by his father, parental disapproval did not deter him from the role of sub-warden at Tonybee Hall in London's East End. The experiences and contacts that he made there opened many doors; he was employed as a leader-writer by the *Morning Post* and aired his views on social questions. In 1908 Churchill personally recruited him as a civil servant to work on proposals that Beveridge had been developing since he began work at Toynbee Hall in 1903.

Beveridge's most important ideas for social and economic reform concerned the labour market and social insurance. Aged just twenty-nine, he was presented with an extraordinary opportunity. Churchill, one of the most energetic ministers in the radical Liberal administration, made him a non-established civil servant and gave him the lead in setting up a national system of labour exchanges, the very thing Beveridge had called for as a leader-writer. He gained public recognition as an exponent of the case for reasoned and expert public policy-making. He seemed well placed to take on an overarching role in shaping government plans for social reform, but the Great War frustrated many of his policy ambitions – even as it furthered his career as a civil servant.

He was moved, first to work on munitions and later on food supply. He was knighted for his public service and, shortly after the war ended, appointed as a permanent secretary. Despite this his optimism about the benefits of intelligent interventionist government suffered a sharp decline, largely because of intense and often very personal conflicts with union leaders and others over the wartime emergency measures for which he was responsible. He acquired a reputation for bossiness that remained with him for the rest of his life. Intellectually he began to row away from New Liberal (q.v.) and Fabian notions supporting state action, and became increasingly sympathetic to laissez-faire economics (q.v.). It was time for a change of environment. An opportunity to leave the civil service and take the helm of the London School of Economics (LSE) proved irresistible.

In 1919 Beveridge became director of the LSE, then a small specialist institution which had been established by the Webbs in the 1890s, dedicated to the proposition that the social sciences could be developed to guide and inform public policy-making. For almost two decades, as director of the LSE, Beveridge's energy and ability to attract both money and scholars enabled it to expand and build an international reputation. However, his autocratic management style and preference for an uncompromisingly empiricist approach to social science did not endear him to his colleagues. Conflicts with senior members of the School's staff explain why there was general relief when he moved to University College, Oxford, in 1937.

As the international situation deteriorated and war between Britain and Germany appeared inevitable Beveridge lobbied hard, but unsuccessfully, to gain a place in government. He was adamant that his special talents should be put to good use. He wanted a leading role in government in order to mobilise economy and society for the struggle. A year after the outbreak of war he was invited to work with the Minister for Labour, Ernest Bevin. Bevin, a Labour heavyweight in every sense, had reservations about working with him, however, and Beveridge was offered what he regarded as a marginal appointment, the chairmanship of an interdepartmental inquiry into social insurance. He accepted the appointment with tears in his eyes, believing that it was designed to sideline him.

If that was the objective it failed spectacularly. The inquiry became a wide-ranging examination of British social policy, and the interdepartmental inquiry team a secretariat for what was in effect a one-man Royal Commission. The final report, *Social Insurance and Allied Services*, was published in December 1942 and outlined a vision of society's battle against 'the five giants': want, disease, ignorance, squalor and idleness. The report proposed a system of comprehensive social insurance delivered through cash benefits, financed by equal contributions from the worker (though Beveridge proposed that married women should be offered an opt-out), the employer and the state, together with a public assistance safety net.

The Beveridge Report met with a cool initial response from the government, but was immensely popular with the British public, and ministers soon found that control of the post-war reform agenda had been wrested from them as Beveridge skilfully popularised his proposals. After a major parliamentary revolt in early 1943, his plan was adopted as the blueprint for the Attlee government's legislation of 1945–48, laying the foundations of the British welfare state for the next forty years.

Beveridge insisted that his scheme needed to be complemented by a national health service available to all, tax-financed family allowances and a commitment to state action to reduce unemployment. These were further developed through his privately funded inquiry into full employment which resulted in 1944 in *Full Employment in a Free Society*. Cabinet papers show that the knowledge that the second report was in preparation added greatly to the urgency ministers felt to publish a White Paper of their own on post-war employment policy.

Beveridge championed an economic approach that he had come to believe was not only vital for social and economic stability but also entirely congruent with individual liberty. He relied, in doing so, on Keynesian (q.v.) ideas and insights presented to him by E. F. Schumacher (q.v.), Nicholas Kaldor and Joan Robinson, all members of the technical committee recruited to support the work of the second inquiry. *Full Employment in a Free Society* remains, as Beveridge undoubtedly intended it to be, one of the strongest statements ever made in support of the mixed economy.

Beveridge served briefly as a Liberal MP (August 1944 to July 1945) but lost his seat, Berwick-upon-Tweed, in the Labour landslide of 1945. In 1946 he entered the

House of Lords as Baron Beveridge of Tug-gal. He retired from public life in 1954.

Beveridge married Janet (Jessy) Mair, his cousin's widow, his secretary in the First World War and his personal assistant at the LSE, just weeks after the Beveridge Report appeared in 1942. An early and successful exponent of the art of spin, she played a leading role in promoting the Report. Jessy died in 1959, and Beveridge four years later, on 16 March 1963, at his home in Oxford.

Ideas

William Beveridge was a quite extraordi-nary combination of moralist and popu-list, public official and social scientist. His enthusiasm for social reform was fused with a commitment to practical action. His approach to both policy and politics places him squarely within a tradition of British empiricism, reflecting the legacy of cam-paigning reformers and public officials such as Edwin Chadwick, John Simon and Flor-ence Nightingale. Although he changed his views about the balance to be struck between the role of markets and govern-ment, he returned, in his work on the Bev-eridge Report and *Full Employment in a Free Society*, to the conviction that good govern-ment had a vital role to play in organising social and economic life. However, his commitment to public action should not be seen as unqualified; he was a determined advocate of both voluntary action and free markets.

The strength of Beveridge's belief in voluntary action can be illustrated in a number of ways. First, by his decision to go and work at Toynbee Hall as a young man; he did so at a time when many highly remunerative opportunities were open to him. Second, the book he wrote about the importance of *Voluntary Action* (1948): it offers a passionate defence of the role of the voluntary sector in the provision of social

welfare. He was known, at the time of its publication, to be angry at the Labour gov-ernment for excluding friendly societies from the new social insurance scheme.

Beveridge's shifting approach to tack-ling social problems, particularly the prob-lems of poverty and unemployment, went through three broad phases. His approach to unemployment serves as a particularly good illustration. Before the Great War he had come to the opinion that the case for far-reaching state involvement was unan-swerable: a free-enterprise economy would be greatly strengthened by interventionist public policies. His subsequent conversion to a laissez-faire approach, including his acceptance of the idea that 'wage rigidi-ties' played an important part in explain-ing unemployment, indicated just how far he shifted his ground. Nevertheless, in *Unemployment* (1930) he hinted at some of the intellectual difficulties created by his acceptance of laissez-faire (against a background of persistent high levels of unemployment). Having attached great importance to 'wage rigidity' and put his faith, for a time at least, in unregulated market adjustments, he began to retrace his steps. He slowly began to accept and adopt the case for counter-cyclical public expenditure and other public interventions to promote fuller employment.

During the 1920s and 1930s Beveridge had, as director of the LSE, found him-self at loggerheads with New Liberals on the School's staff, including L. T. Hob-house (q.v.). A number of his academic col-leagues did not share what they regarded as his naïve empiricism. Others, such as Lionel Robbins, urged Beveridge to put his weight behind attempts to make the social sciences more rigorous and scientific. Bev-eridge himself enthusiastically advocated a 'science of society'. He hoped and expected it would be possible for social scientists to follow in the footsteps of natural scientists. He was suspicious of social studies of a kind that were theoretical, deductive and metaphysical. His personal commitment to an empirical approach to economic and social questions was most clearly reflected in a study of prices he began in 1919. He believed it would be the crowning achievement of his academic career. He could not have been more mistaken. His *Full Employment in a Free Society* and the Beveridge Report itself have attracted vastly more interest than his scholarly investigation of price indices.

His independent study of the case for a full employment policy, meant to rival the government's White Paper on postwar employment policy, owed a great deal to Keynes (q.v.). Beveridge masterfully explored and popularised Keynes's economic theory and underscored its relevance by making a powerful moral and political argument for full employment. It remains the most striking statement of Beveridge's mature social liberalism (q.v.). It is, however, a work that places him at some distance from the opinions he had expressed just two decades earlier about the limitations of public policy in combating unemployment. His leading biographer, José Harris, has observed that: '[Beveridge] had [by the 1940s] reverted to his youthful belief that human institutions were "made by men and could be infinitely improved by them".'

Even when he was expressing scepticism about the ability of public policymakers to improve the economy or lessen unemployment Beveridge remained sanguine about the impact that the best minds could have on society. He told an audience at the LSE in 1934 that he put his faith in 'social doctors' rather than in dictators or parliamentary democracy. The best kinds of professional administrators were the ones

who could 'adjust the economic and social relations of [their] clients so as to produce the maximum economic health'.

Beveridge seems in some ways to have been a man out of time. He was the most notable twentieth-century exponent of a utilitarian (q.v.) liberalism rather than, as some have suggested, an unreliable supporter of late Victorian and Edwardian New Liberalism. When he was convinced of the correctness of his own case, he followed the advice he offered himself in a marginal note to one of the working papers for the Beveridge Report: 'action now not research'. Years later, when speaking in the House of Lords, he said he was 'still radical and still young enough to believe that mountains [could] be moved'.

Key works

- *Unemployment: a Problem of Industry* (1909 and 1930)
- *Planning under Socialism and Other Essays* (1936)
- *Social Insurance and Allied Services* (1942)
- *Full Employment in a Free Society* (1944 and 1960)
- *Why I am a Liberal* (1945)
- *Voluntary Action: A Report on Methods of Social Advance* (1948)

Further reading

- William Beveridge, *Power and Influence* (Hodder and Soughton, 1953)
- José Harris, *William Beveridge: A Biography* (Oxford University Press, 1977)

Ed Randall

Sir William Blackstone   1723–80

The most important British legal writer of the eighteenth century, his works summarised and reinterpreted the English common law tradition. By stressing personal liberty as one of the key elements of common law he not only influenced legal thought in England, but also inspired many of the American founding fathers.

Key ideas

- English law is equal if not superior to Roman law.
- Liberty as an absolute right is the core of English law.
- Catholicism may endanger English liberties.

Biography

Born on 10 July 1723, in London, in the family of a silk merchant, Blackstone was educated at Oxford, where he became a fellow of All Souls College in 1743. In 1746 he started practising law as a barrister, but returned to Oxford in 1758 to take up a professorship. He successfully ran for Parliament in 1761, and later became solicitor to the Queen and judge at the Court of Common Pleas. His fame, however, rests on his writings, especially his *Commentaries on the Laws of England* (1765–69), which became a bestseller (earning the huge sum of £14,000) and one of the classics of English legal thought. Blackstone died on 14 February 1780 in Wallingford, near Oxford.

Ideas

Blackstone never claimed to be an innovative thinker, who came up with grand new ideas on the nature of law. His chief work, the *Commentaries on the Laws of England*, rather, systematised a body of legal thought and practice that was known as the common law. Although there had been other intellectual standard-bearers of the common law tradition (Edward Coke (q.v.) being the most notable), it was Blackstone's systematic approach and his professorial prestige that made it academically acceptable. Until

his work only the more strictly codified Roman law was taught at English universities. He effectively combined the common law tradition with an enlightened Newtonian optimism that was fashionable in these days, arguing that English law and the traditional rights of an Englishman had stood the test of history and were, in many ways, as infallible as the laws of nature.

The *Commentaries* appeared in four volumes, each dedicated to one grand theme. It began appropriately with *The Rights of Persons*, where Blackstone not only explained the British governmental and legal system, but also established individual rights as the basis of English law:

> The absolute rights of man, considered as a free agent, endowed with discernment to know good from evil, and with power of choosing those measures which appear to him to be most desirable, are usually summed up on one general appellation, and denominated the natural liberty of mankind. This natural liberty consists properly in a power of acting as one thinks fit, without any restraint or control, unless by the law of nature: being a right inherent in us by birth, and one of the gifts of God to man at his creation, when he endued him with the faculty of freewill.

In *The Right of Things* (Book II) he supplemented this plea for personal freedoms with a defence of property rights, and in *Private Wrongs* (Book III) with a survey of tort laws. Finally in *Public Wrongs* (Book IV) Blackstone dealt with aspects of crime and punishment. Here his commitment to personal freedom (q.v.) sometimes wavered, especially in his attitude towards Catholicism. Believing that Catholics were more loyal to the Pope than to the British monarchy, he staunchly justified the laws that restricted their civil rights.

Blackstone's complacent optimism about the perfection of the existing laws sometimes aroused the ire of radical reformers, who would maintain that the legal system of England was far from perfect and that there was a need for improvement. Jeremy Bentham (q.v.) in his *Fragment on Government* (1776) fiercely attacked Blackstone's views as a mere vindication of the status quo. Liberal and radical reformers, on the other hand, were often inspired by Blackstone's commitment to absolute personal rights as the core of the English legal tradition. Hence in America Blackstone's *Commentaries* were frequently quoted by the signers of the Declaration of Independence of 1776 and by the architects of the constitution during its ratification process in 1787/88 – both by opponents (e.g. Patrick Henry) and advocates (e.g. Alexander Hamilton) of ratification. Throughout the nineteenth century the *Commentaries* remained a prime source for constitutional lawyers in England and America.

Key works

- *Commentaries on the Laws of England* (1765–69)
- *The Great Charter and Charter of the Forest* (1759).

Further reading

- Albert W. Alschuler, 'Rediscovering Blackstone (William Blackstone's *Commentaries*)', *University of Pennsylvania Law Review* (11/1/1996)
- David A. Lockmiller, *Sir William Blackstone* (University of North Carolina Press, 1938)

Detmar Doering

Barbara Bodichon   1827–91

One of the founders of the British women's rights movement, she established the Langham Place Group, and was a prolific writer

and editor of the first British political magazine for women, *The Englishwoman's Review*. Bodichon contributed much to the ideological underpinnings of the women's movement in the nineteenth century, and her Women and Work also established her reputation as one of the most significant female economic writers of her time.

Key ideas

- Women should enjoy the same legal status as men with respect to property and marriage.
- Women should possess the right to vote and the right to work.
- Women who work contribute to the wealth of all.

Biography

Barbara Leigh Smith Bodichon was born in Whatlington, near Battle, on 8 April 1827, the daughter of Benjamin Leigh Smith and Anne Longden; her father, a member of parliament, came from a well-known radical family. At the age of twenty-one Bodichon set up a non-denominational and coeducational school. From the 1850s onwards, however, she began to engage herself in politics. She campaigned for the removal of women's legal disabilities by writing articles and organising petitions, contributing to the passage of the Matrimonial Causes Act, which allowed divorce through courts. In 1857, shortly before her marriage to French radical Eugene Bodichon, Barbara published her best-known work, *Women and Work*, in which she demanded full access to the labour market for women.

A year later Bodichon began the publication of *The Englishwoman's Review*, the first British journal to devote itself to the cause of women's politics. In 1859, she started an office in Langham Place in London to help women find work. The office soon became the meeting place for a group of women intellectuals like Bessie Rayner Parkes and Emily Davies, later known as the 'Langham Place Group'.

One of the group's prime targets soon became women's right to vote. In 1866, Bodichon and her friends formed the first British Women's Suffrage Committee, which organised a petition on the right of women to vote, which attracted thousands of signatures. The petition was presented in the House of Commons by John Stuart Mill (q.v.), though the move was subsequently defeated, with even a majority of Liberals voting against it. Defiantly, Bodichon continued to write in favour of women's suffrage, but she also returned to her first theme, the improvement of education for women. Together with Emily Davies she helped in setting up Girton College, the first women's college in Cambridge, in 1873.

A stroke in 1877 left Bodichon paralysed and no longer able to play an active role in the women's rights movement that she had helped create. She died on 11 June 1891; in her will she left a substantial bequest to Girton College. Having also been a talented and renowned artist, most of this money derived from the sale of her paintings.

Ideas

Women's rights formed the central issue of Bodichon's writings. Her most mature and thorough-going statement on this topic can be found in her *Brief Summary, in Plain Language, of the Most Important Laws Concerning Women* (1854). In this pamphlet, Bodichon briefly explained the legal status of women in Britain and undertook a critique of the discrimination embodied in the laws relating to property and marriage. Married women, in particular, were deprived of all property rights and therefore fell under the complete legal control of their husbands. Divorce could only be obtained by an Act

of Parliament. The fact that women had no right to vote made things worse. The solution to these problems, Bodichon argued, was the abolition of all laws that discriminated against women. She maintained that the individualist and non-interventionist creed of liberalism had to be taken seriously and to be applied to women, not just to men.

Liberating women also meant that they had to be able to become economically independent – but the law restrained women from gaining access to paid work. In her best-known book, *Women and Work* (1857), Bodichon countered the Malthusian (q.v.) idea of over-production as the cause of unemployment that was commonly deployed to support barriers to employment for women; women, it was argued, would only take away jobs from poor working men. In an original adaptation of Say's Law – supply creates its own demand – Bodichon argued that the introduction of women to paid work would stimulate growth and create more employment opportunities for all. She proved that the argument for liberal free-market economics was, in fact, also one for the emancipation of women. Thus Bodichon provided the women's movement with an important argument within the liberal mainstream.

Bodichon had also noted earlier that even otherwise liberal economists such as John Stuart Mill (who later became a convert) in his *Principles of Political Economy* (1848) had quite consistently ignored the problems arising from the lack of economic rights for women. However, it is only recently that Bodichon's contributions to economics with respect to women's rights have been properly acknowledged. Her economic views were not one-sided and a strong moral and religious undertone can also be found in her book *Women and Work* (1857): 'No Human Being has the Right to be Idle ... Women must, as children of God, be trained to do some work in the world.' Work, she argued, was not only a necessary precondition for economic independence but was also necessary for personal development: 'women want work for both the health of their minds and bodies', she wrote. Thus, most of her articles in *The Englishwoman's Review* were dedicated to the improvement of women's chances to gain access to work and vocational training.

Key works
- *A Brief Summary, in Plain Language, of the Most Important Laws Concerning Women* (1854)
- *Women and Work* (1857)
- *The Englishwoman's Review* (ed.) (1858ff)

Further reading
- Pam Hirsch, *Barbara Leigh Smith Bodichon 1827–1891: Feminist, Artist and Rebel: A Biography* (Chatto & Windus, 1998)
- Candida Lacey (ed.), *Barbara Leigh Smith Bodichon and the Langham Place Group* (Women's Source Library; Routledge, 1987)
- William D. Sockwell, 'Barbara Bodichon and the Women of Langham Place', in Dimand, Dimand and Forget, *Women of Value: Feminist Essays on the History of Women in Economics* (Edward Elgar, 1996)

Detmar Doering

Bernard Bosanquet 1848–1923
Helen Dendy Bosanquet 1860–1925

Bernard Bosanquet's idealist philosophy reconceptualised the orthodox liberal understanding of the relationship between individuals and the state by regarding society as a moral organism with a 'general will', which gave legitimacy to government action. The prominent place his analysis accorded to charitable action complemented his wife Helen's interests in the work of the Charity Organisation Society and the development of social work.

Key ideas
- Society as a moral organism composed of 'ethical individuals'.
- Liberty as essential for the development of 'citizen character' and social progress.
- The state as reflecting a society's 'general will' and as seeking the 'common good'.
- Enhancing 'responsible citizenship' as a fundamental philosophical principle of charitable rather than state action, and the development of related practical guidance for 'social work'.

Biography
Bernard Bosanquet was born on 14 June 1848 at Rock Hall, near Alnwick, Northumberland, the youngest son of a clergyman. He was educated at Harrow from 1862 and then at Balliol College, Oxford, where the teaching and practical social commitment of Thomas Hill Green (q.v.) were significant influences. Bosanquet remained at Oxford as a fellow of University College until 1881, but then gave up teaching the history of philosophy in favour of writing. Once in London, and with the Charity Organisation Society (COS), administration rather than practical work with poor people became Bosanquet's main focus. He also undertook university extension teaching, lecturing at Toynbee Hall, and was involved in the London Ethical Society. His philosophical publications appeared from the early 1880s, initially in the new specialist periodical *Mind*.

Helen Bosanquet (née Dendy) was born on 10 February 1860 in Manchester, to a nonconformist family. She was educated first at home, and then at Newnham College, Cambridge, where, in 1889, she was awarded first-class honours in the moral sciences tripos. As no permanent post in academic life appeared available, she followed her sister Mary's example and took up social work in London with the COS. She became district secretary in Shoreditch, and her intellectual abilities, allied to her social work, won her notice in leading COS circles. She also attended the sessions of the London Ethical Society, where she met Bernard Bosanquet in 1891. He encouraged her in university extension lecturing, arranged for her to translate from German Sigwart's *Logik*, and wooed her into contributing seven articles on social conditions and charity to *Aspects of the Social Problem* (1895), of which he was editor. They married on 13 December 1891.

Between 1894 and 1898 Bernard was president of the Aristotelian Society. From 1903 to 1907 he returned to academic life as Professor of Moral Philosophy at St Andrews, though the couple retained their Oxshott house. His final academic appointment was as Gifford Lecturer at the University of Edinburgh in 1911–12. Following a period as vice-chairman, he was chairman of the Council of the COS from 1916 to 1917.

Helen continued to support the COS through her own writing, including *The Strength of the People* (1902) and *The Family* (1906). She also collaborated with her husband, and translated German philosophy. In 1905 she was appointed to the Royal Commission on the Poor Laws, and drafted the largest share of the eventual majority report. She edited the *Charity Organisation Review* from 1909 to 1921.

Bernard Bosanquet died on 8 February 1923, Helen on 7 April 1925. They had no children.

Ideas

Bernard Bosanquet contributed substantially to the British 'school' of idealist philosophy. Plato, Rousseau, Hegel (q.v.) and Kant (q.v.), and his own contemporaries, especially T. H. Green and F. H. Bradley, were his inspiration; Bentham (q.v.), Mill (q.v.) and Spencer (q.v.) his targets for criticism.

A key component of his idealist thought on social life was that a community or a society was a moral or spiritual organism, a unity and a whole. Reason and morality, and therefore meaning and purpose, were distinctively shared human characteristics The individual could not be contrasted with society or the state in the 'atomistic' way that, it was argued, Spencer assumed: a person was an 'ethical' individual embedded in social and moral relations with others, which brought mutual responsibilities. Beings aware of this possessed a will that reflected their sociality, and a society of such beings, for Bosanquet (taking a lead from Rousseau), possessed a 'general will'. This general will also embodies what is the 'common good'.

The state has legitimate authority and acts morally provided it reflects these ideas. 'Civilised society', he wrote in 1895, has the right and duty to act through the state 'with a view to the fullest development of the life of its members', but responsibility for one's own and one's family's existence should be left 'to the uttermost extent possible' with that individual and family. To act otherwise 'is an abuse fatal of character and ultimately destructive of social life'. The state's place is to restrain hindrances to personal and social development: it cannot make people moral, though it can engender a sense of dependence.

'Character' was important. Rich and poor could have flawed 'characters', though poor people received most attention from both Bernard and Helen. Careful and well-informed charitable (or 'social') work, involving personal and befriending contact, could nurture a sense of responsibility and of fulfilment through understanding the obligations of citizenship. Charitable activity thus enhanced the 'character' of both giver and receiver and was a powerful engine of social improvement. This was the philosophical basis that the Bosanquets offered the Charity Organisation Society, and it underpinned the strong emphasis placed on the front-line role for voluntary organisations in alleviating destitution in the Poor Law Commission majority report of 1909. In such circumstances Bernard had pointed to a 'defect in the citizen character', not necessarily as a cause of destitution but as a feature in an individual's response to a predicament – the 'moral' of the family and the 'whole' person required consideration.

The Webbs and the Bosanquets disagreed over their vision of the 'common good' and how to secure it, but they shared the idealist characteristic of a commitment to the direct attainability of such a goal. Others who owed debts to idealist thought also criticised the Bosanquets: in 1896 J. A. Hobson (q.v.) maintained that economic reform must precede moral reform, and L. T. Hobhouse (q.v.) complained that their German Hegelianism left the authority of the state inadequately checked (a powerful theme in the context of the First World War).

The most systematic expression of Bernard Bosanquet's political thought was *The Philosophical Theory of the State* (1899), but he published widely and wrote on a broad range of topics related to idealism (q.v.) and understanding society. Thus he sought to accommodate Darwin's theory of natural selection within an idealist approach to social life. He also criticised economics and Spencerian sociology as 'materialist' in failing to acknowledge the morally interconnected nature of individuals in society.

It has been argued that the Bosanquets' idealist social thought in general rests on normative foundations and that an enduring impact of their thought is that social policy and the people it serves can be viewed as means to achieving directly the 'good society', thus constraining freedom of choice by constraining behaviour. There is currently a revival of interest in the Bosanquets and other idealists, and their impact on New Labour.

Key works
- Bernard Bosanquet (ed.), *Aspects of the Social Problem* (1895)
- Bernard Bosanquet, *The Philosophical Theory of the State* (1899)
- Helen Bosanquet, *The Family* (1906)

Further reading
- A. M. McBriar, *An Edwardian Mixed Doubles: The Bosanquets versus the Webbs* (Clarendon Press, 1987)
- James Meadowcroft, *Conceptualising the State: Innovation and Dispute in British Political Thought 1880–1914* (Clarendon Press, 1995)
- Peter P. Nicholson, *The Political Philosophy of the British Idealists* (Cambridge University Press, 1990)

John Offer

Charles Bradlaugh   1833–91

Liberal MP for Northampton 1880–91, an outspoken atheist and republican, a prominent radical journalist and a popular orator whose campaign to take his parliamentary seat after being disbarred because of his atheism lasted over five years and became one of the great democratic struggles of the nineteenth century.

Key ideas
- The law must safeguard the rights and liberties of the individual without prejudice.

- The individual is sovereign and may exercise freedom of thought, expression and action within the law.
- Democratic republicanism based on natural rights offers the best guarantee of individual liberty and justice.
- Economic freedom and minimal government interference provide the best conditions for political, economic and social liberty.
- Religion is a delusion, and atheistic materialism based on science provides the only valid basis for human conduct and understanding.

Biography

Born in Hoxton, London, on 26 September 1833 into a poor family, Bradlaugh received only an elementary education. He attended Sunday school until he developed heterodox ideas upon religion, leaving home in 1850 to lodge with Elizabeth Sharples, widow of the freethinking publisher Richard Carlile. Business failure then drove him into the army; he was posted to Ireland where he witnessed starvation and evictions. Returning to civilian life in 1853, he became a solicitor's clerk and in 1854 married Susannah Lamb Hooper.

Bradlaugh was emerging as an expert in the law and an able public speaker. In 1860 he became editor of a new radical paper, the *National Reformer*, with which his career was henceforth identified. He founded the National Secular Society in 1866 to unite popular freethought, agitated for an extension of the suffrage and helped draft the Fenian Manifesto. However, his personal finances were precarious and his home broke up, his alcoholic wife taking their three children to live with her parents.

Bradlaugh now devoted himself full time to public life. He unsuccessfully contested Northampton as an independent at the general elections of 1868 and January 1874 and in a by-election in August 1874. The National Secular Society had become moribund while Bradlaugh concentrated on the republican movement during the early 1870s but, helped by Charles Watts (secretary) and Annie Besant, he revived it in 1874. In 1877 he and Besant then controversially reissued an American birth-control work, Charles Knowlton's *The Fruits of Philosophy*, for which Watts had been prosecuted for obscenity. In the midst of a celebrated trial in which Bradlaugh focused on freedom of publication, Mrs Bradlaugh died. Bradlaugh and Besant were obviously close friends and publicly associated with birth control but their relationship was probably innocent.

The 1880 general election saw Bradlaugh adopted as an official Liberal candidate for Northampton where he was duly elected. An application to the Speaker to affirm instead of taking the oath was refused but then the House also refused him the oath, the opposition being orchestrated by Lord Randolph Churchill. Four times between 1880 and 1883 Bradlaugh spoke at the Bar of the House. He was imprisoned overnight in the Clock Tower on 23 June 1880 for refusing to withdraw, and was physically ejected from the House on 3 August 1881. Four times from 1881 to 1885 he was re-elected for Northampton. He behaved as an unsworn MP but this left him liable to crippling financial penalties against which he defended himself in a series of cases until 1883, when the House of Lords rejected the suit against him, with costs.

Following the general election of 1886, Bradlaugh was permitted the oath and became an unusually hard-working backbencher, opposing privilege, championing the underdog, and in 1888 securing an act to permit affirmations instead of oaths. He was recognised as the unofficial 'member for India', supporting native rights and self-government for India, which he visited in 1889. He died of Bright's disease on 30 January 1891.

Ideas

Politically Bradlaugh was a republican, advocating democracy and the rights of man: every citizen to have equal opportunity, right and duty under the law. He advocated the abolition of the monarchy on the death of Queen Victoria by repealing the Acts of Settlement, his justification being the history of the royal family since 1714 and the size of the Civil List. For Bradlaugh republicanism also meant a wholesale attack on privilege, the hereditary principle and the monopoly of landed wealth that underlay aristocratic political power. He proposed to weaken the House of Lords by restricting future creations to life peerages given for great national service, and excluding those hereditary peers who habitually failed to attend. He regarded government as a necessary evil and thought cheap, minimal government the best. Socialism was anathema to him, since it was identified with foreigners and violent revolution, it sapped individual initiative and it gave too much power to the state. On the other hand he supported the co-operative movement as homegrown, voluntaristic and liberal. Like J. S. Mill (q.v.), he opposed state intervention in matters of belief, favouring freedom of thought, expression and publication, secular education and a separation of church and state.

On religion, Bradlaugh went further than many secularists, arguing not merely for the secularisation of the law and morality, the abolition of compulsory oaths and all privileges enjoyed by religious bodies, but also against the very idea of God. Adopting the ideas of Spinoza (1632–77), he argued against the dualism of body and spirit and for a unified material view of the universe – what his German contemporary, Ernst Haeckel (1834–1919), called 'monism'. Mind was thus a function of the body and gods were mere fabrications of the human mind, whose alleged power was used to support unjust political and social systems and to persecute freethinking.

Bradlaugh's economic thought was libertarian (q.v.), free market and minimal state. Government's role was to ensure legal equality between employers and employees. In 1888 he opposed a bill to enforce an eight-hour day but supported the idea of conciliation councils in industry. He gave evidence to the Royal Commission on Market Rights and Tolls, which he saw as restrictive monopolies; and as a member of the Royal Commission on Vaccination in 1889 his sympathies were against compulsion. His thinking derived from the classical political economy of Malthus (q.v.) as modified by Mill, and he attributed poverty not to capitalism but to the number of children born to poor families due to their lack of knowledge of birth prevention; with fewer children in working-class families, the market would push wages up as well as limiting the essential outgoings of the poor. Persuaded that sexual abstinence was both impracticable and unnatural, he thus favoured making birth control knowledge available to the married poor as both a necessity and a right.

Key works

- *Jesus, Shelly and Malthus; or, Pious Poverty and Heterodox Happiness* (1861)
- *A Plea for Atheism* (1864)
- *The Land, the People and the Coming Struggle* (1871)
- *The Impeachment of the House of Brunswick* (1872)
- *Has, or Is, Man a Soul? Verbatim Report of a Two Nights' Public Debate at Burnley*

between the Rev. W. M. Westerby and Charles Bradlaugh (1879)

- *Will Socialism Benefit the English People? Verbatim Report of a Debate between H. M. Hyndman and Charles Bradlaugh* (1884)

Further reading

- W. L. Arnstein, *The Bradlaugh Case: A Study in Late Victorian Opinion and Politics* (Oxford University Press, 1965)
- Edward Royle, *Radicals, Secularists and Republicans: Popular Freethought in Britain, 1866–1915* (Manchester University Press, 1980)
- J. Saville (ed.), *A Selection of the Political Pamphlets of Charles Bradlaugh* (Augustus Kelley, 1970)
- David Tribe, *President Charles Bradlaugh, MP* (Elek Books, 1971)

Edward Royle

Sir Samuel Brittan   1933–

One of Britain's most distinguished economic journalists and commentators, whose many published works expound a combination of social and economic liberalism.

Key ideas

- Critique of the Keynesian orthodoxy in contemporary economic policy-making.
- Importance of political, economic and social liberty to a free society.
- Governments, even democratic ones, almost always get it wrong.
- Minor redistribution is permissible.
- The necessity for morality, but not moralising, in social and economic life.

Biography

Samuel Brittan was born, on 29 December 1933, to parents of Lithuanian Jewish extraction; his father was a general

practitioner and his brother is Leon (now Lord) Brittan, the former Conservative Cabinet minister and European Commissioner. He was educated at Kilburn Grammar School and Jesus College, Cambridge, where among his economics teachers were Peter Bauer and Milton Friedman (q.v.).

In 1961 he was appointed economics editor at the *Observer* and in 1965 worked as an adviser to Harold Wilson's Labour government at the newly established Department of Economic Affairs. In 1966 he joined the *Financial Times* where he has remained for most of his working life. He has also taught at universities in Britain and the US, notably Oxford and Chicago. He was knighted in 1993 for services to economic journalism.

Ideas

What is remarkable about Brittan is his incorporation of the general social sciences into his economics so that the whole corpus of his work represents something of which an orthodox university professor would be proud. It covers not just economics but political science, sociology and philosophy and displays a high level of scholarly rigour.

Brittan's early works, deriving from his close observations of government policy, were on macroeconomics, chronicling governments' largely unsuccessful attempts to 'manage' the economy following Keynesian (q.v.) methods. In the *Treasury under the Tories* (1964) and *Steering the Economy* (1971), these efforts are described in exquisite detail and despite his critique of the Treasury, under Labour and the Conservatives (this was the age of the 'consensus'), he still thought it an institution that did to an extent restrain the madness of politicians. But throughout the 1970s Brittan shifted subtly away from the orthodoxy, producing some radical ideas. As Britain's self-destructive agreement on the wrong policies reached its apogee under the 1970–74 Heath government, Brittan perceptively saw that the consensus was damaging the private economy. One example: convention held that there was a trade-off between inflation and unemployment so that government could choose an acceptable level of inflation to boost demand so as to reduce unemployment; this was called the 'Philips curve'. But, as Brittan learnt from Friedman, the Philips curve is ultimately vertical, so that repeated attempts to macromanage the economy produced inflation *and* unemployment. Brittan came round to the view that the private enterprise economy itself was self-correcting and did not need 'managing'.

Brittan's first comprehensive onslaught against the consensus came with the publication of *Capitalism and the Permissive Society* (1973). He had always been mildly pro-Labour and favoured the liberalisation of divorce, censorship and homosexuality that came in the 1960s. But he had also always thought that Labour was economically illiterate. The Tories might occasionally get the economics right but were always too authoritarian in regard to personal morality to appeal to him. In his book Brittan demonstrated the ultimate symmetry of economic and personal liberty. A belief in freedom (q.v.) must encompass the right to trade, to acquire property, to write without government restraint and to engage in unconventional sexual practices. This is not just a matter of verbal consistency, for Brittan has always believed that economic liberty is as important for self-development as all the liberties favoured by John Stuart Mill (q.v.). In this enterprise Brittan also resurrected a morally acceptable notion of self-interest, so often calumnied as 'greed'. This is consistent with a related theme, expressed in *Left or Right: The Bogus Dilemma* (1968), that political parties rarely

have neat consistent ideologies and an anti-conservative, like Brittan, must be critical of all unjustified restraints on personal freedom. Thus he is as censorious of Tory attacks on individual sexual freedom as he is of barriers to economic liberty.

In *Capitalism and the Permissive Society* Brittan first wrestled with the problem of the philosophical foundations of liberty and he considered utilitarianism (q.v.) along with the more strident libertarians' (q.v.) natural rights demonstration of the value of freedom. Here Brittan was very much influenced by Hayek's (q.v.) writings on liberty and the rule of law (q.v.). He agreed that socialism, and other forms of economic interventionism, tend to operate by arbitrary command; law ceases to be a protection for the citizen but becomes the oppressor itself. In sum, Brittan's complex defence of liberty is of a modest utilitarian type; and owes a lot more to economics than to Mill's defence of liberty.

Brittan over the years has been a believer in some redistribution. But it is emphatically not egalitarianism, the deadening effects of which on progress and freedom he has been anxious to expose. However, he has not been opposed to using the tax system to extend economic liberty to a wider part of the population. He has been a long-standing advocate of a guaranteed minimum income, displeasing some libertarians. However, there is another way of bringing about these ends. Brittan, in his journalism but not in his formal treatises, has occasionally referred to the advantages of a Henry George (q.v.)-type site value land tax. He has been distressed at the vast increase in wealth enjoyed by lucky owners of land whose property swells in value through the economic efforts of others. Administered properly, this could replace all the other taxes, with no adverse effects on productivity.

All the time, Brittan has maintained his pre-eminence as a pure economic commentator. But as he said, he ended up with 'egg on my face' over his support for the European Exchange Rate Mechanism, from which Britain was ejected in 1992. But even here, his most ignominious economic policy stance, his position was consistent with his earlier monetarism: the Tories had defeated inflation in the early 1980s only to see it return under Nigel Lawson, so why not have an external constraint on government's power over money? All his life Brittan has always been highly critical of politics and the attempts of government to manage the economy.

It was this scepticism about politics that led Brittan to American public choice theory. From people like James Buchanan (q.v.) and Gordon Tullock he learned that even under favourable circumstances democratic systems rarely produce the 'public good', whatever that means. Politicians and bureaucrats are as self-interested as any market trader, but operate without the constraints of the competitive market, and successful action in democratic politics depends on politicians constructing coalitions of interest groups who capture income created by the private sector. As he demonstrated, in his *The Economic Consequences of Democracy*, perhaps his most brilliant single essay, it had produced inflation, excess public spending, trade unions above the law and general economic malaise in Britain in the 1970s.

Key works
- *The Treasury under the Tories* (1964)
- *Left or Right: The Bogus Dilemma* (1968)
- *Steering the Economy: The Role of the Treasury* (1971)
- *Capitalism and the Permissive Society* (1973)

- 'The Economic Consequences of Democracy', *British Journal of Political Science* 5:2 (1975)
- *The Role and Limits of Government: Essays in Political Economy* (1984)
- *A Restatement of Economic Liberalism* (1988)
- *Against the Flow* (2005)

Norman Barry

James Bryce   1838–1922

Achieving distinction in five fields – as jurist, historian, politician, diplomat and traveller – Bryce's reputation might have been higher if his contribution had been more selective. Nevertheless, he held several Cabinet positions, including Chief Secretary for Ireland. His knowledge of world politics, derived from both study and observation, gave him a distinctive position both at home and abroad.

Key ideas
- Historian of the Holy Roman Empire (and thus of supranational authority).
- League of Nations advocate.
- (Ulster Presbyterian) supporter of home rule for Ireland.
- Foremost interpreter of American politics and society to the UK.

Biography
James Bryce was born in Belfast on 10 May 1838. His early years were divided between Ulster and Glasgow, where his father was rector of the high school. A Glasgow University graduate at nineteen, he then proceeded to Trinity College, Oxford where he gained firsts in Classical Moderations and Greats. He was elected to a fellowship at Oriel in 1862. He became president of the Union in 1863 and mingled in literary circles in the university. His *The Holy Roman Empire* (1864) – originally an Oxford prize

essay – was to go through many editions over subsequent decades. Called to the bar in 1867, he joined the northern circuit. His interest in secondary education began at this time, eventually leading to his chairing of the Royal Commission on the subject in 1894–96. He also started contributing to liberal periodicals on European politics and history and was active in the life of literary London. In 1870 he was appointed Regius Professor of Civil Law at Oxford, a position he held until 1893. A keen advocate of research, he was active in the movement for university reform. He married Elizabeth Ashton, daughter of a Manchester mill-owner, in 1889.

After playing a leading part in the Eastern Question agitation of 1876–78, Bryce entered the Commons as MP for Tower Hamlets in 1880, transferring to Aberdeen South in 1885. The following year he became the mouthpiece in the Commons of Rosebery, the Foreign Secretary. In 1892 he became Chancellor of the Duchy of Lancaster and two years later President of the Board of Trade. All the while, he travelled widely and published his impressions of countries he visited. He was a strenuous mountaineer and became, in 1876, the first European to climb Mount Ararat. During the Boer War he was critical of the government but not a 'pro-Boer'.

If global knowledge equipped a person to be Foreign Secretary, Campbell-Bannerman would have appointed him in 1905. Instead, he became Chief Secretary for Ireland. Although his Belfast childhood was by now far in the past, he had earlier canvassed support from Presbyterians, like himself, for home rule. In 1907, however, he was made ambassador to the United States, as it was thought that his understanding of the US would be invaluable in easing Anglo-American-Canadian relations. Moreover, as Lord Hardinge of the Foreign Office

remarked, Bryce's ability to make long and rather dull speeches would 'go down well with the American masses'. In this capacity he was able to bank on his status as author of *The American Commonwealth* (1888), the work that made his name. In due course it went into three editions and was still in print on his death. Its picture of a vibrant civil society – which derived from Bryce's vast network of academic and political contacts – presented an essentially optimistic view of American democracy. As usual, he continued to travel, to South America as well as to every state in the US.

He became president of the British Academy in 1913 – which body he had helped to found in 1902 – and accepted a peerage in 1914, becoming Viscount Bryce. His role (1914–15) as chairman of a committee to investigate German behaviour in occupied Belgium was controversial; critics thought that he had too easily given credence to stories which had not been sufficiently substantiated. He also chaired a joint conference of both houses on the future of the House of Lords. He continued to write on issues of international relations. Active to the last, he died on 22 January 1922.

Ideas

Bryce was not a speculative thinker. He was a relentless accumulator of knowledge, either at first hand or through massive correspondence. It would be unconvincing to suppose that he presented a comprehensive philosophy of liberalism. He rested on convictions, which stemmed from his own background and experiences.

Throughout his life he had a deep devotion to the benefits both for the individual and for society to be gained from secondary and higher education. His love of the open air (and of flora and fauna) made him an early and enthusiastic parliamentary supporter of 'access to the countryside'. While he had once seemed to be keen to advance women in public life, as in membership of the Royal Commission he chaired, he remained to the end opposed to female suffrage. Neither was he in sympathy with New Liberalism (q.v.) after 1906. His academic aura could easily be criticised; Arthur Balfour, for example, described him as a standing instance of the uselessness of 'the higher education'. His fact-filled mind made him a walking encyclopaedia, useful to colleagues for consultation but not for inspiration. Even so, however, his most important and to some extent most influential intellectual contribution is to be found in his prolonged reflection, as a liberal of his generation, on the relationship between nationalism and internationalism.

On the one hand, from his undergraduate days in Oxford to his reflections at the end of the First World War, he had shown active support for 'nations struggling to be free'. He might at one point even have joined Garibaldi in Italy. How, and with what consequences the Ottoman Empire would come to an end, was a deep interest over many decades. He was an ardent advocate for the Armenians and one of the founders of the Balkan Committee in 1902.

Liberals should support national freedom. On the other hand, nationalism could be nasty. The Balkan peoples seemed as anxious to fight each other as to unite to throw off the Ottoman yoke. While Bryce did not suppose that the Holy Roman Empire, the subject of his first book, could be resuscitated, it was an example of a kind of supra-nationality. In 1914 he had been shocked by German behaviour – having studied in Germany and greatly benefited from German legal and constitutional thinking. Unbridled nationalism was awful. It was right that Ireland should have home rule, but separation would be a retrograde step. His experience of South Africa and

Australia led him to recognise the reality of dominion nationalism but it would be folly if the British Empire were to dissolve entirely. He further thought that it might be possible for the United Kingdom and the United States to draw together again in some kind of loose political association. This simultaneous recognition of nationalism and search for its harmonious containment found its final expression in the work of the 'Bryce Committee' on a League of Nations. The League represented the climax of a lifetime's reflection on these matters; he did not live to see its failure.

Key works
- *The Holy Roman Empire* (1864)
- *The American Commonwealth* (1888)
- *Studies in History and Jurisprudence* (1901)
- *Essays and Addresses in War Time* (1918)
- *Modern Democracies* (1921)
- *International Relations* (1922)

Further reading
- Christopher Harvie, *The Lights of Liberalism: University Liberals and the Challenge of Democracy, 1860–1886* (Allen Lane, 1976)
- Hugh Tulloch, *James Bryce's* American Commonwealth (Royal Historical Society/Boydell Press, 1988)

Keith Robbins

James M. Buchanan   1919–

The founder of public choice theory, the academic school that applies economic principles and analysis to the study of government and politics. Public choice theory tends to lead to scepticism as to the ability of government to achieve its intended ends and thereby provides theoretical and empirical justification for the classical liberal principles of constitutionally limited government and free markets.

Key ideas

- Most scholars and government actors under-estimate the pervasiveness of government failure.
- Democratic governments are frequently captured by minorities, notably special interest groups, who use government as a means of achieving their own ends.
- There is no normative basis for privileging simple majority rule in democratic decision-making, but a strong normative case does exist for unanimous decision-making or qualified majority rule.
- Legislation should always be generally applicable – it should not discriminate against particular groups or categories of people.
- Democratic government must be constitutionally protected and constrained.

Biography

James McGill Buchanan was born on 3 October 1919, in rural Tennessee, to a family of relatively poor farmers, although his grandfather had been a one-term Governor of the state. With the exception of a period of military service in the Second World War – when by his own description he had an 'easy war', working at US fleet headquarters at Pearl Harbor and at Guam – Buchanan's biography is that of an extremely prolific academic; the list of his career publications collected in the final volume of his *Collected Works* runs to forty-five pages.

Buchanan took a PhD in economics at Chicago University, but he is most closely associated with Virginian institutions of higher education, having established the Center for the Study of Public Choice first at Virginia Tech University and then transferring it to George Mason University in Fairfax, West Virginia. Indeed, Buchanan's own brand of public choice (which has strong institutional and qualitative dimensions) is known as Virginian public choice,

in contrast to Chicagoan public choice (which is almost entirely quantitative).

Buchanan's achievement as the founder of public choice theory received the highest possible recognition when he was awarded the Nobel Prize in Economics in 1986. From 1999 to 2003 his *Collected Works* were published in twenty volumes by Liberty Fund of Indianapolis.

Ideas

Buchanan has defined public choice theory as 'the theory of government failure', in the same sense that neo-classical economics may be understood as 'the theory of market failure'. Like markets, governments never produce perfect outcomes. Yet in considering public policy proposals, politicians, civil servants and academics rarely consider the possibility of government failure: policy proposals tend to be evaluated in terms of whether the intended ends *should* be achieved rather than whether they *can* be achieved. Public choice theory has shown, however, that there are good reasons to believe government failure to be endemic, because, *inter alia*, public officials may act in their own self-interest rather than in the public interest, government actors may not possess the knowledge required to design successful policies and the vagaries of democratic decision-making may mean that flawed policies are chosen.

Probably the most important cause of government failure identified in the work of Buchanan and other public choice theorists is the ability of minorities to capture government and use it for their own ends. In Buchanan's most famous work, *The Calculus of Consent*, co-authored with Gordon Tullock and first published in 1962, formal models were constructed to show that an organised coalition of a quarter of the electorate is sufficient to control a bicameral legislature elected by simple majority voting and hence impose its will on the rest of the population.

The pressures on government to support special interests will almost always outweigh countervailing demands because of the distribution of the costs and benefits that arise from such subsidies. In the UK, for example, an annual subsidy of £30 million can be funded at a cost to each taxpayer of £1 per year, an extra burden that is unlikely to lead to mass demonstrations. Yet for those groups that are able to secure such subsidies the rewards are significant. Public choice theory predicts that political agitation for special privileges is likely to prove successful despite the burdens that such subsidies impose on the rest of the economy because of the way the costs and benefits tend to be distributed.

Buchanan's work contains a strong normative commitment to democracy, but it is nevertheless extremely critical of the privileging of simple majority rule in contemporary democratic polities. For Buchanan, there is no normative or logical reason why simple majority voting should have become the norm within democracies; it is a decision-making rule that incurs high decision-making costs and imposes high external costs (externalities) on those forced to act contrary to their own wishes. Buchanan has argued that a much stronger case can be made for privileging the rule of unanimity, the only decision-making rule that ensures that the external costs of decision-making are zero. In *The Calculus of Consent* Buchanan and Tullock argued that if a rational, utility-maximising individual were asked to devise a democratic constitution from scratch in ignorance of their own future interests they would select a constitution that enshrined unanimous decision-making, or at the very least some form of qualified majority voting, rather than simple majority rule.

Buchanan has proposed two principal escape routes from the public choice dilemmas that seem to bedevil democracy. First, the generality principle: all legislation should be generally applicable. That is, legislation must not discriminate against people on the basis of personal characteristics, such as sex, race, religion, age, income or wealth. This would mean that one group which controlled the legislature could not target legislation against another group, whether defined by race, income, wealth or some other characteristic. Second, democratic government must be set within clear constitutional boundaries that include a clear separation of powers, federalism and guaranteed periodic elections.

Buchanan's work, and public choice theory more generally, clearly sit within the Madisonian American federalist (q.v.) tradition. It has been hugely influential in academic political science and political theory; Rawls's (q.v.) *A Theory of Justice* is one notable work that bears the imprint of *The Calculus of Consent*. But public choice theory is probably not well known outside academia, despite the fact that it offers important insights to any liberal grappling with the complexities and ambiguities of democratic governance.

Key works

- *The Calculus of Consent* (with Gordon Tullock, 1962)
- *The Limits of Liberty* (1975)
- *Politics by Principle, Not Interest* (with R. D. Congleton, 1998)
- *Why I, Too, Am Not a Conservative* (2005)

John Meadowcroft

Edmund Burke   1730–97

One of the most distinguished parliamentarians and publicists of the eighteenth century,

Burke's importance to the history of political thought stems largely from his eloquent and reflective contributions to the major debates of his time. His most notable work took shape as responses to the outstanding events in British, imperial and international politics from the 1760s to the mid-1790s. He raised political discussion to a level of philosophical analysis scarcely rivalled since, advancing an understanding of the conditions which promote political liberty in modern societies and providing a complex defence of the value of liberty before liberalism as such emerged either as a doctrine or as a party creed.

Key ideas

• Liberty is conditioned by historical and political circumstances.
• Liberty requires the protection of authority.
• Political authority is moderated by trust.
• Trust is disabled under conditions of revolution.
• Politics are circumscribed by conquest and rebellion.

Biography

Edmund Burke was born in Dublin on 12 January 1730. He received his undergraduate education at Trinity College, Dublin, before moving to London to study for the bar at Middle Temple. By the mid-1750s he had resolved to thwart his father's expectations by staying in London to pursue a career in journalism and letters instead of becoming a barrister in Dublin. By 1765 Burke's ambitions had yet again been transformed: he entered political life as private secretary to the Marquis of Rockingham, securing a seat in Parliament in January 1766 as a member for Wendover.

The crisis in colonial America plunged Burke into the thick of affairs from the start. His great speeches on the approaching breach with the mother country propelled him into the political limelight. His final decade, down to 1795, saw him rise to a peak of devastating rhetorical power and the publication of his most original works. India, and then France, absorbed his attention above all else in this final period.

Burke's involvement with the affairs of India at this time was focused on the impeachment of Warren Hastings, the Governor-General, for corruption. The proceedings against Hastings were originally expected by Burke to last only a year, but they carried on until April 1795, when Hastings was acquitted. By then, Burke was five years into a consuming preoccupation with the affairs of France. The great British continental rival had been driven from reform to revolution, culminating in European war. Throughout this time, Burke's invective – some times stirring, other times disturbing – grew Manichean and then apocalyptic. A sense of purpose animating him to the end, he died at Gregories, his Buckinghamshire estate, on 9 July 1797.

Ideas

Burke developed his political ideas by continually placing his interpretation of events in dialogue with the results of extensive reading and wide reflection. Early in the 1750s he acquired a lasting interest in the systematic study of political processes by the application of the historical method exemplified by the work of Montesquieu (q.v.), whose *Spirit of the Laws* (1748) fascinated him. An historically rooted science of politics facilitated Burke's examination of the conditions and mechanisms which determined political relationships. Burke realised early, by comparing his direct experiences of political arrangements in Ireland and Britain, that the systematic organisation of public power determined the character of social life, making available the enjoyment of security and freedom (q.v.) which was its consummation. The balance of forces in Britain after 1688 had freed society and politics from the destructive effects of party strife. But in the same period, factional antagonism in Ireland brought home to Burke how regimes of conquest subverted social trust and cohesion.

Burke derived from Montesquieu an understanding of the extent to which modern European social order was formed through a process of consolidation, pacification and the stabilisation of social relations in the aftermath of the waves of conquest that followed the fall of Rome. However, as the Reformation had demonstrated, social equilibria would always be vulnerable to shocks to their smooth working. In the final analysis, a harmony of social forces could only be sustained on condition that the dominant beliefs among its participants supported respect for social arrangements.

The first great breakdown in political trust to which Burke was exposed came with the crisis in America, beginning in 1765, the steady escalation of fear and wilfulness on both sides underlining the typical means by which the routine conduct of policy could be drawn into a deteriorating spiral of rebellion and conquest. But if the use of British power in America grew inadvertently despotic during the course of ill-advised attempts to force through national policy, a posture of overbearing presumptuousness had characterised the conduct of East India Company affairs since the middle of the 1750s.

In his analysis of the progress of despotic power in India, Burke became increasingly absorbed by the spectacle of an ancient system of regulated liberty being extinguished on the pretext of a British right of conquest. But as he perfected his account of the death of freedom in the East, he was suddenly captivated by developments in France. As the revolutionary character of the agenda of reform in Paris became clearer in Burke's mind, he set about publicising his evolving sense of how anarchy and then military oppression would come to prevail in the heart of Europe on the pretence of a programme of liberation.

In Burke's account, liberty could only flourish as a 'rational', socially responsible freedom. It could only be secured within a framework of established social relationships. This did not mean that the value of liberty was entirely relative to circumstances. Political arrangements prejudicial to freedom could and should be progressively reformed. But it did mean that reform itself was obliged to preserve the conditions without which the pursuit of liberty would threaten to dissolve the existing balance of social forces into internecine conflict. This commitment pitted Burke against the kind of revolutionary freedom sought in France after 1789 under the general rubric of the 'rights of man'. It also divided him from his former political allies when he split from his Foxite Whig friends in 1791.

Burke's opposition to the revolutionary doctrine of egalitarian freedom cast a long and ambiguous shadow over attempts to employ his arguments in subsequent political struggles. However, the meaning of his career is best understood in terms of an ambition to found a science of politics on the principles of justice and liberty, as exemplified by Montesquieu, and it should be evaluated in the context of his attempts to understand the dynamic relations between conquest and rebellion in European politics in the 1750s and 1760s. With this foundation in systematic political analysis, involvement in the affairs of America, Ireland, India and France enabled Burke to produce a succession of controversial yet classic statements – political arguments which continue to generate debate and commentary today.

Key works

- *Speech on American Taxation* (1774)
- *Speech on Conciliation with America* (1775)
- *A Letter to the Sheriffs of Bristol* (1777)
- *Speech on Opening the Articles of Impeachment of Warren Hastings* (1788)
- *Reflections on the Revolution in France* (1790)
- *A Letter to Sir Hercules Langrishe* (1792)
- *Appeal from the New to the Old Whigs* (1791)
- A new, authoritative, edition of Burke's works is virtually complete as *The Writings and Speeches of Edmund Burke* (ed. Paul Langford, Oxford University Press, 1981–)

Further reading

- C. B. Cone, *Burke and the Nature of Politics* (2 vols, University of Kentucky Press, 1957–1964)
- Isaac Kramnick, *The Rage of Edmund Burke: Portrait of an Ambivalent Conservative* (Basic Books, 1977)
- F. P. Lock, *Edmund Burke* (2 vols., 1 volume published to date, Clarendon Press, 1998–)
- Conor Cruise O'Brien, *The Great Melody: A Thematic Biography of Edmund Burke* (University of Chicago Press, 1992)

Richard Bourke

Edward Caird   1835–1908

An ethicist, Kant scholar, political philosopher, theologian, political radical and social activist with a particular interest in the rights of women and the poor. He held the prestigious Chair in Moral Philosophy at the University of Glasgow for nearly thirty years, before becoming Master of Balliol College, Oxford in 1893. Caird was influenced strongly by Hegel and was one of the founding figures of the British idealist movement.

Key ideas

- The world is guided by a process of spiritual evolution or 'History'.
- One should look to the writings of Kant and particularly Hegel in order to understand the coherence and rationality of the development of human societies in all their aspects (religious, artistic, civil and political).
- The good society is founded upon the equality of all persons irrespective of their gender, class or race.
- The human good is achieved through participation by active citizens in a decentralised form of representative government.

Biography

Edward Caird was born in Greenock, near Glasgow, on 23 March 1835, to a devoted Free Kirk family. He studied at Greenock Academy, before going up to the University of Glasgow in 1850. Even though his studies at Glasgow were hindered by ill-health, he still achieved many notable honours for his classical scholarship. In October 1860, he entered Balliol College, Oxford as a Snell Exhibitioner.

He became great friends with noted radicals in the college, including Thomas Hill Green (q.v.) and John Nichol, sharing their fascination for Thomas Carlyle, Immanuel Kant (q.v.) and particularly the absolute idealist philosopher Georg W. F. Hegel (q.v.). Like Green, Nichol and the other members of the college's Old Mortality Club (of which Caird was a very active member), he was a fervent supporter of Giuseppe Garibaldi's uprising against the Austrians in April 1859 and of the Northern cause in the American Civil War. He admired in particular Abraham Lincoln's stand against slavery. As one might expect, at home he hated Conservative figures such as Lord Palmerston for what he saw as their immoral foreign adventures.

Caird graduated with a double first in 1863, and worked for a year as a private tutor before taking up a fellowship at Merton College, Oxford in 1864. He resigned his fellowship with effect from 6 May 1866 in order to marry (T. H. Green was his best man), and was immediately appointed as Professor of Moral Philosophy at the University of Glasgow. Caird held this important post for the next twenty-seven years, during which time he became widely regarded as one of the world's leading Kant scholars.

Caird was made Master of Balliol in 1893, following Benjamin Jowett's death on 1 October. He held this post until shortly before his own death, from Bright's disease, on 1 November 1908.

Ideas

Caird's conviction that the world is in a constant process of spiritual evolution dominated his philosophical writings, including his works on Kant, on Hegel, on the theory of knowledge and especially on the philosophy of religion. (His major theological writings, for example, were entitled *The Evolution of Religion* (1893) and *The Evolution of Theology in the Greek Philosophers* (1904).) In his essay on 'Reform and Reformation' (written ca. 1866), Caird argued that the citizen manifested 'his own deepest nature' by playing an active part in the progressive movements of his society. Such a life allowed the citizen to 'attain a certain useful command over [his] faculties and attainments' and tended to 'draw out the deepest voices of his being', while 'reveal[ing] to himself and to others the full scope of his capacity'. In his late address 'Two Aspects of College Life', he characterised his guiding ideal of civic and political virtue as '[a] double ideal of unity, brotherhood, passionate enthusiasm for humanity and readiness to give up everything for the weal of the community on the one hand, and manly independence, free acceptance of responsibility, and willingness to undertake all the cares and difficulties of an individual life upon the other hand'.

Politically, Caird charted a path between the socialist planning of the Fabians and the heartlessness of unfettered individualism. The state had a duty to protect workers, for example by protecting their terms and conditions at work and providing a welfare net where the voluntary sector failed to catch the vulnerable. Caird condemned the artificial and outmoded class distinctions of his time, and advocated the active participation of all sectors of society, through a diversity of voluntary organisations and representative political institutions. With his brother, Principal John Caird, Edward was a very vocal advocate of the admission of women to British universities, and of the settlement movement, as well as working actively for a number of other progressive causes.

In party terms, Caird was an advanced Liberal. His radicalism attracted a devoted following among his students, who included idealist philosophers such as Sir Henry Jones, A. D. Lindsay and William Wallace. Internationally, he was active in the protests against British atrocities in the Transvaal during the Boer War, and made himself particularly unpopular by joining the campaign against the granting of an honorary Doctorate of Civil Law to Cecil Rhodes, the perpetrator of the Jameson Raid of 1899. In this and in other ways, Caird applied British idealist philosophy to practical political matters long after the death of the movement's greatest exponent and Caird's close friend, T. H. Green.

Key works

- *The Moral Aspect of the Economical Problem* (1887)
- *Individualism and Socialism* (1897)

(Both reprinted in C. Tyler (ed.), *The Collected Works of Edward Caird* (12 vols., Thoemmes, 1999)

- *Lay Sermons and Addresses* (1907)
- 'Reform and Reformation' (ca. 1866), in C. Tyler (ed.), *Unpublished Manuscripts of British Idealism* (2 vols., Thoemmes, 2005)
- 'Lectures on Moral Philosophy: Social Ethics' (ca. 1877–80), ibid.

Further reading

- A. D. Lindsay, 'The Idealism of Caird and Jones', *Journal of Philosophical Studies*, vol. 1, no. 2 (1926)
- William J. Mander, 'Caird's Developmental Absolutism', in W. J. Mander (ed.), *Anglo-American Idealism, 1865–1927* (Greenwood Press, 2000)
- Colin Tyler, *Idealist Political Philosophy: Pluralism and Conflict in the Absolute Idealist Tradition* (Thoemmes Continuum, 2006), ch. 3

Colin Tyler

CentreForum (previously Centre for Reform)

A Liberal Democrat-inclined think-tank established in 1997, the Centre for Reform / CentreForum has had some success in floating new ideas and widening the policy debate.

Think-tanks associated with the Conservative and Labour parties mushroomed in the 1980s and early 1990s, with the support of wealthy donors, companies and banks, and trade unions. With scarce resources concentrated on campaigning, the Liberal Democrats lacked any comparable organisation to float new ideas and widen the policy debate. Following the party's success in the 1997 general election, however, Paddy Ashdown's desire for such a think-tank to help develop the party's credibility came together with an offer from Richard Wainwright (MP for Colne Valley until 1987) to support a new initiative, and the Centre for Reform was established in the autumn of 1997, with its formal launch taking place at the spring 1998 Liberal Democrat conference.

Richard Grayson was the Centre's first director, his salary accounting for half its income. His priority was to establish the Centre for Reform as a think-tank with a high profile within the Liberal Democrats, but also one that was recognised as a serious national player in a crowded market. To this end, there were two particularly significant publications under Grayson's directorship: *Funding Federalism* and *A New Future for the Basic State Pension*, which was influential on future Liberal Democrat policy. The Centre developed a lively programme of meetings in party conferences, and additional sponsorship supported an annual lecture at Westminster, given by Charles Kennedy, Chris Patten and Leon Brittan, amongst others.

Anthony Rowlands succeeded Grayson as director in November 1999, when the latter became the party's policy director; it was now possible to employ a second paid member of staff. The Centre courted controversy with pamphlets outlining the case for the legalisation of cannabis (by a former chief constable), and arguing that increases in the number of asylum-seekers presented an opportunity not a threat. Liberal Democrat MPs used the Centre as a forum for floating new policy ideas, including Edward Davey on the role of Parliament, Andrew Stunell on energy policy and Vince Cable on regulating modern capitalism. Nicholas Bromley and James Stibbs carried out significant research on health systems in different countries; their analysis of the problems of health insurance was influential on the Liberal Democrats' rejection of the idea in their 2002 policy review.

The Centre effectively took over *The Reformer* magazine, through which short reports and articles reached a wider audience. From 2002 it has joined forces with the Liberal Summer School (q.v.; now Keynes Forum) to organise an annual conference.

The death of Richard Wainwright in January 2003, however, threatened the Centre's fragile financial viability. In spite of converting to charitable status and raising some additional corporate subscriptions, it looked by the end of 2004 as if the Centre would have to close within months. Paul Marshall, chair of the Liberal Democrat Business Forum and editor of *The Orange Book*, then offered to underwrite the budget of an expanded Centre while more ambitious fund-raising was pursued. The renamed entity was relaunched in November 2005, as CentreForum, signifying the think-tank's intention to provide a forum for debate in the broad centre of politics; it possesses a larger staff, now under Jennifer Moses.

CentreForum's first papers covered educational deprivation, identity and citizenship, and social exclusion. It sponsored a number of debates with think-tanks close to the Labour and Conservative parties on cross-party issues, and launched breakfast meetings in the City to attract corporate attention to Liberal Democrat approaches.

From the outset, the Centre was close to the party leadership, but formally independent, and thus able to float ideas without committing the party to them. Its trustees (originally Nick Harvey MP, Archy Kirkwood MP, Lord Newby and Lord Clement-Jones), its executive board (chaired by

Duncan Greenland) and its advisory board (chaired by William Wallace) brought together people directly involved with party policy-making with intellectuals sympathetic to Liberal ideas.

Key publications

- Richard Grayson, Jay Liotta, Nicholas Bromley and Margaret Sharp, *Funding Federalism: A Report on Systems of Government Finance* (1999)
- Steve Webb and Alison Dash, *A New Future for the Basic State Pension* (1999)
- Francis Wilkinson, *The Leaf and the Law: The Case for the Legalisation of Cannabis* (2000)
- Edward Davey, *Making MPs Work for Our Money: Reforming Parliament's Role in Budget Scrutiny* (2000)
- Nicholas Bromley and James Stibbs, *Universal Access – Individual Choice* (2001)
- Francis Wilkinson, *Heroin: The Failure of Prohibition and What to Do Now* (2001)
- John Lotherington (ed.), *The Seven Ages of Life* (2002)
- Vince Cable, *Regulating Modern Capitalism* (2002)
- Paul Burstow, *When I'm Sixty-Four: The Case for a New Approach to Ageing* (2003)
- William Goodhart and Paul Tyler, *Britain's Democratic Deficit: Constitutional Reform – Unfinished Business* (2004)
- Julian Astle, David Laws, Paul Marshall and Alasdair Murray (eds.), *Britain after Blair: A Liberal Agenda* (2006)

William Wallace

Joseph Chamberlain   1836–1914

Businessman, social reformer, radical politician – first at the local, then at the national, level – and ardent imperialist, Chamberlain was an authoritarian democrat, wanting to expand state powers greatly. Initially he tried to achieve this through the Liberal Party, but broke with Gladstone over Irish home rule and, as a Liberal Unionist, spent the remainder of his political career in alliance with the Conservatives.

Key ideas
- Enlarging the powers of local and national government to bridge the socioeconomic divisions in urban, industrial Britain.
- Preventing devolution of national powers to Ireland.
- Reinforcing the cohesion of the British Empire through the restoration of a tariff against foreign countries, and imperial preference for the colonies.

Biography
Born on 8 July 1836, in Camberwell, to a family of cordwainers, Joseph Chamberlain was brought up for a career in business. He received a good education, particularly at University College School, but did not go to university. After a brief apprenticeship in his father's establishment in the City of London, he moved to Birmingham to look after his father's investment in his uncle's screw-manufacturing business. Under Chamberlain, who made a substantial personal fortune, the firm secured a monopoly of the manufacture of screws in Britain, establishing the price structure of this market world-wide.

Chamberlain entered public life as a local leader and national spokesman for the National Education League, demanding universal, secular and free elementary education to give rise to a literate and numerate working class. Having learned in business how reducing the hours of his workers could increase their productivity, he sought election to Parliament in 1874 at Sheffield as a workingman's representative. But after his defeat there, it was as mayor of Birmingham that he made his most

distinctive mark on the political scene. He deployed his business skills to bring the gas and water companies of Birmingham under municipal control, providing the town with better service at lower prices: municipal, or 'gas-and-water' socialism, as it was called. Then, driven by environmentalist (q.v.) rather than religious conviction, he tore down the worst slums in the centre of Birmingham and replaced them with an airy avenue for commerce which he named after the institution that created it: Corporation Street.

Chamberlain entered Parliament as MP for Birmingham in 1876. Rising rapidly, he became President of the Board of Trade in 1880 in Gladstone's (q.v.) second ministry. Along the way, he brought the party organisational skills that he had developed in Birmingham to bear upon the country as a whole, with the formation of the National Liberal Federation in 1877. But as an advocate of imperial unity Chamberlain opposed Gladstone's policy of Irish home rule, contributing to the party's nearly fatal split in 1886. In anomalous alliance with his usual Whig and Conservative opponents, Chamberlain did perhaps more than anyone else to defeat home rule, first in the House of Commons and, by a still wider margin, in collaboration with other Liberal Unionist (q.v.) defectors, in the ensuing general election. In 1895, Chamberlain joined Salisbury's Cabinet as Colonial Secretary. He was an enthusiastic supporter of the Boer War but resigned from the government in 1903 over tariff reform and imperial unity.

Although re-elected in Birmingham as a Unionist against the Liberal tide in 1906, in July that year he suffered a paralytic stroke that left him an invalid. He eventually died of a heart attack on 2 July 1914. His two sons, Austen and Neville, both became leaders of the Conservative Party.

Ideas

As Unitarians of an insistently rationalist stripe, the Chamberlains were keenly interested in ideas about bettering society. Chamberlain realised that the kind of large enterprise he had built in Birmingham was undermining the social cohesion that the town had derived from the prevalence of small businesses that kept masters and men in touch with each other. This recognition led him to look for ways through which local and national government could bridge the widening gap between capital and labour and enhance the wealth and well-being of industrial Britain, to the benefit of both.

In his Liberal days he was unable to devise ways for Britain to pursue the socio-economic objectives that he advanced so effectively in Birmingham. His attempt to stop the scandal of merchant shippers profiting, through insurance, from the death of the men they sent out in vessels that were not seaworthy was defeated by the shipowners. The Radical Programme that he announced for the electorate widened by the Third Reform Act of 1884/85 made more enemies than friends and divided Liberal support. He proved able as a Unionist to secure more social legislation than he had as a Liberal – or at any rate, so he claimed, and old Tories grudgingly conceded. His crowning achievement in this regard was the Workmen's Compensation Act of 1897, to recompense workmen injured in industrial accidents, compensation paid at little cost to the Treasury through insurance taken out by the industrial owners. Chamberlain proved unable to discover any similar mechanism to provide old age pensions.

His social agenda was overtaken after the home rule split by preoccupation with the Empire, a mounting concern he shared with the Conservatives. He pressed the Treasury to invest in the undeveloped estates of the Empire overseas, but to little avail. His first attempts to protect colonial agriculture, particularly West Indian sugar, from foreign competition were similarly frustrated. Finally in 1903 he erupted with proposals to abandon the national commitment to free trade (q.v.) and reimpose tariffs to protect British business against foreign competition, tariffs that would be lowered to benefit the colonies and draw them closer, through solid bands of economic interest, to the mother country. This policy fragmented the Unionist alliance and reunited the opposition Liberals, who regained power. Chamberlain emerged over the rest of his life as the driving spirit in an increasingly close but never solid alliance of Conservatives with Liberal Unionists, most of them closer to the Whig Duke of Devonshire than to Chamberlain's radical adherents.

Key works
- Charles W. Boyd (ed.), *Mr. Chamberlain's Speeches* (2 vols., 1914)
- D. A. Hamer (ed.), *Joseph Chamberlain & Others, The Radical Programme (1885)* (1971)

Further reading
- David Cannadine, 'Locality: The "Chamberlain Tradition" and Birmingham' in *In Churchill's Shadow, Confronting the Past in Modern Britain* (Allen Lane, 2002)
- E. H. H. Green, *The Crisis of Conservatism: The politics, economics and ideology of the British Conservative Party, 1880–1914* (Routledge, 1995)
- Denis Judd, *Radical Joe, A Life of Joseph Chamberlain* (University of Wales Press, 1993)
- Peter Marsh, *Joseph Chamberlain, Entrepreneur in Politics* (Yale University Press, 1994)

Peter Marsh

Winston Churchill   1874–1965

The most famous British statesman of the twentieth century. Switching his party affiliation between Tory and Liberal parties and back again, Churchill always remained an eloquent champion of liberal democratic values and institutions in an age when liberalism was on the defensive.

Key ideas

- Centrality of constitutional gradualism in the development of liberal society.
- Exceptionalism of the Anglo–American liberal experience.
- The British Empire as an instrument of civilisation.
- The righteous use of force throughout history in defence of liberal institutions and liberal states.
- Assertion of the counter-intuitive compatibility of efficiency with liberal democracy.

Biography

Grandson of the seventh Duke of Marlborough, Winston Leonard Spencer Churchill was born at Blenheim Palace on 30 November 1874. His mother's American origins fuelled a life-long affection for the United States.

A mediocre student at Harrow, Churchill was dispatched to Sandhurst by a father convinced that his son was ill suited to the academic rigour of Oxford or Cambridge. Churchill always remained something of the autodidact, trying as a young cavalry officer to fill the gaps in his education by reading from politics, economics and history while stationed in India and Egypt. His first successes as an author came through journalistic accounts of his exploits along the North-West Frontier and in the Sudan and the Boer War.

In 1900 Churchill used his newfound celebrity to gain election to Parliament, where he quickly displayed his father's maverick tendencies and a weak allegiance to party. Though Tory by inheritance, the young Oldham MP had confessed to his mother four years earlier, 'I am a Liberal in all but name.' In 1904 Churchill crossed the floor, ostensibly because he disagreed with Conservative policy on free trade (q.v.), but also because the Liberal Party offered the best prospects for a rising political star. In the pre-war Liberal governments Churchill served as Under-Secretary of State for the Colonies, President of the Board of Trade, Home Secretary, and First Lord of the Admiralty. During this period he was identified with the New Liberal (q.v.) wing of the party, classified as a protégé of the radical David Lloyd George (q.v.), influenced by the Fabians Sidney and Beatrice Webb, and drawn to the bipartisan reformism of the National Efficiency Movement.

Blamed for the 1915 Gallipoli debacle, Churchill left the cabinet briefly for active duty on the Western Front. Upon his return as Munitions Minister in 1917, he sided with the Liberal rump supporting Lloyd George against the Asquithian opposition. The collapse of the Lloyd George coalition in 1922 left Churchill out of office and out of Parliament for the only time between 1900 and 1964. It was during this personally discouraging hiatus that he began work on his history of the Great War, *The World Crisis*.

Churchill regained his Commons seat as an independent in 1924. The collapse of the Liberal Party and the rise of Labour soon led him to rejoin the Conservatives, where his reputation and experience ensured Cabinet office as Chancellor of the Exchequer in the Baldwin administration of 1924–29. However, as a two-time turncoat, Churchill was distrusted by most of the party rank and file, perhaps with good reason, since as late as 1937, he declared privately, 'I believe in Liberalism. I am still a Liberal.' The Labour victory of 1929 ushered in his 'wilderness years', though without the burden of Cabinet office, the 1930s proved to be his most fruitful period as an author, witnessing the completion of his massive biography of the Duke of Marlborough, along with most of the manuscript of the four-volume *A History of the English-Speaking Peoples* (although this was not published until 1956).

Churchill enjoyed a triumphant Second World War, beginning as First Lord of the Admiralty in the Chamberlain government, then steering Britain to victory as head of the National Coalition. Surprised and hurt by his rejection in the 1945 general election, he spent the next six years leading the opposition and composing his six-volume *Second World War*. The record of his final stint as Prime Minister (1951–55) was decidedly mixed.

Churchill was awarded the Nobel Prize for Literature in 1953. He died on 24 January 1965, only a few months after leaving Parliament.

Ideas

Churchill never wrote a formal statement of his political philosophy. His principal contribution to the development of liberal ideas came via his histories: somewhat solipsistic multi-volume accounts of the two world wars, his sweeping *History of the English-Speaking Peoples*, and the personally revealing biographies of his father Lord Randolph Churchill and that other illustrious ancestor, John Churchill, first Duke of Marlborough. A collection of liberal themes provides the consistent theoretical foundation for these narratives written across the span of a half-century.

One of Churchill's greatest strengths as a stylist was his moral clarity. While his histories embraced the traditional Whig

view of progress through constitutional gradualism, he also freely employed the moral vocabulary of nineteenth-century liberalism to frame the wars conducted by the British state against a succession of autocratic threats, folding together the defeat of the Armada with resistance to Louis XIV, Bonaparte, Wilhelm II, and Hitler. Churchillian prose succeeded in making squeamish twentieth-century liberalism more comfortable with hard-edged power, legitimising through historical example the principled use of force in the defence of freedom (q.v.) and liberal values.

Despite the apparent superiority of authoritarian regimes in preparing for and prosecuting war, history demonstrated that liberal democratic (q.v.) states were actually more efficient in mobilising the sinews of power from the products of industry and the enthusiasms of their citizenry. There was no need to sacrifice the core values of liberalism. Churchill was 'convinced that with adequate leadership democracy can be a more efficient form of government than Fascism ... It may be that greater efficiency in military preparations can be achieved in a country with autocratic institutions than by the democratic system. But this advantage is not necessarily great, and it is far outweighed by the strength of a democratic country in a long war.' Here was the sub-text to Churchill's two long narratives of the two world wars. Here also was his rebuttal to the socialist inclinations of Britain's home-grown National Efficiency advocates. Despite the claims of Halford Mackinder, H. G. Wells and the Webbs, liberalism squared well with the remorseless demands of modern efficiency.

Thus, Churchill provided new life for decaying Whiggish (q.v.) history. By the early twentieth century the traditional version of the national saga, organised around the story of constitutional evolution, was under fire from multiple sources. Every hero of Churchill's modern narratives of power was a liberal constitutionalist: Marlborough, Wellington, Washington, Lincoln and, most often, Winston Churchill himself. He tells the tales of heroes acting within the confines of constitutional constraints, benevolent agents of liberalism employing power judiciously to combat tyranny. In the process, he generated a version of liberal national history more serviceable to the exigencies of the twentieth century; one that broadened the sweep of the old, insular Whig historiography by fusing the idiom of power with the moral lexicon of Whiggism.

Churchill's parliamentary speeches also contributed to his liberal vision. During his first two years as Prime Minister his oratory was ennobling, heroic and galvanising to all who heard it. He frankly admitted the nation's dire situation, yet provided reassurance and courage to the British people by connecting the current peril to the grand epic of liberal democratic struggle. Churchill's idiosyncratic synthesis of Whiggish constitutionalism, imperial grandeur, liberal efficiency and the legitimate use of military force, all presented in a dramatic cadence employing a starkly moral vocabulary, made his mythic speeches of 1940–41 such a significant moment in the history of the liberal idea.

Key works
- *Lord Randolph Churchill* (1906)
- *The World Crisis* (1925–31)
- *Marlborough: His Life and Times* (1933–38)
- *The Second World War* (1948–53)
- *A History of the English-Speaking Peoples* (1956–58)

Further reading
- Maurice Ashley, *Churchill as Historian* (Secker and Warburg, 1968)

- David Cannadine, *In Churchill's Shadow: Confronting the Past in Modern Britain* (Oxford University Press, 2003)
- Victor Feske, *From Belloc to Churchill: Private Scholars, Public Culture, and the Crisis of British Liberalism, 1900–1939* (University of North Carolina Press, 1996)
- Roy Jenkins, *Churchill* (Macmillan, 2001)
- John Lukacs, *Churchill: Visionary, Statesman, Historian* (Yale University Press, 2002)
- John Ramsden, *Man of the Century: Winston Churchill and His Legend Since 1945* (Columbia University Press, 2003)

Victor Feske

Anders Chydenius   1729–1803

The epitome of a man of the Enlightenment in the Finnish context, a radical statesman and political writer with an overwhelming desire to free people from the guardianship of others and to establish a society and economic order based on trust in the ability of individuals to take responsibility for their own actions. His particular concern was for the status of the working classes, unprivileged members of society who were deprived of personal or political rights. He was a significant pioneer of European democracy.

Key ideas
- The highest ideals of the Enlightenment: progress, freedom, democracy and human rights.
- If freedom of trade prevails, a natural balance will arise out of the acts of every producer, worker, consumer and trader in advancing his own interests, and this is also in the interests of society as a whole, i.e. the greatest 'national gain' will be achieved.

- Economic freedom must be freedom at the grassroots level, the right of individuals to fulfil their own ideals in life.
- Openness and public accountability are essential for a free, stable society.

Biography

Anders Chydenius was born in Sotkamo in Finland (part of Sweden until 1809) on 26 February 1729 and spent his youth in the impoverished, barren surroundings of north-eastern Finland. He attended grammar school in Oulu and studied privately in Tornio, gaining entry to the Royal Academy in Turku in 1745. He also studied at Uppsala University. His main subjects were mathematics, natural sciences, Latin, philosophy and theology.

After graduating, Chydenius was appointed preacher to the parish of Alaveteli in Ostrobothnia in 1753. In the true spirit of Swedish utilitarianism (q.v.), he was active in many practical projects during his years at Alaveteli, especially concerned with agricultural innovations. He also practised medicine.

Chydenius's first writings were concerned with practical matters, but he soon moved on to social questions and was acclaimed as a writer and speaker. He was dispatched to the Stockholm Diet in 1765–66 with a commission to obtain free trading rights for the towns of Ostrobothnia. He participated actively in the work of the Diet, and published several articles criticising the dominant mercantilist economic doctrines based on regulation, rationing and monopolies. The concrete results of his activities included stricter supervision of the national economy and an extension of the freedom of the press.

Following his appointment as vicar of Kokkola in 1770, Chydenius began to concentrate more on parish work, which he considered his most important task.

He participated once again in the Diet in 1778–79, at a time when it was considering the status of hired labour. He was an ardent champion of the rights of servants, and called for the creation of an open labour market. He also introduced a bill, on the initiative of King Gustavus III, by which foreigners were to be granted limited rights to practise their own religion.

Chydenius returned to the Diet in 1792 and remained active as a writer, dealing with topics such as the development of agriculture, the burning of saltpetre, inoculations against smallpox and the settlement of Lapland. He died on 1 February 1803.

Ideas

Chydenius's views on society were grounded in the Enlightenment philosophy of the natural rights of man, as expressed in particular by John Locke (q.v.) and Samuel von Pufendorf. The rights of the individual were of fundamental importance, and although some of these had been surrendered to those in power under the existing social contract, he firmly believed that this contract could be annulled; the state existed for the benefit of its citizens and not vice versa. At the same time, Chydenius's social thinking was based on Christian ethics, to which he appealed when calling for social justice (q.v.), for instance.

When the long period of domination of the Diet by the 'Hats' party came to an end in 1765, a political orientation derived from the ideals of the Enlightenment occupied a prominent position among the members of the 'Caps' party that came to power. This implied a concentration on the needs of agriculture and the peripheries, in contrast to the Stockholm-centred industrialisation policies of the 'Hats', and a more favourable attitude towards personal freedoms and social justice. It was among this group that Chydenius found persons of like mind.

Chydenius's writings were mostly pamphlets on the political issues of the day, in which theoretical discussions were of less importance. His booklet *Den Nationnale Winsten* (The National Gain), on the other hand, was an attempt at a more general examination of the economic principles that he had adopted. In his opinion the planning and direction of a national economy was an impossible task, and production and trade should be allowed to operate freely, letting the laws of supply and demand guide the economy into the appropriate channels. People will naturally pursue their own interests, and even though individuals may strive in directions that are not in the national interest, it is possible to assume, given free competition, that a state of equilibrium will ensue which is the most desirable from the point of view of the whole system and which will generate the maximum 'national gain'. Thus, by exploiting the profit motive of free individuals, a society could achieve a harmony of the same kind as that which, in the scientific world view that prevailed at the time, held good in the natural sphere.

Chydenius is often viewed above all as a pioneer of liberalism and occupational freedom. The occupational freedom that he espoused, however, was only one part of a more extensive radical political programme aimed at a society based on equality (q.v.) between citizens. One step in this direction was dissolution of the economic hegemony achieved by the nobility and influential merchant class through the existing system of monopolies and trade restrictions. It was essential that the economy should serve the needs of all the people and not only of a small minority.

In addition to equality and fundamental rights, Chydenius's model of democracy included the opportunity for exercising political influence. In common with other radicals among the 'Caps', he advocated more extensive powers for the other estates as opposed to the nobility. One of the crucial requirements for social progress, in his view, was a system of public accountability, comprising both freedom of speech and openness in governance. Chydenius was instrumental in bringing about the introduction of liberal legislation on the freedom of the press in Sweden in 1766.

Key works

- *The Source of Our Country's Weakness* (1765)
- *The National Profit* (1765)
- *Assisting the Kingdom through a Natural Monetary System* (1766)
- *Thoughts upon the Natural Rights of Masters and Servants* (1778)

Further reading

- Juha Mustonen (ed.), *The World's First Freedom of Information Act: Anders Chydenius' Legacy Today* (Anders Chydenius Foundation, 2006)
- Bo Sandelin (ed.), *The History of Swedish Economic Thought* (Routledge, 1991)
- Carl G. Uhr, *Anders Chydenius 1729–1803: A Finnish Predecessor to Adam Smith* (Åbo, 1963)
- Pentti Virrankoski, 'Anders Chydenius and the Government of Gustavus III of Sweden in the 1770s', *Scandinavian Journal of History* vol. 13, 1988:2–3
- Chydenius Foundation (www.chydenius.net)

Pertti Hyttinen

Classical Liberalism

The meaning of the term 'liberalism' has become increasingly diffused and has been subject to many changes and interpretations over time. In the Anglo-Saxon world, 'classical liberalism' is the term often used by those who want to preserve the original ideas of liberalism, based on individual freedom, the rule of law and free markets; they support a reduction in the role of the state, particularly in economic and welfare policy.

In the course of its history the term 'liberalism' has undergone many changes and reinterpretations. Those of today's liberals (especially in the Anglo-Saxon world) who see themselves as the heirs of the 'original' tradition of liberalism often call themselves 'classical liberals'. Neither this 'original tradition' nor the term 'classical liberalism' can be defined with absolute precision, but there is a rough consensus. Today's 'classical liberals' agree that individual freedom (q.v.) ranks above material equality, that the state's sphere has to be more strictly limited than it is today and that freedom is the guarantor of wealth for the people. The following political creed can be extracted from their writings:

- Freedom is the leading principle of liberal politics. Freedom means individual liberty or self-determination under the rule of law (q.v.) in the sense of what Isaiah Berlin (q.v.) called negative freedom, i.e. the absence of obstacles, barriers or constraints.
- The state has to be limited in order to protect individual liberty, the rule of law and the functioning of the market economy. Thus, constitutionalism (often based on constitutional economics) is high on the classical liberal agenda. This constitutionalism aims at a new framework for policy-making that makes it more difficult to widen the scope of state action, e.g. by introducing a rigid 'competitive federalism' with strong tax competition that puts pressure on politicians to lower taxes.

- Free markets and free trade (q.v.) are more efficient than any form of state planning and interventionism.
- The welfare state has to be scaled down, or at least reconstituted, to make it work better. While a few classical liberals (e.g. Robert Nozick (q.v.)) are 'minarchists' who see internal and external security as the only legitimate tasks of the government, the majority is more pragmatic in its approach. They mostly try to limit public spending to a sustainable level, to privatise sub-systems of the welfare state or to introduce more market-compatible mechanisms into the system. An example of the latter would be Milton Friedman's (q.v.) proposal of a negative income tax that would gradually replace all other welfare and assistance programmes, thereby making the social policy system more efficient and simple.

Classical liberalism, however, is not such a coherent body of thought as it sometimes appears to be, partly because the 'original' liberal tradition was also one of considerable diversity. Although more sceptical of state coercion than the new liberals in general, the old liberals held widely differering views about the state's responsibilities. For instance, even radicals such as Richard Cobden (q.v.) and the British free traders believed in state-financed schools, while others (their French counterparts like Frédéric Bastiat (q.v.), for example) abhorred the idea. There were also divisions over the theoretical basis of liberalism; liberal theorists included advocates of natural-rights theory (John Locke (q.v.)), utilitarianism (q.v.) (Jeremy Bentham (q.v.)), romanticism (Wilhelm von Humboldt (q.v.)), Catholicism (Lord Acton (q.v.)) and evolutionism (Herbert Spencer (q.v.)).

Modern classical liberalism reflects this pluralism. Hence contractarians (Robert Nozick), utilitarians (Ludwig von Mises), critical rationalists (Karl Popper (q.v.)) and positivists (Milton Friedman) can be found among them. While all of them are generally critical of socialism and the welfare state, there is a great variety of opinions about the extent of the 'roll-back of the state' – often depending on how radical or pragmatic the chosen approach is.

Why is the adjective 'classical' necessary? The reason is historical. As Friedrich August von Hayek (q.v.) in 1973 remarked:

> But though the last quarter of the nineteenth century saw already much internal criticism of liberal doctrines within the liberal camp and though the Liberal Party was beginning to lose support to the new labour movement, the predominance of liberal ideas in Great Britain lasted well into the twentieth century and succeeded in defeating a revival of protectionist demands, though the Liberal Party could not avoid a progressive infiltration by interventionist and imperialist elements. Perhaps the government of H. Campbell Bannerman (1905) should be regarded as the last liberal government of the old type, while under his successor, H. H. Asquith, new experiments in social policy were undertaken which were only doubtfully compatible with the older liberal principles.´

This change from 'old' liberalism to the new social or interventionist type of liberalism was not confined to Britain. In America, for instance, where the term 'liberalism' was hardly used in the nineteenth century, the word 'liberal' became more or less synonymous with leftist or social democratic statism, with an over-reaching welfare state.

In Europe, where 'liberalism' has been associated with a long-standing tradition of political thought and practice since the early nineteenth century, the term has undergone changes in meaning and interpretation. Especially in the later decades of the nineteenth century, theorists and politicians such as Friedrich Naumann in Germany broke with certain liberal ideas about the limits of state power and called for a more interventionist and redistributionist agenda in order to solve the 'social question'. This 'New Liberalism' (q.v.) or 'social liberalism' (q.v.) quite often advocated a closer relationship with the new labour unions and emerging socialist parties.

Not all liberals, however, followed that trend. The extension of coercive power, the fiscal irresponsibility and the inability of the welfare state to preserve its own economic basis always found critics within the liberal movement, who often called themselves 'classical liberals'. Hayek's book *The Road to Serfdom* (1944) gave much of the impetus for the revival of classical liberal ideas in Britain. Anti-market interventionism, he argued, would erode not only economic freedom but other civil freedoms too in the long run; and the basis of wealth and progress would similarly be undermined. At the time he was swimming against the tide, as socialism and social democracy (q.v.) of all sorts formed the political mainstream. This has changed since.

The crisis of the welfare state that began in the 1970s reinforced that tendency. As it became harder to ignore the economic problems market solutions became more and more an intellectually and politically acceptable trend, not only in the Anglo-Saxon world, but – to a lesser degree – in most parts of the world. No longer was it the domain of a few maverick intellectuals; in the 1980s and 1990s it underpinned the practical reform agenda for many governments around the world.

Since then the revival of 'classical liberalism' has played a role in reforming welfare states and restoring economic prospects in many countries, including Britain and New Zealand. Countries that resisted the trend toward 'classical liberalism' in recent years, like most of continental Europe, today tend to suffer from low growth rates and high unemployment.

Further reading

- Norman Barry, *On Classical Liberalism and Libertarianism* (Macmillan, 1987)
- David Conway, *Classical Liberalism: The Unvanquished Ideal* (St Martin's Press, 1995)
- Friedrich August von Hayek, 'Liberalism' (1973), in Hayek, *New Studies in Philosophy, Politics, Economics and the History of Ideas* (Routledge & Kegan Paul, 1978)

Detmar Doering

Richard Cobden   1804–65

Arguably the most important nineteenth-century British statesman never to hold political office. As the principal leader of the Anti-Corn Law League and trenchant opponent of Palmerstonian foreign policy, he was a consistent promoter of the classic liberal tenets of free trade, peace, retrenchment and reform and exercised a lasting influence over British liberalism.

Key ideas

- The free market as providentially ordained and essentially benign; monopoly and protectionism as intrinsically damaging.
- Universal free trade as the first step towards universal peace.
- Non-intervention in foreign affairs, and the rejection of war as an instrument of foreign policy; industry, commerce and moral authority, rather than military might, as the true basis of state power.
- Financial retrenchment, particularly in military expenditure, which should be for defensive purposes only.

Biography

Richard Cobden was born on 3 June 1804, in Heyshott, West Sussex, one of eleven children of a local farmer. His grandfather had been bailiff of the nearby borough of Midhurst, but the family had fallen on hard times and were forced to give up on the land. In 1814 Cobden was sent to Bowes Hall, a 'Dotheboys Hall' in Yorkshire (William Shaw, the original of Wackford Squeers in *Nicholas Nickleby*, had briefly been a master there). He left in 1818 to become a clerk in the London calico warehouse of his uncle, Richard Ware Cole.

Given this inauspicious start, Cobden's rise is remarkable. As a commercial traveller in the 1820s he developed enormous admiration for the dynamism of the industrial districts, and in 1828 he went into partnership with Francis Sherriff and George Gillett, setting up a business in Manchester and London as distribution agents for calico goods. In the early 1830s Cobden settled in Manchester as a calico printer, a business that provided the foundation of his personal fortune and a springboard to public life.

During this period, Cobden read voraciously. The influence upon him of Adam Smith's (q.v.) *Wealth of Nations* is well known; less appreciated is his interest in the phrenologists, particularly George Combe, whose *The Constitution of Man* was first published in 1829. Cobden, who first met Combe in 1836, was a convert to the Scot's pioneering educational ideas, in particular the notion that phrenology could allow the development of a scientific approach to education based on the encouragement of desirable character traits and the discouragement of undesirable ones. *The Constitution of Man* was in fact less a phrenological text than a treatise on society and politics, and its imprint is clear throughout Cobden's thought.

During the 1830s, Cobden established himself in public life in Manchester, through involvement in local voluntary associations and his pivotal role in the campaign for Manchester's Charter of Incorporation in 1837. He also published his first political pamphlets, *England, Ireland and America* (1835) and *Russia* (1836), which set out the basic tenets of 'Cobdenism'. The pamphlets combined classical political economy with a social and political reform agenda that would have been familiar to contemporaries steeped in the eighteenth-century radical tradition, with its hatred of 'Old Corruption' and aristocratic privilege. In 1838, after returning from a tour of the German states (he had already toured the United States), Cobden was persuaded to join an association that had been set up in his absence to campaign for a repeal of the Corn Laws, which he now identified as the keystone of aristocratic power and a major brake on Britain's economic development. The following year, the Manchester Anti-Corn Law Association became the Anti-Corn Law League (q.v.), and Cobden eventually emerged as its effective leader.

The triumph of the anti-Corn Law campaign in 1846 made Cobden an international celebrity, but he found it difficult to repeat the League's success. After unsuccessfully championing financial reform he became involved in the international peace movement, as the logical corollary to free trade (q.v.). For a while peace principles seemed in the ascendant, but the situation was reversed by the outbreak of the Crimean War in 1854. Many of Cobden's colleagues supported the war as a means of encouraging liberal nationalism in Poland and Hungary, isolating Cobden and his close friend, John Bright, who opposed it. Cobden, along with many of his supporters, was defeated at the polls in the election of 1857 and withdrew from public life,

a decision made easier by the death of his only son in April 1856 and the subsequent illness of his wife.

This self-imposed exile ended in 1859, when Cobden returned from a tour of the United States to find himself MP for Rochdale with an offer of a place in Palmerston's Cabinet. This he declined, preferring to maintain his status as the independent MP *par excellence*. He used this position to good effect, negotiating the Cobden–Chevalier commercial treaty with France in 1860, and attempting to smooth Anglo-American relations at crucial points during the American Civil War.

His later years were marred by poor health. In the autumn of 1864 he suffered an acute bout of illness after speaking at an outdoor meeting in Rochdale in November; the following March he felt well enough to travel to London to speak in a debate on Canada, but died at lodgings in Suffolk Street on 2 April 1865.

Ideas

Cobden was notable for the consistency of his major ideas across the whole of his life, and his early pamphlets comprise a manifesto for an impressively coherent and systematic political ideology. Between them, *England, Ireland and America* (1835) and *Russia* (1836) contain an almost complete statement of 'Cobdenism': a rejection of the traditional concern of British foreign policy with the European balance of power; a call for non-intervention in foreign affairs and a concentration on much-needed domestic reform; the primacy of trade over military might and colonial possessions as the measure of national power; and free trade (q.v.) as the first step toward universal peace. Despite their respective titles, both works were actually interventions in the debate over the decline of the Ottoman Empire and the territorial expansion of

Russia which collectively made up the so-called 'Eastern question'. Since the Napoleonic Wars, British policy in the Levant had been to preserve the Ottoman Empire from Russian encroachment. In 1834 David Urquhart, the maverick diplomatist and Turkophile, had written the pamphlet *England, France, Russia and Turkey,* calling for British military intervention in the eastern Mediterranean as a means of restraining Russia. It was this pamphlet that inspired Cobden's first intervention in public life.

In *England, Ireland and America,* Cobden argued that the greatest threat to Britain's global superiority came not from the Cossack hordes, but from the commercial development of a peaceful, industrious United States. Cobden saw the US, with its democratic institutions and non-interventionism, as a model for Britain. He developed this point in *Russia,* arguing that any 'balance of power' which ignored the US was a nonsense, and concluding that the whole notion was simply a spurious justification for British interference in continental affairs. Instead of meddling abroad, Cobden believed that reformers should dedicate themselves to sorting out domestic abuses, and pointed to Ireland as evidence of Britain's unfitness to dictate how other countries should run their affairs. More controversially, he contended that Russian expansion in the east would actually make her less of a threat, as she would be too busy trying to absorb these new territories and establishing internal order to bother her European neighbours. This was Cobden's earliest statement of his view that state power flowed not from the possession of extensive territories, but from volume of trade – a view that formed the basis of his anti-imperialism, and which later influenced the work of economist and anti-imperialist J. A. Hobson (q.v.). These ideas provided the impetus for Cobden's

political campaigns and future writings, including pamphlets on Anglo-French relations (*1793 and 1853* and *The Three Panics*), the Crimean War (*What Next? And Next?*) and Britain's imperial expansion (*How Wars Are Got Up in India*). They also formed the basis of Cobden's long crusade against the interventionist policies of Palmerston, who dominated British foreign policy for almost three decades.

Though Cobden's ideas remained remarkably constant, the very unity of his thought created problems when events brought two or more elements of his system into conflict. The most obvious example of this was the outbreak of the American Civil War in 1861. Not only did this threaten the very survival of the great Republic, it also brought a conflict between his beliefs in peace and free trade and his hatred of slavery, as a protectionist, free-labour North fought desperately to prevent the secession of a free-trading but slave-owning South. This explains Cobden's lukewarm support of the Northern cause in public, and his refusal to acknowledge the necessity of the North's use of blockade as a strategy of war. However, he did campaign against any recognition of the South, and exerted himself to keep Britain from entering the war in the Southern interest.

During his lifetime, Cobden fought to rescue political economy from the stigma of the 'dismal science' disseminated by Benthamites like Edwin Chadwick. It is therefore a harsh irony that he himself became associated by future generations with support for unrestrained capitalism and naked laissez-faire (q.v.). However, this is to misunderstand and misrepresent Cobden's views. First, Cobden was quite prepared to set limits to the operation of the free market when it was found wanting, particularly in the provision of universal education, which he saw as the first step toward the achievement of true democracy. Second, though no Evangelical, Cobden was a devout Christian who believed that free trade had been providentially ordained by a benign deity. Any state intervention therefore contravened the will of God, while its providential nature made a free market the best means of supplying the needs of all. Understanding these beliefs helps to rescue Cobden from those who accuse him of a callous indifference to the plight of the poor. Finally, Cobden's campaign for free trade was motivated not by the profit motive, but by his belief that as nations became more closely bound by ties of trade, war would cease to be an acceptable instrument of foreign policy. It should also be noted that Cobden's ideal society was one based on small units of production, whether industrial or agricultural; the idea that unregulated capitalism would lead eventually to monopoly was one he found difficult to accept.

Cobden's strength as a thinker lay not in originality, but in his ability to systematise a wide body of radical political thought and political-economic theory into a unified and coherent manifesto for reform. However, he was no impractical theorist, and his impact on Victorian politics stemmed from his great abilities as a practical politician. Indeed, as our knowledge of his ideas comes not from any single abstract political treatise, but from pamphlets, speeches and letters written in the moment, in response to rapidly changing political events, the unity of the whole becomes even more impressive. His greatest limitation was an inability to modify some of these core beliefs in the light of contrary evidence.

The impact of Cobdenism on the development of liberalism is difficult to assess. The repeal of the Corn Laws in 1846 inaugurated an extended period of free trade which lasted until 1932, and while repeal owed more to Peel than Cobden, it was Cobden's name that was deployed to defend that legacy from early twentieth-century tariff reformers. However, British liberals proved ready to compromise on the principles which underpinned Cobdenite free trade, particularly those of peace and non-intervention. Despite Gladstone's (q.v.) claim that Cobden was one of his most important influences, Peter Cain is surely right in his assessment that the real significance of Cobden for the development of British liberalism was as a source of ideas to be dipped into, rather than as the originator of a guiding philosophy.

Nevertheless, Cobden's influence was as broad as it was diffuse, extending across Europe, where he established important political friendships with French economists such as Claude Bastiat (q.v.) and Michel Chevalier, and where he met many future Liberal revolutionaries during his tour of 1846–47. Today, Cobden's non-interventionism and vision of peaceful globalisation seem as relevant as ever in the context of contemporary debates over the ethics of military intervention overseas, global poverty and fair trade. There is much in the argument that Cobden was the first proponent of an 'ethical' foreign policy. Unfortunately, decades of vilification as a symbol of exploitative capitalist greed mean that the influence of his ideas and name is now largely restricted to the libertarian (q.v.) fringes of progressive politics.

Key works
- Cobden's pamphlets are collected in *The Political Writings of Richard Cobden* (1867)
- J. E. Thorold Rogers (ed.), *Richard Cobden: Speeches on Public Policy* (1870)

Further reading
- N. Edsall, *Richard Cobden: Independent Radical* (Harvard University Press, 1986)

- W. Hinde, *Richard Cobden: A Victorian Outsider* (Yale University Press, 1987)
- J. A. Hobson, *Richard Cobden: The International Man* (T. Fisher Unwin Ltd., 1918)
- A. Howe and S. Morgan (eds.), *Rethinking Nineteenth-Century Liberalism: Richard Cobden Bicentenary Essays* (Ashgate, 2006)
- J. Morley, *The Life of Richard Cobden*, 2 vols. (Chapman & Hall, 1881)

Simon J. Morgan

Cobden Club *see* Free Trade Union

Sir Edward Coke   1552–1634

An Attorney-General, judge, and parliamentarian, who modernised medieval legal learning and laid the foundations for the common law of the emerging modern era. He pioneered judicial review and is remembered, despite his long service to the crown, as a leading figure of resistance to Charles I.

Key ideas

- Law defined as the professional consensus, the 'artificial reason', of lawyers and judges, rather than the command of the sovereign.
- Common law and parliamentary independence validated by their consistency with the mythical 'ancient constitution' of England.
- Common law upheld against ecclesiastical tribunals and prerogative courts.
- Judicial independence in the face of royal pressure.

Biography

Edward Coke was born in the village of Mileham, Norfolk on 1 February 1552. His family was of the minor gentry, his father a common lawyer and landowner, his mother the daughter and granddaughter of locally prominent lawyers. He was educated at the Norwich grammar school and at Trinity College, Cambridge, which he left in 1570 without taking a degree. Protestant sentiments were prominent in Coke's native shire and in his years at Cambridge, and personal links bound him to England's community of Puritan believers, connections whose radical sentiments he did not fully share, but to whose cause he often inclined.

A member of the Inner Temple, called to the bar in 1578, Coke was one of the most prominent common lawyers of Elizabeth's reign. In 1592 he became Solicitor-General and in 1593, when Parliament sat, he served as Speaker of the Commons. In 1594 he was named Attorney-General. He held this post until 1606, being continued in office by King James I, at whose accession a windfall in fees from coronation pardons made Coke a rich man. James knighted him in May 1603. Coke served as Chief Justice of the Common Pleas from June 1606 to October 1613, and Chief Justice of King's Bench from November 1613 until November 1616, when the King removed a judge with whom he had finally lost patience.

Coke's years on the bench were marked by controversy. He resisted the claim that only church tribunals could interpret ecclesiastical law. He insisted that statutes passed by Parliament limited the powers granted by Royal Commissions, the authority relied upon by the Court of High Commission, the Council in the North, and the Council in the Marches of Wales. In *Bonham's Case* (1608), he went further, giving judges the power to overrule statutes: 'for when an act of Parliament is against common right or reason … the common law will control it, and adjudge such act to be void'. Coke once told the King, face to face, that despite

James's native intellect, he lacked the professional training necessary to rule on legal questions. In 1615–16, finally, the friction became intolerable. The King sought, before trial, to poll the judges *seriatim* as to how each would rule, and to have judicial decisions postponed until he could make his wishes on these cases known. Coke resisted unflinchingly. After he refused to back down, and after he refused the King's request to censor his *Reports* ('wherein', the government observed, 'there be many dangerous conceits of his own uttered for law'), Coke was removed from the bench.

Too useful a servant to be cast aside, Coke soon regained a place on the Privy Council. In the parliament of 1621, he was returned to the Commons. When the Commons turned against monopolists such as Sir Giles Mompesson, Coke helped retrieve from medieval obscurity the device of parliamentary impeachment. His long-time rival Sir Francis Bacon was among those impeached and ruined, but the session ended in frustration; an angry monarch sent Coke to the Tower of London. In the parliament of 1624, Coke seemed chastened and cooperative, but during the parliament of 1625 he slowly turned against the Crown. In the parliament of 1628, Coke led those who distrusted Charles I, and was a principal author of the Petition of Right. Ostensibly, the Petition merely reconfirmed Magna Carta, but to reaffirm medieval liberties represented a new assertion of subjects' rights and parliamentary power.

After this parliament, Coke retired from public life. He died on 3 September 1634, as the King's men were carting away his papers. The royal triumph was only temporary. In 1641, the Long Parliament ordered Coke's manuscripts to be published. The cases reported in Coke's *Reports* and *Institutes* provided a critical mass of precedents and doctrine for the emerging common law.

Ideas

In his master work, *The Commentary upon Littleton* (1628), Coke wrote: 'Reason is the life of the law, nay the common law itself is nothing else but reason; which is to be understood of an artificial perfection of reason, gotten by long study, observation, and experience, and not of every man's natural reason.' The common law was to be trusted 'because by many successions of ages it hath been fined and refined by an infinite number of grave and learned men, and by long experience grown to [such] perfection, for the government of this realm'. This defined law not as the command of the sovereign (as King James believed), nor in terms of natural reason (for which Thomas Hobbes (q.v.) would take Coke to task), but as the professional wisdom of the judges.

The archetype of the common law judge, 'one of the symbolic figures of England,' was unforgettably sketched by George Orwell: 'The hanging judge, that evil old man in scarlet robe and horsehair wig, whom nothing short of dynamite will ever teach what century he is living in, but who will at any rate interpret the law according to the books and will in no circumstances take a money bribe.' This portrait, with its caricaturist's accuracy, is one for which the Lord Chief Justice might have sat. Coke was a fierce and tireless prosecutor. He argued that the common law had not changed since the days of the Druids. Yet his work and *oeuvre* were part of the Elizabethan effort to carve out, as Edmund Spenser put it, 'a kingdom of our own language' – to challenge the heritage of the classical world, the Roman church and the civil law. Moreover, to identify the common law and political institutions with the mythic past, the 'ancient constitution' of the realm, was to privilege them against royal intervention. From *Bonham's Case*, in the United States and elsewhere in the world of the Anglo-American common law, has descended the doctrine of judicial review; any modern-day court decision that strikes down an insupportable law ultimately rests on Coke's authority.

Key works

- *Reports* (thirteen parts, 1600–59)
- *Institutes of the Laws of England* (1628, 1642–44)

Further reading

- Catherine Drinker Bowen, *The Lion and the Throne: The Life and Times of Sir Edward Coke* (Little, Brown & Co., 1957)
- Allen Boyer, *Sir Edward Coke and the Elizabethan Age* (Stanford University Press, 2003)
- Christopher Hill, 'Sir Edward Coke – Myth-Maker', in *Intellectual Origins of the English Revolution Revisited* (Clarendon Press, 1997)
- Sir William Holdsworth, *History of English Law*, vol. 5, pp. 423–80 (Methuen & Co., 1903–72)

Allen D. Boyer

Community Politics

Community politics encompasses a restatement of the intellectual basis for liberalism, based on devolving power to communities, and a strategy for winning elections, particularly focusing on local government. It emerged as a concept in the late 1960s, and was officially adopted by the Liberal Party at its 1970 assembly.

The theory of community politics emerged from the intellectual ferment of the Young Liberal movement (q.v.) during the late 1960s. Young Liberal leaders drawn to the Liberal Party by Jo Grimond (q.v.) sought to rethink the intellectual case for liberalism, earning the nickname 'Red Guards' because their radicalism (q.v.) conflicted with the more staid orthodoxy of the party leadership. After the Red Guards disintegrated following a series of doctrinal disputes, those members who remained with the Liberal Party set out 'a restatement of Liberalism in a new synthesis to meet the changed perspectives of a new generation'. Bernard Greaves (1942–), Tony (now Lord) Greaves (1942–), Gordon Lishman (1947–) and Michael Meadowcroft (q.v.) were among its main proponents.

The basis of community politics was the traditional liberal concern with the individual, and the importance of enabling each person to fulfil his or her own potential. What distinguished community politics from earlier thinking was the focus on the communities to which individuals belong – in particular, geographic and economic communities – and the importance of individual self-fulfilment occurring in conjunction with, and in support of, the development of vibrant, self-confident communities. Community politics rejected the out-and-out individualism of the libertarian (q.v.) right, which had not been short of champions in the postwar Liberal Party, but was also a deliberate challenge to socialism and the bureaucratic centralisation which had come to characterise the welfare state. Community politics was intended to 'reverse the trends towards centralisation and uniformity and to encourage decentralisation and variety'. The job of the community politician was to help foster and maintain a community's identity and to create a habit of participation so as to 'bind a community together in a constant relationship with power and decision-making'. The ultimate aim was for new political structures to emerge based on communities in which individuals were fully involved.

John Stuart Mill (q.v.), T. H. Green (q.v.) and Lord Acton (q.v.) have all been claimed as fathers of community politics. Robert Owen (q.v.) and the Levellers have been cited as early practitioners, and links to libertarian (q.v.) and anarchist (q.v.) thinkers have also been claimed. Closest to the mark was David Thomson's assessment that 'Britain ... lacks a decentralist, communitarian and co-operative tradition' and that inspiration for community politics came principally from the French student riots and US counter-culture of the 1960s.

Community politics was a theory concerned with process – how communities could take power to pursue their own aims – rather than with ends. An obvious danger was that communities would seek empowerment to pursue illiberal objectives. In their influential exposition of the theory of community politics, Lishman and Bernard Greaves suggested that the application of community politics would not degenerate into unrestrained populism because 'with the exercise of power goes an increasing responsibility for its application' and 'in a society based on active consent, tyranny is impossible'. Nevertheless, advocates of community politics argued that the Liberal Party should take a 'dual approach' to politics – seeking to win elections and, at the same time, organising and assisting communities to exercise power for themselves.

The dual approach to politics was mentioned in the first paragraph of the resolution on community politics passed at the 1970 assembly, by 348 votes to 236. The resolution stated that the role of Liberal activists was to organise people in communities to take and to use power and to help redress grievances. It also called for

Liberals to build power bases in the major cities and to identify with the under-privileged. In hindsight, it was remarkable that the Young Liberals should have been so successful in convincing the Liberal rank and file of the need for such a bold statement of strategic intent, although the appalling result of the 1970 general election no doubt convinced many activists that a new approach was required. Also influential was the Liberal success in the Birmingham Ladywood by-election the previous year, which had been based on community politics techniques.

The aspect of community politics most enthusiastically embraced by the Liberal leadership and the party at large was the identification and redress of local grievances, strongly promoted as a campaigning tactic by the Association of Liberal Councillors (q.v.). Community politics very quickly became associated with 'pavement politics'. *Focus* leaflets were used to highlight local grievances – cracked pavements, faulty street lights, dog dirt and so on – and to ask residents to raise issues of concern. This proved immensely successful in local government elections in some areas, particularly the suburbs, though less so in parliamentary elections.

Although the techniques of community politics became a defining feature of the Liberal Party it is questionable whether the theory was widely understood or fully implemented where Liberals took power. It was difficult to prevent a genuine philosophy morphing into a technique simply to win local seats and to being caricatured as 'mindless activism'. Little attention was paid to empowering members of non-geographic communities, such as workplaces, and the Liberal Party's focus on the least well-off was not always evident. The theory was vague about how to determine at which level decisions should be taken and there was little to explain how conflicts within and between different communities might be resolved. The assumption that everyone would automatically seek to participate in political decision-making if given the chance was untested. Community politics encouraged participation by vociferous individuals, and the more articulate and middle-class elements, without engaging those groups most in need of help. A telling criticism of community politics techniques was that they tended to encourage people to look to elected politicians to deal with grievances, instead of helping people to help themselves. Also, it could be difficult to establish a national policy on issues such as transport or housing development if Liberals locally took opposing views on particular schemes. Another problem was that the techniques could be, and increasingly were, aped by other parties.

Although the theory of community politics was a new contribution to Liberal thinking, the techniques with which the theory was associated had developed in a number of places in the late 1950s and early 1960s. Roy Douglas has gone as far as describing community politics as 'a restatement in contemporary terms of practices which were applied by Liberals in Birmingham in the 1870s'. The techniques remain central to the Liberal Democrats' campaign strategy but their theoretical underpinnings are now infrequently cited.

Further reading
- *The Future of Community Politics*, Liberal Democrat consultation paper, 1994
- Bernard Greaves and Gordon Lishman, *The Theory and Practice of Community Politics* (ALC Campaign Booklet No. 12, 1980; reprinted in ALDC, *Community Politics Today*, 2006)
- Peter Hain (ed.), *Community Politics* (John Calder, 1976)

- John Meadowcroft, 'The Origins of Community Politics', *Journal of Liberal Democrat History* 28 (autumn 2000).
- David Thomson, *The Shocktroops of Pavement Politics?* (Hebden Royd Paper No. 1, 1985)

Robert Ingham

Marquis de Condorcet   1743–94

A mathematician, social scientist and political thinker who became deeply involved in the French Revolution of 1789; he served as a secretary to the Legislative Assembly and took a leading role in drafting the republican constitution. His remarkable paean to progress and human reason, *Sketch for a Historical Picture of the Progress of the Human Mind*, was published posthumously in 1795.

Key ideas
- For all practical purposes the scope for developing and improving the human mind and human society is unlimited.
- Reason should be regarded as humanity's greatest asset in fashioning arrangements for good and representative government.
- Mathematical ideas and methods have a very wide application to the study and improvement of human society.
- Slavery is wrong and damaging to society and should be abolished.
- Female emancipation is in the best interests of men as well as women.
- Human beings cannot escape or avoid uncertainty but uncertainty should not be allowed to act as a brake on human progress.

Biography
Marie-Jean-Antoine-Nicholas de Caritat, Marquis de Condorcet, was born into the titled Caritat family at Ribemont near

Saint-Quentin, in Picardy, on 17 September 1743. His education was overseen by his mother, a deeply religious woman, who sent him to the Jesuit College in Reims and then on to the College of Navarre in Paris. In 1765 he published his first work on mathematics; his extraordinary intellect and precocious mathematical talent were widely recognised and he was elected to the Academy of Sciences in 1769, later becoming its secretary. Further recognition for his intellectual distinction came with his subsequent election to the Academy of France. The publication of his work on calculus was welcomed by no less a figure than Lagrange, who described his mathematical investigations as sublime and full of fruitful ideas.

Condorcet's thoughts were not restricted to the production of mathematical treatises. In 1770 he began a correspondence with the economist Turgot, who, as Louis XVI's Controller of Finance, recommended his appointment as Inspector-General of the Mint, a position he retained until 1791. His intellectual circle included Voltaire (q.v.) and d'Alembert, as well as Turgot. Before the Revolution Condorcet and his wife, Sophie de Grouchy, who he married in 1786, established a salon for the liberal intellectual elite of Paris, who were fascinated by the development of republican government in America; it became the place to discuss issues such as the reform of criminal justice, religious toleration and the abolition of slavery. Condorcet himself wrote biographical works about both Voltaire and Turgot, making clear his anti-clerical views (in the former work) and his support for liberal economics (in the latter).

In the wake of the 1789 Revolution Condorcet was elected as a member of the Legislative Assembly and became one of its secretaries and later its president. He gained a reputation as a moderate whose sympathies lay with the liberal republican Girondins. He used his position in the Assembly to champion the cause of state education and drew up plans for a public education system; his proposals profoundly influenced future educational developments in France.

As divisions in the National Convention, which replaced the Assembly in 1792, grew, Condorcet made his opposition to regicide and his sympathy with Girondin positions unmistakeable. His opposition to the King's execution led to him being attacked as a traitor by Jacobins such as Robespierre, and they also targeted him because of his vocal opposition to plans to refashion the republican constitution that he had played a key role in drawing up. Orders were issued for his arrest and he went into hiding – but left his place of concealment in Paris only to be arrested and imprisoned. Within two days of his arrest, he was dead, on 29 March 1794; it is not clear whether he was murdered, committed suicide or died of 'natural causes'.

Ideas

Condorcet's breadth of knowledge and range of interests are amongst the most striking things about him. He was above all else, from a liberal perspective, an ardent proponent of human rights and representative government. He wrote about the abolition of slavery, repeal of the corn laws, probability theory and the design of voting systems, the emancipation of women, liberal economic theory and the significance of the American revolution for European systems of government. At almost every point, when writing about these and many other subjects, Condorcet argued that reason and science could and should play a central role in improving the human condition and organising and driving the government of society.

His most important work on probability and voting systems, published in 1785 (entitled *Essay on the Application of Analysis to the Probability of Majority Decisions*), is one of a number of works where his mathematical knowledge and expertise were used to interrogate political and social questions. His faith in and optimism about the role of reason in human affairs is the most striking thing about Condorcet's diverse, extensive and highly sophisticated writings. While he was in hiding from the Terror, in fear of his life, he wrote what is probably his best-known work, the *Sketch for a Historical Picture of the Progress of the Human Mind*. An outline for a much more extensive work that he never had the opportunity to complete, he put forward in the *Sketch* what, in the opinion of Keith Michael Baker, one of his most noted academic assessors, could be considered 'the most influential formulation of the idea of progress ever written'.

Condorcet's *mathematique* is a one of the greatest examples of Enlightenment rationalism and a forerunner of what many consider the best that modern academic social science has to offer. He sought to make social and economic behaviour more comprehensible by utilising statistical methods and relying on mathematical ideas. He found Rousseau's notion of a general will and emphasis on the role of sentiment in human affairs troubling and argued that what was needed in human affairs was a greater use of reason and evidence rather than a greater reliance upon metaphysics. As Acton (q.v.) observed, he 'sought to extend the empire of reason to social affairs'.

Condorcet was a champion of democratic and accountable government but, in one of the many ironies that attach to his life, he is most widely remembered for his discovery of the voting paradox that now bears his name, which disturbed belief in the possibility of majority rule. *Condorcet's paradox* shows how it is possible for decisions made by majorities to produce inconsistent (circular or intransitive) results. Whatever his findings about the problems encountered in designing voting systems, however, Condorcet should be remembered as one of the most powerful proponents of the liberal case for equality of civil and political rights and the pursuit of what remains for many an impossible but inspiring dream: the perfectibility of the human race.

Key works

- *Reflections on Black Slavery* (1781)
- *Essay on the Application of Analysis to the Probability of Majority Decisions* (1785)
- *Life of M. Turgot* (1786)
- *Life of Voltaire* (1789)
- *On the Admission of Women to the Rights of Citizenship* (1790)
- *Sketch for a Historical Picture of the Progress of the Human Mind* (1795)

Further reading

- Keith Michael Baker, *Condorcet: From Natural Philosophy to Social Mathematics* (University of Chicago Press, 1975)
- Keith Michael Baker (ed.), *Condorcet: Selected Writings* (Bobbs-Merrill, 1976)
- David Williams, *Condorcet and Modernity* (Cambridge University Press, 2004)

Ed Randall

Benjamin Constant   1767–1830

One of the key liberal philosophers between Locke and Hayek, a well-known novelist as well as a challenging political writer, engaged in political activity in France after the French Revolution. Constant was a fierce opponent of Jacobinism and other kinds of usurped power and tyranny, advocating instead a system of liberal democracy, safeguarded by the 'neutral power' of a constitutional monarch.

Key ideas

- Liberty is the most important human value; it consists of both active political participation and inviolable individual freedom.
- All legal rules must be universal, general and non-arbitrary; courts must be independent and bureaucracy has to be neutral.
- All power needs to be limited; neither a sovereign ruler nor the people as a whole are entitled to violate the rights of the individual.
- Government should be constituted by representation; there should be two different houses, and ministers should be personally liable.

Biography

Henri Benjamin Constant de Rebecque was born in Lausanne, Switzerland, on 25 October 1767. His parents, Henriette-Pauline de Chandieu and Colonel Juste Constant de Rebecque, were both of Huguenot origin. The mother died two weeks after his birth. Benjamin was first looked after by his grandmothers and then started moving around Europe with his father, a military official, when he was seven years old; their itinerary took him to the Netherlands, Belgium and Britain.

At age fifteen, this cosmopolitan boy was placed at the Count of Ansbach-Bayreuth's court in southern Germany and took up studying law at the University of Erlangen. A year later, his father brought him to Scotland where, at the University of Edinburgh, he came in touch with the Whigs and other proponents of political liberalism. A member of the 'Speculative Society', he participated in discussions about questions raised by David Hume (q.v.), Adam Smith (q.v.) and Adam Ferguson, and grew fully acquainted with the Anglo-American tradition of political thought. When visiting Paris, he also benefited from discussions within intellectual circles, such as the 'Idéologues', pertaining to the tradition of the French Enlightenment; Turgot, Condorcet (q.v.) and Siéyès were among the minds that shaped his thinking. A couple of years later, his father finally placed him as a chamberlain at the Count of Brunswick's court in Germany. Here, Constant began his political and religious writings, and married Wilhelmine von Cramm, a lady-in-waiting.

In 1793, Constant returned to Switzerland, where he met Germaine de Staël, daughter of the French minister Jacques Necker and wife of the Swedish ambassador to France. The intense intellectual exchange with this independent, cultivated and challenging lady, well integrated in a stimulating network of thinkers such as Jean-Jacques Rousseau and the Schlegel brothers, soon also turned into a turbulent romantic affair that lasted more than fifteen years. In 1794 Constant moved in at Château Coppet, where the Necker family lived, and obtained a divorce from his wife. During this period, he also produced *De la force du gouvernement* (*On the Power of Government*) and *Des réactions politiques* (*On Political Reactions*). He also became engaged politically and ran as a candidate for the parliamentary elections in 1797. That same year, Madame de Staël gave birth to Albertine, presumably Constant's daughter.

When Napoleon rose to power in 1799, the well-connected Madame de Staël managed to have Constant included in the Tribunate, a group of advisers to Napoleon. Constant at first supported him, given that after the dreadful years of the Terror, Napoleon seemed committed to securing the original liberties brought about by the Revolution. But soon Napoleon became corrupted by his own power. Constant was seen as a nuisance and was removed from the Tribunate in 1802; both he and Madame de Staël had to quit political activity and were forced to leave France for Germany. In 1804, Napoleon was crowned as Emperor. In 1806, Constant wrote down his *Principes de politique* (*Principles of Politics Applicable to All Representative Governments*) and started his romantic novels *Adolphe* and *Cécile*. In 1808, he secretly married Charlotte von Hardenberg, though it was only in 1811 that he really broke up with Germaine de Staël and moved to Germany to live with his second wife. In Göttingen, Constant wrote *De l'esprit de conquête et de l'usurpation* (*On the Spirit of Conquest and on Usurpation*).

When Napoleon was dethroned in 1814, Constant returned to France and became again involved in politics, trying to help the country become a constitutional monarchy under Louis XVIII. On Napoleon's return from exile in Elba, however, Constant again switched sides and became a Privy Counsellor. After Napoleon's defeat at Waterloo, however, Constant prudently retreated to England. Upon his return to France in 1816, he became one of the leaders of the liberal party, wrote extensively for the newspaper *Mercure de France* and published another important work, *De la liberté des anciens comparée à celle des modernes* (*The Liberty of Ancients Compared with That of Moderns*). In 1819, he was again elected a deputy.

Constant sided with King Louis-Philippe after the revolution of July 1830, being appointed President of the Council of State. He died soon afterwards, however, on 12 December 1830, in Paris, and was given a state funeral at the famous Père Lachaise cemetery.

Ideas

If Benjamin Constant is not well known nowadays, this is probably due to the lack of a clear structure in his works of political philosophy, unlike his novels. The common trait of his literary work and his writings in political philosophy is his impressive humane sensitivity, allowing him to fully concentrate on the individual. Constant was an outspoken non-collectivist.

In one of his most important works, *Principes de Politique*, Constant developed a fully fledged political philosophy and a theory of government, ranging over the necessity for a freedom-guaranteeing constitution to the practical set-up of representative government and the principle of subsidiarity in administration. Most important, he produced a novel theory of *sovereignty* and the legitimacy of government that ran entirely contrary to Rousseau and the unlimited power that, according to the latter, a 'social contract' is able to bring about. According to Constant, even if all power is necessarily popular, that does not imply that it should therefore be unlimited. Unlimited power is evil, whoever holds it. As soon as any government, even if democratically elected, impinges upon the individual spheres of its citizens, it becomes illegitimate.

Constant emphasised the role of *individual rights*:

> The option to do anything which does not hurt others, or in freedom of action, in the right not to be obliged to profess any belief of which one is not convinced, even though it be the majority view, or in religious freedom, in the right to make public one's thought, using all the means of publicity, provided that that publicity does not harm any individual or provoke any wrong act, finally in the certainty of not being arbitrarily treated, as if one had exceeded the limits of individual rights,

that is to say, in being guaranteed not to be arrested, detained, or judged other than according to law and with all due process. Constant justified all these *individual liberties* in both a practical and a philosophical way. Practically, he claimed that they were necessary to provide for a population capable of understanding, supervising and correcting the functioning of the political mechanisms to which they delegate power. Besides that, they made private actions efficient. From a moral point of view, he argued that individual liberties also promoted general progress, by providing individual minds with insight, characters with strength and spirits with elevation.

On the question of how the state should be organised, Constant developed his theory of *representative government*. In *De la liberté chez les anciens comparée à celle des modernes*, he explained that in ancient times, the Greeks viewed liberty mainly as the right to participate actively in political decision-making – which, however, did not protect the individual against arbitrary political measures. In modern times, liberty was seen, rather, as a personal concept aiming to preserve the individual. Constant tried to combine the two. Imposing constitutional limits to state action was to be the safeguard against encroachments in the personal sphere – while representative government, where the citizens delegate their power to Parliament for a given period of time, is a system that calls for the practical involvement of each citizen in political matters, without, however, requiring too much individual time and energy that could more usefully be employed in other ways.

Notwithstanding this, Constant was an advocate of *constitutional monarchy*. As he explained in *Principes de Politique* and other works, he was convinced that every government needed a 'neutral power' stabilising it by balancing the different sub-powers,

and one itself sufficiently independent not to be biased by self-interest. In Constant's view, a hereditary monarch could play such a role, achieving his status by birth alone rather than by struggle. Idealistically, Constant believed that monarchs also tended to be somewhat morally 'noble' by tradition and could therefore in reality be valuable arbiters. The only concrete effective power that the constitutional monarch should preserve was the power to dissolve the parliament; this ultimate threat was needed to contain the government which, once in place, might otherwise extend and ultimately misuse its powers.

In this context, Constant warned that there could easily be a proliferation of laws: 'The proliferation of the laws flatters the lawmaker in relation to two natural human inclinations: the need for him to act and the pleasure he gets from believing himself necessary … Lawmakers parcel out human existence, by right of conquest …' Constant clearly determined the limits of what should be regulated by law: on the one hand, legal regulation was needed for intrinsically harmful, criminal acts which should be punished, and on the other hand, the state should sanction private agreements according to their proper terms. Any intervention in private matters beyond that would corrupt morality. To stem the proliferation of laws, he proposed a kind of 'inverse sunset' provision, through which government would periodically re-endorse existing laws. Given that some of them would be too embarrassing to re-endorse, he imagined, their number would inevitably shrink.

An elaborate body of law was necessary, however, in order to avoid arbitrariness. In what reads very much like a modern theory of *law*, Constant urged that all legal rules should be general and universally applicable. Every citizen was equal before the law. Furthermore, laws only became really binding when they were adopted by tradition. If they were clearly contrary to general notions of justice, they must not be obeyed. Enforcement must be carried out by independent, non-partisan courts of justice only.

Constant also established a whole series of notions that are today essential to economics. For example, inspired by authors like John Locke (q.v.), David Hume and Adam Smith, he emphasised the role of *private property* and *the division of labour*. Unlike Locke, he did not view property as a natural right, but as a pure social convention fostering the division of labour. While for Locke, life, liberty and property were inseparable, Constant saw a qualitative difference between life and property – just as there is a difference between crimes against life, e.g. murder, and crimes against property, e.g. theft. And yet, the state had no right to infringe on private property; and in particular, every non-necessary tax was such an infringement. Constant also feared that an infringement on property would soon be followed by an infringement on the person.

By clarifying some of the most important concepts of political philosophy, Benjamin Constant laid the groundwork for the development of modern political and economic theory. Many of the ideas that can later be found in the writings of Friedrich August von Hayek (q.v.) and his liberal followers can be traced back to Constant's broad and creative thinking. Constant's influence on liberalism will be long-lasting.

Key works
- *On Political Reactions* (1797)
- *On the Power of Government* (1796)
- *On the Spirit of Conquest and on Usurpation* (1814)

- *Principles of Politics Applicable to All Representative Governments* (1815)
- *Course of Constitutional Politics* (1818–19)
- *The Liberty of Ancients Compared with That of Moderns* (1819)

Further reading
- G. Dodge, *Benjamin Constant's Philosophy of Liberalism* (University of North Carolina Press, 1980)
- S. Holmes, *Benjamin Constant and the Making of Modern Liberalism* (Yale University Press, 1984)
- A. Pitt, 'The Religion of the Moderns: Freedom and Authenticity in Constant's *De la Religion*', *History of Political Thought* xxi, 1 (2000)
- D. Wood, *Benjamin Constant, A Biography* (Routledge, 1993)

Karen Horn

Tony Crosland   1918–77

The leading social democratic thinker of the 1950s and 1960s, Crosland drew on a range of liberal ideas, straddling libertarian and egalitarian beliefs, and influenced a generation of politicians who went on to found the SDP and the Liberal Democrats.

Key ideas
- Equality and social justice, with an emphasis on their role in promoting individual freedom.
- Economic growth, especially its role in funding welfare provision.

Biography
Born on 29 August 1918 at St Leonards, Sussex, Charles Anthony Raven Crosland was educated at Highgate School and then studied classics at Trinity College, Oxford. In 1940, he interrupted his studies to enlist in the army, eventually serving in

the Parachute Regiment. On his post-war return to Oxford as a rather glamorous ex-serviceman, he changed subjects, securing a first in politics, philosophy and economics in 1946, and soon became an economics fellow at Trinity.

In 1950, Crosland was elected as Labour MP for South Gloucestershire. He worked closely with Hugh Gaitskell, while publishing his first book, *Britain's Economic Problem* (1953), but was defeated at the 1955 election due to boundary changes. Out of Parliament, Crosland completed his seminal *The Future of Socialism* (1956). This challenged nationalisation and bureaucratic socialism, and on Keynesian (q.v.) assumptions, emphasised the power of economic growth to deliver social benefits.

In 1959, Crosland returned to Parliament as MP for Grimsby and was a leading moderniser, also publishing *The Conservative Enemy* (1962). When Labour entered government in 1964 he was briefly minister of state in the Department of Economic Affairs, but soon became Secretary of State for Education and Science. A strong advocate of comprehensive education, he issued Circular 10/65, 'requesting' local authorities to move to a comprehensive system. Aspiring to be Chancellor of the Exchequer, Crosland agreed to move to the Board of Trade in 1967, remaining there until near the end of the government when he was briefly Secretary of State for Local Government and Regional Planning.

In opposition, Crosland wrote *Socialism Now* (1974), and in the 1974 Wilson government, returned to local government issues with a new title, Secretary of State for the Environment. He came fifth of five candidates for the Labour leadership in 1976, but was still made Foreign Secretary by James Callaghan. He died in office on 19 February 1977 after a cerebral haemorrhage.

Crosland married twice, in 1952 to Hilary Anne Sarson (marriage dissolved in 1957) and then in 1964 to Susan Barnes Catling, a marriage which brought two step-daughters.

Ideas

The Future of Socialism was a key development in British political thought, as the first significant post-war statement of the differences between socialism and social democracy (q.v.), with the book firmly in the social democratic camp despite both its title and Crosland using the term 'socialism' throughout. The book had five parts. The first examined changes in the British economy, arguing that issues of ownership were now irrelevant because evidence suggested that state ownership did not necessarily lead to greater social justice (q.v.). The second section analysed socialist traditions, attacking Marxists and Fabians for being more interested in bureaucratic means than ends. The third section argued that the provision of 'welfare' or public services should be the main focus of socialism, and part four examined the need for greater equality (q.v.), especially in education. Part five made the case for a mixed economy and argued that only economic growth could provide the basis for social progress and the delivery of high standards of welfare.

In terms of liberal thought, it is striking that *The Future of Socialism* is imbued with the language of individual freedom (q.v.). Although there is much collectivism in the book, Crosland's main aim was to increase the life chances of individuals; indeed, his first definition of 'the ethical basis for being a socialist' was that 'further change will appreciably increase personal freedom'. Moreover, he sought a more socially just society so that political attention could then turn to 'in the long run more important spheres – of personal freedom, happiness, and cultural endeavour'. In a section entitled 'Liberty and Gaiety in Private Life', he argued for a series of reforms, ranging from 'more open-air cafés' and 'later closing-hours for public houses' to greater freedoms on divorce, abortion, homosexuality, censorship and women's rights. In a famous passage attacking Fabianism, Crosland argued: 'Now the time has come for ... a greater emphasis on private life, on freedom and dissent, on culture, beauty, leisure, and even frivolity. Total abstinence and a good filing-system are not now the right sign-posts to the socialist Utopia: or at least, if they are, some of us will fall by the wayside.' In other words, *The Future of Socialism* contained the core political arguments that would inform the liberalising legislation of the 1960s.

If Crosland was essentially pursuing liberal goals, some of his thinking remains challenging for some liberals, especially his emphasis on the need for greater equality. But in arguing for that, Crosland was clear that he was not seeking, for example, 'complete equality of incomes, since extra responsibility and exceptional talent require and deserve a differential reward'. Instead, he sought to promote the social justice funded by a thriving economy that has been a hallmark of social liberalism (q.v.). One can therefore see a direct line from Hobhouse (q.v.) to Crosland, to the SDP, and to current Liberal Democrat policy on public services. All have aimed to increase individual freedom through measures of greater equality funded by economic growth. A challenging thought for Liberal Democrats, however, is that despite the demise of Lib-Labbery, a similar direct line stretches from Crosland to Gordon Brown.

Key works
- *The Future of Socialism* (1956)
- *The Conservative Enemy* (1962)
- *Socialism Now* (1974)

Further reading
- Susan Crosland, *Tony Crosland* (Jonathan Cape, 1982)
- Kevin Jefferys, *Anthony Crosland: A New Biography* (Politico's, 2000)
- Giles Radice, *Friends and Rivals: Crosland, Jenkins and Healey* (Little, Brown, 2002)

Richard S. Grayson

Ralf Dahrendorf   1929–

An academic, trained as a sociologist and initially focusing on class, Dahrendorf has written extensively, including books on liberalism and, increasingly, on European politics. Aside from his scholarly endeavours, he has also been active in German, European and British politics.

Key ideas
- The importance for liberty of regulating conflict, with democracy as a way of organising conflict.
- The importance of a limited state; a deep-seated commitment to individual rights.
- A firm belief in European cooperation, albeit tinged with some scepticism about the process of European integration.

Biography
Ralf Gustav Dahrendorf was born in Hamburg on 1 May 1929, the son of the Social Democrat politician Gustav Dahrendorf, who opposed Nazism and communism in equal measure. Ralf Dahrendorf's early years were coloured by the totalitarianism of the first half of the twentieth century, by imprisonment and by liberation, all of which were to have a profound effect on his beliefs and attitudes.

Dahrendorf had a broad academic training. He initially read classics and philosophy at the University of Hamburg, where he took a doctorate in philosophy. He then took a PhD in sociology at the London School of Economics; here he was to be taught by Karl Popper (q.v.), who greatly influenced his later work, as did the monetarist economist Milton Friedman (q.v.), who taught him in California.

Dahrendorf began his professional career as a sociology professor in Germany before entering politics as a Free Democrat in 1967. He served as deputy Foreign Secretary to Walter Scheel and from 1970 to 1974 was one of Germany's two European Commissioners. After this interlude in practical politics, Dahrendorf became director of the LSE (1974–84) and then Warden of St Antony's College, Oxford (1987–97). He was knighted in 1982 and, having taken British citizenship, was created Baron Dahrendorf of Clare Market in 1993. For some years he took the Liberal Democrat whip in the House of Lords before moving to the cross benches. He has been married three times and has three daughters from his first marriage.

Ideas

Dahrendorf's deep-seated beliefs about liberalism owe much to his formative years and to his incarceration by the SS. Both Ralf and Gustav Dahrendorf were interned during the Second World War; Ralf, still a child, was initially sent to prison and later to a concentration camp east of the River Oder for opposing the SS. In his Reith Lectures, Dahrendorf said that 'it was during the ten days in solitary confinement that an almost claustrophobic yearning for freedom (q.v.) was bred, a visceral desire not to be hemmed in, neither by the personal power of men nor by the anonymous power of organisations'.

Ralf was released by the SS when the Russians reached the Oder, while his father was liberated by the Russians. When Gustav rejected the merger of the Social Democrats with the Communist Socialist Unity Party in East Germany in 1946, the British and Americans became fearful for his safety, and airlifted both men to Hamburg, where the young Dahrendorf's life-long Anglophilia was fostered.

Dahrendorf's first major work, *Class and Class Conflict*, looked at social conflict, assessing class and critiquing the work of Karl Marx. Dahrendorf believed that it was important to accept differences rather than to try to overcome them, arguing that 'Democracy ... is not about the emergence of some unified view from "the people", but it's about organising conflict and living with conflict'. In *Society and Democracy in Germany* he considered the problems associated with embedding liberal democracy (q.v.) in his homeland. He later argued that Germany is 'institutionally social democrat', whereas Britain is 'institutionally liberal', citing this as one of his reasons for emigrating.

Dahrendorf considered liberalism and liberty explicitly in several of his lectures and publications, most notably, perhaps, in his 1974 Reith Lectures, *The New Liberty – Survival and Justice in a Changing World*, which he built upon in *Life Chances – Approaches to Social and Political Theory*. Dahrendorf is committed to the idea of 'individual life chances', something that separates him from the social democrat tradition in which he had been raised. He believes firmly in choice for the individual and, along with Milton Friedman, questions the need for large state provision of services. He is also anxious about the influence of major organisations, business and trade unions. Yet he is aware that it may not be possible to expand life chances or choice inexorably, as some choices will inevitably impact on the world around.

Dahrendorf learned from Popper that 'we cannot know ... we can only guess' and this led him to argue that liberty derives from this uncertainty: 'Since nobody knows all the answers, let us make sure above all that it remains possible to give different answers.' Reading his Reith Lectures in the first decade of the twenty-first century, one is struck by his prescience. While the specific context of his lectures was the socioeconomic climate of the 1970s, characterised by the energy crisis and high unemployment, Dahrendorf raised much wider issues relating to the survival of the planet, which he saw as being jeopardised by the increase in life chances. He also noted a paradox, 'of a need for devolution in order to allow people to participate, and a need for wider international action to safeguard survival'.

Dahrendorf was prolific both in scholarly and journalist endeavours, frequently writing about Europe and the European Union from the 1980s onwards. While he was clearly committed to the European ideal and its importance for Franco-German reconciliation, he was nevertheless often critical of the mechanisms of European integration and, unlike many committed Europhiles, also believed in the importance of good trans-atlantic relations.

Dahrendorf is a leading European thinker on liberal matters and a patron of the Liberal International (q.v.). However, his impact on British liberal politics has been, perhaps, less profound. He was never a member of the Liberal Democrats, although he took the party whip from 1993 until 2004. His views increasingly diverged from the Liberal Democrat mainstream, especially on matters of foreign policy, and his decision to move to the cross benches

was in part, at least, the result of his desire to put forward his own views on Europe. He remains, however, a deeply committed 'small-l' liberal.

Key works

- *Class and Class Conflict in Industrial Society* (1959) (a slightly different German version, *Klassen und Klassenkonflikt in der industriellen Gesellschaft*, was published in 1957)
- *Society and Democracy in Germany* (1967)
- *The New Liberty: Survival and Justice in a Changing World* (1974 Reith Lectures, published 1975)
- *Life Chances: Approaches to Social and Political Theory* (1979)
- *After 1989: Morals, Revolution and Civil Society* (1997)

Further reading

- *Straddling Theory and Practice – Conversation with Sir Ralf Dahrendorf by Harry Kreisler, 4 April 1989* (available at http://globetrotter.berkeley.edu/Elberg/Dahrendorf/dahrendorf0.html)
- House of Lords Hansard, 24 November 2004 (cols. 67–73)
- 'Liberals in the Wilderness', *The Economist*, 25 August 2005

Julie Smith

David Davies   1880–1944

Parliamentary private secretary to David Lloyd George in 1916–17, the passion of Davies's life was the creation and preservation of world peace, for which he campaigned relentlessly through the League of Nations Union and later the New Commonwealth Association, which he established in 1932. A multi-millionaire from his youth, Davies made use of his massive wealth to finance an array of philanthropic initiatives.

Key ideas

- The creation and maintenance of world peace and stability.
- The need to set up an impartial tribunal to resolve disputes, and an international police force.
- The setting up of a Federation of the United States of Europe.

Biography

David Davies was born on 11 May 1880 at Llandinam, Montgomeryshire, the son of Edward Davies (1852–98) and the grandson of the first David Davies (1818–90), popularly known as 'Top Sawyer', an enormously successful capitalist and philanthropist who had amassed a huge personal fortune from the collieries, railways and docks of south Wales. Edward Davies's death in 1898 left his son and his two sisters as heirs to an estate exceeding £2,000,000 and an array of industrial and commercial concerns.

Davies was educated at Merchiston Castle, a public school near Edinburgh, and at King's College, Cambridge. He travelled widely before returning to Wales to run the Llandinam estate. In 1906 he became chairman of the Ocean Colliery group, and also entered Parliament as Liberal MP for Montgomeryshire (with local Unionist support). Immensely popular in his constituency, he soon displayed a marked distaste for parliamentary procedure and political life.

At the beginning of the First World War, Davies served in the South Wales Borderers and the Royal Welch Fusiliers, but in June 1916 was recalled to England to become parliamentary private secretary to David Lloyd George (q.v.), whose accession to the premiership in the following December he facilitated. His dismissal from the Cabinet Secretariat in June 1917 led to a permanent rift with the Prime Minister. Following a further split with Lloyd George over the contentious 'Green Book' proposals in

1926, Davies retired permanently from Parliament in May 1929.

Davies maintained an array of business commitments which provided him with a most substantial income. He felt impelled to make use of his vast wealth to follow the family tradition of public service and benefaction. This explains his unstinting support of the University College of Wales, Aberystwyth, the National Library of Wales and the Presbyterian Church in Wales. In 1910 he made available £150,000 to found the Welsh National Memorial Association, to combat the scourge of tuberculosis in Wales. He also established the Welsh Town Planning and Housing Trust, and in 1938 he was primarily responsible for financing the Temple of Peace and Health in Cathays Park, Cardiff.

His foremost preoccupation, however, was the creation and preservation of world peace. He was a stalwart supporter of the League of Nations Union (q.v.), but by the 1930s he was dismayed by the relative impotence of the League of Nations, and set up the New Commonwealth Association in 1932. In the same year he became the first Baron Davies of Llandinam. During the 1930s he pressed for an international tribunal and police force, and spared no effort to build up the New Commonwealth Association. At the end of the decade he fought for an 'United Front' of progressive forces in British public life to counter the appeasement policies of the Chamberlain government. He died at Llandinam on 16 June 1944.

Davies's undoubted generosity and public-spirited nature, manifested above all in his great crusades for world peace and health, were to some extent undermined by an impulsive, imperious, impatient personality, reflected in a belief that wealth alone could decide the course of events. He was, therefore, inclined to attempt to steamroller his colleagues and opponents alike into submission, an attitude which created as many enemies, repelled by his impatience and reliance on wealth, as it made friends, attracted by his charisma and vision.

Ideas

The experiences of the First World War had a profound impression upon David Davies. The horrors which he witnessed, and the massive loss of life in the trenches, convinced him that war must be avoided at all costs. From 1917 his thinking revolved around these themes: how to make peace, how to keep the peace, how to deal with threats to peace. Hence his involvement with groups set up to prevent a recurrence of the holocaust of 1914–18, among them the League of Nations Society, the League of Free Nations Association and the New Europe Society.

Davies became convinced of the need for a concerted effort to make war impossible; hence his support for the League of Nations, and the League of Nations Union, which became the main vehicle for popular support for the League. Davies was a vice-chairman of the British LNU from 1918 and a stalwart of the Welsh LNU. The promotion of peace and harmony among nations was his primary goal in the 1920s. He endowed the Wilson Chair at Aberystwyth in 1919 and convened a series of conferences on international education at Gregynog Hall, his mansion-like Montgomeryshire home.

Two issues vexed Davies particularly: the problem of decision-making by the League, especially in a crisis situation, and the question of the enforcement of decisions once made. He advocated the need for an impartial tribunal to resolve international disputes and an international police force to carry out the resolutions of the tribunal. These ideas were advocated in his tome *The Problem of the Twentieth Century* (1930). Davies's doubts about the League were confirmed by the events of the Russo-Chinese war of 1929, the Japanese invasion of Manchuria in 1931–33, and the failure of disarmament negotiations by the early 1930s. His intense disillusionment led to the establishment of the New Commonwealth Society in 1932 and the publication of his second volume, *Force* (1934). Events after 1933 convinced Davies that the British government's appeasement policies were totally misguided.

When war broke out again in 1939, Davies grew more certain of the need for a fresh approach to world peace and security. He advocated the setting up of a Federation of the United States of Europe. Sadly, he did not live to see the end of hostilities.

Key works

- *The Problem of the Twentieth Century* (1930)
- *Force* (1934)
- *A Federated Europe* (1940)
- *The Foundations of Victory* (1941)
- *The Seven Pillars of Peace* (1943)

Further reading

- J. Graham Jones, 'Montgomeryshire politics: Lloyd George, David Davies and "the Green Book"', *Montgomeryshire Collections* 72 (1984)
- J. Graham Jones, 'The Peacemonger', *Journal of Liberal Democrat History* 29 (Winter 2000–01)
- Peter Lewis, *Biographical Sketch of David Davies (Topsawyer) 1818–1890 and His Grandson David Davies (1st Baron Davies) 1880–1944* (Newtown, no date)
- David Steeds, 'David Davies, Llandinam and international affairs', *Transactions of the Honourable Society of Cymmrodorion 2002* (New series, Vol. 9, 2003)

J. Graham Jones

Democracy *see* Liberal Democracy

A. V. Dicey   1835–1922

Possibly the leading jurist of his generation (1880–1910), especially renowned for his eminence in the fields of constitutional law and the conflict of laws. Dicey held throughout his life that extension of state action necessarily limited the freedom of the individual.

Key ideas

- The rule of law essential to English constitutionalism.
- Sovereignty of parliament is the key political fact of constitutional law.
- Liberty depends upon the absence of government restraint.

Biography

Albert Venn Dicey was born at Claybrook Hall, near Lutterworth, Leicestershire, on 4 February 1835. His father, Thomas Edward Dicey, was proprietor of the *Northampton Mercury*. His first education came at home from his parents, who impressed upon him that good citizenship required public service. His parents held staunchly liberal values and Dicey embraced the ideas of Jeremy Bentham (q.v.).

At Oxford (Balliol) Dicey graduated in 1858 with a first in Greats and won the Arnold Prize in 1860 with an essay on the Privy Council. He was called to the bar in 1863 at the Inner Temple. He worked briefly as a journalist and practised law with moderate success for the next two decades. In 1882 he was elected Vinerian Professor of English Law at Oxford, and he served in this position with great distinction until his retirement in 1909.

Dicey possessed a keen interest in politics and as a youth he declared himself an individualist, a stance from which he never wavered. He had great faith in the self-regulating beneficence of a market economy and believed that government interference in society diminished individual liberty. Above all other issues, however, Dicey devoted immense energy to opposing home rule, which he criticised in various books from 1886 until his death. For example, when faced in 1903 with a choice between opposing home rule or tariff reform, without hesitation his priority became home rule.

Dicey was remarkably faithful to the liberal values of his youth and his long life transformed a radical of the 1860s into a reactionary in old age. He always thought of himself as a true liberal and never professed Conservative sympathies except on home rule. He died at his home in Oxford on 7 April 1922; he had married Elinor Bonham-Carter in 1872 and the couple had no children.

Ideas

Dicey's great work on constitutional law, *Introduction to the Study of the Law of the Constitution* (1885), explained the three major principles of the English constitution: the rule of law (q.v.), parliamentary sovereignty and constitutional conventions. The rule of law, Dicey wrote, constituted the essence of English liberty, for it ensured all individuals equality (q.v.) before the law and that the state had no special authority exempt from legal control. The sovereignty of Parliament sustained political democracy because politicians were immediately responsible to the electorate. In addition, changing circumstances meant that Parliament might repeal what it had previously approved. No court could invalidate an Act of Parliament; the union of executive and legislative authority in the House of Commons combined legal and political sovereignty. The 'unwritten' constitution also rested on conventions, political understandings that few, if any, would disobey. From this analysis Dicey concluded that the English constitution protected individual rights better than the written constitutions of other countries.

In *Lectures on the Relation between Law and Public Opinion in England during the Nineteenth Century* (1905), Dicey traced the fate of individualism in his lifetime. In a famous tripartite division he rejected the limitations imposed by aristocratic privilege on individual potential under Old Toryism (1800–30); he extolled the period of Benthamite ascendancy (1825–70), when individual liberty reached its zenith; and then he lamented the era of collectivism (1865–1900) in which what he called socialism led to increased government activism and a consequent loss of liberty. His tenacious adherence to classical liberalism (q.v.) never waned and a long introduction to the second edition (1914) contained a bitter jeremiad against the rejection of ideas he held dear.

Dicey was a dedicated Liberal Unionist (q.v.), consistently producing polemics against home rule for Ireland. In *England's Case against Home Rule* (1886) and later books, Dicey presented the constitutional dangers that home rule entailed. He believed passionately that all schemes for Irish home rule would damage constitutional principles and destroy the work of centuries that had created the extant configuration of the United Kingdom. A subsidiary Parliament in Dublin would repudiate parliamentary sovereignty and any form of federal arrangement was inherently a weak form of governance. Hopes for the preservation of the union with Ireland ended in 1921, a result that intensified his pessimism about the changes in public policy that he had witnessed.

Dicey's books still repay reading, for they were written with verve, aimed at a wide audience, and presented arguments clearly. He believed completely in the classical liberal ideas and values that he had embraced as a young man. A true Victorian liberal, Dicey exemplified the commitment to limited government, individual liberty, and an unfettered market economy that would benefit all society. He possessed no sympathy for the New Liberalism (q.v.) that appeared before the First World War. Dicey remained, in his own mind, a true liberal to the end.

Key works
*   *Introduction to the Study of the Law of the Constitution* (1885)
*   *England's Case against Home Rule* (1886)
*   *A Digest of the Law of England with Reference to the Conflict of Laws* (1896)
*   *Lectures on the Relation between Law and Public Opinion in England during the Nineteenth Century* (1905)

Further reading
*   Richard A. Cosgrove, *The Rule of Law: Albert Venn Dicey, Victorian Jurist* (University of North Carolina Press, 1980)
*   Stefan Collini, *Public Moralists: Political Thought and Intellectual Life in Britain, 1850–1930* (Clarendon Press, 1991)
*   Julia Stapleton, 'Dicey and His Legacy', *History of Political Thought* 16 (summer 1995)
*   Ian Ward, *The English Constitution: Myths and Realities* (Hart Publishing, 2004)

Richard Cosgrove

Sir Charles Dilke   1843–1911

A radical politician noted for his ideas on social, political, imperial and military reforms. In the first half of his career he was particularly concerned with democratising Parliament by way of the secret ballot, extending the vote to women and working men, ending corrupt practices and equalising constituencies; the second half saw a marked shift towards support for labour causes and to promoting closer imperial ties and the creation of a powerful navy.

Key ideas

• Injecting a social dimension into orthodox radicalism.
• Reconceptualising empire in terms of a 'Greater Britain'.

Biography

Charles Wentworth Dilke was born on 4 September 1843 in Chelsea, the son of a wealthy periodical publisher. His mother, who died when he was barely ten, was the daughter of an Indian Army captain. His grandfather had the most direct influence on his upbringing, encouraging his radical republicanism and his passion for literature.

He was educated privately and afterwards read law at Trinity Hall, Cambridge, where the ideas of Leslie Stephen, a practitioner of muscular Christianity, and Henry Fawcett, the Benthamite intellectual, rubbed off on him. By this time, he was a thoroughgoing democrat. On leaving Cambridge, he embarked on a global tour. He recounted his experiences in *Greater Britain*, a best seller that led to friendship with J. S. Mill (q.v.). In 1868 he was elected MP for Chelsea. His capabilities were soon in evidence but his reputation with the Liberal establishment was tarnished by his uncompromising radicalism (q.v.), including the promotion of republican ideas.

On the death of his father in 1869, he succeeded to the baronetcy and the considerable family fortune. Two years later, he married Katherine Sheil; she died in 1874, after giving birth to a son. Following a second world tour in 1875, he set about rebuilding his reputation with a series of trenchant speeches critical of Disraeli's imperial policies. He also began forging a formidable alliance with Joseph Chamberlain (q.v.).

In 1880, Dilke was appointed Under-Secretary for Foreign Affairs, a post which involved him in largely fruitless commercial negotiations with France. Promotion to the cabinet in 1882 to the Local Government Board began a period of considerable personal achievement, including chairing the Royal Commission on the Housing of the Working Classes and skilfully steering through the Redistribution of Seats Act (1885), perhaps the most democratising piece of legislation in the whole of the nineteenth century.

Dilke was now at the peak of his influence and was widely regarded as Gladstone's (q.v.) likely successor. The radicals were confident that they would shortly displace the Whigs at the heart of the Liberal Party. Within months, these prospects were shattered by two momentous events: Dilke's fall from grace, when he was cited as co-respondent in an unsavoury divorce case, and the great schism in the Liberal Party over home rule.

Dilke was defeated at Chelsea in 1886 and the rest of his career is usually seen as a minor coda to what had gone before. However, in some respects, it was the more fruitful. First, it saw a prolific output of publications, especially on military and imperial questions. Second, his marriage to Emilia Pattison in 1885 (until her death in 1904) and his return to Parliament in 1892 for the Forest of Dean, a mining constituency, deepened his feminist and labour politics. If we are to believe his own testimony, he was offered, but declined, the leadership of the fledgling Independent Labour Party. He died in London on 26 January 1911.

Ideas

Dilke was in many ways an orthodox radical, supporting 'reform' and 'retrenchment', but he was never a Little Englander or 'peace-at-any-price' radical.

His radicalism was partly a product of his education at the hands of several committed Benthamites: especially his grandfather, who had known Bentham (q.v.), and his Cambridge tutors, Fawcett and Stephen. Although he was a theoretical republican throughout his life, it was only a significant part of his politics during the republican upsurge of 1869–72 and even then was largely about the cost and duties of monarchy rather than its abolition. Of much more significance was his development of a social radicalism. Friendship with Mill drew him into the critical debates over Benthamite individualism and the role of the state. Mill's elaboration of collectivist ideas persuaded Dilke, who was afterwards in the vanguard of attempts to move the Liberal Party towards more interventionist policies, especially after the democratic reforms of 1883–85, when he realised that the Liberal Party might soon lose the allegiance of the working classes. Whether, but for his fall, he could have taken the party in a collectivist direction early enough to have pre-empted the rise of Labour is one of those tantalising imponderables with which history is strewn.

His views on defence and empire alone make this unlikely as they were unacceptable to most Labour (and many Liberal) supporters. *Greater Britain* marked a shift away from the anti-imperialism of the Manchester School (q.v.). In it, Dilke distinguished between 'colonies' and 'dependencies'. The former, areas of white settlement (like Australia), were ripe for independence and incorporation into a voluntary, mutually beneficial confederation (a sort of proto-Commonwealth). By contrast, 'dependencies' (such as India) required a period of benign rule and reform preparatory to independence. This belief in a responsible trusteeship for the undeveloped areas of empire put him ahead of his time. *Greater Britain* is

often seen as encouraging the scramble for territory, but Dilke was resolutely opposed to further annexations; 'Greater Britain' referred to the racial, cultural and ideological superiority of Anglo-Saxons, not to territorial expansion. Twenty years later, in *Problems of Greater Britain,* Dilke returned to considering the value of the colonies as laboratories for social experiments. He had by now shifted his position on the desirability of retaining the empire – it was necessary in order to compete with the US and Russia – but he still believed that it was best held together by cooperation, not control.

Its survival was also dependent upon effective defence. Dilke had always been interested in military reform but after 1886 he promoted it through a stream of publications. He advocated separation of the army into short-service home, and long-service Indian, divisions and the creation of an expeditionary force. He was also converted by Spenser Wilkinson to the importance of maintaining British naval supremacy – the so-called 'blue-water school'.

While Dilke's ideas on social radicalism, empire and defence were not unique, the way in which he combined them was.

Key works
- *Greater Britain* (1868)
- *The British Army* (1888)
- *Problems of Greater Britain* (2 vols., 1890)
- *Imperial Defence* (with S. Wilkinson, 1892)

Further reading
- Stephen Gwynn and Gertrude M. Tuckwell, *The Life of Sir Charles W. Dilke* (2 vols., John Murray, 1917)
- Roy Jenkins, *Sir Charles Dilke: A Victorian Tragedy* (Collins, 1958)
- David Nicholls, *The Lost Prime Minister: A Life of Sir Charles Dilke* (Hambledon Press, 1995)

David Nicholls

Distributism

A non-party-political movement that grew up in the 1920s and 1930s, dedicated to small-scale mass ownership of land and property as a bastion against collectivism, big business and big institutions, which its founders believed led inevitably to slavery. Distributism flourished under the early leadership of former Liberals Hilaire Belloc and G. K. Chesterton, became associated with radical Catholicism and arts and crafts pioneers like Eric Gill, and disintegrated in the 1940s – but was later influential on key Liberal Party policy-makers in the 1950s and green economics pioneers in the 1970s.

The immediate influences on distributism were the ideas of Hilaire Belloc (q.v.), especially in his book *The Servile State* (1912), and the prolific journalism of G. K. Chesterton (1874–1936). According to its proponents, it was an economic doctrine, but much of what they wrote was also historical criticism and profoundly spiritual.

After the departure of its founding figures from the Liberal Party, mainly over the issue of financial corruption in politics – which they believed reached a symbolic apotheosis over the Marconi insider-trading scandal of 1912 – the movement was politically non-aligned, but its main focus of campaigning was anti-Fabian, anti-modernist and anti-corporate.

The broader influences behind distributism also lay in:

- Roman Catholic social doctrine, the political radicalism (q.v.) of Cardinal Henry Manning (1807–92) and Pope Leo XIII's encyclical *Rerum Novarum* (1891), which first propagated the idea – at the heart of distributism – of 'subsidiarity'.
- English agrarian campaigners in the tradition of William Cobbett (1763–1835) and Jesse Collings (1831–1920).
- The arts and crafts movement's critique of industrialism and the ideas of John Ruskin (1819–1900) and William Morris (1834–96).
- Guild socialism as propagated by the journalism of A. R. Orage (1873–1934) and other anti-Fabians of the left, around the newspaper *New Age*.

Distributists tended to be vague about what they were campaigning for. At heart, the movement was a critique of prevailing state socialism, industrialisation and monopolistic commercialism. They proposed the widespread distribution of land and property and looked forward to a revival of the values of small-scale agriculture and crafts, which they regarded as an urgent bastion to defend the human spirit – and distributism was overwhelmingly a spiritual creed – against the slavery of corporatism of right or left.

Apart from Belloc and Chesterton, who remained somewhat apart from the organisation of the Distributist League – founded in 1926 by architect and former Fabian Arthur Penty (1875–1937) and others – the leading figures of distributism were extremely diverse. They ranged from arts and crafts pioneers like Eric Gill (1882–1940) and journalists like 'Beachcomber' (J. B. Morton, 1894–1979), to agrarian campaigners like H. J. Massingham (1888–1952), as well as Catholic apologists and land reformers. In some ways, the sheer diversity of the movement militated against its effectiveness, certainly its coherence in the public's mind.

On the face of it, distributism petered out in the 1940s and 1950s with no lasting political legacy. The whole tenor, certainly of Chesterton's contribution, was melancholic, nostalgic and almost entirely lacking in detailed proposals. There was an implied pessimism in much distributist writing, about the inevitability of change, centralisation and giantism. Their practical projects, including challenging monopolistic bus-operators in London in the 1920s, and advocating land reform as a solution to unemployment in Birmingham in the 1940s, did not take root.

They were more obviously influential on the prevailing culture, with the founding of the distributist crafts community in Ditchling in Sussex, and were undoubtedly an influence which fed into the post-war English romantic revival.

Distributism came to be increasingly identified, not just with extreme romanticism, but also with a particular kind of Catholic radicalism that looked to Franco and Mussolini as defenders of European Catholicism. Their links to more reactionary agrarian groups in the 1930s meant that distributism sometimes provided a route to the far right at that time.

Distributists were uncommitted on the issue of free trade (q.v.), but they were implacable in their opposition to modernism, or what they called 'commercial values'. Although most distributist thinkers rejected the link, in practice there were informal connections with the social credit movement that also emerged from guild socialism.

But there are ways in which distributists managed to make a longer impact on liberal politics. Their critique of mainstream Fabianism was available for those post-war political thinkers searching for alternatives to collectivism and corporatism. There were formal discussions between the League and the Liberal Party in the 1950s, and they were an acknowledged influence on Liberal Party industrial policy from 1937 onwards, especially in the writings of the party on ownership and industrial democracy in the Jo Grimond (q.v.) years.

When the influential book *Small is Beautiful* was published in 1973, author E. F. Schumacher (q.v.) included a critical chapter entitled 'Chestertonian Economics' which had a major influence on the emerging field of green economics. There was also an unacknowledged influence on some of the more radical aspects of Thatcherism, including the 1979 decision to sell council houses to their tenants. There may also, arguably, be deeper and more pervasive influences on modern journalism, building on the original influence of Morton and his associates on the concerns of the popular press – for individuals against the big institutions – which is often dismissed as populism.

Further reading
- Hilaire Belloc, *The Servile State* (1912; reprint, Liberty Fund, 1977)
- Hilaire Belloc, *Economics for Helen* (1924; reprint, Ihs Press, 2005)
- Hilaire Belloc, *An Essay on the Restoration of Property* (1936; reprint, Ihs Press, 2002)
- G. K. Chesterton, *An Outline of Sanity* (1926; reprint, Ihs Press, 2002)
- John Sharpe (ed.), *Distributist Perspectives: Essays on the Economics of Justice and Charity* (Ihs Press, 2004)
- Herbert Shove, *The Fairy Ring of Commerce* (Distributist League, 1930)

David Boyle

Elliott Dodds　　　　1889–1977

An influential communicator of Liberal thought during the middle decades of the twentieth century (the bleakest period in the Liberal Party's history), and closely associated with the party's policy on profit-sharing and co-partnership in industry.

Key ideas
- Liberalism concerned with men and women as persons, not just as units in the economic system.

- Decentralisation – politically and economically – vital to maintain and increase freedom.
- Widespread diffusion of personal ownership of property and business as foundation of liberty ('Ownership for All').
- Liberal Party more radical than main parties rather than situated centrally on a left-right spectrum.

Biography

George Elliott Dodds was born in Sydenham, Kent on 4 March 1889, the son of George William Dodds, a tea merchant originally from Berwick-upon-Tweed, and his wife, Elizabeth Anne. He was educated at Mill Hill School and Oxford University, where he took a first in history and edited *Isis* magazine.

He worked for a time as private secretary to Herbert Samuel (q.v.), taught at a school in Jamaica, and read for the bar, but in 1914 he joined the staff of the *Huddersfield Examiner*, as a leader-writer and literary assistant, beginning a connection with the newspaper which lasted for sixty years. He edited the *Examiner* from 1924–59, infusing the paper with his own liberal values and undoubtedly helping the Liberals retain considerable support in the town into the 1950s and beyond. He stood for Parliament on five occasions in the 1920s and 1930s, contesting York in 1922 and 1923, Halifax in 1929, and Rochdale in 1931 and 1935, but was unsuccessful each time.

Dodds's influence within the Liberal Party stemmed primarily from his writing, commencing with *Is Liberalism Dead?* in 1920. He examined the nature of the division between the Liberal and Labour parties and sought to reconcile contemporary support for increased state involvement in the economy with the Liberal Party's traditional caution in countenancing such an approach.

In 1938 he chaired the Liberal Party's 'Ownership for All' committee, whose report, which emphasised the role of property ownership as the 'bedrock of liberty', was accepted by that year's Liberal Assembly but disputed thereafter by many on the left of the party. Despite emerging as a leader of the right wing of the Liberal Party, Dodds was instrumental in ensuring that the party gave its overwhelming support to the Beveridge Report. He also changed his view on whether or not co-ownership should be voluntary or statutory, backing compulsion after 1945.

Dodds was president of the Liberal Party in 1948, and in 1953 became chairman of the Unservile State Group (q.v.). He was appointed CBE in 1973, finally retired from writing for the *Examiner* in 1974, and died on 20 February 1977.

Ideas

Dodds's political thinking was a product of the era in which he wrote and his northern Nonconformist background. The Liberal Party, dominant before the First World War, was on the retreat during the 1920s as Labour became established as the main challenger to the Conservatives. Dodds spent little time examining the distinctions between the Liberal and Conservative parties – to him the differences between Britain's established political ideologies were too obvious and fundamental to require further explanation. His focus was on the fault lines between the Liberal and Labour parties, as he sought to maintain a philosophical justification for liberalism despite the decline of the Liberal Party's electoral fortunes.

For Dodds, the mainspring of liberalism was a concern for men and women as persons rather than as economic units or cogs in the industrial machine. Personality – the quality of being a person as distinguished from a thing – was best developed by a person's free response to his environment. Dodds was not an unbridled individualist: personal freedoms could only be exercised by all if the interdependence of individuals within society was recognised. From this analysis Dodds drew the conclusion that decentralisation was vital to maintain and increase the freedoms exercised by persons:

> Liberals value the 'small man' not mainly because he represents something indispensable in our national life. He is a person; he renders personal service; he manages his own business; he knows and is known by his customers; he lives where he makes his livelihood; he belongs to the local community and contributes to its life.

Dodds pressed for the Liberal Party to develop policies aimed at the 'small man' and the party's interest in small business was particularly evident in the 1940s and 1950s. His conviction that decentralisation was necessary to promote liberty also influenced his thinking on local government, devolution for Scotland and Wales, and foreign policy. He was a strong supporter of the League of Nations in the 1930s and wrote in support of the rights of small nations. It was in relation to home ownership and the ownership of industry, however, that his thinking was most distinctive and influential.

The development of 'personality' and, therefore, the enhancement of liberty, depended, in Dodds's view, on making more widespread the ownership of property of all sorts. If every person owned, and consequently had some control over, property they would be more secure economically and more likely to participate in, and enhance, the civic society of their community. Tackling the grossly unequal distribution of property in the United Kingdom provided the answer to the dilemma facing the Liberal Party since the later decades

of the nineteenth century: how to ensure people enjoyed economic freedom without excessive state intervention.

The 1938 *Ownership for All* report set out the mechanisms by which property could be redistributed. These included the restoration of free trade (q.v.); the prohibition of price-fixing and other restraints of trade and a tougher line against monopolies; the rating of site values rather than buildings; and changes to the taxation of inheritances. Most striking was the report's emphasis on profit-sharing and co-partnership in industry, whereby workers would have a say in the management of their firms. This built on existing Liberal policy for the establishment of forums in which workers and management could discuss common problems and also drew on the experience of profit-sharing schemes such as that pioneered by former Liberal MP Theodore Taylor at his textiles firm. The 1938 report stated that the effect of such schemes had been:

> to promote a 'saving sense of proprietorship', increase interest in daily work, knit closer the bonds between employer and employed, educate the workers in industrial citizenship, and weaken the tendency towards class distinction.

Profit-sharing, co-partnership and co-ownership – the terms came to be used interchangeably – were a main feature of Liberal policy in the 1940s and 1950s, popular with activists and clearly distinct from the economic thinking of the main parties.

Dodds had also developed a coherent alternative to the ideas promoted by Lloyd George (q.v.) and Keynes (q.v.) in the late 1920s, particularly those encapsulated in *Britain's Industrial Future* (the Yellow Book). Whereas the Yellow Book had envisaged an enhanced role for the state in economic matters, Dodds suggested that a radical redistribution of income could arise from the state creating an appropriate legal framework and then standing back to let the market do the rest. Predictably, Dodds came under attack from the left wing of the Liberal Party at successive Liberal assemblies in the early 1940s. In 1942, for example, Liberal MP Tom Horabin called for the appointment of a Minister of National Planning and an Economic General Staff. In reply Dodds rejected the suggestion that he was harking back to mid-Victorian laissez-faire (q.v.):

> We are advocating State action of the most drastic and radical character to disestablish privilege and abolish the barriers which prevent the gains due to industrial progress from being shared by the whole people. We seek to plan – yes, to plan – a framework in which freedom may flourish.

Having emerged as a standard-bearer of the Liberal right, it is perhaps surprising that Dodds was later to embrace enthusiastically the Beveridge Report and the imposition of co-ownership on large firms by legislation. Although both views could be justified from first principles they also reflected Dodds's role as a politician rather than simply as a liberal thinker. His backing for the details of the Beveridge Report was distinctly lukewarm, but he was unequivocal in his support for its broad thrust: 'Will more people enjoy greater liberty as a result of this policy? ... I, as a libertarian, give an unhesitating affirmative.'

He rejected the concept of the 'welfare state' in favour of a 'welfare society' in which state intervention to help the least well off would generally diminish as private endeavour and voluntary organisations became better able to provide assistance themselves. As for compulsory co-ownership, Dodds considered that the harm caused by state intervention would be outweighed by the benefits of kick-starting the redistribution of property he was so keen to promote.

Dodds's ideas were not original – in calling for a redistribution of property, he was following in the tradition of Belloc (q.v.) and Chesterton, for example – but he had a knack for explaining complex arguments clearly and with reference to contemporary issues. Although Keynes and Beveridge (q.v.) were the outstanding liberal thinkers of the mid-twentieth century, Dodds did more over a longer period to carve out a philosophical niche for the Liberal Party at a time when it was being buffeted from left and right.

Dodds recognised the importance of linking philosophy to concrete policy proposals – well exemplified by the *Ownership for All* package. He showed how liberals could remain radical without accepting the left-wing agenda of increased state involvement in the economy, industry and welfare provision. His conception of liberalism, perhaps unfairly often regarded as right-wing because of its focus on the market, was to predominate in the Liberal Party until the late 1950s.

Key works
- *Is Liberalism Dead?* (1920)
- *Liberalism in Action* (1922)
- Liberal Party Organisation, *Ownership for All* (1937)
- *Let's Try Liberalism* (1944)
- *The Defence of Man* (1947)
- 'Liberty and Welfare', in George Watson (ed.), *The Unservile State: Essays in Liberty and Welfare* (Allen & Unwin, 1957)
- *The Logic of Liberty* (with E. Reiss, 1966)

Further reading
- Donald Wade and Desmond Banks, *The Political Insight of Elliott Dodds* (Elliott Dodds Trust, 1977)
- Dodds's papers have been deposited with the University of Sheffield

Robert Ingham

Ronald Dworkin 1931–

One of the most influential English-language political and legal theorists of his generation, he has put forward a liberal theory of law, rights and distributive justice, and is a prominent defender of the right to free speech, abortion and assisted suicide among others. For the last four decades Dworkin has been setting the terms of debate among legal and political philosophers as well as reaching out to a wider audience through his regular contributions to the *New York Review of Books*.

Key ideas

- To determine what the law requires it is necessary to interpret legal materials in the light of moral principles.
- Rights should be thought of as trumps over collective goals.
- Legitimate government must treat citizens with equal concern and respect.
- Justice requires equality of resources between people.

Biography

Dworkin was born on 11 December 1931 in Worcester, Massachusetts. He received undergraduate degrees from Harvard College and, as a Rhodes Scholar, Oxford University (Magdalen College); an MA from Yale University; and an LLB from Harvard Law School.

Following a prestigious clerkship and career as an associate at the renowned law firm Sullivan & Cromwell, since 1962 Dworkin has held various academic positions, including the Wesley N. Hohfeld Chair of Jurisprudence at Yale; the Chair of Jurisprudence at Oxford, in which position he succeeded H. L. A. Hart; and the Quain Chair of Jurisprudence at University College London.

He is currently Bentham Professor of Jurisprudence at University College London, as well as Professor of Philosophy and Frank Henry Sommer Professor of Law at New York University.

Ideas

Dworkin's writings in legal, political and moral philosophy are notable not just for their influence and originality but also for their internal coherence; they elaborate the idea that governments should treat people with equal concern and respect.

Within the domain of legal philosophy, Dworkin offered a critique of H. L. A. Hart's version of legal positivism. This critique developed into a complex theory of law, set out in *Law's Empire* (1986). One crucial claim made by Dworkin is that the law consists not only of rules adopted or identified by appropriate institutions (for example parliaments and courts) but also of moral principles. Even when there is no immediately relevant statute, judicial decision or constitutional provision (legal materials) regulating a given case, it does not follow that the law is silent on an issue. This is because once we accept that the purpose of law in liberal societies is to constrain as well as to justify state coercion, we must also ask which moral principles are expressed by the legal materials. Dworkin argues that those principles of justice, fairness and due process that simultaneously cohere with the legal materials and provide the most morally compelling reading of them should be accepted as legal principles. The process of finding such principles, and thus what the law requires, is necessarily interpretative; Dworkin therefore offers us a theory of law as interpretation. Importantly, it is also a liberal theory of law since, according to Dworkin, it recognises the values of a liberal community and accords adequate protection to rights. Rights are protected since judges in reaching decisions are seen and expected to interpret legal materials precisely through the prism of justice, fairness and due process rather than to engage in 'strong discretion' that might lead them to privilege other considerations.

Dworkin has famously captured the special status that rights are thought to have in liberal societies by suggesting that we should think of rights as trumps – as claims that override competing claims supported by collective justifications that would normally be decisive. Having a right to something therefore means that the government should not deny it to the right-holder even if denying it would be in the general interest. It is the fundamental commitment to equality of concern and respect that, according to Dworkin, can ground particular rights.

It is also in this fundamental commitment to equality of concern that Dworkin aims to ground his theory of distributive justice, which he developed in a series of articles in the early 1980s before elaborating and defending it further in *Sovereign Virtue* (2000) and subsequent writings. Central to the theory is the claim that how people fare in life should, as far as possible, depend on their ambition (personality) but not on their endowment (circumstances).

Realising this ideal requires a number of steps. First, people should be provided with an equal amount of external resources. How would we know if this has been achieved? When the distribution of resources satisfies the envy test: when people do not envy each other their holdings. Only markets – and indeed only fair markets – can, according to Dworkin, deliver such a distribution. Second, differential physical and mental abilities and talents should not be allowed to determine how people fare in life to the extent they normally do. Dworkin suggests that in order to determine the extent of compensation owed to those born with lesser abilities and talents we should ask how much insurance

people would purchase to guard against disability and lack of talent, had a fair insurance market of this type existed. We should then use the results of this hypothetical exercise to determine the extent of compensation. Finally, people should be made to bear the real costs of their choices (ambition) so that these are not, unfairly, borne by others.

Dworkin's proposals for endowment-insensitivity and ambition-sensitivity have been variously characterised as an improvement or a step backwards from Rawls's (q.v.) proposals in *A Theory of Justice* (1971) and have generated one of the most significant debates in English-language political theory of the last two decades: the debate over the desirability of compensating people for their bad brute luck and holding them responsible for their choices (including choices over risky outcomes, which Dworkin famously called option luck).

Dworkin's theory of distributive justice calls for, among other things, progressive taxation, unemployment insurance and universal health provision. In addition, through his writings Dworkin also offers a novel defence of political obligation; of democracy; of the idea that when properly understood, liberty does not conflict with equality; and of a range of liberal rights. In essence, Dworkin has written on practically all the central questions of political theory and well deserves his reputation as one of the most important contributors to the revival of liberal theory in the second half of the twentieth century.

Key works

- *Taking Rights Seriously* (1977)
- *A Matter of Principle* (1985)
- *Law's Empire* (1986)
- *A Bill of Rights for Britain* (1990)
- *Life's Dominion* (1993)
- *Freedom's Law* (1996)

- *Sovereign Virtue* (2000)
- *Justice in Robes* (2006)

Further reading
- Justine Burley (ed.), *Dworkin and His Critics* (Blackwell, 2004)
- Marshall Cohen (ed.), *Ronald Dworkin and Contemporary Jurisprudence* (Duckworth, 1984)
- Stephen Guest, *Ronald Dworkin* (Edinburgh University Press, 2nd edition, 1997)

Zofia Stemplowska

Economic Concepts: Markets and Prosperity

Liberals accept the use of the market mechanisms because they decentralise power, reinforce diversity, respect individuals and generate prosperity. Nevertheless, liberals recognise that market mechanisms by themselves cannot deliver every desirable outcome, and therefore usually take them to be means, not ends in themselves.

The most fundamental proposition of market economics is that free exchange creates value. When someone voluntarily swaps something for something another person has, both people end up better off. If one adds in the observation that, at least for adults of sound mind, other people are unlikely to know what a person wants more accurately than that person, it follows that market transactions tend to deliver what people want better than other conceivable mechanisms of the allocation of resources.

More formally, the free exchange of goods and services tends to push resources not only towards those who value them most, but also towards those in whose hands they are most productive for the purpose of satisfying other people's desires.

The price mechanism allows those who are most willing to sacrifice what they have to outbid others for what they want. It also signals to producers what others desire and delivers the highest profit to those producers who produce at least cost. The market thus delivers what people want at the least possible cost. This is the basic reason markets produce prosperity. There might be situations in which markets fail to produce what people want (situations of 'market failure' such as those produced by information imbalances and high transactions costs), but even in those cases the fact that the market fails does not automatically mean that some other mechanism will succeed. Even if we know that it is theoretically possible for the government to do better, we often cannot identify the right action or else cannot trust the government to take it.

In addition, markets also encourage innovation and technological change. Although anti-market societies have produced significant technical improvements (for example, the Soviet Union and fifteenth-century Imperial China), their achievements are tiny compared with those of the US and western Europe. Moreover, even though, in theory, perfect markets might not generate incentives to innovate (since in a truly perfect market any advantage for an innovator would be instantly removed by imitation), in practice, real-world markets, with their inevitable imperfections, especially in terms of information, provide much better incentives to innovate than state-controlled economies.

The lesson of the transition of the former communist economies to market economies, however, is that free markets are not simple institutions and that 'free' is not the same as 'lawless'. Very simple market transactions ('those carrots for these potatoes') can take place without any institutional framework. Even quite sophisticated transactions can take place between traders who want to repeat their trading indefinitely into the future, even if the traders do not particularly trust one another – as elementary game theory can show. But where indefinite repeat trading is not likely (the most obvious example in present conditions is buying a house), exchange needs trust, and social and, ultimately, legal institutions become necessary if markets are to exist at all. Without stable expectations guaranteed either by social ties or by the rule of law (q.v.), one cannot expect much in the way of investment in infrastructure, for example. The most obvious such institution is a functioning and respected system of property rights, but the point can extend to the political system as a whole: where people expect political power to be used to transfer resources to those who have power, incentives to invest are destroyed. The result is that a liberal market economy is a delicate set of social and political institutions, often difficult to create (though perhaps easier to destroy). It is not merely the absence of state control over market transactions.

The best balance between social and legal elements in the institutions of a market economy, although a matter of great political controversy even among liberals, is not easy to specify, and indeed there might be no ahistorical answer to the question. Undoubtedly, as the number of people involved in trading grows, the ability of purely social mechanisms – network connections, reputation, voluntary associations – to maintain trust must decline and the space for the role of law will increase. But other factors, including the degree to which we can expect strangers to comply with norms of honesty and fair dealing, are important. A society of rogues requires more legal intervention than an equally sized society of saints.

In addition, legal institutions bring their own problems – for they are political institutions liable to misuse. The separation of courts from other political bodies might bring some protection, but even that depends on the honesty of judges. All institutions, including legal institutions, are social and all social institutions ultimately depend on the morality of those who operate within them. The market cannot develop very far in societies wracked by deceit and dishonesty.

Finally, there are limits inherent in the notion of 'prosperity'. There are two sorts of limit: those related to what counts as prosperity and those related to how important prosperity is compared to other goals.

In the first category come limitations imposed by the physical carrying capacity of the planet. Although the creation of value is not necessarily, as some seem to believe, a physical act subject to the laws of physics, most economic activity does use up physical resources or produce physical effects. In some cases, these physical effects have the potential to produce intolerable costs on the entire population of the planet. Climate change is the most obvious example.

Also in the first category come doubts about whether, after a certain point, satisfying preferences makes people any happier. 'Happiness' economics suggests that increases in overall satisfaction with life are strongly associated with increases in income only over an initial part of the income scale and that, after that point, happiness is associated with satisfactions that are not available from the market, for example personal relationships and feelings of belonging to a community.

In the second category comes the classic problem of the difference between 'allocation' and 'distribution'. Markets are good at what economists call 'allocation' – the matching of resources with people to optimise production and the satisfaction of preferences – but that does not mean that markets are good at 'distribution', how the benefits of production are spread across society. The relationship between efficient allocation and fair distribution is complex. At a technical economic level, according to the Second Fundamental Theorem of Welfare Economics, under certain restrictive conditions, the two are completely independent of one another. But in the real world, for example where information is not perfect and taxes are not all of the lump-sum variety, they are not independent. Looked at more practically, on the one hand, measures taken to improve allocation might interfere with fair distribution, because matters often taken to be relevant to fair distribution (e.g. need, citizenship and place of residence) are not relevant to allocation. On the other hand, there are situations in which creating a distribution that is felt to be fairer can improve productivity, for example by reducing resentments. The balance between the two is an empirical matter.

The relationship is even more complicated because, technically, 'allocation' depends on 'distribution', in the sense that one can only say that an allocation is efficient given a specific distribution of income and wealth. That is because people in different income bands might have different preferences for types of goods and services, so that changing the distribution of income might change the combination of goods and services that would best satisfy preferences. Distribution is thus prior to allocation.

More broadly, unequal distribution can have political consequences the need to avoid which, from a liberal viewpoint, trumps allocative efficiency. According to the Rawlsian (q.v.) political liberal position, for example, wealth maximisation is to be pursued only if the conditions exist to create and maintain a fully working liberal democracy (q.v.), conditions that include a distribution of wealth compatible with the functioning of a democratic society.

Also in the second category are limitations that arise from the fact that the market delivers strictly what people want. It ignores the important question of whether people should want what they happen to want. We all recognise that certain sorts of desire are wrong. Indeed, morality itself is often about what it is right, or good, to want. Morality is not, however, the same as politics. Nevertheless, although there are libertarians who believe that it is never right for the state to proscribe desires, liberals tend to the view that acting on certain forms of desire should be legally barred (on the basis, for example, of the 'harm principle', although the scope of that principle is controversial).

These limitations illustrate the point that although market mechanisms are plausibly seen as inherently liberal, because they decentralise power, reinforce diversity and respect individuals, liberals usually take them to be means, not ends in themselves.

Further reading
- Robert Axelrod, *The Evolution of Co-operation* (Basic Books, 1985)
- James Buchanan, *The Limits of Liberty* (University of Chicago Press, 1975)
- Daniel Finn, *The Moral Economy of Markets* (Cambridge University Press, 2006)
- Friedrich Hayek, *Law, Legislation and Liberty* (3 vols., University of Chicago Press, 1973–79)
- Richard Layard, *Happiness* (Penguin Books, 2006)
- Mancur Olsen, *Power and Prosperity* (Basic Books, 2000)
- John Rawls (ed. Erin Kelly), *Justice as Fairness* (Belknap Press, 2001)

David Howarth

Economic Concepts: The Welfare State

The British welfare state was very largely a liberal creation, the product of Asquith's New Liberal government and of the political tradition it created, culminating in Beveridge's Report. Liberal support for the welfare state has not derived from a single principle or argument, with both arguments of fairness and arguments of efficiency advanced for its continuation or development. Nevertheless, modern liberal justifications would benefit from being grounded more clearly in principle – for example, the Rawlsian position that each citizen should be guaranteed sufficient income that their participation in politics is not excluded purely through the exigencies of poverty, and, beyond that, participation is not prevented by unnecessary ill-health or made meaningless by lack of education.

The political impetus for the creation of welfare states came from different directions in different countries: in Germany, the Bismarckian right, in many other countries the social democratic left. But in Britain, it was a liberal idea, the product of Asquith's New Liberal (q.v.) government and of the political tradition it created, culminating in Beveridge's (q.v.) Report. Indeed, as George Watson has shown, the British Labour Party consistently opposed moves towards a welfare state for the whole of the inter-war period, fearing that it would merely prop up capitalism and undermine both the trade unions and the case for socialism. Despite its subsequent propaganda, Labour was the last major political party to sign up to Beveridge's plan and experienced considerable internal opposition to the idea of a comprehensive National Health Service. The idea that socialism means welfare and welfare means socialism, as opposed to socialism meaning state control of the economy, is a convenient but false historical myth, albeit a myth on which the Labour Party still relies for its self-image.

British Liberal support for the welfare state has not derived from a single principle or argument. The motives of the 1906 government, for example, included a humanitarian impulse to rescue the unfortunate from misery and to provide them with a life of basic dignity, but also included a desire to improve national efficiency to fight off international competition. The same blend continues to this day, with both arguments of fairness and arguments of efficiency advanced for the continuation or the development of the welfare state.

Within the fairness justification a further distinction can be drawn between a desire to protect those who fall into misfortune through no fault of their own and a desire to prevent material degradation regardless of how it came about. The former position seeks to preserve a space for individual responsibility for how a person's life turns out, the latter to guarantee each individual a standard of life which, to quote Lloyd George (q.v.), 'no country can lay any real claim to civilisation' if it fails to provide. Both positions can claim some liberal justification, and, indeed, they are not entirely incompatible with one another, since one might guarantee a basic level regardless of the recipient's conduct but offer more to those who comply with behavioural conditions (as in 'workfare'). Nevertheless, the latter view, because it requires the state to be more neutral about individuals' lifestyles, is arguably more liberal than the former, which is why many liberals have been attracted to the basic or 'citizens' income' approach – under which the state guarantees every citizen a sufficient income (for example through an integrated income tax and benefit system) regardless of their behaviour. The advantage of such an approach from a liberal point of view is that the state maintains a strict neutrality about citizens' lifestyles. The basic income is equivalent to a property right with which citizens can do whatever they want. Questions remain, however, about the practicality of such a scheme.

The efficiency arguments for the welfare state are themselves various: that welfare provision involves the production of goods and services that have positive externalities – for example that health and education spending can raise the productivity of labour in ways that individuals do not themselves capture in wages, that stopping destitution prevents crime, which in turn helps to make property rights more secure and hence encourages investment, that inequality causes resentment that undermines incentives to cooperate and thus reduces productivity, and that informational problems mean that market mechanisms underinsure people against misfortunes such as unemployment and illness.

The efficiency arguments are inherently vulnerable to empirical refutation, and evidence for them, although not entirely absent, is sporadic. On the other hand, attempts to show that welfare spending has the opposite effect – that it is not productive and reduces investment and thus undermines economic prosperity – have themselves found far less success than generally believed. Despite much research effort, the fundamental position is still as Jonathan Temple stated it in 1999:

> In political discussion it is common to hear claims that a high ratio of social security transfers to GDP and a high level of government consumption can be damaging to growth prospects. The evidence is not strong. Some researchers find a negative link between government consumption and growth, but overall studies disagree, and it would be wrong to argue that a correlation between small government and fast growth leaps out from the data.

Work continues on whether particular types of government expenditure are likely to have positive or negative effects on conventional economic growth, but industrial subsidies seem to be a more likely source of economic failure than social security payments. Even if a negative link exists between growth and welfare state expenditures, the role of other factors, especially institutional factors, in promoting or hindering growth are likely to be far more important.

Another, largely conservative or communitarian, line of attack against the welfare state, especially in its liberal form, is that it has undermined informal social solidarity, in the form of family or voluntary sector support. The argument is that, by removing personal responsibility for others, the welfare state has promoted individualism and selfishness, or that, by transferring responsibility to the state, people assume that there is no need for them to help. This criticism is sometimes associated with calls for a 'welfare society' in which responsibility for caring for the poor and ill is transferred back to families and the voluntary sector, including religious organisations – a position liberals have long resisted on the grounds that, in the words of J. S. Mill (q.v.), 'charity gives too much and too little: it lavishes its bounty in one place, and leaves people to starve in another'.

There is also a countervailing argument that the welfare state encourages pro-social attitudes, either by reinforcing the idea that we are responsible for what we allow to happen to others or by reinforcing feelings of mutuality and community (the former being a more liberal argument than the latter). This argument is the basis both of a moral attack on attempts to reduce welfare spending and of an explanation of repeated funding crises in which cuts in spending undermine the legitimacy of the remaining spending by encouraging asocial, individualistic public attitudes.

Evidence can be adduced on both sides of the controversy about the effect of the welfare state on social values, but the current state of play is that there is little sign of an overall effect either way. Although advocates appeal to particular examples, social attitudes, at least in Europe, to informal social support seem largely unconnected with the degree or style of welfare provision, apart, perhaps, for a small effect in the direction of assuming that if the state is helping others effectively there is less need for individuals to help. On the other hand, high welfare spending does seem to be connected with high levels of social capital – for example with social interconnectedness and trust in neighbours – but the direction of causation is unclear.

The connection between social capital and welfare spending has suggested to one *soi-disant* social democratic commentator, David Goodhart, that, as the solidarities of social class decline and as ethnic and religious diversity increases, support for the welfare state will weaken unless a new source of solidarity is found. Goodhart suggests that the new source should be nationalism, albeit in its civic rather than its ethnic guise. This discovery of a British form of Gaullism has had little appeal to liberals, for whom support for the welfare state never arose from class solidarity in the first place. It is, furthermore, far from clear that there is evidence for the suggestion that diversity threatens the legitimacy of the welfare state. As Philippe Legrain points out in a comment on Goodhart's thesis, support for the welfare state seems historically to have been greater in ethnically diverse cities such as London and Toronto than in ethnically homogeneous country areas.

Nevertheless, liberal justifications for the welfare state are in need of clarification. Humanitarian sentiment backed by empirical arguments that turn out to be far from secure looks too weak a base from which to withstand conservative or communitarian attacks on the welfare state. Liberalism in the future needs to develop arguments more grounded in principle. For example, Rawlsian (q.v.) political liberalism offers the perspective of relating the degree and composition of government spending back to the requirements of a functioning democracy in which each citizen has the means to participate in democratic politics on reasonably fair terms. That means, at the very least, securing for each citizen sufficient income that their participation in politics is not excluded purely through the exigencies of poverty, and, beyond that, participation is not prevented by unnecessary ill-health or made meaningless by lack of education.

Further reading

- Wil Arts, Loek Halman & Wim van Oorschot, 'The Welfare State: Villain or Hero of the Piece?' in W. Arts, J. Hagenaars and L. Halman (eds.), *The Cultural Diversity of European Unity* (Brill, 2003)

- Nicholas Barr, 'Economic Theory and the Welfare State: A Survey and Interpretation', *Journal of Economic Literature* 30 (1992)

- *Commission on Wealth Creation and Social Cohesion, Report on Wealth Creation and Social Cohesion in a Free Society* (1995) (the Dahrendorf Report)

- David Goodhart, *Progressive Nationalism* (Demos, 2006)

- David Howarth, 'Three Forms of Responsibility', *Cambridge Law Journal* 60 (2001)

- Jonathan Temple, 'The New Growth Evidence', *Journal of Economic Literature* 56 (1999)
- George Watson, 'Take Back the Past', *European Review* 10 (2002)

David Howarth

Economic Liberalism

In political terms, economic liberals proclaim their belief in individual freedom and free markets; they support a reduction in the role of the state, particularly in the spheres of economic management and social welfare. The term is often used interchangeably with classical liberalism (q.v.) and that entry should be referred to for a summary of the economic liberal position.

The term 'classical liberalism' itself tends to be associated with nineteenth-century approaches to political and economic questions, such as that of the Manchester School (q.v.). The label 'economic liberal' has been more commonly used in modern times, in particular to contrast such individuals' views with those of social liberals (q.v.), who are more willing to accept the case for state intervention as a means of promoting freedom. Economic liberals point to the dangers inherent in such state action, including the growth in bureaucratic power, the threat to civil liberties from an overweening state, and the potential reduction in economic competitiveness.

Although the British Liberal Party/ Liberal Democrats are in general viewed as a social liberal party, there have been and remain some tensions between social and economic liberals, explored in the entry on social liberalism. That entry also explores why continental European liberal parties tend to be more likely to identify themselves as 'economic liberal', although

several European countries possess both social liberal and economic liberal parties.

The term 'economic liberal' – or 'neo-liberal' (q.v.) – has also been used to describe the economic and trade liberalisation policies of the 'Washington consensus' promoted in particular by the International Monetary Fund, involving a withdrawal of state involvement in the economy and a reduction in trade barriers.

Duncan Brack

Environmentalism

A political and ethical set of values that seeks to improve and protect the quality of the natural environment through changes to environmentally harmful human activities, through the adoption of forms of political, economic, and social organisation necessary for the benign treatment of the environment by humans, and through a reassessment of humanity's relationship with nature.

Concern for humanity's impact on the natural environment dates back at least to Roman times, when deforestation in Italy caused irreversible soil degradation and contributed to serious food shortages in the third and fourth centuries AD. Soil conservation was practised in China, India and Peru as early as 2,000 years ago, and in medieval times pollution was associated with the spread of epidemic disease in Europe. In general, however, such issues did not give rise to public activism or much activity by government.

Contemporary environmentalism arose primarily from concerns in the late nineteenth century over the protection of the countryside in Europe and the wilderness in North America, and the health consequences of pollution following the Industrial Revolution. Observing human impacts on the natural environment, the American writer Henry Thoreau (q.v.), amongst others, argued for a duty to preserve areas of unspoiled wilderness. Environmental organisations, established from the late nineteenth century onwards, were primarily middle-class lobbying groups concerned with nature conservation, wildlife protection, and industrial pollution, though a wider concern with the effect of the natural and built environment on human happiness helped drive the garden city movement in Britain in the early twentieth century.

The 1960s and '70s, however, brought a much wider realisation that environmental degradation was an inevitable outcome of modern (or at least Western) patterns of society and economic activity, and could not be halted simply by protecting endangered species, or setting aside land for national parks. Works such as Rachel Carson's *Silent Spring* (1962), Paul Ehrlich's *The Population Bomb* (1968) and the Club of Rome's *The Limits to Growth* (1972) suggested that the planetary ecosystem was reaching the limits of what it could sustain. Further unchecked economic development would, through overwhelming natural ecosystems with pollution, exhausting stocks of natural resources and causing the extinction of species, restrict severely the chances of prosperity, or even of safe and secure livelihoods, for subsequent generations.

The concept of 'sustainable development', expressed most famously in the Brundtland Report (1987) as development 'that meets the needs of the present without compromising the ability of future generations to meet their own needs', became widely accepted, at least in principle, and has subsequently been incorporated into many national action plans and international treaties. Yet, despite some successes, particularly in reducing local air

and water pollution in developed countries, and reducing the use of the chemicals that destroy the Earth's protective ozone layer, the overall record is not encouraging. In 2003, the first report of the UN's Millennium Ecosystem Assessment showed that 60 per cent of the basic ecosystems that support life on Earth are being degraded or used unsustainably. Although catastrophic climate change, caused primarily by the burning of fossil fuels for energy, is increasingly recognised as the most serious current threat to the survival of human societies, action to counteract it has been very limited.

Schools of environmentalist thought

These developments have led to the emergence of a wide variety of schools of environmentalist thought and activism, influencing a huge range of campaigning non-governmental organisations, charitable foundations, scientific bodies and political parties (including explicitly 'green' parties) and ideologies. What follows is a brief sketch, though it should be emphasised that, as in other schools of political thought, environmental thinking is constantly evolving and shifting, and the divisions outlined below are by no means hard and fast.

Environmental thought and the various branches of the environmental movement are often classified into two intellectual camps: *anthropocentric*, or 'human-centred', and *biocentric*, or 'life-centred'; other descriptions of the same divide include 'light green' versus 'dark green', 'shallow ecology' versus 'deep ecology' and 'technocentrism' versus 'ecocentrism'.

The defining feature of *anthropocentrism* is that it considers the moral obligations humans have to the environment to derive from obligations that humans have to each other – including to future generations

– rather than from any obligation to other living things or to the environment as a whole. Anthropocentric approaches therefore focus mainly on the negative effects that environmental degradation has on human beings and their interests; while wildlife and landscapes are afforded value, and their protection is a desirable objective, this is measured in relation to their worth to human societies.

Within this broad heading, there is a variety of viewpoints. *Apocalyptic environmentalism*, common in the 1960s and '70s, suggests the incompatibility of current human lifestyles with long-term survival. It tends to argue for increasing the powers of government to restrict environmentally harmful activities, a viewpoint expressed most vividly in Robert Heilbroner's *An Inquiry into the Human Prospect* (1974), which argued that human survival ultimately required the sacrifice of human freedom (q.v.).

In contrast, so-called *emancipatory environmentalism*, which began to take root in the 1970s and '80s, took a more optimistic approach, emphasising the potential of technological progress to reduce humanity's environmental impact. An important aspect of this approach is the effort to promote an ecological consciousness and an ethic of 'stewardship' of the environment. Individuals are encouraged to live less unsustainably, for example by recycling their waste, or reducing their energy consumption; governments are encouraged towards making the necessary long-term investments, for example in renewable electricity generation or public transport, and altering the framework within which the market operates, for example by taxing energy, to make it more likely that individuals will make more environmentally sensitive choices.

One form of emancipatory environmentalism, *human-welfare ecology* – which aims to enhance human life by creating a safe and clean environment – is part of a broader concern with distributive justice and reflects the 'post-materialist' tendency of citizens in advanced industrial societies to place more importance on quality-of-life issues than on traditional economic concerns. Emancipatory environmentalism also tends to place an emphasis on developing small-scale systems of economic production, more closely integrated with the natural processes of surrounding ecosystems. Important in this strand of environmentalist thought was the German economist Ernst Friedrich Schumacher (q.v.), who emphasised, particularly in *Small is Beautiful* (1973), the need for productive processes that work with nature, not against it.

Critics of anthropocentrism point to its typically Western view of nature as merely a resource to be managed or exploited for human purposes – a view they argue is responsible for centuries of environmental destruction. In contrast, *biocentrism* claims that nature has an intrinsic moral worth that does not depend on its usefulness to human beings; humans are morally bound to protect the environment, as well as individual creatures and species, for their own sake, not for their utility to human society.

Within this general heading, the school of thought known as *social ecology* traces the causes of environmental degradation to the existence of unjust hierarchical relationships in human society, which it sees as endemic to the large-scale social structures of modern capitalist states. The most environmentally sympathetic form of political and social organisation is thus one based on decentralised small-scale communities and systems of production. Similarly, *ecofeminism* asserts that there is a connection between the destruction of nature by humans and the oppression of women by men: both arise from political theories and social practices in which both women and nature are treated as objects to be owned or controlled.

The more radical doctrine of *deep ecology* builds on preservationist themes from the early environmental movement. It shares with social ecologists a distrust of capitalism and industrial technology and favours decentralised forms of social organisation. More than this, however, it claims that humans need to regain a 'spiritual' relationship with nature; by understanding the interconnectedness of all organisms in the ecosphere and empathising with non-human nature, humans can develop an ecological consciousness and a sense of ecological solidarity. In particular, James Lovelock argued in *Gaia: A New Look at Life on Earth* (1979) that the planet is a single living, self-regulating entity capable of re-establishing an ecological equilibrium, even without the existence of human life. The biocentric emphasis on intrinsic value and the interconnectedness of nature has also been important in the development of the animal rights movement.

Liberalism and environmentalism

Liberals in many countries, including in particular the UK, have successfully incorporated many elements of environmentalist thinking into their ideology and political programmes; pollution and resource depletion are clearly major impediments to the liberal aims of freedom (q.v.) and self-realisation. It is still open to question, however, whether they (along with other mainstream politicians) have really appreciated the drastic measures that may ultimately be necessary to avert environmental catastrophe.

Classical liberalism (q.v.) is often blamed for the roots of the environmental crisis, in its promotion of free enterprise, free markets and free trade (q.v.) as necessary conditions for the realisation of individuals' plans of life. The environmental impacts of economic decisions – for example, the production and consumption of fossil fuels – are seldom borne directly by those involved in the market transactions; nevertheless, they are real, even though the resulting climatic change may take many years to develop and impact mainly on people living thousands of miles away. In its failure to internalise such environmental externalities, the free market, the underpinning of modern capitalism, has been blamed for much environmental degradation.

Yet political liberals never accepted unlimited freedom of enterprise, always understanding that intervention in the market was justified in order to prevent harm to others – for example, by forbidding slavery. It is not conceptually difficult to extend this principle to altering the parameters within which the market operates, for example through informational tools (e.g. ecolabelling), green taxes or tradable permit systems, to attempt to internalise these environmental costs and benefits and to steer the market and its participants towards more environmentally sensitive outcomes. This can be seen as an attempt to correct a major market failure, the lack of the exercise of property rights over commonly held resources, such as the atmosphere or the oceans. The economist's parable of the 'tragedy of the commons' (the tendency towards over-exploitation of land held in common and owned by no one individual) demonstrates how free access and unrestricted demand for a finite resource ultimately dooms the resource through over-exploitation; if this was not a practical concern for nineteenth-century liberals, this was only because in general they did not conceive of the limits to natural resources that have become obvious only in the last twenty or thirty years.

In fact, even some classical liberals did recognise the problems of unlimited economic growth; most notably John Stuart Mill (q.v.), who, in his *Principles of Political Economy* (1848) argued that: 'It must always have been seen ... by political economists, that the increase in wealth is not boundless: that at the end of what they term the progressive state lies the stationary state, that all progress in wealth is but a postponement of this, and that each step in advance is an approach to it.' Although Mill, following Thomas Malthus (q.v.), was concerned with the limits to resources and the dangers of over-population (and, like Malthus, hugely under-estimated the potential of technological innovation to improve the efficiency with which resources can be utilised), his advocacy of the stationary-state economy was primarily concerned with the damaging effects on human character of the unremitting pursuit of possessions. In welcoming this condition as an opportunity for a large-scale transformation in social values – where intellectual and moral growth continued but without the need to despoil the natural world – Mill can perhaps be seen as a forerunner more of the post-materialist concern with quality-of-life issues than of the Club of Rome's warnings of resource depletion.

The environmentalist approach probably fits most easily into the social liberal (q.v.) strand of liberalism, always readier to accept the necessity for the state to interfere in the rights of contract and property, and the operations of the market, in the interests of enlarging liberty for individuals – in this case, those affected by environmental degradation outside their ability to counter directly. The extension of this concept to the enlargement of the liberty of future, as well as present, generations also fits fairly straightforwardly into modern social liberal thinking, particularly in its idea of 'stewardship', of the natural environment held as a 'trust' by the present for future generations. John Rawls (q.v.), in *A Theory of Justice* (1972), expressed his so-called 'just savings' principle, which required present generations to save some of their resources and achievements for future ones; this was modified, in *Political Liberalism* (1993), to fit more comfortably into the concept of limits to growth, to become the principle that requires present generations to take the welfare of future generations into account in any circumstances.

It is, therefore, perhaps not surprising that the Liberal Party / Liberal Democrats, in the main a social liberal party for over a century, has been able to claim, with reasonable justification, that it has become the greenest of the main British political parties. The Liberal 'Yellow Book', *Britain's Industrial Future* (1928), contained a strong defence of the countryside, advocating the establishment of National Parks. In the wake of the upsurge of environmental concern later in the century, the Liberal Party published a comprehensive *Report on the Environment* in 1972, and in 1979 the Liberal assembly adopted a resolution declaring that 'economic growth, as measured by GDP, is neither desirable nor achievable'. Liberal support for environmental causes, and in particular the party's opposition to nuclear power, was a source of some tension with their more technophile SDP partners in the Alliance of the 1980s.

Despite tensions caused by the disproportionate representation of rural constituencies in its parliamentary party, the merged party, the Liberal Democrats, has consistently adopted a strongly environmental approach, its election manifestos being rated (by environmental NGOs) just behind those of the Green Party, and well ahead of those of the Conservative and Labour parties. The Liberal Democrat thinker Conrad Russell (q.v.) has argued, consistently with his view of liberalism as being concerned primarily with the control of the exercise of power, for liberal environmentalism as stemming from the concept of power held as a trust. The power is not the trustee's own, it comes from the people; trustees do not hold power for their own benefit, but exercise it on behalf of the people; and – crucially for environmentalism – the duty of the trustees is to hand on the inheritance to the next generation in as good a shape as they can leave it: 'in fact, sustainability is the trustee's essential duty'.

As noted above, though, it is not clear, and will not become so until the Liberal Democrats participate in government, whether the party's approach is really robust enough (and electorally acceptable enough) to cope with the increasingly urgent challenges posed by the current environmental crisis. The balance between the liberal adherence to individual freedom, of non-interference in people's choices and lifestyles, and their desire to limit the environmental consequences of those choices, seems likely to become increasingly difficult to strike.

It should be noted, further, that it is not inevitable that liberals will adapt themselves to environmental programmes, and liberal parties have not always done so. There is some evidence to suggest that where they have failed to take up the environmental agenda, they have allowed the growth of explicitly green parties, most notably in Germany. In contrast, where liberals have 'greened' themselves, green parties have tended to remain marginal – for example in the UK or Denmark.

It should also be clear that liberal environmentalism fits squarely into the anthropocentric school of environmentalist thought. Liberalism is primarily concerned with humans, though, as we have seen, not only those alive in the present. Liberals have, in general, not accepted the biocentric insistence that non-humans, such as animals, or the environment as a whole, must be protected regardless of their value to human beings. For a liberal, the concept of intrinsic value can only be sensibly applied to humans, whereas all else that is valued must by definition be instrumentally valuable in some way (i.e. because of the purposes it serves).

It is possible to edge these two concepts together, for example by arguing, as does Andrew Dobson in *Citizenship and the Environment* (2003), that if liberals value choice for the sake of autonomy, then they should value the existence of as wide a range of 'life environments' as possible. This approach does not presume that nature is always already imbued with value – rather, it is valuable because it is there as an option, to be appreciated or not. This is something of an abstract argument, however, and, as Marcel Wissenburg has observed, 'the reasons motivating ecologists and liberals may differ, but the results would be the same: maximised protection of ecological diversity combined with maximum freedom for humans to pursue a green life'. As the direct impacts of environmental degradation on human societies become steadily more serious, the distinction between protecting the environment for its own sake and protecting it for humanity's sake are likely simply to disappear, for all practical purposes, and liberal (and other political) parties will face the increasingly urgent challenge of living within the planet's means.

Further reading

- Tony Beamish, 'The Greening of the Liberals?', *Journal of Liberal Democrat History* 21 (winter 1998–99)
- Andrew Dobson, *Green Political Thought* (Routledge, 2000)

- Jonathon Porritt, *Capitalism as if the World Matters* (Earthscan, 2005)
- Marcel Wissenburg, 'Liberalism', in Andrew Dobson and Robyn Eckersley (eds.), *Political Theory and the Ecological Challenge* (CUP, 2006)
- Marcel Wissenburg, *Green Liberalism: The Free and Green Society* (UCL Press, 1998)

Duncan Brack

Equality

A concept which is more often associated with socialists and social democrats than with liberals, but which is crucial to all liberals in terms of equality before the law. The broader relationship between equality and liberty is also important to liberals who believe that inequality in the socioeconomic sphere can be a barrier to self-realisation and consider that the pursuit of greater material equality in order to advance freedom and demonstrate equal concern for all citizens can be justified.

Liberals are committed to equality, but in a very different sense to the socialist or communist aim of equality of *outcome*; rather, liberals are committed to equality of *justice*. As the constitution of the British Liberal Democrats expresses it, the party exists 'to build and safeguard a fair, free and open society, in which we seek to balance the fundamental values of liberty, equality and community, and in which no one shall be enslaved by poverty, ignorance or conformity'.

This liberal commitment to equality derives from the liberal commitment to freedom (q.v.), and the corresponding belief in a diverse and tolerant society, where individuals are able to exercise freedom of choice, conscience and thought. Since such a society cannot exist where individuals are treated differently by the law or by government institutions because of their nature, 'equality before the law' has been one of the great rallying cries of liberalism from the earliest days of the Whigs (q.v.). In modern times, the work of John Rawls (q.v.) on social justice (q.v.) and Ronald Dworkin (q.v.) on equal concern as a sovereign liberal virtue have been important in providing a theoretical basis for the concept.

This liberal belief in equality before the law has been constrained in terms of its practical application, and in some cases liberals have been prepared to tolerate specific differences in the law in the name of freedom. For example, for much of the nineteenth and early part of the twentieth century, many liberals (though a diminishing proportion) were prepared to restrict the suffrage on the basis of property holding, the value of a rented dwelling or, most obviously, gender – on the grounds that only citizens who had a stake in the country (through the ownership of property) and were truly independent (women, it was argued, were too easily influenced by their husbands, fathers or brothers) could be expected responsibly to exercise the right to vote. Until the late twentieth century, some liberals were slow to support an equal age of consent for all people regardless of sexuality.

However, laws which specifically allow or require the different treatment of different groups of people are relatively rare in the UK. More of an issue since the 1960s has been legislation specifically to protect individuals against discrimination, for example on the grounds of gender or race or, more recently, age. On these issues, and in line with the concept of equality before the law, liberals have been strongly supportive.

More contentious is what might be described as the 'next stage of equality', measures aimed at tackling inequality through positive discrimination. On this issue, liberals have been split: some have seen positive discrimination as necessary to ensure that ingrained inequalities are tackled, others have seen defining people as members of groups rather than as individuals, and giving them advantages over others on that basis, simply as another form of discrimination. These debates are difficult for liberals to resolve on the basis of the principles of either liberty or equality because they involve not merely conflicts between the two values, but sometimes conflicts between competing liberties or competing equalities. This reflects difficulties in resolving conflicts between equality as an abstract concept and equality as a tangible outcome, on the basis that to ensure true equality, and thus greater freedom, it might be necessary to treat some people unequally.

The question of economic inequality has tended to divide liberals along the social liberal–economic liberal axis. At least since the late nineteenth century, social liberals (q.v.) have recognised that state intervention to redress the impediments of poverty, sickness, unemployment and ignorance is necessary to ensure that people are genuinely free to exercise control over their own lives and destinies. A clear statement of this is to be found in L. T. Hobhouse's (q.v.) *Liberalism* (1911), which argued that:

> ... the struggle for liberty is also, when pushed through, a struggle for equality. Freedom to choose and follow an occupation, if it is to become fully effective, means equality with others in the opportunities for following such occupation. This is, in fact, one among the various considerations which leads Liberalism to support a national system of free education, and will lead it further yet on the same lines.

This approach led social liberals to advance the cause of progressive taxation and state-financed public services throughout the twentieth century. In an abbreviated form 'the struggle for liberty is the struggle for equality' has informed recent Liberal Democrat policy statements, and Charles Kennedy as leader cited it regularly, along with Hobhouse's most famous quotation, 'liberty without equality is a name of noble sound and squalid result'.

More recently, the philosopher and economist Amartya Sen's 'capabilities' view of freedom expresses a similar idea: 'There is a strong case for judging individual advantage in terms of the capabilities that a person has, that is the substantive freedoms he or she enjoys to lead the kind of life he or she has reason to value.' And Ronald Dworkin argued a similar case when he argued that 'equal concern requires that government aims at a form of material equality that I have called equality of resources'.

In contrast, economic liberals (q.v.) have tended to regard state intervention of this magnitude as too great an interference with freedom to justify – though it is worth noting that even the leading economic liberal thinker F. A. von Hayek (q.v.) argued that a guaranteed minimum income providing something akin to a subsistence-level existence for those with no resources of their own could be justified as part of the framework provided by a minimal state.

Clearly, for all liberals, equality is not the end point, as it is for socialists and, to a lesser extent, social democrats. Liberals have profound objections to measures designed to ensure equality of outcome, for example in wealth or educational attainment, because they can only involve unacceptable restrictions to freedom inimical to a commitment to diversity and reward for individual endeavour.

For example, no liberal could support a tax system which redistributed income or wealth to such an extent that all ended up with the same income or wealth, as this would entail a very substantial restriction of individual initiative and effort. The challenge is to strike the right balance between the degree of state intervention and the level of inequality one is prepared to accept; and there is a spectrum of points at which a balance can be reached, rather than one extreme or the other.

Furthermore, those, such as social liberals, who argue a case for state action to reduce inequality remain clear that equality is important as a means to secure freedom, not as an end in itself. As the Liberal Democrats' 2002 values statement, *It's about Freedom*, said:

Equality can be of importance to us in so far as it promotes freedom. We do not believe that it can be pursued as an end in itself, and believe that when equality is pursued as a political goal, it is invariably a failure, and the result is to limit liberty and reduce the potential for diversity. What Liberal Democrats focus on is the extent to which poverty and lack of opportunity restrict freedom.

What has been and remains controversial among liberals is precisely how much equality this commitment actually entails.

Further reading

- Ronald Dworkin, *Sovereign Virtue: The Theory and Practice of Equality* (Harvard University Press, 2000)
- L. T. Hobhouse, *Liberalism* (1911; many reprints)
- Will Kymlicka, *Contemporary Political Philosophy: An Introduction* (Oxford University Press, 2nd edn., 2002), ch. 3, 'Liberal Equality'
- Liberal Democrats, *It's about Freedom* (Liberal Democrats, 2002)
- Amartya Sen, *Development as Freedom* (Oxford University Press, 1999)

Richard S. Grayson and Duncan Brack

The Federalists:
Alexander Hamilton 1755–1804
John Jay 1745–1829
James Madison 1751–1836

A group of American writers and politicians who argued, in 1787–88, for the new US constitution enshrining a strong central – but federal – government. The series of essays they published – *The Federalist Papers* – have become classics of western constitutionalism, laying out the doctrine of limited government, representative democracy and federalism.

Key ideas
- Federalism as the basis for the new United States, with a strong but limited federal government.
- The separation of powers between executive, legislature and judiciary.
- No need for a bill of rights.

Background and biographies
While today the Constitution of the United States of America is the undisputed source of legitimisation for the American federal state, this was not the case when it was ratified in 1787–88.

In 1786 a convention of delegates from the thirteen states which had won their independence from Britain in 1775–83 was held in Annapolis to deal with questions of interstate commerce. The convention saw that this topic had wider political implications and called a Constitutional Convention, ostensibly to amend the Articles of Confederation under which the new nation had operated since 1781. The 1787 Philadelphia Convention in the end agreed upon a document that went far beyond the original intentions; its final outcome was the draft of an entirely new Constitution of the United States of America.

The new constitution had to be ratified by at least nine of the thirteen states. It was opposed by several eminent politicians and publicists, among them some of the heroes of the struggle for independence, including Patrick Henry and George Mason. These so-called Anti-Federalists argued that the Philadelphia Convention had had no mandate to write a constitution, that the new draft would override rights enshrined in the already existing state constitutions, that democracy was only for small states and could not survive in a big federal state, and that rights were endangered by too much centralised power.

In 1787–88, in an effort to persuade New York to ratify the constitution, a series of eighty-five essays on the constitution and republican government were published in New York newspapers. The work was collected and published in book form as *The Federalist* (1788), becoming a classic exposition and defence of the constitution.

All the essays appeared under the pseudonym 'Publius'. The identity of the authors in fact became clear only in 1792. Alexander Hamilton (1755–1804) was a New York delegate to the Constitutional Convention and later became first Secretary of the Treasury (1789–95); he was killed in a duel with a political rival in 1804. John Jay (1745–1829) was a New York attorney who had helped negotiate the 1783 peace treaty with Britain and was then Secretary for Foreign Affairs (1784–90); he later became the first Chief Justice of the Supreme Court. James Madison (1751–1836), another lawyer, later became the fourth President of the United States (1809–17).

All three were members of the Federalist Party, which won the first elections both to Congress and the presidency (with John Adams), in 1789, and shared a conservative and centralist outlook. Some of its members, including Hamilton, were considered as crypto-monarchists by their opposition. Their main concern, however, was that the previous institutional arrangements would lead to increasing economic instability and would invite the European powers to regain influence over the former British colonies.

Madison, the most liberal-leaning of the authors, left the Federalists in 1798 in protest against the Alien and Sedition Act which curtailed the freedom of the press. Together with Thomas Jefferson (q.v.), he formed the Republican Party, which accepted the constitution but interpreted it in a less centralist way than the Federalists had done. In their 'Kentucky and Virginia Resolutions', Jefferson and Madison argued for so-called states' rights – the right of the states to nullify federal laws on their territory if they were thought to violate fundamental rights.

The Federalist Party lost power in 1801, and never regained it, though much of their approach was adopted by the Republicans. Their accomplishments, including the establishment of the administrative machinery of national government, were significant.

Ideas

The *Federalist Papers* laid the theoretical foundations for modern democratic constitutionalism. Most earlier writers on the subject, with the notable exception of David Hume (q.v.), who influenced Madison, had thought that democracy was only practicable in small city-states and that bigger territories needed centralised monarchical rule.

The Federalists argued that a federal state combining a strong, but limited, federal power with reserved powers for the states could also combine representative democracy with a large territory. This argument proved to be correct in historical perspective; for instance, the authors quite rightly argued that a genuine federal government – as opposed to the previous confederalism – would make the republic less vulnerable against the threats of foreign powers.

As Madison explained in *Federalist No. 51,* next to the decentralised federal structure, the separation of powers was the core principle of the constitution:

> In order to lay a due foundation for that separate and distinct exercise of the different powers of government, which to a certain extent is admitted on all hands to be essential to the preservation of liberty, it is evident that each department should have a will of its own; and consequently should be so constituted that the members of each should have as little agency as possible in the appointment of the members of the others.

Thus the *Federalist Papers* outlined a theory of a constitutionally limited democracy that soon became a model for others.

The *Federalist Papers* were not always correct, however, in their predictions about the effects of the constitution. Madison thought that the bureaucracy of federal government would always be smaller than the bureaucracy of any single state, but as early as the middle of the nineteenth century, critics such as John C. Calhoun (in *Disquisition on Government*, 1851), were arguing that the centralising tendencies of federal government had been underestimated. Today the federal government employs more civil servants than all the state governments put together.

Similarly, the constitution did not settle the balance between federal and state power – for example in states' rights to secede from the union – and this was not resolved until the American Civil War of 1861–65.

The Federalists also opposed the need for any declaration or bill of fundamental human rights – which only served to strengthen the Anti-Federalists' suspicion of their centralising tendencies. Although Hamilton argued strongly against any enumeration of rights in *Federalist No. 84*, in this struggle the Anti-Federalists finally gained the upper hand. A set of ten amendments – today known as the Bill of Rights – was added to the constitution in 1791; the former Federalist Madison was a sponsor.

These subsequent disagreements among their authors did not, however, challenge the importance of the *Federalist Papers* as the primary source for the interpretation of the constitution. As such a source they still enjoy widespread judicial use – a rare case of political campaign pamphlets turned into legal classics.

Further reading

- Gottfried Dietze, *The Federalist: A Classic on Federalism and Free Government* (Johns Hopkins University Press, 1960)
- David E. Epstein, *The Political Theory of the Federalist* (University of Chicago Press, 1984)
- Herbert J. Storing, *What the Anti-Federalists Were For* (University of Chicago Press, 1981)

Detmar Doering

Federal Union

Founded in 1938 with a view to attracting support for the creation of a federation of European democracies that would serve to curb the ambitions of the Third Reich and fascist Italy and act as a replacement for the League of Nations, which in the eyes of the founders of Federal Union had failed to prevent war because of the maintenance of national sovereignty.

The founding fathers of Federal Union were the three young men who launched the organisation in the autumn of 1938. Derek Rawnsley (1912–42), 'a young man of abounding energy and determination to take action', and Charles Kimber (1912–), a Macmillanite Conservative, knew each other from Eton and Oxford. They recruited, in turn, Patrick Ransome (1902–54), a journalist with a Cambridge degree in international law, who developed the federalist ideas of the group. The three were convinced that it was necessary to do something to prevent a war that seemed inevitable. They therefore called the inaugural meeting of 14 September 1938, which resulted in the circulation of a refined statement of aims to leading figures in British public life. Among its recipients were the Liberal peer Lord Lothian (q.v.), who had from 1910 advocated federalising the British Empire as a prelude to world federation, and his friend Lionel Curtis, a fellow of All Souls, Oxford. The statement was headed 'Federal Union'.

The central message of Federal Union was – and still is – the belief that war can only be eliminated if the sovereign rights of nation-states are curbed. For Federal Union sovereignty is the single most potent cause of war and federalism the only antidote. To this day the fundamental text justifying the organisation's existence remains Lothian's Burge Memorial Lecture of 28 May 1935, 'Pacifism is not enough, nor patriotism either'. In it he argued that:

> War is inherent and cannot be prevented in a world of sovereign states … until we succeed in creating a federal commonwealth of nations, which need not, at the start, embrace the whole earth, we shall not have laid even the foundation for the ending of the institution of war upon earth.

Lothian repeated these ideas in a pamphlet published by Federal Union in 1939 entitled *The Ending of Armageddon*.

The focus on federalism was suggested by Ransome, and was well received by Lothian and Curtis, who were both enthusiastically committed to the concept. In this way Federal Union received expert help and grew rapidly. By June 1940 it had 12,000 members and 225 branches. Lothian and Curtis were founder-members of Chatham House (the Royal Institute of International Affairs) and used that organisation to give Federal Union respectability. It attracted the support of some of the most distinguished minds in Britain, among them Lionel Robbins, Cyril Joad, Ivor Jennings, J. B. Priestley, Henry Brailsford, Sir William Beveridge (q.v.) and Barbara Wootton. All were to contribute to the work of the Federal Union Research Institute, which was established in Oxford in March 1940 under Beveridge's chairmanship.

The literature disseminated by the Research Institute was very influential, especially W. B. Curry's *The Case for Federal Union*, published in 1939. Equally important was R. W. G. Mackay's book, *Federal Union* (1940), which outlined a federal constitution for Europe (Mackay later became chairman of Federal Union). The tracts and pamphlets published by the Research Institute were vital to the debate on federalism. They even reached the European resistance movements during the war, inspiring the publication in 1941 of the *Ventotene Manifesto* by Altiero Spinelli and Ernesto Rossi, regarded as one of the basic documents of the European federalist movement.

However, as the war progressed the output of the Research Institute diminished, and by 1943 it was effectively moribund. Nevertheless, Federal Union continued and despite the efforts of Lionel Curtis, who wanted to give it an Atlanticist slant, it remained committed to the idea of a European federation. An aspiring Liberal politician and indefatigable worker for a federal

Europe, Miss Frances Josephy, served as chairman of Federal Union from 1941 to 1945, and sat on the Executive Committee for many more years; she was also prominent in the European Movement and the European Union of Federalists. Together with Cyril Joad, she was known as one of the 'heavenly twins' of Federal Union.

The contribution of Federal Union and the role of British federalists have generally been overlooked. Federalism has never been popular with either the Conservative or Labour parties, although it remained influential in the Liberal Party and Liberal Democrats. Federal Union was active in promoting Britain's entry into the European Community, collaborating with such bodies as Britain in Europe; federalists supported the successful campaign for British membership in the early 1970s and its confirmation in the referendum of 1975. To the extent that Britain remains a member of the European Union, the objectives of Federal Union might be said to have been achieved. However, the failure of federalism to seize the imagination of the British public in general, and the policy-making elite in particular, must register as a disappointment.

Federal Union embraced members of all political parties, but, nonetheless, represented a fundamentally liberal principle in relation to international affairs.

Further reading

- Andrea Bosco, *Federal Union and the Origins of the 'Churchill Proposal': The Federalist Debate in the United Kingdom from Munich to the Fall of France 1938* (Lothian Foundation Press, 1992)
- Sir Charles Kimber, 'Federal Union', in Peter Catterall and C. J. Morris (eds.), *Britain and the Threat to Stability in Europe, 1918–1945* (Leicester University Press, 1993)
- Walter Lipgens (ed.), *Documents on the History of European Integration: Volume 2, Plans for European Union in Great Britain and in Exile 1939–1945* (Walter de Gruyter, 1986)
- Richard Mayne and John Pinder, *Federal Union: The Pioneers, A History of Federal Union* (Macmillan, 1990)

A. J. Crozier

H. A. L. Fisher   1865–1940

A historian, educationalist and Liberal politician, in that order of significance. More engaged intellectual than original thinker, his public career exemplified Gladstonian faith in progress, internationalism and rationality; moral purpose and liberal values underpinned his historical writings.

Key ideas

- The vital need for education and active citizenship.
- The value of local variety and self-government.
- The common heritage of European civilisation.

Biography

Herbert Albert Laurens Fisher was born, on 21 March 1865, into a comfortable 'establishment' public-service family. His education took him via Winchester to Oxford, where Irish home rule stirred student passions. Fisher's family became Liberal Unionists (q.v.), but Fisher chose national self-determination. T. H. Green's (q.v.) moral philosophy influenced his idealism, particularly the *Prolegomena to Ethics*, which he thought a 'rich, earnest, difficult book'.

A first in Greats in 1888 led to a New College fellowship. Though tempted by a career studying Greek antiquity, Fisher started teaching philosophy, in which he had excelled as an undergraduate. Seeking an intellectual vocation closer to his sense of public commitment, he chose modern history, though Hellenism continued to inspire him. To prepare professionally he chose postgraduate training in Paris (where he was influenced by Taine and Renan) and Germany. He was struck both by the greater seriousness and breadth of French university education and by the dangerous militaristic trend in German intellectualism. He returned to Oxford with a good grounding in historiography and a clear sense of the challenges facing Europe in the twentieth century.

At Oxford, Fisher taught history to much of Britain's future governing elite. That he taught every one of Milner's 'kindergarten', the group of ambitious, brilliant young men including Philip Kerr, Lord Lothian (q.v.), was a personal claim to fame. A wider public knew him better for popular narrative history (e.g. *Early Tudors* or *Napoleon*).

Fisher's public career ran from 1912, when appointed to the Royal Commission on Public Services in India, to his resignation as a Liberal MP in 1926, after returning to Oxford as Warden of New College. He was President of the Board of Education throughout the Lloyd George coalition government, from 1916–22, his most notable achievement being the 1918 Education Act. He was MP for Sheffield Hallam (1916–18) and then the Combined English Universities (1918–26). Presidency of the British Academy (1928–32) and the Order of Merit (1937) recognised him as one of Britain's leading intellectuals; chairmanship of the Appellate Tribunal for Conscientious Objectors (1940) his humanitarian integrity.

His crowning achievement was *A History of Europe* (1935), a 1,300-page popular bestseller. This highly readable, comprehensive narrative, embracing bold, stimulating generalisations and moral judgements,

became, as his *Dictionary of National Biography* entry put it, 'a staple in the diet of schoolchildren ... for thirty years', helping one generation understand better Britain's place in Europe.

Ideas

The Common Weal (1924), originally lectures on 'Citizenship' delivered after leaving the Cabinet, did not make the impact of his historical writings or public service but it usefully sets out the political thinking underlying his more significant achievements. He denied expounding a systematic philosophy, talking rather of comments on current topics. Nonetheless, his comments were bound together by a systematic view: anything done about such problems necessarily assumes 'some theory of human nature and of human destiny'.

The slightly archaic title captured Fisher's theory: man is a social animal, so individuals need each other and should work together, just as nations need internationalism. His language harked back to Aristotle, Edmund Burke (q.v.) and J. S. Mill (q.v.), but his thinking anticipated 'community politics' (q.v.). He argued for local feeling as the basis of education in citizenship; affection for school, village, town or county is the basis from which loyalty to society and patriotism develops. He praised a French writer for his 'gospel of provincial culture' against the stultifying uniformity of French education and rejoiced in the local autonomy entrenched in his Education Act.

Condemning 'professors of class-consciousness', Fisher defied the dominance of economic theories in intellectual debate. In *A History of Europe*, he refused to treat communism as an expression of socioeconomic forces; rather he identified it as a new religion, with Lenin its prophet, the party its church and Marx's writings its Koran. Fisher, the agnostic, fully appreciated the force of religious ideas in history, understanding the appeal of communism as a belief-system but denying its claim to be a form of science.

The economics chapter in *The Common Weal,* 'The Ethics of Wealth', questioned the measurement of human happiness in financial terms, attacking the sharply opposed debate between individual ownership and nationalisation. Fisher approved private property as 'social convenience', not absolute principle, offering empirical judgments industry by industry on what should be part of the state sector. If the level of public expenditure decided local election outcomes, it was a superficial choice – 'the real question … [being] whether the community as a whole will benefit by the expenditure'.

This reasoned approach gave way to passion when he denounced the two social evils injuring British society – the threat of unemployment and the state of secondary education. The Industrial Revolution had had a debasing effect; 'enlightened posterity' would have contempt for how youth had been seen as factory fodder; education for all young people could reconcile industrial society with self-respect.

Faith in the continuity of a civilisation under threat, and of the civilising effect of education, runs through his magnum opus. *A History of Europe* is the tale of European culture and identity, originating in ancient Greece, transmitted and developed through the Roman Empire, kept alive during the medieval age principally by the church, to be rediscovered, reinterpreted and further developed in modern times. Fisher believed in the superiority of this civilisation, whilst acknowledging its debt to Babylon and Egypt and the significance of the other 'chief civilisation', China. He acknowledged Christianity's contribution to 'the fellowship of the European nations', but considered that its Jewish roots had been

profoundly modified by Greek thought. He discerned a 'deep inner sense of unity which persists at the heart of European turmoils', and was in no doubt of Britain's part, weaving British history throughout the European fabric.

In *The Common Weal*, Fisher wrestled with whether history demonstrated the inevitability of war, and how to reconcile national self-determination with international order. He criticised many arguments for maintaining peace: balance-of-power theory, the deterrent effect of new devastating weapons or that a well-armed confident state could restrain itself from war. Presciently, he saw such a nation saturated with the spirit of conflict, becoming 'the more ready to believe in force as the normal arbiter of serious disputes'. He thought effective powers for the League of Nations (on whose general assembly he had served 1920–22) a necessary but not sufficient condition for world peace. Ultimately it would depend on leaders and public attitudes; *The Common Weal* ended with a plea for wise and far-sighted leadership to persuade nationalism of the danger it posed to the 'great cause of human solidarity'.

For H. A. L. Fisher, people and ideas determined human destiny.

Key works
- *The Common Weal* (1924)
- *A History of Europe* (1936)

Further reading
- David Ogg, *Herbert Fisher, A Short Biography* (Arnold, 1947)

Michael Steed

Charles James Fox   1749–1806

Leader of the Whigs during the late eighteenth and early nineteenth centuries and the first acknowledged 'leader of the opposition' in Parliament. Fox consistently argued in favour of the preservation of individual liberties at a time when Britain was frequently at war and there were many concerns about treasonous plots. Although not an original thinker himself, his dedication to the cause of individual liberty provided an important lead for his party then and subsequently.

Key ideas
- Support for civil liberties.
- Backing for much of the revolution in France and for American independence.
- Religious toleration and opposition to the slave trade.
- The supremacy of Parliament, which needed to be kept free of control and corruption.

Biography
Charles James Fox was born into the political establishment, in London on 24 January 1749. His mother was the great-granddaughter of Charles II and his father had served Prime Minister Walpole. The key traits of his life were present from an early age: a willingness and aptitude for hard work, heavy drinking and gambling, accompanied by a talent and intelligence that charmed many. One of his close friends, the Duchess of Devonshire, described how 'his conversation is like a brilliant player at billiards, the strokes follow one another piff puff'.

Regardless of the law that one had to be twenty-one to be an MP, he was first elected to Parliament for Midhurst, in Sussex, in March 1768. By the time he achieved the legal age, he was not only an MP but also a serving Lord of the Admiralty.

His early political views were conservative, and he made his name as a parliamentary orator in 1769, opposing the free-speech *cause célèbre* of the time, John Wilkes. Matters started to change when he fell out with George III over the Royal Marriage Bill. This was intended to restrict the rights of the monarch's sons to marry and was a sensitive issue for Fox, whose mother has suffered strong disapproval from her family over her own marriage. Then came the War of American Independence, when he backed the colonists.

By the late 1770s Fox was clearly a Whig, regularly attacking the conduct of the war in America and opposing restrictions on civil liberties such as the 1777 suspension of the Habeas Corpus Act. He became Foreign Secretary but was in a minority in the new Cabinet in supporting independence for the American colonies and reforms in the public finances and administration. He soon, therefore, returned to opposition, splitting his Whig colleagues in the process. He subsequently regained office in coalition with the Tories under Lord North. Their somewhat unlikely coalition proved deeply unpopular, and was hindered by the King's opposition, caused in part by his dislike of the fact that Fox, with his dissolute lifestyle, was a poor influence on the King's eldest son. When it fell, William Pitt became Prime Minister and, through assiduous work and astute politics, gradually established himself in power.

Revolution in France and the subsequent war marked out the dividing lines for the rest of Fox's career. Fox was greatly excited by the French Revolution, praising it long after many other people in Britain had began to temper their views in the face of its growing extremism and fears of revolution at home. It followed that Fox was not keen on war with France either. Both views kept the Whigs fractured, with many backing the war and the government. Only Fox and a small band of supporters were left to carry the flame, opposing restrictions on civil liberties, questioning the conduct of the war and supporting reform at home.

Political manoeuvrings as governments came and went did not result in Fox regaining office – particularly because of the continued hostility of the King. However, on Pitt's death in 1806, Fox finally returned to office as Foreign Secretary. He had only a few months in office before his death on 13 September 1806.

Fox married his mistress, Elizabeth Armitstead, in 1795, although their marriage was kept secret until 1802. He had one son, who was deaf and dumb and only lived until fifteen.

Ideas

Fox believed in Parliament being both dominant and free. For most of his years this therefore meant opposing the powers of the monarch and supporting reform. However, it was therefore not inconsistent of him early in his career to have opposed the rights of the press (as they were seen as interfering with the free exercise of judgement within Parliament) nor to be opposed to more radical democratic notions such as those in Tom Paine's (q.v.) *Rights of Man* – which would have weakened Parliament by giving, in Fox's view, too much power to the public.

His major contributions were not as an original thinker, but as a leader and an orator. As an orator the force of his speeches was based more on clear arguments and nimble debate rather than original thought, great eloquence or rhetoric. His success as a leader is highly debatable – he never became Prime Minister, his band of followers in the Commons was frequently very small and he did not have any sustained success in uniting the various Whig factions – but he did ensure that the case for the defence of civil liberties, support for moderate reform and the restriction of the powers of the monarchy was consistently argued.

Though his gambling made him a somewhat disreputable figure in the eyes of many, Fox was also principled, standing by his views rather than desperately seeking power and the money that could come with it, even when his large gambling debts would have tempted many others into going for the money. Even the apparently cynical power-seeking coalition with North was motivated largely by a shared hostility to the monarch.

The War of American Independence and then the French Revolution created a clear ideological gulf between Fox and his followers, and the Tories. For Fox, the correct response to trouble was toleration and liberalism rather than repression. He believed that the latter was more likely to trigger revolution than the former. In addition, he believed that it was important to restrain the power of the monarchy, not just because of any monarch's potentially despotic tendencies but also because financial waste and corruption could too easily follow.

He doubted much of the evidence presented by the government as to plots and treasonable activity in Britain in order to justify a range of repressive acts, such as the suspension of Habeas Corpus in 1794. It was in a failed attempt to oppose this that Fox warned of the 'despotism of monarchy' and that 'we were to be put under the dominion of wild passion, and when our pretended alarms were to be made the pretexts for destroying the first principles of the very system which we affected to revere'.

Whether or not Fox was right in his views that revolution was not being seriously plotted is an issue which historians have debated. What is clear, though, is that he left the Whigs with a clear legacy in support of civil liberties, which was in turn to become a defining feature of the Liberal Party when it emerged later in the nineteenth century. Indeed, increasingly during his life Fox became associated with views that modern liberals would recognise – belief in power stemming from the people, desire for wide-ranging reform, strong preference for peace rather than war and an optimistic belief in progress through appropriate policies.

Further reading

- Stanley Ayling, *Fox* (John Murray, 1991)
- John Derry, *Charles James Fox* (Batsford, 1972)
- Leslie Mitchell, *Charles James Fox* (Oxford University Press, 1992)
- David Powell, *Charles James Fox: Man of the People* (Hutchinson, 1989)
- David Schweitzer, *Charles James Fox 1749–1806: A Bibliography* (Greenwood, 1991)

Mark Pack

Free Trade

The cause of 'free trade', the removal of barriers to international trade in goods and services, played an important part in British politics in the nineteenth and early twentieth centuries. For much of its life, the fortunes of the Liberal Party were closely tied to the strength of popular feeling for free trade.

The theory of free trade was developed by the liberal economists Adam Smith (q.v.) and David Ricardo (q.v.) in opposition to the mercantilist orthodoxy prevalent since the sixteenth century. Mercantilists held that the total volume of world trade was fixed, and it was therefore in nations' interests to dominate as great a share as possible, partly by tariffs aimed at discouraging imports and partly by military action and colonial ventures designed to gain control of markets. In contrast, Smith argued that free markets – international as well as

domestic – would promote enterprise and growth, pointing to the trade-based prosperity of the ancient civilisations of Greece and Rome, and, in more recent times, of Bengal and China.

Ricardo took up Smith's concept of the specialisation of labour and developed the theory of comparative advantage, the idea that nations can maximise their output and wealth by specialising in the production of goods at which they are relatively most efficient, trading with other countries to realise the gains from such specialisation. Again in contrast to prevailing orthodoxy, Ricardo held that even the unilateral removal of trade barriers by only one trading partner would benefit both parties.

In the early nineteenth century, the theory suggested that Britain should concentrate on manufactured goods, selling them abroad to purchase food. Also, as Smith had pointed out, the country with the largest volume of world trade would naturally benefit most from open markets – and until the 1880s, Britain was that country. Furthermore, with its rapidly growing population, it had to trade to survive.

These arguments reached the political scene with the campaign to abolish the Corn Laws (the high duties on the import of grain established after the Napoleonic Wars in order to protect British agriculture from foreign competition) spearheaded by the Anti-Corn Law League (q.v.) in the 1840s. Manchester, the centre of the cotton industry, whose products were denied access to overseas markets because of continental grain-growers' inability to export to Britain, became the headquarters of the League, and the radical liberals Richard Cobden (q.v.) and John Bright were its leaders. The term 'Manchester School' (q.v.), coined by Benjamin Disraeli in 1846 to describe the League's leaders, came in time to stand for a free-trade classical liberal (q.v.) agenda which influenced liberals throughout Europe.

The League achieved its aim in 1846 when the Tory Prime Minister Robert Peel abolished the Corn Law, splitting the Conservative Party and helping to drive some of his supporters (including W. E. Gladstone (q.v.)) towards the Liberals in the process. After Gladstone's budget of 1860, only sixteen dutiable articles remained in the British tariff, compared to more than a thousand in 1852. The subsequent growth in British exports, particularly of manufactured products, formed the basis of the long mid-Victorian economic boom.

As lower tariffs meant cheaper food, together with higher employment and bigger profits in manufacturing, the doctrine of free trade appealed to the growing manufacturing and business interests, precisely those groups most attracted to the nascent Liberal Party – and was opposed by the predominantly Tory land-owners whose estates produced the grain. Liberals, however, always saw much more than economic justification for open markets. Abolishing protection for agriculture was part of the process of tearing down the remnants of the feudal order and putting an end to the special treatment enjoyed by the land-owners. Cobden and the League argued, by extension, for an end to special treatment for *any* industry; commercial success should be the outcome of hard work and natural talent alone, not the protection of vested interests. The campaign for free trade formed an important part of the liberal assault on economic, and therefore political, privilege.

The removal of tariff barriers also had benefits on the international scene. Liberals looked to free trade as the agency which would promote internationalism and end war. 'For the disbanding of great armies and the promotion of peace', wrote Bright, 'I rely on the abolition of tariffs, on the brotherhood of the nations resulting from free trade in the products of industry.' Trade promoted interdependence and a sense of international community, building links between peoples and nations and rendering conflict less likely.

Free trade remained an article of liberal faith for decades, even after British pre-eminence in world markets began to wane in the 1870s. As the trade balance grew steadily worse, pressure for protectionism mounted, most notably from the former radical leader Joseph Chamberlain (q.v.). But free trade had too great a grip on the national mind, and Chamberlain's Imperial Preference campaign (protectionism for domestic industry and preferences for the self-governing dominions), launched in 1903, split the Conservative/Unionist Party and reunited the Liberals after their post-Gladstonian divisions. Businessmen and manufacturers, fearing a trade war, came back to the Liberal fold they had deserted over the previous twenty years, and working-class support grew at the prospect of dearer food. Liberal candidates habitually appeared on election platforms with two loaves of bread, contrasting the Liberal 'big loaf' with the Tory 'little loaf' which would follow the imposition of grain duties. Coupled with the other failures of Balfour's ministry, the result was the Liberal landslide of 1906.

The cause of free trade was to perform much the same function in 1923, when the Liberal Party, split between its Asquith and Lloyd George (q.v.) wings after wartime divisions, was reunited by the Conservative Prime Minister Baldwin's sudden conversion to tariff reform and his decision to call an election on the issue. The result was an interruption of the inter-war decline in Liberal fortunes, with an increase in seats from 116 to 159.

The Liberal faith in free trade, however, wavered under the strains of the Great Depression. The downwards spiral of ever-higher tariffs and ever-lower trade that overtook the world in the wake of Wall Street's Great Crash of 1929 was impossible for any single country to resist. The coalition National Government's introduction of a general tariff in February 1932 produced the 'Agreement to Differ' under which the Liberal leader Herbert Samuel (q.v.) and his colleagues were permitted to remain in government even while opposing its policy; but the Ottawa Agreements entrenching protection within the Empire finally forced them out in September, ending the last peacetime participation in UK government by the Liberal Party. Sir John Simon's Liberal National (q.v.) faction endorsed protection, stayed in government and eventually merged with the Conservatives.

The cause of free trade and the Liberal Party both seemed to be doomed. An opinion survey in 1942 showed that the only Liberal policy the public could identify was free trade, but that the vast majority had no idea what the party stood for; like free trade itself, it seemed a relic of a bygone age. The end of the Second World War, however, brought comprehensive change, with the creation of new international institutions aimed at avoiding a repeat of the disastrous trade wars of the 1930s. The liberal John Maynard Keynes (q.v.) was partly responsible for the plans for an International Trade Organisation alongside the World Bank and International Monetary Fund. Although the proposal was vetoed by the US, its 'provisional' substitute – the General Agreement on Tariffs and Trade – was able, over the following forty years, to coordinate successive rounds of tariff reductions and its own transformation, in 1995, into the World Trade Organisation.

The moral argument for trade was still powerful; the 1959 Liberal manifesto ended with the slogan: 'exchange goods, not bombs'. In 1956 the Liberals became the first party to argue for British participation in the European Common Market: the Cobdenite vision of trade building links between peoples was an important factor, overriding concerns over potential European protectionism against the rest of the world. Liberal parties throughout Europe share this vision, however much they may be divided over the details of economic and social policy.

In more recent times, Liberal Democrats have expressed concern over some of the negative aspects of globalisation, including the elevation of trade liberalisation over other goals of international policy, such as environmental protection, and the growth in inequalities of wealth between developed nations and the poorest countries. The central belief in the freedom to exchange goods and services across international borders has remained, however, not just for the economic benefits, but for wider reasons: the extension of opportunity to every individual, every enterprise and every country, no matter how small; and the building of relationships between peoples and nations, pulling communities together rather than driving them apart.

Further reading

- Jagdish N. Bhagwati, *Free Trade Today* (Princeton University Press, 2003)
- Anthony Howe, *Free Trade and Liberal England 1846–1946* (Oxford University Press, 1998)
- Joseph Stiglitz and Andrew Charlton, *Fair Trade for All: How Trade Can Promote Development* (Oxford University Press, 2005)

Duncan Brack

Free Trade Union and Cobden Club

These two small organisations, closely associated with the Liberal Party, acted as lobbies campaigning in defence of the political legacy of Richard Cobden, and in particular free trade, until after the Second World War. Together they promoted the ideology of Cobdenism, which continued to influence the Liberal Party profoundly during this period.

Cobden Club

The Cobden Club was founded in 1866 following Cobden's (q.v.) death, and held regular political dinners and published pamphlets to advance his ideas. It was particularly active in the 1870s and '80s when free trade (q.v.) was challenged by the Conservative campaign for what the Tories called 'fair trade' – denounced by Gladstone (q.v.) and others as no different from traditional protectionism – and during the tariff reform controversies before 1914. Its membership was open to free traders and internationalists of all parties and all countries, although in practice British Liberals dominated the Club. In its latter years it was largely a mouthpiece for Leif Jones, F. W. Hirst (q.v.) and other Liberal traditionalists on the strict free trade wing of the party.

Free Trade Union

The FTU was established in 1903 as a campaigning organisation to oppose Joseph Chamberlain's (q.v.) bid for tariff reform, and remained active in the cause of free trade until the early 1970s, when its journal *The Free Trader* ceased publication. Ostensibly non-partisan, for much of its history it was more or less an arm of the Liberal Party with many prominent Liberals and only a small number of Conservative free traders sitting on its executive (it had absorbed the Unionist Free Trade Club in 1910).

After its most active phase in the battle with tariff reform, in the 1920s the FTU became an establishment lobby representing the economic orthodoxy shared by the Liberal and Labour parties, much of business and finance, and the vast majority of professional economists. The free trade consensus broke down in the 1931 crisis when the FTU lost some of its hitherto most stalwart supporters, including Sir John Simon and Walter Runciman, who, with the other Liberal Nationals (q.v.), accepted protection and aligned with the Conservatives. From the 1930s onwards the FTU was a voice in the wilderness, kept going by stalwarts such as Hirst and Sir George Paish, but also attracting some younger free-market campaigners including Arthur Seldon (q.v.) and Oliver Smedley. Its presidents included Arnold Morley (–1916), Lord Beauchamp (1916–), Henry Bell (–1935), R. D. Holt (1936–41), W. Rea (1941–48) and Sir A. MacFadyean (1948–59).

In 1959 the moribund FTU (which had merged with the Cobden Club earlier in the decade) was taken over by Lord Grantchester, Oliver Smedley and S. W. Alexander as a platform for their hard-line free trade and anti–Common Market views, and its connections with the Liberal Party were loosened. Its name was changed to the Free Trade League in 1962.

Further reading

- Cobden Club, *A History of the Cobden Club* (Cobden-Sanderson, 1939)

Jaime Reynolds

Freedom

By freedom or liberty we mean the absence of coercion. Human beings are free to the extent to which they are able to take their own decisions. A state of freedom, or liberty, provides the conditions which minimise coercion.

Liberalism aims to bring about a maximum of freedom under given constraints.

The modern concept of freedom has two distinctive characteristics: it applies to individuals and aims to be universal. Only individuals can be free. It is metaphorical language to speak of a 'free people' or a 'free country' unless one refers explicitly to the 'constitution of liberty'. All individuals are entitled to be free. Although Aristotle was one of the first thinkers to advocate freedom as the purpose of politics, his distinction between the 'naturally free' and those who are 'by nature slaves' shows a pre-modern mode of thought. All humans are beings with a life of their own to live. 'This is liberty as it has been conceived by liberals in the modern world from the days of Erasmus to our own.' (Isaiah Berlin, q.v.)

Freedom as the absence of coercion is the core of the concept, but it is only the starting point of the (political) theory of freedom. Even apart from constraints on human behaviour that are not social but natural, coercion by others is a fact of life, and thus a necessary element of the social contract. Much of the debate on freedom notably in the last two centuries is therefore concerned not with the idea of freedom but with its uses in the application to the real world. This is where ambiguities and hence disputes about freedom have their origin. Five subjects of such disputes deserve special attention.

The constitution of liberty

The first issue is that of unavoidable limitations of freedom in human society. At what point does the freedom of one person conflict with the freedom of others? What restrictions on unlimited freedom will therefore have to be accepted and how can they be made acceptable to those who value freedom above all? Questions of this kind underlie the old debate about the 'social contract'. Authors since the seventeenth century have, for purposes of this debate, assumed very different 'states of nature', from Thomas Hobbes's (q.v.) 'war of all against all' which needs to be curbed, to Jean-Jacques Rousseau's arcadian condition which needs to be re-established by dismantling the impediments of civilisation ('Men are born free, but everywhere they lie in chains').

Whatever one's preference – and of course all 'states of nature' are fictions for purposes of analysis – it is clear that freedom has to be bounded in a *Constitution of Liberty*. This is the title of Friedrich von Hayek's (q.v.) major treatise on the subject. For him, the constitution of liberty is that basic agreement in human societies which defines the boundaries of freedom. It may be a written or an unwritten constitution, but in terms of freedom it must make sure that coercion is kept at an acceptable minimum.

The constitution of liberty has two main elements. One is the law, and more precisely the rule of law (q.v.). All laws introduce elements of coercion. All laws are therefore restrictions on freedom. The test of their acceptability is whether such restrictions are kept to demonstrably necessary elements or extended beyond these. The notion of the rule of law adds to such substantial requirements the formal, yet crucial insistence on the supreme legitimacy of the law. Nobody is above the law; the law 'belongs' to all free citizens.

However, where there is law there is power. Laws have to be promulgated and enforced. They do not emerge or exist in a power vacuum. The second main element of the constitution of liberty is therefore the way in which power is organised and, importantly, reined in. This is the link between freedom and democracy (q.v.).

Democracy defines legitimacy by popular assent – or at least absence of majority dissent – guaranteed by such institutions as elections, parliaments, possibly referendums. It makes change possible without violence. It is therefore a useful instrument for constraining the power needed to uphold the rule of law.

Absolute freedom is anarchy. An anarchic streak is present in all notions of freedom. But for freedom to be effective and real it needs to be constituted. Government – 'civil government', to use John Locke's (q.v.) phrase – is necessary. There is no real freedom without the state. The question then is: how much state, and how is it to be organised? This is the institutional side of the other question: how much coercion can be justified? This takes one back to concepts of freedom.

Two concepts of liberty

Isaiah Berlin's essay entitled *Two Concepts of Liberty* (to which he added important embellishments and caveats in the book *Four Essays on Liberty*) has influenced debate not just in the Anglo-Saxon world. The section on what he calls 'negative liberty' is an excellent, and to some extent original, summary of the idea of freedom in the tradition of John Locke and John Stuart Mill (q.v.), Benjamin Constant (q.v.) and Alexis de Tocqueville (q.v.). Absence of coercion means that there is a strictly 'private' sphere 'which must on no account be violated'. It is in principle outside the sphere of public authority. Beyond that, individual liberty is defined by Berlin in ways similar to those proposed here.

Berlin adds one point which cannot be pursued here, but is of significance. He argues that 'negative liberty' has not often 'formed a rallying cry for the great masses of mankind. The desire not to be impinged upon, to be left to oneself, has been a mark of high civilisation both on the part of individuals and communities.' Perhaps, Berlin should have added: in normal times. When totalitarian states began to crumble (as in 1989) elementary freedom certainly was a rallying cry for many.

However, Berlin's main point is the distinction between 'negative' and 'positive freedom'. Advocates of positive freedom have, for Berlin, a different conception of human beings. For them, people are not masters of themselves, constrained only by natural limits (like the inability to jump ten feet high), but part of a larger whole, a tribe, a nation, or bound by the course of history, by the 'world spirit'. Their freedom consists in acceptance of the demands of these 'higher' forces, thus in the insight into necessity Berlin rejects this notion, as does Karl Popper (q.v.) in his devastating critique of Plato, Hegel (q.v.) and Marx (*The Open Society and Its Enemies*). Such tribalism, or historicism, in fact served to justify the abolition of democracy and the rule of law, the destruction of what Popper calls the 'open society' of freedom.

On social freedom

One may regret that Berlin called his preferred concept of freedom 'negative' liberty. It suggests something undesirable when in fact it is the positive idea advanced by all in the tradition of enlightened thinking in seventeenth-century England, eighteenth-century Scotland, France and America, and the great theorists of liberty in the nineteenth and twentieth centuries. The latter in particular had to struggle with another notion of 'positive freedom' (which is often confused with Berlin's), arising from the conviction that freedom from coercion is somehow not enough. More is needed to be free. The extreme version of this view was President Roosevelt's inclusion (in the Atlantic Charter, issued jointly with Winston Churchill (q.v.) in August 1941) of 'freedom from fear' and 'freedom from want' in the list of objectives for the post-war world. Here, insecurity and poverty are regarded as violations of freedom.

The debate on this issue has continued to the present day, and is very much a matter for dispute. What are often called social rights are by many regarded as demands of freedom. In fact, such notions divide 'liberals' (nowadays often called 'neo-liberals' (q.v.)) from 'social liberals' (q.v.) and 'social democrats' (q.v.). In international affairs, the link of social rights with freedom is used to defend authoritarian regimes which argue that they may restrict freedom of speech, but at least nobody is poor. Even democratic politicians have described 'freedom from fear of terrorism' as the first and most important freedom.

This is a very unhelpful debate to which one might well reply with Isaiah Berlin that 'nothing is gained by a confusion of terms'. 'Everything is what it is: liberty is liberty, not equality or fairness or justice or culture, or human happiness or a quiet conscience.' Two kinds of confusion must be avoided. One arises from the fact that freedom is not the only value. Indeed, it is possible to regard it as a rather limited value, and there are certainly those who prefer welfare, prosperity, even happiness to freedom. The other confusion is due to failure to distinguish between freedom and the conditions under which freedom flourishes. It may well be that extreme poverty makes freedom illusory (though India at the time of forced sterilisation provides a counter-example in that the Congress Party under Indira Gandhi and her son Sanjay was not re-elected despite its economic and social record). Freedom in the elementary, strict sense remains a value even at times of fear and in circumstances of want.

Liberties

For real people in the real world (rather than political philosophers) freedom becomes relevant through particular freedoms or liberties. Three sets of these have been particularly important in the last two hundred years.

The first is the elementary freedom of 'free men' or citizens. Even for Adam Smith (q.v.) the end of villainy and slavery defines Freedom with a capital F. The end of slavery certainly marked important progress in the history of freedom. Other forms of dependence followed; some persist to the present day in many parts of the world. Moreover, it would be wrong to assume that the abolition of physical dependence is ever achieved once and for all. Mass migration has brought to light new kinds of unfreedom, notably in the form of forced labour, including the semi-enslavement of women. Such forms of coercion deny individuals the status of persons able to take their own decisions and thus their freedom.

A second set of freedoms concerned, and continues to concern, economic activity. Historically it involved the abrogation of rules inimical to setting up and conducting businesses, the ability to own property, and then increasingly the creation of conditions for 'free trade' (q.v.). Such freedoms were fought for, gained, then abused by some, restricted by political measures, and fought for in a new form. The mantra and the reality of free trade tell the story. At the end of the twentieth century, globalisation has led to the rewriting of the rule book of economic freedoms, or at any rate to the scrapping of much of the old rule book. The attempt to extend the range of permissible decisions for individual economic actors by reducing the rules to which they are subject is part of the 'neo-liberal' creed. It is much criticised, but also widely accepted that the market economy (q.v.) with its large liberties is the most effective framework for advancing prosperity.

Since the dark totalitarian days of the twentieth century, a third set of liberties has gained increasing dominance. It dates back to John Stuart Mill (q.v.) and beyond and can be described by the general notion of freedom of expression. This includes freedom of speech, of opinion, of religion and creed, of publication and other means of disseminating views, of the arts, of scientific research, and also freedom of association. Many authors have shown that these liberties are by no means luxuries for a small intellectual elite. They are at the basis of the political constitution of liberty. (It was no accident that President Gorbachev began his programme of liberalisation in the Soviet Union with *glasnost*, that is freedom of expression.) They inform, as the social liberals following John Stuart Mill have shown, well-functioning (social) market economies. They even have direct social effects, if we follow the argument of Amartya Sen in his *Poverty and Famines*, which suggests that where there is freedom of expression, famines are less likely and poverty is more effectively fought. Freedom of expression is of course the lifeblood of civil society. For such reasons, it is rightly regarded as the core of the practical pursuit of liberty.

Freedom and ...

Freedom (as we argued, following Isaiah Berlin) is not the only value. It is part of the human predicament that we have to live with a plurality of often conflicting values. It is not helpful to try and cover this fact by extending the concept of freedom or seeking harmony of incompatibles. We have to accept that there are more values than just one, and that they can be in conflict. Two examples are particularly relevant for the discourse on freedom.

One is the relation between freedom and equality (q.v.). The two appear – along with the third, fraternity – in the famous programme of the French Revolution. They are often said to be complementary if not identical. While it is true that the universal nature of freedom implies equal rights for all citizens, it is still clear that such equal citizenship involves a sacrifice of freedom for some (if not all). More generally, freedom and equality lead to different approaches to politics. Inequality of status, insofar as it is not entrenched in privilege, is arguably compatible with freedom. It may indeed be an expression of freedom. Equality as a dominant value always involves a sacrifice of freedom. There may be times when the freedom party and the equality party form coalitions, but when they merge, a hybrid is created which promises above all confusion. This may be bearable in the real world of politics, but must be exposed as such in the world of ideas.

Another complex relationship is that between freedom and responsibility. Freedom is not just a condition, a state of affairs, but requires a certain kind of behaviour. Men and women have to act in a certain way to keep freedom alive; in that sense at least they have to act responsibly. Freedom survives only if it is active freedom. This is a relatively new discovery. Most theorists of freedom have assumed that humans will naturally strive for freedom. They have discounted human apathy. Yet as normal times extend to long periods, socio-political (as well as economic) conditions tend to become rigid, and participation by citizens declines. Mancur Olson has foreseen this condition in his *Rise and Decline of Nations*.

Olson has also advocated rather drastic remedies, like war and revolution. A responsible approach to freedom can help avoid such extreme events. This will have to be based on the insight that freedom is a civilised rather than a natural state of affairs. It has to be created and kept alive by the activity of enlightened human beings. When freedom ceases to be an active endeavour, it is at risk.

Contemporary threats to freedom

The battle for freedom has accompanied modern history since the days of Erasmus, if not earlier. When it seemed to be winning in the early twentieth century, however, new threats to freedom emerged. The greatest of these was totalitarianism, which appeared in two guises, communism and fascism. The former took its extreme form as Stalinism, that is when Stalin ruled the Soviet Union and its empire, the latter as National Socialism under Hitler's rule over Germany and large parts of Europe. Leadership, ideology and mobilisation are the hallmarks of totalitarianism, and all three are in extreme conflict with freedom. The resulting regimes were murderous; they may be said to have needed war; they were also catastrophic so that they could not last; initially small groups of defenders of freedom, helped by outside forces committed to this value, eventually prevailed. 1945 and 1989 are dates which mark milestones on the road to freedom.

It is an open question whether totalitarianism can happen again. There have certainly been, and there still are, vicious dictatorships in many parts of the world. Some intellectuals argue that a new, 'third' totalitarianism threatens from militant Islamism; though one may wonder whether this is not a defensive posture of the losers of modernity, which has great nuisance value but no future.

Arguably the more serious threat to freedom in the twenty-first century is that of authoritarianism. This is the combination of rule by a small group – a *nomenklatura*, a bureaucracy – with public apathy by the many. Such authoritarianism may well be coupled with economic prosperity, as in parts of south-east Asia. It may also develop in small, almost unnoticed steps ('creeping authoritarianism'). The fight against terrorism has favoured such tendencies even in the old democracies. Rising executive power is coupled here with reduced civil rights and declining political participation. Freedom becomes a minority concern, and defenders of freedom find themselves under attack.

Perhaps such trends should not be overrated. They are, however, a reminder of the fact that freedom is neither given by human nature nor there for good once it has been won. Fighting for the life chances of individuals against coercion by others is a battle that never ends.

Further reading

- Isaiah Berlin, *Liberty* (incorporating *Four Essays on Liberty*), ed. Henry Hardy (Oxford University Press, 1969)
- F. A. Hayek, *The Constitution of Liberty* (University of Chicago Press, 1960)
- John Stuart Mill, *On Liberty* (Longman, Green and Company, 1865)
- Karl R. Popper, *The Open Society and Its Enemies* (Routledge, 1945)
- Amartya Sen, *Rationality and Freedom* (Harvard University Press, 2002)

Ralf Dahrendorf

Milton Friedman   1912–2006

One of the most influential figures on economic policy in the late twentieth century, his teaching that 'inflation is always a monetary phenomenon' is now established economic orthodoxy. As his work became more influential he advocated a number of libertarian social policies and became a major figure in the popularisation of the case for economic liberalism.

Key ideas

- Restated and popularised case for economic liberalism, free markets and free trade.
- Emphasised the importance of monetary rules for central banks.
- 'Inflation is always a monetary phenomenon'.
- Advocated abolition of military conscription, use of vouchers in education and legalisation of recreational drugs.

Biography

Milton Friedman was born on 31 July 1912, in Brooklyn, New York, the fourth child and first son of immigrant parents from an area of Eastern Europe now in Ukraine. They were a working-class family and both parents worked. When Friedman was aged one his parents moved to New Jersey where he was educated and won a scholarship to Rutgers University, achieving a BA in economics in 1933. His father had died during his later high school years, so he was supported by his family and worked throughout university. He gained a further scholarship to Chicago to study for an MA in economics, which he achieved in 1935. Though he returned to New York to study for a PhD at Columbia University (awarded in 1946), he was most closely associated with Chicago University, where he held a professorship in economics from 1948 until his retirement in 1976, when he joined Stanford University's Hoover Institute.

He was awarded the Nobel Prize in Economics in 1976. He was actively involved in Republican Party politics, working for Barry Goldwater's unsuccessful 1964 presidential campaign and Richard Nixon's successful campaign four years later, although his political beliefs were libertarian (q.v.) rather than conservative. He died on 16 November 2006.

Ideas

Friedman is most remembered for his contribution to monetarist theory which he popularised in his later career. After the Second World War, most Western governments accepted Keynes's (q.v.) theories of achieving the level of demand which would maintain full employment. This was to be reached through adjusting government expenditure and tax levels, with increased government borrowing if necessary. As time went by it was found that inflation was gradually rising and to try to restrain price rises governments interfered with the market mechanism and introduced prices and incomes policies. Nevertheless, inflation kept rising, to the extent that at the end of the 1960s inflation rates of around 7 per cent were common and by 1975 the UK rate of inflation reached 25 per cent.

As President of the American Economic Association in 1967 Friedman used his presidential address to explain the error of the Keynesian (q.v.) policies used to minimise unemployment since 1945. Keynesians had believed that the rate of change of money wages varied inversely with the rate of unemployment, as shown by the Phillips curve, so that inflation was explained by the rate of unemployment falling too low. Friedman was adamant that 'inflation is always a monetary phenomenon': control of the money supply was the key variable if inflation was to be controlled.

Friedman used his address to show the problem with the Phillips curve. If unemployment fell below the 'natural' rate, as determined by inflexibilities in the labour market, the demand for labour would cause money wages to rise. If the money supply then rose to accommodate the rise in wages, inflation was the result. In fact, at the 'natural' rate of unemployment the Phillips curve becomes vertical and money wages could spiral out of control. (This insight into the problem of the Phillips curve was also identified at the same time by another US economist, Henry Phelps.) The UK experienced just such a wage–price spiral during 1974–75, which led to a draconian prices and incomes policy in 1975–79. Friedman's arguments built upon his previous work, *A Monetary History of the United States, 1867–1960*, written with Anna Schwarz, in which the authors identified a monetary contraction by the monetary authorities as a major cause of the Great Depression in the 1930s.

The success of monetarist policies – such as those implemented by Margaret Thatcher in the UK in the early 1980s and General Pinochet in Chile in the 1970s – remains a matter of dispute. Monetarist policies appear to have been successful in lowering inflation, but they also caused high levels of unemployment as the economy contracted – a phenomenon generally deemed by monetarists to be an unavoidable part of the 'shock therapy' necessary to bring inflation under control.

While much of the detail of Friedmanite monetarism is rejected or questioned by contemporary economists, the general thrust of Friedman's ideas has been widely accepted. Today, all central banks use monetary policy as the primary tool for controlling inflation – something that would have been unthinkable before Friedman's contribution.

Friedman was also a powerful advocate of a number of libertarian social policies. He was an influential advocate for the abolition of military conscription in the US (which happened in 1973), and consistently argued for the legalisation of all recreational drugs and the introduction of school vouchers as a means of ensuring that parents rather than bureaucrats controlled the education of their children and to create incentives to improve the general quality of schools.

Friedman was also a great populariser of the case for economic liberalism (q.v.). In 1962 he published *Capitalism and Freedom*, a book that underlined the importance of economic freedom to underpin political freedom; aimed at a popular audience, it sold more than 500,000 copies. It also introduced other aspects of Friedman's work to a wider audience, including occupational licensure (which explains how groups such as doctors can exploit a monopoly position) and the importance of free trade (q.v.) and free exchange rates.

This was followed in 1980 by *Free to Choose*, written with his wife, Rose, and based on a successful television series. This book sold more than one million copies in English and was translated into a dozen foreign languages. As in his previous work, *Free to Choose* restated the case for economic freedom, free trade and individual liberty at a time when the merits of such policies were widely disputed.

The association of Friedmanite monetarism with conservative political figures and movements may mean that many British liberals are reluctant to accept Friedman as a liberal thinker. If approached free from the baggage of 'guilt by association', however, Friedman's work can be seen to make a powerful case for economic liberalism, individual liberty and personal responsibility squarely in the classical liberal (q.v.) tradition.

Key works
- *Capitalism and Freedom* (1962)
- *A Monetary History of the United States, 1867–1960* (with Anna Schwarz, 1963)
- *Essays in Positive Economics* (1966)
- *The Role of Monetary Policy* (1969)
- *Free to Choose* (with Rose Friedman, 1980)

Further reading

- Samuel Brittan, *Capitalism with a Human Face* (Edward Elgar, 1995)
- Milton Friedman, *Inflation and Unemployment* (1976 Alfred Nobel Memorial Lecture) (IEA Occasional Paper 51, 1977)

Roger Fox and John Meadowcroft

J. K. Galbraith   1908–2006

Widely recognised as the most prolific and accessible academic economist of the twentieth century, he acquired a reputation for making the 'dismal science' comprehensible and politically relevant. Following his introduction to Keynes, Galbraith became a leading exponent of Keynesianism and one of the most challenging and liberal voices in American public life.

Key ideas

- The inevitability of economic concentration and the need for liberals to face up to its consequences.
- The notion of 'countervailing power'.
- The existence of a 'dependence effect' (manufactured demand in consumer societies).
- The importance of measures of the good society that capture social harmony, not just economic outputs as conventionally defined.
- The paradox of public squalor co-existing with unprecedented private affluence.
- The importance of integrating the study of economics with that of politics, and questioning the 'conventional wisdom'.

Biography

John Kenneth Galbraith was born, on 15 October 1908, at Iona Station, Ontario, and brought up on a small farm in Dutton close to Lake Erie. In 1926 he began a degree in agriculture at the Ontario Agricultural College. He was dismissive about its academic standards but, whatever its shortcomings, it enabled him to study agricultural economics, and that led on to a research fellowship at the Giannini Foundation, University of California at Berkeley.

Moving to California in the summer of 1931, Galbraith was able to combine his fellowship in agricultural economics with an eclectic study of the social sciences. His Berkeley student transcripts show that he was an exceptional student and his professors recognised that he would have a great future. During this period he came across the work of Thorstein Veblen (1857–1929), author of *The Theory of the Leisure Class*. Veblen supplied an enduring and telling critique of neo-classical economics and Galbraith's life parallels Veblen's in a number of respects.

Galbraith was ambitious and set his sights on going to Harvard. By the autumn of 1934 he had gained both a doctorate from Berkeley and a teaching post at Harvard. With the aid of John D. Black, a Harvard professor, he won an introduction to J. M. Keynes's (q.v.) circle at Cambridge. When he left for England in September 1937 Galbraith did so with a Rockefeller fellowship, a new wife and American citizenship. In Europe he not only built up a great circle of friends and academic colleagues but developed a taste for the good life.

Shortly after his return to Harvard, in the autumn of 1938, and seeing little prospect of a permanent academic position there, Galbraith accepted an invitation to lead a government-sponsored research project assessing Roosevelt's New Deal (q.v.) programme; it proved a stepping stone to a career in the public service. He became deeply involved in the federal government's machinery for 'economic planning and controls', being hired as America's 'price czar' at the Office of Price Administration (OPA). In 1941 he was quite literally put in charge of running the American wartime command economy; aged thirty-two, he directed 1,000 OPA employees in Washington and over 2,000 more across the US. He was not simply an economist who theorised about the American economy, he ran it.

Despite making enemies in the process and being fired (in 1943), Galbraith was able to move on to work as a journalist and to communicate his own economic analyses rooted in Keynesian theory (q.v.). He retained friends and supporters in government and in 1945 was invited to join an investigation into US strategic bombing in Europe. His findings – that bombing had failed to inhibit German war production – were not well received; they reinforced his reputation as a maverick and independent thinker and prompted him to develop his notion of the 'conventional wisdom'. Nevertheless, against some opposition, he was appointed to a chair in economics at Harvard in 1948; he held it for nearly fifty years.

Galbraith remained deeply engaged with US politics throughout his life. In the 1960s, John F. Kennedy appointed him US ambassador to India. This did not prevent him becoming a fierce critic of the war in Vietnam. He later became a television personality when, in the 1970s, he wrote and presented a series of television programmes on 'The Age of Uncertainty', dealing with the relationship between ideas and economic change. Galbraith's intellectual battles with rival economist Milton Friedman (q.v.) over economic policy continued in the 1980s, when he appeared to be on the losing side of a clash between exponents of Keynesianism and monetarism. Galbraith remained a regular contributor to public debate over economic issues until shortly before his death, on 29 April 2006, and continued to lament the widespread acceptance of erroneous ideas, the theme of his *Economics of Innocent Fraud* (2004).

Galbraith had, by all accounts, a happy personal life. His marriage to Catherine Atwater lasted almost seventy years until his death. The Galbraiths had four sons, three of whom survived their father.

Ideas

In the course of his long career Galbraith often found himself at odds with academic and political establishments. He was rarely restrained in expressing his doubts about the worth of rival economic analyses, especially those dependent upon the fabrication of complex mathematical equations. The advanced mathematics that has come to symbolise excellence in academic economics held little interest. He was one of the few eminent economic scholars to write about economics and politics in ways that are not only comprehensible but intellectually engaging to non-specialists. Time and again in his published works, most notably in *American Capitalism*, *The Affluent Society* and *The New Industrial State*, Galbraith set out to explain how and why public policy-makers, and the economists who advise them, have mistaken or misrepresented the most important goals of economic policy. Leading members of his own profession had, in his view, a great deal in common with the economists Keynes criticised in the 1930s: they were so wedded to solving abstract puzzles that they permitted real-world issues to pass them by. As he explained in *The Affluent Society*, the problems of expanding production should not be considered the most pressing in the world's wealthiest societies; attention should be focused instead upon the quality of what is produced, its distribution and its impact on the world around us. This was an important part of what concerned Galbraith when he contrasted private affluence with public squalor.

In *American Capitalism* Galbraith proposed a more realistic model of modern capitalism in which the consequences of oligopoly and the erosion of consumer sovereignty become the prime subjects of economic enquiry. While his professional colleagues were desperately trying to eject politics from economics he was insistent that politics was becoming ever more important to economics. Those who really wanted to understand how the interests of consumers and firms were balanced should be prepared to look beyond the neo-classical synthesis. In his opinion, students of modern economies needed to make an especially close study of 'countervailing power'. Capitalist societies had become arenas in which organised interests ('countervailing powers') battled each other. Professional economists might want to behave as though modern economies were a triumphant realisation of economic and political theories from an earlier age, but the idea that modern economic actors (including major producers and resource-owners) were so insignificant that their utility- and profit-maximising behaviour made no difference to market equilibriums, political processes or consumer choices was simply laughable.

The significance of Galbraith's economics for liberals and for those who want to understand contemporary political and economic systems is profound. He challenged classical liberals and his fellow economists. He called on both to recognise that if theory and practice are out of alignment the unrealistic assumptions that underpin classical liberalism (q.v.) and neo-classical economic theory should be questioned and, if necessary, abandoned. He was insistent

that a much more sophisticated and realistic view of the modern world, directly relevant to public policy-making, needed to be fashioned. Those who accepted conventional wisdom uncritically might not be guilty of any crime but were responsible for a kind of fraud which, however innocent their motives, was likely to prove enormously damaging to the interests of ordinary people.

Key works
- *American Capitalism* (1952)
- *The Great Crash, 1929* (1954)
- *The Affluent Society* (1958)
- *The New Industrial State* (1967)
- *The Age of Uncertainty* (1977)
- *Annals of an Abiding Liberal* (1979)
- *The Good Society: The Humane Agenda* (1996)
- *The Economics of Innocent Fraud* (2004)

Further reading
- Richard Parker, *John Kenneth Galbraith: His Life, His Politics and His Economics* (Farrar Straus Giroux, 2005)

Ed Randall

Henry George   1839–97

Nineteenth-century America's most influential radical theorist, his claim that the God-given land, the source of all wealth, had been unjustly usurped by landlords, and that the situation could be remedied by a tax on the unimproved value of land, inspired a generation of radical and socialist politicians in the English-speaking world and Europe.

Key ideas
- Land is the source of all wealth.
- God gave the land to the people, so its appropriation as private property was theft.

- This can be remedied by taxing away the value of rents paid on land and minerals.
- This 'single tax' would eliminate the monopoly power of landowners to exploit wage-earners and allow for the abolition of other taxes.

Biography

Henry George was born in Philadelphia on 2 September 1839, the second of ten children in a devout Episcopalian family. At sixteen, he went to sea and spent ten years drifting from job to job until, with a wife and young family, he settled in San Francisco, where he discovered a talent for journalism and, by 1871, became the editor and co-owner of the *San Francisco Daily Evening Post*.

An active Democrat, he attacked railroad and land speculators and their corrupt political allies, and in an 1868 article, 'What the Railroad Will Bring Us', he first suggested that, far from reducing poverty, industrialisation and urbanisation were increasing impoverishment despite the rapid creation of wealth. He explained this paradox in *Our Land and Land Policy* (1871) as due to the monopolistic exactions of landlords, which could be remedied by a tax on the rent of land and minerals. He further elaborated his ideas in *Progress and Poverty* (1879), which, with its evocative, almost religious, language and its tone of moral outrage, was an unexpected and sensational success, selling millions of copies world-wide.

George moved to New York in 1880, where he took an interest in Irish-American affairs. He wrote a pamphlet, *The Irish Land Question*, and was commissioned to tour Ireland as a correspondent for the *Irish World*. During the trip, in 1881–82, he spoke on radical platforms – often with the Irish Land League's Michael Davitt, or with the English socialist H. M. Hyndman. George's notoriety was assured when he

was arrested by an over-zealous policeman, who thought him a 'suspicious character'.

With his radical credentials burnished by the tour, and two further British trips in 1883–84 and 1885, George ran as the United Labor Party candidate for mayor of New York in 1886. He came second to the Democrat Abram S. Hewitt, beating the Republican hopeful, Theodore Roosevelt, into third place.

Such was the success of *Progress and Poverty* that by the late 1880s a network of Single Tax associations had spread throughout America, the British Empire and Europe. George toured Britain again in 1888 and 1889, and visited Australia and New Zealand in 1890. The following winter he suffered a stroke, yet ran again for the mayoralty of New York in 1897, this time as an independent Democrat. A further stroke killed him just before the election, on 29 October. His death prompted tributes from around the world, and his supporters claimed that over 100,000 attended his funeral procession.

Ideas

Late nineteenth-century radicalism (q.v.) was underpinned by an anti-aristocratic tradition dating back to the seventeenth century, which held that the land was the property of the people. Henry George gave a moral and intellectual justification for this claim. His idea, based partly on Ricardo (q.v.), Cobden (q.v.), and J. S. Mill (q.v.), was that land, which God had created for the whole community, was the essential prerequisite to the creation of all other forms of wealth. For those who owned no land, rent was a tax on their production. As the population grew, competitive pressure bid up rents and so tended to suppress wages to subsistence levels. Landlords further exploited their power by withholding land from the market in anticipation of higher prices, so further increasing over-crowding and destitution.

George's remedy was to take as tax the rental value of the underlying land and minerals, but not any rent due to 'productive' improvements made to the land, such as buildings. Rises in land value due to growth in the community would thus be reclaimed for the community; land speculation would become pointless; and the under-use of land would be discouraged. George argued that the ending of the 'land monopoly' would give every man the option of setting up as a smallholder, so breaking the power of employers to set unfairly low wages, while capital would not suffer because the tax on land would produce enough revenue to allow for the abolition of all taxes on productive enterprise (hence 'single tax').

This would have more than economic consequences, as George argued that once the evil of the land monopoly was removed social harmony and economic well-being would prevail without the necessity for collectivism or other socialist palliatives. Rather, and following Herbert Spencer (q.v.), he thought that the end of both economic monopoly and state interference would allow for the full development of the moral potential of the individual.

George's emphasis on the special nature of landed property, his lack of formal education and his cavalier attitude to statistics meant that his ideas were accepted by few economists in his own day or since, while land-owners saw him as the 'apostle of plunder'. Yet for a generation after his death his theories had a significant influence on progressive politics in the English-speaking world and beyond (see also entry on the Henry George Foundation).

Key works
- *Progress and Poverty* (1879)

Further reading
- Charles A. Barker, *Henry George* (Oxford University Press, 1955)
- Elwood P. Lawrence, *Henry George in the British Isles* (Michigan State University Press, 1957)
- Antony Taylor, *Lords of Misrule* (Palgrave Macmillan, 2004)

Paul Mulvey

William Ewart Gladstone   1809–98

As a long-serving Chancellor of the Exchequer and four-term Prime Minister, Gladstone dominated Victorian Liberal politics. He embodied the ideals of the party and was responsible for many of its most notable achievements, including free trade, disestablishment of the Church of Ireland, electoral reform and state primary education. His Irish home rule policy split the party, however, depriving it of office for nearly two decades, but remains part of the British Liberal heritage.

Key ideas
- The progressive incorporation of all classes within the political community.
- Free trade, to redistribute the burden of taxation away from the lower classes and to stimulate consumption.
- Efficient administration, to minimise the cost of government and promote personal responsibility.
- The 'right principles' of foreign policy based on the equal rights of nations and the promotion of joint international action.
- Devolution of Irish legislation to a subordinate parliament in Dublin.

Biography
William Ewart Gladstone was born in Liverpool on 29 December 1809, the fifth child of Sir John Gladstone, a wealthy

trader, and Anne Robertson. He was educated at Eton (1821–27) and Christ Church, Oxford (1828–31) where he was awarded a double first in mathematics and classics. Gladstone regularly participated in the Union debates, notably one opposing the 1831 Reform Bill.

When Sir John vetoed his son's ambition to enter the church, his friend Lord Lincoln arranged with his father, the Duke of Newcastle, for Gladstone to stand for Parliament for Newark, where he was elected in 1832. He was given junior office in Peel's short-lived Tory ministry of 1834, and while in opposition published *The State in Its Relations with the Church*, outlining the responsibility of the state, as a moral agency, to support the established Church of England and to advance its truths. In 1839 he married Catherine Glynne.

In Peel's second government of 1841, Gladstone was appointed to the Board of Trade, entering the Cabinet in 1843. Here, he became converted to free trade (q.v.) but his chief accomplishment was the Railway Act, celebrated in Gilbert & Sullivan's *Mikado*. Gladstone resigned when Peel increased the grant for the Roman Catholic Maynooth seminary, in contradiction to his church/state sentiments. In 1845, he was reappointed to the Cabinet that repealed the Corn Laws, but vacated the Newark seat in deference to Newcastle's protectionist views. Consequently, Gladstone was not in Parliament to help defend Peel from Disraeli's attacks during the Corn Law debates that broke up the Conservative Party in 1846 and unsettled party alignment for the next decade and more.

Gladstone became MP for Oxford University in 1847. When the minority Whig government fell in 1851, Lord John Russell (q.v.) was succeeded by Derby, with Disraeli at the Exchequer. Although Disraeli soon abandoned protectionism to hold on to office, Gladstone helped to destroy his 1852 budget proposals, accusing him of failing to provide for a surplus and subsidising agricultural interests at the expense of the professional classes who paid income tax. Gladstone succeeded Disraeli as Chancellor in the short-lived Aberdeen Peelite/Whig coalition. In his own budget he set out a strategy for extending free trade and the eventual abolition of income tax. This plan was disrupted by the Crimean War, however, as the government fell when the inadequacies of its war departments were exposed.

In 1859, Palmerston again brought together the Whigs, Peelites and Radicals, united as the Liberal Party in support of Italian nationalism. As Chancellor of the Exchequer, Gladstone completed the programme of tax simplification and free trade, abolished paper duties to facilitate the growth of the press and established the Post Office Savings Bank. The political instability of the 1850s partly reflected disagreement over further electoral reform; in 1864 Gladstone signalled his conversion to extending the franchise and after Palmerston's death in 1865, he introduced a moderate Reform Bill on behalf of Russell's government, which failed when the Liberals split. Disraeli exploited the Liberal disarray to pass the more radical 1867 Reform Act giving household suffrage to the boroughs. On Russell's retirement, Gladstone was the inevitable leader and he was able to reunite the Liberal Party in a campaign to disestablish the Church of Ireland.

Gladstone's first government of 1868–74 reflected his energetic personality, delivering Forster's 1870 primary education Act, abolishing the sale of military commissions, instituting the secret ballot and ending religious tests for university fellowships as well as disestablishing the Irish church. Failure to carry Irish university reforms and the enmity of the brewing interests cost Gladstone the 1874 election, despite his belated promise to abolish income tax.

Gladstone resigned the leadership of the party early in 1875, but when, in 1876, he believed his successors had failed adequately to oppose Disraeli's pro-Turkish policies, he published *The Bulgarian Horrors and the Question of the East* to condemn the massacre of Bulgarian Christians. This was followed by his 1879 Midlothian campaign, which further damned Disraeli's exploitative 'balance-of-power' foreign policy. The Grand Old Man proclaimed an alternative set of 'right principles' for Liberal foreign policy, promoting equal rights for all nations and joint action by the 'concert' of European powers to preserve peace. With his victory at the 1880 election in Midlothian, Gladstone's comeback was complete.

Despite Queen Victoria's attempts to appoint Lord Hartington, Gladstone became Prime Minister again in 1880. His second government was less successful than his first. Irish MPs obstructed parliamentary business while the government's Irish land reforms failed to end rural discontent. In contravention of Gladstone's Midlothian principles, Britain invaded Egypt, showing little respect for the 'equal rights of all nations' or Egyptian 'love of freedom' and without waiting for the authority of the concert of Europe. Later, the death of Gordon at Khartoum was blamed on Liberal incompetence. Nevertheless the government did pass major reform and redistribution acts in 1884–85, which extended household suffrage to the counties and created mostly single-member constituencies. In the summer of 1885 the government fell, the victim of internal splits.

When the 1885 general election left Irish Nationalist MPs holding the balance of power, Gladstone surprised his party by proposing home rule, an extensive scheme of devolution to a powerful but subordinate Irish parliament. He was defeated by an alliance of Conservatives and dissident Whigs and Radicals who feared that home rule prefigured Irish independence and the break-up of the Empire. The dissident Liberal Unionists (q.v.) supported the Conservatives in office between 1886 and 1892. Gladstone used his only substantive period as leader of the opposition to convert the country to his Irish plans, becoming the first party leader to speak regularly at national party conferences and the first to endorse a manifesto proposed by party activists. The Newcastle Programme, as it was known after the 1891 conference venue, promised reform of the Lords, payment for MPs, elected district and parish councils, disestablishment of the Welsh and Scottish churches, compulsory purchase powers for local authorities to create smallholdings and limitations on working hours, as well as home rule.

The Liberals defeated the Tories in the 1892 general election but were reliant on Irish MPs for a majority in the Commons. Gladstone's second home rule bill passed the Commons but was swiftly rejected by the Lords. Gladstone resigned in 1894, after failing to convince the Cabinet to reduce military expenditure, though publicly blaming ill-health. He died in May 1898 of cancer of the face at Hawarden, his wife's ancestral home.

Catherine and William Gladstone had four sons and four daughters. Herbert later became Chief Whip of the Liberal Party and Helen Vice-Principal of Newnham College, Cambridge.

Ideas

Gladstone absorbed ideas from a multitude of sources. His library (preserved at St Deiniol's, Hawarden) and his diaries suggest that he read around 20,000 books. However, the keys to understanding his political ideas are his evangelical Christian upbringing, his love of the classics (particularly Homer), and the administration of Robert Peel.

His Christianity gave him the strong sense of moral purpose, which powered his campaigning oratory and strengthened his public appeal, particularly to Nonconformists. He believed that all his actions, including those as a politician and statesman, were to be held accountable to the Almighty. This was combined with a Peelite drive for efficiency in government and a recognition that conservative ends in government often required radical reforms.

Gladstone's early period as a Conservative MP allowed him to stand outside the Whig–Radical dichotomy of the Victorian Liberal Party, reassuring the Whigs by his moderate objectives while delivering reforms embraced by the Radicals. Key features of Gladstone's liberalism were his search for signs of responsibility among the lower classes, which signified that they could be trusted to play a greater civic role, and the use of timely reform to introduce flexibility into the constitution as a means of forestalling any prospect of revolution. This trust in the people informed his conversion to extending the franchise, the creation of the Post Office Savings Bank and home rule for Ireland. While Gladstone's Homeric studies constituted primarily a means of serious relaxation, his reading and writing on the subject provided a framework against which the British political system could be judged and analysed.

Gladstone envisaged a hierarchy in which the prime mover was the individual within a family that was part of a local community, and in which the church and local aristocracy played a role commensurate with the extra resources that were their birthright. In later years, elected local government superseded this aristocratic role.

This somewhat paternalistic view informed Gladstone's church and state writings and it is a measure of his movement towards liberalism that he undertook the disestablishment of the Church of Ireland – its separation from the state. Central government undertook only the limited functions that could not be performed lower down the hierarchy, and in turn the nation-state formed part of a concert of nations.

Personal responsibility and the limited role of government combined with the pressure of accountability required that the fewest resources should be taken from individuals; taxes were to be minimised. Ministers had an obligation to prune ruthlessly all wasteful expenditure – retrenchment. This should not be confused with a laissez-faire (q.v.) approach to government; while he opposed the government constructively taking over responsibilities that should remain with the individual and the family, Gladstone was always a government activist willing to expand the role of the state as a regulator (e.g. through the 1844 Railway Act, or Irish land reform) and as a provider where voluntary means were inadequate, as in education. The search for a level playing field, equality of burden between the social classes and efficiency in taxation were strong drivers towards free trade. Gladstone was never an enthusiastic imperialist, not only out of respect for the rights of other communities but because he feared that colonies represented needless expenditure by the metropolitan government.

The six right principles of the Midlothian campaign extended this philosophy into the international sphere. Like the individual citizen, each nation or empire had a responsibility to foster its strength by just legislation and economy at home. The aim of foreign policy should be to preserve peace, which was best achieved by the powerful European states acting in concert and by avoiding needless, wasteful entanglements. States should acknowledge the equal rights of all nations and, above all, the foreign policy of England should 'always be inspired by the love of freedom'.

Key works

Gladstone contributed voluminously to the periodic literature of the Victorian era but was primarily an orator and he may perhaps be best sampled through Tilney Basset's selection of speeches. His early work reflects his position as a Conservative and *A Chapter of Autobiography* seeks to explain the subsequent development of his thinking preparatory to Irish disestablishment.

- *The State in Its Relations with the Church* (1838, revised 1841)
- *Church Principles Considered in Their Results* (1840)
- *A Chapter of Autobiography* (1868)
- *Bulgarian Horrors and the Question of the East* (1876)
- *Special Aspects of the Irish Question* (1892)
- A. Tilney Basset (ed.), *Gladstone's Speeches* (Methuen, 1916)
- *Midlothian Speeches 1879* (reprinted with an introduction by M. R. D. Foot, Leicester University Press, 1971)

Further reading

- David Bebbington, *The Mind of Gladstone: Religion, Homer, and Politics* (Oxford University Press, 2004)
- Eugenio Biagini, *Gladstone* (Macmillan, 2000)
- Colin Matthew, *Gladstone 1809–1898* (Clarendon Press, 1996)
- John Morley, *Life of Gladstone* (Macmillan, 1903)
- Richard Shannon, *Gladstone: Peel's Inheritor* (Penguin, 1999)
- Richard Shannon, *Gladstone: Heroic Minister* (Penguin, 1999)

Tony Little

John Gray   1948–

Initially a defender of a version of J. S. Mill's liberalism, Gray became one of the foremost theorists of the revival of the economic liberalism associated with Thatcherism in the 1980s. He subsequently became one of its most powerful critics, defending instead a modus vivendi liberalism based on a form of value-pluralism, and marked by scepticism towards all universalistic projects for human improvement.

Key ideas

- The critique of contemporary liberal political philosophy as unpolitical and intolerant.
- The articulation of a form of value-pluralism as the moral basis for politics.
- The defence of a politics of modus vivendi as an alternative to currently dominant forms of liberalism.

Biography

John Gray was born in 1948 in South Shields, the son of a shipyard joiner. He was educated at South Shields Grammar School, and read philosophy, politics and economics at Exeter College, Oxford, on a scholarship, where he received his BA and DPhil degrees.

At Oxford he came to know Isaiah Berlin (q.v.), who had a lasting influence on his thought. Other influences include F. A. von Hayek (q.v.), and subsequently Michael Oakeshott, George Santayana and, most recently, James Lovelock. After briefly teaching at the University of Essex, he was fellow in politics at Jesus College, Oxford from 1976 until 1998, when he was appointed Professor of European Thought at the London School of Economics. He has held several visiting professorships, including at Harvard and Yale, and lectured widely across the world.

Gray has never held any formal political position, although he was an active participant in informal intellectual groups involved in the development of the Thatcherite project in the late 1970s and early 1980s. He later became estranged from them, and after a brief flirtation with groups formed around New Labour, he has subsequently kept his distance from any political associations, increasingly mixing with a diverse range of writers and intellectuals.

Ideas

Gray first achieved scholarly recognition for his original and ingenious attempt to reconcile J. S. Mill's (q.v.) utilitarianism (q.v.) with his defence of the liberty principle in *On Liberty* (*Mill on Liberty: a Defence*, 1983). He achieved wider recognition, however, as one of the leading intellectuals associated with the revival of economic liberalism (q.v.) which accompanied the rise of Thatcherism. In a series of scholarly and popular writings, Gray was a coruscating critic of the post-war political consensus, and an advocate of economic and (unlike Thatcher) moral liberalism.

However, from the mid-1980s he became disenchanted with the Thatcherite project, becoming critical of its destruction of the social fabric and insensitivity to the diversity of social and cultural formations. While remaining consistently hostile to Marxism as a social theory and communism as a political system, he nonetheless became fiercely critical of Western triumphalism over 'global capitalism' and 'liberal democracy' (q.v.) in the wake of the fall of communism (*False Dawn*, 1998). He has increasingly defended the need for political regimes to take account of local history and culture, without ever embracing a communitarian conception of politics These radical shifts have led to charges that his politics are chameleon and unserious; but these shifts have been underpinned by a consistent and firmly held conviction about the limits of politics, and a scepticism towards all utopian political projects.

Gray's conception of politics stresses the fundamental roles of diversity and conflict, although elaborating and explaining what this means has become a central focus of his thought since the 1990s. In particular, he has come to embrace a strong form of value-pluralism, which asserts the fundamental incommensurability of many human values. Although this idea has its roots in the work of his mentor, Isaiah Berlin, Gray draws from it very different conclusions. Whereas Berlin saw value-pluralism as essentially supporting Enlightenment liberalism, for Gray this form of liberalism is but one competing conception among others of the good life, representing only a limited range of human values. While all worthwhile political regimes must meet certain minimal standards of human decency, Western liberal democracy cannot be demonstrated to be uniquely the best of them.

This critique of the dominant form of contemporary liberal political theory is, however, also conducted in the name of liberalism. In *Two Faces of Liberalism* (2000) Gray defends an alternative understanding of liberalism, one that grows out of the wars of religion in the sixteenth century and is concerned above all with mutual toleration and peaceful coexistence through a politics of *modus vivendi*. This is contrasted with what he sees as the deformation of liberalism in the work of Rawls (q.v.), Dworkin (q.v.) and others, which is vitiated by an excessive rationalism in its emphasis in the primacy of individual rights, and a misguided universalisation of the historically specific political practices that have emerged in the West.

Gray's most recent work has become still more pessimistic, and also moved in an explicitly anti-humanist direction, as he has adopted a broader ecological perspective, particularly influenced by James Lovelock's *Gaia* hypothesis (*Straw Dogs*, 2002). There has also been a shift towards a more aphoristic written style. There is a sense that Gray's interests have moved away from politics and political thought, or at least that those interests have become absorbed within a broader form of cultural criticism, and an increasingly bleak view of human life and its prospects in which the significance of the political is diminished yet further.

Key works
- *Liberalisms: Essays in Political Philosophy* (1989)
- *Post-liberalism: Studies in Political Thought* (1993)
- *Beyond the New Right: Markets, Government and the Common Environment* (1993)
- *Enlightenment's Wake: Politics and Culture at the Close of the Modern Age* (1995)
- *Isaiah Berlin* (1995)
- *Endgames: Questions in Late Modern Political Thought* (1997)
- *False Dawn: The Delusions of Global Capitalism* (1998, revised edn., 1998)
- *Two Faces of Liberalism* (2000)
- *Straw Dogs: Thoughts on Humans and Other Animals* (2002)
- *Al Qaeda and What It Means to Be Modern* (2003)

Further reading
- J. Horton and G. Newey (eds.), *The Political Theory of John Gray* (Routledge, 2006)

John Horton

T. H. Green   1836–82

An ethicist, political philosopher, philosopher of religion, social reformer and political radical, Green was active in temperance reform and had a strong influence on the British idealist movement. His political thought grew out of the writings of St Paul, Aristotle, Kant and Hegel. He called upon English philosophers to study Kant and Hegel and turn away from the tradition of John Stuart Mill and Herbert Spencer. He was a significant influence on the New Liberals, especially L. T. Hobhouse.

Key ideas
- That the Kantian belief in human reason and goodness should be combined with an Aristotelian belief in human potential and that liberalism should be reformulated in line with these insights.
- That the state should actively foster the conditions in which individual citizens can fulfil their potentials as autonomous agents, rather than limiting its actions to supplying a legal framework in which citizens are treated simply as workers and consumers.
- That the true patriot serves the nation by helping others to live virtuous and fulfilling lives.
- That liberals should do all they can to promote active citizenship and ensure that it occupies a place at the very centre of British public life.

Biography
Thomas Hill Green was born on 7 April 1836, the son of the rector of the hamlet of Birkin in West Yorkshire. He was educated at home until he was fourteen years old and then entered Rugby School in 1850, where he first met Henry Sidgwick. Even at this young age he showed a great concern for many of the things that were important to him as an adult: Christian Nonconformity, idealist philosophy (q.v.), the exploitation of the poor and social reform. His fellow students thought of him as a very serious, intelligent and pious student.

He went up to Balliol College, Oxford in 1855 where he came under the tutelage of Benjamin Jowett. Jowett was not a typical

Victorian. First, he held markedly unorthodox religious beliefs, which became most
evident during his involvement with the
Essays and Reviews controversy of the early
1860s. Second, at this time at least, Jowett
was a great admirer of the latest German
philosophy and especially of the absolute
idealism (q.v.) of Georg Wilhelm Friedrich
Hegel (q.v.) and his followers. Green was
profoundly influenced by both of these
things and came to hold Jowett in near
reverence until the end of his (Green's) life.
He also became great friends with Edward
Caird (q.v.) and A. V. Dicey (q.v.) at this
time. Nevertheless, Green's habitual lazi-
ness ensured that he failed to get a first in
Classical Moderations, in 1857. He applied
himself in his next studies and achieved the
highest class in *Literae Humaniores* in 1859.
Another six months of hard work earned
him a respectable third in law and modern history, which in turn qualified him to
work as a temporary college tutor at Balliol
in 1860. He was made a fellow of Balliol
towards the end of that year.

At this time, Green vacillated between
an academic life and a more directly socially
useful career. He took up a position as an
inspector with the Schools' Inquiry Commission in 1865, but returned to his fellowship at Balliol the following year. From this
time, he committed himself to philosophy
and the life of the college. His influence on
his students grew, partly as a result of the
force of his lectures but also because of his
very evident religious and moral depth.

It was at this time that Green became
more involved with the Oxford Liberal
Party. He had been well known among
successive peer groups as a radical in religious and political matters, and this was
reflected in the stances that he took as a
member of the party. He was an advanced
liberal, although his great admiration for
John Bright, the Manchester School (q.v.)

liberal, did not reflect support for free trade
(q.v.). He seems also to have seen Gladstone
(q.v.) as too conservative. He was a forceful advocate of the radical extension of
the franchise in the run-up to the Second
Reform Act in 1867, and always stressed the
interlinking of franchise reform and wider
constitutional changes. For example, he
concluded a speech to the radical Reform
League on 25 March 1867 by arguing that
'if the reform of Parliament, for which we
wait, brings with it a free Church, free land,
and free education, we shall rejoice to have
refused all half measures, and shall feel that
we have not waited and laboured in vain
(loud and continuous cheering)'. He spoke
on several occasions to the Agricultural
Labourers' Union and various temperance societies and local schools, as well as
the local Liberal Party and in support of
numerous radical causes, such as the protests against Turkish atrocities of 1876 and
the Contagious Diseases Act of 1874.

Green died unexpectedly from blood
poisoning on 26 March 1882, a few days
short of his forty-sixth birthday.

Ideas

Green was elected as a Liberal member of
Oxford City Council on 1 November 1876
and again in 1878 (he died in office). His
political speeches show his intense dislike
for the Conservative Party and in particular
their aggressive foreign policies and their
corruption of the ideals of citizenship in the
service of vested interests. In the notes of a
speech to be made toward what became the
end of his life, Green observed that:

> There is a false patriotism and a true. The
> false patriot is a man who clamours for dis-
> play of national strength without consid-
> ering whether the cause in which strength
> is to be displayed is just or no. Who seeks
> to gratify passion for excitement by call-
> ing for wars, in which he will not shed his

blood, without considering their effect on [the] permanent good of his nation. The true patriot is a man who will sacrifice [himself] … to serve his nation not merely in war, … but by making the people more virtuous and contented, and therefore greater and stronger with only true greatness and strength. Those who talk most about patriotism are not best patriots.

Green was made Whyte's Professor of Moral Philosophy in 1878, and began to write his major philosophical work, *The Prolegomena to Ethics*, which was published posthumously in 1883. His political activism intertwined with his political philosophy, and he founded both upon his ethics. (His pupil David G. Ritchie (q.v.) once noted that he 'went straight from declaration of the poll, when he was elected town councillor, to lecture on *The Critique of Pure Reason*'.) Green's fundamental value throughout was a profound respect for 'a free life'. In the posthumously published *Lectures on the Principles of Political Obligation*, he observed that:

If there are such things as rights at all, then, there must be a right to life and liberty, or, to put it more properly, to free life. No distinction can be made between the right to life and the right to liberty, for there can be no right to mere life – no right to life on the part of a being that has not also the right to direct the life according to the motions of his own will.

Green argued that this made it incumbent upon the state to foster the conditions for the development of the effective freedom of its individual citizens rather than merely providing a legal framework in which they could exist as workers or consumers. It was this belief that led Green to justify the more interventionist turn that the Liberal Party had taken, a direction which in the late 1870s and early 1880s superseded the Manchester School (q.v.) liberalism

of Bright and Cobden (q.v.). Then as now, Liberals were asking whether the party should pursue greater state intervention in at least nominally free relations between individuals. Green himself wrote against the background of the Education Acts of 1876 and 1880, the Ground Game Act, the Employers' Liability Act and various other interventionist Liberal measures. In the famous 'Lecture on Liberal Legislation and Freedom of Contract', which he gave to a meeting of working men in Leicester in 1881, Green observed that:

Our modern legislation then with reference to labour, and education, and health, involving as it does manifold interference with freedom of contract, is justified on the ground that it is the business of the state, not indeed directly to promote moral goodness, for that, from the very nature of moral goodness, it cannot do, but to maintain the conditions without which a free exercise of the human faculties is impossible.

Green called such 'free exercise' of one's innate capacities 'positive freedom' (now we call it 'personal autonomy'). This is the ability to reflect upon and rank one's desires, to choose rationally which desires to seek to satisfy, and to pursue that satisfaction in the surest and most efficient manner possible given the particular circumstances of one's life. Philosophically, Green combined a Kantian (q.v.) belief that the individual's highest good was to live as a rational being (a being who uses her reason to regulate her desires) with an Aristotelian belief that we are all beings with under-developed and yet inherently valuable intellectual, artistic, civic and political capacities that we should develop as fully as we can. Hence, Green argued that the satisfaction of some desires offered a more profound and lasting sense of fulfilment than others. One of the most important of these in a time of social inequality and widespread squalor and oppression was the desire to help others to develop their own higher capacities. In Green's terminology, these were desires to serve 'the common good'.

Precisely what we should do is an inescapably personal matter, heavily dependent on one's particular character and circumstances. It is founded also upon the particular nature of the society in which we as unique individuals are raised. It is the individual's society that starts to make her an intelligent, self-conscious being; in other words, to make her a particular person. We come to understand the world in certain ways because of the ideas that our society gives us. We come to value certain things because of the values we are raised with as children. Yet it is a mark of adulthood that each of us can stand back from these given meanings and values, criticise them and seek to reform them where our conscience tells us that is necessary. Our capacity for autonomous action must gain substance from our upbringing in other words, but it is the mark of our humanity as intelligent beings that we use our (Kantian) rationality and our awareness of our (frequently rather latent Aristotelian) capacities to judge and reform these meanings and values and the collective practices, norms, conventions, and institutions which they underpin.

The individual's capacity for an autonomous or free life grows through debate and contestation in our private lives, our civic engagements and our political battles. These conflicts force us to articulate ourselves more clearly and to justify our positions more persuasively to others. The more sections of society that can enter these debates, the more rounded and coherent will be the public life of the nation and the personal lives of the citizens. This was the main reason why Green pushed for the radical extension of the franchise to all urban

working men in 1866–67 and, with a little more caution due their then lower level of education, to the agricultural poor.

We have seen that Greenian positive freedom requires each individual to be able to think rationally about their particular situation. As has just been indicated also, this means that he or she must possess a certain level of education (which Green held it was the state's duty to provide when the cost of instruction was beyond the individual's finances). It also requires that the individual be free from addiction. Green himself had failed in his attempts to help his brother to overcome alcoholism and subsequently spent a great deal of time making a liberal case for the placing of certain restrictions on the drinks trade. Positive freedom also requires the state to enable the individual to escape grinding poverty. It was for this reason, Green held, that the state had a duty to set legal limits on the appropriate terms and conditions of employment that workers could 'freely' enter into with employers.

Yet, all state intervention was valuable only to the extent that it enabled individuals to be active and intelligent members of their communities. Green held that even the regulation of the sale of alcohol should be trusted to ordinary citizens. He placed a great deal of faith in the ability of working people to control their own lives and the lives of their own communities. For Green the heart of democracy lay in the locality and the municipality. Moreover, in many ways the most important areas of legislation and political action were those of 'low' policy – public health, education, transport and so on – rather than the more glamorous concerns of 'high' policy, such as international statesmanship and war. The heart of true citizenship coincided with the nature of true patriotism. Green stated while an undergraduate at Balliol that he would 'let the flag of England be dragged through the dirt rather than sixpence be added to the taxes which weigh on the poor.'

Green's followers, who have come to be called the British idealists, represented one of the most influential ethical and political movements of the late nineteenth and early twentieth centuries. His thought had a profound effect on the New Liberalism (q.v.) of L. T. Hobhouse (q.v.). He has also been claimed as a precursor of New Labour. There are great problems however, defending the latter claim in an age of 'constrained discretion' and a naïve faith in the efficiency and equity of the impersonal free market. Nevertheless, Green's radicalism (q.v.) does continue to offer an alternative future for liberal politics, one that calls for the active citizen rather than the consumer to stand at the heart of British public life.

Key works

- *Prolegomena to Ethics* (1883)
- *Lectures on the Principles of Political Obligation* (1886)
- 'Different Senses of "Freedom" as Applied to Will and the Moral Progress of Man' (1886)
- 'Lecture on Liberal Legislation and Freedom of Contract' (1881)

Further reading

- Olive Anderson, 'The Feminism of Thomas Hill Green: A Late-Victorian Success Story?', *History of Political Thought*, vol. 12 (1991)
- Matt Carter, *T. H. Green and the Ethical Socialist Tradition* (Imprint Academic, 2003)
- Peter Nicholson, 'T. H. Green and State Action: Liquor Legislation', *History of Political Thought*, vol. 6 (1985)
- Peter Nicholson, *Political Philosophy of the British Idealists: Selected Studies* (Cambridge University Press, 1990)

- Albert de Sanctis, *The 'Puritan' Democracy of T. H. Green* (Imprint Academic, 2005)
- Colin Tyler, *Liberal Socialism of T. H. Green* (Imprint Academic, 2007)

Colin Tyler

Jo Grimond   1913–93

From 1956 until 1967 Grimond led the Liberal Party, spearheading its revival to become once again a significant force in British politics. A charismatic figure, his legacy is a rich seam of ideas and a commitment to the realignment of the centre-left that was later to find expression in the creation of the Liberal Democrats.

Key ideas

- Individualism within a social framework of common values, endorsing positive as well as negative liberty, including human rights.
- Preference for voluntary cooperation and civil society over statist solutions, while recognising that the state can promote liberal conditions.
- Qualitative interpretation of democracy, embracing active citizenship and participation.
- Kantian tradition of 'moral means' in denial of utilitarian consequentialism.
- Internationalism.

Biography

The son of a wealthy Dundee jute manufacturer, Joseph Grimond was born on 29 July 1913 in St Andrews. Having attended two London prep schools, he went first to Eton and then Balliol College, Oxford, where he was a Brackenbury scholar. There he took a first in PPE, subsequently being called to the bar at Middle Temple.

In 1937 he married Laura Bonham Carter, daughter of Lady Violet Bonham

Carter and granddaughter of Liberal premier H. H. Asquith. Thus sustained and strengthened in his liberal convictions, he sought election to Parliament as the war came to an end, while still serving as a major in the army. Narrowly defeated on that occasion, he was successful five years later (February 1950) in the same constituency of Orkney & Shetland that he was to represent for the next thirty-three years until his retirement from the House of Commons in 1983.

At the height of the Suez crisis in November 1956, Grimond succeeded Clement Davies as leader of the Liberal Party. In over ten years at the helm he reestablished the party's position at the heart of British politics. While during this time the Liberals' presence in the Commons advanced only modestly from six to twelve MPs, there were some spectacular by-election successes, notably at Orpington in March 1962. There was a sustained heightening in the Liberal popular vote. More importantly, with Grimond as its leader the Liberal Party was taken more seriously than at any time since Lloyd George (q.v.).

Grimond led from the front, providing inspiration both by his personal magnetism and by the defining ideas that he promulgated or endorsed. And where he chose not to lead from the front, he lent his imprimatur for others to revitalise the management of the party. With his youthful vigour and sometimes contentious policies such as (multilateral) nuclear disarmament, membership of the EEC and quasi-dirigiste economic policies, Grimond during the first half of the 1960s promoted a radical progressivism which, to some of his critics, seemed more akin to social democracy (q.v.) than to traditional liberalism. But he was rebuffed when he tried to effect a realignment of the centre-left, though his efforts perhaps tilled the soil for the 1980s'

Alliance and subsequent merger of the Liberal Party and the Social Democratic Party. Roy Jenkins described him as the 'father of the Alliance'.

Grimond himself, however, came to regard his political career as a failure. Certainly it was only after his retirement from the party leadership in January 1967 that the Liberals made more significant headway in national elections, holding the balance in the Commons during much of the Wilson/Callaghan premiership in 1974–79. But when his successor Jeremy Thorpe was forced to resign, Grimond enjoyed a two-month spell as caretaker leader from May to July 1976. Thereafter freed from the responsibilities of leadership, he further enhanced his reputation as something of a maverick, becoming increasingly disenchanted with what he (and others) saw as an excessive though often ineffective state bureaucracy.

Upon his retirement from the Commons he became Baron Grimond of Firth, continuing until his death on 24 October 1993 to expound a wide variety of ideas in a steady output of books, pamphlets and journalistic articles as well as speeches.

Ideas

Three factors complicate any simple account of the ideas associated with Jo Grimond. First, he was, in Isaiah Berlin's (q.v.) terms, a fox not a hedgehog – that is, one who had many relatively small ideas rather than one big idea. Second, the emphasis of his thinking shifted down the years, partly in response to changing circumstances. Third, he was an active politician; as such he was often obliged to offer instant responses to particular issues of the day, sometimes inviting apparent contradictions. That said, Grimond, more than most politicians, explicitly traded in and promulgated ideas that can scarcely be dismissed as ephemeral.

A number of common themes are evident in his thinking, even if there were variations of inflection. These ideas can best be outlined under five headings: the state; civil society; participatory democracy; morality; and internationalism.

Grimond was broadly anti-statist, becoming more so with the passage of time. During the early and middle years of his party leadership he seemed almost uncritically to champion the welfare state and the managed economy, associated with William Beveridge (q.v.) and Maynard Keynes (q.v.) respectively. In the tradition of T. H. Green (q.v.) he believed that the state possessed unique potential as an enabler, as a positive agent for the common good. But pursuit of the common good as a legitimate object of state activity did not, for Grimond, extend to the more abstract, reified notion of a Rousseau-type general will. The state, he insisted, is a human construct, manifest in its institutions, activated by its functionaries. And, since human beings are fallible so, too, is the state. It possesses no superior moral wisdom or authority, though Grimond did acknowledge as a matter of fact that the man in Whitehall may sometimes be right. He thought that liberal values could be placed in jeopardy as much by a weak state as by a strong one. Equally, the state should never be seized by sectional interests; all should be apprised of its bounty, just as none should be crushed by its yoke.

Here there was a perceptible shift of emphasis down the years. Earlier in his career he was adamant that all should have access to the state's largesse; later he tended to underline the need to ensure that none should fall under its yoke. By the late 1960s and '70s, he was asserting that the state had become captured by big business and big unions, and that state functionaries had become a self-serving oligarchy,

insufficiently accountable. To that extent he held common cause with the public-choice school of libertarian (q.v.) thinkers. He feared that the ideals of Beveridge and Keynes had been subverted. He drew a distinction, borrowed from Alan Peacock, between the welfare state and the welfare society. He thought that the state should do less but do it better. The state should withdraw from some of its activities, especially those where market solutions were more appropriate. But while he wanted a more efficient state, he did not seek market solutions for their own sake, nor did he call for the state to ape the private sector in the conduct of public business.

Closely related to Grimond's ideas about the state is his reverence for civil society. In Tocquevillian (q.v.) terms, he saw great virtue in intermediate, non-state institutions that provided both a focus – a leavening of 'social glue' in a potentially anomic world – and a buffer between state and citizen. He adopted the classic liberal precept that the individual matters – or at any rate ought to matter. But it was very much the social individual that Grimond had in mind – one whose fulfilment necessitated concert with other individuals or groups of individuals. Thus the spirit of community and of localism was of cardinal importance. In his maiden parliamentary speech, he expressed strong support for devolution, though he criticised the ill-fated proposals of the Callaghan government in the 1970s, claiming that they offered not devolution but an additional tier of government.

Grimond's long-standing advocacy of devolution speaks to his ideas about representative government and participatory democracy. He was a committed parliamentarian. Yet he did not accept the exclusive, absolutist notion of parliamentary sovereignty associated with A. V. Dicey (q.v.). Sovereignty could and should be shared between Parliament and other institutions, be they organs of state or of civil society. Moreover, he drew attention to the limitations of representative government as an instrument of democracy. Here his ideas seemed on occasion controversial, as when he professed understanding of the frustrations that led the excluded to engage in various forms of direct action, sometimes culminating in violence – which, of course, he abhorred. Representative institutions were deficient, he argued, to the extent that certain sections of society felt themselves to lie beyond the pale, and to the extent that they failed to provide a mechanism for deeper, more qualitative exchange that would engage the citizen. Democracy was about active participation, not just a vicarious affair. It was essential to the health of the body politic that citizens should be involved in areas in which they could readily relate and connect – the workplace, the local community. He upheld a Millite (q.v.) position in advocating participation as an agent of improvement. In what he came to regard as an age of numbing conformity and moral turpitude he worried not that citizens would demand too much freedom but that they would be satisfied with too little.

There is a strong stripe of moralism in Grimond's liberalism. He did not believe that morality could or should be imposed, by the state or any other agent. And he upheld traditional notions about free expression in a genuinely pluralist society. But he was not a moral relativist; he believed in value judgements. In the traditions of Kant (q.v.), Mill and T. H. Green, he believed in the promise if not the inevitability of some sort of 'good life' rooted in common values. He rejected utilitarian (q.v.) consequentialism, instead following the Kantian precept that a superior end cannot justify an ignoble deed. He lamented what he judged to be the decline

of 'conscience politics'; he feared that the liberal society was in danger of going the way of the Roman Empire – decay from within. While he never sneered at the need to attend to the mundane practicalities of politics, there was more of the Greek than the Roman in the temper of his thinking. Yet he came increasingly to see that strong vision and active advocacy were needed to sustain liberalism against its enemies.

Vision was a feature of Grimond's internationalism, too. Under his leadership the Liberals became the first mainstream party to call for Britain's membership of the EEC. Grimond went further than most in seeing virtue in the promise of reduced national sovereignty, rather than in trying to obscure or deny the fact. He wanted a world in which nations were locked, so far as possible, into a common cause rather than one marked by the potential combat of competitive, independent states. Thus he questioned the need for Britain to maintain its own nuclear arsenal, believing that too much foreign and defence policy was driven by empty notions of national prestige. Yet he was not in the strict sense a federalist. He saw validity in moderate nationalism and the nation state, and he came to question the wisdom of some of the integrationist policies emanating from Brussels. He remained a robust advocate of the Atlantic alliance, both as regards NATO during the Cold War years and in Anglo-American relations. In the last analysis, he found it difficult to reconcile the diktat of national self-determination with the implications of a fully blown internationalism.

Key works
- *The Liberal Future* (1959)
- *The Liberal Challenge: Democracy through Participation* (1963)
- *The Common Welfare* (1978)
- *A Personal Manifesto* (1983)

Further reading

- Peter Barberis, *Liberal Lion – Jo Grimond: A Political Life* (I. B. Tauris, 2005)
- Jo Grimond, *Memoirs* (Heinemann, 1979)
- Michael McManus, *Jo Grimond: Towards the Sound of Gunfire* (Birlinn, 2001)

Peter Barberis

R. B. Haldane   1856–1928

One of the leading figures in the Liberal Imperialist strand of thought within late nineteenth- and early twentieth-century liberalism, Haldane combined a serious interest in philosophy with a range of achievements as a Liberal Cabinet minister, especially as Secretary of State for War in 1905–12.

Key ideas

- Reconciliation of the ideas of the German philosopher G. W. F. Hegel with British liberalism.
- Combination of social reform with a robust stance on national defence.
- Advocacy of a positive attitude towards the Empire and its evolution towards greater imperial unity.
- The need for a national system of education as the agent of moral and economic progress.

Biography

Richard Burdon Haldane was born in Edinburgh on 30 July 1856. Both his parents' families were prominent in the fields of evangelical religion and the legal profession. He was educated at Edinburgh Academy and the University of Edinburgh, though in 1874–75 he spent some time at the University of Gottingen, thus confirming a life-long interest in Germany and idealist philosophy. Haldane's earliest and most important influences were the German philosopher G. W. F. Hegel (q.v.) and the Oxford University idealist, T. H. Green (q.v.), though he also translated the works of another German thinker, Arthur Schopenhauer.

Haldane was called to the bar at Lincoln's Inn in 1879 and became a QC in 1890, building up a profitable equity practice which concentrated on appeals to the House of Lords and the judicial committee of the Privy Council. He was a convinced liberal from an early age and became Liberal MP for Haddingtonshire in 1885, keeping the seat until 1911, when he went to the Lords as Viscount Haldane of Cloan. In the Commons in the late 1880s he formed a close friendship and working relationship with H. H. Asquith and Sir Edward Grey and together they formed the nucleus of the future Liberal Imperialist (q.v.) grouping within the party. Like his friends, Haldane believed that only by promoting enthusiasm for an active foreign policy, the Empire and social reform could Liberal fortunes be revived in the aftermath of the party split over Irish home rule in 1886.

In 1905–12 Haldane served as Secretary of State for War in the Liberal governments of Campbell-Bannerman and Asquith, rising to be one of the five or six leading ministers in the Cabinet. His crucial achievement was the 1907 Territorial and Reserve Forces Act, which reorganised the existing part-time home defence forces, leaving the regular army free to be sent abroad in wartime. In 1912–15 Haldane served as Lord Chancellor, without making any great impact in that office. He lost his place in May 1915 when the coalition government was formed and the Tories insisted he be sacked as a Germanophile.

Haldane became alienated from liberalism after his dismissal and served as Lord Chancellor and Labour leader in the Lords in Ramsay MacDonald's first Labour government of January – November 1924. He died at his home at Cloan in Scotland on 19 August 1928. He never married.

Ideas

Haldane was an unusual figure in British politics and in liberalism: while he was a professional politician, he was also a knowledgeable and well-published philosopher. He was only denied a doctorate in philosophy at Edinburgh because the Dean of the Faculty of Science objected to his religious unorthodoxy, and he was later offered the Chair of Moral Philosophy at St Andrews. Haldane was particularly interested in German philosophy, spoke German well and was a regular visitor to that country before 1914. Throughout his life he remained a passionate advocate of the ideas of Hegel. He believed that the political policies that he espoused were the outcome of the general principles he enunciated in his philosophy. In particular, he believed that humanity was progressing towards the self-realisation of reason and freedom (q.v.), through the evolution of the 'World Spirit' (or God), who was gradually revealed in men's evolving ideas and institutions.

Because he believed in progress Haldane had no doubt he was a liberal. But he had little time for many nineteenth-century liberal traditions precisely because he believed that they had been superseded by new and 'higher' developments. Most importantly, Haldane lacked earlier liberals' suspicion of the state. Like many committed Hegelians he tended to emphasise man's social and political relationships, rather than individual liberty, and to point to how freedom could be promoted by the state, which represented one of the most important contemporary expressions of the 'World Spirit'. As Haldane put it, the rights of individuals had to be balanced by 'the equally real life of the common whole'. He insisted that liberalism should embrace social reform, and helped to popularise the term 'the New Liberalism' (q.v.) in an article in the *Progressive Review* in 1896. Throughout the 1905–15 governments Haldane was a key supporter of their progressive legislation, including the budgets of 1909 and 1914 which raised the money to pay for the programme.

But Haldane also followed Hegel in believing that the state had the right to defend its interests, and he fully supported increased naval expenditure, the secret military discussions with France in 1905–14 and the decision to declare war on Germany in August 1914. He also detected the 'World Spirit' in the evolution of the British state into the centre of a world-wide Empire, and was one of the most enthusiastic liberal backers of the Boer War of 1899–1902. Haldane even flirted with the idea of turning the Lords into an imperial senate.

His other great enthusiasm was for a system of national education, led by a greatly expanded university system. He had no time for the Anglican v. Nonconformist battle that obsessed educational politics in the early 1900s, and argued that education was crucial to an enlightened democracy, equality of opportunity and economic efficiency – all key components of progress towards individual and collective self-realisation. To the horror of many liberals these views led Haldane to support the Tories' 1902 Education Act; he also spent much of his time promoting higher education, playing a crucial role in the founding of Imperial College in London.

Haldane's interest in philosophy made him the nearest thing Liberal Imperialism possessed to an intellectual apologist. But his devotion to abstract thought and the obscurity of his mode of expression made him ill suited to explain Liberal

Imperialism to a wider audience. Moreover, his willingness to jettison traditional liberal icons made him an object of suspicion to many liberals; but Haldane's thought represented an important attempt to reconcile liberalism with the increased role of the state in the early twentieth century.

Key works

- *Essays in Philosophical Criticism* (1883)
- *The Pathway to Reality* (2 vols., 1903–04)
- *Education and Empire* (1902)
- *Army Reform and Other Addresses* (1907)
- *Autobiography* (1929)

Further reading

- H. C. G. Matthew, *The Liberal Imperialists: The Ideas and Politics of a Post-Gladstonian Elite* (Oxford University Press, 1973)
- Geoffrey Searle, *The Quest for National Efficiency: A Study in British Politics and Political Thought, 1899–1914* (Blackwell, 1971)
- Andrew Vincent and Raymond Plant, *Philosophy, Politics and Citizenship: The Life and Thought of the British Idealists* (Blackwell, 1984)

Ian Packer

Lord Halifax 1633–95

A politician and writer who started out as a respected supporter of the English monarchy but became one of the architects of the 1688 'Glorious Revolution' which replaced the Catholic James II with the Protestant monarchs William and Mary.

Key ideas

- Views should be based on practical experience rather than abstract theory.
- Moderation and seeking the middle course in politics.

Biography

George Savile, Lord Halifax was born, on 11 November 1633, into the political establishment, though there are significant gaps in our knowledge of his early years. He certainly spent considerable time being educated abroad, and was married in 1656 to Dorothy, sister of the 2nd Earl of Sunderland.

He was initially a political protégé of the 2nd Duke of Buckingham and sat in the Privy Council for several years from 1672. He left office after opposing the government, but regained it in 1679 when the King was seeking to broaden his support.

In 1680 an epic debating duel took place in the House of Lords between Halifax and his uncle, Lord Shaftesbury, over a Bill to exclude King Charles II's Catholic brother, James, from the throne. Halifax spoke sixteen times in a seven-hour debate, and was credited with the Bill's defeat – though it seems likely that the Bill would have failed anyway. Having alienated many Whigs with these speeches, he then alienated many Tories by insisting that any future Catholic monarch should have strict limitations placed on their power and by asking for leniency for Whigs caught plotting against the monarchy. When James did ascend to the throne, as James II, in 1685, Halifax was only briefly in power before he was ousted for opposing James's pro-Catholic policies.

A cynical and caustic wit, he bequeathed a range of biting quotations (some of which display what would become a typically liberal approach), including: 'Men are not hanged for stealing horses, but that horses may not be stolen', and: 'They who are of the opinion that Money will do everything, may very well be suspected to do everything for Money'. A more general cynicism ran through many of his other comments, as with: 'Laws are generally not understood by three sorts of persons, viz., by those who make them, by those who execute them, and by those who suffer if they break them', and: 'Malice is of a low stature, but it hath very long arms'.

During the early stages of the Glorious Revolution he did not support the overthrow of James II. Indeed, when William of Orange launched his invasion in 1688, Halifax tried to negotiate a compromise. In the turmoil caused by James's attempt to flee, Halifax rapidly assumed a position of importance and it was he who both told James that he had to go and issued the formal invitation to William to take the throne.

Despite this key role in James's replacement, his subsequent political career was brief: he became Chief Minister in 1689, but had little support in Parliament and quit in 1690. He died on 5 April 1695.

Ideas

Though Halifax frequently found politics distasteful, his active participation in it differentiates him from other political thinkers of the time such as Locke (q.v.) and Hobbes (q.v.). By contrast with their abstract arguments, his views were closely related to his practical experience of politics.

He saw political disagreement as inevitable, and stressed the importance of taking a middle course rather than succumbing to extremes. He believed in a balance between liberty and power, seeing dangers in either extreme. For him, there had to be a supreme power, but it should not be lodged in the potentially despotic hands of one person. He both frequently opposed the line taken by his friends and surprised opponents by agreeing with them. Many contemporaries interpreted his moderation as constant untrustworthiness, no firm beliefs and unscrupulous jettisoning of principles.

His main work, *The Character of a Trimmer*, was published in 1688 (four years after being written and not initially published under his name); it was a work of political thought of some note. (He also wrote a series of other pieces but, deeply rooted in the disputes of the time, they failed to have a lasting impact.) The book was triggered by Tory attacks on the idea of moderation. It defended a strategy of a shifting set of allies and opposed the rigidities of party politics, which Halifax saw as being inimical to debate and discussion. It argued for restrictions on the power of the monarch, toleration of nonconformists – though not of Catholics – and a foreign policy aimed at ensuring no one power dominated Europe. During Halifax's career, he often feared the consequences of war with France, believing that the needs of war would allow the King to amass political and financial power. This opposition to foreign adventures for their impact on domestic liberty was one that recurs throughout subsequent liberal thought.

Halifax's political legacy was limited for a number of reasons: he ended his career unpopular; his family line died out after his son; his speeches were not published and his other works were only briefly in print after 1700; and some of the most influential eighteenth-century thinkers had little kind to say about his views, even whilst admiring his intelligence and oratory – David Hume (q.v.), for example, describing him as 'always, with reason, regarded as an intriguer rather than a patriot'. Only with Thomas Macaulay (q.v.) in the nineteenth century did his reputation markedly improve as someone who had played a key part in the Glorious Revolution, an event that had by then become a key component of the Whig tradition and mythology.

Key works

- *The Character of a Trimmer* (1688)

Further reading
- Hilda Foxcroft, *A Character of the Trimmer* (Cambridge University Press, 1946)
- J. P Kenyon, *Halifax: Complete Works* (Penguin, 1969)

Mark Pack

J. L. Hammond   1872–1949
Barbara Hammond   1873–1961

The husband-and-wife team of J. L. and Barbara Hammond exerted enormous influence as social and economic historians during the first half of the twentieth century. Their works concentrated upon the effects and costs of the decline of the traditional village and the rise of industry. As New Liberals, the Hammonds offered an original critique of classical liberalism that often overshadowed their subtler defence of liberalism's redemptive virtues.

Key ideas
- Insistence upon moral and psychological effects as the proper criteria for judging the agricultural and industrial revolutions, rather than statistical measurements of productivity and prosperity.
- A reorientation of the study of English history to introduce greater complexity and tension into the standard celebratory Whig version of constitutional development.
- The civic impulse grew directly from liberal values; liberalism therefore possessed the insight to recognise its blemishes, and then reform itself in pursuit of a just and humane society.
- Abiding belief in the unique role of liberalism to mediate between socialism and conservatism during the inter-war years.

Biography
John Lawrence LeBreton Hammond was born in 1872. From his father, a Yorkshire vicar, Lawrence imbibed a strong dose of radical, Gladstonian Liberalism. Educated at Bradford Grammar School and St John's College, Oxford, Hammond earned a second in classics. Beaten by Hilaire Belloc (q.v.) for President of the Union, Hammond later collaborated with 'Six Oxford Men', a sextet that included Belloc, to publish *Essays in Liberalism* (1897), a pointed expression of New Liberal (q.v.) sentiments. He then began a career in journalism, becoming editor of the liberal weekly the *Speaker* from 1899–1907.

Born in 1873, Lucy Barbara Bradby was the daughter of the headmaster of Haileybury College. She was a brilliant student, first at St. Leonard's School, St Andrews, followed by Lady Margaret Hall, Oxford, where she earned a first in classics.

Lawrence and Barbara were married in 1901. Lawrence briefly considered a parliamentary career but instead joined the Civil Service Commission. Thus insulated from the partisan political world where neither felt comfortable, the couple relocated from London, eventually settling in Hertfordshire. Here they developed a strange ascetic lifestyle that included gardening, long walks, and sleeping outdoors.

From the solitude of their rural outpost emerged a fruitful collaboration in history-writing. Barbara performed most of the research at the British Museum or the Public Record Office, while her husband assumed the bulk of the writing. Their first book together was *The Village Labourer* (1911); *The Town Labourer* appeared in 1917, followed by *The Skilled Labourer* (1919). This trilogy examining the disappearance of traditional rural England and its replacement by urban, industrial society generated enormous interest, sparking as much discussion about the contemporary health and future trajectory of British society as it did regarding the events of the eighteenth century.

Discouraged by the demise of the Liberal Party, the Hammonds hovered between liberal and socialist sympathies at the beginning of the inter-war period. But they publicly reasserted their liberal credentials by jointly publishing *Lord Shaftesbury* in 1923; and in 1938, Lawrence published, under his name alone, *Gladstone and the Irish Nation* – his last major book. For the duration of the war, the couple moved to Manchester where Lawrence became a more frequent contributor to the *Manchester Guardian*. Lawrence died in 1949 leaving a partial manuscript, *Gladstone and Liberalism;* M. R. D. Foot completed the task and published the book in 1952. Barbara lived on until 1961.

Ideas

The historiography of the Hammonds recapitulates their political evolution. At its best, their prose strikes a balance between the traditional Whiggish (q.v.) history of constitutional progress and socialist anti-liberal revisionism, perhaps a classic New Liberal position. But the couple were dissatisfied with the party of Campbell-Bannerman and Asquith, noting the chasm between the reformist agenda of New Liberal theory and the practice of Liberal politics-as-usual at Westminster.

Despite this frustration, Lawrence's research for *Charles James Fox* (1903) reassured him of the virtuous, even heroic, roots of the modern variant of liberalism. On the surface, *The Village Labourer* seemed to contradict such optimism. Like its two sequels, the book was written in part because the Hammonds judged as too narrow the boundaries of available national histories. What was missing was a 'life of the poor' detailing what happened to the labouring classes 'under a government in which they had no share'. Based almost entirely upon untapped primary sources, *The Village Labourer* was a recitation of the steps in the break-up of the ancient village community, the degradation of labourer and family. It chronicled the death of an old civilisation. *The Town Labourer* and *The Skilled Labourer* described the painful birth of a new one, the social and economic exploitation of the labouring classes during the early phase of rapid industrialisation.

The Hammonds aimed at the general reader rather than the specialist. The reception of their works by the academic world was generally hostile. Their methodology was attacked as partial and misleading, neglecting the crucial issue of productivity, which in turn hinged upon a sophisticated analysis of economic data. Drawing upon their training in the classics, Lawrence and Barbara argued that the moral element must always take precedence in historical assessment; their primary concern was to catalogue the human costs of the 'new civilisation'. The standard Whig version of British history linked constitutional progress to the moral development of the nation. The Hammonds' preoccupation with the moral effects of economic change situated them well within this liberal historical tradition. Yet a fixation on moral issues frustrated academic economic historians, while the naked appeal to their readers' emotions exaggerated the apparent subversiveness of the Hammonds' critique of capitalism.

The appearance of *The Skilled Labourer* in the wake of the First World War represented the high-water mark of the Hammonds' tentative migration towards socialist politics. At the time the couple was often compared to Sidney and Beatrice Webb, but Lawrence and Barbara never strayed far from their liberal roots. They politely ignored invitations to join the Fabian Society and Labour Party, all the while mourning the impotence of inter-war liberalism.

The Hammonds' research reinforced their contemporary political allegiance. Work on a biography of Lord Shaftesbury reassured them of the ethical core of Victorian liberalism; a humane sense of compassion and an unshakeable commitment to justice, a liberal conscience that eventually tamed the 'savage logic' of the Industrial Revolution. At the moment of Labour's great electoral triumph in the summer of 1945, the Hammonds voted Liberal.

Key works: J. L. Hammond
- *Charles James Fox: A Political Study* (1903)
- *Gladstone and the Irish Nation* (1938)

Key works: J. L. and Barbara Hammond
- *The Village Labourer, 1760–1832* (1911)
- *The Town Labourer, 1760–1832: The New Civilisation* (1917)
- *The Skilled Labourer* (1919)
- *Lord Shaftesbury* (1923)
- *The Rise of Modern Industry* (1925)
- *The Age of the Chartists, 1832–1854* (1930)
- *The Bleak Age* (1934)

Further reading
- Peter Clarke, *Liberals and Social Democrats* (Cambridge University Press, 1978)
- Victor Feske, *From Belloc to Churchill: Private Scholars, Public Culture, and the Crisis of British Liberalism, 1900–1939* (University of North Carolina Press, 1996)
- Stewart Weaver, *The Hammonds: A Marriage in History* (Stanford University Press, 1997)

Victor Feske

Friedrich von Hayek   1899–1992

Widely considered as the leading theorist of classical liberalism in the twentieth century, his research covered an extensive range of topics and his work has had an important and lasting impact on the academic as well as the political landscape.

Key ideas
- Price mechanism as a conveyor of dispersed knowledge, thereby coordinating economic activities; hence the impossibility of central planning due to knowledge problems.
- Theory of spontaneous order, according to which highly complex orders can arise endogenously out of social interactions; and the need for intellectual humility, as spontaneous orders cannot be fully understood, predicted or fine-tuned, due to their complexity.
- Critique of the notion of social justice, insofar as justice is not applicable to a spontaneous order that has not been designed by anyone; justice can only be attributed to the actions of individuals.
- Liberty as the absence of coercion that can be achieved by the rule of law based on general rules that regulate other-regarding behaviour, thereby minimising arbitrary and discretionary use of force.

Biography
Friedrich August von Hayek was born on 8 May 1899 in Vienna. Following military service in World War One, he studied law at the University of Vienna, gaining a PhD in law in 1921 followed by a PhD in political sciences in 1923. While at university, he attended courses by Friedrich von Wieser. As a result of a letter of introduction by Wieser, Hayek attended the private seminars organised by Ludwig von Mises which gathered together a number of prominent intellectuals, including Oskar Morgenstern, Gottfried Haberler and Fritz Machlup. Having finished his studies, Hayek went on a one-year visit to the United States made possible by a grant from the Rockefeller

Foundation. After returning to Austria, he became the first director of the Austrian Institute for Business Cycles Research, founded by Ludwig von Mises, in 1927.

In 1930 Hayek was invited by Lionel Robbins to give a series of lectures at the London School of Economics, later published as *Prices and Production* (1931). As a result of these lectures, Hayek was offered the Tooke Professorship in Economic Science and Statistics at the LSE, which he took up in 1931. He gained international prominence through the publication of *The Road to Serfdom* in 1944, together with a condensed version produced by *Reader's Digest*. In 1947 he founded the Mont Pelerin Society (q.v.) for the purpose of bringing together classical liberal (q.v.) scholars.

In 1950 Hayek went to Chicago to become the Professor for Social and Moral Sciences on the Committee on Social Thought. This was a productive time for him, including the publication of his masterpiece, *The Constitution of Liberty* (1960). In 1962 he went to Freiburg in Germany where he stayed until 1968, followed by nine years at the University of Salzburg.

In 1974, Hayek gained a Nobel Prize in Economics, shared with Gunnar Myrdal. He was awarded the US Presidential Medal of Freedom in 1991. He died on 23 March 1992, in Freiburg.

Ideas

In *The Road to Serfdom* (1944), Hayek warned against the political consequences of centralised economic planning, identifying a slippery slope that could lead from good intentions to a totalitarian regime. His argument establishes a link between political and economic freedom, arguing that the lack of economic freedom is likely to put at risk our political freedom – a connection deriving from the dangerous

tendencies inherent in political power. Centralised economic control requires vast amounts of centralised political power, which Hayek criticises as dangerous due to the likelihood and magnitude of abuse. By controlling the economy, the government is essentially taking control over the lives of the people, given that the economic sphere represents an important sector of human life and given that 'it is the control of the means for all our ends'. Centralised political power is likely to be misused because, as Lord Acton (q.v.) observed, 'Power tends to corrupt, absolute power corrupts absolutely'. Moreover, it is not only that power corrupts, since, due to the nature of the political system, one mostly must already be corrupt in order to reach positions of power. Hayek argues that the 'worst' people have a competitive advantage in the struggle for political power and are therefore more likely to get to the top. There is thus a need to limit power and to prevent the government from controlling the economic sphere.

In *The Constitution of Liberty* (1960), Hayek provides a positive account of the aims and spheres of a liberal government. He defines liberty as the absence of coercion, and claims that one should try to achieve a state of affairs in which coercion is minimised. Accordingly, he advocates a constitutionally limited government that must respect the rule of law (q.v.), thereby reducing the use of discretionary power. The most important aspect of the rule of law for Hayek is equality before the law. Laws must be general and should not discriminate between people. A liberal government should also provide a safety-net to ensure that no one falls below a minimum standard of living. Hayek recognises that market processes often involve luck and that people sometimes fail due to no fault of their own.

This conception of the role of government is often criticised on the basis that it does not lead to social justice (q.v.). In the second volume of *Law, Legislation and Liberty* (1976) Hayek criticises the concept of 'social justice', arguing that it is a vacuous notion that is not applicable to the outcome of market processes. Justice, for Hayek, is an attribute of individual action. An *action* can be just or unjust, but not, however, a market outcome which is the result of the interaction of a vast number of economic agents. The distribution of goods produced by a market cannot be attributed to any particular individual and consequently no one can be held responsible for it.

A prominent aspect of Hayek's work is his concern with knowledge. In particular, he focuses on the coordination of knowledge, the limits of knowledge and the discovery of knowledge. Hayek himself claims that his greatest discovery is that the price mechanism coordinates the dispersed knowledge possessed by economic agents. This insight forms the basis of his critique of central planning. It is impossible for a central agency to collect all the knowledge required to determine an adequate allocation of resources. This is because of both the quantity and the quality of the relevant information, since much knowledge is of a subjective nature, is held tacitly and cannot be articulated, and has only a time-bound validity given that the economy is in a constant flux. Instead, one has to rely on the price mechanism to ensure economic efficiency. Prices convey information and coordinate the dispersed knowledge of vast numbers of individuals.

As regards the limits of knowledge, Hayek argues for a form of humility based on the insight that many social phenomena are too complex to be fully understood by our finite and limited minds. Our cognitive abilities place restrictions upon what we can comprehend. Based on this argument he criticises what he terms 'rationalistic constructivism', that is, the attempt to plan and direct society rationally. This constructivism is not possible, according to Hayek, because society is too complex. As in the case of the price mechanism, there is too much knowledge for any individual to comprehend and utilise through rational deliberation. Instead, we have to rely on invisible-hand processes to create spontaneous order.

Hayek's focus on the dynamic aspect of knowledge is evident in his portrayal of the market mechanism as a discovery procedure. An economic system must give individuals the freedom to compete and experiment; it must leave room for entrepreneurs to be innovative and try out new things. The market mechanism then provides entrepreneurs with signals in the form of profits and losses, informing them whether these new ideas are economically feasible. This feasibility can often only be established by means of trial and error, since knowledge problems can make a priori assessments impossible.

Hayek agues that not all order must be planned or constructed. Instead, many ordered phenomena, such as language, money and the common law, have arisen spontaneously and evolved over time. A spontaneous order is, in the words of Adam Ferguson, the 'result of human action, but not the execution of any human design'. The actions and interactions of a variety of people can produce an order that arises spontaneously. This is an unintended consequence of the actions of individuals; the order is endogenous to the phenomenon and does not have to be exogenously imposed. These spontaneous orders can surpass the complexity of any order that human beings can design, because construction is limited by the cognitive limits of the human mind. Thus the fact that no one controls, plans and directs the economy does not mean that it is a chaotic system. Instead the economy is a highly complex order that has arisen spontaneously. It is a different type of order – what Hayek calls *cosmos*, as opposed to *taxis* – but it can, of course, only arise and will only be fully beneficial when individuals can act freely and when the market principles that bring about this order are free from interference. Individuals must be able to respond to price signals and prices must be allowed to adjust freely so that they can reflect economic reality.

His theory of spontaneous orders led Hayek to re-evaluate his earlier conception of the philosophy of social sciences. In *The Counter-Revolution of Science* (1952), he still placed great emphasis on the difference between social sciences and natural sciences, arguing that intentionality characterises the social sciences, thereby entailing the need for a specially adapted methodology. This was the basis of his attack on what he labelled 'scientism', by which he meant the attempts of social scientists to use the methods of the natural sciences. In his later works, however, in particular in his essay 'The Theory of Complex Phenomena' (1964), Hayek changed his position. He then argued that the dividing line was not provided by intentionality but by the complexity of the phenomena that were to be explained. Complex phenomena are those that are more complex than our cognitive structures can handle. We are not able to make predictions about the progression of complex phenomena, but are only able to understand the underlying principles which govern them. The subjects of the social sciences are mostly issues regarding complex phenomena. However, there are also natural phenomena, like evolution, that are so complex that we can only

understand their guiding principles, without being able to make any precise predictions. The goal of the social scientist, then, is to try to discover the principles underlying spontaneous social orders, while at the same time having enough humility to recognise that these phenomena are too complex to be fully understood and that they can consequently not be planned or fine-tuned. Accordingly, his conception of 'scientism' can be understood in his later terminology as the attempt of social scientists to treat complex phenomena as if they were simple phenomena. This lack of intellectual humility is the essence of what Hayek terms the 'abuse of reason'.

Key works

- *The Road to Serfdom* (1944)
- *The Counter-Revolution of Science: Studies on the Abuse of Reason* (1952)
- *The Constitution of Liberty* (1960)
- *Law, Legislation and Liberty* volumes I, II and III (1973, 1976, 1979)
- *The Fatal Conceit: The Errors of Socialism* (1988)

Further reading

- Norman Barry, *Hayek's Social and Economic Philosophy* (Macmillan, 1979)
- Bruce Caldwell, *Hayek's Challenge: An Intellectual Biography of F. A. Hayek* (University of Chicago Press, 2003)
- John Gray, *Hayek on Liberty* (Blackwell, 1984)
- Chandran Kukathas, *Hayek and Modern Liberalism* (Oxford University Press, 1989)

Ralf Bader

G. W. F. Hegel   1770–1831

The major philosopher of German idealism. The interpretation of his political thought has always been controversial, but many now see him as committed to liberal ideals and concerned with the social, cultural and historical conditions of their realisation.

Key ideas

- History as the development of free and rational institutions.
- Individuality and civil society as positive achievements of modernity.
- Individual freedom also depends upon family, civil associations and membership of a political community.
- Corporatism, bureaucracy and constitutional monarchy as key components of a rational state.

Biography

Georg Wilhelm Friedrich Hegel was born in Stuttgart on 27 August 1770 to a middle-class family, the product of a Lutheran upbringing and a classical education. He studied at a seminary in Tübingen with F. W. J. Schelling and Friedrich Hölderlin, with whom he shared enthusiasms for Kant (q.v.) and the French Revolution. Hegel worked as a private tutor in Berne and Frankfurt, and in 1801 sought an academic career in Jena, where Schelling was already a professor. They co-edited a journal in which he published his first philosophical works.

In time Hegel's thought took its own course, culminating in the *Phenomenology of Spirit*, famously completed as his hero Napoleon rode through Jena's streets in 1806. Hegel briefly edited a small-town newspaper and in 1808 took a job as headmaster of a *Gymnasium* in Nuremburg. There he married, fathered two children, and continued to develop and publish his new idealist system. He finally obtained a professorship at Heidelberg in 1816 and in 1818 was invited to take up the important chair in philosophy at Berlin.

Now at the pinnacle of his profession, Hegel began to gather a school of committed followers around him. He maintained outward loyalty to the Prussian King Friedrich Willhelm III but sympathised with the goals of the Prussian Reform Movement, which hoped to place the state on a more constitutional footing. His last publication before his death, on 14 November 1831, was a sceptical essay on the English reform Bill. His lectures on history, religion, aesthetics and the history of philosophy were published posthumously by his students.

Ideas

Hegel's idealist philosophy is notoriously obscure, and opinions still differ as to its meaning and value. Roughly speaking, Hegel argued that because all knowledge and agency is conceptually mediated, we must think of reality itself as fundamentally conceptual in nature. His 'dialectic' described the process by which any particular concept revealed itself to be only a partial or 'contradictory' aspect or 'moment' of a greater or more complex whole, leading us ultimately towards a holistically interconnected conceptual totality or 'Absolute Idea'. As well as being logically demonstrable, this progression could be seen to be playing itself out in human experience and world history, with changing cultural attitudes and social institutions the medium through which the Absolute Idea was coming to consciousness of itself as 'Spirit'.

Hegel's philosophy has often been viewed as an extravagant attempt to translate an idiosyncratic religious outlook into an ambitiously all-encompassing system of rationalist metaphysics. But many find in his writing a subtle and sophisticated exploration of the insight that we always think and act within a shared fabric of concepts that develops progressively in time through socially situated practices of reasoned argument and inquiry.

His major political work, *Elements of the Philosophy of Right* (1821), presented a philosophical argument for the rational necessity of a certain kind of state, whose main components were a constitutional monarchy, a professional bureaucratic administration and representative estates based upon the corporate organisations of civil society. Its broad outlines unmistakeably resembled the Prussian status quo; but it was more liberal in its detail – specifying, for example, public trial by jury, civil service careers open to talents, and a written constitution.

The meaning of Hegel's political thought became a matter of intense controversy almost as soon as he had died. A new generation of radical 'Young Hegelians', of whom Marx and Engels would become the most famous, viewed Hegel's accommodation with the Prussian state as a reactionary perversion of the revolutionary essence of his philosophy. For others he inaugurated a problematic tradition of statist nationalism in Germany with tragic historical consequences – L. T. Hobhouse (q.v.) famously blamed the First World War on 'the Hegelian theory of the god-state'. Karl Popper (q.v.) held Hegel responsible for *both* of the two great totalitarian doctrines of the twentieth century, Soviet Marxism and National Socialism.

But there have always been others who see Hegel as deepening and strengthening liberal principles. 'British idealists' such as T. H. Green (q.v.) and D. G. Ritchie (q.v.) contributed to the development of New Liberalism's (q.v.) realisation of the dependence of individual freedom (q.v.) on social and state action. More recent political theory has seen Hegel less as an anti-liberal thinker than one who recognised that a liberal culture and liberal institutions can only be the product of a long historical development.

Fundamental to this reading of Hegel is his lifetime goal of reconciling Kantian (q.v.) principles of freedom and rationality (q.v.) with a richer account of human nature, social interdependence and historical change, influenced by classical philosophy and German historicism. Hegel's earliest writings can seem nostalgic for the tight social integration of the Greek *polis* or traditional religious communities. But he came to see the development of individuality – or 'the principle of subjectivity', the ability to stand back and reflect upon one's social involvements – as a positive and irreversible achievement of modern European history. This was reflected in the institutions of bourgeois 'civil society' – private property, free trade (q.v.) and the rule of law (q.v.), all of which Hegel defended. And yet he maintained that the simple assertion of 'abstract' freedom or individualism was empty, unsatisfying, potentially destructive – as the French Terror had shown. His hope was that Prussia was discovering a more mature, gradualist realisation of a liberal society, recognising that we can only develop our individual characters, and our very ability to reason independently, within a social context – the shared values and practices of 'ethical life', as found in the family, civil associations and membership of a political community. Hegel's intention was not that these institutions replace the domain of individual freedom, but that they provide its necessary support and framework, and should be rationally justifiable to each and every individual on that basis.

Key works

• *Elements of the Philosophy of Right* (1821)

Further reading

• Paul Franco, *Hegel's Philosophy of Freedom* (Yale University Press, 1999)

- Terry Pinkard, *Hegel: A Biography* (Cambridge University Press, 2000)
- Allen Wood, 'Editor's Introduction' to *Elements of the Philosophy of Right* (Cambridge University Press, 1991)

Martin McIvor

Henry George Foundation

A charity that promotes the theories of Henry George, the Foundation is the principal supporter in the UK of taxes on the value of land (and other natural resources) as a means to promote social justice, alleviate poverty and increase economic efficiency.

Concerned about urban overcrowding and the plight of the poor, in February 1884 the British followers of Henry George (q.v.) established the Scottish Land Restoration League in Glasgow, with 1,800 members. Three months later they captured the London-based Land Reform Union (LRU) and renamed it the English Land Restoration League.

The Georgeite leagues were soon strongly connected with the Radical (q.v.) wing of the Liberal Party, and in 1894, the now-renamed United Committee for the Taxation of Ground Rents and Values started a journal, *The Single Tax* (later renamed *Land Values* and still extant as *Land and Liberty*), which by 1896 had a circulation of 5,000.

Most supporters of land value taxation saw it as a mildly progressive way to redistribute land-owners' wealth. At the core of the movement, however, were the Single-Taxers, who in the years before 1914 included the MPs Josiah Wedgwood, Philip Morrell and Charles Trevelyan, the Scottish Lord Advocate Alexander Ure, and the American soap millionaire Joseph Fels, along with several thousand activists nationwide — mostly in the large cities — who, enthused by George's mixture of simple economics and pseudo-religious moral certainty, wanted a radical reformation of economics, politics and morality.

A combination of the House of Lords' recalcitrance, the reform's inherent complexity and the advent of the First World War, however, meant that attempts to introduce taxes on land values were frustrated before 1914. And while the minority Labour government did enact rating based on site values in 1931, that government's prompt fall, and the general Conservative dominance of inter-war politics, meant that land value taxes were never actually implemented.

Perhaps more significantly, the land-taxers were never again the force they had been before 1914, both because their aristocratic *bête noire* had lost much of its potency and because their own activists had splintered along with the Liberal Party. After 1945, collectivism — not least in the form of subsidised council housing — seemed to relegate George's ideas to a historical footnote, where they stayed even when more libertarian (q.v.) economic views were revived by British governments after 1979.

The Henry George Foundation (the name it adopted in 1920) mirrored the decline of wider support for George's ideas. It still survives, but its supporters now number in the hundreds, while its funds have declined until it can no longer afford any full-time staff. And yet it continues to keep the message of Henry George alive, at least on the internet, encouraged by the occasional support that taxes on land and other 'common resources' receive from academia or economic commentators, and a recent revival in political interest in land value taxation, including the Liberal Democrat proposal to base local business taxes on site value.

Further reading

- Roy Douglas, *Land, People and Politics* (Allison & Busby, 1976)
- Dominic Maxwell & Anthony Vigor (eds.), *Time For A Land Value Tax?* (IPPR, 2005)
- Paul Mulvey, *The British Liberal Party and the Taxation of Land Values, 1906–1914* (www.schalkenbach.org/scholars-forum/Radicalisms-Last-Gasp.html, 2006)

Paul Mulvey

Auberon Herbert   1838–1906

Although briefly a Liberal MP in the 1870s, Herbert's main significance is as an ardent advocate of individual freedom. 'Voluntaryism' was the true route to advancement; action by the state, except to protect against aggressions on freedom, hindered variety and competition, essential for progress. Herbert thus criticised both New Liberalism and state socialism.

Key ideas

- Voluntary action by individuals, not 'forced' action, as the key to progress.
- Liberty would benefit working men and the economy as a whole.
- Taxation should be voluntary, not compulsory.
- Opposition to idealist social thought, New Liberalism, state socialism and imperialism in all forms.

Biography

Auberon Edward William Molyneaux Herbert, third son of the third Earl of Carnarvon, was born on 18 June 1838, and spent most of his early childhood at the family estate at Highclere. He was educated at Eton and St John's College, Oxford and served in the 7th Hussars in India. He graduated in civil law in 1862 and became a lecturer in history at his college. He resigned his fellowship in 1869, giving as a reason his distaste for the restricted competition under which he himself had been appointed.

In the 1860s he was also developing a career in politics. He leant initially towards the Conservatives, standing for Parliament in 1865. In 1866 he was appointed private secretary in the Conservative government to Sir Stafford Northcote at the Board of Trade, resigning in 1867 to pursue an independent line, particularly over the disestablishment of the Irish church, which he advocated. In 1868, with Goldwin Smith's support, he stood unsuccessfully as a Liberal for Berkshire. He was elected as a Liberal MP at a by-election at Nottingham in February 1870. In 1871 he married Lady Florence Cowper (she died in 1886).

By the close of 1872 Herbert was already disillusioned with party politics, and left Parliament in 1874. In the same year he met Herbert Spencer (q.v.): the conversation led to a profound and permanent distrust of the 'great law-making machine'. In 1882 he commenced the essays which became *A Politician in Trouble with His Soul*, praised by Spencer. He established a Party of Individual Liberty to galvanise popular support for voluntary cooperation and 'justice' as interpreted by Spencer, and wrote articles for the *Newcastle Weekly Chronicle* which formed *The Right and Wrong of Compulsion by the State* (1885).

In 1890 he became the founder and editor of the paper *Free Life*, which lasted until 1901. Both Herbert and Spencer contributed to *A Plea for Liberty* of 1891 (edited by T. Mackay), a publication associated with the Liberty and Property Defence League. Herbert was named the first of three trustees of Herbert Spencer, who died in 1903; one responsibility became the administration of the Herbert Spencer Lectures at Oxford. Herbert himself was asked to deliver the second Lecture in June 1906, which he entitled 'Herbert Spencer and the Great Machine'. He died on 5 November of the same year.

Ideas

In his brief stint in Parliament, Herbert supported republicanism, the protection of wild birds, proportional representation, the need to secularise compulsory state education, women's suffrage and reform of the House of Lords. However, it was subsequent to his encounter with Spencer that his thought crystallised; virtually all his political writings date from after this time.

While Herbert acknowledged Mill's (q.v.) *On Liberty* as setting out a moral case for freedom (q.v.), he believed that Spencer had provided a more comprehensive, compelling and robust justification for it as the *sine qua non* for the advance of social, political and moral life. However, Spencer's general theory of evolution is not evident in the detail of his thought; it was Spencer's political 'derivations', developed in various essays (and most clearly displayed in his slightly later *The Man versus The State* of 1884), that most influenced Herbert. In his *A Politician in Trouble About His Soul* 'Markham' is mostly a mouthpiece for Spencer's ideas. Government should defend individuals from rather than subject them to force and coercion. Variety and competition are the conditions of advance and necessitate liberty. Infringements tend towards uniformity and hinder advance. Majorities possess no rights over individuals. However, Herbert also advocated voluntary taxation, recognised as a step too far by Spencer; they diverged also over the practicability of Herbert's proposal to broaden the base of land ownership.

Herbert characterised his individualist position as 'voluntaryist': in a free world there could be 'voluntary social-ism', entered into freely as representing the interests of those concerned. 'Force social-ism' was entirely different: it trampled individual freedom. The life of a nation could not be moved in a mass or manufactured by Parliament; it could be moved only by acting through the living energies of free individuals left to combine in their own ways, aiming at the ends that they shared in common and respecting their own freedom and the freedom of all others. This was the central message of his Spencer Lecture in 1906 and *The Voluntaryist Creed*, which contained the Lecture, posthumously published in 1908.

The launch of *Free Life*, founded to propagate radical and conservative ideas, provided an occasion for Herbert to identify the substantive positions associated with voluntaryism. It was opposed to hereditary privilege, religious establishments, artificial regulations tending to monopoly in land, attacks on property, bureaucracy, and a centralised system of compulsory education. It deprecated enslaving education to examinations. It also criticised growing taxation and sought to popularise instead the idea of voluntary national subscriptions. It praised efforts by labour to improve its condition by voluntary methods, alongside opposition to state socialism and its imitations. In a nutshell, the aim was to make the country 'the freest, the most tolerant, the most enterprising, and, economically, the cheapest country a man can live in'. The delusions of governments too were to be exposed: in 1893 the *Nineteenth Century* published his 'A Cabinet Minister's *Vade-mecum*', a lampoon on the dynamics of parliamentary party politics. Herbert's voluntaryism was sometimes construed as anarchism (q.v.), to which he demurred. The following year the *Contemporary Review* published his 'The Ethics of Dynamite', critical of anarchist violence, to clear the air.

In 1898 and 1899 he crossed swords with J. A. Hobson (q.v.) in *The Humanitarian* on the merits of socialism. Herbert aimed to undermine the foundations of New Liberal (q.v.) thought, which drew on idealist philosophy as developed in the hands of T. H. Green (q.v.) and Bernard Bosanquet (q.v.) out of Plato, Rousseau and Hegel (q.v.). For Herbert, Hobson had reduced the individual to nothingness in glorifying the 'social organism'. Moreover, to contrast the 'social entity' to an individual is only to contrast an individual with other individuals. Interdependence does not extinguish the individual. Hobson's universal scheme of compulsory organisation represents forced action: 'the unity of unrestrained difference is a far truer unity than the unity of compulsory sameness'.

Key works
- *A Politician in Trouble about His Soul* (1884)
- *The Right and Wrong of Compulsion by the State* (1885)
- *The Voluntaryist Creed* (1908)

Further reading
- S. Hutchinson Harris, *Auberon Herbert: Crusader for Liberty* (Williams and Norgate, 1943)
- Auberon Herbert, *The Right and Wrong of Compulsion by the State, and Other Essays*, edited by Eric Mack (Liberty, 1978)
- John Offer, *An Intellectual History of British Social Policy* (Policy Press, 2006)

John Offer

Francis Hirst   1873–1953

The leading critic – from a traditional radical viewpoint – of war, protectionism and collectivism in Britain from the 1900s to the 1940s, and the foremost ideologist of free-trade ideas within the Liberal Party during this period. His career connected the liberalism of Cobden, Gladstone and Morley with the renaissance of economic liberal ideas after 1945.

Key ideas
- 'The great watchwords of Liberalism – Peace, Liberty, Free Trade, Public Economy, and Good Will among Nations'.
- Dispute resolution through international law and arbitration, not collective security.
- Opposition to militarism and arms expenditure and the Boer, First and Second World Wars, on both economic and civil liberty grounds.
- Traditional economic liberalism, often described as 'laissez-faire'.
- Support for return to the pre-1914 gold standard, based on a metallic currency.

Biography
Francis Wrigley Hirst was born on 10 June 1873, near Huddersfield, into a wealthy mill-owning family with deep Nonconformist (q.v.) and Liberal roots. His uncle, William Willans, was the leading figure in Huddersfield Liberalism and Nonconformity and grandfather of Herbert Asquith.

Hirst studied political economy at Oxford under the neo-classical economists Alfred Marshall (q.v.) and F. Y. Edgeworth, obtaining a double first and serving as president of the Union. After helping John Morley (q.v.) to research his biography of Gladstone (q.v.), Hirst became Morley's protégé. In 1903 he married Helena Cobden, great niece of Richard Cobden (q.v.). They later lived in Cobden's old home, Dunford House in Sussex, turning it into a shrine to the great free trader and his ideas.

Hirst was editor of *The Economist* from 1907 until 1916, when the owners tired of his outspoken opposition to the war and conscription. In 1915, in perhaps the most celebrated civil liberties case of the First World War, he defended Arthur Zadig, on trial for 'hostile origin and associations', before the House of Lords. He edited the radical free-trade journal *Common Sense* from 1916–21.

Hirst was a life-long Liberal, despite his increasing distaste for the party's economic policies. He unsuccessfully contested Sudbury in January 1910 and Shipley, Yorkshire, in 1929. As chairman of the Liberal Free Trade Committee from 1931, he led the defence of free trade (q.v.) in the party. He was also a moving force in the Free Trade Union (q.v.), the Cobden Club (q.v.) and the Public Economy League. Hirst was involved with Ernest Benn's Individualist movement but split away in 1944, claiming that the Individualists were too close to the Tories and neglected civil liberties issues.

Hirst died on 22 February 1953.

Ideas

Hirst was not an original thinker; he is interesting for producing a neo-Cobdenite critique of Britain's development between 1914 and 1945, and for propagating traditional Liberal ideas within and beyond the party.

Hirst's views remained constant from his earliest writings in *Essays in Liberalism* (1900), which reasserted classical liberal doctrines then under increasing attack from Fabians and New Liberals (q.v.), to his final attacks on expenditure and bureaucracy in the 1940s. He is usually regarded as a 'laissez-faire Liberal', although he rejected the term if it meant that 'government should abstain inertly from constructive work'. He certainly favoured a limited role for the public sector and strict economy in public expenditure, and attacked the growth of the state, especially during wartime. He considered that the state should be responsible for defence and police, education and the provision of municipal services. However, it should take responsibility only for services 'plainly beneficial to society which cannot be left to private enterprise'. Nevertheless he wrote positively of the progress in education, public health, old-age pensions, and other public services in the years before 1914. He rejected narrow individualism, and called for the active participation of the citizen in the management of local and national affairs, and public-spiritedness. He wanted to return to what he called 'the long reign of economic liberty' between 1846 and 1914, when, as he pointed out, both Liberal and Conservative governments promoted social reforms involving large expenditure.

Sound money occupied a central place in Hirst's economic thinking. He favoured a gold standard with a metallic gold and silver currency of the sort that existed in Britain from the early nineteenth century until 1914, arguing that the temptation to inflate paper currencies for political reasons would be irresistible.

Hirst blamed the Liberal government for the slide to war in 1914. He later wrote that 'the death of Campbell-Bannerman made way for Mr Asquith and so gave the Liberal Imperialists (q.v.) a free hand in foreign policy and at the same time opened the door to a great expansion of armaments'. Hirst's opposition to war was, to a significant degree, budgetary. He later wrote that 'the Great War [was] the most tremendous economic catastrophe recorded in history', setting out his case in several of his books. He wrote in 1947 that two world wars had left Britain 'shorn of its liberties, in a state of bankruptcy and serfdom, oppressed by ruinous taxation, overwhelming debt, and conscription, manacled by more and more inflation, entangled in new alliances … and with military commitments in all parts of the world'.

Hirst's interpretation of Britain's decline, and his political and economic doctrines, were set out most definitively in his books *The Consequences of the War to Great Britain* (1934), *Economic Freedom and Private Property* (1935) and *Liberty and Tyranny* (1935). The last influenced Walter Lippmann's (q.v.) *The Good Society* (1937), which inspired efforts at the end of the 1930s by Hayek (q.v.) and others to revive liberal thinking in Europe. Hirst also promoted classical liberalism (q.v.) at the London School of Economics, the seedbed of the anti-Keynesian academics and students who formed the vanguard of the neo-liberal (q.v.) revival after the war.

Hirst was an orthodox Cobdenite in international affairs, favouring international law and arbitration rather than collective security and the League of Nations. He was one of the few Liberals to support the Munich agreement in 1938. He was not, however, a pacifist (q.v.) and accepted that the defence of freedom (q.v.) justified the use of force both at home and abroad against its enemies.

Though an indifferent politician, Hirst was the leading ideologue of traditional Liberalism in the first four decades of the twentieth century, a viewpoint that saw economic liberalism (q.v.), civil liberties, peace and internationalism as an indivisible whole. He was unashamedly backward-looking and nostalgic: for him Victorian Liberal England truly represented the golden days. He insistently restated Cobdenite and Gladstonian principles and sought to show how their abandonment lay behind the troubles of his times.

Key works
- *Adam Smith* (1904)
- *Life and Letters of Thomas Jefferson* (1925)
- *Early Life and Letters of John Morley* (1927)
- *Gladstone as Financier & Economist* (1931)

- *The Consequences of the War to Great Britain* (1934)
- *Liberty and Tyranny* (1935)
- *Economic Freedom and Private Property* (1935)

Further reading
- G. P. Gooch et al, *F. W. Hirst by His Friends* (Oxford University Press, 1958)
- F. W. Hirst, *In the Golden Days* (Frederick Muller, 1947)
- J. Reynolds, 'The Last of the Liberals' – Francis Wrigley Hirst (1873–1953), *Journal of Liberal History* 47 (summer 2005)

Jaime Reynolds

Thomas Hobbes   1588–1679

One of the great philosophers, Hobbes's profound and original political theory is strikingly illiberal in most respects, but helped to lay some of the intellectual foundations for liberalism.

Key ideas
- Self-preservation and self-interest are the keys to human motivation.
- War of all against all exists in the state of nature – ended by a social contract which creates a legitimate government.
- An absolute sovereign (preferably a monarch) is needed to maintain peace.
- Defence of a fundamentally illiberal 'negative' idea of liberty.

Biography
Born on 5 April 1588, Thomas Hobbes later joked that his mother went into labour on hearing of the Spanish Armada's arrival, giving birth to twins: 'me, and fear'. Fear was his constant companion. Fear of violent death was central to his political theory: to avoid the bloodshed of a war of all against all, he argued, we need an absolute sover-

eign – preferably a monarch. Fearing that Parliament would arrest him after he presented these views in his 1640 tract *The Elements of Law*, he fled to self-imposed exile in France.

In 1642 Hobbes published *De Cive* ('On The Citizen'), which he saw as the first example of a genuine science of politics: influenced by Euclid's geometry, he sought to argue step by step from clear definitions to undeniable political conclusions. After working on physics and logic, he returned to political theory following King Charles I's execution in 1649, and in 1651 published the philosophical and literary masterpiece for which he is now best known: *Leviathan*. He returned to England in 1652, this time for fear of royalist reprisal: *Leviathan* had implicitly accepted the new parliamentary regime, and outlined religious and clerical doctrines that affronted many royalists in Paris. Hobbes continued to write about science and politics, remaining intellectually active until his death on 4 December 1679.

Aside from his time in France, Hobbes spent most of his life as tutor and secretary to aristocrats, serving the Cavendish family for four generations after graduating from Oxford in 1608. He met the aged Galileo, sparred with Descartes, and briefly worked for Francis Bacon. He was a profoundly original thinker; it is astonishing how much intellectual baggage he was able to discard. A leading European thinker of the day, he remains one of the great philosophers, and a political theorist of the first order.

Ideas

Hobbes believed that there are no moral absolutes, 'nothing simply and absolutely so', no 'common rule of good and evil' that exists independently of what we agree on. The state of nature which exists before society and government, or when they break down, is a state of equality (q.v.) between men – Hobbes largely neglected women – competing for scarce resources. Despite a common fear of death, aggressive action is needed to maintain one's resources, producing a 'war of every man against every man', such that life becomes 'solitary, poor, nasty, brutish, and short'. To escape the state of nature, a social contract is devised to create a sovereign with absolute power to decide on what is good and bad, to resolve disputes, and to enforce laws. Anything less would lead back to a state of nature, which no one wants: provided the sovereign does not try to kill them, citizens are always better off under an absolute sovereign.

Scholars have written much about whether individuals could actually escape the state of nature. Hobbes himself wrote far more about how to avoid returning to it. The sovereign must shape men's dispositions and opinions, moulding obedient citizens who are taught not to confuse apparent, short-term goods with their real, long-term good (self-preservation). Only civic-minded, peaceful actions are permitted; Hobbes was not a simple egoist defending self-interest. Subversive doctrines should be banned; Greek and Roman republican tracts, including the works of Aristotle and Cicero, are like 'the biting of a mad dog', producing rabid hatred of monarchy.

Hobbes was not a liberal, then. He placed no institutional limits on governmental powers: there are no checks and balances, no separation or sharing of powers, and the only accountability of officials is to the sovereign, who answers only to God. Citizens have no rights against the state, and although citizens retain the right to self-preservation, this amounts to little more than the right to kick and scream on the way to the gallows. Freedom of speech is limited to opinions which are conducive to civic peace, and the sovereign's educational invasiveness would undercut free thought.

These fundamentally illiberal prescriptions have often been glossed over. Bentham (q.v.) interpreted Hobbes in a more liberal way, as did a string of nineteenth- and twentieth-century misinterpreters like Michael Oakeshott. Philosophers like David Gauthier, Jean Hampton and Gregory Kavka argue that Hobbes's principles should have pushed him towards the liberalism of Locke (q.v.) or Kant (q.v.), but we should not forget that Hobbes's actual conclusions were mostly illiberal.

Nor should liberal ideas of liberty be read into Hobbes's strongly 'negative' notion of liberty, which he defined as the absence of external impediments to motion. On this definition, laws do not restrict liberty, as they do not physically prevent us from doing anything: all actions which we take for fear of breaking the law are actions that we were also free not to take, says Hobbes. Even someone who must choose between life or death faces a free choice.

Yet some of Hobbes's arguments point *towards* liberalism. He wanted more freedom of religion than many of his contemporaries, and attacked the persecution of heretics; he had himself feared persecution for his unorthodox religious views. Hobbes rested the sovereign's authority not on divine right but on consent, which many people read (questionably) as a democratic argument. And while he presented illiberal theories of rights and of the social contract, he gave both ideas a more central place in political theory. So, Hobbes may have helped to lay some of the intellectual foundations for liberalism. But anyone who describes Hobbes simply as a liberal is either misled or is an opponent of liberalism who is disingenuously painting an unpalatable picture of it.

Key works
- *The Elements of Law* (1640)

- *De Cive* (1642)
- *Leviathan* (1651)

Further reading
- K. C. Brown (ed.), *Hobbes Studies* (Basil Blackwell, 1965)
- G. A. J. Rogers and Alan Ryan (eds.), *Perspectives on Thomas Hobbes* (Clarendon Press, 1988)
- Quentin Skinner, *Visions of Politics. Volume III: Hobbes and Civil Science* (Cambridge University Press: 2002)
- Richard Tuck, *Hobbes* (Oxford University Press, 1989)

Adrian Blau

L. T. Hobhouse   1864–1929

One of the leading social theorists of his generation, noted for his prominence in the fields of liberalism and sociology, Hobhouse was a major exponent of the New Liberalism, developing ideas on the enabling purposes of state power to further liberty.

Key ideas
- Liberty is essential to self-development, which cannot be achieved by coercion.
- The 'enabling' role of the state in maximising liberty.
- The rejection of Fabian statism and conformist egalitarianism.
- Gladstonian radical views on international issues.

Biography
Leonard Trelawney Hobhouse was born on 8 September 1864 at Liskeard, Cornwall, where his father was the local rector, the latest of a long line of Anglican clerics in the family. His mother was a Trelawney from the prominent West Country family. Although his immediate family were narrow Tories, Hobhouse became a committed

Radical and firm agnostic while a school-boy at Marlborough College. His boyhood heroes included Morley (q.v.), Bradlaugh (q.v.) and Bright. He also greatly admired John Stuart Mill (q.v.) and read Spencer (q.v.) and Mazzini (q.v.).

At Oxford (Corpus Christi) he was influenced by Green (q.v.) and Toynbee. He became increasingly concerned with social questions, especially the plight of the rural poor, and was active in organising unions for agricultural labourers. His radical opinions, in favour of home rule, temperance and the abolition of the monarchy, brought him notoriety and the presidency of the Oxford Radical Club. He graduated in 1887 with a first in Greats and immediately won a prize fellowship at Merton. He was made a full tutorial fellow in 1894 and until 1897 taught philosophy, specialising in epistemology. At this time Hobhouse was close to the Fabians, although he never joined the Society and later became a fierce critic of its elitism, imperialism and opportunism.

From 1897 to 1903 he was a leader-writer for the *Manchester Guardian*, taking a 'pro-Boer', anti-imperialist line. Throughout this period his productivity as a journalist and as an academic was quite staggering. In 1903, before he left the *Guardian*, he wrote 322 full-length book reviews or long articles at the same time as he continued with academic work and political campaigning. He left the *Guardian*, intending to concentrate on academic work, but financial pressures caused him to take up the post of secretary and organiser of the Free Trade Union (q.v.), which was in the forefront of the campaign against Joseph Chamberlain's (q.v.) tariff reform crusade.

In 1905 he left the FTU and became the political editor of a new London-based Liberal-inclined newspaper, the *Tribune*. He resigned when the paper moved to a

populist jingoist line to attract readers. He had kept up his academic writing on the new subject of sociology, and on the basis of this work, in 1907 he secured an academic post at the London School of Economics, thus becoming the first (and for many years the only) professor of sociology in Britain. Hobhouse retained the White Chair of Sociology until his death. He continued sporadically to contribute leaders to the *Manchester Guardian*, but declined offers to stand for Parliament.

Hobhouse remained active in Liberal circles and briefly took part in the preparation of Lloyd George's (q.v.) 'coloured books' of the late 1920s. He died in Alençon, France on 21 June 1929. He had married Nora Hawden in 1891, and was the father of three children.

Ideas

Hobhouse's first major political work, *The Labour Movement* (1893), was strongly collectivist, calling for the profits of industry to be appropriated to consumers in the form of the cooperative movement, trade unions and local and national government. It advocated a steeply graduated income tax, higher death duties and the taxation of ground rent. Its political doctrine was closer to Green's organicism than to Mill. But Hobhouse soon saw that collectivism in its Fabian form was liable to turn into the glorification of the state and the pursuit of conformity in the name of equality (q.v.). Hobhouse was also deeply internationalist and was revolted by the Fabian endorsement of the Boer War. His New Liberalism (q.v.) was, above all, the result of his disillusion with Fabian socialism.

His sociological works included *The Mind in Evolution* (1901) and *Morals in Evolution* (1906). In these works, rejecting Spencer and social Darwinism, Hobhouse attempted to establish, both theoretically and empirically, that progress in human thought and conduct was inevitable not as the result of biology or instinct but as the result of self-conscious intelligence.

Hobhouse's Radical journalism followed an orthodox Gladstonian (q.v.) line of moral rectitude in foreign policy, attacking the ideas of Joseph Chamberlain and the Fabians which combined collectivism with imperialism. For all his objections to laissez-faire economics (q.v.), Hobhouse's rejection of imperialism drove him back to the Radical Liberal camp. He subsequently sought to combine Mill's devotion to individuality, his own commitment to social justice (q.v.) and Gladstonian morality in international politics into a theoretical whole.

It was during this period that Hobhouse's mature political and economic thought emerged, culminating in his extraordinary little book, *Liberalism* (1911). In it he sought to explain the social programme and taxation policies of the Liberal government as an extension, not a reversal, of the economic principles of earlier Liberals such as Mill. His underlying theory, difficult to apply in practice but clear enough in theory, was that wealth was created by a combination of individual effort and social organisation, and that the state was entitled to redistribute for the common good that part which arose from social organisation. He also distinguished between property held 'for use' and property held 'for power', recognising the need for the former but not the latter to be protected by a system of rights. Out of the combination of these ideas, Hobhouse developed Liberal justifications for a guaranteed minimum income funded by income tax.

Given his love of individual liberty the strength of Hobhouse's egalitarianism is particularly striking. He argued that 'full liberty implies full equality' and believed that liberty could not be reconciled with persistent social and economic inequalities. He was particularly adamant that a society that truly valued liberty would strive and succeed in overcoming all those social and economic privileges that impeded equal access to and representation in the courts.

Hobhouse developed a distinctive view of liberty and the proper purposes of state power. He maintained, against what we now call libertarianism (q.v), that liberty depended on restraint – that 'every liberty depends on a corresponding act of control'. He followed Mill in pointing out the many forms of coercion in social life, including features of existing social and economic conditions. His conclusion was that the proper role of the state was to maximise the availability of liberty by reorganising the existing constraints. But Hobhouse differed from Mill in explaining why paternalism should be opposed. Whereas Mill starts with the harm principle, that no one should be coerced except to prevent harm to others, Hobhouse says that we should refrain from coercing people for their own good 'not because [their] good is indifferent to us but because it cannot be furthered by coercion'. He believed that the value of liberty lies precisely in its role in human self-development. In what many regard as his clearest statement of this view he wrote:

> Liberalism is the belief that society can safety be founded on [the] self-directing power of personality, that it is only on this foundation that a true community can be built, and that so established its foundations are so deep and so wide that there is no limit that we can place to the extent of the building. Liberty then becomes not so much a right of the individual as a necessity of society. It rests not on the claim of A to be let alone by B, but on the duty of B to treat A as a rational being.

In *Liberalism* Hobhouse advanced the view, useful in the political situation of the time, that 'socialism' could be subsumed within Liberalism, though not if 'socialism' were understood in its Marxist or bureaucratic-elitist forms. He also advocated a 'Progressive Alliance' between the Liberal Party and the Labour movement, a hope he maintained throughout the 1920s when despair at the divisions in the party separated him from membership of it. Unlike other New Liberal intellectuals, however, Hobhouse did not join the Labour Party. He was hostile to class-based politics, and although a supporter of trade unionism, opposed the idea of a political party based on sectional interest. In the last month of his life, following the election of 1929 which had seen a Labour minority government come to power, he wrote that he was 'sorry that the Liberals did not get more seats, as I think (I know it's blasphemy) they carry more brains to the square inch than Labour, most of whose men are merely dull and terribly afraid of their permanent officials'.

Hobhouse sought to reformulate and revive Liberal thought and politics not only by distancing Liberalism from some aspects of its classical ancestry but also by challenging the English idealists, particularly those led and most strongly influenced by T. H. Green: people to whom he looked as the members of a liberal generation he believed were capable of championing social reform. He was keen to see them become more deeply engaged in the practical pursuit of social justice. His *The Metaphysical Theory of the State: A Criticism* (1918) was a reply to Bernard Bosanquet's (q.v.) Hegelian (q.v.) *The Philosophical Theory of the State* (1899) and a response to the authoritarian characteristics of idealist philosophising, which he opposed at the same time as he championed and supported the development of a state that could serve as an instrument for social development and improvement.

Reading Hobhouse's work remains a rewarding experience. He invested an enormous part of his very considerable intellectual energies in exploring the relationships between social, economic and political liberty. He argued passionately in favour of a practical view of liberty in which he insisted that there would be a close correspondence between individual freedom (q.v.) and the acceptance of restraints on individual action. He was prepared to take on an extraordinarily diverse range of thinkers and schools of thought in order to promote his brand of socially responsible liberalism, including German idealism (q.v.), the Manchester School (q.v.), naturalist/evolutionary social theories, and Marxism. His published works continue to provide readers with a remarkably eclectic appreciation of the evolution of liberal political thought and its principal contenders. His writings also serve to remind readers of the great variety of political ideas that cohabit within liberalism and the strength of the case for constantly re-evaluating 'liberal' ideas that may have come to be accepted uncritically as falling within the canon of liberal political thought.

Key works

- *The Labour Movement* (1893)
- *Democracy and Reaction* (1904)
- *Liberalism* (1911)
- *The Metaphysical Theory of the State: A Criticism* (1918)
- *The Elements of Social Justice* (1922)

Further reading

- Stefan Collini, *Liberalism and Sociology: L. T. Hobhouse and Political Argument in England 1880–1914* (Cambridge University Press, 1979)
- Alan P. Grimes, 'New Introduction' to *Liberalism* (Oxford University Press, 1964)

- James Meadowcroft (ed.), *L. T. Hobhouse: Liberalism and Other Writings* (Cambridge University Press, 1994)

    David Howarth and Ed Randall

J. A. Hobson   1858–1940

A radical journalist, economic thinker and critic of imperialism, Hobson was, along with L. T. Hobhouse, the most important contributor to the development of the New Liberalism. He was active in both Liberal and Fabian circles in late Victorian and Edwardian Britain.

Key ideas

- Economics should be part of a broad enquiry into social conditions, informed and complemented by politics and ethics, and dedicated to the improvement of the human condition.
- Capitalist economies are prone to general failures of demand; such failures, caused by under-consumption and over-saving, give rise to a maldistribution of purchasing power which is the real and remediable cause of unemployment and poverty.
- Imperialism serves many different purposes but has an important role in enabling capitalists to find new markets and overcome the economic problems that arise from under-consumption and excessive saving in the home economy.
- Government action is needed to overcome the problems generated by excessive saving and under-consumption; appropriate government action includes progressive taxation, income redistribution and the control of monopolies.
- Although governments should be democratically accountable 'disinterested experts' have a vital role to play in providing good government.

Biography

John Atkinson Hobson was born in Derby on 6 July 1858, into a well-to-do Derbyshire family, the second son of William and Josephine (née Atkinson) Hobson. His father was part-owner and editor of the *Derbyshire Advertiser* and a substantial figure in Derby politics, becoming mayor of Derby twice in the 1880s. Having attended a local grammar school Hobson won an open scholarship to Oxford, from where he graduated in 1880, having read classics and *Literae Humaniores*, though his performance as a sportsman was rather more impressive than his academic achievements. This may help to explain his decision, on leaving Oxford, to pursue a career as a school teacher rather than in academia.

Having moved to Exeter to teach classics, in the early 1880s he met and married Florence Edgar, an American writer, poet and campaigner for women rights. Hobson also met and formed a close intellectual partnership with the businessman and mountaineer A. F. Mummery. In his autobiography (*Confessions of an Economic Heretic* (1938)), he acknowledges the encouragement that Mummery gave him in developing and publishing what were decidedly heterodox views on economics in the late 1880s. The book they wrote together, *Physiology of Industry* (1889), appears to have offended the economics establishment of the day, and may, as Hobson suggests in his autobiography, have severely damaged his prospects of ever achieving academic respectability and obtaining a university post.

In 1887 the Hobsons moved to London and he joined the university extension movement, becoming an extra-mural lecturer in English. Responding to a rapidly growing and only partially satisfied demand for higher and further education, the extension movement offered a wide range of courses and intellectual experiences to the late Victorian and Edwardian public. Hobson was thus able to share his ideas with large numbers of people whose only route into higher education was the extra-mural system. His unconventional economic views meant that he encountered opposition to his teaching economics in London for many years, though he was offered the opportunity to lecture on political economy in Oxford.

Nevertheless, working as an extra-mural lecturer and a journalist, Hobson enjoyed many opportunities to express his ideas and win public recognition for his views and expertise. Since he lived in London he was also able to build intellectually rewarding relationships with other radicals, and he became a prominent member of the Rainbow Circle, established in 1894. Bringing together both Fabians and Liberals, the Circle served, in Michael Freeden's words, as a 'crucible for the welfare-oriented liberal-social ideas which inspired both the Liberal and the Labour parties in the early twentieth century'; it also became 'an incubator for ethical foreign policy views which were to be heard during the First World War'.

In 1899 Hobson travelled to South Africa as a special correspondent for the *Manchester Guardian* to report on the conflict with the Boers. His experiences as a war correspondent, and his disgust at the way in which imperial power was being exercised, led him to develop an analysis of imperialism that included its interrelationship with capitalism. On his return to Britain he won a large audience for his ideas and a public reputation as an exceptionally well-informed critic of the war in South Africa, and of British imperialism in general. His radicalism (q.v.) attracted the support of leading members of the Liberal Party and cemented his reputation for

economic heterodoxy. He became, along with L. T. Hobhouse (q.v.), the most widely read and influential proponent of the New Liberalism (q.v.). He was almost certainly the most prolific liberal exponent of interventionist and egalitarian public policies in Edwardian Britain. The quantity of his published work on social, political and economic subjects is staggering; one biographer, Peter Cain, has calculated that he was the author of no less than fifty-four books and 700 substantial articles.

Hobson's support for the Liberal Party was profoundly shaken, however, by the party's decision to take Britain to war in 1914. The war swept away the hopes of the liberal and radical generation for whom Hobson had been a prominent spokesman, along with hopes for international cooperation and the peaceful resolution of international disputes and economic rivalries. Hobson himself became a driving force behind the Union of Democratic Control, a cross-party progressive organisation that brought together Liberal and Labour intellectuals in shared opposition to the war and to government policy. One historian, David Blaazer, has described the UDC as 'conveying Liberal opponents of the war into the Labour Party', and that was Hobson's experience. He stood, unsuccessfully, for Parliament as an independent at the 1918 general election, and shortly afterwards became a supporter of the Independent Labour Party and then, in 1924, a member of the Labour Party. However, as he explained in his autobiography, he never felt entirely at home 'in a body governed by trade union members and their finance, and intellectually led by full-blooded Socialists'.

Hobson continued to engage in popular and academic debates, and contributed extensively to policy analysis. In 1919 he gave evidence to the Sankey Commission on the coal industry, and in the 1920s he served as a member of the Colwyn Committee on national debt and taxation. His interest in economic and political issues did not wane during the inter-war years and, in 1938, aged eighty, he issued a revised edition of his most famous work, *Imperialism*. He died in Hampstead on 1 April 1940.

Ideas

Hobson was a fervent critic of classical economics, attacking the work of those who attempted to present economics as an objective and independent social science, able to make sense of social and economic phenomena without reference to human values and politics. He argued that any worthwhile social study called for an understanding of relationships between individual human beings and the society of which they were a part. He was, in this sense, an organicist, concerned – as liberal idealists (q.v.) such as T. H. Green (q.v.) had been – with the interaction and interdependence between individual human beings and the communities of which they were members. Political programmes, intended to guide and inform economic policy, needed to take account of ethical goals, not just empirical findings about individual economic behaviour and theoretical speculations about the operation of economic systems. What was the point of economics if it did not embrace a commitment to improve the lives of human beings, particularly those who were unable to share in the prosperity of capitalist and industrial societies? Hobson's humanism and strong beliefs in the need for an ethical approach to economics are readily apparent in his published works, including *The Social Problem* (1901), *Work and Wealth* (1914) and *Wealth and Life* (1929).

Hobson went in search of a synthesis between the individualistic tenets of classical liberalism (q.v.) and the collectivist concerns of liberals, such as himself, who were deeply disturbed by the poverty they observed around them. Laissez-faire (q.v.) appeared incapable of addressing the social and economic problems of a highly industrialised nation, and could not meet the reasonable expectations of a growing body of politically active citizens. Hobson's thoughts on capitalism and poverty appeared mainly in *Problems of Poverty* (1891), *Evolution of Modern Capitalism* (1894), *Problem of the Unemployed* (1896) and *The Economics of Distribution* (1900). In 1909, in *The Crisis of Liberalism*, he explained why it was imperative for liberalism, both as a political philosophy and as a political movement, to support radical social and economic change in order to win popular backing for an active state capable of radically reforming social and economic life and achieving greater social justice (q.v.).

In the course of more than two decades, before the First World War, Hobson developed a radical new political economy in which he set out to explain what he identified as the fundamental weaknesses of unreformed capitalism. Capitalism was susceptible to general economic failures, attributable to over-saving and under-consumption, and reflected in a maldistribution of purchasing power and in general failures of demand; these general failures could only be remedied by extensive state activity and intervention. This theory of failures of demand contradicted Say's law, an axiom of conventional economic thought, but conventional theory was clearly in error; there could be no excuse for failing to take action to reduce unemployment and poverty.

Hobson in fact anticipated a good deal of Keynesian (q.v.) economic theory, something that Keynes (q.v.) himself acknowledged in his *General Theory of Employment, Interest and Money* (1936). The policies

Hobson advocated implied a critical corrective or compensatory role for government economic policy, including progressive taxation, redistributive fiscal policy and the public control of monopolies.

Hobson was not only the scourge of the economics establishment of his era, he was also the leading critic of British imperialism. His study of *Imperialism* (1902) was wide-ranging and well integrated with the political economy he had developed as the theoretical foundation for the New Liberalism. Imperialism was not only a manifestation of national arrogance and national rivalries, which fuelled military conflicts, but also the chief means by which capitalists attempted to lessen or elide the problems created by inadequate demand or under-consumption at home. Imperialism opened up new markets for manufactured goods and new avenues for the investment of economic surpluses. Empire also appeared to offer capitalists opportunities for obtaining higher rates of return than could be found at home. Hobson argued that by overcoming the maldistribution of purchasing power in the home economy, it would be possible to reduce or even eliminate the pressure for imperial adventures and expansion.

In addition to his political economy Hobson developed firm views about the role of 'disinterested experts' in governing and managing a decent society. His support for and recognition of the value of expert knowledge, which he favoured over common sense and individual choice in a range of circumstances, distinguishes him from other liberal thinkers, who have typically been much less willing to qualify or modify their commitment to individual choice and self-determination. Hobson came to the view, clearly expressed in his autobiography, that the complexity of industrial societies made it essential to approach the state 'not as a nest of bureaucrats or of interest politicians, but as a body of experts on matters where we can have little personal knowledge'.

Hobson did not live to see his most important political and economic ideas embraced by government, but many of his key ideas won general acceptance and were reflected in British public policy in the late 1940s and 1950s, including, most strikingly, demand management, redistributive public policy and the renunciation of empire. The New Liberal ideas he had long advocated had become part of the new post-war conventional wisdom.

Key works
- *Evolution of Modern Capitalism* (1894)
- *Problem of the Unemployed* (1896)
- *Imperialism* (1902)
- *The Industrial System* (1909)
- *The Crisis of Liberalism* (1909)
- *Towards International Government* (1914)

Further reading
- John Allett, *New Liberalism: The Political Economy of J. A. Hobson* (University of Toronto Press, 1981)
- Peter Cain, *Hobson and Imperialism: Radicalism, New Liberalism and Finance 1887–1938* (Oxford University Press, 2002)
- John Atkinson Hobson, *Confessions of an Economic Heretic* (George Allen and Unwin, 1938)
- John C. Wood and Robert D. Wood, *John A. Hobson* (Routledge, 2003)

Ed Randall

Wilhelm von Humboldt   1767–1835

A political writer, educationalist and statesman in Prussia whose work influenced, among others John Stuart Mill. Not only Germany's most important liberal thinker, Humboldt was also a practical statesman who reformed the Prussian educational system.

Key ideas
- Self-education and self-realisation are the goals of man.
- Freedom is the precondition for self-education.
- The state must be limited to its essential tasks, such as internal and external security.
- Reform, not revolution, is the path to a liberal society.

Biography
Wilhelm von Humboldt was born on 22 June 1767, in Potsdam, to a family of the lower aristocracy; he was brought up with his equally famous brother, the explorer and scientist Alexander von Humboldt. In 1788 Wilhelm began studying law and classical literature at Göttingen University. A year later, when the French Revolution broke out, he undertook a journey to Paris on the invitation of Mirabeau in order to watch the 'funeral ceremony of French despotism'. He came back somewhat disillusioned. In his *Thoughts on Constitutions, Suggested by the New French Constitution* (1791), Humboldt declared his sympathy with the liberal ideals of the Revolution, but doubted whether these ideals could be maintained through its course. A more gradualist approach would have produced less dangerous results.

Humboldt's political ideas were more elaborately outlined in his *The Limits of State Action* (1792). Only a few sections of this book were published during Humboldt's lifetime, but it became an instant classic of political philosophy when it was published posthumously in 1851.

Humboldt's intellectual interests went far beyond that of political philosophy; his writings cover a wide range of subjects including linguistics. However, it was practical politics, rather than theory, that became the focus of his life over the following years. Prussia's failure to defeat Napoleon made it necessary to carry out long-needed and thorough-going reforms within the state. A peculiar brand of liberalism came into existence that was typical of Prussia: *Beamten-Liberalismus* (civil servant's liberalism), where enlightened persons from the royal bureaucracy tried to modernise the country in a 'top-down approach'. Among them were Baron vom Stein, the father of German local self-government.

Humboldt became Minister for Public Instruction in 1809. His reforms proved to be outstandingly efficient and durable and today Humboldt is best remembered for them. A multi-tiered system of educational institutions was introduced throughout the land, covering elementary schools to universities; universal education beyond a narrow subject was achieved. As Humboldt had already outlined in his *Limits of State Action*, self-development and individuality were the central goals of education.

From 1810 to 1813 Humboldt was the chief Prussian diplomat in Vienna; he later became ambassador in London. In 1819 he became the Minister for Estate (Diet) Affairs, but soon resigned in protest against Metternich's Karlsberg Decrees, which introduced greater censorship of the press and other repressive policies. He never re-entered public life, and until his death on 8 April 1835 in Tegel (near Berlin), he devoted himself to his family and to academic research.

Ideas
The most comprehensive statement of Humboldt's political thinking can be found in his book *The Limits of State Action*. His basic premise is that:

The true end of Man, or that which is prescribed by the eternal and immutable dictates of reason, and not suggested by vague and transient desires, is the highest and most harmonious development of his powers to a complete and consistent whole. Freedom is the first and indispensable condition which the possibility of such a development pre-supposes; but there is besides another essential – intimately connected with freedom, it is true – a variety of situations. Even the most free and self-reliant of men is hindered in his development, when set in a monotonous situation.

Out of this premise he concluded that only a minimal state that secured internal and external peace and security was legitimate. A state that provided for more would inevitably encourage and foster conformism and uniformity. Humboldt's concept of self-education can be distinguished from similar traditional Aristotelian concepts. While Aristotelian essentialism aimed at humans developing themselves as the ideal realisation of a general ideal of mankind, Humboldt, as a romanticist revolutionary, believed in the development, with all its peculiarities, of the individual.

This idea deeply impressed the English philosopher John Stuart Mill (q.v.), who learned about Humboldt after the first translation of *The Limits of State Action* appeared in 1854. In his classic defence of individual freedom (q.v.), *On Liberty* (1859), Mill constantly refers to Humboldt as his intellectual precursor and inspiration, who helped him to overcome his narrow utilitarian (q.v.) philosophy.

Some critics of Humboldt tried to see a contradiction between the author of *The Limits of State Action*, who denied any responsibility of the state for education, and the educational reformer of 1809. Was Humboldt an inconsistent liberal?

There is little reason to doubt Humboldt's liberal convictions in his later life. He never turned fiercely nationalist, unlike some of his previously enlightened liberal contemporaries like Fichte, but always maintained contact with liberal circles, especially in France. Benjamin Constant (q.v.) and the 'deologues' always remained politically close to him. With his educational reforms Humboldt simply had to accept certain constraints. Although he could not privatise the whole system, he managed to make it accessible to everyone and removed from it privilege and patronage. The autonomy and freedom of all educational institutions was the cornerstone of his reforms, the best he could do under the circumstances. All this was compatible with Humboldt's early liberal ideas, fairly radical in vision, but also gradualist and reformist in practical outlook. Self-organisation, based on a peaceful intellectual exchange, was, of course, more desirable than compulsory state-dominated association.

Humboldt's individualism was by no means atomistic. In the process of self-education, he maintained, one learns and rises to the level where cultivated voluntary self-organisation is possible. Therefore a liberal order could never be imposed on the people; it would grow with their capabilities. Such ideas were also the theme of his later publications, such as his *Memorandum on the German Constitution* (1813). In this memorandum he warned of the nationalist enthusiasm for a centralised unitary state and advocated a decentralised constitution that would grant freedom and cultural diversity to its citizens.

Key works
- *Thoughts on Constitutions* (1791)
- *The Limits of State Action* (1792)
- *Memorandum on the German Constitution* (1813)

Further reading

- Joachim H. Knoll and Horst Siebert: *Wilhelm von Humboldt: Politician and Educationist* (Inter Nationes, 1967)
- Paul R. Sweet, *Wilhelm von Humboldt: A Biography* (Ohio State University Press, 1978)

Detmar Doering

David Hume   1711–76

Known to his contemporaries primarily as an essayist and historian, Hume owes his posthumous fame among philosophers to his defence of empiricism and his sceptical positions on a number of key metaphysical issues. While he was cautious about the risks of radical social change, he was also an energetic promoter of what he saw as the hallmarks of civilised society: open commerce, basic civil freedoms and an equitable system of law.

Key ideas

- Government exists to serve the public good, primarily by enforcing laws to protect property but also by promoting commerce and performing public works.
- Free and open commerce has 'civilising' effects both on the people and their governments.
- Political actors must balance the competing claims of public liberty and state authority, while acknowledging the necessity of both.
- Although people are entitled to freedom of conscience, religious belief is a potent source of social instability that must be controlled.

Biography

David Hume was born on 7 May 1711, the second son of a minor Scottish gentry family, the Homes of Ninewells, a modest estate near the English border. (While in his twenties, he changed the spelling of his name to what he believed to be a more ancient orthography.) His father died young, and, as he put it in his autobiography, 'my family was not rich'. His mother tolerated her son's passion for study and reflection, but spent the rest of her life gently prodding him to find a stable profession. He never managed to do so.

Hume attended Edinburgh University, from which he graduated at age fifteen, after which he began a period of private study. He read widely among contemporary philosophy, including the writings of Shaftesbury and Francis Hutcheson, in whose 'moral sense' theory he heard echoes of Cicero and the classical moralist writers he loved. He lost his religious faith during this period, and remained a sceptic his entire life. While still a teenager, he embarked on the philosophical project that, after nearly a decade of work, became *A Treatise of Human Nature*.

The book was published when Hume was only twenty-seven. It attempted to systematise the new 'science of man' he associated with Locke (q.v.), Mandeville, Shaftesbury, Hutcheson and Butler, and which he considered the extension of Bacon's experimentalism into the human sciences. For all its brilliance, the *Treatise* was poorly received on its initial publication, and sold very few copies. Within two years, however, Hume found the popular success he craved with the first of several collections of essays on various topics. From this point on, his writings were always directed to a broad audience.

Despite being little read and still less understood, Hume's sceptical metaphysical theories were sufficiently notorious to bring him into confrontation with the orthodox faction of the Presbyterian Church, who (correctly) interpreted them as evidence of the author's religious heterodoxy. His reputation as an unbeliever prevented him ever attaining the academic posting he desperately wanted. However, he benefited from the rapid modernisation of Scottish society that followed the Union of 1707, and (more specifically) from his friendship with the brilliant and ambitious Edinburgh Moderate circle of church reformers. The zealots' attempt to excommunicate Hume failed, and he was able, in spite of his public defiance of church orthodoxy, to live a comfortable life in Edinburgh. This would have been impossible even fifty years earlier.

Hume's greatest fame came with his monumental *History of England*, published between 1754 and 1764. The *History* provides a narrative of political events beginning in Roman times and ending with the Glorious Revolution – a narrative which Hume interrupts frequently to offer overviews of the nation's economic, cultural and intellectual development, as well as character studies of England's different monarchs. The overall picture is of a people rising from an early period of barbarism to one of cultural and political refinement, with liberty guaranteed by established structures of law. The book's success finally gave its author the financial security he had always sought.

The accession of George III in 1760, and the consequent ascension of Lord Bute as chief minister, brought a number of Hume's friends into positions of power. In 1763, following the Seven Years' War, he obtained a diplomatic posting as personal secretary to England's ambassador to France, Francis Seymour Conway, the Earl of Hertford. Hume was lionised in Paris, and (his diplomatic duties being light) he spent his time as a sought-after guest at the city's leading salons. He formed close friendships with many of France's leading intellectuals. During his three years in Paris, Hume ascended to the position of secretary to the embassy and served briefly, after Hertford's recall to London, as its chargé d'affaires.

In 1767 Hume was appointed Under-Secretary of State, serving under General Henry Seymour Conway (Hertford's brother). However, he lost the office on Conway's resignation in January 1768. (Conway was an 'old Whig' who fell out with the government over its imposition of external taxes on the American colonies, among other issues.) He retired to Edinburgh in 1769, embittered by what he saw as rising levels of anti-French and anti-Scottish sentiment among the English public. Though he wrote little after the completion of his *History*, he continued to revise and republish his various works. Thanks to the numerous editions he saw through the press, by the end of his life even his purely philosophical writings had begun to find a broader audience.

Hume died peacefully on 25 August 1776, without recanting his infidelity – to the amazement of observers such as James Boswell, who could not conceive of facing death without the comfort of the afterlife. In his last days Hume joked with Adam Smith (q.v.) that he should plead with Charon, the boatman charged with taking him to the underworld, for extra time on earth, that he might 'have the satisfaction of seeing the downfall of some of the prevailing systems of superstition'. But he expected the boatman would see through the ruse, since it was clear 'that will not happen these many hundred years'.-

Ideas

Hume's earliest work, the *Treatise of Human Nature*, contains a lengthy discussion of political philosophy. This discussion is entirely theoretical, in the tradition of Hobbes (q.v.) and Locke (q.v.) – to both of whom it owes many of its key ideas. The relevant sections are devoted to analysing the foundation of government and the source of its legitimacy. Hume argues that political society is established in order to realise the benefits, apparent to all, that result from rules governing the protection and transfer of property. We maintain our allegiance to a particular regime because of its ability to execute an effective and equitable system of property laws. Where it fails at this basic task, this allegiance is dissolved. Hume differs from his predecessors in arguing that the rules governing property are the result not of a specific (even hypothetical) 'promise' or contract. Rather they are a 'convention', our commitment to which (as with two men rowing a boat) we constantly reaffirm through our behaviour. This is because we see that it is in the ongoing interest of ourselves and others to do so; they are rooted in 'a general sense of the common interest'.

Hume stresses that, except in cases of extreme tyranny or incompetence by the magistrates, we must defer to established laws and established governments. He thinks that rebellion against authority always risks creating a situation where order breaks down altogether and property is left unprotected, the worst possible outcome. But his political theory by no means terminates in this Hobbesian doctrine. He clearly hopes that his works will inspire enlightened law-givers to undertake projects for social reform, and emphasises that in disputed questions of policy, 'public utility' or 'the true interests of mankind' must provide the ultimate standard for decision.

Hume's later, more extensive writings on politics, history and government are much less abstract than the *Treatise*. They take as one of their central tasks to identify what distinguishes a 'civilised' nation from a 'barbarous' one, and what enables the former to evolve from the latter. Hume thinks civilised societies are characterised by greater levels of both 'knowledge' and 'humanity'. This means, first of all, that there is greater interest in both technical and artistic innovation; and, second, that the sentiments of sociability and 'fellow feeling', which lie at the basis of moral behaviour, become more widespread. He further thinks that knowledge and humanity are both the products of increased commercial activity, and of the wealth that invariably results. He challenges the equation, common during his era and argued vigorously by both classical and contemporary republican theorists, of 'luxury' (in other words, the desire for material prosperity) with languor and moral corruption. Hume believes that greater commerce, in addition to making people happier and more moral, promotes peaceful international relations by (as he puts it) binding together 'the most distant nations' in a 'close chain'.

Hume thinks that good government is a prerequisite to commercial development. However, after it has established an effective legal system, the chief service a government can do to promote commerce is to remove barriers to trade and, that done, to keep out of its way. He is emphatic in his rejection of all forms of mercantilism and protectionism. However, he is by no means a pure laissez-faire (q.v.) liberal in the Victorian mould. He looks to the state to provide a variety of public works, such as the construction of bridges and canals. Its ability to perform such improving tasks makes government 'one of the finest and most subtle inventions imaginable'.

For Hume, the history of Britain reveals a slow evolution towards what he calls a 'regular and equitable plan of liberty'. During the feudal era, the execution of the laws depended on the personal power and prestige of the monarch, with the higher aristocracy always ready to take advantage of any period of royal weakness to spread disorder. Regular liberty was only achieved when the power of the state came to depend as much on the commons as on the monarch. The rise of the commons was gradual, but accelerated during the Tudor period, due to the dramatic increase in commercial wealth brought on by overseas trade, as well as by Henry VII's statute of alienations, which through a byzantine legal manoeuvre, unintended by the law's author, allowed small landowners finally to free themselves from the remaining vestiges of feudal obligation.

There is an undeniable tension in Hume's writing between its conservative and reforming aspects, and this has led to ongoing disputes about his legacy for political philosophy. He has been called both the 'creator of the Liberal reform programme' and the 'first conservative philosopher'. Such disagreements might not have displeased Hume, who prided himself on standing above the partisan disputes of his era. 'I have the impudence to pretend that I am of no party', he boasted, 'and have no bias.' He attempts to refute what he sees as the philosophical bases of both the Tory and Whig parties: the doctrine of passive obedience and the belief in an unchanging ancient constitution, respectively.

Against those, however, who hoped for the dissolution of factional division under the benign rule of impartial 'patriots', Hume accepts the inevitability, and indeed the advantages, of ongoing partisan disagreement. 'In all governments,' he says, 'there is a perpetual intestine [i.e. internecine] struggle ... between AUTHORITY and LIBERTY; and neither of them can ever absolutely prevail in the contest' – nor, he thought, ought either to do so. He thinks that the authority of government, while necessary to preserve society,

should never be left unrestricted. Hume is an eloquent advocate for liberty, which he calls 'the common right of mankind' and 'the perfection of civil society'. The political parties in Britain do the nation a service when they each advocate one of these principles, while acknowledging the claims of the other.

Hume insists that everyone should possess, among other fundamental freedoms, the liberty of religious conscience. However, he also considers religious opinion a potent source of social disorder. For this reason, he advocates strict control of the clergy by civil magistrates. Ideally, he thinks Britain should possess a single national church, regulated by the state, which would tolerate dissenting opinions and curtail the enthusiasms of its followers.

Though Hume is now remembered less as a political thinker than as a metaphysical and religious sceptic, his ideas about government, law and economics were widely known and discussed during the eighteenth century, and his *History of England* remained the standard work on the subject until Thomas Macaulay's (q.v.) rival treatment appeared in the mid-nineteenth century. The narrative of the *History* allowed debate to move beyond the narrow partisan accounts of royalists and parliamentarians, and convinced many that England's political development was the result of a complex process of give-and-take between competing, but legitimate, interests.

Hume's influence can be detected in the writings of Adam Smith, James Madison (q.v. Federalists) and Jeremy Bentham (q.v.), among others. Smith found in him a mentor who shared his faith in the benefits of free trade (q.v.) and the division of labour, and in economic growth as a means of liberating people from barbarism. Crafting a constitution for the new colonies, Madison drew on his model for a form of representative government that could operate in a large state. And Bentham, who credited Hume with removing the scales from his eyes, learned from him that the chief end of government policy should be to promote the public interest or 'utility'. In general Hume stood before subsequent generations as a man of the Enlightenment, who was a tireless advocate for the general good and who had the courage to speak out against what he saw as the destructive prejudices of the past.

Key works

- *A Treatise of Human Nature* (1739–40)
- *Essays, Moral and Political* (1741–42)
- *Enquiry Concerning the Principles of Morals* (1751)
- *Political Discourses* (1752)
- *The History of England* (1754–64)

Further reading

- Nicholas Capaldi and Donald W. Livingston (eds.), *Liberty in Hume's* History of England (Kluwer Academic Publishers, 1990)
- Eugene Rotwein, 'Introduction', in *David Hume: Writings on Economics* (University of Wisconsin Press, 1955)
- John B. Stewart, *Opinion and Reform in Hume's Political Philosophy* (Princeton University Press, 1992)
- John B. Stewart, 'The Public Interest vs. Old Rights', *Hume Studies* 31.2 (November 1995)

Neil McArthur

Idealism

A philosophical position in epistemology and metaphysics. In epistemology, idealism holds that only mental states or ideas can be truly known, not external things 'in themselves'. In metaphysics, idealism holds that only minds truly exist. Idealism is usually considered in opposition to materialism.

Idealism is a very broad tradition encompassing several different variants – including subjective idealism, objective idealism and panpsychism – with a complex history reaching from Plato until the current century. However, in the context of British liberal thought, philosophical idealism was most influential through the 'British idealism' movement in the late nineteenth century which was linked to the rise of the New Liberalism (q.v.). Leading figures in the movement included T. H. Green (q.v.), F. H. Bradley (1846–1924), Bernard Bosanquet (q.v.), Edward Caird (q.v.) and J. M. E. McTaggart (1866–1925).

In the eighteenth and early nineteenth centuries, empiricism had been the dominant strand in British philosophy, providing the philosophical underpinning for the development of classical liberalism (q.v.), but in the late nineteenth century British philosophers became strongly influenced by German idealism, in particular the work of Hegel (q.v.). Benjamin Jowett, the Master of Balliol College, Oxford, in the mid-Victorian era, was an early exponent of these ideas in England, and many of the leading figures of both British idealism and New Liberalism were educated at Balliol in this period.

Although there were a number of differences in the beliefs of the British idealists, and they certainly did not accept Hegelian ideas uncritically, some general common features can be described. These include a belief in an 'Absolute' (a single all-encompassing reality that in some sense formed a coherent and all-inclusive system); the importance of reason as both the faculty by which the Absolute's structure is grasped and as that structure itself; the doctrine of internal relations (all relations are internal to their bearers, implying that everything has some relation, however distant, to everything else); and a coherence theory of truth (someone's belief is true if and only if it is *coherent* with all or most of his other beliefs).

Taken together, this cluster of ideas clearly lends itself to an organic conception of society and the state. In politics and political economy, the British idealists were therefore dissatisfied with what they considered the atomistic individualism of the classical liberals, especially the 'survival of the fittest' doctrine propounded by Herbert Spencer (q.v.). In their view, humans were innately social beings and could only fulfil their potential as individuals in a social context. Bosanquet in particular believed that social relations and institutions were not ultimately material phenomena, but were best understood as existing at the level of human consciousness. He saw a relation between the 'real' or 'general will' and the 'common good': 'The General Will seems to be, in the last resort, the ineradicable impulse of an intelligent being to a good extending beyond itself.' This 'good' is nothing other than 'the existence and the perfection of human personality' which he identifies with 'the excellence of souls' and the complete realisation of the individual. It is insofar as the state reflects the general will and this common good that its authority is legitimate and its action morally justifiable; Bosanquet describes the function of the state as 'the hindrance of hindrances' to human development.

The British idealists always retained a strong sense of the importance of individuals – Green in particular spoke of the individual as the sole locus of value and argued that the state's existence was justified only insofar as it contributed to the realisation of value in the lives of individual persons.

The linkage of this kind of philosophy of the state and the more practical New Liberal writings of J. A. Hobson (q.v.) and L. T. Hobhouse (q.v.) on positive liberty and the enabling state is clear. Not all New Liberal political thinkers were uncritical supporters of idealist philosophy, however – Hobhouse in particular perceived a danger of authoritarian statism within Hegelian idealism. Also, the party-political allegiances of the British idealist philosophers were not exclusively liberal – McTaggart was a political Conservative and although Bradley was not active politically he appears to have held broadly Conservative views. There are also links between British idealism and ethical socialism, and indeed the 'Third Way' communitarianism of the 1990s might not have been uncongenial to some of the British idealists.

The dominant position of idealism among Britsish academic philosophers eventually came under sustained attack from the new analytic school, starting with G. E. Moore's *The Refutation of Idealism* in 1903, and culminating in the devastating polemic of A. J. Ayer's *Language, Truth and Logic* in 1936. Idealism was marginalised in British philosophy for most of the twentieth century, although there were always a few supporters, such as Timothy L. S. Sprigge, the author of *The Vindication of Absolute Idealism* (1984), and there has been some revival of interest in recent years.

Philosophical idealism should be distinguished from the general use of the terms 'idealism' and 'idealistic' to describe the holding of strong and possibly utopian principles.

Key works
- T. H. Green, *Prolegomena to Ethics* (1883)
- F. H. Bradley, *Appearance and Reality: A Metaphysical Essay* (1893)
- Bernard Bosanquet, *The Philosophical Theory of the State* (1899)

- J. M. E. McTaggart, *The Nature of Existence* (1921 and 1927)

Further reading
- G. A. Kelly, *Idealism, Politics and History* (Cambridge University Press, 1969)
- Peter P. Nicholson, *The Political Philosophy of the British Idealists* (Cambridge University Press, 1990)

Christian Moon

Institute of Economic Affairs

The Institute of Economic Affairs (IEA) is a UK-based think-tank dedicated to the promotion of economic or classical liberalism. It describes its mission as 'to improve understanding of the fundamental institutions of a free society by analysing and expounding the role of markets in solving economic and social problems'. The IEA is one of a small number of think-tanks world-wide that can claim to have had a significant impact on public policy, both in terms of contributing to a transformation of the general climate of opinion in the UK and the implementation of specific policies.

The IEA was founded in 1955 by Sir Antony Fisher (1915–88), a former Battle of Britain pilot and founder of Buxted Chickens, following the advice of F. A. Hayek (q.v.). Fisher had sought out Hayek at his office at the LSE at the end of the war after reading *The Reader's Digest* condensed version of Hayek's *The Road to Serfdom*. Fisher told Hayek that he intended to go into politics to put right the wrongs that Hayek had identified in his book. However, Hayek counselled Fisher that future government policy would be determined by the intellectuals – academics, teachers, journalists and other opinion-leaders – whose ideas politicians would ultimately follow. Hayek advised Fisher to establish a research institute dedicated to the promotion of classical liberal (q.v.) ideas among the intellectuals rather than pursue a career in politics.

Ten years after that meeting the commercial success of Buxted Chickens put Fisher in a position to act on Hayek's advice and establish the IEA. Fisher quickly recruited two young economists, Ralph Harris (1924–2006; later Lord Harris of High Cross) and Arthur Seldon (q.v.), to run the institute, a management team that was to remain in place for the best part of thirty years. During their collaboration Harris and Seldon established the IEA's wide-ranging publication programme that continues to this day, consisting of monographs and, since 1980, the journal *Economic Affairs*. IEA authors, principally recruited from academia, are required to apply classical liberal principles and economic analysis to particular policy areas and to ignore questions of practical or political feasibility. Topics covered have included standard economic concerns, such as monetary policy and utility regulation, as well as more unusual subjects, such as markets in animal semen for the artificial insemination of cattle and in human blood for transfusion.

Judging the impact of a think-tank is notoriously difficult. For the first twenty years of the IEA's existence its success in influencing public policy was probably limited to the outlawing of resale price maintenance by the Heath government – a policy that can be argued to be contrary to the classical liberal principle of freedom of contract. However, from 1979 onwards a myriad of policies advocated in IEA publications and often initially thought politically impossible have been implemented, including abolition of exchange controls, the ending of incomes and prices policies, the cessation of regional policy, the introduction of road charging, privatisation of the major utilities, bus deregulation and central bank independence. Indeed, it seems reasonable to judge that the IEA and its authors were among the key architects of the transformation of UK public policy after the collapse of the post-war consensus.

The IEA is a non-partisan think-tank independent of all political parties. Although MPs of all parties have written for the institute, its influence has undeniably been greater on the Conservative Party than the Liberal Party or Liberal Democrats. While this may be a source of chagrin to those connected with the IEA who consider themselves liberals rather than conservatives, it has nevertheless meant that classical liberal policies (or neo-liberalism (q.v.)) have been implemented in the UK – in contrast to most of continental Europe where liberal parties, and hence classical liberal ideas, have remained marginal.

Further reading
- John Blundell, *Waging the War of Ideas* (Institute of Economic Affairs, 2nd edn., 2003)
- Richard Cockett, *Thinking the Unthinkable* (Fontana, 1995)
- John Meadowcroft and Jaime Reynolds, 'Liberals and the New Right', *Journal of Liberal History* 47 (summer 2005)

John Meadowcroft

Internationalism see Liberal Internationalism

Thomas Jefferson   1743–1826

Principal author of the American Declaration of Independence in 1776 and US President from 1801–09, Jefferson was considered as one of the greatest intellectuals of his age. His political philosophy centred on a radical vision of individual liberty, limited government and anti-centralism.

Key ideas
- 'Life, liberty, and the pursuit of happiness'.
- Natural rights are inalienable.
- Limited government is necessary to protect freedom.
- Anti-centralism is a safeguard against tyranny.

Biography
Thomas Jefferson was born on 13 April 1743 in Albemarle County, Virginia, the son of a rich tobacco planter. He studied law at William and Mary College and soon entered public life in local government and later in the Virginia House of Burgesses. As tensions arose between Britain and the American colonies, Jefferson sided with the supporters of independence. He became a member of the Continental Congress and was chosen to draft the Declaration of Independence of 1776, the founding document of American freedom.

Afterwards he served in the Virginian legislature, becoming Governor from 1779 to 1781. From 1784–89 he was appointed US ambassador to France, and on his return became Secretary of State under President George Washington. In 1796 he was defeated by John Adams in the presidential election, but won the following election, in 1800, and was re-elected in 1804. The Louisiana Purchase (1803), the war against the Barbary pirates (1803), his policy of neutrality in the Napoleonic Wars and the marked reduction of the public debt were the most remarkable features of his presidency.

After he left office, he retired to Monticello, the country house he had designed for himself, and devoted himself to scientific studies and the promotion of learning.

A man of vast intellect, he excelled as a philosopher, statesman, architect, scientist, educator, farmer and writer. He died in Monticello on 4 July 1826, on the fiftieth anniversary of the signing of the Declaration of Independence which he had written.

Ideas

In 1962, at a White House dinner for Nobel Prize winners, President John F. Kennedy observed: 'I think this is the most extraordinary collection of talent, of human knowledge, that has ever been gathered together at the White House, with the possible exception of when Thomas Jefferson dined alone.' Jefferson has always been seen, rightly, as the greatest American intellectual of his age. It is therefore surprising that he never wrote a systematic treatise on his political philosophy, which has instead to be distilled from his public papers and his voluminous correspondence, an extraordinarily rich source of stimulating and innovative ideas. His book, *Notes on the State of Virginia*, treats politics only as a side-issue among a list of topics embracing almost every branch of knowledge from architecture to climatology.

Much of Jefferson's political thought is encapsulated in the famous phrase from the Declaration of Independence, that it is government's sole task to defend the individual's unalienable and natural rights to 'life, liberty, and the pursuit of happiness'. Throughout his life he pursued this idea with increasing radicalism. He always remained a staunch republican and an advocate of religious tolerance and the complete separation of church and state.

The state, to him, was at best a cruel necessity and a constant threat to individual liberty. Hence he always regarded – more than most of the political thinkers of the day would have allowed – popular resistance

against the state as an essential right; his ideas inspired Henry David Thoreau's (q.v.) famous essay *On Civil Disobedience* of 1849. Not only the authorship of the Declaration, but also his support for the French Revolution, including even some of its more violent aspects, point in this direction. He was in full sympathy with militant uprisings in his own country, such as Shay's Rebellion of 1786 and the Whiskey Rebellion of 1794, that had otherwise put the political establishment in a state of panic. In a letter written in 1816, he even advanced a theory of 'permanent revolution', because he feared that every government would abridge the freedom (q.v.) of its citizens once it has become too consolidated: 'Each generation is as independent of the one preceding, as that was of all which had gone before. It has then, like them, a right to choose for itself the form of government it believes most promotive of its own happiness.'

There was clearly an anarchist (q.v.) streak in his thought: 'I would rather be exposed to the inconveniences attending too much liberty than to those attending too small a degree of it,' he wrote in 1791. His scepticism of consolidated state power led him to advocate a radical type of democratic anti-centralism. If federal government violated elementary human rights, the states could simply ignore federal laws and nullify them on their territory. Later in the nineteenth century his doctrine of states' rights became a tool of the Southern states in their defence of slavery (toward which Jefferson had an ambiguous attitude, being against it in principle, but being a slave-holder himself). Until the 1960s some Southern states used this argument to combat federal civil rights legislation. Jefferson, however, used it as a bulwark of civil rights, believing that some sort of grassroots democracy offered better protection for freedom than any centralised and less democratic institution, such as the 'aristocratic' Supreme Court.

When Congress voted for the Alien and Sedition Act in 1789, which curtailed the freedom of the press and immigration in reaction to the French Revolution and the alleged danger of Jacobinism unsettling the country, Jefferson decided to resist. Together with James Madison (see Federalists) he authored the Kentucky and Virginia Resolutions, passed by the legislators in both states; although never put into practice, these acts nullified the Alien and Sedition Act. This was based on an extreme and controversial interpretation of federalism and the US constitution. Contemporary critics always had some doubts about his attitude toward the constitution, especially after the purchase of Louisiana in 1803 under his presidency, which was not only held unconstitutional by many of his contemporary critics, but is still so by many legal experts today.

Jefferson, a humane intellectual, was never as dogmatic in practice as his radical ideas could sometimes suggest. As the founder of the University of Virginia and the Library of Congress, he allowed government to be active in the field of higher education and for the promotion of science.

Key works
- Declaration of Independence (1776)
- *Notes on the State of Virginia* (1787)
- Kentucky and Virginia Resolutions (1798)

Further reading
- Joyce Appleby, *Capitalism and a New Social Order: The Republican Vision of the 1790s* (New York University Press, 1984)
- David N. Mayer, *The Constitutional Thought of Thomas Jefferson* (University Press of Virginia, 1994)

- Albert J. Nock, *Jefferson* (Kessinger Publishing, 2004, originally published 1926)

Detmar Doering

Roy Jenkins   1920–2003

Not only a leading politician, but also a distinguished writer and biographer. Jenkins played a significant role in developing a new progressive vision for social, political and constitutional change. As Home Secretary, he was responsible for reforms that helped to transform Britain into a more modern, more civilised society; he played a key role in taking Britain into Europe; and he was a co-founder of the SDP.

Key ideas
- The state should try to reduce the gap between the wealthiest and poorest. Everyone should have the opportunity to lead a full and satisfying life.
- At the same time, people must be free to pursue their own aspirations and to run their own lives without undue interference from the state.
- Post-imperial Britain's influence was dependent on being part of Europe.
- The need for a new political force of the 'radical centre', to work with the Liberal Party for all sections of society and achieve real economic, social and constitutional change.

Biography
Roy Harris Jenkins was born on 11 November 1920 in Abersychan, Monmouthshire. He gained a first in PPE at Balliol College, Oxford and from 1943–45 worked on intelligence at Bletchley Park Headquarters Staff. After demobilisation, he worked in the City as an economist. At a by-election in April 1948, Jenkins held Southwark Central for

the Labour Party, and at the 1950 general election, he became MP for Birmingham Stechford.

Jenkins became a significant figure in Harold Wilson's 1964–70 Labour government. As Home Secretary (1965–67), he was responsible for reforming the laws on abortion, homosexuality, race relations and theatre censorship. Following the 1967 devaluation crisis, he became Chancellor of the Exchequer, where his two years of tough economic medicine restored the balance of payments and made the pound stable.

Jenkins was elected as deputy leader of the Labour Party in July 1970. In October 1971, defying a three-line whip, he led sixty-nine Labour MPs to vote for the terms of entry into the European Economic Community (EEC) negotiated by the Conservative government. The following April, he resigned the deputy leadership when the shadow Cabinet promised a referendum on whether Britain should stay in Europe.

Labour regained office after the February 1974 general election and Jenkins returned to the Home Office. In the run-up to the 1975 referendum on Britain's membership of the EEC, he joined politicians from other parties to campaign for a 'Yes' vote. After Wilson resigned in April 1976, he came third in the subsequent leadership ballot, won by James Callaghan. After Callaghan failed to make him Foreign Secretary, Jenkins left British politics to become president of the European Commission (1977–81), where he took a leading role in establishing the European Monetary System.

In 1981 Jenkins joined forces with David Owen, Shirley Williams and Bill Rodgers to become part of the 'Gang of Four' who founded the Social Democratic Party (SDP). In March 1982, he won the Glasgow Hillhead by-election and went on to defeat David Owen (q.v.) in the election to be the SDP's first leader. But he did not have a happy time in that role and resigned soon after the 1983 general election. He lost Hillhead in 1987 and went to the House of Lords, where he led the Liberal Democrats from 1988 to 1998.

Jenkins wrote numerous political biographies, including *Asquith* (1964), *Gladstone* (1995) and *Churchill* (2002). In 1986, he was elected chancellor of Oxford University. He was awarded the Order of Merit in 1993. He died at his Oxfordshire home, East Hendred, on 5 January 2003.

Ideas

Roy Jenkins was frequently accused of lacking a coherent political philosophy; and, indeed, his politics tended to be guided by a liberal state of mind rather than driven by ideology. He was much more concerned with practical measures than with realising utopian visions. In his autobiography, Jenkins himself debated whether he was really an 'establishment Whig' or a 'perpetual radical'. He opted for the latter, though many disagreed.

Still, Jenkins had a major influence on modern liberal thinking. Far more successfully than anyone else, he synthesised the principles of liberalism and social democracy (q.v.) in a late twentieth-century context. He was one of the first leading British politicians to become an enthusiast for Europe.

During the Labour Party's internal battles of the 1950s, Jenkins forged some of the revisionists' intellectual ammunition. In *The Labour Case* (1959), he described the party's ultimate goal as being 'a society … in which everyone will have the opportunity for a full and satisfying life'. Labour, he said, was 'a practical party … as much concerned with immediate reforms as practical purposes'. He did not see totemic policies, such as the further nationalisation of industry, as ends in themselves. Instead, he viewed sustained economic growth in a mixed economy as the best way of achieving progressive aims. The role of government was to manage fiscal and incomes policies to underpin a strong economy.

Jenkins's approach to politics was aimed at enabling people to enjoy 'a rapidly rising standard of living', as members of a 'civilised society'. His efforts as a backbench MP to reform the law on obscene publications sparked a deep interest in libertarian (q.v.) reform. In *The Labour Case,* he called on his party to 'be on the side of those who want to be free to live their own lives, to make their own mistakes, and to decide in an adult way and provided they do not infringe the rights of others, the code by which they wish to live'. This presaged his ground-breaking social reforms at the Home Office.

Jenkins became an avowed internationalist, supporting alliance with the United States and believing it would be unrealistic to pursue a 'socialist foreign policy' in a world where Britain's influence was greatly reduced and the United States and the Soviet Union were the dominant powers. By 1960, he was also arguing passionately that the UK could only exert a positive influence on world affairs as part of a united Europe. He believed that the 'adventure of going into Europe' would prevent Britain from becoming an isolated, introverted and declining nation. The cause of Europe defined his political outlook and persona and became the main influence on his career. As Labour drifted to the left in the early 1970s, Jenkins defended the mixed economy and the European ideal against ever-stronger opponents within his own party. It was these differences that led him to leave Labour and, eventually, to co-found the SDP.

In 1979 Jenkins brought these opinions up to date with his Dimbleby Lecture, 'Home Thoughts from Abroad'. This criticised the false choices, see-saw politics and broken promises of the two-party system, advocated electoral reform and called for a new political force of the 'radical centre' that would appeal to all sections of society. This would recognise that the private sector in a market economy would generate the most wealth but that the state should work to prevent the gap between the wealthiest and poorest from growing too large. Whilst it should try to promote equal opportunities, the state should 'know its place' in society. The party of the 'radical centre' would also pursue policies for constitutional reform, devolution, partnership in industry, equality for women, the environment and third world concerns.

Jenkins's Dimbleby Lecture was the SDP's philosophical foundation and much of it has stood the test of time as a statement of the shared political credo of modern liberals and genuine social democrats. The Liberal Democrat leader Sir Menzies Campbell has observed that the speech, like many that Jenkins made, still reads as a powerful statement of why the Liberal Democrats exist.

Key works
- *The Labour Case* (1959)
- *What Matters Now* (1972)
- 'Home Thoughts from Abroad': The Richard Dimbleby Lecture (1979)
- *Partnership of Principle: Writings and Speeches on the Making of the Alliance* (1985)
- *A Life at the Centre* (1991)
- *The British Liberal Tradition* (2001)

Further reading
- Andrew Adonis & Keith Thomas (eds.), *Roy Jenkins: A Retrospective* (Oxford University Press, 2004)

- John Campbell, *Roy Jenkins: A Biography* (Weidenfeld & Nicolson, 1983)
- Ivor Crewe & Anthony King, *SDP: The Birth, Life and Death of the Social Democratic Party* (Oxford University Press, 1995)
- Giles Radice, *Friends & Rivals: Crosland, Jenkins and Healey* (Little, Brown, 2002)
- Neil Stockley, 'Writing about Roy: Obituaries and Appreciation', *Journal of Liberal History* 38 (spring 2003)

Neil Stockley

Joseph Rowntree Reform Trust Limited

Established in 1904 by the Quaker confectionary manufacturer and social reformer Joseph Rowntree, the Joseph Rowntree Reform Trust promotes political reform, constitutional change and social justice; it has been by far the largest single donor to the Liberal Party and its successor, the Liberal Democrats.

Joseph Rowntree (1836–1925) was born into the family of a Quaker grocer in York. He built his younger brother Henry's small cocoa business into a major manufacturer of sweets, chocolate and cocoa, employing nearly 7,000 people by the time of his death. His Quaker faith motivated him to show a genuine concern for his employees and their welfare; Rowntrees was one of the earliest companies to develop a pension scheme, in 1906, and profit-sharing, in 1923.

Rowntree's Quakerism led him into various forms of social service and contact with York's poor, and his flair for accountancy, which partly lay behind the success of his company, was part of a passion for statistics which led him to collect figures about the wider context of social conditions. Although his son Seebohm's study of poverty in the York slums was to make

him better known as a social researcher, his work drew on Joseph's earlier studies of pauperism, illiteracy and crime. Like many late Victorian Nonconformists, Joseph was a total abstainer from alcohol and a passionate believer that drink was the major cause of poverty and misery.

Rowntree was a committed Liberal and, together with other members of his family and associates, effectively controlled the local association and the Liberal group on York council in the Edwardian era. Unlike many other wealthy Liberal businessmen, however, he did not give large sums to the party's central organisation, probably because he was not interested in securing any honours for himself or his family. Instead, he used his wealth to establish, in 1904, the three trusts that still bear his name, in the firm belief that money should be spent on projects of social use rather than for one man's benefit. The Joseph Rowntree Charitable Trust mainly concerned itself with grants to various Quaker activities, while the Joseph Rowntree Village Trust (now the Joseph Rowntree Foundation) was established initially to create a model housing estate, at New Earswick, as an ideal community of all classes.

The third of the trusts, the Joseph Rowntree Social Service Trust Ltd (now the Joseph Rowntree Reform Trust Ltd), was explicitly set up with a view to influencing political debate, and was deliberately not made a charity in order to pursue this goal. Rowntree was determined that the high-minded Liberal press should not be squeezed out by its Tory rivals, and the Trust's most famous acquisition was the weekly the *Nation*, which it owned from 1907 to 1923. Under its editor H. W. Massingham, it promoted not just liberalism, but the New Liberal (q.v.) social reform agenda that Rowntree supported; it effectively became the house journal of New Liberal intellectuals such as L. T. Hobhouse (q.v.) and J. A. Hobson (q.v.).

The Trust also bought and supported regional Liberal newspapers, such as the *Northern Echo* and *Yorkshire Gazette*, though a foray into Fleet Street was less happy. After heavy losses during the First World War, the Trust's newspapers were merged into the Westminster Group in 1921. After Seebohm became chairman of the Trust in 1938, he scaled down its subsidies to the papers and initiated direct grants to the ailing Liberal Party, starting a tradition that continues to this day and making the Trust the party's largest long-term benefactor in the post-1945 era.

The Trust also, however, continued its focus on social research. After the war, the Acton Society Trust was created to analyse the implications of the burgeoning welfare state for liberty and the individual. Support was also forthcoming for the development of the university in York.

The Trust's links with the Liberal Party were strengthened through some of the directors who were influential in the 1960s and '70s, including Richard Wainwright and Jo Grimond (q.v.), both Liberal MPs, and Pratap Chitnis, former head of the Liberal Party Organisation. In order to improve the quality of parliamentary opposition, in the early 1970s the Trust introduced a scheme for financing assistants for leading frontbenchers in the House of Commons. Known as the 'chocolate soldiers', most of the appointees were later to make significant contributions to public and parliamentary life. The Wilson government formally incorporated the scheme into the workings of the Commons in 1974.

In the 1970s the matter of media ownership and control was a major issue, and a number of pressure groups, concerned to defend the principle and standards of public service broadcasting, were brought together under the aegis of the Standing Conference on Broadcasting, which played an important part in the subsequent appointment of the (Annan) Royal Commission and its deliberations.

The Trust took on an international dimension when it initiated a series of grants to liberation movements in Africa; the political and welfare wings of such movements were assisted in Rhodesia, Mozambique and Guinea-Bissau. Similarly, fledgling democrats behind the Iron Curtain were later to receive grants, including Solidarity in Poland, for whom a printing machine was purchased.

Another successful innovation was the taking on of 9 Poland Street in the West End of London, to provide accommodation for many of the small single-issue pressure groups that were mushrooming at the time. Described in the press as the centre for 'the counter-civil service', 9 Poland Street provided a home for Friends of the Earth, the Low Pay Unit, the Campaign for Press and Broadcasting Freedom, the Tory Reform Group and the 300 Group, among many others.

Since the 1970s one of the main interests of the Trust has been constitutional reform. Progressive elements in most of the political parties in Britain have been assisted and many pressure groups aided in their endeavours – including the Scottish Constitutional Convention, which spearheaded the case for a Scottish Parliament, and Charter 88, the most successful pressure group of the 1990s, according to the *Sunday Telegraph*. A series of 'State of the Nation' surveys was initiated to monitor public opinion on a range of democratic issues.

Collaboration with the Joseph Rowntree Charitable Trust has extended to the struggle against racism and the re-emergence of extreme right-wing elements in

British politics, and the co-founding and funding of the Power Inquiry in 2004, which continues the efforts to foster and extend the realisation of a modern, inclusive participatory democracy in the UK.

Further reading

- Tony Flower, *Trusting in Change: A Story of Reform* (Joseph Rowntree Trust Ltd, 2004, available from www.jrrt.org.uk)
- Ian Packer, 'Joseph and Seebohm Rowntree', *Journal of Liberal History* 45 (winter 2004–05)

Trevor Smith

Immanuel Kant   1724–1804

Widely recognised as Germany's leading philosopher of the late Enlightenment and one of the most influential thinkers in Europe; some rank him among the greatest philosophers ever.

Key ideas

- Categorical imperative – a rule or command of the kind: 'Act only on that maxim by which you can at the same time will that it would become a universal law.'
- Hypothetical imperative – a practical law that states that something is good as a means to something else, rather than being a good in itself.
- Sapere aude! – the injunction to think for yourself; 'Have courage to use your own reason!'
- Synthetic truths a priori – truths regarding the empirical world that can be known independently of experience.

Biography

Immanuel Kant was born on 22 April 1724, in Königsberg, Prussia (now Kaliningrad in Russia), the fourth of the nine children of a craftsman and his wife. He became a student at the local Albertina University in 1740 and from his mid-twenties earned his living as a private tutor in and around his home town. After receiving his doctorate in 1755, Kant taught at his alma mater, but it was only in 1770 that he was appointed to the chair of logic and metaphysics. He joined the prestigious Academy of Sciences, but declined calls from other universities, preferring the peace and quiet of his native Königsberg. He suffered under the increasingly oppressive censorship of the Prussian monarchy after the death of Frederick the Great in 1786.

Kant steadily became a renowned local celebrity and an enormously popular lecturer. His famous punctuality and well-organised daily routine (citizens of Königsberg were supposed to have been able to set their clocks by his appearance for his daily walk) left the impression of a typical donnish Prussian, an image supported by his rigorous moral maxims, most notably his famous 'categorical imperative'. Although he spent his entire life in and around Königsberg, he was extremely well read; he corresponded with almost every renowned European thinker of his time and influenced many of them, especially Hegel (q.v.), Fichte and Schelling.

Kant never married, and died at the age of eighty, on 12 February 1804. His funeral was attended by thousands.

Ideas

Influenced by Copernicus and Newton, Kant developed his own cosmology (*Universal Natural History and Theory of Heaven*, 1755), which in turn led him to his so-called 'transcendental idealism' – perhaps a misleading term, because Kant never was an idealist, despite later claims for him as the first representative of German idealism (q.v.). He did not question reality, but used the term 'transcendental idealism' to characterise his view that space and time are forms of intuition rather than mind-independent features of reality. In his *De Mundi Sensiblis atque Intelligibilis Forma et Principiis* of 1770 we find the more general assumption that sensory experience is not about the things as they are in themselves, but as they appear to us as phenomena (as opposed to *noumena* – things as they are perceived by reason through cognition). The denial of empirically acquired synthetic knowledge of the world led Kant to assume some synthetic statements to be a priori true and made him move towards metaphysics. Synthetic statements are those that do not merely elucidate the meaning of the words by means of analysis, but that are informative and provide us with new knowledge; they do not merely highlight something that is already contained in a concept but add something new by connecting and synthesising different concepts.

His greatest work, *The Critique of Pure Reason* (1781), can be seen as the résumé of his aprioristic epistemology. In it, Kant proposed categories that allow for a priori true synthetic statement prior to all empirical experience. In a nutshell, Kant's epistemology is an attempt to bridge continental classical rationalism and Anglo-Saxon empiricism. Whether his attempt was convincing is disputed, to put it mildly. Kant himself conceded that he was initially awakened from his dogmatic slumber by David Hume (q.v.); many ridiculed his 'critical philosophy', i.e. his combination of Leibniz's rationalism and Hume's scepticism, by saying that he fell asleep again quickly afterwards. In *The Critique of Pure Reason* Kant outlines and defends his theory of transcendental thought. It incorporates rationalistic strands by allowing for synthetic a priori truths that can be known independently of experience, while at the same time avoiding the rationalistic dogmatism of Descartes and Leibniz by placing strict limits on knowledge insofar as the bounds of knowledge are set by the bounds of possible experience. Only that which can be a possible object of experience can be known to us and we are accordingly ignorant of that which transcends all experience. As a result, traditional disputes about the immortality of soul and the existence of God become moot since we are unable to settle them either way.

While his epistemological treatises still are hard to understand and usually intelligently debated only in scholarly circles, his ethical writings were and are studied by non-philosophers. The *Groundwork of the Metaphysics of Morals*, first published in 1785, became famous because of the 'categorical imperative' – later simplified by others as a secular version of the golden rule, i.e. the rule that you should do to others what you would have them do unto you. Though formulated in several ways by Kant, the most widely known definition of the categorical imperative runs as follows: 'Act only in that maxim by which you can at the same time will that it would become a universal law.'

It is this very idea of universalisability that has divided the adherents and opponents of Kant's moral theory. While defenders praise the relentlessness of Kant's principles, critics were and are alienated by some of its putative consequences – for instance that you should betray your friend to the bloodhounds if they are after him, because you wish the maxim 'to say the truth' to become a universal law without exemptions. While the categorical imperative remained questionable, his conception of the 'hypothetical imperative' as a rule for prudential behaviour was more readily adopted. The hypothetical imperative, of the form 'if you want to achieve A, you should do X', is, according to Kant, not justified in itself, but is a means to an end.

Rather than appealing to hypothetical imperatives, Kant argued that every man is an end and that one should act 'in such a way that you always treat humanity, whether in your own person or in the person of any other, never simply as a means, but always at the same time as an end'. On the basis of this guideline for all moral behaviour, he ended up with the idea that freedom (q.v.) is nothing else than the autonomy to set for oneself moral laws: 'Thus a free will and a will under moral law are one and the same.' Therefore, acting morally well is a duty, a duty perceived in the face of moral law. Moral laws in turn can be perceived by every man, in principle. Kant viewed the Enlightenment as the process whereby people begin to use their own reason to discover moral truths, rather than accepting moral rules dictated by an external authority. Kant's ethics thus provided for peaceful interactions among free individuals.

Kant's political philosophy can be placed in the tradition of classical liberalism (q.v.). In his *Metaphysics of Morals* (1796) he extensively explores the requirements for safeguarding property in a political body. Originally accepting Locke's (q.v.) theory of first possession, he later argued against legitimate appropriation via mixing unowned natural goods with one's labour. Kant concluded that labour may establish property in what it gives rise to but not in the material with which it was originally mixed. To Kant legitimate appropriation is caused by the exercise of man's will alone. However this idea is understood it should not be interpreted as opening the way to or justifying the Marxian labour theory of value.

Kant had little interest in economics and his economic views were dominated by his ethical convictions. (His admiration for Adam Smith (q.v.) was grounded in *The Theory of Moral Sentiments* rather than *The Wealth of Nations*.) Kant's view that man should be viewed as an end in itself gave rise to his reservations about the morality of human services. His application of his moral law may strike the modern reader as distinctly odd – making a distinction, for example, between those, such as barbers, who sell their services, and wig-makers, who sell a good. Although he considered that the distribution of goods arising from market exchange was probably unjust, Kant was not an advocate of redistribution, because it could not be reconciled with his universal moral law, which entailed the acceptance of private property.

Beside his main works, which were often hard to comprehend, Kant published many short booklets that contain plain but nevertheless influential ideas, such as the *Idea of a Universal History Based on the Principle of World-Citizenship*, *Response to the Question: What is Enlightenment?* (both 1784), *Groundwork of the Metaphysics of Morals* (1785), *On the Proverbial Saying: 'All Is Very Well in Theory, but No Good in Practice'* (1792) and *Perpetual Peace* (1795). The latter became famous for Kant's claim that democratic societies are less likely to enter into war. In the light of recent findings about the bellicosity of democracies this seems wishful thinking. However, there still seems to be much truth in Kant's well-known phrase that 'enlightenment is man's emergence from his self-imposed immaturity'.

Key works

- *Universal Natural History and Theory of the Heavens* (1755)
- *Inaugural Dissertation on the Form and Principles of the Sensible and Intelligible World* (1770)
- *Critique of Pure Reason* (1781)

- *Idea of a Universal History Based on the Principle of World-Citizenship* (1784)
- *Response to the Question: What Is Enlightenment?* (1784)
- *Groundwork of the Metaphysics of Morals* (1785)
- *Critique of Practical Reason* (1788)
- *Critique of Judgement* (1790)
- *Perpetual Peace* (1795)
- *Metaphysics of Morals* (1796)

Further reading

- Henry E. Allison, *Kant's Theory of Freedom* (Cambridge University Press, 1990)
- Paul Guyer (ed.), *The Cambridge Companion to Kant* (Cambridge University Press, 1996)
- Manfred Kuehn, *Kant: A Biography* (Cambridge University Press, 2001)
- Hans Sauer, *Kant's Political Thought: Its Origins and Development*, trans. E. B. Ashton (University of Chicago Press, 1973)
- Susan Meld Shell, *The Rights of Reason: A Study of Kant's Philosophy and Politics* (University of Toronto Press, 1980)
- Howard Williams, *Kant's Political Philosophy* (Basil Blackwell, 1985)

Hardy Bouillon

John Maynard Keynes 1883–1946

The most influential and important economic thinker of the twentieth century, Keynes's most important academic works were concerned not only with challenging accepted economic theory but also with finding solutions to real economic problems; his ideas came to underpin the post-war economic strategy of Western governments. He was an active Liberal and contributed to Lloyd George's reshaping of Liberal Party policy in the 1920s; he also helped to found the Liberal Summer School.

Key ideas

- Human decision-making under uncertainty is necessarily based on subjective expectations of utility (this reflects the fact that human beings lack a sound basis for calculating probabilities).
- Economic recovery from war requires great magnanimity in order to fashion a programme of economic assistance and cooperation that serves the best interests of victors and vanquished alike.
- A stable world requires the strong to help the weak, and intelligent international cooperation is essential in order to build the foundations for general prosperity and diminish the risks of future conflict.
- It is possible that where an economy's aggregate output is below its potential, it will suffer an extended period of high unemployment and depressed output; public policy should therefore be designed so that government is equipped to raise effective demand in such circumstances.
- The need for an international reserve currency, managed by an international clearing union.

Biography

John Maynard Keynes was born in Cambridge on 5 June 1883. His father, John Neville Keynes, was a Cambridge don who taught logic and economics; his mother, Florence, was an author and social reformer and the first woman to be elected to Cambridge Borough Council; she became mayor of Cambridge in 1932. While John Maynard, the eldest of the Keynes children, had no children of his own, his brother, Geoffrey, and sister, Margaret, continued a family line that includes many distinguished academics and researchers.

Educated initially at Eton, Keynes graduated from King's College, Cambridge in 1906. He was a physically striking man, standing over 6′ 5″ tall. He had limited regard for social convention, and became one of the best-known members of the Bloomsbury group, which included Virginia Woolf, Clive Bell, E. M. Forster and Duncan Grant, the painter, with whom Keynes had an intimate personal relationship in his twenties. He later married the Russian ballerina Lydia Lopokova, with whom he appears to have had a happy marriage.

Keynes was first employed at the India Office, but in 1908 became a fellow of King's College with responsibility for teaching economics (established as a subject there in 1905). He joined the Treasury in January 1915 and advised Lloyd George (q.v.) on war finance and at the Versailles peace settlement negotiations until his dramatic resignation over the terms of the settlement in 1919.

His academic work as a Cambridge economist did not prevent him from pursuing a wide range of other interests. He was an avid collector of books and an exceptionally generous supporter of the arts, most notably as a patron of the Cambridge Arts Theatre, which, with his support, became one of the most successful provincial theatres in Britain. It was his success as an investor that enabled him to fund such artistic endeavours, a success he shared with his Cambridge college, King's, as the manager of its investment portfolio. He left King's one of the best-endowed university institutions in Britain.

Keynes was noted as a keen controversialist and rarely passed up opportunities to engage in public debate. His reputation is said to have dissuaded Friedrich von Hayek (q.v.) from meeting him to debate economic theory and policy. Bertrand Russell, no mean debater, regarded Keynes as the most intelligent person he had known, observing: 'Every time I argued with Keynes, I felt I was taking my life in my hands.' Keynes's broad range of interests and willingness to become directly involved in the formulation of public policy reflected a highly instrumental view of economics, which he regarded, for all its intellectual fascination, as subordinate to the pursuit of the good life. The role of economics was to help create and maintain the conditions in which human beings could live truly civilised, creative and passionate lives.

In the final years of his life Keynes became a prominent public figure. He was the leading economic adviser to the British Treasury in 1940–46, and Britain's most important international representative in economic matters; this was despite a marked decline in his health in 1938. He was made a peer in 1942, taking the title Baron Keynes of Tilton.

Keynes headed the British delegation to the Bretton Woods talks in 1944, where he presented his own proposals for an international reserve currency. Although his ideas for an international clearing union were not accepted, Bretton Woods led to the establishment of the World Bank, the International Monetary Fund and the General Agreement on Tariffs and Trade (GATT), laying the foundations for an international financial and trading system that contributed strongly to post-war prosperity. Keynes's enormous personal effort in helping to shape the post-war international economic architecture almost certainly contributed to his death, on 21 April 1946.

Ideas

Any assessment of Keynes's contribution to the development of economic thought is certain to be contested. He has been described as the founder of macroeconomics, and a revolutionary thinker who saved capitalism from itself. His critics, amongst them some of the world's best-known liberal economists, most especially Hayek and Milton Friedman (q.v.), have argued that Keynes founded a school of economic thought that encouraged extravagant government intervention in economic life and promoted an approach to economics that was not only fundamentally illiberal but ultimately self-defeating. Keynes's many admirers strongly disagree, arguing that he upheld the finest of liberal traditions: a willingness to learn when things go wrong and change and adapt economic theory and policy in the light of changing circumstances.

Keynes's mathematical abilities were recognised early in his school career. He was encouraged by his teachers to specialise exclusively in mathematics, but rejected this advice and pursued interests in monetary reform as well as probability theory. The former led to his first book, published in 1913, on *Indian Currency*, and the latter, many years after his student work on the subject had been completed, to the *Treatise on Probability* (1921). This work not only issued a remarkable challenge to classical probability theory but also provided the foundations for much of his later economic theorising in which uncertainty plays a central role. What has been described by Will Hutton as Keynes's shocking finding that 'capitalist economic systems are inherently unstable' is a notion strongly linked to and dependent on his earlier work on probability theory; it is one the most poorly appreciated aspects of his economic thought.

Keynes's determination to undertake work that not only interested him but was strongly linked to practical questions of policy won him a substantial and appreciative public audience. In 1919 he published *The Economic Consequences of the Peace*, a fiery denunciation of what he regarded as the folly of the Allies' approach to the Versailles Treaty. He argued that their insistence on punitive levels of war reparations would ruin the German economy and contribute to future international instability.

Keynes's place as a leading British economist had been assured some years earlier by his appointment as the editor of the *Economic Journal* in 1912. He followed the noted economic theorist F. Y. Edgeworth in holding the post, and retained it until March 1945. It was a position that gave him immense influence, reinforced when, in 1913, the role of editor was combined with that of secretary to the Royal Economic Society. Nevertheless, in the inter-war years, Keynes found himself increasingly at odds with many members of Britain's political, financial and economic establishments.

Keynes's academic reputation was secured by his *Tract on Monetary Reform* (1923), in which he declared his support for flexible exchange rates. Soon afterwards he publicly nailed his colours to the mast as a forthright critic of laissez-faire (q.v.) and an opponent of Britain's return to the gold standard. His growing belief in the need for more government intervention in the economy was reflected in his membership of Lloyd George's Liberal Industrial Inquiry (1926–28), and his considerable contribution to its outcome: *Britain's Industrial Future*, the famous Liberal 'Yellow Book' (1928). It advocated a substantial increase in public spending to stimulate economic activity and reduce unemployment. Keynes also contributed to the 1929 Liberal manifesto, and published the pamphlet *Can Lloyd George Do It?*, which appeared just before the 1929 election to explain the party's approach to reducing unemployment. He was one of the most important moving spirits in establishing and supporting the Liberal Summer School (q.v.), and Chairman of the (Liberal) *Nation and Athenaeum* until he arranged its merger with the *New Statesman* in 1931.

Keynes's academic renown and involvement in public controversy seem to have been mutually reinforcing; his publication of a two-volume *Treatise on Money* in 1930, for example, which set out his theory of the credit cycle, attracted a good deal of criticism from eminent members of the economics profession, among them Hayek. However, Keynes enjoyed the enthusiastic support of a rising generation of economists, a group known as 'the circus', mostly made up of young Cambridge economists, including Richard Kahn, James Meade, Austin Robinson, Joan Robinson and Piero Sraffa. They worked to help him revise and strengthen his new economic theories. Kahn has been credited with providing Keynes with several of the critical insights that enabled him to write his most famous work of economic theory, *The General Theory of Employment, Interest and Money* (1936). Kahn proposed an income–expenditure multiplier that appeared to offer Keynes a way of overcoming many of the objections raised to his notion of failures in aggregate demand. It was one of a number of theoretical developments that helped Keynes to explain weak demand and account for its damaging consequences for the economy as a whole.

The *General Theory* was truly revolutionary. Controversial at the time, Keynes described the economic system as a whole in a way that clearly implied that governments could and should intervene to mitigate the consequences of low levels of economic activity, most especially unemployment. He showed that the price system could not necessarily be relied upon to achieve an equilibrium that made full use of the human resources available to an economy; aggregate demand reflected such things as uncertainty and shifting human expectations. Economic unpredictability

and human responses to it were fundamental to an understanding of capitalist economies. Human behaviour, Keynes asserted, did not always accord with the market-clearing assumptions of classical or neo-classical economics. He also argued that a realistic model of the economy needed to take account of the 'stickiness' of prices in the labour market and fluctuating preferences for holding money. The notion of 'liquidity preference', and its importance in accounting for changes in effective demand, provided him with yet another way of taking issue with the assumptions that underpinned the work of his neo-classical opponents. Although many of his ideas have been greatly modified and absorbed into a modern neo-classical synthesis, Keynes was recognised as the creator of a new branch of economics: macroeconomics. His ideas – labelled 'Keynesianism' (q.v.) – came to underpin the post-war economic strategy of Western governments for three decades.

Keynes was also the author of proposals for the *bancor*, an international reserve currency, together with an international clearing union to manage it. His proposals were designed to facilitate international trade by entrenching a system of stable exchange rates and balanced trade. His attempts at Bretton Woods, in 1944, to persuade his American counterparts of the need for such a system met with only partial success; a fervent internationalist, he had to settle for what he regarded as very much second best. Nevertheless, he helped lay the foundations for the international economic system that made it possible to consolidate the peace and build post-war prosperity through rapid growth in international trade.

John Maynard Keynes was, in the words of one biographer, 'born into a traditional haute bourgeois Cambridge academic family'. The economist, Harry Johnson, in his assessment of Keynes's economic thought, concluded that his social origins and path in life helped instil an extraordinary self-confidence and optimism in him that were strongly reflected in his work as an economist: Keynes was born to believe that government – in the hands of the right men and women – could lead the rest of humanity to a much better place. Johnson compared Keynes with Milton Friedman, the 'scion of penniless emigrants from the Hapsburg Empire', who was, understandably, a sceptic and pessimist when it came to judging what governments, as opposed to individuals, could be expected to achieve. Personal outlook and style are undoubtedly important factors in shaping the ways in which different individuals espouse and express their political beliefs. Keynes's liberalism was much more than an expression of his party allegiance or even his economic views; his social position, enormous appetite for friendship, conversation and the arts, not just his prodigious talent, were all reflected in the way he lived his life and gave expression to his political beliefs.

Key works

- *Indian Currency* (1913)
- *The Economic Consequences of the Peace* (1919)
- *Treatise on Probability* (1921)
- *Tract on Monetary Reform* (1923)
- *Am I a Liberal?* (1925)
- *Treatise on Money* (1930)
- *The General Theory of Employment, Interest and Money* (1936)
- *How to Pay for the War* (1940)
- *Essays in Persuasion* (Royal Economic Society and Macmillan Press, 1972)

Further reading

- Roy Harrod, *The Life of John Maynard Keynes* (Norton, 1982)
- Robert Skidelsky, *John Maynard Keynes 1883–1946: Economist, Philosopher,*

Statesman (compiled and abridged single-volume edition, Macmillan, 2003)

Ed Randall

Keynes Forum *see* Liberal Summer School

Keynesianism

A school of economic thought inspired by the work of John Maynard Keynes, especially his *General Theory of Employment, Interest and Money*. Keynes's challenge to the ideas underpinning classical and neo-classical economics, and in particular to the proposition that market economies would always find an equilibrium consistent with the highest possible level of economic output, became the foundation for macroeconomics, and Keynesian ideas came to underpin the economic policy of Western governments for the three decades following the Second World War.

In the *General Theory*, first published in 1936, John Maynard Keynes (q.v.) challenged the majority of his peers in the economics profession, who had steadfastly rejected his notion that there was any need for a branch of economics that distinguished between the behaviour of individual economic actors and the operation of the economy as a whole.

Keynesians generally support the following three propositions: (a) aggregate demand plays a central role in determining the level of real output; (b) economies can remain for a long period in a state where there is substantial under-utilisation of both capital and labour; and (c) government, principally though not exclusively through its fiscal policies, can influence aggregate demand and thus help bring about significant reductions in unemployment.

Keynesianism came to dominate economic policy-making after 1945 when the reflationary actions of the US government, principally designed to boost the production of munitions and weapons, appeared to confirm Keynes's theoretical arguments about the fundamental importance of government taking the initiative in overcoming failures in aggregate demand. The general acceptance of the three Keynesian propositions seemed to have been confirmed when Richard Nixon observed that 'we are all Keynesians now'. However, critics of Keynesianism, most notably the American economist Milton Friedman (q.v.), began a counter-revolution in economic thought that attracted political leaders and economic policy-makers from the mid-1970s onwards, including James Callaghan and Margaret Thatcher in Britain, whose statements and policy decisions appeared to reject all or part of Keynesianism.

British economic policy-makers were confronted in the 1970s by 'stagflation': low or no growth accompanied by inflation. This was taken as evidence that Keynesian policies for combating unemployment could no longer be expected to work. Friedman argued that government action to boost demand in order to reduce unemployment below its 'natural rate' was counter-productive: it would simply raise inflation and add to inflationary expectations in economies.

The counter-revolutionary policy prescriptions offered by Friedman and his colleagues were tested (some say to destruction) in Britain, where the Conservative governments of the 1980s adopted a monetarist strategy. They failed, however, to produce either the stable monetary environment or the economic recovery that had been expected. Friedman himself declared, in June 2003, that 'use of the quantity of money as a target has not been a success ... I'm not sure I would as of today push it as hard as I once did'.

Keynesianism has enjoyed something of a revival since the 1980s, although it has undergone considerable development and reformulation in an effort to integrate Keynes's theoretical ideas about the operation of the economic system as a whole with classical and neo-classical ideas about the behaviour of individual consumers and producers. In particular, Keynesians have accepted that while human beings are not perfectly rational, human behaviour sufficiently approximates rational behaviour – of the kind hypothesised by economists – so that it is possible to develop models of the economy that can handle long lags between changes in output, employment rates, inflation and interest rates.

Some Keynesians have tried to take account of the growth of international trade and increasing economic interdependence in their economic theorising, and to make the case for internationally coordinated economic policy treating the whole world as a single global economic system. Whether their economic and political ambitions have any real prospect of success is arguable. Perhaps the most important element of the Keynesian legacy is the conclusion that market economies are inherently unstable and that there can be no guarantee that they will, unaided, find a balance that makes full use of the economic resources, including labour, that are available to them. What Will Hutton has described as Keynes's 'very shocking' finding – that capitalist economic systems are inherently unstable – is rightly regarded as a watershed in the development of economic thought.

Further reading
- Will Hutton, *The Revolution That Never Was: An Assessment of Keynesian Economics* (Vintage, 2001)

- John Maynard Keynes, *The General Theory of Employment, Interest and Money* (1936)
- Charles P. Kindleberger, *Keynesianism vs Monetarism* (Routledge, 2005)

Ed Randall

Will Kymlicka   1962–

The author of several major works of normative political theory, his work on culture and group rights has strongly influenced the development of liberal theory and contemporary debate about liberal notions of equality, autonomy, and justice.

Key ideas

- Support for liberal egalitarianism, rather than classical liberalism or libertarianism.
- Preference for personal autonomy over 'negative' freedom.
- Recognition of cultural membership as a prerequisite for personal autonomy.
- Liberal states should afford 'group rights' to cultural groups.
- Distinction between and importance of 'external protections' and 'internal restrictions'.

Biography

Will Kymlicka was born in Winnipeg, Canada on 22 October 1962. His parents moved almost immediately from Winnipeg to London, western Ontario, where his father was a professor in politics at the University of Western Ontario. Kymlicka grew up and went to elementary and secondary school in London, before going on to Queen's University (Kingston, Ontario) to study for his first degree. He subsequently travelled to Oxford University to pursue graduate studies. After lecturing in Canada, the US and Europe he became the Canada Research Professor in Political Philosophy at Queen's University, in 2003.

Ideas

At the time of Kymlicka's first book, *Liberalism, Community, and Culture* (1989), egalitarian liberal theory – most closely associated with the work of John Rawls (q.v.) – was attracting significant criticism from a growing communitarian movement. Kymlicka's aim was to resolve the tension between liberalism and communitarianism by arguing that culture should be understood as one of Rawls's 'primary goods' (one of the background conditions that needs to be satisfied if individuals are to lead valuable and rewarding lives and pursue goals they have chosen for themselves). Kymlicka claimed that culture provided the 'context of choice' in which individuals were enabled to decide what was and was not worthwhile.

The notion of a 'context of choice' underpins Kymlicka's criticisms of classical liberal (q.v.) and libertarian (q.v.) conceptions of freedom (q.v.); it also has important implications for public policy. Philosophically, it suggests that the 'negative' conception of freedom is inadequate because it severely and arbitrarily restricts the kinds of choices and circumstances conducive to advancing individual freedom. Choices made by individuals who have been divorced from their culture, and hence the framework of values and meanings that shape their human understanding of what is worthwhile, cannot be said to be autonomous.

Politically, Kymlicka's claims about the links between autonomy and culture imply that liberal states should protect cultural minorities from any requirement to 'assimilate' to the wider political community. If liberalism is committed to securing individual autonomy for all members of society, and one's membership of a secure, historically resilient cultural group is crucial to one's autonomy, then it follows that liberal states should do what they can to allow different cultures to flourish.

Kymlicka's theory was received as a new and subtle attempt to dissolve the liberal–communitarian debate. By showing that a broadly communitarian understanding of community and culture was necessary to realising the core liberal principles of freedom and autonomy, Kymlicka was able to strengthen the case for egalitarian liberalism while addressing the complaints of critics who argued that liberalism presupposed an atomistic society of unencumbered selves. However, Kymlicka's claims about culture and freedom invited many questions. How, for example, might we define a *cultural* group as distinct from any other kind of group? Is it really true that membership of a cultural group contributes to personal autonomy? What about groups that reject core liberal values and *deny* the importance of personal autonomy; or groups requiring individual members to show an absolute, unquestioning, obedience to cultural or religious norms? The existence of religious and cultural groups that strongly discourage personal autonomy and embody deeply patriarchal norms and practices was not in dispute. How could members of such groups be said to be more autonomous by virtue of their group membership? Wouldn't individual members of such groups be better off, from a liberal perspective, if they were encouraged to break away and live utterly different kinds of lives?

Kymlicka's responses to these and other questions are found in his book *Multicultural Citizenship* (1995). The cultures Kymlicka is most interested in defending are national or *societal* cultures – i.e. 'an intergenerational community, more or less institutionally complete, occupying a given territory or homeland, sharing a distinct language and history'. Kymlicka believes that immigrant members of diverse 'polyethnic' societies such as Britain and the US will inevitably become integrated into the wider political community as they learn the language, absorb wider norms and practices, and avail themselves of the benefits of living in the wider community. The measures needed to secure meaningful cultural membership for immigrants will be modest, as the culture to which they belong adapts and changes and participation in the wider community increases. Members of minority groups have a duty to integrate because they chose to join an already-existing society. However, real problems can arise when minority groups, with a strong sense of identity and a distinct history, aspire to nationhood and are thwarted. From the Basques in Spain and the Québecois in Canada, to indigenous peoples in Australia and elsewhere, he says, there is evidence of groups whose claim to a distinct national identity goes unrecognised and remains unsatisfied. Such peoples are, at least potentially, being robbed of the societal culture they need to be autonomous. In such circumstances their shared nationality should be recognised by the states in which they live and they should enjoy political autonomy.

Kymlicka's argument for culture is, ultimately, an argument for nation-states and against those univeralist liberals and cosmopolitans who downplay the importance of national boundaries and cultures in their quest for universal liberal values. This raises the question of how liberalism should respond to cultures or nations that do not respect liberal values. Do groups that flout liberal principles, undermine personal freedom and demonstrate indifference to notions of fairness, nevertheless have a claim to cultural protections of the kind Kymlicka advocates? Kymlicka thinks not. He makes a critical distinction between groups which practice 'internal restrictions' and those which require 'external protections'. Liberal states, he believes, have a duty to recognise and protect cultures which are subject to external pressures: social and political pressures to conform that threaten a distinctive way of life. Laws should not undermine the rights of members of minority groups to practice their beliefs freely and openly. Indeed, states have a duty to lift external restraints on the practice of cultural beliefs, providing such practices do not contravene broadly liberal principles. However, there is no duty to facilitate illiberal cultural practices or norms which impose 'internal restrictions' on their members. Consequently, while liberal states have a duty to ensure that members of religious minorities are not denied the same opportunities as other members of the community, on account of their observance of cultural beliefs, they do not have a duty to uphold such cultural practices as ritual scarring, or overtly sexist practices which undermine equal dignity or freedom. The distinction between the wearing of turbans by Sikhs when riding motorbikes, and the circumcision of girls and young women, appears clear from this perspective.

This last point has led critics to question how genuine Kymlicka's commitment to culture and cultural diversity really is. After all, his position on illiberal cultures seems to suggest that it is not membership of a culture *in and of itself* that is crucial to individual autonomy, but membership of a culture which respects and encourages individual autonomy. This appears tautological: cultural membership is important to individual autonomy only if that culture respects individual autonomy. Some critics have suggested that in differentiating

between cultures Kymlicka's defence of culture is rendered hollow. The real challenge for liberal theory, it has been argued, remains formulating a liberal response to cultures that reject or contravene liberal principles.

Key works
- *Liberalism, Community, and Culture* (Oxford University Press, 1989)
- *Multicultural Citizenship* (Oxford University Press, 1995)
- *Contemporary Political Philosophy* (Oxford University Press, 2nd edn., 2002)

Phil Parvin

Laissez-faire

The French words *laisser faire* mean 'to let things go their own way' or 'to leave things alone'. In the realm of politics and economics, laissez-faire refers to economic liberalism's general preference for individual initiative and free markets over central planning and state intervention. It is based on the belief that the economy produces the maximum well-being for individuals and society if governmental policy does not disturb the proper functioning of the market mechanism.

The term 'laissez-faire' was first used by the Physiocrats (a group of economists who argued that wealth derived from productive work, chiefly in agriculture) in the eighteenth century, to contrast their new liberal creed from the then orthodox doctrines of mercantilism that favoured an active role for the state in directing trade and industry (see Adam Smith). In this original meaning, laissez-faire simply denotes liberalism's general belief in the greater efficiency of free markets in guiding production and consumption through the operation of the price mechanism. In this sense, all liberals can be said to subscribe to the basic idea of a laissez-faire economy. As Adam Smith argued in his *Wealth of Nations* (1776), if individuals are left to pursue their own personal preferences, the market will order their interactions to promote both individual gain and the common good, as if they were guided by an 'invisible hand'.

Laissez-faire ideas strongly resonated with nineteenth-century liberal thinkers such as Jeremy Bentham (q.v.) and John Stuart Mill (q.v.), who emphasised the concept's close connection with individualism and utilitarian (q.v.) ethics. Applied to the realm of international relations, liberals also advocated a system of laissez-faire as the best way to deter war and secure peace. Richard Cobden (q.v.) and others popularised the 'peace-through-trade' idea in their campaign to repeal Britain's Corn Laws, arguing that free trade (q.v.) would increase economic interdependence between societies and promote their mutual interest in world peace.

Although gaining widespread recognition in the second half of the nineteenth century, laissez-faire principles were never fully applied even in Britain. The rise of the New Liberalism (q.v.) at the beginning of the twentieth century gave way to a modified liberal tradition that envisaged a larger role for the state in economic and social affairs. Economic non-interventionism continued to shape governmental policy in Europe and North America but suffered a severe blow from the economic crisis of the 1920s and 1930s, which was widely blamed on inadequate governmental responses to the economic dislocations caused by the First World War. The Great Depression helped to usher in a new era of macroeconomic stabilisation and welfare policies, culminating in Roosevelt's New Deal (q.v.) and the rise of the welfare state in Europe.

Ideas associated with the laissez-faire tradition in economic policy made a comeback in the 1960s and 1970s, though more in conservative than liberal circles. Led by liberal thinkers such as Friedrich Hayek (q.v.) and Milton Friedman (q.v.), the revival of neo-liberal (q.v.) economics helped to undermine the Keynesian (q.v.) consensus in economic policy and provided the intellectual basis for the neo-liberal policy reforms under Margaret Thatcher in the UK and Ronald Reagan in the US. Laissez-faire ideas were less successful elsewhere in Europe, but have contributed significantly to the growing acceptance of privatisation and trade liberalisation policies around the world.

Further reading
- Milton Friedman, *Capitalism and Freedom* (University of Chicago Press, 1962)
- David Harvey, *A Brief History of Neo-Liberalism* (Oxford University Press, 2005)
                                    Robert Falkner

Walter Layton   1884–1966

Best known as a major figure in inter-war journalism, Layton was also an influential thinker in inter-war liberalism, with his ideas on 'interdependency' particularly important.

Key ideas
- The 'interdependency' of the world with regard to social, cultural and economic issues, its relationship to free trade, and the need to develop political institutions to match such links.
- European unity post-1945 as a fulfilment of his commitment to political interdependency.
- The relationship between wages and prices and their impact on the wider economy.

Biography

Walter Thomas Layton was born on 15 March 1884, in Chelsea, to musician parents. After gaining a third in history at University College, London, Layton enjoyed greater success in economics at Cambridge, gaining a double first in 1907. Over the next seven years, he combined a Cambridge fellowship with lecturing at UCL and for the Workers' Educational Association. At the same time, he was an assistant editor of *The Economist*, and wrote his first and best-known book, *An Introduction to the Study of Prices* (1912), a ground-breaking study of the link between wages and prices.

In 1914 Layton joined the wartime civil service, eventually participating in the negotiations over the military and economic clauses of the Treaty of Versailles. Layton had acquired an international reputation as an economist statistician, which led to brief post-war positions with the Iron and Steel Federation and as director of the Economic and Financial Section of the League of Nations. He then moved full time to journalism as editor of *The Economist* in 1922–38 and, in 1930–40 and 1944–50, as chairman of the *News Chronicle* and the *Star*. Under Layton's hands-on editorship, *The Economist* acquired a reputation for authority on international economic issues. During this time he was one of the founders of the Liberal Summer School (q.v.) and he remained a key figure in its work throughout the inter-war years.

Layton was an unsuccessful Liberal parliamentary candidate for Burnley (1922), Cardiff South (1923), and London University (1929), but his journalism put him at the heart of national Liberal politics, and brought influence on wider political and public opinion. He even advised the Conservatives on India in 1927–29, and Labour on reparations in 1929–31. Layton's highest-profile role in developing Liberal policy was as chairman of the Executive Committee of the Liberal Industrial Inquiry, which produced the 'Yellow Book' of 1928. In this, Layton did not so much provide the ideas as the contacts and drive which underpinned the project.

During the Second World War, Layton was again a civil servant, working principally on planning and production issues. He resigned in 1943, partly due to his health, but also to speak publicly about war aims, and returned to *The Economist* and the *News Chronicle* in 1944, where he was a keen supporter both of the United Nations and European unity. As Baron Layton from 1947, he was Liberal spokesman on economic affairs and the Council of Europe, and in 1952–55, was deputy Liberal leader in the Lords.

Layton died on 14 February 1966 in Putney. He had married (Eleanor) Dorothea Osmaston (1887–1959), with whom he had seven children (three sons and four daughters).

Ideas

Layton's influence on Liberal thought stemmed from a number of sources. He was a regular speaker at meetings of both the Liberal Summer School and the National Liberal Federation. His most important work was his writing on international policy in *The Economist*, especially with the idea of 'interdependency'. Layton was not remarkable as a Liberal in supporting free trade, but his particular take on the issue was that that free trade was effective because the world was interdependent. In promoting this idea, *The Economist* was a valuable platform, and the first clear statement on 'interdependency' in any publication of the time came in a leader article written by Layton in April 1929. Layton was responding to recent criticisms of free trade (q.v.), attacking the concept as a 'political Shibboleth', possibly relevant to the nineteenth century, but no longer valid. Layton argued in response: 'Circumstances, it is true, have changed since the nineteenth century. But the main trend of change is in the direction of the enormously greater interdependence of nations; and the trend has served, not to destroy, but to reinforce every argument against trade restriction.'

While it was not new to see *The Economist* arguing the free trade case, it was less common for anyone to be justifying it on the basis of an 'interdependence of nations' that went beyond economics to include politics and culture. The implications of this for foreign policy were twofold for Layton: first, governments must maintain a tariff-free economic policy; second, the League of Nations must develop. As Layton argued in *The Economist*: 'It is only possible to develop a policy of political cooperation between nations if there is some degree of economic cooperation. Free Trade in economic affairs is the counterpart of the work of the League of Nations in political matters. They stand as a joint policy against the alternatives of Protection, competition in armaments and aggressive nationalism.'

Layton and *The Economist* returned to interdependency in several leader articles throughout the economic crisis of 1929–31. In October 1930, when free trade still prevailed, at least in British policy, a leader article argued that the 'supreme difficulty of our generation' was 'that our achievements on the economic plane of life have outstripped our progress on the political plane to such an extent that our economics and our politics are perpetually out of gear with one another'. This remained the core of the interdependency argument.

Layton was not the only Liberal figure to promote the idea of 'interdependency'. Ramsay Muir (q.v.) was a major proponent, but Layton developed it first, provided it with an intellectual foundation, and gave

it a solid platform of publicity. Through *The Economist*, Layton showed how political and economic issues were related, and how the emergence of a global economic system had important implications for the political organisation of the world; this informed his commitment to European unity after the Second World War. That approach has remained at the heart of Liberal policy from Layton's day until the present.

Key works
- *An Introduction to the Study of Prices* (1912)
- *The Relations of Capital and Labour* (1914)
- *The British Commonwealth and World Order* (1944)
- *How to Deal with Germany: A Plan for European Peace* (1945)

Further reading
- Ruth Dudley Edwards, *The Pursuit of Reason:* The Economist, *1843–1993* (Hamish Hamilton, 1993)
- Richard S. Grayson, *Liberals, International Relations and Appeasement: The Liberal Party, 1919–39* (Frank Cass, 2001)
- David Hubback, *No Ordinary Press Baron: A Life of Walter Layton* (Weidenfeld & Nicolson, 1985)

Richard S. Grayson

League of Nations Union and United Nations Association

Founded in 1918, the League of Nations Union was a significant part of the inter-war peace movement in the UK, playing a role both in political campaigns and education, working in support of the goals of the League of Nations, and informing the policy of the Liberal Party. Its defining moment was the organisation of the 'peace ballot' in 1934–35. It transferred its membership to the United Nations Association in 1945.

The League of Nations Union was formed in 1918 from the merger of the League of Nations Society and League of Free Nations Association. It operated as a pressure group in support of the ideals of the League of Nations. To this end it sought to influence British public opinion and government policy so that a League-based approach would be at the heart of British foreign policy in the 1920s and 1930s. Robert Cecil, Viscount Cecil of Chelwood (1864–1958) was its president from 1923 to 1945, during which time he sat in the House of Lords as a Conservative, and was a Cabinet minister in 1924–27. Notwithstanding Cecil, one of the Union's great successes was in influencing the Liberal Party's policy and there was often little to distinguish the LNU from the party. Gilbert Murray (q.v.), a leading classical scholar and Liberal, was chairman of the LNU's executive council in 1923–38, and was also president of the United Nations Association in 1945–57.

By 1931, the Union had over 3,000 local branches and more than 400,000 individual members. The peak of its activity came in 1934–35 with the 'peace ballot'. Over a period of eight months, LNU members canvassed 38 per cent of the UK's adult population, and found that 95 per cent of those said that they were in favour of the League of Nations. Economic sanctions against aggressors were backed by 87 per cent and military sanctions by 54 per cent. It is widely believed that these results influenced the government's decision to impose economic sanctions on Italy after the invasion of Abyssinia in October 1935.

As rearmament and collective security became more widely advocated among progressives in the late 1930s, however, the LNU struggled to retain support. When the United Nations came into existence in 1945, a new body, the United Nations Association, was formed to provide support for the UN cause in the UK in the same way as the LNU had done for the League. The LNU transferred its membership to the UNA, though it remained in operation for financial reasons until the mid-1970s when it was wound up.

The UNA has never aroused public enthusiasm in the way that the LNU did in its heyday, but it remains active. The Association aims to lobby the UK government and educate the public in support of the UN, for example by helping to organise 'model UN' events. It has four current policy programmes: implementation of the UN Millennium Development Goals; peace, security and disarmament; human rights and humanitarian affairs; and UN reform.

Further reading

- Donald S. Birn, *The League of Nations Union, 1918–45* (Clarendon Press, 1981)
- Martin Ceadel, *Semi-Detached Idealists: the British Peace Movement and International Relations, 1854–1945* (Oxford University Press, 2000)
- Martin Ceadel, 'The First British Referendum: The Peace Ballot, 1934–35', *English Historical Review*, 95 (1980)
- United Nations Association: www.una-uk.org

Richard S. Grayson

Liberal Democracy

Liberal democracy, otherwise known as constitutional and representative democracy, is the form of government espoused by liberals. Many liberal thinkers, including John Stuart Mill, recognised the dangers inherent to democracy stemming from poorly educated electors, tyrannous majorities and demagogues. They therefore argued for democratic forms of government to be accompanied by limits to state power, protection of individual rights, the separation of powers, and an active political culture with an educated and engaged electorate. Mill's hope was that democratic government would prosper in a liberal society and that liberty and democracy would become and remain mutually reinforcing: a liberal democracy.

The defining characteristic of democratic society is that 'the people' decide. Of course such a definition of democracy begs all kinds of questions, not least who are 'the people'? and what do 'the people' really decide?

Governments in 'democratic societies', including the member states of the European Union, amongst whom the commitment to democracy is a defining characteristic, claim that they possess legitimacy and political authority because 'the people', typically defined as the whole of the adult population (with some exclusions) are entitled and empowered to decide who enters government.

However, the majority of electors believe (and are surely right to believe) that their direct and personal influence over government is vanishingly small. Democracies are, in recognition of the occasional and highly attenuated influence that individual electors exercise through the ballot box, said to be representative rather than direct democracies. Indeed, beyond the act of voting, modern democracies, including liberal democracies, operate with very small numbers of people – elected representatives and government officials – becoming deeply involved in the business of government.

Political theorists, including the distinguished writer on democracy Robert A. Dahl, recognise that most modern states are simply too large, and public policy-making too complex, to involve more than

a very small number of people directly in the detailed formulation, approval and implementation of public policy. It is for this reason that the political authority and legitimacy of those who govern is said to rest primarily on the results of elections, in which rival teams of would-be representatives compete for the people's votes. Yet, while fair and free elections are generally regarded as the linchpin of legitimate democratic government, it is important to acknowledge that in recent years the electoral processes at the heart of democratic societies have often become the focus of intense criticism, including in particular their failure to motivate, inform and accurately reflect the wishes of their citizens.

While liberals have long been supporters of democracy their support has almost always been qualified and conditional: liberty, rather than democracy, is the core liberal value. The anxiety that the great liberal thinkers, such as John Stuart Mill (q.v.) and James Madison (see Federalists), expressed about the possibility that democracy might extinguish liberty led them to invest considerable intellectual energy in specifying the institutional, legal, social and economic requirements for establishing and maintaining democratic systems of representative government. They were both certain that it would require a great deal of hard work to foster societies that were both liberal and democratic. Mill and Madison were not alone in recognising and warning of the threat that poorly educated electors, tyrannous majorities and demagogues posed to individual liberties and to the integrity and longevity of democratic institutions.

Liberal democracy calls for much more than a majoritarian electoral system. Liberal enthusiasm for self-determination can only be reconciled with support for a system of elections and government driven by the will of the people if there are limits to what can be done in their name; and it is vital that these limits are clear to all. A written constitution and a system of common law and/or precedent that entrenches individual rights are key features in virtually all versions of liberal democracy.

This liberal armoury, deemed essential for liberal democracy, is multi-faceted. As Madison and his fellow Federalists – framers of and propagandists for the American constitution – recognised, a clear statement of individual rights is unlikely to be sufficient to protect personal liberty. A free and democratic society needs to be supported by institutions strong enough to uphold personal liberties. Those who interpret and apply statute and common law – and whatever other statements of rights and entitlements a free society promulgates – should be separated from and unmistakeably above the partisan interests that might, from time to time, affect the judgement of elected representatives and members of the executive. A liberal democracy is a society of laws, not just of votes, that are applied consistently without fear or favour.

This framework of liberal democracy is intended to impede all attempts to concentrate power in any single part of government. The executive is answerable to and balanced by the powers accorded to the public's elected law-makers. The legislature is required to conduct its business publicly and in ways that ensure that law-making is undertaken thoughtfully and deliberatively. Legislature and executive are held in check by an independent judiciary. Liberal democracy, in short, is defined by a system of checks and balances and also by its openness. Each branch of government is accountable, by one means or another, to 'the people', to civil society. Constitutional freedoms, the cornerstones of liberal democracy, empower citizens to speak and assemble freely and are meant to serve as a bulwark against attempts to curb basic liberty. Freedom of conscience is one amongst a number of constitutional entitlements, including the right to a fair trial and to due process, intended to give liberal democracy its special liberal character.

True democracy also depends, in the minds of liberals at least, on the viability and vitality of a liberal political culture. John Stuart Mill, an enthusiastic supporter of female emancipation and proportional representation, was an even stronger supporter of educational ideals and the universal provision of educational opportunities. He was wedded to the proposition that the health of democratic societies depended upon their ability to develop the intellectual faculties of their citizens; an educated and engaged electorate was the ultimate assurance that democratic, representative and efficient government would prosper and survive. Winning and retaining the consent of the governed, once the mass of the public was well educated and well informed, would be an intellectually exacting task. As educational opportunities grew, Mill anticipated that civil society would become better equipped to maintain a political climate in which public judgements about the great questions of the day were well informed and rational.

Advocates of liberal democracy continue to attach, as Mill did, particular importance to developing the capacity of electors to understand and participate in the public discussion of political issues. The quality and maturity of public debate in a liberal democracy is generally regarded as the key to assessing its health and durability. While there is less agreement about how far it is necessary or, indeed, possible to go in strengthening civil society in order to meet the requirements of liberal democracy, most liberal political thinkers agree that informed consent and political participation depend upon the existence of a free and diverse press, legal guarantees affording citizens unimpeded access to official information and the existence of extensive educational opportunities. The latter is deemed to be particularly important, especially so when it comes to the education of citizens in the making; most supporters of liberal democracy have come to believe that popular education should include an introduction to the values and mechanics of liberal and democratic systems of government.

Nevertheless, supporters of constitutional or liberal democracy have little option but to acknowledge that, even in those societies where educational opportunities have been developed most strongly and successfully, political *equality* (q.v.) – even of the limited kind envisaged by Madison – remains an elusive goal, primarily because of the imbalances consequent upon economic *inequality*.

As early as the seventeenth century, liberal writers such as John Locke (q.v.) identified the importance of the right to enjoy private property, which played a critical role in securing economic independence and thus the opportunities needed for self-determining citizens to develop as political beings. In the eighteenth and nineteenth centuries, Adam Smith (q.v.), Richard Cobden (q.v.) and others extended this to the right to free exchange of goods and services unhindered by privilege, and the right of every individual to use their talents in an open economy. Economic independence and the self-determination that went with it were the hallmarks of liberal society: freedom (q.v.), enterprise and democracy went together.

Liberals expected concentrations of wealth and therefore power to diminish in such a free society. Modern democracies, however, are very far from being equal

societies: economic and social inequalities persist (and in some countries are growing) and significantly affect life chances. Economic power feeds through to political power: persistent and deeply entrenched social and economic inequalities, concentrated media ownership and the privileged position of producer groups all lead to political distortions where elected representatives are more attentive to the needs of some groups than to those of others. Particularly in the United States, where the escalating costs of running election campaigns and the failure to cap campaign contributions trap politicians in an endless round of fund-raising, money clearly buys influence in the political system. Liberal democrats believe in the need to establish a 'level playing field' but recognise just how difficult this is to achieve in societies where economic inequalities go deep. However, it is undeniable that concentrations of economic power continue to unbalance political competition in Western democracies.

Similarly, many developing countries have failed to strike the balance needed between capitalism and democracy which is required to establish liberal democracy – notably in Latin America, as pointed out by José Nun. As Nun argues, Europe's capitalists accepted a compromise that enabled democratic governments to formulate citizenship rights and fabricate welfare states. By comparison, in Latin America, national and international investors, bolstered by the neo-liberal (q.v.) ideology of the 'Washington consensus', have been unwilling to accept such a political settlement. Nun's conclusion is that liberal democracy can only succeed in Latin America if it becomes more egalitarian.

Liberal or constitutional democracy makes many assumptions about the practicability and desirability of marrying liberalism with democracy. Liberal democracy is championed, by liberals, as the best way of reconciling respect for individual rights with the political choices of majorities, of accommodating highly divergent majority and minority interests, of overcoming disagreements and moderating conflicts, and of promoting compromise and mutual understanding, facilitating or requiring peaceful arbitration and assisting in the identification of common interests. The preservation and promotion of liberal democracy, both domestically and internationally, requires that those who are in the majority accept that they cannot always get their own way and recognise and willingly bow to the need for change. Indeed, it is the opportunities that liberal democracy affords for learning and for reform that make it the most attractive form of government available to human society, from a liberal point of view. Managing conflicts peacefully and persuading majorities that their interests are not always paramount also presents liberal democracies with the opportunity to show just what they are capable of.

The need to demonstrate the ability of democratic societies to overcome or, at the very least reconcile, differences, including those between religious and ethnic groups, has become increasingly pressing for the European Union and the United States. Both seek to promote democracy throughout the world and to make the world safe for democracies. Such goals make it especially important to strive to establish a moral and philosophical basis for mutual respect between democratic and undemocratic, liberal and illiberal states.

The need to open and sustain a true dialogue between liberal democratic states and societies, and states and peoples who did not share or accept liberal and democratic ideals, preoccupied the liberal political philosopher John Rawls (q.v.) towards the end of his life. In *The Law of Peoples*

(1999) and *The Idea of Public Reason Revisited* (1999) Rawls explored an enduring concern for liberal democrats: how to persuade others of the good sense and necessity for toleration between states and peoples. He was motivated by a conviction that democratic and liberal societies needed not only to work together but with their erstwhile opponents in order to sponsor values that appealed to liberals and to others. Belief in *public reason* and a *just world order* are indispensable if the world is to be safe for liberal democracies and more welcoming to emergent liberal and democratic states.

Liberal thinkers, most notable amongst them Condorcet (q.v.), Tom Paine (q.v.) and John Stuart Mill, and Liberal political leaders, among them Lord John Russell (q.v.) and William Ewart Gladstone (q.v.), can be counted amongst those who were most instrumental and most determined to advance the cause of democratic government. All of them insisted on the importance of allying liberalism and democracy in order to build societies in which democracy was informed and secured by liberal values. All of them believed liberal values to be indispensable, not only to the realisation of democratic societies but to liberal democracy's prospects and very survival. Though liberals put liberty first, they are true champions of democracy in the modern world.

Further reading
- Robert A. Dahl, *On Democracy* (Yale University Press, 2000)
- David Held, *Models of Democracy* (Polity Press, 3rd edn., 2006)
- Barry Holden, *Understanding Liberal Democracy* (Harvester Wheatsheaf, 2nd edn., 1993)
- Steven Lukes, 'Epilogue: The grand dichotomy of the twentieth century', in Terence Ball and Richard Bellamy (eds.), *The Cambridge History of Twentieth-*

Century Political Thought (Cambridge University Press, 2003)

- John Stuart Mill, *On Liberty* and *Considerations on Representative Government* (1859 and 1861; many reprints)
- José Nun, *Democracy: Government of the People or Government of the Politicians?* (Rowman & Littlefield, 2003)

Ed Randall

Liberal Imperialists

A moderate, centrist faction within the Liberal Party during the late Victorian and early Edwardian period, Liberal Imperialism was less an intellectual movement than an expression of a strategy for reviving the party's electoral fortunes and ensuring the success of future Liberal governments. Liberal Imperialists argued for a more positive attitude towards empire and imperialism, ending the overriding commitment to Irish home rule and distancing themselves from 'faddist' minority causes. They supported the idea of 'national efficiency' as an organising principle for domestic policy.

The origins of Liberal Imperialism lie in the differing views within the Liberal Party of Gladstone's (q.v.) adoption of Irish home rule in 1885 and of the future of the party after his resignation in 1894. Rosebery, Gladstone's successor, wanted the party to govern from the political centre, with 'continuity' in foreign and imperial policy between Unionist and Liberal governments. By contrast, other leading figures, such as Sir William Harcourt and John Morley (q.v.), often dubbed 'Little Englanders', saw this as pandering to jingoism and alien to the high-minded traditions of Gladstonian Liberalism.

These divisions were brought to a head in 1899 by the outbreak of war between Britain and the South African republics of Transvaal and Orange Free State. Those Liberals who supported the war became known as Liberal Imperialists, and members of the rival faction were often referred to by Unionist opponents as 'pro-Boers'; the party leader, Campbell-Bannerman, attempted to steer a middle course between the two. During the war, the Liberal Imperialists increasingly feared, with some justification, that Campbell-Bannerman's real sympathies lay with the pro-Boers, and they formed a succession of ginger groups to protect their position and promote their views.

The most important was the Liberal League, founded in March 1902; Rosebery was president and its members included some of the most talented and best-known Liberal politicians of the day, including H. H. Asquith, Sir Edward Grey and R. B. Haldane (q.v.). The main initial purpose of the League was to promote the policies outlined by Rosebery in his much-publicised speech at Chesterfield in December 1901. This at first appeared to offer the prospect of conciliation within the party, as Rosebery advocated a negotiated peace with the South African republics; but over the subsequent months the divisions widened.

The Chesterfield speech is the probably the clearest and best-known exposition of the Liberal Imperialist view of politics. It advocated the idea of the 'clean slate' with the party abandoning historic commitments, now out of keeping with the spirit of the times. Rosebery criticised the party's 1891 'Newcastle Programme', which included a range of reforms: Irish home rule, Scottish and Welsh disestablishment, temperance reform (a local veto on alcohol sales), land reform and 'mending or ending' the House of Lords. Rosebery believed that this programme would saddle Liberal governments with an impossible legislative agenda, alienate sections of the electorate the party needed to win over and lead to disappointment among Liberal supporters.

The Liberal Imperialists, in contrast, believed that the party should concentrate on judicious and gradual reforms that the majority of voters would support. As Rosebery argued, 'If you move far in front of the nation to which you look for support, you find yourself isolated.' By implication, this meant that Liberal leaders should use their own judgement on what measures to present, depending on political circumstances rather than being bound by the views of the party caucus.

The Liberal Imperialists also supported the concept of 'national efficiency'. This was never clearly defined (as Campbell-Bannerman sneered, 'Who is against it?'), but the examples specifically cited by Rosebery were reform of the War Office and a national system of education. This implied that the party should support state action to improve social conditions and the administration of government so that Britain could remain economically and militarily competitive.

Unsurprisingly, the Liberal Imperialists wanted the party to take a positive view of empire and shed its perceived image of being unpatriotic and unreliable in defending British interests overseas. Rosebery admitted: 'To many, the word "Empire" is suspect as indicating aggression and greed and violence,' but argued that it should instead be regarded as 'a passion of affection, of family feeling, of pride and of hopefulness'. Allied to this was a wish to distance the party from the cause of Irish home rule – reinforced by overt opposition to the British war effort displayed by many Irish nationalists during the Boer War. Even among Liberal Imperialists, views varied about how far home rule should be repudiated. Rosebery became an outright opponent, whereas Asquith and others wanted a step-by-step approach that was less than, but did not preclude, ultimate home rule.

Implicit in the Liberal Imperialist approach was that British foreign policy should be above party politics; as Foreign Secretary in 1886 and 1892–94, Rosebery had committed himself to the notion of 'continuity' in foreign policy. Above all, the Liberal Imperialists believed that unless the Liberal Party adopted their approach, there was little chance of it winning an election and returning to power.

It was initially unclear whether the Liberal League was intended to be a putative breakaway movement or a faction within the mainstream of the party. Its attempts to wrest control of the Liberal leadership proved unsuccessful and Campbell-Bannerman remained leader with the support of the bulk of Liberals in Parliament and the country. The end of the Boer War in 1902 removed the main source of internal division, and the course of political events then served to unify rather than divide Liberals. The whole party rallied to oppose the Unionist government's 1902 Education Act and to defend free trade (q.v.) after Joseph Chamberlain (q.v.) launched his tariff reform campaign in 1903. In the following three years, divisions within the Unionist parties increased, leading to the Liberal landslide in the 1906 general election. Campbell-Bannerman took office as Prime Minister, thwarting Liberal Imperialist attempts to persuade him to accept a peerage and allow Asquith to lead in the Commons. Rosebery remained outside the government and his semi-detached relationship with the party increasingly became one of complete estrangement.

In view of their inability to win control of the Liberal Party, it is tempting to dismiss the Liberal Imperialist project as a failure. However, Liberal Imperialism did have an impact on the party and, as a result, on the course of British politics. Some of the main Liberal Imperialist policies found their way into the party's official programme for the 1906 election. Campbell-Bannerman pledged that his government would not put forward an Irish home rule Bill in its first term. The party quietly abandoned any commitment to prohibitionist temperance legislation. During its first term of office the party made no move towards Scottish or Welsh disestablishment. And Campbell-Bannerman explicitly committed the party to continuity in foreign policy, appointing Sir Edward Grey as Foreign Secretary.

Liberal Imperialists played leading roles in the 1905–15 administrations: Asquith as Chancellor and then Prime Minister, Grey as Foreign Secretary and Haldane as Secretary of State for War and then Lord Chancellor. Government was conducted in the style advocated by Liberal Imperialists: rational, slightly patrician executive government rather than rule by the mob or by party caucus. The radical reforms the government implemented were a response to events rather than part of a comprehensive programme.

The Liberal Imperialists can be placed within a clear tradition in British politics: the progressive centre-left, advocating gradual rather than root-and-branch reform. Liberal Imperialists continued the Whig (q.v.) tradition of acting at once as a brake on radicalism (q.v.) and a progressive alternative to Toryism. They were also forerunners, variously, of the Gaitskellites in the Labour Party of the 1950s who resisted the challenge of the party's left, of Harold Wilson's attempt to rebrand Labour as the party of technology and innovation in the 1960s, and of Tony Blair's creation of 'New Labour' in the 1990s, all of them a response to prolonged periods of Conservative government.

Further reading

- D. A. Hamer, *Liberal Politics in the Age of Gladstone and Rosebery* (Clarendon Press, 1972)
- H. C. G Matthew, *The Liberal Imperialists: The Ideas and Politics of a Post-Gladstonian Elite* (Oxford University Press, 1973)
- Rosebery's Chesterfield speech is included in Duncan Brack and Tony Little (eds.), *Great Liberal Speeches* (Politico's, 2001)

Iain Sharpe

Liberal International (World Liberal Union)

Established in 1947 to bring together liberal parties and individuals internationally and to foster liberal parties and governments across the world, Liberal International has proved a useful vehicle for networking and exchanging best practice among liberals, particularly in emerging democracies.

Liberal International was established in the aftermath of the Second World War, at a time when the forces of liberalism had come under threat from extremism of the right and left and, paradoxically, from the moderates, who were adopting many of the tenets of liberalism within their own political parties. Anti-totalitarianism was thus a defining characteristic of LI from the outset.

LI's origins were essentially European, with an Anglo-Norwegian initiative instigated by John MacCallum Scott, a liberal on the fringes of the British Liberal Party, who sought like-minded people when he was posted to Norway in 1945, and an initiative of Belgian Senator Roger Motz on the hundredth anniversary of the Belgian Liberal Party in 1946. The upshot was a conference held in Oxford in May 1947, which launched the Liberal International (World Liberal Union). At the time the vast majority of participants were Europeans, either from liberal democracies or exiles from countries such as Hungary and Czechoslovakia that were to spend the next forty years behind the Iron Curtain.

The challenges to liberalism aside, a major problem facing LI was how to define liberalism. The divisions between social and economic liberals which characterise liberal politics in many European states ensured that from the outset LI was subject to pressures from differing liberal factions, frequently from within a country. The problem was exacerbated by the fact that the very term 'liberalism', not to mention the apparent association with the British Liberal Party, which had been in decline for the previous three decades, was anathema across much of the United States, where it was often conflated with the left, or even socialism. Thus, any links with Americans tended to be on an ad-hoc basis. While there was no such concern about the nature of liberalism in Canada, where the Liberal Party was in office, its leaders were reluctant to associate with Europeans who were not in office. Thus, representatives from both North American countries tended to be like-minded individuals rather than representatives of political parties, at least until the Trudeau (q.v.) government took office in Canada.

Elsewhere liberalism was weak: Latin America, Africa and Asia, not to mention some southern and many east European states, had yet to make the transition to democracy. Thus membership of LI was patchy for its first three decades, often relying on a few liberals in a country, such as Minoo Masani in India, to found groups that persisted for a while and then typically withered. Despite periodic suggestions that LI should become a global movement, little progress was made until the 1980s.

LI was deeply wedded to the ideal of European integration, which in many ways shared the same values of peace through cooperation. Europe was the theme of almost every Congress until the mid-1970s when, with the prospect of direct elections to the European Parliament, LI and its member parties pushed for the creation of the Federation of Liberal and Democratic Parties of the European Community (later the ELDR Party), which would be a vehicle to fight European parliamentary elections. Thereafter LI sought a more global role, albeit without a clear mission at first.

In the 1970s, LI was important in the development of Spanish democracy, though no Castillian liberal party was to emerge. After 1989, the collapse of communism in Eastern Europe ensured the emergence of a wealth of new parties claiming liberal credentials and seeking membership of LI. Some vanished almost immediately, while others became solid members. Moves to democracy elsewhere enabled LI to expand, although, as might have been predicted, expansion would again raise the question of what it means to be a liberal.

In the 1980s Latin America began to embrace democracy and LI began to forge links with some of the emerging parties. In 1986, a Central American grouping, the *Federación Liberal Centroamericana y del Caribe* (FELICA) was established and granted observer status of LI. FELICA was heavily dependent on funding from the German Friedrich Naumann Stiftung and gradually declined during the 1990s.

LI expanded into South America, thanks to Adolfo Suárez, president from 1989–91, and Count Lambsdorff, who succeeded him as president from 1991–94.

Liberalism in South America tends to be centred on think-tanks and liberal parties remained weak, not least because the term is often associated with economic liberalism (q.v.), which was not widely accepted in a region that had suffered under the so-called Washington Consensus in the 1990s. Nevertheless, in 2005, a Liberal Network of Latin America (*Red Liberal de América Latina*, RELIAL) was granted cooperating organisation status of LI.

Several Asian parties have embraced certain aspects of liberalism and in 1993 a Council of Asian Liberals and Democrats (CALD) was set up. CALD was self-financing and established itself as a regional grouping. However, not all member parties affiliated to LI, some rejecting the word 'liberal' because of the connotations of economic liberalism, which many in Asia distrust, believing it benefits the West disproportionately. Thus, Asian liberals tend to emphasise the human and civil-rights aspects of liberalism.

Democracy and hence liberalism has taken longer to become embedded in Africa, where clientalist politics remain to the fore. Nevertheless, through the 1990s, liberal parties emerged in several states, notably Senegal, where President Abdoulaye Wade represented Africa alongside Thabo Mbeki at the G8 summit in 2005, as well as Malawi and Ghana, whose Presidents called themselves liberal. An Organisation of African Liberal Parties was established in 1995, becoming the Africa Liberal Network in 2001. As elsewhere, the aim of the network was to bring together liberal parties from across Africa which were committed to freedom (q.v.) and democracy.

Initially, LI brought together as many individuals as it did parties, either as individual members of LI or as members of affiliated groups such as the Liberal International (British Group). Under Giovanni Malagodi (LI president 1958–66 and 1982–89) there was a move to strengthen the role of political parties within LI, a development which strengthened under the Lambsdorff presidency, when individual membership ceased. The country groups and, especially, such cooperating organisations as the Friedrich Naumann Stiftung, the National Democratic Institute of the US and the Swedish International Liberal Centre, remain important, however, not least because they frequently provide financial resources to enable LI to complete its objectives of sharing electoral know-how in emerging democracies.

Liberal International was originally established to bring together liberal parties and individuals internationally and to foster liberal parties and governments across the world. It proved a useful vehicle for networking and exchanging best practice among liberals, particularly in emerging democracies. LI has not exported the values of Western liberalism so much as endeavoured to create a network of liberals around the world. It has worked with political parties in emerging democracies to help foster grassroots liberalism and has offered political know-how in many countries. Its member parties differ in their conceptions of liberalism but all focus on the ideals of liberty, human rights and anti-totalitarianism as the founding fathers did in 1947.

Further reading

- Liberal International: www.liberal-international.org
- John MacCallum Scott, *Experiment in Internationalism: A Study in International Politics* (George Allen and Unwin, 1967)
- Julie Smith, *A Sense of Liberty: The History of the Liberal International* (Liberal International, 1997)

Julie Smith

Liberal Internationalism

The term 'internationalism' came into use in the English-speaking world in the mid-nineteenth century and was soon identified with the liberal desire to promote international cooperation, law and peace. Liberal internationalism has since become a powerful force in international affairs, challenging *realpolitik*'s gloom and cynicism with the antidote of hope and idealism and shaping the theory and practice of foreign policy in the West and beyond. Today, liberal internationalism continues to represent a political and moral commitment to active engagement in international affairs and the pursuit of liberal values worldwide, most importantly individual freedom and human rights, democracy and the rule of law, and a market economy.

Liberal internationalism builds on a long tradition of liberal thinking on international affairs, arguably stretching back as far as sixteenth-century humanism. The different strands that make up liberal internationalism share a belief in core liberal values and ideas that they apply to the realm of international relations. These include:

- The idea of progress, and the belief that human agency can shape history for the better, even in a world seemingly characterised by recurrent conflict and war.
- The belief in an underlying harmony of interests, be it within societies or among them.
- The value of individual liberty and the need for creating political institutions, both national and international, that protect individuals' freedom (q.v.) and human rights.

Liberals have, of course, put different weight on these elements of liberal thought and have come up with a distinctive emphasis on core values, stressing either market-liberal or social-justice (q.v.) models of liberalism.

Liberal internationalism represents a particular way of applying liberalism to international affairs. While some define it more broadly as comprising all varieties of liberal international thought, it is preferable to distinguish it from other, related, traditions, especially *liberal pacifism* and *liberal imperialism*. Although sharing a desire with pacifism (q.v.) for the eradication of war, liberal internationalism accepts the principle of self-defence and considers the use of military force to defend liberal values as legitimate. Unlike liberal imperialism, however, it values the norm of national sovereignty and rejects the systematic use of force to spread liberal ideals abroad.

Beyond sharing a commitment to an activist foreign policy and the promotion of liberal values, however, liberal internationalists differ with regard to the means by which liberal principles can be promoted in international affairs. Broadly speaking, liberal internationalists fall into three categories, emphasising democracy (q.v.), free trade (q.v.) and international law as the main vehicles with which to create a peaceful and liberal international order. The intellectual sources of these three varieties of liberal internationalism are to be found in the canon of liberal philosophy, and are most closely associated with Kant, Smith and Bentham.

Immanuel Kant (q.v.) provided one of the first and most coherent blueprints for a liberal international order in his *Perpetual Peace* (1795). Kant argued that the spread of republican constitutions would help to eliminate war. He called upon republics – states based on constitutional, representative government and a separation of powers – to create a federation of liberal states that would outlaw wars of aggression and maintain an open system of international exchange. Since Kant, democratisation and the emergence of a global society and economy have been considered as the two key liberal transformations that may bring the world closer to lasting peace. In the twentieth century, the 'democratic peace' thesis gained widespread acceptance, according to which liberal states do not go to war with other liberal states, although they may be as aggressive as any other state in their relations with non-liberal states.

Following in the footsteps of Adam Smith (q.v.), economic liberals (q.v.) in the nineteenth century shifted the focus to international economics, asserting that it was free trade and prosperity that would turn states away from territorial expansion and the use of force. As Richard Cobden (q.v.) and John Bright (1811–89) argued, David Ricardo's (q.v.) theory of comparative advantage had shown that in a world of free trade all nations could realise their full economic potential. Once nations adopted the market economy and international economic integration, they would develop an interest in settling their disputes peacefully so as not to disrupt the free flow of goods and capital on which their wealth rested. The close nexus between free trade and peace became a popular theme in liberal internationalism in the late nineteenth and early twentieth century. Norman Angell (q.v.) took this to its logical end by asserting in *The Great Illusion* (1909) that wars no long made economic sense and that the progress of commerce would reduce the chances of future war.

The challenge posed by the rise of nationalism in the nineteenth century led liberal thinkers such as John Stuart Mill (q.v.) to embrace the principle of national self-determination in international affairs. Only a state that was ruled by a government based on the consent of the people could be considered legitimate, and it was the right of every people to form a nation, free from domination or interference by other nations.

National self-determination became one of the key principles of Gladstonian (q.v.) liberalism in foreign affairs during the late nineteenth century. After the First World War, American President Woodrow Wilson (q.v.) emerged as the leading proponent of self-determination and liberal democracy (q.v.) which he intended to form the basis of a new international order. Wilson sought to commit the United States to an activist foreign policy and support for international institutions such as the League of Nations, on which his ideas and statesmanship were a foundational influence. His ideas became the major reference point in the subsequent development of American liberal internationalism.

Liberalism's embrace of nationalism, however, created new dilemmas for liberal internationalism. When applied in reality, the principle of self-determination often caused more problems than it solved, for it could not answer the question of which groups could legitimately claim the right to form their own nation-state. Only in rare cases could geography, ethnicity, religion, culture and/or language establish indisputable claims to nationhood. For as the experience of the twentieth century showed, with every new nation arises a new minority problem. Moreover, if national self-rule and liberal self-government were two sides of the same coin, then peoples wishing to become independent would be morally entitled to receive the help of existing liberal nation-states. But support for independence struggles would clash with the idea of national sovereignty, the founding principle of the modern states system. Should liberals abandon the norm of sovereignty and come to the aid of all those seeking national self-determination? Overzealous support for self-determination could easily become a source of conflict and instability in the international system.

Twentieth-century debates on liberal internationalism saw a shift in focus to the creation of international law and institutions, based in part on ideas developed by Jeremy Bentham (q.v.). Calls for the creation of a fully fledged world government never enjoyed much success, though. Instead, liberals such as W. E. Gladstone made more modest arguments for the centrality of international law in creating international peace, and twentieth-century liberals concentrated their energy on the creation of the League of Nations (1919) and the United Nations (1945). Of course, both the League and the UN had their deficiencies and represented a compromise between the liberal desire to transform international affairs and the reality of power politics. Liberals therefore argued for the continued growth of international law and the enmeshing of nation-states in a web of international institutions and treaties, ranging from the World Trade Organisation to human rights conventions and international environmental regimes. At the beginning of the twenty-first century, multilateralism remains central to the liberal internationalist vision of a society of states governed by international law.

Contemporary liberal internationalism continues to reinterpret the philosophical tenets of liberalism and apply them to international affairs, responding also to the specific historical circumstances and experiences of nations. In Britain, liberal internationalism is most closely associated with support for international institutions and law, European integration and the pursuit of human rights and global justice in world affairs. Mindful of their country's imperial past, British liberal internationalists wish to see their country play an active role in world politics while ensuring it acts within the multi-layered institutional framework of the UN, the European Union

and international law more generally. In contrast, Americans view liberal internationalism primarily as an expression of the Wilsonian commitment to an activist foreign policy that seeks to use the preponderance of American power to promote liberal values in the world. Unencumbered by an imperial past and inspired by America's unrivalled power, their liberal internationalist vision is more assertive and calls for a more radical remodelling of the international order. In Canada, liberal internationalism is interpreted as a more limited effort by a middle power to promote multilateral institutions and peaceful conflict resolution, as advocated and practiced by Lester Pearson, Canada's Prime Minister from 1963 to 1968.

How pronounced an impact has liberal internationalism had on the practice of foreign policy? For much of the history of the modern state system, diplomacy followed the rulebook of *realpolitik* as described by Machiavelli and practised by Bismarck. But with the spread of democracy and the growth of an embryonic global society, especially in the twentieth century, most Western states have come to pursue foreign policy objectives more in line with their domestic liberal values. Foreign policy today may still be constrained by the imperative imposed on it by an anarchic international environment and the sheer complexity of the international scene, but can no longer simply ignore domestic demands for the pursuit of human rights, international justice and the protection of the global environment.

Measured against the success of domestic liberalism, however, the record of liberal internationalism remains uneven and is in many ways disappointing. Still, since the end of the Cold War, the renewed interest in human rights and the link between democracy and peace has had a profound impact on the praxis of foreign policy in the West and beyond. Led by the United States, Western powers have actively sought to promote political liberalisation and democracy around the world. Recent US diplomacy under Bill Clinton and George W. Bush saw democracy promotion elevated to a strategic imperative, and the neo-conservative revolution in American foreign policy at the beginning of the twenty-first century is in part influenced by liberal internationalist ideas. Reawakened from its Cold War slumber, the UN has adopted a more activist interpretation of its security mandate in the form of humanitarian interventionism, but is often held back by the conflicting interests of the five permanent members of the UN Security Council.

The revival of a more assertive US foreign policy intent on using force to protect human rights (e.g. Kosovo, 1999) and export democracy (e.g. Iraq, 2003) has brought into sharper relief the deep divisions and contradictions that afflict liberal internationalist beliefs. Liberal states are usually peaceful in relations with each other, but may confront illiberal states with the full force of their military might. Humanitarian intervention may be required to protect the lives and freedom of the oppressed, but is not always carried out in a consistent manner, leading to accusations of hypocrisy and self-interested behaviour. While seeking to promote democracy and human rights, the new interventionism risks destroying respect for national integrity and undermining international security. As in the era of nineteenth-century imperialism, liberal zeal in foreign policy may end up threatening to undermine core liberal values and the foundations of international order and peace.

Nonetheless, as the contours of the new international relations are slowly emerging after the end of the Cold War, liberal internationalism continues to provide essential guidance in the search for a peaceful and just international order. If anything, its importance has increased over the last two centuries, as democracy and liberalism have spread and globalisation is creating new levels of connectedness. As before, however, the challenge is to relate its enduring principles and aspirations to the reality of a less then perfect world.

Further reading

- Michael W. Doyle, *Ways of War and Peace: Realism, Liberalism, and Socialism* (W. W. Norton & Co., 1997) (chs. 6–8)
- Stanley Hoffmann, 'The Crisis of Liberal Internationalism', *Foreign Policy* 98 (spring 1995)
- Carsten Holbraad, *Internationalism and Nationalism in European Political Thought* (Palgrave, 2003)
- Michael Howard, *War and the Liberal Conscience* (Oxford University Press, 1981)
- David Long and Peter Wilson (eds.), *Thinkers of the Twenty Years Crisis: Interwar Idealism Reassessed* (Clarendon Press, 1995)
- Nicholas J. Wheeler, *Saving Strangers: Humanitarian Intervention in International Society* (Oxford University Press, 2003)

Robert Falkner

Liberal Nationals (National Liberal Party from 1948)

The Liberal Nationals began life with the defection of around two dozen MPs from the parliamentary Liberal Party in the autumn of 1931. They subsequently took on the apparatus and organisation of a political party, damaging the Liberal Party when it was already in a state of serious decline, while helping to 'liberalise' the image of the Conservatives, with whom they acted in close political and electoral collaboration. They eventually merged into the Conservative Party in the 1960s.

Following the initial parliamentary rebellion the Liberal National Organisation was established at the beginning of 1933, with headquarters in Old Queen Street, under the direction of the chairman of the Liberal National Council, Lord Hutchison, a former Liberal chief whip. The style 'Liberal National' rather than 'National Liberal' was adopted to avoid confusion with the Lloyd George Coalition Liberals of an earlier era.

The party regularised its relationship with the Conservatives under the Woolton–Teviot Agreement of May 1947, which led, in effect, to the amalgamation of the two parties at constituency level. In Parliament the National Liberals maintained a nominally independent existence throughout the 1950s with their own chairman, vice-chairman, chief whip and Scottish whip. They also held an annual conference and issued their own manifesto at each general election. But the diminishing band of MPs became increasingly difficult to distinguish from the Conservatives and, after the 1966 general election, they relinquished the room assigned to them in the House of Commons. Finally, in May 1968, the Liberal National Council was disbanded and the party became fully integrated inside the Conservative ranks.

From 1931 to 1940 the party was led by Sir John Simon (1873–1954), who occupied leading positions within the National Government, serving successively as Foreign Secretary, Home Secretary, Chancellor of the Exchequer and Lord Chancellor. Other leading Liberal Nationals of this period included Walter Runciman (1870–1949), Leslie Hore-Belisha (1893–1957) and Leslie Burgin (1887–1945). Upon Simon's elevation

to the Woolsack in May 1940, leadership of the party passed, after a short interregnum, to Ernest Brown (1881–1962). Brown lost his parliamentary seat in the general election of 1945, after which a succession of figures including Jack Maclay (1905–92), a Cabinet minister under Churchill and Macmillan, served as chairman of the parliamentary party. The party's last leader, David Renton (1908–), who took the initiative in disbanding the National Liberals, was a junior Home Office minister in the Macmillan government.

In 1931 two key ideas divided Liberal Nationals from the mainstream Liberal Party. The first was a conviction that socialism represented the ultimate political danger against which Liberals must guard. The second was a readiness to consider all remedies, including tariffs, to deal with the balance of payments crisis which confronted the newly formed National Government. Reviled by orthodox Liberals as self-serving renegades whose ambitions and principles did not extend beyond the preservation of their own parliamentary seats, the Liberal Nationals presented themselves as the exponents of a liberalism that was ready to adapt to changing circumstances. Dropping the traditional Liberal commitment to free trade (q.v.) was part of this process. 'The abandonment of the practice of non-interference in international trade', declared Hore-Belisha, 'is in itself no more derogatory from essential Liberalism than was the earlier abandonment of the doctrine of non-interference in domestic contract … It is our belief, the belief of Liberal Nationals, that the creation of our movement was not fortuitous – that it was not a mere flash thrown out from the burning Liberal torch – a flash that was to be bright for a moment and then dimmed for ever – but rather it was the real light itself, preserved and sheltered when the torch was dying.'

But there was also a very practical consideration. The last purely Liberal government had come to an end in 1915 and Liberal Nationals were convinced that there was no foreseeable likelihood of the Liberal Party regaining power. Participation inside the National Government offered a practical opportunity to exert Liberal influence over government policy rather than dream idly of the day when liberalism on its own would recover the power it had enjoyed under Gladstone and Asquith. The Liberal Nationals' pre-war journal *The Liberal* coined the slogan 'Be an Effective Liberal and join the Liberal National Organisation'.

Precisely how much influence the Liberal Nationals exercised over what was overwhelmingly a Conservative government is difficult to assess. Certainly, they were stronger in the upper reaches of the MacDonald, Baldwin and Chamberlain Cabinets than their parliamentary numbers justified. Successive Prime Ministers were keen to maintain the government's 'National' credentials, for which purpose the Liberal Nationals were indispensable. The best assessment is probably that their presence enabled both Baldwin and Chamberlain to move the centre of gravity of their administrations towards the political centre, in line with their own instincts as progressive Tories. This made possible the effective sidelining of the Conservative right wing. Such a strategy was particularly effective in easing the Government of India Bill on to the statute book in 1935.

In the post-war era those who strove to maintain the National Liberals as a separate force used much the same arguments as had their predecessors in the 1930s. National Liberalism, they suggested, was the balm which served to moderate the more extreme elements of the Conservative Party and the conduit through which Liberal influence could permeate a Tory government. One National Liberal publication, *If You're a Liberal*, suggested that many Liberal policies, including the abolition of identity cards and the adoption of the principle of equal pay for men and women, had been implemented by the Conservative government elected in 1951. The argument is, however, unconvincing. The post-war Conservative Party, the party of Eden, Macmillan and Butler, probably did not need much prodding to move in directions for which the National Liberals claimed credit. Rather it was a case of Conservatives tolerating their allies because they believed they helped to attract Liberal votes which, particularly in marginal constituencies, could be vital to electoral success. Had the Liberals reunited, however, the Conservatives' loss of the National Liberal vote might have been enough to give Labour a working majority in 1950, sufficient for it to survive a full parliament. From the point of view of the mainstream Liberal Party, it has also been argued that the continuing split in the ranks of British liberalism cost it several key seats, including that of its leader, Archibald Sinclair, in 1945.

Perhaps the most interesting development came in 1954 with the emergence of the so-called Hastings Group, reflective of a strand of opinion among National Liberals that too much of their identity had been sacrificed after Woolton–Teviot. There followed a series of articles and pamphlets whose free-market ideas seemed to hark back to an earlier era of Liberalism and to anticipate the Conservatism of a later generation – this at a time when leading Tories were striving to occupy a consensual, sometimes corporatist, centre ground.

It is revealing that David Renton, who joined the Liberal Nationals soon after their formation and who, more than three decades later, finally wound the organisation up, doubts in retrospect whether his party ever achieved very much. This assessment is perhaps harsh. Liberal Nationals espoused a more coherent political creed than their critics allowed. They at least gave a clear answer to the question which confounded so many liberals in the interwar years of whether their inclination, particularly in the event of a hung parliament, was to lean to the left or to the right. Furthermore, their readiness to accept political reality and work with other parties to try to secure Liberal policies anticipated the electoral strategy of a later generation of Liberal leaders from Jo Grimond (q.v.) onwards.

Further reading

- N. Cott, 'Tory Cuckoos in the Liberal Nest?', *Journal of Liberal Democrat History* 25 (Winter 1999–2000)
- D. Dutton, 'John Simon and the Postwar National Liberal Party: An Historical Postscript', *Historical Journal* 32:2 (1989)
- D. Dutton, *Simon: A Political Biography of Sir John Simon* (Aurum Press, 1992)
- D. Dutton, *Liberals in Schism: A History of the National Liberal Party* (I. B. Tauris, 2007)
- G. Goodlad, 'The Liberal Nationals, 1931–1940: The Problems of a Party in Partnership Government', *Historical Journal* 38:1 (1995)

David Dutton

Liberal Summer School (now Keynes Forum)

Founded in 1921 as an annual week-long residential school to develop innovative Liberal policies, domestic and international, for the post-war world, the Liberal Summer Schools were the source of the Liberal 'Yellow Book' and helped to develop the thinking behind Beveridge's proposals for the reform of welfare provision. The School now survives as an annual one-day seminar, in 2004 renamed the Keynes Forum, and run by CentreForum.

The Liberal Summer Schools movement in the 1920s originated in the apparently disparate strands of Nonconformist (q.v.) Manchester liberalism, as represented by Ernest Simon (q.v.) and C. P Scott (1846–1932), social and industrial reformers from Toynbee Hall and the LSE (including William Beveridge (q.v.) and Seebohm Rowntree (1871–1954)); and John Maynard Keynes's (q.v.) Cambridge- and Bloomsbury-based circle of young economists (including Hubert Henderson (1890–1952), Walter Layton (q.v.) and Dennis Robertson (1890–-1963)).

In 1920 Liberals were simultaneously faced with a world that seemed both dangerously disintegrated and full of exciting promise, and with the disastrous Asquith–Lloyd George (q.v.) split. Recognising the urgent need for positive Liberal polices to fill this vacuum, the powerful Manchester Liberal Federation under Ernest Simon and the chief national party agent, Thomas Tweed, initiated the movement which 'recruited intellectuals to the Liberal Party, and provided a forum at which experts could float their ideas about contemporary economic, social, and industrial questions'.

The first Summer School was held at Grasmere in 1921, on the lines of the Fabian Summer Schools. The founders included the historians Ramsay Muir (q.v.) and Philip Guedalla (1889–1944), and the economists Keynes, Henderson and Layton, supported by Simon's friend and Lloyd George loyalist, C. P. Scott of the *Manchester Guardian*. Eleanor Rathbone (1872–1946), herself from a Manchester Nonconformist Liberal dynasty, spoke on 'Women and the Family'. 'What a party!' Simon noted in his diary at about this time: 'No leaders. No organisation. No policy. Only a Summer School!'

The format, retained for many years, was a residential 'school' where Liberals and sympathisers met in a university setting to hear and discuss lectures on topical issues, domestic and international. The 'school' structure remained through the 1920s and '30s; the programme was described as a 'Syllabus', with the emphasis on discussion rather than received wisdom, and a recommended reading list. The week included cultural excursions, concerts, a dance, a garden party and sometimes a satirical revue by School members.

From 1922 to 1939 the Schools were held annually, alternately at Oxford and Cambridge. They were a uniquely Liberal combination of distinguished speakers and rank-and-file party members and supporters, meeting and debating on equal terms in a relaxed setting. The lectures, the discussions, and the interaction within the influential group behind the Schools, developed and influenced Liberal Party thinking throughout the 1920s and '30s, and disseminated ideas through the other parties, both in Britain and the US.

The pre-war Summer Schools were supported by a powerful press network, finally ending with the death of the *News Chronicle* in 1960. Keynes augmented the *Manchester Guardian* connection by buying the weekly *Nation & Athenaeum* in 1923, appointing Henderson as editor. The Cadbury-owned *Daily News*, which merged with the *News Chronicle*, the *New Statesman* (which later absorbed the *Nation*), *Tribune, The Economist,* the *Westminster Newsletter* and *The Liberal Magazine* all had active Summer School connections. Wilson Harris, editor of the *Spectator*, was on its ruling council.

Facing political eclipse in the 1920s, Lloyd George used the Schools for his 'crusade' to galvanise Liberal policies with new, radical solutions. His research department, at 41 Parliament St., SW1, operated through the Summer School organisation to produce a series of 'coloured books' on industrial and social issues. The most famous was the 'Yellow Book' (*Britain's Industrial Future*), whose principal contributors – Keynes, Beveridge, Henderson, Layton, Jules Menken, Ernest Simon and Sir Herbert Samuel MP (q.v.) – were Summer School members.

The 'coloured books', especially the Yellow Book, supplemented by Keynes's and Henderson's pamphlet *Can Lloyd George Do It?*, offered a novel and dynamic programme for the 1929 election. However the Liberals were defeated by the electoral system – a 2½m rise in votes only increased the number of MPs from forty to fifty-nine – and the Liberals' adventurous policies did not suit Baldwin's 'safety first' approach.

Beveridge was a member of the Summer Schools Council and its executive committee from 1924 to 1935, and his long association with Keynes and Seebohm Rowntree (a Summer School Council member until 1939) arguably influenced his subsequent proposals for overcoming the 'five giants of want, disease, ignorance, squalor and idleness'. His 1942 and 1944 Reports show his move from belief in a self-regulating free market towards Keynesian-style (q.v.) fiscal regulation and state support for 'all social contingencies from the cradle to the grave'.

The Schools' approach to internal politics was broad-church. In spite of their strong Lloyd George connection, Herbert Asquith (1852–1928) addressed Schools in the 1920s; his son-in-law Sir Maurice Bonham Carter (1880–1960) was on the council, as was his wife Lady Violet (later Lady Asquith, 1887–1969), before and after the Second War. Runciman and Sir John (later Viscount) Simon (1873–1954) attended regularly until the political and economic crises of the Labour government of 1929–31 opened up the possibility of a revival in Simon's career, and he and Runciman left to form the Liberal National Party (q.v.).

Sir Herbert (later Lord) Samuel, former Home Secretary and a social reformer – vilified by Lloyd George for his attempts to hold the party together in the 1930s (though Samuel had stuck with the official Liberal Party during the divisions of 1931) – nevertheless attended Summer Schools regularly until well into his eighties.

The 1939 School was held in Cambridge from 3–8 August, under the shadow of war. Some Czecho-Slovaks had attended the 1938 School – 'to join with us in upholding the dignity and ideals of free Democracy', as the secretary wrote. 'This year these friends will not be with us. We do not know how dearly they may be paying for the beliefs which we and they have voiced in common ....' But, memorably, the School was addressed by ex-President Beneš. Before the School met again after the war, he was to have been murdered by the Communist regime.

The Liberal Summer Schools had a lasting influence on political thinking, domestically and abroad. Exact quantification is impossible, partly because it was achieved through a network of like-minded economists, historians, philosophers, social reformers and politicians, and partly because the party's parliamentary decline meant the influence had to be Maquisard in nature, stealthily working in the undergrowth of conservative thought. It is widely believed that Keynes, together with his Gordon Square coterie, which included Layton, Beveridge and Arthur Salter (1881–1975) (later known as the 'Old Dogs'), influenced President Roosevelt's thinking before and during the Second World War.

The Schools' heyday lasted from 1922 to 1939. After the war they continued in more or less the same form, though Keynes, Guedalla and Muir had died. By the late 1950s increasing costs of travel and accommodation reduced the Schools to a long weekend, Oxbridge being replaced by provincial venues. Although their influence as a creative source of Liberal political philosophy was reduced, the Schools continued to attract distinguished lecturers, and the participants greatly valued the opportunity for free discussion and debate with the speakers, a 'High Table' mentality being discouraged.

In the 1990s, as 'Summer Schools' went out of fashion, and costs continued to rise, they could not be financially sustained in their original form. The Liberal Summer School is now run by CentreForum (q.v.) as the Keynes Forum, a one-day autumn seminar with invited speakers on topical political themes.

Ann Moore

Liberal Unionists

The Liberal Unionist Party was founded in 1886 by Liberal politicians who opposed Gladstone's policy of granting home rule for Ireland and wanted to defend the Union. It operated in informal alliance with the Conservative Party until 1895, when Liberal Unionists entered formal coalition and accepted ministerial office in Lord Salisbury's second administration. It was largely composed of figures from the moderate, Whig section of the Liberal Party, most prominent of whom was the party leader Lord Hartington; more surprisingly, it also included the radical leader Joseph Chamberlain and a number of his followers. The distinctions between Liberal Unionists and Conservative parties increasingly ceased to have any real meaning and the two organisations formally merged in 1912.

The home rule question led, in 1886, to many academics and public intellectuals defecting from the Gladstonian (q.v.) Liberal Party to the Liberal Unionists. Most prominent among these were the jurist and constitutional theorist A. V. Dicey (q.v.) and the leading Irish historian, W. E. H. Lecky, both of whom became leading anti-home rule propagandists. There is a sense in which the 1886 split separated the Liberal Party from Britain's intellectual elite, a factor that doubtless indirectly contributed to the party's relative electoral failure in the subsequent two decades. For example, whereas before 1886 a majority of the British press supported the party, enough editors and proprietors opposed home rule to put Liberal newspapers in a minority thereafter.

Although the Liberal Unionists were a breakaway party whose separation from their erstwhile colleagues was very rapid, arguably their Irish policies were more directly in the traditions of the Liberal Party than were those of the Gladstonians. Until Gladstone's conversion to home rule, nearly all British Liberals supported the Union and opposed the Irish parliamentary party's wish for legislative independence. Moderate Liberals believed that if Ireland was fully integrated into the United Kingdom this would reduce the negative influence on the Irish population of the Roman Catholic Church, whose beliefs they saw as backward and superstitious.

There were a number of dimensions to the Liberal Unionists' objections to home rule. In the first place, they were concerned at the nature of Gladstone's leadership of the Liberal Party, in particular what they saw as his overt religiosity and demagoguery. They felt that this ran counter to the distinctively rational view of politics which they saw as being at the heart of liberalism. This was particularly so on the issue of home rule, because they felt that the Irish parliamentary party was inextricably linked with the political violence of the Fenian movement and the Land League and at the same excessively influenced by the Roman Catholic clergy. As a result they believed that creating an Irish parliament would reduce the chances of reform and progress in the way Ireland was governed and would instead reward lawlessness and lead to chaos.

Liberal Unionists believed that Irish nationalists would not be content for long with a parliament subordinate to Westminster and that home rule would soon be followed by a complete political separation of Ireland and Great Britain – leading in turn to the dissolution of the United Kingdom and the destruction of the integrity of the British Empire. The perceived hostility of Irish nationalists towards Britain meant that an independent Ireland might in future enter into an alliance with Britain's enemies, and Ireland would become a staging post for a potential invasion.

By no means all Liberal Unionists were completely opposed to an increased measure of self-government for Ireland, but they believed that this should stop short of legislative independence. Prior to Gladstone's adoption of home rule, Joseph Chamberlain (q.v.) had promoted a scheme for greater local government powers, with an all-Ireland dimension, known as the 'central board scheme'. The Liberal Unionists supported measures of land reform, in particular government-sponsored land purchase. The aim was to create a class of land-owning farmers who would have a vested interest in the maintenance of law and order and in defending property rights. The reliance of the Conservatives on Liberal Unionist support during the 1886–92 and 1895–1905 administrations acted as an impetus for the passing of successive land purchase acts, as well as a comprehensive scheme of democratic local government for Ireland in 1898 – the strategy of 'killing home rule with kindness'.

The presence of Joseph Chamberlain and his small band of radical followers within the Liberal Unionist coalition also encouraged Salisbury's governments to support measures of social reform within Britain, including free elementary education, a new system of elected county councils and payment to employees for injuries sustained at work. While there was already an element of support within the Conservative Party for such measures, sceptics of state action in social issues were won over by the need to defend the Union and therefore to keep the Unionist coalition together. While he was able to work within the constraints of a Conservative-dominated administration, Chamberlain remained a radical, however, in his campaigning methods; his public campaign for tariff reform after 1903 was divisive within both parties of the Unionist coalition.

The main impact of the Liberal Unionist Party on Liberal politics was to weaken the Whig or moderate section of the party for the two decades after 1886. This gave greater influence to single-issue enthusiasts (or 'faddists') within the Liberal Party. In the twenty years after 1886, the Liberals were out of office for seventeen, and dependent on Irish nationalist support for a Commons majority during the short-lived 1892–95 ministry. This weakness in the Liberal Party during the late Victorian period led to the party's moderates, most notably Rosebery, Asquith, Grey and Haldane (q.v.), promoting the concept of 'Liberal Imperialism' (q.v.), an attempt to force the party back towards the political centre. This included a move away from explicit commitment to Irish home rule. As part of its platform for the 1906 general election,

in which it won a famous landslide victory, the Liberal Party explicitly pledged itself not to introduce a home rule bill in the subsequent parliament. It was only with some reluctance and in very changed political circumstances that the party again attempted to legislate for Irish home rule, after the Irish parliamentary party held the balance of power in the House of Commons after the 1910 general elections.

Further reading

- A. V. Dicey, *England's Case against Home Rule* (John Murray, 1886)
- John D. Fair, 'From Liberal to Conservative: The Flight of the Liberal Unionists After 1886', *Victorian Studies* 29:2 (winter 1986)
- Richard Jay, *Joseph Chamberlain* (Clarendon Press, 1981)
- T. A. Jenkins, *Gladstone, Whiggery and the Liberal Party 1874–1886* (Clarendon Press, 1988)
- Patrick Jackson, *The Last of the Whigs: A Political Biography of Lord Hartington* (Fairleigh Dickinson University Press, 1994)

Iain Sharpe

Liberalism: Pre-Enlightenment and non-Western

Often thought of a child of the European Enlightenment, liberal attitudes and beliefs can be identified in many pre-Enlightment and non-Western traditions, thinkers and political leaders. Liberals and liberalism should acknowledge and be more willing to draw upon the intellectual, moral and political resources that they embody.

Very few of the sources likely to be consulted by modern readers searching for information about either the origins or the meaning of liberalism suggest that it is anything other than the product of an exclusively Western tradition of political thought rooted in the Reformation, the Enlightenment and the rise of possessive individualism, all three partnered by the growth of market exchange in sixteenth-, seventeenth- and eighteenth-century Europe. Readers of popular and well-established introductions to political thought are likely to be informed that the Englishman John Locke (q.v.) made the decisive intellectual contribution to the establishment of truly liberal political thought; Locke is credited with giving liberalism its distinctive and radical character and setting forth its core notions: the importance of individual freedom (q.v.) and unfettered exchange in both goods and ideas, opposition to censorship, support for religious tolerance, private ownership of property, accountable government and, ultimately, the right to resist and overthrow a tyranny.

However, the history of liberal notions of freedom, which rest upon an uncompromising faith in the priority of individual liberty and respect for each person's notion of the good life, have a longer and richer history than the focus on Locke's liberal treatises suggests – a proposition from which Locke himself would have been unlikely to dissent. Lord Acton (q.v.), addressing precisely that point in his *History of Freedom in Antiquity* (1877), wrote that liberty, like religion, had long been a 'motive for good deeds [as well as a] ... pretext for crime'. Acton was in no doubt that the seeds of liberty (and liberalism) had been sown in Athens nearly 2,500 years earlier.

While some of the propositions advanced in this entry might have prompted a lengthy and possibly heated discussion with Lord Acton, they build upon the insights contained in his account of liberalism's intellectual roots in the ancient world. Indeed, liberal notions of freedom have grown, been nurtured and taken root (often only shallowly and briefly) in many different parts of the world.

In his *Universal Truths: Human Rights and Westernising Illusion* (1998) Amartya Sen asks: 'How much truth is there [in a] grand cultural dichotomy between Western and non-Western civilisations on the subject of liberty and rights?' His answer is: not much. He has no difficulty in identifying great leaders and thinkers who have been committed to liberal values drawn from the East. While some of the figures he identifies proffered only a highly conditional support for individual freedom, he recognises that there is little new or surprising in that. Alongside Confucius and Aristotle, both equivocal in their support for human freedom, there are others, from almost every part of the globe and representing many different periods in human history, who should be acknowledged as enthusiastic proponents of individual liberty, unfettered economic exchange and religious toleration.

Sen identifies, among others, the Indian Mughal Emperor Akbar (1543–1605) '[who, when] the Inquisitions were still in full bloom in Europe ... was making it a state policy to tolerate and protect all religious groups'. Other proponents of liberal values, such as the Jewish scholar Maimonides (1135–1204), found a haven in Islamic society, in Maimonides' case in twelfth-century Cairo. Sultan Saladin's protection is said to have made it possible for him to pursue his work as a Jewish religious thinker and philosopher unmolested, something that had not been possible while he lived in Europe. The Persian mathematician and thinker Al-Biruni (973–1048) is described, by Sen, as having been amongst the 'earliest of anthropological theorists', a determined advocate of religious toleration and an equally firm opponent of xenophobia.

Much earlier, in ancient China, Lao Tse (thought to have lived in the sixth century BC), the author of the *Tao Te Ching*, had given expression to a political philosophy that encouraged scepticism about those in authority and, most especially, about the capabilities of those in government. Lao Tse was convinced that governments could undermine and stifle prosperity by regulation: 'The more prohibitions there are, the poorer the people will be,' he wrote. He also posed a fundamental question about the legitimacy of claims made by those in power upon the labours of ordinary people. Those who inherited wealth and position should be told: 'I dig the well for water; I plough the field for food' and then asked: 'What use do I have for the emperor's power?' Some commentators have suggested that, in his ethical and philosophical writings, Lao Tse anticipated the work of Adam Smith (q.v.) by more than two millennia.

Emperor Ashoka (third century BC) has been credited with the 'first serious attempt to develop a Buddhist polity'. Ashoka's empire extended from modern-day Bangladesh to Afghanistan; he is known to have set up universities and hospitals, pursued an ethical foreign policy and introduced non-sectarian government. Ashoka, who issued edicts in both Aramaic and Greek, appears to have been a willing and able student of government; perhaps he can be regarded as one of the first internationalists, keen to apply what he had learnt from abroad within his own Mauryan empire. Sen points to Ashoka as a particularly good example of an Asian ruler and champion of religious toleration whose liberalism can be confirmed by the existence of 'inscriptions in favour of tolerance and individual freedom'. The archaeological evidence is consistent with Ashoka having made the equality of his subjects 'state policy' with the establishment of a 'domain of toleration [in the Mauryan empire including] ... everybody without exception'.

The North African Ibn Khaldun (1332–1406), like Lao Tse, is believed to have anticipated the development of classical liberal (q.v.) thought and economics (as well as the discipline of sociology). His writings, including the *Muqaddimah*, were 'rediscovered' by Arab and European scholars at the beginning of the nineteenth century and have been acclaimed as examples of an open, scholarly and liberal tradition that flourished in Islamic societies in the thirteenth and fourteenth centuries. Born in the territory of modern-day Tunisia, Ibn Khaldun served a number of Arab rulers as an adviser before writing a 'universal history' of human society, of which the *Muqaddimah* is a part. His commitment to the publication of his ideas about economy and society in order to invite and stimulate debate surely serves to underscore his credentials as a liberal thinker.

If Sen was concerned with bringing champions of liberty in the East to the attention of a wider audience, then Lord Acton aimed, in his *History of Freedom*, to persuade a Victorian audience that ancient Greeks and Romans had made vital contributions to the development of their liberal and democratic institutions as well as to the exposition of the ideas needed to establish and sustain a free society. By understanding how the case for liberty and democratic institutions had been made and developed in ancient Greece and Rome, Acton hoped to inspire and strengthen the liberalism of his own time.

Pericles (495–429 BC), whom Acton praises to the high heavens, must count as one of the most remarkable exponents of liberal and democratic values in the whole of human history. He had, as Acton put it, 'struck away all the props that ... sustained the artificial preponderance of wealth' in Athenian society, and declared it to be tyrannical if 'one part of the community should govern the whole'. Pericles relied upon his powers of persuasion, in public debate, to make the case for a polity in which the constitution's role was 'not to confirm the predominance of any interest ... but to preserve with equal care the independence of labour and the security of property, to make the rich safe against envy, and the poor against oppression'. We know that Pericles and his fellow Athenians failed to fashion a liberal and democratic society with true staying power; oratory alone was insufficient to meet the many threats to freedom, including those posed by the tyranny of majorities or the institution of slavery. Majorities, in ancient Athens, trampled upon individual liberty. Nevertheless, Acton is unequivocal about what Pericles and his fellows bequeathed: persuasive arguments in favour of a democratic polity and an extraordinary, if short-lived, example of how an open society could be made to work.

Pericles had been preceded by Solon (638–558 BC), who proposed and won the support of his fellow Athenians for a constitution. The record of that constitution and the law-making its acceptance made possible stand as a remarkable memorial to the political inventiveness and skill of the man and the society of which he was a part. In creating a society in which citizens elected rulers, laws were openly debated before they could be agreed and applied, taxes were levied according to the ability to pay and trials conducted with juries, Athenians were responsible for a political bequest that enabled others to have faith in the human capacity to change society peacefully, construct a polity of their own and choose and shape the institutions required for effective and accountable government. In Acton's own words, the Athenians, led by Solon,

'inaugurated the reign of moral influence where all political power had [previously] depended upon physical force'. Lord Acton wanted his audience to know that the ancient Greeks had refused to accept that 'the only recourse against political disorders ... was the concentration of power'. Solon had overcome disorder and conflict by promoting cooperation and by winning popular support for a constitution that distributed power more widely.

If the fleeting grip of Athenian society on its own democratic institutions prompts awkward questions about the durability of liberty in democratic societies, it also invites a challenge to democrats who insist that individual freedom is necessarily compatible with majoritarian forms of government. How great is the risk that democracy, without restraint, will create a monster, an over-mighty and instrusive state? In the history of liberal thought, the ancient Roman Republic, the forerunner of the Empire, sought to fashion a polity dedicated to a rather different notion of liberty from that which animated and inspired Solon and Pericles. Theirs has been described as the republican conception of liberty, embodying an abiding and quintessentially liberal anxiety about government taking and using excessive powers.

Romans knew that individual liberty was the antithesis of slavery and could only be enjoyed by those who were not slaves. Avoiding their own enslavement was their paramount political goal. They understood that avoidance of servitude and subjugation was vital in order to enjoy personal freedom and required all those who were free, wanted to remain free or sought freedom, to oppose any power or interest that threatened to enslave them. An over-mighty government and domination by a rival state were perceived as the greatest threats to individual liberty by those who upheld this liberal republican tradition. Governments were not to be trusted and must not be permitted to become too powerful. Those who occupied the most eminent positions in government must not be allowed to threaten the liberties of free men, and foreign states must always be regarded as potential enemies and a threat to liberty. Enemies, including rival states, should never be permitted to grow so strong that they endanger either the government of the republic or the liberties of its citizens.

Quentin Skinner, in his *Liberty before Liberalism*, is one of the most widely read and persuasive advocates of the 'neo-Roman theory of free citizens and free states'. Skinner is an admirer of Roman law and a persuasive advocate of the case for firmly entrenched limits to the powers of the state. Acton, an enthusiast for the Greek rather than the Roman tradition, admired the vitality and spontaneity of Greek democracy and was much less impressed than Skinner with the Roman tendency to give greater weight to precedent and example rather than to the 'spirit of the moment'. Their differences are reflected in the contemporary liberal argument about the weight that we should attach to the different ingredients that are undoubtedly needed to sustain liberal and democratic societies. Skinner gives voice to the fear that the modern champions of liberty have made poor choices and are easily seduced by the idea of a potent, socially just and efficient state that promises the earth to the people. He urges us to focus our attention on the dangers of the state over-reaching itself and the need to guard against this, however good the cause it espouses. We are all, of course, well aware of what the Roman Republic became: a monarchy.

The historical and philosophical enquiries undertaken by both Acton and Skinner should serve as reminders of just

how deep differences over the origins and constitution of liberty go. While Skinner urges us to be vigilant and to regard the state with the greatest possible scepticism, Acton's disciples suggest that the pursuit of private interests, especially by the wealthiest and most powerful citizens, represent a most potent threat to individual freedom. Indeed, explanations of the fall of the Roman Republic focus our attention on the greed and power of Rome's wealthiest families and the weakness of its institutions.

If Liberal International's (q.v.) Hall of Freedom was open to the greatest pre-Enlightenment advocates of liberty and democracy it is unlikely that any of the great orators and political leaders of ancient Rome would be admitted. Amongst the most eminent – Cicero (106–43 BC), Seneca the Elder (54 BC – 39 AD), Seneca the Younger (4 BC – 64 AD) and Pliny the Younger (63–113) – none are truly notable for their unqualified support for either human rights or representative government. Nevertheless, their insistence that individual liberty and self-determination depend upon eternal vigilance and individual courage does speak strongly to the liberal tradition. To most contemporary liberals the great flaw in the political system and culture to which they belonged was that it concentrated power in the hands of a small number of Rome's elite families and had little time for social justice (q.v.) or freedom of expression beyond its own membership. As Acton observed, 'That which ... ingenious Athenians ... carried forward by the spell of plausible argument, was in Rome a conflict between rival forces ... Speculative politics had no attraction for the grim and practical genius of the Romans.' Despite this, liberals should not lose sight of the fact that liberalism has drawn and can draw inspiration from the actions and ideas of those who were serious in their pursuit of efficient and effective government while at the same time determined to set clear limits to government's powers. Despite the fact that the commitment of ancient Romans to core liberal values was both incomplete and highly conditional their jurisprudence and strength of civic purpose remains a source of inspiration to many liberals.

It is the opinion of this author that modern liberals should be willing to look to all parts of the globe as well as to other political traditions. Indeed in modern times, the actions and philosophy of that great twentieth-century champion of self-determination and religious toleration, Mohandas K. Gandhi (1869–1948), whose battle against colonialism exemplified a non-violent path to political reform, demonstrate just how much liberals and liberalism can draw upon intellectual, moral and political resources that exist outside the canon of the European Enlightenment.

Further reading

- Lord Acton, *The History of Freedom* (1877; many reprints)
- Cicely Buckley (ed.), *Thoughts for the Free Life: Lao Tse to the Present* (Oyster River Press, 1997)
- Ibn Khaldun, *The Muqaddimah: An Introduction to History* (N. J. Dawood (ed.), Princeton University Press, 2004)
- Amartya Sen, 'Universal Truths: Human Rights and the Westernising Illusion', *Harvard International Review* 20:3, summer 1998
- Quentin Skinner, *Liberty before Liberalism* (Cambridge University Press, 1998)

Ed Randall

Liberation Society

The Liberation Society campaigned for the disestablishment of the Church of England. Founded in 1844, as 'The British Anti-State Church Association', the name was changed to the more constructive 'The Society for the Liberation of Religion from State Patronage and Control' in 1853 but became generally known as the Liberation Society. Although it survived into the second half of the twentieth century, its work and achievements belong to the Victorian era.

As a result of the religious struggles in Britain during the Tudor and Stuart periods, the Church of England held a unique position, 'established' under state control, privileged above other Protestant denominations and Catholicism. Although the eighteenth century brought some de facto toleration, discrimination against Nonconformists (q.v.) remained. All taxpayers, whether Anglican or not, paid towards the upkeep of the established church; Oxford, Cambridge and Durham (though not the London or Scottish universities) restricted admission to degrees; certain occupations were reserved for Anglicans; and Anglican burial grounds were denied to other denominations.

The repeal of the Test and Corporation Acts in 1828 raised hopes that Nonconformist complaints would be quickly resolved, hopes that were reinforced by the 1832 Reform Act but dashed by the reluctance of the Whigs to embrace further reform in the 1830s. Local campaigns against church rates helped to radicalise individuals such as Edward Miall (q.v.), a Congregationalist minister. The disruption of the Church of Scotland and the attempt to incorporate provisions for an Anglican education into the 1843 Factory Bill further stimulated efforts to create a national Nonconformist campaigning organisation. Miall organised a successful conference in London in 1844 and founded the British Anti-State Church Association shortly afterwards, run by a council of 500 and a management committee of fifty with three national secretaries. In 1847, (John) Carvell Williams was appointed as a permanent salaried secretary; he was to become its most significant leader after Miall's retirement in the late 1870s until his own departure in 1906.

The 1853 name change heralded a more effective campaigning strategy. A press and publishing committee was established in 1854, together with a parliamentary subcommittee to provide whipping services for sympathetic MPs. The Society established its own journal, the *Liberator*, in 1855 and in the same year created an electoral subcommittee to stimulate lobbying in local constituencies. While it was backed by some Anglicans (mainly High Churchmen), it drew support mainly from Nonconformists, particularly from the more radically minded Congregationalist and Baptist groups; enthusiasm was lower among the Wesleyan Methodists. In 1868 there were an estimated 10,000 subscribers.

The Society's core belief was that the establishment not only discriminated against Protestants outside the Church of England but obstructed the church in its Christian mission by imposing controls in the interest of worldly government not religion. Liberationists argued that:

- Religion should be a matter of conscience between man and God, not of control by law.
- The state should recognise all equally in matters of conscience.
- All laws which conferred privilege or disability in ecclesiastical matters should be repealed.
- Public funds should not be compulsorily collected on behalf of or paid for religious purposes.
- Church property should be disendowed from the Anglican church and diverted to other national purposes.

The Liberation Society undertook all the usual activities of a Victorian campaigning group — lecture tours, the publication of tracts and the employment of a full-time researcher, H. S. Skeats — but what made it different was the determination behind its electoral activities. The Liberationists recognised that their best hopes lay with the Whig/Liberal Party, but the Society was nevertheless willing to run its own candidates at by-elections against the official Liberal candidate where it received unsatisfactory responses to test questions or where a Liberal MP did not live up to his promises. This strategy never delivered a Liberationist MP but did cost the Liberal Party seats from time to time. Discipline among Liberation Society supporters was never strong enough to enforce the policy consistently — most preferred a weakly sympathetic Liberal to a completely hostile Tory — but was sufficient to win consideration from Liberal organisers. More positively, the Society identified areas with significant Nonconformist communities and campaigned to register them on the electoral roll while seeking, in such areas, to influence the local party into selecting candidates favourable to disestablishment. By these methods the number of Nonconformist MPs gradually grew and their case received more vocal backing in Parliament.

Over time, the minor Nonconformist disabilities were eliminated. In the 1850s the ancient universities were reformed and the arrival of Gladstone (q.v.) as Liberal leader accelerated the process. Although he remained a High Church Anglican, his moral crusading style resonated strongly with the Nonconformists. In 1868, the church rate was abolished and in 1880 a Burial Act was passed.

During Gladstone's first government (1868–74), the Church of Ireland was disestablished and disendowed. The church establishment was difficult to defend when around 80 per cent of the Irish population was Catholic, and the balance divided between Anglicans and the other Protestant denominations. Emboldened by this success, Miall, now an MP, introduced motions for the disestablishment of the Church of England each year from 1871 to 1873. However, he never mustered more than ninety-four MPs on his side and support tailed off after Gladstone rebuked him, requiring him to demonstrate sufficient public support for further legislation. For England, Liberationists never provided convincing evidence and the case for Scottish disestablishment was complicated by the splits within its church. But the strong Nonconformist Liberal presence in Wales, aided by the Liberation Society's campaigning, was another story.

Forster's Education Act of 1870, which continued reliance on Anglican schools, annoyed and disappointed Nonconformists, diverting their campaigning energies into Chamberlain's (q.v.) National Education League. Further dilution was occasioned by Gladstone's crusades against Bulgarian atrocities in 1876 and for Irish home rule during the 1880s. Disestablishment was part of Chamberlain's 'Radical Programme' in 1885 and disestablishment for Scotland and Wales formed an element of the Newcastle Programme for the 1892 election, but Tory rather than Liberal governments dominated the final years of the century.

Asquith's government passed a Bill to disestablish the Church in Wales in 1914, which, delayed by the Great War, came into operation in 1920. While the Liberation Society could count this as another success, its own role in the lengthy campaign had been a dwindling one. From about 1906, membership declined and, although the Society survived until 1958, there was no revival. The elimination of the substantive injustices suffered by Nonconformists and the disestablishment of the Church in Wales and Ireland left insufficient capacity for a successful campaign against the much stronger Church of England.

Further reading

- D. W. Bebbington, *The Nonconformist Conscience: Chapel and Politics 1870–1914* (Allen & Unwin, 1982)
- D. A. Hamer, *The Politics of Electoral Pressure* (The Harvester Press, 1977)
- W. H. Mackintosh, *Disestablishment and Liberation: The Movement for the Separation of the Anglican Church from State Control* (Epworth Press, 1972)
- Ian Machin, *Politics and the Churches in Great Britain*, 2 vols.: *1832 to 1868* (Oxford University Press 1977) and *1869 to 1921* (Oxford University Press, 1987)

Tony Little

Libertarianism

Libertarianism is a variant of liberalism that values the rights of individuals above all other considerations. For libertarians, the rights of individuals, including their rights to their justly acquired income and wealth, trump all other considerations, including the claims of distributive justice or the state provision of public goods.

Libertarian ideas can be traced back to the classical liberalism (q.v.) of John Locke (q.v.) and John Stuart Mill (q.v.), but it was the key contributions of F. A. Hayek (q.v.) and Robert Nozick (q.v.) in the twentieth century that shaped contemporary libertarianism.

The starting point of libertarianism is the belief that each individual has a complete right of self-ownership: each individual person and her property are believed to be sacrosanct and cannot be violated by anyone else except where that person has first violated the property rights of another. This position was classically set out as far back as the seventeenth century in Locke's *Second Treatise of Government* and was restated in part in John Stuart Mill's *On Liberty*, where Mill wrote that 'over himself, over his own body and mind, the individual is sovereign'.

The principle of self-ownership implies that each individual possesses inviolable moral rights over her own body, faculties and talents, and the use to which they are put, and hence all individuals are of separate and irreplaceable moral importance. Accordingly, it is judged that individuals should be free to determine and pursue their own ends. In the words of Hayek, it is believed that 'people are and ought to be guided in their actions by *their* interest and desires ... they ought to be allowed to strive for whatever *they* think desirable', rather than have ends imposed upon them by others, whether politicians, bureaucrats, gangsters or majorities.

Some libertarians have drawn a distinction between the right of self-ownership over one's person and the right of self-ownership over one's property. It is argued that rights to the ownership of property, or to certain types of property, or to the income derived from certain types of property, do not have the same moral status as ownership of one's self. It is contended that while an individual may be entirely sovereign over her body, the external resources of the world are another matter entirely, so that, 'perhaps even if we possess a libertarian right of ownership over ourselves, we can only ever come to have a less full right of ownership over land and other worldly resources' (Otsuka). On this basis, what have become known as 'left-libertarians'

have claimed that redistributive taxation and even egalitarianism may be reconciled with the principle of self-ownership and libertarianism.

The majority of libertarians, however, have argued that the right to dispose of one's own property as one sees fit is an integral part of the moral status that should attributed to human beings. It is contended that the right to self-ownership extends to a person's property because of the connection between the acquisition of property and one's person. In the classical Lockean sense, a property right is established when a person applies their labour to a natural resource in the state of nature. It is because each individual has a property right in her own person that when the labour of her body is mixed with the natural products of the earth that which is produced is legitimately her property. In a contemporary context, this means that we acquire property rights via our labour indirectly by earning money. Whether a person earns money by working in an office or by investing their capital wisely, for example, it is argued that there is still an intrinsic connection between ownership of one's person and ownership of one's property.

The policy positions that libertarians advocate are logically derived from the principle of self-ownership and involve a rejection of government action beyond the maintenance of a minimal state required to protect private property rights and ensure the rule of law (q.v.). Compulsory taxation is usually regarded as unacceptable and, indeed, tantamount to slavery, as it involves forcing people to work for others potentially against their will. However, it is worth noting that some libertarians, notably Hayek, have argued that a guaranteed minimum income providing something akin to a subsistence-level existence for those with no resources of their own may be justified as part of the legal and political framework provided by a minimal state.

The principle of self-ownership also implies that people have a right to engage in any activity so long as it does not harm others. Hence, libertarians would argue for the legalisation of all activities without direct third-party victims, including recreational drug use, prostitution and gun ownership.

Libertarians have also argued that only the market provision of goods and services is compatible with the principle of self-ownership. It is claimed that when goods are supplied in private markets, every individual has the option to 'exit' from a particular transaction if it is not congruent with their ends. Hence, if an individual does not approve of a firm's employment practices she can choose to frequent their competitors; if she is a vegetarian she can choose not to buy meat, and if she does not like the taste of a particular soft drink she can purchase an alternative. By contrast, when goods and services are supplied by non-market means, that is, as public goods provided by the state and funded from general taxation, no such exit option exists. Unless collective decisions are unanimous, the majority has the power to force its ends upon the minority and the minority has no exit option. In such a situation, pacifists must pay for nuclear weapons, environmentalists must contribute to the construction of new motorways and vegans are required to fund live animal experiments in government laboratories. It is claimed that when goods and services are provided by non-market means people are required to work towards ends that they do not share.

There are undoubted tensions within libertarianism. For example, how can the revenue required to fund even a minimal state be raised without compromising the principle of individual self-ownership? At what point does a child subject to parental authority become a self-commanding adult? It is also true that from a relatively straightforward starting point (that each individual has a complete right of self-ownership) libertarianism quickly leads to conclusions that many people find uncomfortable or objectionable: namely, that almost all government activity is morally unjustifiable. This may explain why although it represents an important and challenging strand of liberal thought, the influence of libertarianism on political parties like the Liberal Democrats has been limited.

Key works

- F. A. Hayek, *The Constitution of Liberty* (Routledge, 1960)
- F. A. Hayek, *Law, Legislation and Liberty* (3 vols., Routledge, 1973–79)
- Robert Nozick, *Anarchy, State, and Utopia* (Blackwells, 1974)
- Michael Otsuka, *Libertarianism without Inequality* (Oxford University Press, 2003)

John Meadowcroft

Liberty see Freedom

Walter Lippmann   1889–1974

American philosopher and journalist who veered, in the course of his long career, from progressive idealism to sceptical elitism. An elegant prose stylist, Lippmann's early work made a profound contribution to progressive thought, most notably in *Drift and Mastery* (1914), but exposure to foreign relations and, later, to totalitarianism, made him doubt the viability of sustaining liberal values in modern mass democracies. His *The Good Society* (1937) is sometimes seen as the genesis of the post-war revival of European neo-liberal thought.

Key ideas

- Sceptic about decision-making by mass democracy; looked to liberal elite to lead public opinion.
- The importance of civil society based on the rule of law.
- Collective security, based on the League of Nations and later the Western Alliance.

Biography

Walter Lippmann, the son of affluent second-generation German-Jewish parents, was born in New York City on 23 September 1889. He became a socialist while at Harvard University, where he co-founded the Harvard Socialist Club and edited the *Harvard Monthly*. As an undergraduate, he attracted the attention of William James and George Santayana. Lippmann's knack for ingratiating himself into the company of older men was a striking feature of his early career.

After brief spells working for muck-raking journalist Lincoln Steffens, Lippmann wrote his first book, *A Preface to Politics* (1913). It was a publishing sensation. His second, and arguably finest, book, *Drift and Mastery* (1914), soon followed. In 1914, at the behest of Herbert Croly, Lippmann joined the staff of the new political weekly, the *New Republic* (associate editor 1914–21).

During the First World War, Lippmann gained an extraordinary political education. His writing for the *New Republic* led Woodrow Wilson's (q.v.) aide, Edward M. House, to bring Lippmann into the government. He acted as an assistant to Secretary of War Newton D. Baker, as an editor and analyst for the Inquiry (the clandestine agency set up to formulate the peace), and for the army's propaganda unit in Europe. At the Inquiry, he drafted much of the material Wilson would incorporate into the Fourteen Points. After the war, he was part of the US delegation to the Paris Peace Conference and helped draw up the covenant of the League of Nations.

Lippmann left the *New Republic* in 1921 to work for the *New York World*, serving as its editor from 1929 to 1931. When the *World* collapsed he joined the *New York Herald Tribune*, where he began 'Today and Tomorrow', the nationally syndicated column he wrote until 1967. He ended his journalistic career at the *Washington Post*, which he had joined in 1963.

An early supporter of the New Deal (q.v.), by the end of 1935 Lippmann had grown suspicious of F. D. Roosevelt, voting for his opponent, Alfred Landon, in the 1936 presidential election. His perception that the New Deal was authoritarian informed *The Good Society* (1937). This work contributed to the revival of European liberal thought through 'Le Colloque Walter Lippmann'. This meeting, convened in Paris in August 1938, is sometimes regarded as the starting point for the development of post-war neo-liberal (q.v.) ideas by von Mises, Hayek (q.v.), Ropke and others. However, after the Second World War, in domestic policy at least, Lippmann inclined to a more mainstream US-style liberalism.

Ideas

Lippmann's early attachment to socialism was fleeting, but he was deeply influenced by the ideas of Graham Wallas (q.v.), the renegade Fabian whom he encountered at Harvard. Wallas's *Human Nature in Politics* (1908) questioned the capacity of ordinary citizens to make informed political judgements. If anything Lippmann's scepticism about the capabilities of the masses increased as he matured. His social theories grew to depend on the intervention of experts. His work in propaganda during the First World War perhaps further contributed to his pessimism about the ability of the public to understand complex political issues.

The other major influences on Lippmann's ideas were William James and Sigmund Freud. James's fascination with uncertainty was the prime preoccupation of *Drift and Mastery* (1914). The great challenge of politics, Lippmann contended, was how to reconcile the need for effective human direction with the inescapable uncertainty of man's epistemological predicament. He took from Freud the notion that all humanity is ill-informed, subject to partiality, and driven by irrational impulses. Both *Public Opinion* (1922) and *The Phantom Public* (1925) explore this terrain.

Lippmann came to believe that civil society depended on the capacity of people to sublimate their aggressive impulses through the adoption of a rule of law (q.v.). A life-long religious sceptic, he nevertheless recognised the void created by the absence of religious faith, a theme he pursued in *A Preface to Morals* (1929). He accepted as unavoidable the role of business organisations and their dominant place in industrial societies, adopting a form of corporate collectivism: a state with a strong executive composed of private corporate entities managed by experts. He never wavered from these elitist ideas and continued to take a dim view of popular government dependent on legislative procedures, a view developed in *The Public Philosophy* (1955).

Throughout his career Lippmann retained a strong interest in foreign affairs. At the close of the First World War he broke with Woodrow Wilson over the issue of ethnic self-determination, which he predicted would precipitate chaos in central Europe. The rise of totalitarian governments during the 1930s led him to develop his conception of a Western alliance based on Anglo-American solidarity. The Second World War confirmed his belief in collective security. Early in the Cold War he opposed George Kennan's containment policy, arguing it would risk war and undermine American prestige. His last significant public role was as a critic of the Vietnam War, which earned him the enmity of Lyndon Johnson and the admiration of a new generation of American radicals.

Key works
- *A Preface to Politics* (1913)
- *Drift and Mastery* (1914)
- *Public Opinion* (1922)
- *The Phantom Public* (1925)
- *A Preface to Morals* (1929)
- *The Good Society* (1937)
- *The Public Philosophy* (1955)

Further reading
- J. M. Blum (ed.), *Selected Letters of Public Philosopher Walter Lippmann* (Ticknor & Fields, 1985)
- M. W. Childs and J. B. Reston (eds.), *Walter Lippmann and His Times* (Harcourt, Brace & Co., 1959)
- R. Steel, *Walter Lippmann and the American Century* (Vintage, 1980)
- E. W. Weeks (ed.), *Conversations with Walter Lippmann* (Little, Brown, 1965)

Daniel Scroop and Jaime Reynolds

David Lloyd George   1863–1945

The best known and most dynamic Liberal leader of the twentieth century, Lloyd George was Chancellor of the Exchequer under Asquith, implementing an array of New Liberal policy initiatives, and then Prime Minister 1916–22. Although personal rivalries with Asquith split the Liberal Party in the 1920s, his accession to the leadership brought an influx of radical ideas and a brief Liberal revival in 1929.

Key ideas

- Rejection of English authority and dominance over Wales – aim of Welsh equality within the United Kingdom, at least until about 1896 (less so thereafter).
- A more active role for the state to help the poor, the elderly and the down-trodden and by increasing freedom of opportunity in education.
- The redistribution of wealth by increasing taxation on the rich.
- The need to persecute 'total war' during the First World War.
- Advocacy of radical, progressive social and economic policies and reviving production in the 1920s and the 1930s.

Biography

David Lloyd George was born at Manchester on 17 January 1863, but was brought to Llanystumdwy in Caernarfonshire by his recently widowed mother the following year. He received only an elementary education, qualified as a solicitor in 1885, became an alderman of Caernarvonshire County Council in 1889, and entered Parliament as the Liberal MP for the Caernarvon Boroughs in a fiercely contested by-election in April 1890. Until the collapse of the *Cymru Fydd* ('Young Wales') movement in January 1896, he was closely associated mainly with Welsh issues and grievances and was very heavily influenced by the Nonconformist (q.v.) ethos in Wales.

Thereafter Lloyd George came to national prominence as one of the leading opponents of the Boer War and as a leader of the campaign against the Balfour Education Act of 1902. He first entered the Cabinet as President of the Board of Trade in December 1905, and later succeeded Asquith as Chancellor of the Exchequer in April 1908. In this position he was responsible for the introduction of an array of highly radical, New Liberal (q.v.) initiatives such as the

payment of old age pensions in 1908 and national health insurance in 1911. The need to pay for these audacious initiatives (and to finance a far-reaching programme of naval construction) led to the introduction of the famous 'People's Budget' of 1909, the ensuing struggle with the House of Lords and the holding of two general elections in 1910. In 1913 Lloyd George, forever innovative in policy, initiated a new rural land campaign.

After reluctantly coming around to the necessity for total war, Lloyd George became Minister of Munitions in May 1915 and Secretary of State for War in July 1916; he finally succeeded Asquith as Prime Minister in December. At this critical juncture he undoubtedly displayed the crucial resourcefulness and the resolute leadership needed to win the war. But the manner of his succession to the premiership split the Liberal Party into two distinct groups, a fatal fissure perpetuated further by the 'coupon' general election of December 1918. Lloyd George remained Prime Minister of a Conservative-dominated administration from 1918 until 1922, during which period he managed to bring about a lasting solution to the Irish problem, in 1921. He fell from power, permanently as it so happened, in October 1922, and was destined to spend the rest of his days firmly on the sidelines of British political life.

Lloyd George returned to the leadership of a reunited Liberal Party in 1926 and made a determined effort to return to power in the 'We Can Conquer Unemployment' general election of 30 May 1929; the Liberal manifesto, according to the historian Robert Skidelsky, was the most intellectually distinguished programme ever put before British voters. The dazzling campaign with its catchy slogans was, however, a relative failure, as the Liberals won no more than fifty-nine parliamentary seats. He became one of a tiny group of just four 'independent Liberals', all members of his own family, at the time of the formation of the National Government in August 1931, and launched his radical 'New Deal' proposals at Bangor in January 1935. He was soon also to set up a new propaganda body, the Council of Action for Peace and Reconstruction. By this time, however, most of his dwindling energies were being mainly devoted to the preparation of his mammoth *War Memoirs* at his Surrey home.

Lloyd George's last important intervention in political life was his contribution to the removal of Neville Chamberlain from office in an impassioned speech in the Norway debate in the House of Commons in May 1940. He accepted a peerage in the January 1945 New Year's Honours List and died at his North Wales home on 26 March of the same year.

Ideas

Lloyd George's Welsh-speaking, fervently Nonconformist background, together with the influence of his revered uncle, Richard Lloyd (1834–1917), who became almost a kind of adoptive father to the young LG, meant that he instinctively resented English dominance over Wales, notably the influence of the established 'alien church' and the highly anglicised landlord class. Hence his support for the disestablishment and disendowment of the church, radical agrarian reforms, measures to secure educational advance, and some degree of Welsh devolution. As a young up-and-coming solicitor, he gained a reputation as one always willing to defend ordinary people against those in authority.

Lloyd George supported the campaign to end church tithes. His avid support for land reform grew from his reading of the works of Thomas Spence, John Stuart Mill (q.v.) and Henry George (q.v.) and the pamphlets written by George Bernard Shaw

and Sidney Webb of the Fabian Society, which underlined the need to tackle the issue of land ownership. This support was of course firmly underpinned by his Welsh Liberal background. As a young politician, Lloyd George fought for religious equality in Wales, land reforms, the 'local veto' on sales of alcohol, graduated taxation and free trade (q.v.).

Lloyd George was also a vehement opponent of the Poor Law, and was determined to take action to 'lift the shadow of the workhouse from the homes of the poor'. Hence his advocacy of old age pensions and unemployment and sickness benefit to provide safety-nets against misfortune and privation. His 1909 'People's Budget' introduced a new supertax and heavy taxes from the profits gained from the ownership and sale of property and also substantially increased death duties on the estates of the rich. This concerted attempt to redistribute wealth provoked the wrath of the Conservative diehards in the House of Lords, and LG was often accused of socialist policies derived from the works of Shaw and the Webbs; but they can also be seen as the implementation of New Liberal principles. Nominally at least, Lloyd George was a supporter of women's rights, but he did precious little to advance their cause whilst in office and was consequently often hounded by the more militant suffragettes.

Lloyd George's avid support for war in 1914–15, and his eventual advocacy of conscription, after a great deal of agitated soul-searching, in 1916, and a more thorough organisation of the country for the war effort, enraged many fellow Liberals and marked something of a departure from his previous views. As Prime Minister of the post-war coalition government, charged to decontrol the wartime economy and embark upon substantial social reconstruction (powerfully reflected in his avowed determination to make Britain 'a land fit for heroes to live in'), he was strongly in favour of increased state intervention, as was reflected in his support for reforms in education, housing, health and transport. But many of these policies, which marked a return to his image as a social reformer, predictably appalled some of LG's old radical associates who had been affronted by his apparent enthusiasm for conscription, his intolerance of conscientious objectors and his breaking with Asquith in favour of working with Bonar Law and the Conservatives.

Even after his fall from office in 1922, Lloyd George continued to campaign for progressive causes, and was certainly much more alert to new radical, progressive ideas than most contemporary politicians from any party. Hence his use of the infamous Lloyd George Fund to finance a number of autonomous investigations in the mid-1920s, charged to look into the social and economic ills of the nation and evolve progressive policies for their remedy. The fruit of these researches was the series of famous 'coloured books', policy documents such as *Coal and Power* (1924), *The Towns and the Land* (1925) and *The Land and the Nation* (1925).

Undoubtedly the best-known of the coloured books was *Britain's Industrial Future*, the famous 'Yellow Book'. Published in 1928, this was the outcome of the Liberal Industrial Inquiry (1926–28), which involved many of the liveliest Liberal minds, including J. M. Keynes (q.v.), Ramsay Muir (q.v.), Walter Layton (q.v.) and E. D. Simon (q.v.), and discussions at the Liberal Summer School (q.v.). The Inquiry was designed to tackle the problems of British industry: high unemployment, low wages, the depression in staple industries, inefficiency, immobility in the labour market and excessive investment overseas. The proposals it put forward in response chiefly originated with Keynes

and Lloyd George himself; they included government planning, including the establishment of an Economic General Staff, special councils to review pay and conditions in each industry, industry-wide minimum wages, a comminission to review trade union law, public boards as a new way of running public concerns and new controls over monopolies. Most strikingly, the Yellow Book proposed a reflationary financial and fiscal policy, including a programme of investment in roads, housing, electricity, waterways and docks, together with a new emphasis on training. Twenty years ahead of their time, these proto-Keynesian (q.v.) proposals were popularised through the pamphlet *We Can Conquer Unemployment* (the 'Orange Book', 1929).

The radical, progressive ideas embodied in these documents resurfaced yet again in LG's 1935 'New Deal' programme which emulated the policies then being advocated by Franklin D. Roosevelt in the US. During the 1930s Lloyd George was generally opposed to the government's appeasement policies and displayed some sympathy for the aspirations of Adolf Hitler, whom he twice visited during 1936.

According to Winston Churchill (q.v.), Lloyd George 'was the greatest Welshman which that unconquerable race has produced since the age of the Tudors'. A deeply controversial leader, both loved and loathed, his impact on early twentieth-century British politics was immense. Not a particularly original thinker, he adopted and implemented the ideas of others with huge energy; as Charles Masterman (q.v.) admitted when the Liberal Party reunited in 1923, 'I've fought him as hard as anyone but I have to confess, when Lloyd George came back to the party, ideas came back to the party'. It was Britain's loss that the bitter political splits for which he was himself partly responsible left Lloyd George out of power during the late 1920s and early '30s, when his imagination and dynamism might have served the country much better than the policies of the cautious and economically hidebound Labour and National governments.

Key works

- *Better Times* (1910)
- *Through Terror to Triumph* (1915)
- *War Memoirs* (6 volumes, 1933–36)
- *The Truth about the Peace Treaties* (2 volumes, 1938)

Further reading

- Bentley B. Gilbert, *David Lloyd George: a Political Life* (two vols., Batsford, 1987 and 1992)
- John Grigg, *The Young Lloyd George* (Eyre Methuen, 1973); *Lloyd George: The People's Champion, 1902–11* (Eyre Methuen, 1978), *Lloyd George: From Peace to War, 1912–16* (Methuen, 1985) and *Lloyd George: War Leader, 1916–18* (Allen Lane, 2002)
- J. Graham Jones, *Lloyd George Papers at the National Library of Wales and Other Repositories* (Welsh Political Archive, the National Library of Wales, 2001)
- Kenneth O. Morgan, *Lloyd George* (Weidenfeld & Nicolson, 1974)
- Martin Pugh, *Lloyd George* (Longman, 1988)
- Peter Rowland, *Lloyd George* (Barrie & Jenkins, 1975)
- Chris Wrigley, *Lloyd George* (Blackwell, 1992)

J. Graham Jones

John Locke   1632–1704

Often described as the patron saint of liberalism, due to his contention that the natural rights of the individual place a limit on the powers of the state, as well as his defence of the rule of law, liberals also see Locke's remarks on separation of the executive and the legislature and on some form of popular representation within government as a precursor to the liberal democratic institutions that emerged following the American and French Revolutions.

Key ideas

- Legitimate polities are built on consent.
- Human beings have natural rights to life, liberty and property; consequently, state power must be limited.
- A labour theory of value and property.
- The legitimacy of armed resistance against tyrants.
- Religious toleration and the separation of church and state.

Biography

John Locke was born into a Puritan family in Wrington, Somerset, on 29 August 1632. Locke's father, also John Locke, a local justice of the peace, was of limited means but had some influential connections, including Alexander Popham, who had served as an officer in the Parliamentary army and a member of the Long Parliament during the English Civil War. Locke's father had fought as a captain in the Parliamentary cavalry alongside Popham during the war, and it was through this friendship that Locke gained a place at London's prestigious Westminster School.

From Westminster Locke moved to Christ Church, Oxford. There he was trained as humanist, but became more and more interested in the anti-scholastic 'new philosophy'; notably, whilst at Oxford in the 1660s he participated in chemical experiments designed by Robert Boyle, a leading member of the Royal Society and an influential exponent of the emerging experimental method. Subsequently, having left Oxford, Locke worked with

Thomas Sydenham, the famous medical doctor with notable empirical leanings.

In 1666 Locke became a protégé of a wealthy aristocrat, Anthony Ashley Cooper, who was created Earl of Shaftesbury in 1672, becoming a leading political figure. Subsequently, Locke's political fortunes were tied to those of his patron. After Shaftesbury became Lord Chancellor in 1672, Locke served as Secretary of the Board of Trade and Plantations as well as Secretary to the Lords and Proprietors of the Carolinas. Similarly, when Shaftesbury became a leading opponent of Charles II and the succession of the Duke of York (later James II), Locke's work set out the seditious philosophical case for constitutional constraints on executive power, and the right to resist tyrannical government. In the aftermath of the so-called Exclusion Crisis, Shaftesbury was accused of planning a revolution to overthrow Charles II, and had to flee into exile. Locke himself also fled to Holland.

Locke's exile, from 1683–89, was an extremely fruitful period. As he was no longer involved in Shaftesbury's political schemes and intrigues he was able to devote himself to his philosophical work, and completed the works that would later be published as *A Letter Concerning Toleration* (1689) and *An Essay Concerning Human Understanding* (1693).

In 1688 Locke's fortunes changed once again, this time as a result of the Glorious Revolution. The overthrow of James II allowed him to return to England and to publish works that would have been viewed as seditious prior to the Revolution; the works that established Locke's reputation as a thinker were published in the five years following 1688. Locke was also able to return to domestic political life, sometimes as an adviser, but also in a formal capacity as an official on the Board of Trade.

In spite of his renewed influence within government Locke's last years were not free from controversy, as members of the religious establishment attacked his religious and philosophical views. The publication of *On the Reasonableness of Christianity* (1695) led the theologian John Edwards to accuse Locke of anti-Trinitarian heresy of Socinianism. More threatening was the Bishop of Worcester, Edward Stillingfleet's, allegation of the same heresy based on Locke's position in *An Essay Concerning Human Understanding*. Locke's final works attempted to refute these accusations and challenge the religious intolerance that characterised English and European politics during this period.

Ideas

The most important statement of Locke's politics is the *Two Treatises of Government* (1689). The first treatise attempts to show that the doctrine of the divine right of kings has no Biblical warrant. The more influential second treatise describes the emergence and limits of legitimate political authority. Locke begins with the notion that all men are by nature equal. Given that God does not appoint human authority, this means that there can be no rightful basis for political power apart from consent. Locke demonstrates this by considering men in their natural state, that is to say 'a state of perfect freedom' where no one is subject to the will of another. Locke's conception of the state of nature is clearly more tranquil than the 'condition of mere nature' described by Hobbes (q.v.) in *Leviathan*. Locke argued that free action in the state of nature is governed by the law of nature, so men in the state of nature ought not to harm each other; ought to honour their promises; seek the good of others; and respect each other's property. Nonetheless, Locke acknowledges that there will be breaches of natural law. In such cases he argues that the law of nature permits each man to judge and punish others. This, he acknowledges, is an unsatisfactory arrangement as it amounts to each man being judge in his own case. Consequently, he argues, men may seek a way out of the state of nature to secure an impartial judge who can apply the laws of nature dispassionately.

Before considering Locke's discussion of the formation of the state it is worth considering his theory of property, as the accumulation of property is an important impetus for the creation of civil government. Like other natural law theorists, Locke argued that in the beginning God gave the earth to mankind in common. Nonetheless, private property was also part of God's order. Locke claims that God gives each man exclusive ownership of his own body. This in turn means that men own their labour and the product of their labour. Consequently, Locke argues that individuals are able to create private property by mixing natural goods with their labour. Even so, men have no right to hoard possessions that would simply decay while others could use them. Nevertheless, with the invention of money, which does not spoil, men have created a system that permits the accumulation of wealth without limit. Indeed, Locke assumed that although men are naturally equal they would not all become equally wealthy. Thus, the creation of money leads to jealousy and conflict, again necessitating a common power.

Crucially, the move from nature to a body politic arises from the consent of those who chose to establish a political society, and it is this act of giving consent that obliges citizens of the body politic to obey its laws. Clearly, for Locke, this obligation has limits. First, he argues that men in the state of nature form a community with a single government in order to protect their natural rights to life, liberty and property. Consequently, they are not obliged to submit to anything that undermines these rights. Indeed, state action that infringes these rights is illegitimate. Equally, men in the state of nature only surrender those rights that are necessary to ensure their natural rights are safeguarded. Locke's belief that men retain their God-given rights in a body politic and that the object of the state is their protection both place a limit on the power of government.

Clearly, not all citizens are involved in the original compact that creates the state. Nonetheless, Locke argues that we give tacit consent to the government if our property enjoys state protection. This, he claims, is true even if we are merely 'lodging only for a week; or … barely travelling freely on the highway'. Nonetheless, this obligation is not without limitation. Locke clearly endorses the right to resist tyrannical government. Essentially, if a government violates the rights of the governed it has cast off its legitimacy, and the people can use force to restore a just political settlement. Nonetheless, in practice Locke thought that individual injustices would not lead to widespread resistance. Indeed, Locke only foresaw resistance and revolution as a response to a consistently tyrannical government or a regime that threatened the rights of the majority of its citizens.

Locke's arguments for toleration in *The Letter Concerning Toleration* stem from his own religious conviction. Locke states that personal salvation is the result of sincere belief. Consequently, coercion would never lead to salvation as it was unable to generate genuine conviction. Additionally, as government is constituted to protect men's natural rights it has no responsibility for or authority over their supernatural destiny. Indeed, Locke also claims that religious persecution is an affront to natural rights and therefore citizens can legitimately resist such interference. Nonetheless, he argues that toleration must be limited; atheists could not be tolerated for the simple reason that there can be no morality without a belief in God. As a result atheists were unfit for society and the state was justified in acting against them as they were a threat to the natural rights of others. This position is underlined by Locke's last major work, *On the Reasonableness of Christianity*. Here he claims that mankind can have no certain knowledge of the laws of nature. Consequently, we must rely on revelation in order to understand how to live a moral life. Again, this demonstrates that atheists are unable to understand morality, as it is only through faith that we can know natural law. Finally, Locke claims that Roman Catholics should be excluded from the political community as their allegiance was to a foreign sovereign, and their influence tended to the imposition of religious orthodoxy.

Locke's ideas have had an enormous impact on the history of ideas and political practice. While the immediate context in which the *Two Treatises of Government* was written was the English crisis of 1679–83, the work was only published after the Glorious Revolution, and consequently the critique of absolutism and the defence of limited government were read as a defence of the Revolution. There is some justification for this interpretation of the *Two Treatises*, as the preface to the first edition expressed the hope that work would 'establish the Throne of our Great Restorer, Our present King William'. Nonetheless, the absence of fundamental constitutional change meant that Locke was far from satisfied by the settlement that emerged following the events of 1688–89.

Beyond the English context, echoes of Locke's thinking on the role and limits of government can be found in the American Declaration of Independence and constitution. Similarly, writers such as Thomas Paine (q.v.) drew on Locke's arguments on natural rights to help defend the French Revolution. While Locke cannot be justly described as a liberal, his conception of natural rights, toleration and the limits of legitimate authority have had a profound impact on classical liberalism (q.v.).

Key works
- *Essays on the Law of Nature* (1660)
- *A Letter Concerning Toleration* (1689)
- *Two Treatises of Government* (1689)
- *An Essay Concerning Human Understanding* (1693)
- *Thoughts on Education* (1693)
- *On the Reasonableness of Christianity* (1695)

Further reading
- Richard Ashcraft, 'Revolutionary Politics and Locke's *Two Treatises of Government:* Radicalism and Lockean Political Theory', *Political Theory* 1980
- John Dunn, *The Political Thought of John Locke* (Cambridge University Press, 1969)
- John Dunn, *Locke* (Oxford University Press, 1984)
- Ian Harris, *The Mind of John Locke* (Cambridge University Press, 1994)
- John Marshal, *John Locke: Resistance, Religion, and Responsibility* (Cambridge University Press, 1994)
- Richard Tuck, *Natural Rights Theories: Their Origins and Development* (Cambridge University Press, 1979)
- James Tully, *A Discourse of Property* (Cambridge University Press, 1984)
- James Tully, *An Approach to Political Philosophy: Locke in Contexts* (Cambridge University Press, 1993)

Robin Bunce

Lord Lothian   1882–1940

A theorist of international relations, arguing that the ultimate cause of war lay in the absence of an international reign of law applying to individual sovereign nations. Peace therefore requires the creation of an international federal state.

Key ideas

- Peace and the reign of law in society is ensured by the role of the state.
- The absence of such a reign of law applying to states is the ultimate cause of war.
- If war is to be prevented, then an international state is needed.
- The United States and the British Empire should form the basis of the international state.

Biography

Philip Henry Kerr, 11th Lord Lothian, was born into one of Britain's leading Catholic families on 18 April 1882; he was educated at the Oratory School, Edgbaston, and New College, Oxford. Kerr's first professional experience was in the reconstruction of government in South Africa after the Boer War (in Lord Milner's famous 'Kindergarten'). There, he encountered the principles of federal government which were to form the basis of his subsequent political thought. A fellow member of the Kindergarten, Lionel Curtis, became a life-long friend, adviser and collaborator on political issues.

Kerr became the first editor of the *Round Table* quarterly review and wrote prolifically on international affairs, including the idea of converting the British Empire into an English-speaking federation. He served in the private office of Lloyd George (q.v.) from 1916 to 1921 and played an influential role at the Versailles peace conference of 1919.

A devout believer, he left the Catholic Church to become a Christian Scientist in 1923, having been introduced to the sect by Nancy Astor. She was perhaps the second most influential figure in his life; he never married.

Upon acceding to the peerage in March 1930, he joined the Liberal benches in the House of Lords and served as Chancellor of the Duchy of Lancaster and then Under-Secretary for India in the National Government, from August 1931 to September 1932. He was a supporter of Indian self-government within the empire, proposing a federal model for the government of India, drawing on his earlier experience in South Africa.

Lothian became a prominent figure in British public life, enjoying, if that is the word, personal meetings with Stalin, Hitler and Gandhi (did anyone else meet all three?). His final public service found him as ambassador to the United States at the outbreak of the Second World War. He used this position to appeal to American public opinion, explaining the existential threat faced by democracy and paving the way for Roosevelt's steady increase in support for the Allied cause. He died unexpectedly in Washington on 12 December 1940.

Ideas

The central theme of Lothian's work was that peace can be assured and the threat of war averted only through the institutions of a federal state.

His earliest experience of federalism was in the development of government in South Africa after the Boer War. There, the notion of different levels of government to do different jobs became readily apparent to him; he was asked, for example, to investigate how to manage the railway system in the face of conflicting interests among the four colonies. The application of the federal principle to the empire as a whole followed naturally – the dominions should contribute more to the defence of the empire, and

Britain should accept a greater role for the dominions in taking imperial decisions. He became the first editor of the *Round Table*, a 'Quarterly Review of Imperial Politics', and encouraged local circles of readers throughout the empire to discuss and sustain the idea of imperial federation.

The first significant expression of his federalist ideas was in a series of lectures given in 1923 at Yale, *The Prevention of War*. In this work, he argued that the fundamental cause of war was 'the division of humanity into absolutely sovereign states'. He compared the position of states in international society with that of the American West before the arrival of constitutional government, when 'the rights and property of the individual depended fundamentally on upon his own strength and courage, and quickness of hand and eye'. The notion of the 'general good', expressed in the solemn covenant of the Pilgrim Fathers at Plymouth in 1620, was, he said, absent from the international society of states. There had been a limited attempt to bring it into the Versailles peace conference of 1919, but the years since had seen a resumption of the scramble of every nation for itself. Nothing short of a federal democracy was needed if there was not to be a lapse back into war.

Lothian was a prolific writer, but a few works make up the most important reading. The 1935 Burge Memorial Lecture, *Pacifism is Not Enough, nor Patriotism Either*, contains the essence of his thinking. He himself once remarked that it had been the most intense and difficult thing he had ever written, although reading it is neither.

He was critical of the League of Nations and the Kellogg Peace Pact of 1928 (which provided for the renunciation of war as an instrument of national policy), based as they were on the defence of absolute national sovereignty rather than its replacement. Those institutions were flawed because, he said, there was no means of looking at issues from the position of the general good and they lacked the power to make their decisions effective. They were not a substitute for an international state.

Lothian's political judgement was perhaps less sure than his political thinking. Recognising the injustice meted out to Germany in the Versailles treaty, he was a rather late convert from appeasement once it became clear that Hitler's demands went far beyond a simple adjustment of the peace terms of 1919. He may have looked to the United States rather than France as the most immediate and obvious partner for Britain, making him an ideal spokesman for his country at the outbreak of the Second World War, but at the end of the war his thinking was in fact followed most closely in Europe, a continent of which he had little knowledge and interest during his career.

Key works

- *The Prevention of War* (1923)
- *Pacifism is Not Enough* (1935)

Further reading

- *The American Speeches of Lord Lothian* (Oxford University Press, 1941)
- J. R. M. Butler, *Lord Lothian (Philip Kerr) 1882–1940* (Macmillan & Co., 1960)
- John Turner (ed.), *The Larger Idea: Lord Lothian and the Problem of National Sovereignty* (The Historians' Press, 1988)

Richard Laming

T. B. Macaulay　　　　1800–59

A celebrated parliamentary orator, essayist, poet and historian, Macaulay was one of the foremost exponents of Whig principles in the nineteenth century, making the case for a political strategy of timely, cautious reform, in order to forestall the danger of revolutionary change.

Key ideas

- Moderate reform as the means of avoiding revolution.
- Rejection of utilitarian deductive reasoning.
- Elitist distrust of the masses.
- The importance of history for popular education.

Biography

Thomas Babington Macaulay was born on 25 October 1800 at Rothley, Leicestershire, the son of Zachary Macaulay, a prominent campaigner for the abolition of slavery. His early years were spent mainly at Clapham, where the Macaulays mixed with their fellow evangelical 'Saints', such as William Wilberforce. An extraordinarily precocious child, Macaulay was educated by an evangelical clergyman before attending Trinity College, Cambridge, in 1818. His distinguished academic career culminated in a fellowship at Trinity in 1824. Macaulay had grown distrustful of the fervour and simplicity of evangelicalism, and its Tory leanings, and he briefly flirted with the fashionable utilitarian (q.v.) philosophy of Jeremy Bentham (q.v.).

Although he was called to the bar in 1826, it was as an essayist for the *Edinburgh Review* that Macaulay made his mark, attracting the attention of the Whig leaders. In February 1830 he was brought into Parliament for Lord Lansdowne's pocket borough of Calne, and over the next two years his oratorical powers, which electrified the House of Commons, were deployed in support of the Great Reform Bill. Macaulay was appointed to the Board of Control (responsible for the government of India) in June 1832, and later that year became MP for the new constituency of Leeds.

However, he resigned his seat in 1834 to take up a lucrative position on the Supreme Council in India.

Following his return to England, Macaulay was elected MP for Edinburgh in June 1839. Four months later he joined Lord Melbourne's Cabinet as Secretary at War, and held this post until the government's demise in 1841. He served as Paymaster-General in Lord John Russell's (q.v.) Cabinet, formed in 1846, but was a notable casualty of the 1847 general election and subsequently retired from office.

Since 1839, Macaulay had devoted much of his spare time to writing an ambitious *History of England*. The four volumes, published in two instalments (1848 and 1855), only covered the years from 1685 to 1697, but they were a spectacular success, selling many thousands of copies worldwide. Failing health prevented Macaulay from taking his project further.

Edinburgh made amends by re-electing Macaulay in 1852. In 1857 he accepted a peerage, becoming Baron Macaulay of Rothley. He died in London, on 28 December 1859, and was buried in Poets' Corner in Westminster Abbey.

Ideas

Macaulay's intellectual commitment to Whiggism (q.v.) resulted from a journey through competing ideologies. Initially, his political thinking was shaped by the romantic Toryism of Edmund Burke (q.v.) and Sir Walter Scott, with its reverence for traditional ruling institutions. This was tempered by the attraction of utilitarianism, which demonstrated the need to overhaul anachronistic structures and practices. However, in the *Edinburgh Review* in 1829, Macaulay launched a damaging attack on the utilitarians' doctrinaire belief that the blueprint for an ideal political system could be deduced from basic principles of human nature. He relied instead on inductive reasoning, drawing general conclusions from practical experience. Whiggism, the creed of gradual, peaceful reform, offered Macaulay a way of reconciling his desire for both stability and change.

In his speeches defending the Great Reform Bill, Macaulay urged MPs to take counsel from the lesson of history, that 'all great revolutions have been produced by a disproportion between society and its institutions' (5 July 1831). If revolution was to be avoided, the system of parliamentary representation had to be modernised in accordance with 'the spirit of the age'. This meant enfranchising the 'middle classes', whose numbers had grown as a result of economic diversification and rapid urbanisation, so that all the 'property and intelligence' of the country was united in defence of the constitution (2 March 1831). Macaulay wanted enlightened leadership by a carefully expanded political elite, not democracy, and he argued that a timely concession of reform would 'save the multitude from its own ungovernable power and passion', and thus prove to be a 'measure of conservation'.

The key to the future improvement of society lay in education, and Macaulay was particularly anxious that 'the multitude' should be made aware of the nation's past, and imbued with a sense of pride in its achievements. His long-planned *History of England* was deliberately intended to supply a suitable popular text. In describing the events surrounding the Glorious Revolution of 1688–89, the triumph of Protestant libertarianism (q.v.) over Catholic despotism, Macaulay hailed the inauguration of an era of unbroken political, moral and cultural progress, that was still spreading its beneficent effects over the people. The publication of his first two volumes in 1848, the year of revolutions in Europe, was for-

tuitous but highly appropriate, for he was able to explain in his introduction the reason why Britain had been immune from the continental disease: 'It is because we had a preserving revolution in the seventeenth century that we have not had a destroying revolution in the nineteenth.'

Like many Whigs, Macaulay was resistant to extreme laissez-faire doctrines (q.v.). Free trade (q.v.) was an admirable principle when applied to strictly commercial matters, but many issues had a wider relevance for 'the community' as a whole (22 May 1846). Macaulay therefore approved of state intervention to regulate conditions in factories. Similarly, he maintained that the state had a duty to ensure that the people were educated.

Key works
- *History of England from the Accession of James II* (1848–55)

Further reading
- John Clive, *Thomas Babington Macaulay: The Shaping of the Historian* (Harvard University Press, 1973)
- T. F. Ellis (ed.), *Miscellaneous Writings and Speeches of Lord Macaulay* (Longman, 1860)
- Joseph Hamburger, *Macaulay and the Whig Tradition* (University of Chicago Press, 1976)
- T. Pinney (ed.), *Letters of Thomas Babington Macaulay* (Cambridge University Press, 1974–81)
- G. O. Trevelyan, *Life and Letters of Lord Macaulay* (Longman, 1876)

T. A. Jenkins

Thomas Malthus   1766–1834

Malthus' thesis that population will increase in a geometric progression while the means of subsistence will increase at an arithmetical progression, so the population will always expand to the limit of subsistence, have influenced economists and policy-makers of his time and since, including Keynes, and students of population studies.

Key ideas

- Population will increase to the limit of subsistence.
- Poverty is man's inescapable lot.
- Welfare for the poor is to be discouraged.
- Identification of the need to stimulate 'effective demand'.

Biography

Thomas Robert Malthus was born on 13 February 1766 at Dorking, and educated at home. His father was a country gentleman, a friend of David Hume (q.v.) and an admirer of Jean-Jacques Rousseau, so we may assume intellectual influences in his upbringing. He was educated by his father and tutors. He went to St John's College, Cambridge in 1784, and studied mathematics. He also took holy orders, being ordained in 1788, and became a Church of England curate. He was then elected a fellow of St John's in 1793 and employed curates to look after his parish; his fellowship was forfeited when he married, in 1804. He travelled to Germany, Russia and Scandinavia.

Malthus's most well-known work, *An Essay on the Principle of Population*, was first published in 1798, following discussions with his father of the ideas of Godwin and Condorcet (q.v.). Subsequent editions were expanded until the sixth came out in 1826.

In 1805 Malthus was appointed to the chair of political economy at the East India Company's college at Haileybury. He was, therefore, able to concentrate on his interest in population and political economy generally. He became friendly with David Ricardo (q.v.), they debated the issues of the day, and became rivals in the development of economic theory. In 1800 he published *An Investigation into the Cause of the Present High Price of Provisions*, in which the term 'effective demand' was first used, and in 1820 he published *Principles of Political Economy Considered with a View to Their Practical Application*, in which he proposed public works and private luxury investment to increase effective demand.

Malthus's work on population was controversial but as a conservative Whig he influenced policy-makers, particularly over the decision to hold Britain's first census, in 1801, and the Poor Law Amendment Act of 1834. Malthus is considered a classical economist and his ideas were included in Keynes's (q.v.) lectures at Cambridge in the early part of the twentieth century. He died on 23 December 1834, and was buried in Bath Abbey, where there is a memorial to him in the porch.

Ideas

Like most economists, Malthus wrote about the economy which he experienced at the time. When he wrote the thesis for which he is most remembered, it was believed that Britain was experiencing rapid population growth; the working classes were also experiencing poor conditions during the Industrial Revolution. His thesis was that while population increases at a geometric, or exponential, rate (e.g. 2, 4, 8, 16, 32 ...) agricultural production increases at an arithmetical rate (e.g. 1, 2, 3, 4, 5, 6 ...) – thus leading eventually to a subsistence, and then a lower, standard of living, poverty and famine. Malthus's view of the human nature of the poor led him to conclude that if wages rose to permit a higher standard of living then there would be an increase in the birth rate and yet more poverty.

This led directly to the idea that any relief for the poor above that which was given in extreme circumstances would be counter-productive and should be withheld. Consequently the Pitt government shelved an idea of introducing family allowances, and a later proposal for housing for the poor was also withdrawn.

Malthus was a moralist and his own proposal for ameliorating the birth rate was deferment of marriage accompanied by chastity prior to marriage, although he viewed this as unachievable for many men. However, he considered the sexual promiscuity caused by deferred marriage as a lesser evil than the increase in population resulting from earlier marriage. Other of his ideas for curbing the rise in population included 'moral restraint', universal suffrage, state-run education for the poor, elimination of the Poor Laws and an unfettered labour market.

The approach of Malthus to the rise in population was accepted by many writers at the time, but they were more optimistic about the future, suggesting that birth control should be practiced to keep population growth in check. In particular, John Stuart Mill (q.v.) defended the Malthusian theory of population but believed in the capacity of the working class to practice voluntary family limitation. Interestingly, Malthus influenced Charles Darwin when he was beginning to think about natural selection.

In retrospect Malthus had adopted the theory of wages developed by Richard Cantillon, who argued that the wage rate would fall to the subsistence level as the supply of labour increased – but this only ever applied to the unskilled, as was shown by Adam Smith (q.v.). Also, Malthus could not anticipate the technical progress which would occur in agriculture, and has continued to the present day, increasing the supply of food. Among those who study

population the basic proposition that unrestricted growth can lead to a subsistence standard of living lingers on; the leaders of Communist China who enforced a one-child-per-family policy are one example.

Reflecting the economy of his time, Malthus turned his mind to the depression in the world economy following the Napoleonic Wars. The value of British exports fell from an index of 100 in 1815 to 63 in 1823, and the resultant unemployment led to widespread agitation, including the Peterloo Masacre in 1819. Malthus identified a 'general glut', an excess supply caused by insufficient demand and proposed in his *Principles of Political Economy* public works and private luxury investment as palliatives to economic distress to increase effective demand. These ideas were to reappear in Keynes's (q.v.) *General Theory* in 1936.

During the period 1814–15 Malthus entered the controversy regarding the Corn Laws: first he proposed their abolition, and then he changed his mind. At this time he debated this issue, and others such as a theory of rent and 'value', with Ricardo prior to the publication of Ricardo's *Principles* in 1817. Some of Malthus's ideas were incorporated by Ricardo.

Another, not insignificant but undeveloped, idea of Malthus, identified by Keynes, was expounded in his 1800 pamphlet *An Investigation into the Cause of the Recent High Price of Provisions* – that rising prices follow increases in the supply of money, i.e. an endogenous supply of money.

Key works
- *An Essay on the Principle of Population* (1798)
- *An Investigation into the Causes of the Present High Price of Provisions* (1800)
- *Principles of Political Economy Considered with a View to Their Practical Application* (1820)

Further reading

- M. Blaug, *Economic Theory in Retrospect* (Macmillan, 5th edition, 1975)
- J. M. Keynes, *Essays in Biography, The Collected Writings of John Maynard Keynes*, vol. X (Royal Economic Society, Macmillan, 1972)
- G. Routh, *The Origin of Economic Ideas* (Macmillan, 1975)

Roger Fox

Manchester School

Never as coherent a body as contemporaries and subsequent historians often liked to imply, in the narrow sense the term 'Manchester School' was used to denote the leaders of the campaign against the Corn Laws, but in a wider sense has come to refer to the British free trade movement. The School's agenda, which included peace, disarmament and public education, triggered off an era of reform that went far beyond the issue of free trade.

Benjamin Disraeli coined the term 'Manchester School' in February 1846 to describe the leaders of the Anti-Corn Law League (q.v.), who mostly came from the Manchester region. While the League was focused on a single issue (the repeal of the Corn Laws), the term 'Manchester School' soon became associated not only with the movement for free trade (q.v.), but also with a wider reform agenda.

In the minds of many people, the repeal of the Corn Laws in 1846 marked the end of the political stagnation and the misery of the 'hungry forties' (the central topic of many of Charles Dickens's novels). After 1846 the main representatives of the League, Richard Cobden (q.v.), John Bright and others, not only advocated free trade, but fought for a wider range of issues, including international peace and disarmament, anti-

colonialism and anti-imperialism, women's rights and electoral reform and – most significantly – for better education of the poor, which they held to be the key to any improvement of the working classes' lot. Not as dogmatically free market-oriented as is often supposed, many of them advocated a stronger involvement of the state in basic education.

Thus Cobden and his adherents managed to associate the issue of free trade with a consistently radical image in politics. The core of that image was the struggle against the political and economic privileges of the land-owning aristocracy and for the improvement of the conditions of the working classes. As Cobden said: 'Now, the first and greatest count in my indictment against the Corn-law is, that it is an injustice to the labourers of this and every other country.'

Arguably, economic reform policies after the fall of the Corn Laws helped to increase wages considerably in the following decades. When in 1909 the Royal Statistical Society recorded the trend in real wages for nineteenth-century England, it found that they had increased by 18 per cent between 1850 and 1870, and by 1880 they were 38 per cent higher than in 1850. This impact, as well as the personal integrity of the School's leading figures, such as Cobden, contributed much to the historical fame of the Manchester School in Britain itself.

Notwithstanding their support for state involvement in education, the Manchester School's adherents eventually came to be associated with the classical liberal (q.v.) laissez-faire (q.v.) approach to state intervention. Bright in particular opposed government interference in contract, and accordingly tended to be hostile to the Factory Acts. Although the New Liberals (q.v.) of the late nineteenth and early twentieth century moved on from this position, they remained firmly attached to the Manchester School's core legacy, support for free trade. This remained a powerful cause right through to the 1930s; the Liberal Party's election campaign of 1906 successfully used the image of the 'big (free-trade) loaf' versus the 'little (protectionist) loaf' in order to win working-class votes.

Outside Britain the success of the Anti-Corn Law League soon inspired similar movements in most European countries. Although usually well connected with the peace movement and the (voluntary) workers' cooperatives, the European 'Manchesterites' mainly associated themselves with the issue of free trade, and their political outlook was often less radical. Yet organisations like the French Association for Free Trade (founded in 1846 by Frédéric Bastiat (q.v.)) and the German Congress of German Economists (founded in 1858) exercised a considerable influence on their respective governments. It would not be entirely incorrect to talk of the mid-nineteenth century as the time of the European free trade movement. With a series of bilateral treaties, beginning with the Cobden-Chevalier Treaty between Britain and France in 1860, for roughly two decades this movement helped to establish free trade as the guiding principle of economic policy. The volume of trade increased considerably and as a consequence, the standard of living in most industrialised European countries improved substantially.

At the same time, however, the term 'Manchester School' gradually came to acquire a negative image, especially in Germany from 1870 onwards, where *Manchestertum* became increasingly dissociated from the original reformist radicalism (q.v.) of Cobden and his colleagues. Socialist authors, like Ferdinand Lassalle in 1864, attempted to discredit the School by labelling it as an instrument of bourgeois rule and capitalist ideology to exploit the working classes. Ignoring the cosmopolitan and anti-imperialist thinking of the School's exponents, socialist and nationalist writers portrayed the Manchester School as a tool of Britain's economic self-interest, denouncing German free-trade liberals as a 'fifth column' of British imperialism. Anti-Semitic authors like Wilhelm Marr in 1878 soon jumped on the bandwagon and created the image of the 'Manchesterite' as a heartless speculator. Partly because it sounded so foreign, the word 'Manchester' itself became one of the most effective anti-liberal slogans in Germany before the First World War and contributed significantly to the rise of authoritarian statism.

It is only in recent years that German historians have begun to correct the distorted image that had prevailed in Germany for more than a century. This should restore the much-deserved reputation of the Manchester School – the embodiment of true liberal radicalism at its best.

Further reading

- Detmar Doering, *Countering the Myth of Manchesterism: An Essay on Richard Cobden and the Free Trade Movement* (Friedrich Naumann Foundation, 2004)
- William D. Grampp, *The Manchester School of Economics* (Stanford University Press, 1960)
- Francis W. Hirst (ed.), *Free Trade and Other Fundamental Doctrines of the Manchester School* (Harper & Bros., 1903)
- Anthony Howe, *Free Trade and Liberal England, 1846–1946* (Oxford University Press, 1997)
- Anthony Howe and Simon Morgan (eds.), *Rethinking Nineteenth Century Liberalism: Richard Cobden Bicentenary Essays* (Ashgate, 2006)

Detmar Doering

David Marquand   1934–

One of Britain's leading social-democratic thinkers since the 1970s, in a succession of elegant writings Marquand has developed his political ideas, significantly influencing the changing climate of centre-left thought.

Key ideas

- Keynesian social democracy as the governing philosophy of the post-war collectivist consensus.
- Advocacy of a new-model libertarian, decentralist social democracy.
- A developmental state, capable of harnessing market forces to the long-term national interest.
- A communitarian public philosophy, centred on the notion of 'politics as mutual education'.
- Defence of the public domain distinct from the market realm, and nurturing values of public service and citizenship.

Biography

David Marquand was born in Cardiff on 20 September 1934. His father was a Labour MP and minister in Attlee's governments. He was educated at Emanuel School and Magdalen College, Oxford. After teaching politics at Sussex University, he was Labour MP for Ashfield 1966–77. He left Parliament for the European Commission but returned to academia in 1978 as Professor of Politics and Contemporary History at Salford University, and subsequently Professor of Politics at Sheffield University 1991–96. He joined the Social Democratic Party in 1981, becoming one of its leading political thinkers and advisers, continuing in that role in the Liberal Democrats until the 1990s. He was Principal of Mansfield College, Oxford 1996–2002.

Ideas

Until the 1970s, Marquand adhered to the main tenets of what he called the governing philosophy of the post-war collectivist consensus, 'Keynesian social democracy' (see Keynsianism, social democracy). This approach rejected the traditional association of socialism with public ownership and comprised an ethical reformulation of socialist aims, acceptance of a state-regulated yet market-oriented mixed economy, promotion of a welfare state, financed by both economic growth and redistributive taxation, and the pursuit of full employment and sustained economic growth through the application of demand management techniques.

However, in the harsh economic climate of the 1970s, the intellectual and political appeal of Keynesian social democracy began to fade. By the late 1970s, therefore, Marquand stressed the need to amend the fundamental assumptions of that ideological position, and to devise what he called a 'new-model libertarian, decentralist social democracy'. He even indicated, as Roy Jenkins did more explicitly, that a new political vehicle might be needed to achieve that aim.

When that new party emerged in March 1981, in the form of the SDP, Marquand, an enthusiastic founder member, became one of its leading thinkers. In his 1981 pamphlet, *Russet-Coated Captains: The Challenge of Social Democracy*, a personal interpretation of the 'varied ancestry' of the social democratic tradition in Britain, he identified 'three principles of central importance' which it had inherited: an equal commitment to personal freedom (q.v.) and social justice (q.v.); a firm attachment to the distinctive features of the open society; and unequivocal support for the mixed economy.

Marquand's first major work of political theory and analysis, *The Unprincipled Society* (1988), was conceived in the mid-1980s, and 'written in the glare of Thatcherism's high noon'. It examined 'the long hegemony of post-war Keynesian social democracy' and 'the crises which destroyed it', and provided 'a contribution to the search for a new governing philosophy' in the wake of the breakdown of the post-war collectivist consensus. *The Unprincipled Society* contained a critique of neo-liberalism (q.v.), an alternative account both of the rise and fall of the post-war consensus and of the relative decline of the British economy, and the tentative outlines of what Marquand proposed as an 'alternative, communitarian public philosophy', centred on the civic republican notion of 'politics as mutual education'.

In his account of national economic decline, Marquand argued, distinctively and contentiously, that Britain, unlike more successful mixed economies, had failed to evolve a 'developmental state' capable of harnessing market forces to the long-term national interest. The reasons for this deficiency lay, in his view, in a political culture which since the early nineteenth century had been suffused with the individualist attitudes of economic liberalism (q.v.).

Marquand's next major work, *The Progressive Dilemma* (1991), explored, in a succession of elegant biographical portraits, the disturbing historical reality that since 1918 the Labour Party had captured only part of the Liberals' pre-1914 progressive coalition. He examined not only the divorce of the Labour and Liberal parties after 1918 but also the divergence of the democratic socialist and social liberal (q.v.) traditions in British politics, thus revisiting, with a broader focus, territory which he had covered in his 1977 revisionist biography of Labour's first Prime Minister, Ramsay MacDonald.

After rejoining Labour in the 1990s, Marquand published *The New Reckoning* (1997), a collection of essays written between the mid-1980s and mid-1990s,

with an added introduction, entitled 'Journey to an Unknown Destination', consisting of a perceptive and revealing fragment of political and intellectual autobiography. He explained that 'intellectually, even if not chronologically', he had been 'a child of the Keynesian golden age'. But 'the far from golden 1970s and 1980s' had swept him 'from the political moorings to which [he] had been attached for most of [his] life'. In a transformed climate in which 'the tamed welfare capitalism' of the Keynesian era had been superseded by 'the untamed capitalism of today', one of the most serious casualties had been the erosion of 'a public domain, ring-fenced from the pressures of the market place', and in which, since the second half of the nineteenth century, values of citizenship and public service had prevailed.

Marquand developed this observation into the central theme of his next major work, *Decline of the Public: The Hollowing Out of Citizenship* (2004). Here he defined the precarious concept of the public domain in more detail. It was 'a dimension of social life' distinct from the market realm, 'a space, protected from the adjacent market and private domains', where people acted not in response to monetary incentives or on the basis of friendship or kinship ties, but rather from a motive of public service. After tracing its origins and development from mid-Victorian Britain to its zenith in the 1950s, Marquand argued that the public domain was indeed now at serious risk, undermined by what he called the New Right's 'Kulturkampf', the Conservative governments' 'relentless marketisation' in the 1980s and 1990s of intermediate public-service institutions, including local government, the health service, schools, universities and the senior civil service.

Moreover, Marquand noted with regret that the Blair governments since 1997 had not reversed this process. Rather, they had promoted it just as zealously as the Conservatives. That conclusion reflected Marquand's growing disenchantment with the New Labour project, which, he later lamented, had betrayed the heritage of the SDP and jettisoned the version of social democracy that it had been 'founded to save'. In subsequent writings he has sought to address this question with the historical and theoretical insight that has characterised his political thought.

Key works

- *Ramsay MacDonald* (1977)
- *The Unprincipled Society: New Demands and Old Politics* (1988)
- *The New Reckoning: Capitalism, States and Citizens* (1997)
- *The Progressive Dilemma: From Lloyd George to Blair* (1991; 2nd edn., 1999)
- *Decline of the Public: The Hollowing Out of Citizenship* (2004)

Tudor Jones

Alfred Marshall   1842–1924

Playing the leading role in pursuing and winning support for the 'marginalist revolution' in economic thought, Marshall's contribution to economics (and indirectly to politics) has been described as the most sophisticated extension of the work of the classical liberal economists, most notably Adam Smith, David Ricardo and John Stuart Mill.

Key ideas

- Neo-classical economic analysis can provide a coherent and integrated account of supply and demand, marginal utility and production costs.
- Specific economic notions, including elasticity of demand, consumer and producer surplus, quasi-rent and the representative firm.

- Importance, possibility and desirability of providing dispassionate advice to inform public policy-makers and economic decision-makers.

Biography

Alfred Marshall was born, on 26 July 1842, into a respectable middle-class family and grew up in the south London suburb of Clapham. His parents expected him to become a clergyman but he became an academic economist instead, having demonstrated great mathematical ability at Cambridge University. His academic success led to employment as a lecturer in 'moral sciences' at St John's College, Cambridge, when he was just twenty-six years old.

His marriage to Mary Paley in 1877, a Newnham student to whom he had taught political economy, meant leaving St John's because of its celibacy rules. He moved to Bristol where he became Principal of the new University College and Professor of Political Economy. His health became and remained problematic; he suffered greatly with kidney stones and was increasingly frustrated in his intellectual ambitions. He spent time in Palermo in Italy in order to pursue his academic interests and partially recover his health. In 1881 he left Bristol to teach at Oxford University before taking up a chair in political economy in Cambridge in 1884.

Marshall's campaign to establish economics as a discipline in its own right bore fruit in 1903, when a new tripos in economics and politics was introduced. Although his poor health meant that the seeds he planted were largely left to others to nourish, he nevertheless attracted and helped motivate some notable thinkers, amongst them J. M. Keynes (q.v.) and A. C. Pigou, who helped to build Cambridge's international reputation for economic theorising and its influence on economic policy-making.

Marshall retired from his chair in political economy in 1908. His poor health continued to dog his efforts to bring his major theoretical works to completion, and his fastidiousness meant that he was always reluctant to complete and publish his research. His desire to take all possible developments in economic thought into account earned him a reputation as both a difficult and a fussy colleague. His most famous work, *Principles of Political Economy*, first published in 1890, underwent revision after revision, seven revised editions appearing before he died in his Cambridge home on 13 July 1924.

Ideas

Marshall is generally regarded as the most important figure in British economics between 1890 and 1920. The status of his *Principles* as the foundation for modern economics is rarely disputed. His mathematical excellence enabled him to construct the neo-classical economic paradigm, adding substantially to classical economic thought. His theoretical approach shaped the work of almost all those economists who have tried to make sense of the operation of markets containing large numbers of individual economic actors. Marshall was responsible for putting the analysis of supply and demand at the very heart of economics and directing the attention of his successors to the ways in which they intersect to determine price and quantity in the market place.

Marshall's *Principles* became notable for the introduction of a series of new concepts, including 'elasticity of demand', 'consumer's surplus', 'quasi-rent' and the 'representative firm', adding to the armoury of economic thinkers as well as influencing public discussion over economic policy and management. Marshall's major intellec-

tual contribution to the study of economics brought together theories of supply and demand, marginal utility and production costs and organised them into a coherent whole. His recasting of economic thought invited economists to express economic relationships in a sophisticated and specialist language, changing the way in which ideas about economic systems are communicated. Having fashioned an analytical framework and developed a methodology for economic analysis, relying heavily on mathematics and classical mechanics, Marshall was able to convince others that economic analysis could be used to study and measure changes in well-being that followed from alterations in public policies, including taxation and trade policies. The idea that economic analysis could be systematic, dispassionate and objective has proven very powerful indeed.

Because of his status as the most eminent British economist of his era Marshall found himself drawn into the public discussion of economic policy, something that he looked upon with great trepidation. He was concerned about his role as a leader in the economics profession and anxious not to jeopardise the status of the discipline. In 1903 Marshall wrote a private memorandum to the Chancellor of the Exchequer setting out his views on trade and tariff policy and commending the need for public policy-makers to take careful note of economic analysis in formulating policy; his work on *Industry and Trade* was not published, however, until 1919. Earlier, in the 1890s, he had been an expert witness before a number of government inquiries and served as a member of the Royal Commission on Labour (1890–94). His answers to questions about the desirability or otherwise of trade unions being able to redress imbalances in their bargaining power with employers were hedged around with caveats and qualifications. He was far from being a user-friendly figure in the eyes of those whose sectional interests he felt obliged to question.

In an introduction to his *Principles* Marshall wrote that he had come to economics because it entailed a 'study of the causes of poverty [and] … the causes of degradation of a large part of mankind'. He doubted that the lives of those working in poor conditions and with limited means could be improved without great economic advances. And, in this respect, the study of economics had much to offer all those who wanted to understand how markets functioned and learn how they could be made to operate more successfully. It was this perspective that strongly influenced many of those he taught or worked with, most notably Keynes. Marshall was doubtful, however, that better economic conditions would, by themselves, improve human character or behaviour. Income redistribution might be sensible and reasonable but government and, most particularly, those who enjoyed the greatest affluence, had to shoulder their responsibilities, lead by example and avoid ostentatious consumption.

His work stands as a late Victorian bridge between classical and twentieth-century economic and liberal thought.

Key works

- *The Pure Theory of Foreign Trade: The Pure Theory of Domestic Values* (1879)
- *The Economics of Industry* (with Mary Paley Marshall, 1879)
- *Principles of Economics* (1890)
- *Industry and Trade* (1919)
- *Money, Credit and Commerce* (1923)

Further reading

- Peter Groenewegen, *A Soaring Eagle: Alfred Marshall, 1842–1924* (Edward Elgar, 1995)

- John K. Whitaker, *The Correspondence of Alfred Marshall, Economist* (3 vols., Cambridge University Press, 1996)

Ed Randall

Harriet Martineau   1802–76

A life-long radical, Harriet Martineau first became famous as a populariser of Malthusian political economy. Throughout her varied career she espoused classical liberalism, applying its central tenets to many causes including feminism and anti-slavery.

Key ideas

- Belief in Malthusian political economy as a universal law.
- State to facilitate free trade, laissez-faire, a national system of education and universal suffrage for men and women of all classes (all essential to the creation of a meritocratic society).
- Emphasis on the development of reason central to her role in the formulation of early liberal feminism.

Biography

Harriet Martineau was born, on 12 June 1802, into a family of Norwich Unitarians, the sixth of eight children of Thomas Martineau, a cloth manufacturer, and Elizabeth (formerly Rankin), the daughter of a sugar refiner. Educated to a high standard at home, at fifteen years of age she boarded at her aunt's school in Bristol for fifteen months. Here she met the Reverend Lant Carpenter, who introduced her to David Hartley's theory of association and Joseph Priestley's doctrine of necessity. She became increasingly deaf in childhood, and in later life suffered lengthy bouts of incapacity due to an ovarian cyst and heart disease.

In 1822 she began writing for the Unitarian *Monthly Repository*, joining the radical circle around its editor, W. J. Fox. The obligation to earn a living after her father's death in 1826, and the collapse of the family business in 1829, resulted in the *Illustrations of Political Economy* (1832–34), which drew on the work of James Mill (q.v.), David Ricardo (q.v.), Adam Smith (q.v.) and Thomas Malthus (q.v.). She was doctrinaire and radical in her liberalism, and committed to the cause of truth as she saw it – a stance that influenced all her writing. Always a rationalist, in 1851 she publicly declared her break with religion. From 1851 she was much influenced by Auguste Comte's positivist philosophy, though her enthusiasm was not uncritical.

Martineau never married, embracing instead a life of prolific literary endeavour. Besides matters of political economy she published on topics as diverse as mesmerism, religion, the Contagious Diseases Act, women's work, and trades unionism. She worked in a range of genres: her publications included novels, history, sociological travel writing (she visited America, Egypt and the Near East), and journalism for several radical-leaning publications, including the *Westminster Review* and the *Daily News*. She died on 27 June 1876 at her home in the Lake District.

Ideas

The fundamentals of Martineau's radical, reforming liberal thought changed little in the course of her life, and almost all of its key aspects appear in the *Illustrations of Political Economy*. In this series of twenty-five tales she argues against the Corn Laws, slavery and the established church; makes her case for laissez-faire (q.v.) and the lifting of trade barriers within and between nations; and advocates universal education and the widening of the franchise. A fervent Malthusian, she regarded delayed marriage as the solution to working-class poverty. In 'Cousin Marshall' (*Illustrations*, vol. 3) she urged the gradual withdrawal of charitable relief, but did support the New Poor Law of 1834. Her doctrinaire approach led J. S. Mill (q.v.) to comment that she reduced 'the *laissez faire* system to an absurdity as far as the *principle* goes, by merely carrying it out to all its consequences'.

In *Illustrations*, she followed David Ricardo on wages fund theory and rents; took the series' structure from James Mill's political economic school primer; and agreed with Adam Smith and Thomas Malthus that political economy was a system of moral philosophy. Like that of Smith and Malthus, Martineau's work was informed by a four-stages theory of social development. Her utopian belief in unlimited progress and human perfectibility meant that she also envisaged a fifth stage when 'society shall be *wisely* arranged, so that all may become intellectual, virtuous and happy'. Her necessarianism led her to understand Malthusian political economy as one of the natural laws operating in the universe. Man's chances of happiness were maximised if he acted in accordance with these immutable laws. Thus she could support the working man's right to strike for higher wages while simultaneously using Ricardo's wages fund theory to argue that it was probably futile.

Martineau's aim was a society in which individuals advanced through merit rather than privilege, to be achieved by the removal of all restrictive practices – simply expressed as 'an open field and fair play to every one'. This led her to champion anti-slavery and women's emancipation, her support for both causes increasing after her trip to America, where she was radicalised further by the perceptible gap between the republic's founding principles and its actual practices (see *Society in America*, 1837). Central to her arguments for women's legal, social and political equality (q.v.) was an insistence on their capacity for exercising reason if properly educated.

Martineau consistently prioritised the mind over the body, and rationality (q.v.) over feeling. Hence she was always slow to recognise the role of power in relationships, whether between men and women, or worker and employer. Yet she eventually came to support factory legislation for women and children, positing it as a means to protect them from unequal relations within the family. Similarly, although she had decried communitarianism in the *Illustrations* for its eradication of competition and individual incentive, she later changed her mind. Writing in 1837, she described the material prosperity of the utopian socialist communities encountered during her travels in America, and wondered aloud what 'co-operation and community of property' might achieve for the lower classes in England. Thereafter, she was willing to give her support to voluntary workplace and domestic ventures – such as the Rochdale Pioneers and Model Lodging Houses – that were founded on what she termed the 'Economy of Association'.

Martineau's brand of liberalism informed all her writings, but after the *Illustrations* it can be found in most concentrated form in *The History of England During the Thirty Years' Peace 1816–46* (1849–50) – a wide-ranging piece of political partisanship that is thoroughly revealing of her radical-liberal perspective.

Key works

- *Illustrations of Political Economy* (9 vols., 1832–34)
- *Society in America* (3 vols., 1837)
- *How to Observe: Morals and Manners* (1838)
- *Eastern Life: Present and Past* (3 vols., 1848)

- *The History of England During the Thirty Years' Peace 1816–1846* (2 vols., 1849–50)
- *The Positive Philosophy of Auguste Comte* (2 vols., 1853)
- 'Female Industry', *Edinburgh Review* 109 (1859)
- *Autobiography, with Memorials by Maria Weston Chapman* (3 vols., 1877)

Further reading

- Deirdre David, *Intellectual Women and Victorian Patriarchy: Harriet Martineau, Elizabeth Barrett Browning, George Eliot* (Cornell University Press, 1987)
- Elaine Freedgood, 'Banishing Panic: Harriet Martineau and the Popularisation of Political Economy', *Victorian Studies* 39 (1995)
- Michael R. Hill and Susan Hoecker-Drysdale (eds.), *Harriet Martineau: Theoretical and Methodological Perspectives* (Routledge, 2001)
- R. K. Webb, *Harriet Martineau: A Radical Victorian* (Heinemann, 1960)

Ella Dzelzainis

C. F. G. Masterman   1874–1927

Enjoying a considerable reputation in his own lifetime as a journalist, practical politician and thinker, Masterman's retrospective stature is generally considered much less than that accorded by his contemporaries. Within the spectrum of New Liberalism, he supported a qualified and regulated capitalism, as opposed to those liberal collectivisms which shared more common ground with social democracy.

Key ideas

- Christian/humanitarian response to poverty.
- 'Active government' on issues such as unemployment, housing and health.

- Opposed nationalisation of industry but supported land reform.
- Anti-imperialism (before 1914).

Biography

Charles Frederick Gurney Masterman was born in Wimbledon, Surrey, on 25 October in the year following John Stuart Mill's (q.v.) death, 1874 (although some sources say 1873). His family were well-to-do middle class, with farming, banking and Westminster connections. Masterman's political opinions as a schoolboy are not recorded, although his father, Thomas, was a convert to Congregationalism and described himself as a 'Radical Republican'.

Charles matriculated at Cambridge (Christ's College) in 1892, but did not become active in the Union until 1894, where he adopted a liberal and progressive position. He achieved a double first in natural and moral sciences in 1895 and 1896, but the later 1890s were marred by some ill-advised business decisions (which lost a great deal of money) and when he returned to Cambridge as a postgraduate in 1897, he was surprisingly unprolific, although his prize-winning essay, *Tennyson as a Religious Teacher* (1899), was published in book form.

Masterman's Christian commitment was also expressed in the next stage of his career, which we may sensibly call his 'social journalism'. Resident in London from 1900, and inspired by Christian socialism and the university settlement movement, he contributed numerous commentaries on urban poverty and its inhuman effects to the newspapers of the day, as well as publishing two books on the subject: *From the Abyss* (1902) and *In Peril of Change* (1905). During this period he was also associated with the progressive opposition to the Boer War.

Masterman was elected as a Liberal MP in 1906 and served as a loyal but critical

backbencher during the Campbell-Bannerman government, arguing for a more active programme of social reform. A friend of David Lloyd George (q.v.), he became increasingly effective as a 'political networker' and his 1908 marriage to a well-known political hostess, Lucy Lyttleton, created an additional conduit through which he could influence government policy despite the relatively junior posts – Under-Secretary of the Local Government Board (1908–09), Under-Secretary to the Home Office (1909–12) and Financial Secretary to the Treasury (1912–14) – which he held in the Asquith governments. He acquiesced in Asquith's anti-suffragette policy, although he was known to have suffragist sympathies.

Ultimately, Masterman's parliamentary career was severely hampered by his inability to find a 'safe seat'. He served as MP for West Ham (1906–10) and for South-West Bethnal Green (1911–14), but when he was finally appointed to the Cabinet in 1914, the contemporary convention of facing a by-election led to electoral defeat. He failed to find a suitable alternative constituency and eventually resigned as Chancellor of the Duchy of Lancaster in February 1915. Nevertheless, he continued to serve the coalition government as head of the Wellington House wartime propaganda department, a post which he filled with some success.

The post-war period was generally an unhappy one for Masterman. Having split with Lloyd George, he was defeated by a 'coupon' Conservative at the general election of 1918, and although he returned to the Commons as Liberal MP for Manchester Rusholme in 1923, he lost his seat the following year and never returned to front-line politics. He worked for the reunification of the party through the Liberal Summer Schools (q.v.) and made a precarious living from books – *The New Liberalism*

(1920), *How England is Governed* (1920) and *England after the War* (1922) – and journalism. On 17 November 1927, he died of heart failure after several months of illness.

Ideas

Masterman's support for the Liberal Party dated from at least 1895, and although his views on collectivism and individualism evolved throughout his career, it was only for a brief 'moment' in 1923 that he considered joining the Labour Party. During his Cambridge Union period, he moved a motion redolent of the *Fabian Essays in Socialism* (expressing 'satisfaction' with 'the approaching reconstruction of Society in England on a Collectivist basis'), while a few years later he was associated with Beatrice and Sidney Webb (plus H. G. Wells) in person via the 'Coefficients' dining club (1902–08). However, Masterman's contribution as intellectual guru of the 1911 National Insurance Act involved a decisive turn away from crypto-Fabianism, because the scheme enlisted voluntary organisations (mainly friendly and industrial insurance societies) for public, welfarist purposes and involved rejection of the Webbian 'Minority Report' proposals for a much more directive approach to unemployment and poverty.

A strong personal Christian faith was at the root of Masterman's commitment to assisting the poor, and he became increasingly hostile to state socialism in later life. He continued to endorse the social-service, regulative and mildly redistributive functions of government implicit in his earlier support for practical policies such as public works, public housing, state education, wage boards, regulated working conditions, old age pensions and unemployment insurance. Yet, at the same time, he stressed his opposition to both the Bolshevik revolution and more moderate schemes for the nationalisation of industry, arguing instead, in *The New Liberalism*, that true liberalism believed 'in a Capitalism widely diffused amongst a whole community, with each man and family owning a "stake in the country"'.

With reference to 'structural' inequality, Masterman was far more concerned to challenge 'the land monopoly' – echoing an earlier style of radicalism (q.v.), with roots in Paine's (q.v.) *Agrarian Justice*. From 1906 to 1925 (when Masterman contributed to the Liberal 'Green Book', *The Land and the Nation*), policies such as security of tenure, fair taxation of land values and farm colonies for the benefit of the unemployed were recurring themes in his speeches, manifestos and other political writings.

As was noted earlier, Masterman became known for his pro-Boer and anti-colonial views in the early 1900s. For example, in his well-known essay, 'Realities at Home' (in *The Heart of the Empire* (1901)), he condemned the unchristian 'lust for domination' which underpinned contemporary imperialism and asserted that an influx of wealth derived from 'the labour of the inferior races of mankind' would *not* resolve the issue of domestic poverty. Although he failed to apply such an analysis to the First World War, he did criticise the Versailles peace settlement and other aspects of British foreign policy after 1918.

Key works
- 'Realities at Home' in [C. F. G Masterman. (ed.)], *The Heart of the Empire* (1901)
- *The Condition of England* (1909)
- *The New Liberalism* (1920)

Further reading
- E. David, 'The New Liberalism of C. F. G. Masterman, 1873–1927' in K. Brown

(ed.), *Essays in Anti-Labour History* (Macmillan, 1974)

- E. Hopkins, *Charles Masterman (1873–1927), Politician and Journalist, The Splendid Failure* (Edwin Mellen Press, 1999)

Clive E. Hill

Giuseppe Mazzini 1805–72

An Italian republican, patriot and propagandist, founder of various radical societies and journals against occupying foreign armies and in favour of Italian unification. As well as being a leading figure in the Risorgimento, Mazzini was a powerful advocate of universal suffrage and liberal freedoms in the place of monarchical and aristocratic power and privilege.

Key ideas

- Politics should be guided by ethics and based on a faith in God.
- An Italian republic would have a unique historical mission.
- Free republics would foster the development of a free egalitarian Europe and ultimately of a sense of the true worth of humanity.
- Strong republics can only be founded on progressive, popular civil associations.

Biography

Giuseppe Mazzini was born in Genoa on 22 June 1805, the son of a physician and professor of pathology. He graduated with a degree in law from the University of Genoa before attempting to build a career as a literary critic. He became a political radical, seeking Italian unification.

He was exiled from Italy in 1831 and was eventually given the death sentence *in absentia* for his revolutionary activities. The same year he founded the Young Italy movement, whose revolutionary republican aims caused him to be expelled from France and Switzerland before moving to England early in 1837. He found many sympathisers among Chartists and advanced liberals such as John Stuart Mill (q.v.), but in 1840 his post was intercepted on the authority of Lord Aberdeen, who used the information to help the Austrian government suppress their domestic radicals. This caused outrage in Parliament, as well as among leading intellectuals such as Macaulay (q.v.) and Carlyle.

From the late 1840s, Mazzini was involved in various insurrections against foreign occupation of Italian territories, even holding political office in the short-lived Roman republic created in 1849. Often Mazzini was in alliance with Garibaldi, who in 1860, with the help of Cavour, managed to gain control of southern Italy. Mazzini's radicalism (q.v.) meant that even with the victory of his (now former) allies, he was not welcome in Italy. He spent almost all of the rest of his life in England, where he continued to be a great favourite of the radical and liberal elite, admired for his social concern, political passion and personal charm.

In 1872 he returned secretly to Italy, where he died on 10 March.

Ideas

Mazzini stated the fundamental principle of his political thought and action thus, in 1836: 'For us the starting-point is Country; the object or aim is Collective Humanity.' He was emphatic, however, in his rejection of those types of nationalism which repressed minorities at home and sought a deceitful and self-interested policy abroad. Such nationalisms were little more than myths and fictions used by the monarchy and aristocracy to maintain and extend their national domination: 'Their whole doctrine might have been summed up in one proposition – *the weakening of the mass, for the furtherance and security of their own individual interests.'* Yet Mazzini also rejected cosmopolitanism, for which, as he put it, 'the *aim* may be Humanity but the starting-point is the Individual Man'. Cosmopolitanism assumes (often vaguely stated) rights of the individual to constitute the basis of a social life, and is led to use force as the only feasible way of maintaining social order.

Mazzini's alternative was a particular form of republican patriotism. In his most influential and comprehensive statement of his political thought, *The Duties of Man* (1844, 1858), Mazzini traced the contours of this republican vision, focusing on its class basis, divine inspiration and legal form, as well as one's duties to humanity, to one's country, family and to oneself. He drew out the implications for freedom (q.v.), education and what we would call now the principles of social justice (q.v.), particularly in the context of the struggle for Italian unification under a republican government. Throughout, his guiding ideal was a common life structured by a diversity of free civil associations, each dedicated to serving some aspect of the true progress of man.

The dignified self-confidence of the free and active citizen could exist only to the extent that the mass of the population were free from the material and spiritual destitution amidst which monarchical and aristocratic orders flourished. To escape such deprivation, individuals should form associations that would then overwhelm the established order, partly through revolutionary actions, but possibly more importantly through propaganda and non-violent agitation. Ultimately, the citizen's life should be guided by ideals of duty rather than an insistence on their personal rights: the former bound individuals together in the name of a common purpose while the latter divided them through egoistic competition. Mazzini expressed the core of his republicanism in a pregnant passage that opened the tenth chapter of *The Duties of Man* ('Association-Progress'):

> God has created you social and progressive beings. It is therefore your duty to associate yourselves, and to progress as far as the sphere of activity in which circumstances have placed you will permit. You have a right to demand that the society to which you belong shall in no way impede your work of association and progress, but, on the contrary, shall assist you, and furnish you with the means of association and of progress of which you stand in need.

Such civil associations underpinned the life of a free nation. Mazzini went on to stress the role that such nations would play in the development of an egalitarian Europe and ultimately in the development of humanity.

Such beliefs, together with his Christian faith, led him into conflict with many on the more extreme left. Mazzini may have been admired by socialists like Mikhail Bakunin at one time, but by the 1860s even these once good friends had fallen out. In an interview with R. Landor of the New York *World* on 1 July 1871, Karl Marx said of Mazzini, 'We should have made but little progress if we had not got beyond the range of his ideas ... He represents nothing better than the old idea of a middle-class republic. We seek no part with the middle class.' Nevertheless, Mazzini continued to influence many republicans and advanced liberals, including T. H. Green (q.v.) and Edward Caird (q.v.).

Key works
- *Life and Writings of Joseph Mazzini* (ed. Emilie Ashurst, 6 vols., 2nd edn., 1891)

Further reading
- Karl Marx, *Political Writings, volume 3: The First International and After* (Penguin, 1992)

- Denis Mack Smith, *Mazzini* (Yale University Press, 1994)

Colin Tyler

Michael Meadowcroft   1942–

One of the few Liberal thinkers active at a time when the Liberal Party was consumed by debates on the practice of community politics and electoral strategy, Meadowcroft's ideas acquired particular prominence in the party in the decade before the merger with the SDP. He was insistent that what the party did, said and aimed for at local and national level should be grounded firmly in liberal philosophy.

Key ideas

- Liberalism was important, the Liberal Party only its vehicle.
- Politics without firm philosophical roots will fail.
- Liberalism is concerned mainly with freedom, so will always sit uneasily with parties grounded in economics.

Biography

Michael James Meadowcroft was born in Southport on 6 March 1942. On leaving school he worked briefly in a bank, before becoming the Liberal Party's full-time local government officer in 1962. He was elected to Leeds City Council in 1968, where he served until his election as MP for Leeds West in 1983. He lost the seat in 1987.

Meadowcroft was the Liberal Party's president-elect at the time of the 1988 merger with the SDP, which he opposed. Later that year he announced the reformation of the Liberal Party, of which he became president until 2005.

After the fall of the Berlin Wall in 1989 he became an adviser on democratisation and elections in eastern Europe, an activity that led him to similar work in the developing world, where he now spends much of his time.

Ideas

Meadowcroft first put his political thoughts on paper in the quarterly journal of Merseyside Young Liberals, which he joined after being inspired by Jo Grimond.

He describes his self-imposed task as having been 'to produce thorough and dependable booklets to demonstrate that modern Liberalism was coherent, philosophically based, progressive and distinctive, and that Liberals need have no lack of confidence in their "left libertarianism"'. His publications have the common theme that the Liberal Party should not have become so concerned with its tactics that it forgot that its main job was to be a political vehicle for liberalism. That might sound an obvious assertion now, but in the 1980s the very localist emphasis of community politics (q.v.), and the party's attempts to find a short cut to national success (through the Lib-Lab Pact, the Alliance and the merger), served to focus party members on 'power' with little regard to how and why they proposed to use it.

In a party that was just starting to taste electoral success, few wanted to be told by Meadowcroft, or anyone else, that the party's guiding philosophy was more important than winning at any cost. As he wrote in *Liberal Values for a New Decade* (1980): 'The Liberal Party depends on liberalism, rather then the other way round.' In the same pamphlet he noted that 'Liberals' excitement over the development of community politics [has] led to a certain neglect of consideration of the political context in which it has to be placed'.

This was not a popular message; a party with its face, so to speak, turned towards local pavements considered political theory a diversion. Meadowcroft tried to counter this by staging a half-day debate on Liberal philosophy at the 1979 assembly, which he said 'demonstrated the fundamental unity of the Liberal movement' and his *New Decade* booklet grew from that. How this philosophical endeavour might have influenced Liberal politics is a matter for speculation, as it was overtaken by the formation of the Alliance, of which Meadowcroft was greatly suspicious.

In *Social Democracy – Barrier or Bridge?* (1981) he said of the SDP: 'Liberals, who see the key political spectrum running from diffusion of power to corporatism – public or private – always have difficulty in relating to parties who perceive themselves along a different spectrum, from public ownership to private ownership.' The booklet illustrates Meadowcroft's belief that the SDP had minimal philosophical underpinnings with which either to agree or disagree, and so was bound to drag the Liberal Party into that area vaguely defined as 'the centre' in which liberalism could not prosper.

In *Liberalism and the Left*, written at the height of Labour's internecine warfare in 1982, he argued that Labour should not be the automatic home for those who considered themselves on the 'left' because it was dominated by economic issues and gave little attention to freedom (q.v.). *Liberalism and the Right* (1983) attempted a similar exercise for Conservatives who disliked the early Thatcher government. He castigated that government's claims to be interested in liberty by pointing to the impact of its economic policies: 'Increasing liberty is a joke for the 40 per cent or so of British citizens who depend on the dole or on social security. Liberty only really exists for the handful of entrepreneurs who benefit from the economic liberalism to which the present government is committed.'

Meadowcroft might well have interesting things to say on the debates on economic liberalism (q.v.) taking place in the Liberal Democrats in the mid-2000s; that he speaks from off-stage is because of where his convictions took him after 1988. Liberal Party members who saw themselves as centrists were happy to merge with SDP centrists. Meadowcroft was not. He saw liberalism and social democracy (q.v.) as fundamentally different. In a report to the special Liberal assembly of January 1988, which voted for the merger, he wrote: 'The political danger of merger is that it is seen by many as yet another short-cut to electoral success, requiring neither rigorous intellectual commitment nor committed local campaigning.' Soon after, Meadowcroft became president of the separate Liberal Party, before devoting his time largely to the developing world.

His own explanation for why he wrote on Liberal philosophy, and the impact he achieved, is bleak: 'It was lack of intellectual rigour that appalled me and which I hoped to diminish by writing and speaking. I failed, and superficialism, as practised by Steel and the SDP, won.'

Meadowcroft's view, that he failed in trying to influence the Liberal Party, is true if one seeks Meadowcroft 'causes' and policy or strategy 'effects'. It was his misfortune to have been at his most active during an era when the Liberal Party was preoccupied with the politics of splitting the difference in the pact and the Alliance, and at its least receptive to debate about political ideas of any sort. Nevertheless, his work gave some coherence to the left and localist wings of the party when they might have lacked it, and doubtless provoked many individual liberals to think and to question. Meadowcroft's importance lies not only in his ideas but in his having been willing to take on the role of political thinker at a time when few Liberals would.

Key works

- *Success in Local Government* (1971)
- *Liberals and a Popular Front* (1974)
- *Bluffer's Guide to Politics* (1976)
- *Liberal Values for a New Decade* (1980)
- *Social Democracy – Barrier or Bridge?* (1981)
- *Liberalism and the Left* (1982)
- *Liberalism and the Right* (1983)
- *Liberalism Today and Tomorrow* (1989)
- *The Case for the Liberal Party* (1992)
- *Focus on Freedom* (1997)

Mark Smulian

Edward Miall   1809–81

A leading campaigner against the privileged position of the Church of England, Miall was the founder and editor of the *Nonconformist* and a founding member of the Liberation Society.

Key ideas

- Voluntaryism, or the reliance on private rather than state provision, particularly in education.
- Disestablishment of the Church of England to create equal opportunity for every Christian denomination.

Biography

Edward Miall was born at Portsmouth on 8 May 1809. He followed his brother James into the Congregationalist church and was educated for the ministry at the Protestant Dissenters' College at Wymondley, Hertfordshire, becoming minister of the Independent Chapel at Ware in 1831. In 1832 he married Louisa Holmes, the niece of his tutor at Wymondley.

In 1835 he moved to Leicester, where he campaigned against the local taxes levied for the upkeep of the Church of England. Success led the Leicester dissenters to widen their campaign and Miall raised the capital to fund a new national weekly, the *Nonconformist*, which he launched in April 1841. In 1844 he convened a national convention of nonconformists in London, and shortly afterwards the British Anti-State Church Association was formed, with Miall as one of its secretaries. In 1853 the Association changed its name to the Society for the Liberation of Religion from State Patronage and Control – generally shortened to the Liberation Society (q.v.).

Miall showed a wider interest in politics and stood, unsuccessfully, at by-elections in Southwark and Halifax in the 1840s, opposing the church establishment and the increased grant for the Maynooth Catholic seminary. He supported Chartist policies of universal suffrage, annual parliaments, the secret ballot, payment of members and equal electoral districts. Miall's third attempt, in 1852 at Rochdale, was successful. The victory gave him enhanced standing within the Liberation Society, which he used to press the nascent Liberal Party to elect MPs who were Nonconformists or active supporters of Liberation Society policies. Since his tactics included running candidates against local party nominees, he did little to endear the Society to the Liberal hierarchy. In 1856 he proposed a resolution in Parliament for the disestablishment of the Church of Ireland, but this, together with his support for Cobden's (q.v.) attack on Palmerston's Chinese policy, lost him Rochdale at the 1857 general election.

Between 1858 and 1861, Miall served as a member of the Newcastle Education Commission, whose immediate consequence was the payment of teachers by results, but whose longer-term legacy was the Education Act of 1870. Miall submitted a minority report opposing state funding of education.

He rejoined Parliament in 1869 after a by-election in Bradford. The 1868–74 period saw considerable progress for the Liberationists, with Gladstone (q.v.) disestablishing the Church of Ireland and abolishing the compulsory church rate. However, Nonconformists were disappointed by the 1870 Education Bill, proposed by Miall's fellow Bradford MP, W. E. Forster, because it continued to fund church schools. Miall's speeches in favour of secular education and his motions to disestablish the Church of England won only modest support against Gladstone's opposition.

Miall declined to stand at the 1874 general election on health grounds but continued to work for the Liberation Society. His wife died in 1876, and in 1877 he passed on the editorship of the *Nonconformist* to his brother. He died on 29 April 1881, leaving two sons and three daughters.

Ideas

Using the *Nonconformist* and the Liberation Society, Miall led the arguments for religious equality in mid-Victorian Britain. In secular politics, he supported Radical (q.v.) proposals, particularly extension of the franchise, which he anticipated would prepare the way for disestablishment – the separation of the Church of England from the state.

Nonconformists suffered under a variety of disadvantages. They were obliged to pay rates to support an Anglican Church they did not attend, but could not bury their dead in its churchyards. Their national taxes funded Anglican schools and religious tests prevented them from taking fellowships at some universities. Anglican ministers occupied a privileged position in local society, enabling them to discriminate against Nonconformists in the administration of charitable funds and school admissions.

Miall's arguments for disestablishment depended not simply on the negative test of discrimination against dissenters but on a positive theological case. Disestablishment would free the church to undertake God's work, not Whitehall's; a state church was not under the guidance of its members but unavoidably controlled by a worldly government, whose members need not be believers. Disestablishment would remove any restrictions on freedom of conscience. Competition between different denominations would be beneficial both in demonstrating which preached the true gospel and in ensuring that churches would need to proselytise, since to survive they would be reliant on the voluntary contributions of their members.

A true church was composed of those who had freely volunteered to subject themselves to the preaching of the gospel. Individuals could not escape their religious or other moral responsibilities by offloading them on to the state. Consequently, Miall was campaigning not just to take the state out of religion but to prevent the state assuming other responsibilities which belonged to the individual, such as the education or welfare of the family.

Key works

- The *Nonconformist* (journal)
- *The Nonconformist's Sketchbook* (1842)
- *The British Churches in Relation to the British People* (1849)
- *The Title Deeds of the Church of England to her Parochial Endowments* (1862)

Further reading

- Ian Bradley, *The Optimists: Themes and Personalities in Victorian Liberalism* (Faber & Faber, 1980)
- D. A. Hamer, *The Politics of Electoral Pressure* (Harvester Press, 1977)
- Arthur Miall, *Life of Edward Miall* (Macmillan, 1884)

- Edward Miall, *An Editor off the Line: Or Wayside Musings and Reminiscences* (Arthur Miall, 1865)

Tony Little

Nathaniel Micklem   1888–1976

Nonconformist minister and academic, for whom Christian belief and Liberal politics were inextricably linked.

Key ideas

- 'Politics in the Liberal view is a branch of ethics rather than of economics.'
- 'Liberalism aims at the moralising of power through the enlargement of liberty.'

Biography

Nathaniel Micklem was born at Brondesbury, on 10 April 1888, into what might be called the Liberal squirearchy; his father, also Nathaniel, was MP for West Hertfordshire in the parliament of 1906. He was educated at Rugby and at New College, Oxford, and as an undergraduate was president of the Oxford Union. He was to stay in that university town for much of his academic career.

A Congregrationalist, he served as Principal of Mansfield College from 1932 until his retirement in 1953. He played a seminal role in the development of his denomination as his own religious beliefs evolved. It is said that he moved his church to the right, but, all the while, he was a committed lifetime Liberal, active in the Oxford party, and culminating in being president of the national party in 1957–58.

His outlook was also shaped by his own experiences in Germany in the 1930s, seeing at first hand the Nazi persecution of Catholics and of Jews. He wrote widely, on his experiences of Hitler's Germany, on religious belief and the Gospels, and on politics, and composed both prose and verse. He died in Abingdon on Boxing Day, 1976. His wife Agatha, with whom he had three sons, died in 1961.

Ideas

Micklem once commented that 'I was brought up to be concerned with politics, as a citizen in a modern state should be'. A sense of social responsibility informed his career, but it was combined with a disarming diffidence. Late in life, opposing the proposal to hold a referendum on Britain's membership of the European Economic Community as inimical to the tradition of representative government, he commented that the EEC raised complex issues with which 'I have wrestled … in my amateurish way'. Similarly, he had earlier prefaced his best-known work, *The Theology of Politics* (1941), by describing himself as 'a plagiarist, a populariser'. His political writings may not have revealed significant new insights but his emphasis on the moral imperative of politics provided a salutary contribution to mid-century Liberalism.

He described himself as 'a Liberal of ancient vintage'. His statement of his political credo, *The Idea of Liberal Democracy* (1957), written after retirement and in the same year he was president of the Liberal Party, characteristically made no claims to intellectual originality. What is surprising is not its debt to John Stuart Mill (q.v.) but its absence of reference to New Liberal (q.v.) thinkers like Hobhouse (q.v.) or Hobson (q.v.). In differentiating itself from socialism, post-war liberalism was in danger of denying its recent antecedents. Micklem's concern was to apply classic nineteenth-century liberalism to 'the Atomic Age', an age also of atomisation. Micklem penned the conclusion to the 1950s successor to the 'Yellow Book', *The Unservile State* (see

Unservile State Group) and expressed there what he saw as the contemporary challenge to liberalism and to liberty itself: 'The ever-increasing mechanisation of industry which ... ought to mean a great enlargement of human liberty has tended in fact to the depersonalising of man and the reduction of his human status.'

Micklem's own response to this challenge was to reinvigorate politics by reviving its ethical dimension. His political belief in liberty was derived from his Christian faith. It was an association of political commitment with religious conviction which was expressed most fully in his *Theology of Politics*. His ideological terminology was redolent of both classical and Christian traditions, in particular in its emphasis on a term crucial to both Aristotelian and Augustinian discourse: virtue or (as he said) 'to use the modern term, responsibility'.

For him, democracy was based on the three principles of liberty, order and virtue, and 'Liberalism aims at the moralising of power through the enlargement of liberty'. It was an elemental struggle – against totalitarianism, against socialism, and against bureaucracy. Of the last, he commented: 'A Welfare State which inevitably involves very large numbers of ... imperfectly trained minor officials can easily become a tyranny.' In socialism Micklem also saw a threat of tyranny, especially in its attack on private property, since property 'is the bulwark of political liberty'. In contrast, Liberals, he said, want 'the emancipation of workers by making property-owners of them all'. The argument for free markets and free trade (q.v.) was, for him, not just economic but, more fundamentally, moral. This was the key message of Micklem's presidential address to the Liberal assembly of 1957. He ended it with a rallying cry that distilled his outlook: 'We may appeal with good conscience to the country; it is to the conscience of the country that we must appeal.'

Key works
- *The Theology of Politics* (1941)
- *The Idea of Liberal Democracy* (1957)

David Rundle

Harriet Taylor Mill   1807–58

An early advocate of women's rights, her husband, John Stuart Mill, claimed that many of his major works were based on intellectual collaboration with her.

Key ideas
- The right to cheap and easy divorce.
- 'Separate spheres' for men and women to be replaced by equal opportunities for all.

Biography
Harriet Hardy was born on 8 October 1807, the fourth of seven children of her Unitarian parents. From 1831 she wrote book reviews, poems and articles for a Unitarian publication, the *Monthly Repository*. However, she is better known for her life than her writings, and pre-eminently that part of her life that linked her with the great liberal philosopher John Stuart Mill (q.v.). This relationship has particular human interest because of the extent to which it flouted the middle-class norms of the time.

Harriet Taylor was a married woman when she met Mill in 1830. She was nevertheless, one might say, intellectually available, in that she had decided that her husband, the pharmacist John Taylor, who she had married in 1826, was her mental inferior. She bore him two sons and a daughter but he bored her; Mill didn't, so Harriet and Mill became regular companions. Mill dined at the Taylor household once or twice a week. John Taylor was amazingly tolerant of this development, but, unsurprisingly, friends and acquaintances began to gossip. With his denigration of 'animal appetites' and 'lower pleasures' Mill seemed not the most promising candidate for an affair. Carlyle referred to Harriet Taylor as 'Platonica' and noted that Mill, 'who up to that time, had never looked a female creature, even a cow, in the face, found himself opposite those great dark eyes, that were flashing unutterable things'.

Initial development was rapid but then stalled. In 1833 the Taylors began a six-month trial separation; Harriet went to Paris, where Mill soon joined her. She decided on what was, perhaps, for her the best of both worlds: that the marriage and Mill's visits both continue as before. So it went on until 1849, when Taylor died. Two years later Harriet and Mill married. Their time living together was all too brief; Harriet died, of tuberculosis, in Avignon on 3 November 1858.

Ideas

It seems that Harriet Taylor and Mill were both feminists prior to their meeting; indeed that this was one of the reasons for their initial mutual attraction. Among her papers were found a few pages 'On Marriage', usually dated to the 1832–33 period. It is a cry from the heart of an unhappily married and occupationally restricted woman.

Harriet Taylor called for women to be granted complete equality with men and for all occupations to be opened to them. She noted that women were educated for only one occupation, that of marriage; once that is achieved they 'cease to exist as to anything worth calling life'. Furthermore, in very few marriages was there real companionship between the partners. Women's 'minds are degenerated by habits of dependence'. Taylor called for the education of

women and also for the right of divorce 'without any reason assigned'. Divorce should also be obtainable cheaply, in contrast to it then only being available through the costly process of an Act of Parliament.

John Stuart Mill's *The Subjection of Women* is far better known than any writings on that subject by his wife. History has not given proper credit to her earlier and shorter *Enfranchisement of Women*, which was first published anonymously in 1851, but it is a lucid and noteworthy work. Its starting point is the 1848 Women's Rights Convention that met at Seneca Falls, New York State, and produced a Declaration of Sentiments self-consciously modelled on the United States Declaration of Independence of seventy-two years earlier. The new Declaration referred to 'the repeated injuries and usurpations on the part of man towards woman' and asserted that 'we hold these truths to be self-evident … that all men *and women* are created equal'. Harriet points out that so-called universal principles need universal application rather than the denial of rights to half the human species. The division of the sexes into separate spheres is described, polemically yet plausibly, as one of 'caste', for it is a division of power determined biologically at birth. Its basis lies merely, yet powerfully, in custom, a subordination that many women themselves accept. Custom, however, had once sanctioned slavery, monarchical despotism and feudal nobility. Those injustices had been challenged; the same would happen to that of sexual domination.

In time the notion of separate spheres would fall away. Harriet Taylor saw the proper sphere of individuals as being whatever level they were able, by their own efforts, to attain. The limitation of women's prospects to motherhood was conventional rather than necessary. She thought that earning an income would help liberate women from dependence on their husbands. Women's improved education and cultivation would also make them better companions for their husbands. As to women's capacities, Harriet noted that Queen Elizabeth, Isabella of Castille, Maria Teresa and Catherine the Great of Russia had excelled in the highest offices of state. There was no reason why other women should not do so also.

Apart from her feminism, Harriet Taylor was sympathetic to socialistic communities. It was on her insistence that Mill added a chapter 'On the Probable Futurity of the Labouring Classes' to his *Principles of Political Economy*.

Key works

- *Enfranchisement of Women* (1851)

Further reading

- F. A. Hayek (ed.), *John Stuart Mill and Harriet Taylor: Their Correspondence and Subsequent Marriage* (University of Chicago Press, 1951)
- J. S. Mill, *Autobiography*, ch. 6
- H. O. Pappe, *John Stuart Mill and the Harriet Taylor Myth* (Melbourne University Press, 1960)
- Phyllis Rose, *Parallel Lives* (Vintage, 1994), ch. 3
- A. Rossi, *Essays on Sex Equality* (University of Chicago Press, 1970), ch. 1, 'Sentiment and Intellect: The Story of John Stuart Mill and Harriet Taylor'

Michael Levin

James Mill   1773–1836

A noted historian of British India, economist, psychologist, radical liberal thinker and propagator of the utilitarian doctrine of Jeremy Bentham, Mill was a firm believer in the power of education and is remembered for the intense educational regime imposed

on his eldest son, the liberal philosopher John Stuart Mill.

Key ideas

- Imperialism was justified if it brought rationality to backward societies.
- The aristocracy enjoyed privileges they neither earned nor deserved, whereas the hard-working middle classes made the greatest contribution to social progress.
- Representative government was the best safeguard against sectional power.
- Freedom of the press was an essential control on government and the prerequisite for informed electoral choice.

Biography

In eighteenth-century Scotland schooling was available to poor children to an extent not matched in England until very much later. James Mill, born on 6 April 1773 to a Forfarshire shoe-maker, was one of the many beneficiaries. His obvious ability came to the attention of Lady Jane Stuart, who supported a charity to help prepare poor boys for the Presbyterian ministry. After studying at Edinburgh University, and graduating in 1794, Mill was licensed as a preacher in 1798. He failed, however, to secure a position. This was the turning point of his life. He abandoned hopes of a clerical career and, in 1802, left for London in the hope of becoming a writer.

In the early years in London Mill worked for the *Anti-Jacobin Review* and edited the *Literary Journal* and *St James's Chronicle*. His great breakthrough came with his multivolume *History of British India* (1817). This secured him a position with the British East India Company, in whose ranks he rose rapidly, being appointed Chief Examiner at India House in 1830.

Mill first met Jeremy Bentham (q.v.) in 1808 and soon became his friend, neighbour and major advocate of the utilitarian (q.v.) doctrine. It was at Bentham's house that Mill met David Ricardo (q.v.) and encouraged him to write his *Principles of Political Economy* (1817). Mill married Harriet Burrow in 1805; John Stuart Mill (q.v.), named after the husband of his early patron, was the first of their nine children. James Mill died on 23 June 1836.

Ideas

For James Mill it was fundamental that 'superstition necessarily gives way, as civilisation advances', but in India this had not happened. In a manner derived from Scottish political economy, Mill sought to ascertain India's place on the ladder of civilisation. He found that the country was mired in barbarism and despotism and its people were 'the most enslaved portion of the human race'. No improvements had been made; 'the Hindus have been stationary for many ages'. It was, consequently, the task of the British East India Company to raise the country to the higher level it was otherwise unable to attain. The Company had 'maintained a virtue which, under the temptations of their situation is worthy of the highest applause'. This message went down well and the work became a textbook for candidates for the Indian Civil Service.

Comparative advantage, however, did not imply that Britain provided the perfect standard to which other countries or cultures should aspire. Mill and the utilitarians were also critics of the British political system. Its cobwebbed and archaic constitutional remnants required the cold gleam of rational investigation. Mill pointed out that Napoleon had been the first European sovereign to codify the laws of his country; in England, by contrast, the common law remained in an unwritten and barbarous state. This was to the advantage of the landowners who controlled Parliament and

formed a 'sinister interest'; their income and influence was unearned and undeserved.

This was all in line with Mill's rather Hobbesian (q.v.) precept that individuals or groups will always seek to maximise their own power. Mill typified the standard liberal belief that power is to be viewed with suspicion. Representative government, consequently, is the only reliable means of ensuring that government serves the interests of all. This view of human nature destroys any notion of benevolent monarchy and aristocracy and delegitimises notions of honour, altruism or benevolence. The emphasis on representation certainly points in a democratic direction and Mill wanted a wider franchise so that the British Parliament could be more representative. Nevertheless he rejected the idea that India should have representative institutions, suggested that women were adequately represented by their fathers or husbands, and believed that forty was a suitable age for men to get the vote. For those who did have the vote, Mill wanted it made more genuine. He was, therefore, an early campaigner for the secret ballot, which was not made law until 1872. He wrote that open voting led to corruption, as electors were pressured into supporting the preferences of their employers and landlords.

Having first pursued a Presbyterian clerical career, Mill closed a lifetime of writing with a denunciation of the Church of England. He regarded the Dissenters as serious about religion whereas the Church of England was for those who were indifferent to it and belonged for the sake of its worldly advantages. Mill asked whether the opinions of the clergy were justified by evidence and denounced them as 'enemies of all improvement'. He proposed a church without dogmas and ceremonies in which the diffusion of genuine knowledge would have the highest priority. He was, not so surreptitiously, suggesting that a religious institution be transformed into an educational one.

Key works
- *The History of British India* (1817)
- *Essay on Government* (1820)
- *Elements of Political Economy* (1826)
- T. Ball (ed.), *James Mill: Political Writings* (Cambridge University Press, 1992)
- D. Winch (ed.), *James Mill: Selected Economic Writings* (University of Chicago Press, 1966)

Further reading
- A. Bain, *James Mill: A Biography* [1882] (Augustus M. Kelly, 1967)
- R. A. Fenn, *James Mill's Political Thought* (Garland, 1987)
- B. Mazlish, *James and John Stuart Mill: Father and Son in the Nineteenth Century* (Basic Books, 1975), section 2.
- W. Thomas, *The Philosophic Radicals: Nine Studies in Theory and Practice 1817–1841* (Clarendon Press, 1979), ch. 3.

Michael Levin

John Stuart Mill   1806–73

The leading liberal theorist of Victorian Britain, contributing eminent works on philosophy, economics and political theory. He is noted for his adaptation of utilitarianism, his defence of liberty, and his advocacy of representative government.

Key ideas
- Liberty is both a personal need and a condition of social development.
- Liberty and individuality need to be defended against the advance of mass society.
- Advocated proportional representation.
- Campaigned for equality between the sexes.

- Opposed the aristocracy on account of their unearned and undeserved privileges.

Biography
A key aspect of nineteenth-century liberalism was faith in the power and influence of education, concerning which John Stuart Mill was remarkable even before he had published anything. He was the subject, one might almost say the victim, of his father's educational theory. John Stuart Mill was the son of the philosopher James Mill (q.v.) and the friend and populariser of Jeremy Bentham (q.v.), and was trained to be the flag-bearer of utilitarianism (q.v.) for the next generation.

Born on 20 May 1806, John Stuart was educated at home by his father in a regime that involved learning Greek from the age of three and adding Latin when he was eight. At the age of sixteen he produced his first book review, on the rather unyouthful topic of Thomas Tooks's *Thoughts and Details on the High and Low Prices of the Last Thirty Years*.

In 1823 he followed his father into the India Office, where he worked for the next thirty-five years. Mill's hours of employment were from 10 until 4, during which time he not only satisfied the demands of his superiors but also met his friends, completed personal correspondence and engaged in his intellectual pursuits. In 1856 he became the Chief Examiner of India Correspondence, a post previously held by his father. A year later, following the Indian Mutiny, Parliament took over the direct administration of the company's territory. Mill strongly opposed this and chose to go into retirement.

Mill was the Liberal MP for Westminster between 1865 and 1868, during which time he attempted, unsuccessfully, to allow women the vote on the same terms as men. In 1851 he married Harriet Taylor (q.v.), with whom he had been associated for more than twenty years. Mill claimed that *On Liberty* was as much her work as his, a claim that critics have regarded as doubtful. She died in 1858 and was buried in Avignon, where Mill also died, on 8 May 1873. They had no children together.

Ideas

One fundamental aspect of liberalism is its suspicion of the state. Liberal theory has sought to control the state by constitutionalism, disperse its power through federalism, keep it within the bounds of acceptability through government by consent, and limit its economic control by a policy of laissez-faire (q.v.).

In *Principles of Political Economy* (1848) Mill voiced his unease concerning the state. It already had too much power and influence. Officials, even of a liberal state, could be just as tyrannical as those of a despotism. People understand their own business better than the government does, and most things are done worse by government than they would be by the individuals most concerned with the matter. However, in spite of his best endeavours, Mill admitted the impossibility of defining a precise limitation to the functions of government. As he delved more deeply into the issue he found that the area of legitimate state action seemed to grow. Thus he acknowledged that infant industries may need protection, that the currency supply needs to be controlled by the state and that the mentally ill should be cared for. Mill accepted that gas and water belonged to the category of natural monopolies and that, like the paving and cleaning of the streets, were best arranged by the municipal authorities and paid for out of the rates. Roads, railways and canals could be rented and run by voluntary associations; however, they should still be strictly controlled by the government. In such ways Mill can be seen as providing a bridge between classical political economy and the New Liberalism (q.v.) of the later nineteenth century.

At the age of thirteen Mill had been sent for a year to France with the family of Samuel Bentham, the brother of the great philosopher of utilitarianism. Thus began an immersion in French intellectual culture that profoundly influenced the development of his own ideas. From Guizot, Comte and Tocqueville (q.v.), Mill developed a concern with the logic of history, of the process by which the advanced nations had ascended from barbarism to civilisation. Mill's long reviews of Tocqueville's two volumes on *Democracy in America* (1835, 1840) were significant in bringing them to the attention of English readers. Tocqueville's influence is fundamental to what is now Mill's best-known work, the essay *On Liberty* of 1859. It was in Tocqueville's writings that Mill found a concern with mass society as a social change that threatened to undermine liberty even in a democracy. A mass society was one where time-honoured stratifications had broken down. People were now more equal, but sameness produced a social condition in which it was becoming increasingly hard to be different. Thus liberty was under attack from a new direction. In earlier times it had been endangered from above, from the state or the church; but now it was threatened from below, from the mass. The new direction of the threat caught society off its guard. Hence Mill not merely drew attention to the new danger but called for resistance. Individuality should reassert itself; even eccentricity was a service in providing a point of differentiation from an increasingly stifling norm.

The call for individuality was based on both personal and social requirements.

Firstly, 'it is only the cultivation of individuality which produces, or can produce, well-developed human beings'. Secondly, social progress depended upon a plurality of ideas competing for predominance. It seemed to Mill that the rise of conformity might undermine the very conditions that had elevated the European nations above the rest of mankind. His great warning example was that of China, a once-great civilisation which had ossified and been bypassed once conformity had got the better of diversity.

Resistance to mass society required defending the individual against both society and the state. Here Mill attempted to provide principles by which non-interference could be justified. He instanced the supposedly 'very simple principle' that only the threat of harm to others could justify interfering with anyone's liberty of action. This is based on the famous distinction between self- and other-regarding actions. The idea that actions can easily be separated into these two categories no longer carries plausibility, but what remains significant here is less Mill's achievement than his purpose. He was trying to find a principle by which individuality might be defended; by which certain actions could be ring-fenced from the external powers of society and state. One of the appealing aspects of Mill's approach is that he was more than a philosopher; his attempts to work out principles of social action were combined with proposals on their practical application. He argued, for example, against state education, sabbatarian legislation, and restrictions on trade which infringed the liberty of the buyer.

On Liberty has come to be one of the best-known of all liberal texts. In the same way as John Milton's (q.v.) *Areopagitica* served as the symbol of office of the president of the Liberal Party, *On Liberty* serves the same function within the Liberal Democrats, a bound copy being presented to each new incumbent by his predecessor at the party conference.

The issue of liberty was also central to *The Subjection of Women* (1869), for, said Mill, freedom (q.v.) was commonly denied to half the species – to women. He believed that women's inferior legal status was a consequence of their lesser physical stature; it was the sole surviving legacy of the anachronistic law of the strongest and ought to be rejected. Mill saw the power of the husband as analogous to that of the aristocrat in enjoying advantages based on birth rather than merit or achievement. In both cases such a basis of power corrupts the beneficiary and unjustly degrades the victims.

For Mill *Representative Government* (1861) was ideally the best form of rule in that power was ultimately vested in the whole community and so was a check on tyranny. It was, however, only suitable for the more developed societies. Such colonies of British settlement as Canada and Australia might qualify, but definitely not India, which Mill saw as 'not fit to govern itself'. Even within the United Kingdom representative government did not imply democracy, for the suffrage should not extend to those who were illiterate and unable to 'perform the common operations of arithmetic'.

Mill's essay on *Utilitarianism* (1861) is a purported defence that to many critics overcomes some difficulties by landing in still greater ones. Mill here sought to overcome two standard objections to Bentham's formulations. Firstly, it seemed that Bentham had aligned two principles that seemed more obviously divergent, those of pursuing one's own greatest happiness yet simultaneously attaining the 'greatest happiness of the greatest number'. What was at issue, in a nutshell, was the question of whether individual selfishness contributed to the greater good. Adam Smith (q.v.), nearly a century earlier, had imagined an 'invisible guiding hand' mediating between these extremes. Mill was less metaphysically inclined. He believed that in the future cultivated individuals would overcome this disparity by learning to be strictly impartial between their individual desires and the needs of the society. Secondly, Mill faced up to the criticism that utilitarianism was a doctrine worthy only of swine, in that 'low' pleasures could score high on Bentham's 'felicific calculus'. Mill's solution was to complicate the utilitarian arithmetic by adding a quality axis to the quantity one; now happiness was measured not simply by crude amount but also by its quality. This rejection of Bentham's belief that 'pushpin is as good as poetry' gives utilitarianism a developmental aspect. The 'higher pleasures' of educated people are given a weighting denied to the simpler pursuits of the uncultivated. To some critics the elitism of the quality axis seems to qualify Mill's liberalism; to others it also confirms their designation of liberalism as a middle-class creed.

It is clear, presumably, that liberalism then was not the same as it is now and some recent writers have noted limitations to Mill's liberalism. Mill, for example, did not believe that liberty was for all. It was not suitable for barbarians, among whom he included the Indians who were the subject of his employment. He was, then, a liberal imperialist, which now seems an oxymoron but did not then; for Mill, imperialism could be progressive if it helped advance a backward people some further steps up the ladder of civilisation. Mill, then, might be called a developmental liberal. Like Bentham, he did not believe in universal human rights. Mill's liberalism was one that a people developed into by demonstrating the qualities that fitted them for freedom and representative government. Similarly, Mill believed that the franchise was a privilege that could be earned by those achieving the requisite educational standard.

If this is beginning to make Mill sound rather conservative we should note that he took a bold, radical, controversial and uncompromising stance on the following issues:

- Condemning centuries of British misrule in Ireland and putting the case for the Irish poor at the time of the great famine of 1845–46.
- Publicly supporting the 1848 revolution in France at a time when the established order in Britain was still fearful of the example it set.
- Giving a very fair hearing to the case for socialist communities in his *Principles of Political Economy*.
- Condemning the 1865 massacre by Governor Eyre in Jamaica in spite of opposition from the mass of public opinion in Britain.
- Sympathising with the Northern states in the American Civil War, when upper-class opinion was more in favour of the South.
- Combating *The Subjection of Women*, a cause that led to him being subjected to immense ridicule. His book is now acknowledged as the only feminist classic written by a male author.

Perhaps the ultimate accolade to Mill's liberalism is that after his death *The Times* granted him an unsympathetic obituary. Mill's intellectual achievements were probably unmatched in Victorian England. There have always been those who, while respecting his achievements, rejected his conclusions. Nevertheless, in numerous areas, and in particular concerning the vital issue of freedom of speech, Mill's formulations still often set the terms of debate today.

Key works

- *On Liberty* (1859)
- *Considerations on Representative Government* (1861)
- *Utilitarianism* (1861)
- *The Subjection of Women* (1869)

Further reading

- I. Berlin, 'John Stuart Mill and the Ends of Life', in *Four Essays on Liberty* (Oxford University Press, 1969)
- N. Capaldi, *John Stuart Mill* (Cambridge University Press, 2005)
- J. Hamburger, *John Stuart Mill on Liberty and Control* (Princeton University Press, 1999)
- A. Ryan, *J. S. Mill* (Routledge and Kegan Paul, 1974)
- J. Skorupski (ed.), *The Cambridge Companion to Mill* (Cambridge University Press, 1998)

Michael Levin

John Milton   1608–74

Best remembered now as a poet, Milton stands as the father figure of the radical Protestant Dissenting tradition which largely forged the British liberal commitment to liberty, tolerance and open-mindedness. A devout Puritan, he supported the Parliamentary side in the English Civil War but came to oppose Presbyterian narrow-mindedness and the authoritarianism of the period when England was ruled without a monarch almost as much as he did royalist absolutism.

Key ideas

- Only the free exchange of ideas and opinions will allow truth to advance.
- Freedom of the press.
- Religious toleration.
- Advocated divorce 300 years before it became legal in the UK.

Biography

John Milton was born, on 9 December 1608, in Bread Street, London, the son of a scrivener who had abandoned the Catholic faith of his ancestors for Protestantism. He inherited from his father a love of and proficiency in music. Educated initially by a Scottish Puritan friend of his father's, he went to St Paul's School and then to Christ's College, Cambridge, where he was nicknamed 'the lady' on account of his physical beauty and delicacy of mind.

It was as a student that Milton began writing poems. Originally destined for holy orders, he chose rather to devote himself to writing and teaching. In 1638 he travelled through France and Italy, meeting the distinguished legal theorist Grotius in Paris and the astronomer Galileo in Rome. On his return, he settled in London and plunged himself into the political and ecclesiastical controversies of the day, publishing a stream of tracts attacking the Episcopalian government (a church structure governed by bishops) of the Church of England and the absolutist monarchy of the Stuarts. He strongly defended the execution of Charles I in 1649 in his treatise on *The Tenure of Kings and Magistrates* and in the same year became Latin Secretary to the newly appointed Council of State, being responsible for all foreign correspondence.

At the age of thirty-five he married Mary Powell, the seventeen-year-old daughter of an Oxfordshire Cavalier. She found living with the austere intellectual unappealing and left him after only a month or so of married life. This led Milton to write a series of pamphlets advocating that 'unfitness and contrariety of mind' should constitute valid grounds for divorce. In the event, the couple were reconciled and went on to have three daughters. Mary died in 1652 and four years later Milton married Katharine Woodcock, who died in childbirth the following year. In 1663, by which time his long-standing problems with his eyesight had resulted in total blindness, he took as his third wife and helpmate the twenty-five-year-old Elizabeth Minshull, who provided much support in his declining years and survived him for fifty-three years.

As a close aide of Oliver Cromwell, and strong supporter of the execution of Charles I, Milton could have expected to face death himself with the restoration of the monarchy in 1660. He was, however, allowed to retire unmolested and with his daughters reading to him and writing down the blank verse which he composed and carried in his head, he embarked on the most productive period of his literary career. He began dictating *Paradise Lost* in 1658 and completed it in 1663. In 1665 he and his family fled from London during the great plague and settled in Chalfont St Giles, Buckinghamshire. *Paradise Regained* and *Samson Agonistes* were published together in 1671, three years before his death on 8 November 1674. He was buried in the chancel of St Giles' Church in Cripplegate, London.

Ideas

John Milton was a product of both the Renaissance humanist tradition and the radical Protestantism of the Reformation. In *Areopagitica, A Speech for the Liberty of Unlicensed Printing* (1644), he produced one of the most powerful and eloquent apologias ever for religious toleration and the principles of free speech and a free press, valuing 'the liberty to know, to utter and to argue freely according to conscience above all liberties'. He based his argument on the centrality of the Christian concept of free will, the fact that humans are created by God with the freedom to choose between good and ill and that only the free exchange of opinions and ideas will permit the continuing active choice between good and evil and allow truth to advance. Freedom (q.v.), for Milton, is the essential quality for any moral or rational creature.

It is significant that *Areopagitica* was provoked not by the absolutist tendencies of the Stuart monarchs who formed Milton's natural enemies but by the imposition by Parliament of a form of censorship every bit as draconian as that associated with the monarchy. While Milton was a committed Parliamentarian and Puritan, rejecting monarchy, Episcopalianism and the principle of establishment, he also disliked Presbyterianism (the system of church government in which courts decide church policy) because of its dogmatic authoritarianism and emphasised a free Christian Commonwealth. He opened his *The Tenure of Kings and Magistrates* (1649) with the words 'All men were naturally born free, being the image of God', and went on to support the notion of parliamentary sovereignty and the right to remove rulers of any kind when they act tyrannically.

In *A Treatise of Civil Power in Ecclesiastical Causes shewing that it is not lawful for any Power on Earth to Compel in Matters of Religion* (1659) Milton further argued the case for religious toleration and for the non-interference of the state in matters of religious belief and observance. The 'inward man', he argued, can never be reached by force or controlled by authority but only by divine grace. He was prepared to extend the principle of toleration to the Catholic faith but not to the Roman Catholic Church because it put papal authority above individual conscience and denied the free exercise of choice and ideas.

In an interesting recent study, *Reviving Liberty*, Joan Bennett has located Milton in what she calls a radical Christian humanist tradition and suggested that his great poetic works, *Paradise Lost* and *Paradise Regained*, can be read as allegories on the birth of Christian liberty in the mind of its creator who was above all 'Christ our liberator'. It is in that they are born free that humans are most obviously made in the image of God – the exercise of their freedom is the ultimate theological purpose of their human existence and human love is the exercise of human freedom.

Milton's passionate commitment to the principle of liberty and to its unrestricted exercise through the institutions of a free press, a democratic and non-authoritarian political system and an atmosphere of religious tolerance makes him the founding father of the English liberal tradition and the forerunner of John Locke (q.v.) and John Stuart Mill (q.v.). His anchoring of the pursuit of liberty on the rock of Christian doctrine and Protestant theology places him equally as the chief progenitor of the great radical Nonconformist (q.v.) dissenting tradition that has supplied so much of British liberalism with its lifeblood and passion. It is wholly appropriate that a copy of *Areopagitica* was placed on the high altar of Westminster Abbey at the special service to mark the centenary of the British Liberal Party in May 1977 and that the work also served as the symbol of office of the party president, a bound copy being presented to each new incumbent by his predecessor at the annual party assembly.

Key works
- *The Doctrine and Discipline of Divorce* (1643)
- *Areopagitica, A Speech for the Liberty of Unlicensed Printing* (1644)
- *The Tenure of Kings and Magistrates* (1649)
- *A Treatise of Civil Power in Ecclesiastical Causes shewing that it is not lawful for any Power on Earth to Compel in Matters of Religion* (1659)

Further reading
- Joan Bennett, *Reviving Liberty: Radical Christian Humanism in Milton's Great Poems* (Harvard University Press, 1989)
- Roy Flannagan, *John Milton* (Blackwell, 2002)
- Christopher Hill, *Milton and the English Revolution* (Faber & Faber, 1977)
- E. M. W. Tillyard, *Milton* (Peregrine, 1968)

Ian Bradley

Mont Pelerin Society

The Mont Pelerin Society is an international association of classical liberal scholars that meets biennially (with annual regional meetings) to discuss the state and possible fate of liberalism, in terms of both practical social, economic and political changes and developments in liberal scholarship.

The Mont Pelerin Society was founded shortly after the Second World War at the instigation of the economist and political theorist F. A. Hayek (q.v.). With Marxist-Leninism already entrenched in the Soviet Union and various forms of socialism taking root across eastern and western Europe, at the time the prospects for liberalism seemed bleak. The Society was intended to bring together classical liberal scholars from around the world to build an intellectual movement that would challenge the socialist hegemony that appeared to be consuming intellectual and public life.

The first meeting of the then-unnamed society was held at the small Swiss Alpine town of Mont Pelerin in April 1947, and was attended by thirty-nine scholars from ten countries. Among the participants were Milton Friedman (q.v.), Bertrand de Jouvenel, Frank H. Knight, Ludwig von Mises, Michael Polanyi (q.v.), Karl Popper (q.v.), Lionel Robbins and Wilhelm Röpke. Those present agreed a statement of aims which began with the following analysis of the threat to free societies:

> The central values of civilisation are in danger. Over large stretches of the earth's surface the essential conditions of human dignity and freedom have already disappeared. In others they are under constant menace from the development of current tendencies of policy. The position of the individual and of the voluntary group are progressively undermined by extensions of arbitrary power. Even that most precious possession of Western Man, freedom of thought and expression, is threatened by the spread of creeds which, claiming the privilege of tolerance when in the position of a minority, seek only to establish a position of power in which they can suppress and obliterate all views but their own.

To combat the perceived threat to freedom (q.v.) the members of the Mont Pelerin Society undertook a largely academic mission to engage in scholarly analysis of the problems facing contemporary societies and the possible solutions to those problems offered by the principles of classical liberalism (q.v.).

The intellectual mission of the Society reflected the belief of Hayek and others in the power of ideas to change the course of human events. Hayek (like his friend Keynes (q.v.)) believed that the 'common sense' politics of the future would be determined by the scholarly fashions of today: it was the success of socialists in academia in the early decades of the twentieth century that had paved the way for the triumph of socialism in government decades later. Hayek sought to reverse this process by creating institutions to advance the cause of classical liberalism in scholarly debate – the Mont Pelerin Society was one, the Institute of Economic Affairs (q.v.) another.

The Society has greatly expanded from its relatively humble origins and today its biennial meetings are often attended by more than 500 participants. Among its members are the Nobel laureates James Buchanan (q.v.), Gary Becker and Vernon Smith, and the Czech President, Václav Klaus. The climate of ideas has also changed dramatically since the Society was created in 1947; socialism no longer holds sway throughout Europe and the Society is one of a number of organisations that can claim some credit for bringing about this reversal in the relative fortunes of liberalism and socialism.

In the UK context, it is probably true to say that the Mont Pelerin Society has had a greater influence on the Conservative than the Liberal Party; many of the market-based policies introduced by the Conservative governments of the 1980s and 1990s clearly owe a great deal to the work of Society members in the post-war period.

Further reading
- A. Ebenstein, *Hayek: A Biography* (Palgrave, 2001)
- R. M. Hartwell, *A History of the Mont Pelerin Society* (Liberty Fund, 1995)

John Meadowcroft

Baron de Montesquieu   1689–1755

One of the most important and influential figures in the early French Enlightenment, his ideas stimulated both David Hume and Adam Smith, and his theory of the separation of powers inspired the framers of the US Constitution to divide the government into legislative, executive and judiciary branches.

Key ideas
- The importance of explaining and justifying human laws and institutions.

- The need to choose between different forms of government that vary greatly in their attributes.
- The belief that a robust political philosophy requires a well-thought-out theory of liberty.
- The necessity of separating the functions of government.
- A belief that commerce plays a vital role in helping build a better society.

Biography

Charles-Louis de Secondat, Baron de La Brède et de Montesquieu, was born on 18 January 1689, at the Château of la Brède, near Bordeaux. He began his education at the Oratorian Collège de Juill, received a degree in law from Bordeaux and continued pursuing law in Paris.

In 1716 he inherited the title Baron de La Brède et de Montesquieu and the office of Président à Mortier in the Parlement de Bordeaux, which at that time was mainly a judicial and administrative body. From 1716 he was president of the Tournelle, the Parliament's criminal division, where he attended legal proceedings, supervised prisons and administered various punishments. At the same time he was an active member of the Academy of Bordeaux. In 1721 he published *Persian Letters*, anonymously. In 1728 he began his travels to Hungary, Turkey, Italy, Germany and England; in 1738 he was elected a member of the Royal Society in London.

He returned to Bordeaux in 1731. His *The Spirit of the Laws* was published in 1748; it had been twenty years in preparation and appeared in twenty-two editions before the end of his life. In 1750 he published *In Defence of the Spirit of the Laws* to answer his critics. Despite this the Roman Catholic Church placed *The Spirit of the Laws*, along with his many other works, on the *Index Librorum Prohibitorum* in 1751.

On 10 February 1755, Montesquieu died in Paris of a fever. He left unfinished an essay on taste for the *Encyclopédie* of Diderot and D'Alembert.

Ideas

The goal of Montesquieu's *The Spirit of the Laws* is to explain and supply a scientific understanding of laws and social institutions. Whereas physical laws are created and sustained by God, laws of the social world are instituted by man, who is 'a limited being; he is subject to ignorance and error, as are all finite intelligences. As an emotional creature, he falls subject to a thousand passions.' The practical aim is to warn and to advise in the light of this theory of the human condition.

According to Montesquieu there are three kinds of government: republican government (democratic or aristocratic), monarchy, and despotism, a view which is paralleled by David Hume (q.v.) in his *History of England*. All, however, are threatened by potential corruption. Democracy must beware of two excesses: 'the spirit of inequality, which leads it to aristocracy or the government of one alone, and the spirit of extreme equality, which leads it to the despotism of one alone, as the despotism of one alone ends up by conquest'. Aristocracy is corrupted when the power of the aristocrats becomes arbitrary; extreme corruption occurs when nobility becomes hereditary, because then 'the nobles can scarcely remain moderate'. A monarchy is ruined when the prerogatives of the established bodies or the privileges of the towns are removed. Strictly speaking, a despotic government cannot be corrupted because it is corrupt by its very nature: 'Other governments are destroyed because particular accidents violate their principle; this one is destroyed by its internal vice if accidental causes do not prevent its principle from becoming corrupt.'

Montesquieu was, after John Locke (q.v.), one of the greatest and earliest thinkers on liberty (see Freedom) and liberalism. In his view, 'political liberty in a citizen is that tranquillity of spirit which comes from the opinion each one has of his security, and in order for him to have this liberty the government must be such that one citizen cannot fear another citizen'. Therefore liberty is not just unrestricted independence, nor is it mere licence. If we have the liberty to harm others, others will also have the liberty to harm us, and we will have neither tranquillity nor security. Liberty thus understood depends principally on the goodness of the criminal law, but it depends also on certain features of the political constitution.

Montesquieu envisaged an idealised type of constitution developed from his understanding of the English constitution of the early eighteenth century. He identified three separate functions of government: what we today call the legislative, the executive and the judicial functions. Although he does not use the term 'separation of powers' Montesquieu argues that no two functions should be under the control of one branch of government. Alexander Hamilton, James Madison and John Jay, the authors of the *Federalist Papers* (see Federalists) shaped this idea into its modern form. It implies (1) that executive, legislative and judicial powers are distributed among different persons and bodies; (2) that the branches of government have equal responsibilities; and (3) that the judicial power acts independently of political influence.

Montesquieu is also the champion of the 'spirit of commerce', which 'brings with it the spirit of frugality, economy, moderation, work, wisdom, tranquillity, order, and rule'. In addition, commerce 'cures destructive prejudices, and it is an almost general rule that everywhere there are gentle mores there is commerce and that everywhere there is commerce, there are gentle mores'. Commerce also had a beneficial influence on government. Since commerce began to recover after the development of letters of exchange and the reintroduction of lending at interest, he wrote, 'princes have had to govern themselves more wisely than they themselves would have thought, for it turned out that great acts of authority were so clumsy that experience itself has made known that only goodness of government brings prosperity'. From here it is but a short step to Adam Smith's (q.v.) famous view – 'Whenever commerce is introduced in any country, probity and punctuality always accompany it. These virtues in a rude and barbarous country are almost unknown' – similar views underlay the attachment of later generations of liberal politicians, particularly in nineteenth-century Britain, to free trade (q.v.).

Key works

- *Persian Letters* (1721)
- *Considerations on the Causes of the Grandeur and Decadence of the Romans* (1734)
- *The Spirit of the Laws* (1748)

Further reading

- Isaiah Berlin, 'Montesquieu', in *Against the Current* (Princeton University Press, 2001)
- Anne M. Cohler, *Montesquieu's Comparative Politics and the Spirit of American Constitutionalism* (University Press of Kansas, 1988)
- Susan Gordon, *Montesquieu: The French Philosopher Who Shaped Modern Government* (The Rosen Publishing Group, 2005)
- Thomas L. Pangle, *Montesquieu's Philosophy of Liberalism: A Commentary on* The Spirit of the Laws (University of Chicago Press, 1973)

- Judith N. Shklar, *Montesquieu* (Oxford University Press, 1987)

Horst Wolfgang Boger

John Morley   1838–1923

A leading Liberal statesman and moralist who promoted individualism, home rule for Ireland, and a non-interventionist foreign policy. His political biographies and prominent public figure gave the Victorian tradition of Richard Cobden, W. E. Gladstone, and J. S. Mill continuity and popular appeal well into the 1900s.

Key ideas

- Individualism and the doctrine of moral progress.
- Cobdenite economics: free trade, retrenchment, non-interventionism.
- Single-issue politics as a counter to class politics and a way of communicating liberal principles.
- A home ruler and 'Little Englander'.

Biography

John Morley was born in Blackburn on 24 December 1838. His mother was an ardent Wesleyan, his father a surgeon who had turned from chapel to church. Morley attended University College School, London, and Cheltenham College, where he won an open scholarship to Lincoln College, Oxford in 1856. Reading John Stuart Mill (q.v.) and Auguste Comte, he soon became an agnostic. He believed that moral progress in history depended on the improvement of individual 'character', and that the perfection of character should be achieved through public duty.

Refusing to take holy orders, Morley quarrelled with his father and left Oxford with a pass degree in 1859. After some difficult years of 'penny-a-lining' he became editor of the rationalist *Fortnightly*

Review (1867–82), a position establishing him in the centre of London intellectual life. Acquainted with Mill, George Eliot, George Meredith, and Herbert Spencer (q.v.), he supported radical issues such as disestablishment of the church, reform of the House of Lords and female enfranchisement. In 1873 he formed a political partnership with Joseph Chamberlain (q.v.); together they agitated against the moderate Whiggism (q.v.) of Gladstone's (q.v.) first ministry and against the involvement of the church in elementary education.

In 1880 Morley became editor of the *Pall Mall Gazette*, which he turned into a liberal and anti-imperialist newspaper. His campaign against Irish Secretary W. E. Forster, a liberal coercionist, contributed to the latter's resignation in May 1882. In regard to Irish government Morley continued to steer a critical tack once elected as MP for Newcastle-upon-Tyne in February 1883; not only was he convinced of England's historical responsibility to redress Irish grievances, he also believed that the question of Irish government could elevate the electorate into a 'polity of discussion' (the phrase is Walter Bagehot's (q.v.)) and prevent its division over class issues. When Gladstone converted to a home rule solution, Morley's position turned from a liability into an asset for the party; he was made Chief Secretary for Ireland in 1886.

Morley's political career became frustrated, however, during his second tenure of the Irish Office (1892–95). The second Home Rule Bill stranded in the Lords; his role in the Gladstone succession crisis lost him credit among his peers; and his opposition to labour legislation cost him his Newcastle seat in 1895 (he was returned for Montrose Burghs the next year). In the late 1890s Morley's stock rose again as he emerged a critic of Liberal Imperialism (q.v.), but his interventions were few and some felt that he failed to offer practical leadership. His crowning performance as an orator came at Manchester in September 1899, where he gainsaid Britain's *casus belli* against the South African Boers. When the Liberals returned to power in 1905 he served as Secretary of State for India (1905–10) and, having accepted a peerage in 1908, as Lord President of the Council. He resigned from Asquith's Cabinet shortly before war was declared on Germany in August 1914.

In 1870, after several years of cohabitation, Morley had married Rose Mary Ayling, adopting his wife's two children as well as (in 1877) a son of his deceased brother William. He had no children of his own. He died on 23 September 1923.

Ideas

Morley's first books, including *Edmund Burke: A Historical Study* (1867), tried to determine the place of intellectuals in political life. Although Morley accepted Burke's (q.v.) critique of abstract ideas in politics, he sought to remedy the excessive anti-intellectualism which he perceived in British public life by adopting Auguste Comte's vision of a society run by scientific experts and unified by a civic 'Religion of Humanity'.

Morley dissociated himself from 'Comtism' while writing his studies of enlightened French *philosophes* in the early 1870s, realising that Comte's dogmatism stifled free discussion and inquiry, and accepting Mill's view that progress was conditional upon pluralism and the extension of civic liberties. His treatise *On Compromise* (1874) defends Mill's doctrine of liberty against its assailant James Fitzjames Stephen. It probes the limits imposed upon the freedom of expression by the demands of public opinion and considerations of utility, and its final message is gradualist and elitist and not quite free from 'compromise' itself. Its reputation as a Millite tract rests more on its rhetoric and on Morley's public figure than on its message, for Morley conceded to Stephen that the notion of 'negative liberty' was logically untenable, and it is doubtful whether he accepted Mill's postulate that liberty and individuality were ends in themselves. Yet *On Compromise* (in print until the 1940s) inspired men like J. L. Hammond (q.v.), F. W. Hirst (q.v.), L. T. Hobhouse (q.v.), Julian Huxley and Gilbert Murray (q.v.) in their opposition to collectivism, militarism, and religious dishonesty.

While Morley's unbelief rendered the early works controversial, his later biographies – especially the popular *Life of Richard Cobden* (1881), which he dedicated to John Bright, and *Walpole* (1889) – aimed at invigorating the mainstream of national life. The major challenge which Morley identified for England's modern, industrial democracy was to prevent citizens from selfishly identifying with class interests. On this view, to campaign on the 'single issue' of Irish home rule was a way of impressing liberal principles on the electorate. Likewise, Morley's opposition to empire and military conquest evolved from his belief that the true 'expansion of England' was 'within her own shores' as a prosperous, orderly and morally progressive polity. From his rationalist perspective, Morley shared the Gladstonian approach to politics as a branch of ethics.

Morley's essays and lectures of the 1890s are interesting but piecemeal. He refuted pessimistic critics of modern democracy (e.g. Henry Sumner Maine and W. E. H. Lecky), and like T. H. Huxley and L. T. Hobhouse he was uncomfortable with Darwinian evolutionism, which undercut the idea of moral progress and incited a defeatist attitude. But Morley asked more questions than he answered, and some would consider his confidence in progress and ethical living by this time rather contrived. His last biographies were *Oliver Cromwell* (1900), which contested Lord Rosebery's hero-worship of Cromwell, and *The Life of William Ewart Gladstone* (1903), by which he sought to tie his party more firmly to the mid-Victorian liberalism of 'peace, retrenchment and reform'.

If Morley's ideas and politics are sometimes difficult to gauge it is because he adhered to principles at which he had arrived by reason and logic but which were contrary to his sympathies and tastes. In 1885 he told a journalist that 'I am a cautious Whig by temperament, I am a sound Liberal by training, and I am a thorough Radical by observation and experience'.

Key works

- *On Compromise* (1874, second revised edition 1877)
- *Critical Miscellanies* (3 vols., 1886)
- *The Life of William Ewart Gladstone* (3 vols., 1903)
- *Memorandum on Resignation* (1928)

Further reading

- D. A. Hamer, *John Morley: Liberal Intellectual in Politics* (Clarendon Press, 1968)
- Christopher Kent, *Brains and Numbers: Elitism, Comtism, and Democracy in Mid-Victorian England* (University of Toronto Press, 1978)

Marco de Waard

Ramsay Muir   1872–1941

A contributor to key ideas in the development of liberalism in the 1920s and 1930s: on domestic policy through his work on industrial issues, and on international policy through promoting the idea of 'interdependency'. His

impact flowed not just from his thinking but also his political activism. After Muir's death, Ernest Barker described him as 'the scholar-prophet of Liberalism'.

Key ideas

- 'Interdependency', arguing for greater international political co-operation to match the economic and technological interdependency which had developed.
- Industrial cooperation, with government and industry working together to set goals to promote competitiveness and remedy social problems.
- A liberal form of imperialism, in which Britain's obligations to its colonies loomed large, with an emphasis on trusteeship.

Biography

John Ramsay Bryce Muir was born at Otterburn, Northumberland, on 30 September 1872, the son of a Presbyterian minister. He was educated at a small private school in Birkenhead, followed by University College, Liverpool (gaining a first in history, having switched from training to be a Presbyterian minister), and then Balliol College, Oxford (where he gained firsts in Greats and modern history). In 1898, Muir became a lecturer at Liverpool, and was Professor of History there in 1906–13. During this time, much of his historical work focused on local studies of Liverpool, but he also wrote on issues around the constitutional crisis of 1910. Muir spent 1913–14 travelling in India, before taking on the chair of modern history at Manchester, a post he held until 1921, when he resigned to devote himself to politics full time.

Muir had become interested in politics while at Oxford, but the major influence on his early thought was his strong belief in the British Empire, and this meant that he was out of sympathy with many in the

Liberal Party of the 1890s. But in Manchester, Muir became active in the Manchester Liberal Federation. It was in this forum that he began to think seriously about industrial questions, writing *Liberalism and Industry* in 1920. A year later, Muir was one of the founders of the Liberal Summer School (q.v.) with Ernest Simon (q.v.), Walter Layton (q.v.), J. M. Keynes (q.v.) and Hubert Henderson. Muir was active in the School throughout the 1920s and 1930s, when it was a major source of ideas for the Liberal Party. At the same time, Muir was a leading Liberal journalist, as editor of the *Weekly Westminster* from 1923 to 1926, when the paper merged with the *Westminster Gazette*, for which he continued to write articles.

In seeking elected office, Muir stood for Parliament eight times, winning once. His first battle was in Rochdale in 1922, and he took the seat at his second attempt in December 1923. This was an unfortunate time to enter Parliament as MP for a marginal seat, as there was a further election within a year and Muir lost. In March 1926 he then fought the Combined English Universities constituency in a by-election, and again stood in Rochdale in 1929. He fought Scarborough & Whitby at the May 1931 by-election and at the 1935 general election. In the 1931 general election he stood in Louth. However, within the Liberal Party, Muir had more electoral success, as chairman of the National Liberal Federation in 1931–33 and its president in 1933–36. When the Liberal Party's constitution was reformed in 1936 he became vice-president of the Liberal Party Organisation, a post he held until his death in 1941. He was also a key figure in the Liberal policy review of 1934, writing much of the report of the review, *The Liberal Way*.

Muir died on 4 May 1941 at Pinner, Middlesex. He never married and had no children.

Ideas

Ramsay Muir was a prolific political author. In addition to the contents of his weekly journalism in the mid-1920s, covering all the issues of the day, his work in book and pamphlet form was similarly broad in scope. He wrote two general political texts (*Politics and Progress* (1923) and *The Liberal Way* (1934)), one pamphlet on Liberal political philosophy (*The Faith of a Liberal* (1933)), and countless tracts on specific issues ranging from rating reform to whether democracy had a future. He even wrote a mildly humorous political novel based on the events of a hung parliament: *Robinson the Great: A Political Fantasia on the Problems of To-day and the Solutions of To-morrow, Extracted from the Works of Professor Solomon Slack, LL.D.,* (1929). However, his most significant contributions to Liberal thought were in three areas of policy: imperial, industrial and international.

Muir's first passion in politics was the Empire. He recalled that when he first became interested in politics, 'though I was a convinced Liberal, I was also an ardent Imperialist, because the development of the British Empire seemed to me to be a supreme expression of the very spirit of Liberalism'. He developed this interest through some of his historical work, such as *The Making of British India, 1756–1858* (1915) and *A Short History of the British Commonwealth* (1920–22). These portrayed the development of the British Empire (as distinct from other empires) as the perfect combination of nationalism, self-government and internationalism. In *The Character of the British Empire* (1917) he argued that the dominions were clearly in the Empire voluntarily, and that the ancient civilisations of India and Egypt, meanwhile, welcomed the order, peace, and justice that the British had brought with them. Though India sought self-government, he said, 'all the best opinion in India recognises that the progress already made has been due to British rule, and that its continuance depends upon the continuance of British rule'.

Throughout the 1920s and 1930s there is little sign in Muir's work of any sense of injustice in the Empire, or that it should one day end. However, he did advocate 'trusteeship', the widely held view across parties that Britain was holding colonies 'on trust' until 'native peoples' would be 'able' to rule themselves. By 1939, he was arguing for an institutionalised form of trusteeship, with a more formal sharing by European powers of the sovereignty of colonies, writing that a settlement of extra-European problems 'is impossible so long as the principle of unqualified State-sovereignty is maintained by the Western peoples themselves, and is adopted from them by other peoples'. Although it is difficult now to equate liberalism to Empire, Muir was far from alone in inter-war Britain in being a Liberal supportive of Britain's imperial mission.

Even though Muir continued to be an imperialist throughout his time as an active Liberal, his imperial thinking developed little between 1917 and 1939. A more important development in his thought came in industrial policy, where his work can be seen as a precursor to Lloyd George's (q.v.) industrial enquiry and the 'Yellow Book' of 1928. Muir's book *Liberalism and Industry* (1920) was part of a sustained campaign by the Manchester Liberal Federation to persuade the National Liberal Federation to debate and develop a fresh policy on industry and its relationship to social policy. Muir had many ideas on these issues, but five strands of thought emerge most clearly from his writing. First, he was clear that competitiveness was necessary to enable Britain to buy from abroad those goods and materials which it did not produce itself. Second, he believed that friction between

capital and labour damaged competitiveness. Third, he wanted to see much larger investment in the renewal and improvement of machinery. Fourth, he wanted to see new forms of industrial organisation running alongside private enterprise and advocated, for example, public trusts to run the railways, and cooperatives to run factories. Fifth, Muir advocated a National Industrial Council including representatives of management and labour with the aim of reducing conflict between the two. These ideas formed the core of the general approach adopted by the National Liberal Federation in 1921, seven years before the 'Yellow Book'.

Although Muir's thinking in industrial policy was important in its day, his work on international policy is arguably his most important legacy to liberal thought, particularly his book *The Interdependent World and its Problems* (1932). This popularised the idea of 'interdependency', originally developed through the pages of *The Economist* through its editor Water Layton. Muir argued that the world was now interdependent in a way that it had never been before, in three ways: technologically, politically (in that a shot fired in Sarajevo could cause a world war), and culturally (for example, through trade, films and sport). However, in the absence of an effective international system to deal with conflicts, nationalism remained a threat to world peace as it could lead to nations being too assertive and, thus, dangerous. This necessitated internationalism as the true way of safeguarding independence for all nations. Otherwise, the perils of interdependence would become apparent – struggles for self-determination or domination, tariff wars, monetary instability, and social revolution.

Muir's answer was found in limiting state sovereignty, by which he did not mean any form of world government; indeed, in

Politics and Progress (1923), he advocated a relatively limited League of Nations. Instead, Muir wanted a focus on regional pacts in the world's trouble-spots, rather than global obligations, although these should be reached under the aegis of the League. These should be accompanied by steady disarmament and the gradual reduction of tariffs through the establishment of various free-trade areas (q.v.). Two years later, *The Liberal Way* (1934) put forward more details on how the League could be made stronger. It started with the view that effective sanctions were needed if the League was ever to prevent war and set out precise terms for an Act of Parliament establishing which sanctions Britain would enforce and in which circumstances.

Muir's writing put forward ideas drawn from numerous sources, and one can see that he was strongly influenced by people such as Layton, Keynes and Murray. He developed many of their ideas into detailed statements of liberal attitudes, which were accessible to a wide range of people. One of his main contributions to liberal thought was therefore as a publicist as much as a thinker. However, like Walter Layton, he played an important part in developing the idea of 'interdependency', making it the basis of liberal internationalism (q.v.) in the 1930s and beyond. Meanwhile, his role as formulator of ideas which later appeared in the 'Yellow Book' should not be under-estimated.

Key works
- *The Character of the British Empire* (1917)
- *Liberalism and Industry: Towards a Better Social Order* (1920)
- *Politics and Progress: A Survey of the Problems of To-day* (1923)
- *Protection versus Free Imports* (1930)
- *The Interdependent World and its Problems* (1932)

- *The Faith of a Liberal* (1933)
- *The Liberal Way* (1934)
- *Is Democracy a Failure?* (1934)
- *The British Empire: How It Grew and How It Works* (1940)

Further reading
- Richard S. Grayson, *Liberals, International Relations and Appeasement: The Liberal Party, 1919–39* (Frank Cass, 2001)
- Stuart Hodgson (ed.), *Ramsay Muir: An Autobiography and Some Essays* (Lund Humphries, 1943)

Richard S. Grayson

Gilbert Murray   1866–1957

One of the most distinguished classical scholars of his generation, Murray was also a prominent internationalist and advocate of international organisation.

Key ideas
- The centrality of liberality to civilisation.
- The contemporary relevance of Hellenism.
- The importance of rationality, enlightenment and self-sacrifice to progress.
- The importance of the League of Nations and the United Nations to peace.

Biography
George Gilbert Aimé Murray was born into a Catholic Irish family in Sydney, Australia on 2 January 1866, and educated at Merchant Taylors' School, London, and St John's College, Oxford. A scholar of rare ability, he won several university prizes in his freshman year and took a double first in Classical Moderations and Greats in 1888.

At Oxford he became a disciple of John Stuart Mill (q.v.), a supporter of Irish home rule, and an admirer of Gladstone (q.v.), whom he regarded as a modern Pericles in manner, morals and statesmanship. Along with the detestation of cruelty he acquired during his boyhood, these were the foundation-stones of Murray's liberalism.

In 1889 he married Lady Mary Howard, daughter of the Earl and Countess of Carlisle, marrying into one of the great Whig aristocratic families of England. In the same year he was elected Professor of Greek at the University of Glasgow and over the next decade he forged his reputation as the leading interpreter of the Greek world. Following an important period in which he contributed to the revival of Greek drama on the London stage, he returned to Oxford as Regius Professor. Further new translations followed along with several important works of scholarship, notably *Four Stages of Greek Religion* (1912) and *The Classical Tradition in Poetry* (1927). His classic *Euripides and His Age* was published in 1913 for the landmark Home University Library, which he co-founded and co-edited for thirty years.

Murray's hope for a new Hellenistic age was dealt a shattering blow by the First World War. He spent the next thirty years tirelessly campaigning for international peace. He was chairman of the League of Nations Union 1923–38 and president 1938–46, and was chosen by Smuts to represent South Africa in the League Assembly. He was appointed vice-president of the League's International Committee for Intellectual Cooperation at its inception in 1922, becoming its president in 1928. This body, the forerunner of UNESCO, in many ways embodied Murray's high-minded hopes for a better, more civilised world. In works such as *The Ordeal of This Generation* (1928) and *From the League to the UN* (1948), Murray attempted to show how the world could, inspired by the ideals and virtues of fifth-century-BC Athens, retrieve Cosmos from the forces of Chaos.

He stood for Parliament as a Liberal candidate for Oxford University on six occasions between 1918 and 1929, none of them successful, nor too strenuously pursued. He was awarded the Order of Merit in 1940. While steadfast in his commitment to liberal principles, his aristocratic political instincts, paternalist outlook and Eurocentrism led him to distrust non-Western peoples. In old age he publicly supported Eden over Suez. He died in Oxford on 20 May 1957.

Ideas

'Liberalism is what the world needs both at home and abroad,' wrote Murray in 1925. Yet he preferred to talk not of liberalism but of liberality. The word 'liberalism' was too closely associated with the Liberal Party, and while a life-long member, Murray's instincts were bipartisan. He hated extreme partisanship in any form, including the exaggeration, misrepresentation and tribalism of the two-party system. The word 'liberalism' also implied a definite doctrine or set of principles, which Murray doubted existed. Rather, liberalism was a temper, a spirit, or an attitude of mind. When Gladstone wanted to get the measure of a man he would ask: 'Is he a man of real Liberality?' This appealed to Murray's ecumenicalism as it implied that good men could be found in all major political parties.

The notion of liberality also enabled Murray to downplay the traditional liberal emphasis on individual liberty. Following Mill, he believed that liberty did not mean licence. For the mass of men liberty was a destructive principle; only the noblest elements in society, those possessed of considerable powers of self-discipline and self-denial, could enjoy it unfettered.

The goal of liberality was freedom from prejudice, ignorance, self-interest and the passions of class and nation. The man of liberality hated injustice, cruelty, vulgarity and vice – everything that blinded and enslaved humanity – believing in the intimate connection between reason, enlightenment and progress. To this list Murray sometimes added scepticism. The true liberal might believe passionately in something, but he was always aware that he might be wrong. Above all else liberality meant concern for the common good: putting to one side private and class interests and doing what was right for the whole community. Here, as elsewhere, his ideas were moulded by his understanding of classical Greece. Individual freedom (q.v.) and loyalty to one's family or clan were important, but not at the cost of disservice to the *polis*.

To international relations Murray brought much the same progressive Hellenistic vision. Progress depended on developing a sense of the good of the whole international community. It meant above all else the eradication of war. Murray shared all the conventional liberal internationalist nostrums of his age: arbitration, disarmament, collective security, international law, international cooperation – especially via the League. Yet the way in which he arrived at these nostrums differed from his liberal internationalist (q.v.) colleagues. He did not subscribe to the Cobdenite (q.v.) belief in a harmony of interests underlying the relations between superficially antagonistic states. On the contrary, struggle and strife were endemic in social life. But unlike E. H. Carr and other 'realists' he did not believe that this made violent conflict and war inevitable.

Murray viewed social evolution in terms of the Greek concepts of Chaos and Cosmos. The latter was a settled, rational, moral order in which every individual had his due share of privilege and gave his due share of service. Cosmos was not something that arose spontaneously, nor something inherent in Man or nature, it had to be striven for. This sometimes resulted in violence and conflict but Cosmos could be achieved through discussion, argument and negotiation. And peaceful striving, while never easy, was especially important in the age of highly armed nationalist states.

The Victorians, like the Romans and Athenians before them, had built an impressive Cosmos. But it had one great flaw: it left untouched the international anarchy. While government within the state had become progressively more representative and efficient, government between states remained absent. Despite the great changes that had occurred in the nineteenth century in areas such as technology and trade, methods for the conduct of international relationships remained largely untouched. There were no regular procedures for the settlement of disputes, no world court, no system of international conferences, no communal method for deterring or punishing the law-breaker. The result was the First World War and the onset of Chaos. The task, therefore, was to restore the Cosmos enjoyed by the Victorians and rectify its chief fault – a laissez-faire (q.v.) approach to international politics.

Key works
- *The Foreign Policy of Sir Edward Grey* (1915)
- *The Ordeal of This Generation* (1928)
- *Liberality and Civilisation* (1938)
- *From the League to the UN* (1948)

Further reading
- Jeannie Morefield, *Covenants without Swords* (Princeton University Press, 2005)
- Christopher Stray (ed.), *Gilbert Murray Reassessed* (Oxford University Press, 2007)

- Francis West, *Gilbert Murray: A Life* (Croom Helm, 1984)
- Duncan Wilson, *Gilbert Murray, OM* (Oxford University Press, 1987)

Peter Wilson

National League of Young Liberals

The National League of Young Liberals, representing Liberals under the age of thirty years, comprised one half of the young Liberal movement, alongside the Union of University Liberal Societies. It had a history of adopting radical positions that sometimes embarrassed the party leadership but also contributed to the development of party thinking, particularly in the 1960s and '70s.

The National League of Young Liberals (NLYL) was formed in 1903 as part of a wider initiative to reinvigorate the Liberal Party following a long period of electoral weakness. It was intended to bring new voters into the Liberal fold. Its organisation mirrored that of the senior party, with district and constituency Young Liberal Associations, area federations and national institutions, including an annual assembly. There was a separate, but weaker, Scottish League of Young Liberals. NLYL was constitutionally separate from the senior party, which increased the potential for conflict between the two; generally, however, NLYL was a source of considerable support to the senior party, in terms of recruiting new members and providing energetic assistance in election campaigns.

A separate Union of University Liberal Societies (later the Union of Liberal Students) existed alongside NLYL. The two bodies were complementary and efforts were made to ensure that members of UULS joined NLYL on graduation. There were, however, tensions between the two organisations: UULS tended to regard itself as more cerebral and internationalist in outlook than the more parochial, constituency-based NLYL, and there was a suspicion that the party leadership shared this view.

Estimating the size of Liberal organisations is always fraught with difficulty, but it is likely that, after 1945, membership of NLYL peaked at around 15,000 during the early 1960s, while that of UULS was around 4,500 at that time. The Liberal Democrats continued with separate youth and student wings until the early 1990s when the present-day Liberal Democrat Youth and Students (LDYS) organisation was created.

The turnover of membership of the NLYL resulted in the organisation's leadership, image and outlook changing regularly throughout its history. It was most prominent in the years after 1945, and in particular in the decade from around 1966, when it achieved a level of political potency unmatched by the youth section of any other political party before or since.

Immediately after the Second World War, the Liberal leadership made a conscious effort to promote the recruitment of young Liberals, although mostly focusing on university students. NLYL was a beneficiary of the party's successful recruiting campaigns of the late 1940s, and many parliamentary candidates were brought into the party through this route. NLYL leaders such as Roy Douglas were prominent economic liberals (q.v.), supporting free trade (q.v), land value taxation, and stricter controls on monopolies and trades unions. The ideological battles which raged at Liberal assemblies at this time often pitted NLYL leaders against their student counterparts, although both organisations included a broad spectrum of views.

In 1959 a new generation of young Liberals formed the New Orbits group, which grew from a joint committee of NLYL and UULS. It was formed to promote new policy thinking following the accession of Jo Grimond (q.v.) to the leadership of the party. Its main achievement was the publication of a policy document – *New Orbits* – which was the most far-reaching restatement of the Liberal Party's principles and policies for many years. *New Orbits* emphasised the importance of the Liberal Party tackling bread-and-butter economic issues and made what was at the time a bold stand on nuclear disarmament. It also proposed divorce by consent and the abolition of censorship – both of which were rejected by NLYL and UULS as too radical.

The New Orbits group was a strong proponent of the concept of the realignment of the left in British politics. It urged the party leadership to target Labour voters and seats and also to undertake joint campaigns with the Labour Party on issues where the two parties agreed. Finally, it was instrumental in improving the presentation of Liberal assemblies – crucial in the television age – and in bringing modern design ideas to bear on the party's antiquated publications.

The New Orbits group continued into the 1970s but by the mid-1960s it had been replaced at the heart of the Young Liberal movement by a new generation of radicals, nicknamed the 'Red Guard' (after the Red Guards of Mao Zedong's Cultural Revolution), as a result of their antagonistic relationship with the Liberal leadership. By 1970 the Young Liberals came prominently to the fore on the national stage as advocates of radical, direct action politics, most famously playing a leading role in the 'Stop The Seventy Tour' campaign aimed at the South African cricket team.

Throughout the late 1960s and early 1970s NLYL was a constant advocate of radical policy positions, particularly in the field of foreign affairs, with anti-NATO and pro-Palestinian resolutions regularly submitted to the Liberal assembly. Similarly, in the domestic field the League committed itself to the abolition of head teachers and the imposition of time limits on prosecutions. In other areas it proved to be ahead of its time, particularly through its advocacy of environmental politics, gay rights and the withdrawal of military forces from Northern Ireland.

From the late 1960s onwards, NLYL was associated with three key strands of thought influencing both the party's philosophical and strategic thinking.

First, some elements within the League were advocates of Grimond's idea that the Liberal Party should act as an 'umbrella' under whose shade single-issue pressure groups could find a conducive environment in which to flourish, enabling the Liberal Party in turn to construct a wider political base of support and influence. NLYL, through its direct action campaigns and radical stance, was particularly well positioned to cultivate links with groups such as the Anti-Apartheid Movement, the Campaign for Nuclear Disarmament and Friends of the Earth. But whilst this approach provided young radicals with an outlet for their opposition to American policies in Vietnam and eastern Europe, and for their growing support for the green agenda, it did not provide a sufficient base for a growth in Liberal Party electoral support.

Within NLYL there were also a significant number of activists who were proponents of libertarian socialism. They claimed their analysis of capitalism and their commitment to egalitarianism from socialism, their understanding of worker control from syndicalism, their libertarian perspective and commitment to direct action from anarchism (q.v.), and from pacifism (q.v.)

their commitment to non-violence. Again, however, this approach was idealistic but inchoate and was incapable of providing a coherent and sustainable Liberal programme at the national level.

The activities of the more radical 'Red Guard' NLYL leaders – particularly the ripping-up of cricket pitches – were perceived to have put off floating voters, and the Young Liberals were widely blamed for the party's disappointing 1970 general election result. Less than a year later, however, more moderate influences within NLYL prevailed, switching its focus away from direct action politics and towards a strategic concentration on community politics which, the Young Liberals contended, offered the party both a philosophical and an electoral sense of direction.

The third strand of thought within the NLYL – community politics (q.v.) – proved to be the most durable. NLYL leaders such as Tony Greaves and Gordon Lishman were instrumental in developing a philosophical basis for community politics and for ensuring that it was adopted as party strategy at the 1970 assembly. For a time it seemed to some that the Young Liberals had found the elixir by which the Liberal Party could be transformed once again into a party of power. The party's brief electoral revival in 1972–73 was hailed as vindication of the community politics strategy and for NLYL there was particular satisfaction when one of its own leading members, Graham Tope, was elected in Sutton & Cheam. In the late 1970s, however, it became clear that although community politics offered a route to success the road would be slow, and some proponents drifted out of politics or, as with Peter Hain, to the Labour Party.

In subsequent years, NLYL and LDYS were less prominent. LDYS remained capable of discomforting the party leadership, however, by taking radical positions on

issues such as drugs, prostitution and the monarchy and sponsoring debates on such issues at Liberal Democrat conferences.

Further reading
- Ruth Fox, 'Young Liberal Influence and its Effects, 1970–74', *Journal of Liberal Democrat History* 14 (spring 1997)
- Tony Greaves (ed.), *Blackpool Essays: Towards A Radical View of Society* (Gunfire Publications, NLYL, 1967)
- Peter Hain, *Radical Liberalism and Youth Politics* (Liberal Publications Department, 1973)
- Peter Hain, *Radical Regeneration: Protest, Direct Action and Community Politics* (Quartet Books, 1975)
- New Orbits Group, *New Orbits* (1959)
  Ruth Fox and Robert Ingham

National Liberal Party see Liberal Nationals

Neo-liberalism

Neo-liberalism is a term used to describe the thinkers responsible for the revival of classical liberal and libertarian ideas from the 1970s onwards, and the politicians responsible for the translation of some of those ideas into public policy in a number of liberal democracies at about the same time.

Neo-liberals rejected important aspects of the post-war consensus that had existed in most Western liberal democracies from the 1940s to the 1970s. Instead they argued for a return to the principles of classical liberalism (q.v.) similar to those that had guided the nineteenth-century Liberal Party. The key principles of neo-liberalism are:
- The state should have a minimal role in society, principally restricted to

guaranteeing the rule of law (q.v.) and protecting property rights.

- Optimal economic outcomes are most likely to be achieved by the unhindered operation of free markets.
- Generous welfare states generate perverse incentives that lead people who are able to work to voluntarily exit the labour market.
- Attempts to achieve 'social justice' (q.v.) via redistributive taxation necessarily infringe the liberty of those whose income and wealth is redistributed and hence are inherently unjust.
- Corporatism leads to economic decline and social unrest as uneconomic industries and inefficient practices are subsidised and different groups compete for the receipt of special privileges from government.

These ideas can be seen to be an application of the principles of classical liberalism in a contemporary context. The belief in the minimal role of the state and the importance of free markets in producing socially beneficent outcomes can be traced back to the Manchester School (q.v.) traditions of the Liberal Party; suspicion of state welfare and 'social justice' can be linked to the Gladstonian (q.v.) emphasis on self-help and charity, and the rejection of corporatism is consistent with the liberal rejection of a class politics that sees society as being framed by the competing interests of labour and capital.

The three thinkers most closely identified with neo-liberalism are Milton Friedman (q.v.), F. A. Hayek (q.v.) and Robert Nozick (q.v.). Margaret Thatcher (1925–), former US presidential candidate Barry Goldwater (1909–98), Ronald Reagan (1911–2004) and New Zealand's former finance minister Roger Douglas (1937–), the architect of 'Rogernomics', are the politicians most commonly associated with neo-liberalism. Today the term is most frequently used to describe the policies of economic liberalisation implemented in some Latin American countries and advocated by the World Bank and International Monetary Fund in recent decades.

Of all the schools of liberal thought collected in this volume, neo-liberalism is probably unique in being rejected as a label by almost all those described as neo-liberals; it is a term that tends to be used almost exclusively by its opponents. Alleged neo-liberals have preferred to describe themselves variously as 'conservatives' (Reagan and Thatcher), 'libertarians' (Nozick), 'economic liberals' (Friedman), or, uniquely, as 'Old Whigs' (Hayek).

Neo-liberals tend to reject the term because they believe it contains pejorative undertones that imply a qualified or mutated liberalism. As the Peruvian novelist and former presidential candidate Mario Vargas Llosa has written:

> To say 'neo-liberal' is the same as saying 'semi-liberal' or 'pseudo-liberal'. It is pure nonsense. Either one is in favour of liberty or against it, but one cannot be semi-in-favour of liberty or pseudo-in-favour of liberty, just as one cannot be 'semi-pregnant', 'semi-living' or 'semi-dead'.

Neo-liberalism, then, is believed by those described as such to describe a partial or conditional commitment to liberty, as distinct from genuine (or classical) liberalism.

If neo-liberalism describes a return to the liberal principles of the late nineteenth century then it should be asked why the influence of neo-liberalism appears to have been minimal within the Liberal Party and the Liberal Democrats? The Liberal Party was formed in the nineteenth century by a coalition of Whigs, Radicals and Peelites united by Peel's repeal of the Corn Laws and there is good reason to believe that in the mid-1950s the great majority of economic liberals (q.v.) would have been found in the Liberal Party rather than among the Conservatives. Economic liberalism was rejected within the Liberal Party under the leadership of Jo Grimond (q.v.) as he sought to replace the Labour Party as the natural party of opposition to the Conservatives – although Grimond himself was personally sympathetic to economic liberalism and neo-liberal ideas and policies. By the time the neo-liberal revival was under way the Liberal Party had come to embrace the Keynesian (q.v.) post-war settlement – which also represented an important strand in the party's own thinking – and the adoption of many neo-liberal policies by the Conservative Party under Margaret Thatcher seemed to cement Liberal hostility to a neo-liberal approach.

Beyond the Liberal Party and Liberal Democrats, the influence of neo-liberalism has clearly been dramatic and far-reaching. Advocates and opponents would probably agree that neo-liberalism has transformed politics and policy in almost all liberal democracies and has had a significant influence in China, India and many Latin American countries. In the UK, Margaret Thatcher's programme of privatisation, trade union reform and reductions in the higher rates of income tax have transformed the political landscape and have not been repealed by Tony Blair's Labour governments. Today, key aspects of the public policy agenda are characterised by a neo-liberal consensus that challenges the belief that government action always produces the beneficent consequences it intends and believes that private-sector entrepreneurship performs an important positive economic function that government cannot easily imitate.

Key works
- Milton Friedman, *Capitalism and Freedom* (University of Chicago Press, 1962)

- F. A. Hayek, *The Constitution of Liberty* (Routledge, 1960)
- Robert Nozick, *Anarchy, State, and Utopia* (Blackwells, 1974)

Further reading
- Richard Cockett, *Thinking the Unthinkable* (Fontana, 1995)
- Desmond King, *The New Right: Politics, Markets and Citizenship* (Macmillan, 1987)
- John Meadowcroft and Jaime Reynolds, 'Liberals and the New Right', *Journal of Liberal History* 47 (summer 2005)

John Meadowcroft

New Deal

The name given by President Franklin D. Roosevelt to the series of programmes designed to rescue the US economy from the effects of the Great Depression. The New Deal's creation of the social security system, and its belief that government had a duty to ensure high levels of employment, economic activity and personal economic security, in good times as well as bad, came to encapsulate the doctrine of liberalism in the United States.

The Great Depression that wreaked havoc on the economies of the Western world in the decade following the Wall Street Crash of October 1929 hit the United States particularly hard. Between 1929 and 1933 American gross national product fell by 30 per cent, industrial output declined by nearly 50 per cent, and agricultural production by some 60 per cent. Almost a third of the adult workforce was unemployed by 1933. The nation's poorly regulated, ramshackle banking system was near collapse by the time Franklin D. Roosevelt (1882–1945) assumed the presidency that same year. It was in this climate of economic disaster that Roosevelt, addressing his party's national convention in July 1932 after accepting nomination as their candidate for the presidency, stated: 'I pledge you, I pledge myself, to a new deal for the American people.'

This 'New Deal' represented a series of emergency and long-term measures to use the power of government to rescue the economy from recession and to provide a measure of economic security for the American people. The Roosevelt administration's enduring legacy was to create a social security system and to develop the idea that government had a duty to ensure high levels of employment, economic activity, and personal economic security in good times as well as bad. This legacy, often known in the United States as the doctrine of liberalism, would not only help shape American politics in the latter half of the twentieth century, but would also form part of an international movement dedicated to the use of state power to try to ensure a fairer distribution of a nation's resources to all citizens.

It is difficult to encapsulate the basic tenets of early New Deal liberalism, as the policies that made up the first hundred days of the Roosevelt administration between March and July 1933 were formulated by various advisers who sometimes shared little ideological kinship. Measures to stabilise the banking system and regulate securities trading received the blessing of more conservative members of Roosevelt's 'Brains Trust' such as Raymond Moley, law professor at Columbia University and Roosevelt's Under-Secretary of State in his first months in office. More radical advisers like Adolf Berle and Rexford Tugwell pushed for a programme of public works to eliminate unemployment, as well as a system of subsidies to help alleviate the worst of the farming crisis. The National Recovery Administration (NRA) was designed to allow businesses to cooperate to fix prices and production levels and so reduce the impact of cut-throat competition on profits. One thing most of the early New Deal policies had in common was their experimental approach to the problems of the Depression, and their very limited reliance on international precedents and practice. Indeed, Roosevelt withdrew the United States from the London Economic Conference in July 1933, claiming that his administration's commitment to devaluation of the dollar in order to stimulate the economy was at odds with the goal of many other participating countries to maintain currency values and to prop up the Gold Standard.

However, while much of the early New Deal had a limited lifespan – some measures were temporary, whereas others, like the NRA, were declared unconstitutional by the US Supreme Court – legislation passed after 1935 formed an enduring New Deal legacy, and relied increasingly on the sharing of political experience with like-minded thinkers abroad. The Social Security Act of 1935 took shape using the precedent of social insurance schemes for unemployment and old age payments already in place in several American states, and shared many of the contributory mechanisms of the British 1911 National Insurance Act. In the early twenty-first century American workers and employers still contribute part of their payroll in unemployment, disability, and old age insurance taxes. The scheme was later extended to include medical care for the elderly and for poorer citizens.

The National Labor Relations Act of 1935 brought the power of the state to bear on employers to recognise labour unions and to bargain with them over wages and working conditions, a process that had developed much earlier in the twentieth century in many other industrialised states. The Works Progress Administration (WPA) was established the same year to allow the federal government to employ Americans in a variety of public works, ranging from the construction of public buildings to the funding of theatrical productions, writers and artists. The Fair Labor Standards Act of 1938 created a minimum wage for many employees. By 1938 the administration had abandoned its notional commitment to a balanced budget, paving the way for the use of Keynesian (q.v.) deficit financing to promote economic growth late into the twentieth century. A hostile Congress abolished the WPA during the Second World War, but the other principal tenets of later 1930s policy-making remained in place long after the term 'the New Deal' had entered the history books, and were repeatedly expanded in the decades after the war.

The war years saw a massive expansion of the regulatory powers of the federal government as it presided over the country's largest-ever war mobilisation. The growth of the war state in the early 1940s encouraged the Roosevelt administration to become increasingly ambitious in its vision of a new world order in peacetime, reflecting a perceptible shift to the left in the political zeitgeist in Europe and the Antipodes as much as the US. The National Resources Planning Board, a wartime planning agency, produced an agenda for postwar planning which it termed an American 'Second Bill of Rights', in effect a US version of the Beveridge Plan (q.v.), that was circulated to Congress in 1943.

The increasing clout of conservatism in the United States by the late 1940s limited the achievements of the political heirs to the New Deal. Nevertheless, the legislative vision of American liberalism, encapsulated in Roosevelt's 'Economic Bill of Rights'

speech in 1944 that promised Americans 'the right to adequate protection from the economic fears of old age, sickness, accident and unemployment', would help shape social policy in the two decades after the war.

Further reading

- Anthony Badger, *The New Deal: The Depression Years* (Macmillan, 1989)
- Alan Brinkley, *The End of Reform: New Deal Liberalism in Recession and War* (Knopf, 1995)
- Patrick Reagan, *Designing a New America: The Origins of New Deal Planning, 1890–1943* (University of Massachusetts Press, 1999)
- Daniel Rodgers, *Atlantic Crossings: Social Politics in a Progressive Age* (Belknap Press, 1998)
- Fiona Venn, *The New Deal* (Edinburgh University Press, 1998)

Jonathan Bell

New Liberalism

The New Liberals of the late nineteenth and early twentieth century made the case against laissez-faire classical liberalism and in favour of state intervention directed against impediments to freedom such as poverty, ignorance or disease. They saw individual liberty as something to be achievable only under favourable social and economic circumstances. The New Liberal programme came to underpin most of the legislative achievements of the 1906–14 Liberal governments and marked the party's transformation to social liberalism.

The New Liberalism emerged at the end of the nineteenth century (the term was first used by the Liberal MP L. A. Atherley-Jones in 1889) largely as a reaction to the Liberal Party's failure, under W. E. Gladstone (q.v.), to formulate an adequate response to the new social problems of industrialisation. Although radical (q.v.) pressure for 'constructionist' legislation – for example the free elementary education, graduated taxation and land reform of Joseph Chamberlain's (q.v.) 'Unauthorised Programme' of 1885 – had been growing for some time, Gladstone used great moral questions, such as home rule for Ireland, to steer the party away from the state-sponsored social reforms to which he remained firmly opposed.

The departure of the remaining Whigs (q.v.), with Chamberlain, in 1886, Gladstone's retirement in 1894, and the disastrous elections of 1895 and 1900 opened the way to new thinking. Although living standards in general had risen throughout the latter half of the nineteenth century, society was increasingly characterised by the spread of slums, poverty, ignorance and disease, and the ending of the long mid-Victorian economic boom had removed the belief that economic growth would automatically solve such social problems. Just as the emergence of classical liberalism (q.v.) in the early and mid-nineteenth century was closely linked to the emergence of industrial capitalism, so the development of the New Liberalism of the late nineteenth and early twentieth centuries derived from this further evolution of economy and society.

T. H. Green (q.v.) was the first of the liberal thinkers fully to take this growing social inequality into account. Green argued that the unrestrained pursuit of profit had given rise to new forms of poverty and injustice; the economic liberty of the few had blighted the life-chances of the many. Negative liberty, the removal of constraints on the individual, would not necessarily lead to freedom of choice for all; workers, for example, frequently had little if any choice of employer, and no real choice between working or not working, whereas

employers had plenty of choice regarding their employees. The free market therefore often could, and did, lead to exploitation. Green proposed the idea of *positive* freedom: the ability of the individual to develop and attain individuality through personal self-development and self-realisation.

Since much of the population was prevented from such self-realisation by the impediments of poverty, sickness, unemployment and a lack of education, government was justified in taking action to tackle all these conditions. This was not a threat to liberty, but the necessary guarantee of it:

> Our modern legislation then with reference to labour, and education, and health, involving as it does manifold interference with freedom of contract, is justified on the ground that it is the business of the state, not indeed directly to promote moral goodness, for that, from the very nature of moral goodness, it cannot do, but to maintain the conditions without which a free exercise of the human faculties is impossible.

In this extension of the role of the state, Green was in fact reflecting what was already beginning to be common practice amongst Liberals in local government; Green himself was an Oxford councillor, as well as an academic, and Chamberlain's municipal liberalism had showed how councils could run gas, water and sewerage companies to the benefit of the living standards of their citizens.

The members of the Rainbow Circle, a group of progressive politicians and thinkers who started meeting regularly in the early 1890s to discuss social and labour questions, provided much of the intellectual justification for the New Liberal programme. They included almost all of the major New Liberal writers, L. T. Hobhouse (q.v.), J. A. Hobson (q.v.), R. B. Haldane (q.v.), Charles Trevelyan and Herbert Samuel (q.v.), together with many of the leaders of the Fabian Society and the Labour Representation Committee, founded in 1900. In 1896 the group established the *Progressive Review*, dedicated to promoting a 'New Liberalism' based on 'a specific policy of reconstruction, the conscious organisation of society and an enlarged and enlightened conception of the functions of the state'. Their creed was a self-conscious departure from the past; as David Lloyd George (q.v.) put it in 1908: 'The old Liberals used the natural discontent of the people with the poverty and precariousness of the means of subsistence as a motive power to win for them a better, more influential, and more honourable status in the citizenship of their native land. The new Liberalism, while pursuing this great political ideal with unflinching energy, devotes a part of its endeavour also to the removing of the immediate causes of discontent. It is true that man cannot live by bread alone. It is equally true that a man cannot live without bread.'

Although the Liberal government elected in 1906 drew its inspiration from many sources, including, importantly, Bismarck's social reforms in Germany (designed primarily to fend off the rise of socialism), New Liberal thinking came to dominate its programme, particularly after the elevation of H. H. Asquith to the premiership in 1908. Although Asquith himself, a student of Green's at Oxford, was not a consistent radical, his Cabinet contained several who were, notably Lloyd George, Samuel (from 1909) and Winston Churchill (q.v.), and they had many supporters amongst the new and younger MPs. The introduction of old age pensions and national insurance for periods of sickness, invalidity and unemployment, minimum wages for the miners, government grants for maternity and child welfare clinics, compulsory school meals, loans for local

authority house-building, and the establishment of labour exchanges and trade boards and of the Development Commission to provide investment in those sectors of the economy which private capital failed to finance: all marked the acceptance of the New Liberal belief that however much one removed constraints upon individual liberty, there were some things that individuals could not accomplish by themselves – and therefore could not be truly free.

The budgets of Asquith and Lloyd George marked a similar redirection of fiscal policy, abandoning the Gladstonian notion that taxation was merely a necessary evil, and accepting that taxation and expenditure could become positive instruments of social policy. Asquith's 1907 budget not only raised taxation in aggregate, in order to pay for the planned social expenditure of the years ahead, but for the first time differentiated between earned and unearned income, raising taxation on the latter. Lloyd George's 'People's Budget' of 1909, which graduated the income tax structure more progressively, and introduced a new super-tax, higher excise duties and new taxes on cars, petrol and land – all designed to raise revenue for social spending (along with higher military expenditure) – was perhaps the apotheosis of the New Liberal programme.

Tension inevitably existed between the New Liberals and the more orthodox party members who still supplied much of its rank and file; for many of them, New Liberalism seemed little different from socialism. Herbert Spencer (q.v.) in particular, in his exposition of social Darwinism, articulated the antipathy that many liberals felt towards those who championed the state as an essential agent in achieving social progress. Why, then, did New Liberal thinking come to dominate the government's programme so thoroughly? Three main reasons can be identified. First, because there was no alternative agenda on offer: Gladstonianism had clearly run its course, the Conservatives were split over tariff reform and the Labour Party had no distinctive programme of its own.

Second, because the New Liberal agenda met the requirements of the time. The living conditions of the working class, revealed in the poor physical conditions of Boer War recruits and the social surveys of Booth and Rowntree, and highlighted by campaigning journalists, were clearly bad enough to stimulate action of some kind. Many of the New Liberals discovered the realities of poverty and destitution for themselves, through work in 'settlements' such as Toynbee Hall in east London. The programme was also supported by the more radical (usually Nonconformist) industrialists, concerned to see state investment in those sectors of the economy where private finance was lacking.

The third reason was entirely pragmatic: that in electoral terms the New Liberal programme worked. By and large the government's social and economic programme was popular; even the Conservatives accepted the irreversibility of much of its legislation, particularly old age pensions. The Liberal Party looked well placed to win the election due in 1915, had war not intervened.

This New Liberalism which was in so many ways so different from Gladstonian liberalism can still be seen, however, as identifiably liberal. While retaining a firm belief in liberty, it sought a wider definition. 'Liberalism', wrote Hobson in 1909, 'is now formally committed to a task which certainly involves a new conception of the State in its relation to the individual life and to private enterprise ... From the standpoint which best presents its continuity with earlier Liberalism, it appears as a fuller appreciation and realisation of individual liberty contained in the provision of equal opportunities for self-development. But to this individual standpoint must be joined a just apprehension of the social, viz., the insistence that these claims or rights of self-development be adjusted to the sovereignty of social welfare.'

What the New Liberals did was to inject the concept of a community wider than the individual firmly into liberal thinking. The state was entitled to take action on behalf of the community as a collectivity, rather than merely on behalf of individuals as themselves. The New Liberals were quite clear, however, *why* they were advocating such collectivism: for the greater liberty of the individual. 'Liberals must ever insist', wrote Hobson, 'that each enlargement of the authority and functions of the State must justify itself as an enlargement of personal liberty, interfering with individuals only in order to set free new and larger opportunities ... Liberalism will probably retain its distinction from Socialism, in taking for its chief test of policy the freedom of the individual citizen rather than the strength of the State.'

In this way the Liberals evolved from a classical to a social liberal (q.v.) party – unlike many continental European liberal parties of the time. Although the wartime split of 1916 prevented the party from being able to implement the New Liberal agenda further, its legacy can be seen in Lloyd George's 'coloured books', the innovative thinking of Keynes (q.v.) and Beveridge (q.v.), and the welfare state that Labour governments created after 1945.

Further reading
- Michael Bentley, *The Climax of Liberal Politics: British Liberalism in Theory and Practice 1868–1918* (Edward Arnold, 1987)

- Michael Freeden, *The New Liberalism: An Ideology of Social Reform* (Clarendon Press, 1986)
- Martin Pugh, *The Making of Modern British Politics 1867–1945* (Blackwell Publishers, 3rd edn., 2002), ch. 6, 'Edwardian Progressivism'

Duncan Brack

Nonconformity

Generally taken to mean Protestant Dissenters, Nonconformists provided the Victorian Liberal Party with some of its leaders, many of its supporters, and several of its causes. After the First World War, both declined together.

'Nonconformity', in any era, presents itself in opposition to a prevailing 'Establishment'. In British political history its connotation has been primarily religious: Nonconformists (or Dissenters) were adherents of sects or denominations which refused to conform to the established church. Roman Catholics naturally came into this category but it is in terms of Protestant Dissent, as it crystallised in the seventeenth century, that Nonconformity is primarily considered. In England and Wales it embraces Baptists, Congregationalists, Quakers and Presbyterians (many of the latter turning into Unitarians) and, in Scotland, various seceding bodies from the Church of Scotland. The theological differences between them, together with their largely decentralised and non-hierarchical forms of church government, make it difficult to speak about 'the Nonconformist voice' – hence the phrase 'the dissidence of dissent'.

Nonconformists, after the Restoration, had been subjected to periodic bouts of persecution and imprisonment. In 1689, however, the Toleration Act allowed Dissenters the freedom of public worship, so long as their meeting houses were duly registered. Although often regarded as a landmark piece of legislation in this particular, and in other provisions, it was a grudging concession rather than a declaration of principle. Since the Test Acts of the 1670s, which required all civil and military office-holders to take the oaths of allegiance and supremacy, sign declarations against transubstantiation, and receive the sacrament according to the forms of the Church of England, were not repealed, here was no ringing commitment to civic equality (q.v.) (though in practice toleration extended more widely than the Act formally guaranteed).

It was the eighteenth-century pursuit of this goal which led some of their prominent members, the Protestant Dissenting Deputies, to forge political connections with Whig (q.v.) politicians. While the Tory/church and Whig/Dissent equation over-simplifies, it does not do so greatly. However, the extent to which the pursuit of ecclesiastical liberty spilled over into a more full-blown advocacy of liberal notions varied both within and between the sects. There was, for example, considerable Dissenting sympathy with the American colonists and, initially at least, in some quarters, for the French Revolution. The device of 'occasional conformity' had enabled those Dissenters who were so minded to play a part in local political affairs commensurate with the commercial standing which important elements among them possessed.

The separation of Methodists from the Church of England (and in turn the proliferation of a number of different Methodist bodies) raised a further complication. Methodists, though they had to be categorised as Nonconformists, did not possess the same cultural baggage as 'Historic Dissent'. Thus while, taken in the round, the numerical growth of nonconformists made them a substantial presence in English and Welsh life, the extent to which they made common cause varied. The repeal of the Test and Corporations Act in 1828 (together with Catholic emancipation the following year) constituted further landmarks on the road to parity, though equal access had still to be fully achieved. There were, for example, struggles against the continuing requirement that Dissenters should pay the church rate. It was this symbolic issue which brought the young Quaker John Bright into politics in the 1830s. Both locally and nationally, Nonconformity came to constitute a significant element in the constellation which constituted mid and late-Victorian liberalism, though Wesleyans, to some extent, held back.

The classical Nonconformist issue was the very existence of an established church. It was not sufficient, the most vocal declared, to campaign for and then witness the steady elimination of remaining restrictions (for example, making it possible for Nonconformists to enter and/or graduate from the universities of Oxford and Cambridge). The principle of a state church was wrong – and the fact that a substantial body of Christians urged this gave British liberalism, in whose ranks they largely were, a different flavour from continental liberalism where the same issue was largely prosecuted by secularists or anti-clericals. The Anti-State Church Society, later the Liberation Society (q.v.), campaigned vigorously on just this issue.

It was a struggle which came to dominate Welsh politics in the late century and led to the disestablishment of the Church of England in Wales. In England, where there was no comparable Nonconformist majority, establishment survived. Although Gladstone (q.v.) cultivated Nonconformists, and was cultivated by them, he was not to be moved on this issue. The presence by the 1870s

and 1880s of some Nonconformists at the top of the party – men as different as John Bright, Joseph Chamberlain (q.v.) and H. H. Fowler – was testimony to their increasing importance, but they were not dominant. By the end of the century, too, there was an increasing questioning in their own ranks of just what 'nonconformity' amounted to. Exclusions and restrictions had preserved a sense of solidarity, while their substantial removal had the opposite consequence. What was there to be 'nonconformist' about? John Bright, in the end, had been an opponent of Irish home rule. Joseph Chamberlain espoused tariff reform. Nonconformity in itself did not offer a comprehensive political or philosophical package.

One solution was to 'accentuate the positive', that is to say to replace the term 'Nonconformity' by talking instead about 'the Free Churches' and create greater unity among them. The passive resistance campaign mounted against Balfour's 1902 Education Act further showed that there was still substance, though not sufficient substance to be effective, in Nonconformist grievance. The Liberal victory of 1906 brought into the Commons a greater number of Nonconformists, overwhelmingly Liberal, than at any time since Cromwell, it was proudly said; both David Lloyd George (q.v.) and H. H. Asquith had Nonconformist pedigrees (though rather different ones). Yet a common political/philosophical stance was problematic. The 'Nonconformist conscience', a term associated with the Wesleyan preacher Hugh Price Hughes at the end of the century, certainly sought to press the maxim that whatever was morally wrong could not be politically right. What that meant in practice, as the South African War had demonstrated, and 1914 was to confirm, was difficult to discern, notwithstanding a commitment to peace; as it was with the crusade for 'social morality' and the strong advocacy of temperance. It could appear (paradoxically) that the Free Churches were most vocal in seeking to restrict 'freedom'. Some saw a way out in the 'Social Gospel' and in a sympathy for the emphasis to be found in contemporary New Liberalism (q.v.) on 'positive freedom'. It led some prominent preachers into the socialist camp.

Post-1919, the crisis of the Liberal Party and the crisis of Nonconformity appear in retrospect to be two sides of the same coin; both suffered numerical decline and loss of direction. Lloyd George's attempt, with prominent Nonconformists, to rally the two together in the 1930s failed. In the latter half of the twentieth century, men and women of Free Church background or active commitment still played a significant part in Liberal politics, both locally and nationally – and helped the Liberal Party to survive its lowest ebb, in the 1950s and '60s – but Nonconformity had very largely lost such political, philosophical and theological coherence as, for a time, it had possessed.

Further reading

- D. W. Bebbington, *The Nonconformist Conscience: Chapel and Politics 1870–1914* (Allen & Unwin, 1982)
- Dale A. Johnson, *The Changing Shape of English Nonconformity, 1825–1925* (Oxford University Press, 1999)
- Stephen Koss, *Nonconformity in Modern British Politics* (Batsford, 1975)
- E. A. Payne, *The Free Church Tradition in the Life of England* (SCM Press, 1944)

Keith Robbins

Robert Nozick   1938–2002

Probably the most important and influential libertarian philosopher of the twentieth century, Nozick's book *Anarchy, State, and Utopia* (1974), written as a response to John Rawls' *A Theory of Justice* (1971), is widely credited with moving libertarianism from a marginal sub-set of political philosophy to the centre of the discipline as one of the most important critiques of social democracy and egalitarian liberalism.

Key ideas

- Each individual has a complete right of self-ownership that extends to their private property.
- The entitlement theory of justice: each individual is entitled to the (unequal) resources they possess if their acquisition of those resources satisfied the requirements of procedural justice.
- Any preferred pattern of distribution of income and wealth can only be maintained by outlawing capitalist acts among consenting adults and hence by an unacceptable infringement of individual liberty.
- Only a minimal state that protects individual liberty and private property rights may be justified.

Biography

Robert Nozick was born in Brooklyn, New York, on 16 November 1938. His interest in philosophy is said to have been kindled by reading an old paperback edition of Plato's *Republic* while a teenager in Brooklyn. Nozick obtained his first degree from Columbia College in 1959 and was awarded his PhD by Princeton University four years later. He joined Harvard University as a full professor at the age of thirty in 1969 and remained at Harvard until his death after a long illness, more than thirty years later on 23 January 2002.

Ideas

Nozick was an inspirational teacher who eschewed standard pedagogy. His preferred teaching method was to pace the room, speaking without notes, inviting his students to join him in wide-ranging philosophical discussions. In his thirty years at Harvard he is reputed never to have taught the same course twice, choosing constantly to reinvent and innovate rather than recycle old material. He followed a similar approach in his written work, refusing to return to old subjects. Hence, his most famous work, *Anarchy, State, and Utopia* (1974), was his only substantial contribution to political philosophy and he made no attempt to engage directly with its critics.

A friend and colleague of Nozick at Harvard was the liberal egalitarian philosopher John Rawls (q.v.), whose *magnum opus*, *A Theory of Justice* (1971), set out an important new liberal case for state intervention in the name of attaining 'social justice' (q.v.). While on sabbatical leave from Harvard between 1971 and 1972, Nozick began work on his response to Rawls that would become his most famous work.

In *Anarchy, State, and Utopia*, Nozick argued that because the distribution of resources in a market economy arises spontaneously as a result of the voluntary actions of individual men and women, rather than from one individual or group of individuals deliberately deciding who should get what, it is a mistake to seek to evaluate such outcomes according to a deliberative (rather than procedural) model of justice.

Nozick illustrated this argument with an account of the wealth acquired by the basketball player Wilt Chamberlain in a fictional scenario. Taking as a starting point a distribution of resources that is considered just, which Nozick named D1, Nozick supposed that large numbers of people paid twenty-five cents directly to Chamberlain (in addition to the standard ticket price) in order to watch him play basketball. Supposing that one million people came through the turnstiles during the course of a season, Chamberlain would acquire additional personal wealth of $250,000; one individual had amassed a sizeable personal fortune as a consequence of many small and seemingly inconsequential exchanges. As a result of the voluntary actions of a million basketball fans and Wilt Chamberlain, a new distribution of resources has emerged, which Nozick named D2.

For Nozick, the new distribution of resources (D2) must be considered just because it met the criteria of 'justice in acquisition' and 'justice in transfer'. The theoretical starting point of Nozick's example was a distribution of resources that was considered just (it is left to the reader to imagine what such a distribution might be) and then people voluntarily transferred their justly held resources to Chamberlain in return for a service (watching him play) that they considered more valuable than the twenty-five cents each paid. In neither case can an injustice be said to have occurred, and therefore the outcome of the transactions described must logically be considered just:

> If D1 was a just distribution, and people voluntarily moved from it to D2, transferring parts of their shares they were given under D1 (what was it for if not to do something with?), isn't D2 also just? If the people were entitled to dispose of the resources to which they were entitled (under D1), didn't this also include their being entitled to give it to, or exchange it with, Wilt Chamberlain?

Nozick's example of Wilt Chamberlain's acquisition of wealth illustrated how individual liberty upset any preferred pattern of distribution and inevitably produced inequalities. When a musician releases a record that is purchased by a large number of fans, when a firm poaches an employee from a rival with a large salary, or even when people enter a lottery with only one jackpot winner, inequalities of income and wealth emerge as a consequence.

For Nozick, justice in the distribution of resources could only ever be procedural. Because a distribution of resources is (or should be) the unintended consequence of the spontaneous actions of individual men and women, the only criterion of justice that was applicable was that the procedures that governed the steps that led to a particular distribution were just. The distribution of resources itself cannot be considered just or unjust (or fair or unfair), in the same way that the outcome of a football match or the distribution of sexual partners cannot similarly be considered just or unjust – the only ethical consideration is whether the laws of the game have been observed or the people who engaged in sexual relations consented.

Nozick's argument is a particularly powerful critique of those who would advocate the imposition of a particular pattern of distribution upon a society because it appears to demonstrate that any preferred pattern of distribution can only be sustained either by outlawing voluntary exchanges between consenting adults or by seizing the resources that they have acquired in those voluntary exchanges. For Nozick, neither of these courses of action could be taken without creating an injustice by violating each individual's freedom to engage in voluntary exchanges or confiscating their justly acquired resources. Hence, Nozick wrote that 'no end-state principle or distributional patterned principle of justice can be continuously realized without continuous interference with people's lives'.

Nozick's entitlement theory is predicated upon exchanges that arise from an initial allocation of resources that is considered just. While this provides a theoretically robust refutation of the idea that a particular pattern of distribution can be sustained without violating the rights of individuals to engage in voluntary exchanges, it is less clear that it provides a successful defence of the distribution of resources in a real-world market economy, given that many would contend that the private property rights that individuals exchange in contemporary capitalist economies were not originally acquired according to the principle of justice in acquisition.

However, in terms of Nozick's principal aim in *Anarchy, State, and Utopia* of refuting the Rawlsian position this objection must be considered of limited relevance. It may mean, however, that Nozick's argument would logically justify rectification or compensation where it can be shown that private property rights were acquired unjustly, for example in the cases of the European conquest of North America or Australia. In most contemporary market economies, however, it may be argued that the origins of the private property rights that exist are untraceable and any attempt to remedy the wrongs of the past would simply heap injustice upon injustice, notwithstanding the dire social and economic consequences that follow where long-established private property rights are not respected by governments.

It is from this critique of patterned theories of justice that Nozick developed his case for the minimal state. According to Nozick, only a minimal state that restricts itself to the protection of individual liberty and private property rights is compatible with the principle of individual self-ownership that must lie at the heart of a free society. Any state that assumed greater functions than this must inevitably compromise individual liberty as the compulsory taxation needed to fund a larger state involves the requisition of people's justly-acquired resources against their wishes. Hence, for Nozick, 'no state more extensive than the minimal state can be justified'.

As well as providing a powerful critique of Rawlsian liberalism and an enduring defence of free-market capitalism, *Anarchy, State, and Utopia* is also a highly accessible and entertaining book that contains memorable asides on a myriad of topics, including animal rights and welfare, invisible-hand explanations in the social sciences and the labour theory of value. In many respects its lightness of touch and conversational tone make it almost the polar opposite of Rawls's dense and intimidating work in style as well as substance.

Despite the remarkable success of *Anarchy, State, and Utopia*, Nozick did not return to political philosophy. In the introduction to a collection of his essays published in 1997 he explained that this decision was motivated by the desire not to spend the rest of his life 'writing *The Son of Anarchy, State, and Utopia*'. Instead, after 1974 he returned to the analytical philosophy in which he had first established his scholarly reputation, publishing books and papers on numerous topics, including free will versus determinism, the subjective nature of experience and the requirements of analytical proof. Nozick also published a series of short meditations on life, death, sex and art, inter alia, intended for a popular audience (*The Examined Life*, 1989).

Key works
• *Anarchy, State, and Utopia* (1974)

Further reading
• Edward Feser, *On Nozick* (Thomson, 2004)
• John Meadowcroft, *The Ethics of the Market* (Palgrave Macmillan, 2005)
• David Schmidtz (ed.), *Robert Nozick* (Cambridge University Press, 2002)

• Jonathan Wolff, *Robert Nozick: Property, Justice and the Minimal State* (Stanford University Press, 1991)

John Meadowcroft

David Owen   1938–

One of the founders of the Social Democratic Party in 1981, and its leader from 1983 to 1987, Owen was also a leading contributor to political ideas and debate in Britain during the 1980s, within both the SDP and the Alliance, elaborating his views in books, pamphlets and speeches.

Key ideas
• The social market economy, as an approach combining market realism with social justice.
• Emphasis on the decentralist, cooperative and non-statist strand in the tradition of British social democracy.

Biography
David Anthony Llewellyn Owen was born in Plympton, then just outside Plymouth, on 2 July 1938. He was educated at Bradfield College and at Sidney Sussex College, Cambridge, where he read medicine. After training at St Thomas' Hospital Medical School, he later became a neurology registrar at that hospital.

Becoming involved for the first time in Labour Party politics after the 1959 general election, Owen's political and intellectual influences, which were to prove enduring, included R. H. Tawney, G. D. H. Cole, Richard Titmuss, Hugh Gaitskell and Tony Crosland (q.v.). In 1966 Owen was elected as Labour MP for Plymouth Sutton. He was Navy Minister from 1968 to 1970 in the 1966–70 Labour government, and Health Minister from 1974 to 1976, and

Foreign Secretary from 1977 to 1979, in the 1974–79 Labour governments.

A founder of the Social Democratic Party in 1981, Owen led the party from 1983 to 1987. Following the merger, which he opposed, of the SDP with the Liberal Party in 1988, he led the 'continuing SDP' from 1988 until its eventual demise in 1990.

In 1992 he retired as Plymouth's longest-serving MP, subsequently becoming Lord Owen of the City of Plymouth. In August 1992 he was appointed co-chairman of the Steering Committee of the International Conference on the Former Yugoslavia, stepping down in June 1995. He was made a Companion of Honour in 1994.

Ideas

David Owen's first major political work, *Face the Future* (1981), was an attempt to provide the newly founded Social Democratic Party with a clear political and ideological identity. First published early in 1981, before the SDP's launch, and while Owen was, in his own words, 'still nominally a member of the Labour Party', the book was republished in an abridged edition later that year. It soon became, in David Marquand's (q.v.) description, 'the nearest thing to a philosophical credo which the new party had', involving Owen's 'earnest attempt to give policy substance to the co-operative, decentralist, non-statist tradition in British socialism'.

In drawing on that tradition, associated with socialist thinkers such as Robert Owen (q.v.), William Morris and G. D. H. Cole, Owen was developing a critique of the bureaucratic centralism and statism of established Labour policy and thinking in the early 1980s. In place of the 'deeply centralist' tradition of the Fabian collectivism that had dominated the Labour Party for so long, he thus advocated a revival of 'the concept of fellowship and community

within a participatory society'. In practice, he argued, the achievement of that goal would require 'a detailed programme of legislative and administrative reforms to diffuse power in Britain'.

Such a programme would be based, Owen stressed, on the principle of political and economic decentralisation, which had previously been affirmed by social-democratic thinkers such as David Marquand, John Mackintosh and Evan Luard in the late 1970s, and which, as Owen later acknowledged, the Liberal Party had been the first political party in Britain to value and emphasise. This decentralist approach had earlier in 1981 been endorsed by official SDP statements of principle and policy. The original Limehouse Declaration, for instance, underlined the new party's support for 'the greatest practical degree of decentralisation of decision-making in industry and government'.

In *Face the Future*, Owen also emphasised his support for a mixed economy, a stance that remained ideologically contentious in the Labour Party, and yet which had become a widely accepted orthodoxy among European social-democratic parties. Indeed, in continental Europe, the term 'Social Democrat' had become a description, he pointed out, of 'a socialist who worked constructively within the framework of a mixed economy'.

Yet in spite of this declaration of support, Owen gradually came to discard the term 'mixed economy', favouring instead the idea of a 'social market economy' or 'social market' (q.v.). For in his view, the 'mixed economy' had become a broad, imprecise term, 'a portmanteau description to which virtually anyone can subscribe'. From September 1983 onwards, therefore, after succeeding Roy Jenkins as SDP leader, Owen increasingly employed the concept of a 'social market economy' as a means of defining his new party's ideo-logical position. This, he argued, should be based on a combination of market realism and social concern, of competitiveness and compassion.

By 1984 the concept of the social mar-ket economy had become closely identified with Owen's leadership and was officially adopted as a central SDP policy position at the party conference of that year. Yet in spite of its elevated status in SDP strategy, it did not feature prominently in the Alli-ance programme in the run-up to the 1987 general election; the detailed Alliance pol-icy statement, *The Time Has Come*, whilst endorsing the broad underlying approach of the social market economy, contained no references to the phrase itself.

Ultimately, then, the idea of the social market economy exerted little direct influ-ence on Alliance strategy; but it had proved useful, in terms of both policy and rheto-ric, in helping to widen the gap between a more market-oriented SDP and the more collectivist and interventionist approach of social democrats such as Denis Healey, Roy Hattersley and John Smith, who had remained loyal to Labour. More broadly, as David Marquand later observed, on 'the level of emotional and political symbolism', the social market provided both Owen and the SDP with 'a banner, a rallying cry, an assertion of identity'.

As its critics argued, however, both at the time and later, Owen's concept of the social market economy lacked a precise meaning. It was unclear, they claimed, whether the emphasis lay on the 'social' or the 'market' factor in the formula. It was consequently unclear, too, what exactly the economic and social policy implications of the idea were for the SDP's programme and strategy. Nonetheless, through Owen's assiduous advocacy, the social market econ-omy was one of the few distinctive ideas

to emerge from SDP thinking between 1983 and 1987. In its broad commitment to combine an unequivocal recognition of the centrality of the market economy with a concern for social justice (q.v.) and social inclusion, it thereby anticipated later ideological developments on the centre-left during the 1990s and thereafter.

Key works
- *Face the Future* (1981)
- *A Future That Will Work* (1984)
- *Time to Declare* (1991)

Further reading
- Ivor Crewe and Anthony King, *SDP: The Birth, Life and Death of the Social Democratic Party* (Oxford University Press, 1995)

Tudor Jones

Robert Owen   1771–1858

A successful industrialist, Owen became a social reformer noted for his promotion of fac-tory reform, more liberal treatment of the poor and popular education. He was a prominent exponent of cooperation.

Key ideas
- Primacy of education in promoting self-development and a more egalitarian, liberal society.
- Enabling role of the state in maximising social improvement, especially the con-dition of the working class.
- Social and economic cooperation rather than competition.
- Cooperation and consensus on interna-tional issues.

Biography
Robert Owen was born on 14 May 1771 at Newtown, Montgomeryshire. His early

education greatly influenced his ideas. A quick learner, by the time he left school, aged eleven, he had become a mentor to younger pupils. Thereafter he was largely self-taught.

After apprenticeship to a draper in Stamford, he worked in stores in London and Manchester. He used his leisure to read popular Enlightenment works, notably *Robinson Crusoe*, with whom he identified. He shifted to cotton machine-making, then management in spinning. While in Manchester he joined the Literary and Philosophical Society, delivering papers which had some relevance to his later ideas.

In 1799 Owen moved to New Lanark, then one of the largest factories built by his father-in-law. Owen's workplace reforms reduced wastage, improved productivity and enhanced returns. He phased out apprentices, and stopped employing children under ten. He made environmental improvements, introducing better housing, welfare and schooling and thereafter used New Lanark as a test-bed for his ideas.

After 1815 he promoted popular education and factory reform, bringing him into contact with Brougham, the Peels, Ashley and others. He also intervened in the post-war crisis, suggesting planned communities to encourage reconstruction. His 'millennial moment', when he seemed to eschew capitalism for socialism, came in 1817, but in reality he supported public–private partnerships to advance his New System, and this message he carried on a tour to Europe and to the Congress of Sovereigns meeting at Aix-la-Chapelle in 1818. In 1820 he produced his *Report to the County of Lanark*, also standing unsuccessfully for Parliament. Despite aristocratic support he failed to persuade Parliament to act and efforts in Ireland were also abortive. Disillusioned, he left Britain for the US, where he purchased New Harmony, Indiana, for a community of equality. When this failed he made another unsuccessful effort in Mexico.

Owen then associated himself with working-class movements, labour exchanges, cooperatives and trade unions. With John Doherty he led the short-lived Grand National Consolidated Trade Union. The Owenites set up 'Halls of Science' and another community at Queenwood, Hampshire. He was 'Social Father' to Owenism until his death at Newtown on 17 November 1858.

Owen married Caroline Dale in 1799 and had eight children; his eldest son, Robert Dale Owen, became a distinguished US Congressman, diplomat and social reformer.

Ideas

In *A New View of Society* (1813–14), Owen argued that character was formed by environment, suggested a national education system, public works and Poor Law reform. He was alarmed by poverty in the post-war depression. Mechanisation and war demand had generated economic growth, greatly increasing output, but also bringing inflation and social dislocation. He linked the effects of machinery to the labour theory of value, possibly borrowing from Ricardo's (q.v.) *Principles* (1817).

Owen's *Observations on the Effects of the Manufacturing System* (1815) stressed factory reform. Industry had brought 'accompanying evils', the peasant replaced by subsistence workers more degraded than before the factories. Exports were now essential 'to support the additional population which this increased demand for labour had produced'. Rather muddled on the laws of supply and demand, he thought exports would gradually diminish, partly because of a new Corn Law.

Owen's main concern was the eradication of poverty. In 1817 he proposed his village scheme, drawing on New Lanark. With careful husbandry, communities would become self-sufficient; people would be educated and employed according to ability, and at a profit once the capital was recovered, an arrangement that has its resonance in public–private partnerships. Critics condemned the villages as workhouses and a millennialist tone began to creep into the discourse, as the communities became 'Villages of Unity and Mutual Co-operation'.

The *Report to the County of Lanark* (1820) was a significant pre-'socialist' document; Owen's thinking now half-way between two different conceptions of the economy. On the one hand, investors would benefit, the working class would be paid, boosting consumption, and the economy regenerated. On the other, the existing system was based on an 'artificial' notion of wages, which would be replaced by one that was 'equitable'. By rejecting an increasing division of labour and the economic benefits of self-interest, and promoting instead united labour and communal property, Owen moved well beyond accepted solutions to economic problems.

Owen tried without success to get government and fellow capitalists to support his ideas. By 1824 he realised that cooperative communities had to be built anew if they were to achieve his objective; this led to his utopian experiment at New Harmony while others were tried in Britain. None succeeded. Owen failed to realise that New Lanark was an inappropriate model and that its success as a dynamic capitalist enterprise was unlikely to be replicated in contexts where the profit motive was secondary to cooperation and social progress.

Owen's ideas were formed by 1830 and remained unchanged for the remainder of his career: mechanisation devalued manual labour; under-consumption should be promoted by higher wages; society should maximise the number of producers; goods should be valued and exchanged according to the amount of labour contained in them; money should be non-metallic and expand and contract with the volume of production; private property and competition arose from selfishness, and would eventually bring about the demise of the existing system; agricultural and manufacturing labour must be combined; and, contradicting Malthus (q.v.), better agriculture could feed a larger population than previously supposed.

Owen mostly upheld existing political institutions, as much at ease with Tory ministers as with Whigs. He rejected parliamentary reform, seeing no point in it before society had been transformed by his ideas. He thought the working class was generally ignorant, through no fault of its own, and giving workers the vote before their characters had been reformed might generate unrest. He later promoted moderate reform to deliver wider suffrage. However, Owen valued political connections, maintaining contacts with leading political figures in Britain, France and the US.

Owen's ideas are hard to categorise, but his promotion of an alternative view to the dominant ideology was of long-term significance, greatly influencing factory reform, education, welfare and cooperation, and other improvements embraced by radical liberalism later in the nineteenth century.

Key works
- *A New View of Society; or, Essays on the Principle of the Formation of Human Character* (1813–14)
- *Observations on the Effect of the Manufacturing System* (1815)
- *Mr Owen's Proposed Arrangements for the Distressed Working Classes shown to be*

consistent with Sound Principles of Political Economy, in three letters to David Ricardo, MP (1819)

- *Report to the County of Lanark* (1821)
- *The Book of the New Moral World* (1836–44)
- *Home Colonies* (1841)
- *Life of Robert Owen by Himself* (1857)

Further reading

- Gregory Claeys, *Machinery, Money and the Millennium: From Moral Economy to Socialism, 1815–1860* (Princeton University Press, 1987)
- Ian Donnachie, *Robert Owen, Social Visionary* (Birlinn, 2005)
- John F. C. Harrison, *Robert Owen and the Owenites in Britain and America* (Routledge & Kegan Paul, 1969)
- Robert Pearson and Geraint Williams, *Political Thought and Public Policy in the Nineteenth Century* (Longman, 1984)

Ian Donnachie

Pacifism and Pacificism

Pacifism and pacificism have been the two key strands of thought within the peace movement. The former is usually described as an absolute rejection of war, with the latter seen as a more reformist approach proposing the establishment of international legal regimes and structures to end wars. Both reject defencism, which promotes self-defence as the best method for avoiding war. Both, but particularly pacificism, have informed liberal involvement in peace and anti-war movements.

The roots of pacifism in the UK are to be found in Nonconformist (q.v.) groups, such as the Quakers in the eighteenth century; the Nonconformist-led Peace Society (q.v.) was one of its main mouthpieces. The nineteenth and early twentieth

centuries saw a diversity of pacifist views, including the belief that nations which did not engage in war would not be attacked, and the view that individual rejection of war could make an impact on national policy. This underpinned the stance of conscientious objectors during the First World War and after.

Pacificism emphasises the harmony of international interests, arguing that war is the result of elites having too much power and being influenced by vested interests. Pacificists therefore argued for international law upheld by international institutions. Combined with an economic policy based on free trade (q.v.), they believed that this would ensure that nations respected the needs of other nations and did not behave selfishly. Such a system, pacificists believed, would reduce the likelihood of war. During the First World War many Liberal and Labour supporters backed the Union of Democratic Control, which argued that if foreign policy in the UK was subject to greater parliamentary control, war would be less likely. After 1918, pacificists became enthusiastic supporters of the League of Nations. The strength of the League of Nations Union (q.v.) in the 1920s and 1930s marked the zenith of popular support for pacificism.

Prominent pacifists have been distant from formal Liberal politics, and in the twentieth century, many were socialists. The main pacificist thinkers prior to 1914 included the Liberals Richard Cobden (q.v.), J. A. Hobson (q.v.) and Norman Angell (q.v.). Cobden was particularly associated with the promotion of free trade; Hobson saw war as the result of financiers encouraging jingoism in support of wars from which they would make money; Angell made similar arguments but also emphasised the warlike sentiments of the 'mass mind'. After 1918, major pacificist thinkers included Gilbert Murray (q.v.) who dominated the League of Nations Union.

Pacifist thought has had little impact on formal Liberal policy, but the influence of pacificism can be seen in the consistent and outspoken Liberal support for the rule of international law through at least the last hundred years. That has informed Liberal Democrat support for the United Nations, such as during the events leading up to the Second Gulf War in 2003.

Further reading

- Norman Angell, *The Great Illusion* (William Heinemann, 1910)
- Martin Ceadel, *Thinking about Peace and War* (Oxford University Press, 1987)
- J. A. Hobson, *Imperialism: A Study* (1901; reprint, Unwin Hyman, 1988)

Richard S. Grayson

Thomas Paine   1737–1809

One of the most influential radical writers of the revolutionary era, an active participant in both the American and French Revolutions, a champion of democratic republicanism and rational religion, and the author of key propagandist works both during the American War of Independence and in Britain following the French Revolution of 1789.

Key ideas

- Reason and utility should be the guiding principles in all aspects of human affairs.
- Tradition and the hereditary principle are irrational.
- Democratic republicanism based on natural rights is the best form of political organisation.
- Economic freedom and minimal government interference provide the best

conditions for political, economic and social liberty.
- True religion is revealed in the natural world and not the Bible.

Biography

Thomas Paine was born at Thetford, Norfolk, on 29 January 1737, the son of a Quaker stay-maker. He attended Thetford Grammar School but did not remain to learn Latin, was apprenticed to his father's trade, and then went to London where, in 1757, he joined the navy as a privateer.

After a few months at sea and a similar period picking up an interest in science among the skilled artisans of London, he removed in 1758 to Sandwich in Kent where he set up as a master stay-maker and in the following year married Mary Lambert, the daughter of an Excise officer. Within a year she had died in childbirth. Paine now applied to join the Excise service and was sent to Lincolnshire, first to Grantham and then to Alford, where he was dismissed in 1765 for neglecting his duties.

He taught for a while in London before being reappointed in 1768 to the Excise service at Lewes in Sussex. Here he lodged with Samuel Ollive, a retail tobacconist at whose death he took on the shop and, in 1771, married Ollive's daughter, Elizabeth. Meanwhile he joined a local debating society and was elected to his parish vestry. He also took up the cause of the Excise officers' pay, writing a pamphlet, *The Case of the Officers of Excise* (1772), and travelling to London to promote it. This neglect of his affairs at home led to the collapse of his business in 1772 and the failure of his marriage two years later. Influenced by Benjamin Franklin, whom he had met in London, Paine emigrated to America.

Beginning as a journalist on the *Pennsylvania Magazine*, Paine caught the public mood with his pamphlet *Common Sense*

(January 1776), arguing against reconciliation with Britain and for the rejection of monarchical government. During the War of Independence his *Crisis* papers in the *Pennsylvania Journal* (December 1776–April 1783) helped sustain morale, but he was never far from controversy. He was forced to give up his position as secretary to the Committee on Foreign Affairs after disclosing that France was supporting America while still at peace with Britain and alleging (correctly) financial misconduct by Silas Deane, the American agent in Paris. In the struggle over the nature of the new American politics, Paine was a democratic republican, opposed to the more cautious conservatism of John Adams but in favour of a strong federal republic. After the war he retired from politics, devoted himself to science and in 1787 returned to Europe to promote his scheme to build an iron bridge.

The outbreak of revolution in Paris in 1789, which Paine enthusiastically supported, for a time revived reform politics in Britain. When Edmund Burke (q.v.) led the reaction in his *Reflections on the Revolution in France* (1790), Paine immediately responded with his two-part *Rights of Man* (1791 and 1792) in which he developed the ideas set out in *Common Sense*, advocating a democratic republic for Britain. This publication was identified as the most successful expression of extreme 'French' politics in Britain, but with the country now at war with France and an impending prosecution for sedition, in September 1792 Paine left for Paris, where he had been elected to the National Assembly. His parting shot was a *Letter Addressed to the Addressers of the Late Proclamation* in which he called on the British to emulate the French and establish a democratic republic.

In France he joined the moderate Girondins, opposed to the execution of Louis XVI and the increasingly violent extremism of the revolution. Imprisoned for a year during the Terror (1793–94) despite his American (and French) citizenship, he began *The Age of Reason* (published in two parts, 1794 and 1795), his major work challenging Christianity and asserting Natural Religion. After his release, embittered by his neglect by the American government while in gaol, he addressed a *Letter to George Washington* (1796) which completed the destruction of his reputation in America. He also published a development of the ideas in Part 2 of *Rights of Man*, entitled *Agrarian Justice*.

In 1802, he left France for the United States. He died in Greenwich, New York on 8 June 1809. He was buried on his farm at New Rochelle but in 1819 William Cobbett returned his bones to England, where they were subsequently mislaid.

Ideas

Paine's originality lay not so much in his ideas as in the way he developed and popularised them, writing with telling images and humour but without the ornate rhetorical flourishes engendered by a classical education. He could be blunt, and argued as much by analogy as by logic: 'An hereditary governor is as inconsistent as an hereditary author,' he asserted in *Rights of Man*. But his innocence of Burkean rhetoric did not mean that his prose lacked style; the opening passage of the first *Crisis* paper has Shakespearean qualities: 'These are the times that try men's souls. The summer-soldier and the sunshine-patriot will, in this crisis, shrink from the service of their country; but he that stands it now, deserves the thanks of man and woman.'

Paine was the champion of 'the people', by whom he meant all worthwhile citizens as opposed to the lazy parasites who benefited from the inequalities of hereditary society. The objects of his derision were privilege and 'corruption'. His ideal was a career open to talents in a free society based on political equality (q.v.). In *Common Sense* he rejected hereditary monarchy in favour of 'a large and equal representation' and argued that 'where there are no distinctions there can be no superiority'. He wanted citizens, not subjects. But he also advocated a minimalist state: 'government even in its best state is but a necessary evil', its object no more than security at the least expense. These ideas were developed but not essentially changed in *Rights of Man*.

Following John Locke (q.v.), he argued that as property is the guarantee of independence, the first condition of democracy, so government must be subject to all with a stake in it, which meant all taxpayers – and, as a former Excise officer, Paine knew that poor people also paid taxes. Security meant the safeguarding of civil rights. The latter owed their validity to those natural rights that each individual had held in the state of nature. The social contract whereby civil rights had replaced natural rights had to be renewed in each generation, for no generation could bind its successors. Paine's ideal was therefore one of small, independent and roughly equal property-owners with government having no right of interference except to safeguard the civil – and thereby natural – rights of each and all. This was a political theory that assumed the public good would best be advanced by a republic based on an open and representative system such as had been established in America. He did not see the need to confront those doubts about democracy that concerned John Adams, and were later to trouble Tocqueville (q.v.) and J. S. Mill (q.v.). Paine's ideal was a world fit for small shopkeepers and independent artisans, whose experiences he knew and understood.

This political approach carried over into Paine's economics, which were derived from the theories of Adam Smith (q.v.) and his own practical experience. He believed not in equality but in equality of opportunity, private property and the free market. This language infused his politics and economics alike. In the *Crisis* no. 1 he had observed, 'What we obtain too cheap, we esteem too lightly; it is dearness only that gives everything its value'; and in *Rights of Man* he maintained with impeccable orthodoxy:

> All the great laws of society are laws of nature. Those of trade and commerce, whether with respect to the intercourse of individuals or of nations, are laws of mutual and reciprocal interest. They are followed and obeyed, because it is in the interest of the parties to do so, and not on account of any formal laws their governments may impose or interpose.

The most radical part of his economic theory came in *Rights of Man*, part 2, augmented in *Agrarian Justice*. Economic and political inequality resulted from the landed monopoly built up over generations; the solution was a system of redistributive taxation which would ensure to the poor their rightful inheritance of what had been 'the common property of the human race' in the state of nature. Unlike his contemporary Thomas Spence, Paine did not assert the continuation of common ownership into civil society and he was careful to distinguish between the original value of land and the value added by work and talent that created a new form of legitimate private property which, because industry and talent were not naturally equal, would mean that society could never be completely equal.

Paine's approach to economics also applied to finance. As a bankrupted shopkeeper he had experienced aristocrats whose lifestyles exploited credit, and he maintained a stout faith in hard currency and an abhorrence of paper money. So, at the close of the American War, when coinage was short and the elected Assembly of Pennsylvania ordered the Bank to issue paper money, he resolutely defended the Bank's refusal to print it; and in 1796, as the Bank of England was faltering over financing the war against France, in *The Decline and Fall of the English System of Finance* he again attacked paper money (to which the Bank resorted a few months later) because it caused inflation that ate away the rich man's debts and the poor man's limited savings. A sound currency and cheap government were the key to Paine's economics.

Paine was baptised and confirmed in the Church of England, brought up a Quaker by his father, influenced by Methodists in London, and married into a Dissenting family in Lewes, but his mature religious views were pure deism. He believed in God, but his was the remote God of Nature, not the interventionist and irrational God of the Bible. He was not a materialistic atheist like his French contemporary Condorcet (q.v.), though he was accused of the latter by his Christian opponents. As he wrote in *The Age of Reason*: 'The word of God is the creation we behold: it is in this word, which no human invention can counterfeit or alter, that God speaketh universally to man.' As in his politics, though, alongside his positive views he inserted negative, popular criticisms. As he wrote of the Bible *(The Prosecution of the Age of Reason*, 1797): 'For my own part, my belief in the perfection of the Deity will not permit me to believe that a book so manifestly obscure, disorderly and contradictory can be his work. I can write a better book myself.' His objections were based not only on biblical criticism and common sense but also on outraged morality: 'It is a history of wickedness, that has served to corrupt and brutalise mankind; and, for my own part,

I sincerely detest it, as I detest everything that is cruel.' Thus the God of the Bible was despatched with as little ceremony as George III. Indeed, there is an echo of Paine's 'Of more worth is one honest man to society, and in the sight of God, than all the crowned ruffians that ever lived' (*Common Sense*) in his later 'One good schoolmaster is of more use than a hundred priests' (*On Worship and Church Bells*, 1797).

Thomas Paine's political reputation rests on his twice writing a topical popular work at a time of political upheaval. In America he advanced those extreme opinions that were eventually to triumph in the War of Independence. In Britain he inspired opponents of the government and came to symbolise what the British elite feared most about the French Revolution. His religious ideas were less popular, alienating him from supporters in America and making the prosecution of his works and publishers easier in Britain. His economic ideas, when presented in the context of his political and religious views, appeared more threatening than they really were. As a consequence, the Paine whose legacy passed to the nineteenth century was a more formidable figure than an academic reading of his writings might suggest. Political authority rested on mystification, so to lay bare religion was politically threatening. Although politicians in the later twentieth century, from Ronald Reagan to Tony Benn, have felt able to claim part of Paine's legacy for their own, for over a century after his death Paine the liberal economist, rational deist and committed democrat was politically untouchable, the personification of a dangerous, levelling atheist, and a threat to the civilised world.

Key works
- *Common Sense* (1776)
- *The American Crisis* (1776–83)

- *Rights of Man*, parts 1 and 2 (1791, 1792)
- *The Age of Reason*, parts 1 and 2 (1793, 1794)
- *The Decline and Fall of the English System of Finance* (1796)
- *Agrarian Justice* (1797)

Further reading

- Gregory Claeys, *Thomas Paine: Social and Political Thought* (Unwin Hyman, 1989)
- Jack Fruchtman, Jr, *Thomas Paine: Apostle of Freedom* (Four Walls, Eight Windows, 1994)
- David Freeman Hawke, *Paine* (Norton, 1975)
- John Keane, *Tom Paine: A Political Life* (Bloomsbury, 1995)
- Mark Philp, *Paine* (Oxford University Press, 1989)

Edward Royle

Alan Paton   1903–88

Writer and South African liberal leader, Paton achieved world fame in 1948 with his novel, *Cry, the Beloved Country*, which opened the eyes of the world to the consequences of white racial supremacy in his country. He co-founded the Liberal Party of South Africa in 1953 and continued to champion the liberal cause after its forced dissolution in 1968.

Key ideas

- Liberalism should not be seen as the creed of any particular party or country.
- Violence should not be used to achieve political objectives.
- Apartheid should be rejected by the whole human race.
- Liberalism in South Africa has a special character because of its deep and abiding concern with racial justice.
- Liberals must demonstrate exceptional resolution to defeat apartheid.

Biography

Alan Stewart Paton was born on 11 January 1903, eldest of four children of his Scottish settler father and South African-born mother, in Pietermaritzburg, capital of the then British colony of Natal. After school at Maritzburg College and taking a science degree at Natal University College, he taught at Ixopo, where he married Doris, the widowed daughter of a local solicitor; they had two sons. In 1930 he became an Anglican and founded the Student Christian Association boys' camp in Natal, attended annually by Jan Hofmeyr, a leading liberal parliamentarian, through whom he was appointed principal of Diepkloof Reformatory for African boys, in Johannesburg, in 1935.

Paton's Diepkloof experience, and Dorrie Paton's influence, opened his eyes to the plight of the black population, then subject to the colour bar and denied political rights. In 1948, after a European and American study tour, he published his first novel, *Cry, the Beloved Country*; it was an instant world-wide bestseller. It communicated his deep feelings for both black and white South Africans, caught in the racial trap, and his Christian faith in change. He then wrote *Too Late the Phalarope*, which dealt sensitively with the Afrikaner–African relationship. It was published in 1953, the same year that he became a founder member of the non-racial Liberal Party of South Africa. He had despaired of the opposition's capacity to defeat the Afrikaner Nationalist government and its apartheid policy. Paton served as Liberal Party chairman from 1958, then president from 1960 until the party was forced, by apartheid legislation, to dissolve in 1968. He campaigned vigorously as speaker, writer and organiser to spread the liberal ideals that later informed the new South African constitution, after the apartheid regime had conceded power; the constitution was adopted six years after his death on 12 April 1988.

In his last twenty years, after the restoration of his passport, he travelled widely, accepting honours and promoting liberalism in South Africa. Though his political life had reduced his literary output, he wrote great biographies of Hofmeyr and of Archbishop Clayton, who had led the Anglican Church into the anti-apartheid camp.

Ideas

The development of Paton's beliefs went through five stages. First, until his mid-thirties, he lived quite comfortably within the cocoon of white South Africa, aware of his black fellow countrymen principally as servants, labourers or, in Natal, small Indian traders. During the second stage, his main concern was with the English–Afrikaner relationship, the latter winning his sympathy as defeated victims of the Anglo-Boer War. He attended the celebration of the centenary of the Great Trek at the Voortrekker Monument in 1938 and was utterly repelled by the authoritarian, xenophobic, exclusivist face of the new Afrikaner nationalism, which was to achieve power and to introduce the apartheid policy in 1948.

He was then drawn increasingly into confrontation by South Africa's racially divided society, his work with Africans at Diepkloof Reformatory and his membership of the Anglican Church; this was exemplified by his attendance, as a delegate, at a conference convened by Archbishop Geoffrey Clayton in Johannesburg in 1943. Paton emerged from the conference as a convert, rejecting the 'policies of racial separation'. In the fourth stage, he took an increasingly active political role in the Liberal Party of South Africa, especially in his relations with its black members. He adopted a radical position, fully accepting universal suffrage in a non-racial democracy.

With the demise of his party, in 1968, the death of his wife Dorrie, and remarriage later, he moved nearer to the white community and they to him. In the 1980s the abandonment of white supremacy was seen to be inevitable. Paton opposed economic sanctions, as certain to intensify African poverty without political gain, and the 'armed struggle', which, as a Christian, he did not see as a 'just war'. Perhaps this won him more white support and made the transition to the new South Africa easier. He had anticipated that South Africa might reject the Liberal Party but ultimately accept its policies; this was to be so with the Jeffersonian constitution of the 1990s and the establishment of a non-racial liberal democracy (q.v.). Alan Paton was without doubt one of those who, by his writings, his speeches and his example, made this possible.

Paton's liberalism can best be summed up in four core beliefs, to which he gave frequent and uncompromising expression. In 1973, when lecturing at Yale, he explained that liberalism was not the creed of any single party or country: it called for a generosity of spirit, tolerance of others and commitment to the rule of law (q.v.). Many years earlier, when delivering a sermon at St Paul's Cathedral, he sought to convey the intimate relationship he believed existed between Christian morality, opposition to apartheid and his political beliefs: 'How can one help remembering the words of Christ, "whoso shall offend one of these little ones which believe in me, it were better for him that a millstone were hanged about his neck, and that he were drowned in the depth of the sea"?' The duty of Christians, all over the world, was to condemn and oppose apartheid. It was not a matter of domestic politics; it should concern the whole human race.

Paton believed that liberalism in South Africa had one characteristic that was quintessentially its own: a deep and abiding concern with racial justice. He conveyed this conviction particularly powerfully in his 'Hope for South Africa' (1959). Liberals had to fight not only for political rights for all citizens but a basic recognition of the humanity of all South Africans regardless of race. Alan Paton's liberalism was infused with a belief in the justice of his cause, even when the kind of society he wanted appeared distant. For Paton some famous words of William the Silent captured his liberal commitment: 'It is not necessary to hope in order to undertake, and it is not necessary to succeed in order to persevere.'

Key works

- *Cry, the Beloved Country: A Story of Comfort in Desolation* (1948)
- *Hope for South Africa* (1958)
- *Hofmeyr* (1964)
- *Towards the Mountain: An Autobiography* (1981)
- *Journey Continued: An Autobiography* (1988)

Further reading

- Peter Alexander, *Alan Paton: A Biography* (Oxford University Press, 1995)
- Edward Callan, *Alan Paton* (Twayne, revised edition, 1984)
- Randolph Vigne, *Liberals against Apartheid: A History of the Liberal Party of South Africa* (Macmillan, 1997)

Randolph Vigne

Peace Society

A pacifist group, heavily influenced by Quakers, the Peace Society sought to promote the avoidance of war through international arbitration, and held several international peace congresses in the late 1840s and 1850s to this effect.

The Society for the Promotion of Permanent and Universal Peace, generally known as the Peace Society, was founded in London in 1816, one of many such societies organised throughout Europe and the US in response to the Napoleonic wars. Heavily influenced by Quaker pacifism (q.v.), it encouraged international arbitration. The society's first *Address* stated that it was 'principled against all war, upon any pretence' and that it would 'print and circulate Tracts and … diffuse information tending to show that War is inconsistent with the spirit of Christianity, and the true interests of mankind; and to point out the means best calculated to maintain permanent and universal Peace, upon the basis of Christian principles'. A key publication was its monthly journal, *Herald of Peace*, and it used local societies throughout the country to disseminate material.

The peak of Peace Society activity came in the period from 1843 to 1853, with a series of international congresses drawing together campaigners for arbitration, led by Henry Richard (1812–88), a Nonconformist minister and MP for Merthyr who was secretary of the Peace Society from 1848 to 1885. One practical result was a general declaration in favour of arbitration in the Treaty of Paris, which ended the Crimean War in 1856. During the periodic wars which dogged Europe from the 1850s to the 1870s, the cause of arbitration foundered somewhat, but further congresses followed in 1878, 1889 and 1891. At the last, in Rome, the Peace Society fed into the foundation of the International Peace Bureau, which continued to use international congresses to popularise the idea of arbitration until the outbreak of the First World War. During this period, the Peace Society was also active in opposition to the Boer War.

After 1918, liberals became more involved with the League of Nations Union (q.v.) than with other peace bodies and the residual Peace Society ceased to be important in liberal politics. A small residual Peace Society had become the International Peace Society by 1930, having been incorporated into the International Christian Peace Fellowship. There do not appear to be any available records confirming exactly when the Peace Society ceased to operate.

Further reading
- Martin Ceadel, *The Origins of War Prevention: The British Peace Movement and International Relations, 1730–1854* (Clarendon Press, 1996)
- Martin Ceadel, *Semi-Detached Idealists: The British Peace Movement and International Relations, 1854–1945* (Oxford University Press, 2000)

Richard S. Grayson

Michael Polanyi   1891–1976

A Hungarian physical chemist who turned to political, economic and philosophical questions, Polanyi developed his philosophy of personal knowing, tacit integration and freedom as self-dedication to transcendent ideals rooted in tradition, in answer to modern threats to free societies, along with his own arguments for a free economy and adjustment of the money supply to reduce unemployment.

Key ideas
- Knowing as a personal achievement as the 'tacit integration' of 'subsidiary details' into 'focal wholes'.
- Knowing as rooted in authority and tradition.
- Freedom as self-dedication to transcendent ideals, in contrast to the 'the suspended logic of Anglo-American liberalism'.
- The analogy of 'the republic of science': 'spontaneous' versus 'corporate' order, mutual adjustment for the performance of 'polycentric tasks', the limits of the 'span of control' and thus of economic and other planning.
- Government expansion and contraction of the money supply by neutral means to counter unemployment.

Biography
Michael Polanyi was born in Budapest on 11 March 1891, to Mihaly and Cecile Pollasek, non-religious Jews who had Magyarised their surname. He attended the prestigious Minta gymnasium in Budapest, and studied medicine, and then physical chemistry, at the university. He joined Oskár Jászi's Sociological Society, aimed at introducing reforms in Hungary, but he was sceptical of socialism and ambitious political schemes, as seen in his two pamphlets, *To the Peacemakers* (1918) and *New Scepticism* (1919), and always opposed to communism.

Following the declaration of Hungarian independence in October 1919, he served as secretary to the Minister of Health in Count Michael Karolyi's government. When the Communists under Béla Kun took control, he moved to Budapest University, where he was the only one to refuse to serve in the Red Army. Despite this, he was viewed with suspicion by the counter-revolutionary regime under Admiral Horthy, which took power in 1920, and he left Hungary to pursue a scientific career in Germany. In 1923 he became a full professor at the Institute for Physical Chemistry in Berlin. After Hitler seized power in 1933, Polanyi moved to Manchester.

Once he left Hungary, Polanyi was never active politically but remained interested in the cause of freedom (q.v.), its relation to economics and its philosophical presuppositions. In 1941 he was one of the founders of the Society for Freedom in Science and was active from 1953 onwards in the Congress for Cultural Freedom. In 1958 he retired to become a research fellow at Merton College, Oxford, but found more of an audience in America.

In 1921 he married Madga Kemeny; they had two sons, George, who died in 1975, and John, Professor of Physical Chemistry at Toronto, a fellow of the Royal Society like his father, and a joint winner of a Nobel Prize for Chemistry. Suffering from loss of memory, Michael Polanyi died on 22 February 1972, in Northampton.

Ideas

Polanyi was an original thinker but drew on many sources. He rejected the usual Anglo-American utilitarian (q.v.) and sceptical defences of freedom, deriving from Locke (q.v.). He thought they had led, in continental Europe, to openly ruthless totalitarianisms, which also covertly appealed to a secularised Christian thirst for moral perfection. Behind all these political trends is a false ideal of 'scientific' knowledge as impersonal and precise, which results in a devaluation and elimination of the person.

Polanyi's *magnum opus, Personal Knowledge* (1958), presents an alternative philosophy based on the demonstration that all knowing is an essentially tacit integration of subsidiary clues, *from* which we attend, into focal wholes, *to* which we attend. This conception restores the reality, freedom and responsibility of the person for his knowing and life generally, guided by transcendent ideals. It demolishes the dichotomies of 'fact and value' and 'description and evaluation' and the possibility of any 'value-free' study of man and society. Because what is known tacitly can be conveyed only tacitly, general principles can be known and applied, not in the abstract, but only in and through specific beliefs and practices

embodied in a tradition. A free society especially rests upon a tradition of freedom, and hence the problems of transplanting freedom to peoples who have little experience of it. In pre-modern static and modern self-reforming societies, thought and truth are acknowledged as having autonomy and authority, over the rulers and the ruled, although in the former they are confined with a specific set of beliefs, whereas in the latter they form a general authority of ideals and standards embodied in a specific set of beliefs which change as individuals modify them in their own lights. But in modern revolutionary societies, aiming at total transformation, there is no such acknowledgment of transcendent standards above the wills and desires of the rulers and ruled alike.

In *The Logic of Liberty* (1951), Polanyi explicitly dissociated a free society from Popper's (q.v.) 'Open Society', and from the right to do as one pleases so long as one does not impinge on the equal rights of others. Instead a free society is dedicated to a distinctive set of beliefs in 'public liberties' to pursue transcendent ends, such as arts, sciences, religion and charity. Its ideal is to be a good society of people who respect truth, justice and each other. The institutions formed for the promotion of such ends protect individuals from their own vices as much as from those of others. Morally we live by sacrificing ourselves to our consciences, and social responsibilities give us opportunities for this. Hence a free society is an end in itself and so can rightly demand the services of its citizens. The emphasis of sceptical and utilitarian liberalism upon merely 'negative' liberties and rights defeats itself by opening the way to totalitarian claims to deny such merely private and 'selfish' liberties in the name of morally superior collective enterprises controlled by the state. Instead, what

Polanyi emphasises are those institutions, such as families, churches, charitable trusts, institutes of learning and academies of art, which persons freely form and join to achieve transcendent ends.

A free society also rests upon unplanned 'spontaneous orders' formed by the mutual adjustment of its individual and institutional members, as opposed to a 'corporate order' that is planned from a centre. Polanyi uses the analogy of 'the republic of science', a network of overlapping competences and mutually adjusting individual and group efforts procedures. But the mutual adjustments in an economy lack an inherent reference to transpersonal ideals and standards. Hence a society based solely on the principles of a market would have no superior loyalties and dedications, such as to truth, justice and to freedom itself, to hold it together.

Mutual adjustment is the way in which all 'polycentric tasks' are accomplished, that is, ones in which several items have to be determined and fitted to each other by successive approximation. But there is a limit as to how far this can be done, even for static conditions, and that is the designer's or planner's span of attention. So, whereas von Mises thought a centrally planned economy to be possible only if there were also an unplanned one to supply it with the necessary data, Polanyi demonstrated that it would be completely impossible. He also showed that in fact the Soviet economy, which he had studied at first hand on visits there in the mid-1930s, was not centrally planned at all, and that instead the central planners merely set targets for output and the managers of the state enterprises hired workers and traded among themselves.

Polanyi was also concerned with unemployment. Keynes's (q.v.) *General Theory* (1936) was generally interpreted to require direct and particular state interventions in the economy, but Polanyi, in *Full Employment and Free Trade* (1945, 1948), proved that employment had not been increased by these measures but by the increase in the supply of money which had accompanied them. Hence he proposed that the government should directly increase, by budget deficits and surpluses, the supply of money in times of depression to reduce unemployment and that it should reduce it in times of expansion and full employment to prevent inflation.

In summary, Polanyi articulated a traditionalist and 'positive' account of freedom, and of its necessary political, moral, social and economic conditions, which also took full account of the specific features and problems of the modern age.

Key works

- *Full Employment and Free Trade* (1945; 2nd edn., 1948)
- *Science, Faith and Society* (1946; 2nd edn., 1964)
- *The Logic of Liberty* (1951)
- *Personal Knowledge* (1958)
- *The Study of Man* (1959)
- *The Tacit Dimension* (1966)
- *Knowing and Being* (1969)
- *Society, Economics, Philosophy: Articles by Michael Polanyi* (ed. R. T. Allen, 1997)

Further reading

- R. T. Allen, *Beyond Liberalism: The Political Thought of F. A. Hayek and Michael Polanyi* (Transaction Publishers, 1998)
- Struan Jacobs and R. T. Allen (eds.), *Emotion, Tradition and Reason: Essays on the Social, Political and Economic Thought of Michael Polanyi* (Ashgate, 2005)
- W. T. Scott and Martin X. Moleski, *Michael Polanyi: Scientist and Philosopher* (Oxford University Press, 2005)

R. T. Allen

Karl Popper   1902–94

The twentieth century's foremost philosopher of science and the most formidable critic of Marxism when it was at its zenith, Popper showed that human knowledge develops through the free criticism of ideas and used this insight to expose the pretensions of all political philosophies that would curb liberty in the name of reason or science.

Key ideas

- All human knowledge is provisional and open to later correction; therefore, it can only flourish in a free society.
- Democracy is not a luxury that successful societies can afford but a precondition of that success.
- The idea that it is the role of social science or governments to predict the course of history is dangerous and logically confused.

Biography

Karl Raimund Popper was born in Vienna on 28 July 1902 – an era when that city was the world's intellectual capital. His father was a liberal lawyer with wide political and philosophical interests – 'there were books everywhere,' Popper later remembered – and his mother instilled in him a great love of music.

Illness and the First World War disrupted Popper's education, with the result that he left school at sixteen. He attended lectures on a variety of subjects at the University of Vienna while working to support himself and furthering his interest in progressive education, but did not formally enrol there until 1922. He was awarded a doctorate in philosophy in 1928, and taught in secondary schools from 1930 to 1936. In 1930 he married Josefine Henninger, a fellow teacher.

Popper came to prominence as a philosopher of science in 1934 with the publication of his *Logik der Forschung*. Like many intellectuals with a Jewish background (his parents had converted to Christianity), he decided to leave Austria in the face of the rise of Nazism, and in 1937 he took up a lectureship at Canterbury University College at Christchurch in New Zealand. There he completed what he called his 'war work': *The Poverty of Historicism* (though it was not published until some years later) and *The Open Society and Its Enemies*. It was this latter work, an examination of the philosophical roots of tyranny, which made Popper's name. Scandalously to some, it included Plato amongst its villains.

Popper came to England in 1946 to teach at the London School of Economics, and in 1949 he was awarded a chair in logic and scientific method at the University of London. His reputation, particularly as a philosopher of science, continued to grow, and was cemented when *Logik der Forschung* was belatedly translated into English (as *The Logic of Scientific Discovery*) in 1959. Though he was never taken to the bosom of the Oxford and Cambridge philosophical establishment, Popper became an eminent figure in British life. He lived for many years at Penn in Buckinghamshire. He was knighted in 1965, invested as a Companion of Honour in 1982 and elected a fellow of both the Royal Society and the British Academy.

Popper retired from the University of London in 1969, but continued to publish and lecture at an unstinting rate until his death in London on 17 September 1994.

Ideas

Karl Popper's liberalism flowed from his understanding of the way that human knowledge develops. He rejected the conventional wisdom that it grows through the accumulation of observations; instead he saw it as a creative process where bold hypotheses are tested through experiments in an attempt to disprove them. As he famously said, the observation of any number of white swans will never prove the proposition that all swans are white, but the observation of one black swan will disprove it.

Crucially, he argued that it was the nature of good scientific theories to generate predictions that can be tested and, if not fulfilled, can show the theory to be inadequate. Newton's system, for instance, was seen for centuries as the acme of secure scientific knowledge, but it was eventually supplanted by the theories of Einstein. Yet when Popper heard Einstein lecture, he was struck by Einstein's modesty and his awareness that his own ideas might one day be shown to be wrong.

Popper contrasted this view of science with the work of both Marx and Freud, which had attracted him as a young man. He saw them and their followers as attempting to produce theories that could never be refuted – whatever happened in the world would show that Marx or Freud was right. Popper saw that by purporting to explain everything, such theories really explained nothing. He termed them 'pseudo-science'.

It was as a critic of Marxism that Popper was celebrated after he came to London in 1946. The second volume of *The Open Society and Its Enemies* contains his most concentrated critique of Marx's theories, with its central tenets each examined and found wanting, but it was his understanding of the nature of science that was most damning for the Marxists.

Popper also argued strongly that it was not the role of social science to predict the future or of governments to ally themselves with the tides of history. This was a braver and more important argument than it sounds today. as it is easy now to forget how impressed many were in the West by the supposed efficiency of Soviet-style central economic planning. At the heart of Popper's case was the insight that the growth of knowledge is key to the way that society develops, and that it is logically impossible to predict what new things we shall know in the future (otherwise we should know them already).

The 'open society' was perhaps more of a slogan than a fully realised vision of the good society, but then Popper was always insistent that it was dangerous for governments to attempt to impose such blueprints upon their people. His positive views in politics were quite practical: he was impatient of debates about the meaning of words such as 'democracy' or 'freedom', urging people to concentrate instead upon practical questions such as 'how do we get rid of bad governments without violence?' He saw politics, like science, as a process of problem-solving; he believed that government action should be directed towards particular problems. He also believed that free criticism was as crucial to politics as it was to science, so the institutions of a free society were needed to ensure that government action fulfilled its intended aims. This led him to the important insight that democracy is not a luxury that successful states can afford, but is central to their being able to achieve that success in the first place.

Because of his renown as a critic of Marx, Popper is often seen as a right-wing figure. Yet he was no advocate of the untrammelled market, not least because his own father had lost his wealth in the inflation that followed the First World War. Popper's greatest advocate in Britain has been Bryan Magee, who sat in the Commons for Labour and the SDP, and a wide variety of politicians made the pilgrimage to Penn to meet him, including Helmut Kohl, Mario Soares and Václav Havel.

Popper's greatest contribution was made in the fields of the philosophy of science and epistemology, and in an age when Marx's ideas are in eclipse his political ideas may seem less important. Yet his undermining of the pretensions of those who advocate tyranny, and his insight that the institutions of a liberal democracy (q.v.) are essential to the growth of human knowledge and happiness, meant that he will remain an inspiration to liberals everywhere.

Key works

- *The Open Society and Its Enemies* (two vols, 1945)
- *The Poverty of Historicism* (1957)
- *Logic of Scientific Discovery* (1959), first published as *Logik der Forschung* (1934)
- *Objective Knowledge* (1972)

Further reading

- David Edmonds and John Eidinow, *Wittgenstein's Poker: The Story of a Ten-Minute Argument between Two Great Philosophers* (Faber & Faber, 2001)
- Malachi Haim Hacohen, *Karl Popper – The Formative Years, 1902–1945: Politics and Philosophy in Inter-war Vienna* (Cambridge University Press, 2002)
- Roger James, *Return to Reason* (Open Books, 1980)
- Bryan Magee, *Popper* (Fontana, 1978)

Jonathan Calder

Radical Action

Radical Action was established in 1941 by Liberal parliamentary candidates and others to challenge the party leadership's support for the wartime electoral truce and to campaign in favour of imaginative policies for post-war reconstruction. It had a significant influence over the Liberal leadership's decision not to seek to perpetuate the coalition government after the end of the Second World War.

The Liberal Action Group was founded on 19 July 1941, the name Radical Action being adopted in 1943. It aimed to activate and energise the Liberal Party both as regards policy and organisation. The impetus for the establishment of Radical Action came from the refusal of the Liberal Party leadership, during the 1941 assembly, to countenance a discussion of the wartime electoral truce, despite mounting evidence from by-elections that a significant and expanding portion of the electorate was not prepared to back the government when asked to do so. A section of the Liberal Party was uneasy at the prospect of allowing the Munich-tainted Conservative Party to coopt its supporters into Parliament for the duration of the war and saw an opportunity for the Liberal Party to exploit the growing public dissatisfaction with the Conservatives.

Radical Action's founders were Donald Johnson (1903–78), a doctor and publisher, who contested Bury in 1935 and Bewdley in 1937; Honor Balfour (1912–2001), a journalist; and Ivor Davies (1915–86), a publisher. All three came close to capturing seats during the war, in defiance of the electoral truce, Balfour missing out at Darwen in 1944 by only 70 votes. Lancelot Spicer (1893–1979), a company director, replaced Johnson as chairman of the group in 1942. Also prominent in the group were the Liberal MPs Clement Davies (1884–1962) and Tom Horabin (1896–1956).

Radical Action was not concerned only with strategic matters. Throughout 1942 it debated the views expounded in print by Johnson and two Liberal MPs, Sir Richard Acland (q.v.) and Tom Horabin. All three were concerned with the question of how to prevent the re-emergence of mass unemployment, gross inequalities of income and fascism at the end of the war. The Beveridge Report, published in November 1942, provided a focus for Radical Action's attention. The mutual suspicion with which Radical Action and the Liberal leadership regarded each other was intensified by the refusal of the latter to vote in the House of Commons for the immediate implementation of the Beveridge Report, in February 1943.

The initial aims of Radical Action were subtly changed by the influx of new members into the group. It did not support a motion brought by Johnson to the 1942 Liberal assembly opposing the truce, and as a consequence Johnson was replaced by Lancelot Spicer as the group's chairman. Spicer understood that if the Liberal Party formally broke the electoral truce then it would have to leave the government and he was not prepared to recommend this step. Radical Action therefore pressed the Liberal leader, Sir Archibald Sinclair, to define his attitude towards the continuance of the coalition government after the end of the war. Sinclair suggested that political conditions could be very dangerous after the war, with a resurgence of communism and an outbreak of right-wing Conservatism. He suggested that the coalition ought to proceed until international peace, order, justice and commerce were all restored, a process which would take time. This approach was reiterated by Sinclair at the 1943 assembly and by some of his parliamentary colleagues.

In the end, however, Radical Action was effective in achieving its aim of committing the Liberal leadership to fighting the impending general election as an independent organisation, free of coupons and pacts, and staying out of any subsequent coalition administration. Donald Johnson's 1943 assembly motion opposing the continuance of the coalition after the end of the war was passed and subsequently backed by the Party Council. In January 1944 the Liberal candidates also backed Radical Action's stance and in October the parliamentary party announced that the Liberal Party would contest the election with the maximum number of candidates and in complete independence.

Radical Action also claimed success in its aim of encouraging the Liberal leadership to embrace the Beveridge Report and other radical social policies. Beveridge (q.v.) took a prominent part in the Liberal Party's election campaign in 1945 and most Liberal candidates made reference to his report and to the party's commitment to fight want, ignorance, squalor and disease. Spicer felt that Radical Action had infused the Liberal Party with a militant, radical policy. Although Radical Action was outspoken in its support of Beveridge, there was little significant opposition within the Liberal Party to his ideas.

In its third aim, of reviving the party organisation, Radical Action was not successful. The formation of the group reflected the frustration felt by many young candidates at the domination of the Liberal Party by an aristocratic, nepotistic, Asquithian elite. Spicer suggested that Radical Action's immediate goal was to ensure that office-holders and committee members throughout the party were radical in outlook and active during the election. At the national level, the group submitted a slate of candidates to the elections of the party's officerships in 1944, but all were unsuccessful in their challenge. Locally, Spicer claimed that Radical Action was reinvigorating the Liberal challenge in the constituencies, but there is no evidence that Radical Action members performed better than other Liberals in the 1945 election. The group continued to exist until 1948, but its activities petered out after the 1945 election.

Radical Action acted as a safety valve, allowing young Liberal candidates a chance to influence the Liberal leadership at a time when the youth and student wings of the party were virtually inoperative owing to the war. The group gave a first platform for a generation of future party leaders, including Donald Wade (q.v.), Philip Fothergill, Emrys Roberts and Leonard Smith. Radical Action's greatest success lay in encouraging Liberals such as these to challenge received wisdom within the party at a time when such challenges were often construed as disloyal and unpatriotic.

Further reading

- J. Davies, 'Keeper of the Liberal Flame', *Journal of Liberal Democrat History* 34/35 (spring/summer 2002)
- R. Ingham, 'Donald Johnson', *Journal of Liberal Democrat History* 25 (winter 1999–2000)
- D. Johnson, *Bars and Barricades* (Christopher Johnson, 1952)
- 'Odysseus' [Donald Johnson], *Safer than a Known Way* (Jonathan Cape, 1941)
- Honor Balfour's papers have been deposited with the Bodleian Library, Oxford

Robert Ingham

Radical Reform Group

A social liberal pressure group established within the Liberal Party in 1952 to provide a focus for those who feared the party was drifting to the right. After an unsuccessful period in 1954–55 trying to influence all parties from outside, the Group rejoined the Liberal Party and in general can be assessed as having achieved its aims by the late 1950s.

The Radical Reform Group was established in the autumn of 1952 against the background of an ideological debate within the Liberal Party: should it be a party of classical liberal (q.v.) ideas (free trade (q.v.), minimal government and individual liberty) or should it stand for social liberalism (q.v.), in the more recent traditions of Asquith's post-1908 government, the economic thinking of J. M. Keynes (q.v.), the industrial heritage of the 'Yellow Book' and the social welfare programme of Beveridge (q.v.)? The Group provided a focus for those who feared the party was drifting rightwards and was in danger of being captured by the economic liberals (q.v.). It also sought to prevent the growing defection of senior party figures, ordinary members and voters to the Labour Party and to seize upon Labour's own internal struggles, typified by the debates over Clause IV, to attract support from social democrats as well as from liberals in other parties. In this way, the Group not only helped maintain a social liberal ascendancy in the Liberal Party but also anticipated the political and electoral strategy that came to be known as 'realignment of the left'.

The period of the Radical Reform Group's greatest influence was the mid-1950s, although it carried on until the late 1960s when other policy agendas and electoral strategies such as community politics (q.v.) were taking over in relevance. The Group's two main protagonists were Desmond Banks, Baron Banks of Kenton (1918–97) and Peter Grafton (1916–), Liberal candidate for Bromley in 1950. Over the years the group attracted many senior and well-known figures including John Arlott, Peter Bessell, Lady Beveridge, Robin Day, A. J. F. MacDonald, Frank Owen, Nancy Seear and Jeremy Thorpe. For several years up to 1960, Jo Grimond (q.v.) was its president.

The early policy agenda of the Radical Reform Group focused on the proper funding of the welfare state and free health service, the maintenance of full employment, planned production in agriculture and industrial reform, based on profit-sharing and co-ownership. The Group characterised this approach as 'social reform without socialism'. Other policy themes were developed later, notably support for faster decolonisation, overseas aid and the free-trading opportunities of European unity. The Group was also an early advocate of the importance of sustainability, acknowledging the need to conserve the world's material resources for the developing world and future generations.

However, it was always more about political strategy than detailed policy. The Group's founders were motivated by the failure of the existing party system to produce representation in Parliament that accurately reflected the true divisions of opinion in the country. Of course there was an element within this critique of the traditional Liberal call for proportional representation. However the radical reformers felt that a politics based on tribal and artificial divisions was undemocratic and that the existing system hindered the introduction of policies based clearly on the twin pillars of liberty and social justice (q.v.). They argued that the system also acted as a barrier to the emergence of an effective progressive force in British politics to realise these principles.

In the spring of 1954 the Group took a controversial decision to try to maximise the potential for realignment and the creation of a new progressive force. In the hope of recruiting defectors from those in the Labour social-democratic tradition and casting their eye towards liberal Conservatives, the Group moved outside the Liberal Party as an organisation, although most individual members remained in the party. The project was not a success. The

Labour moderates may have felt uneasy during internal clashes between Aneurin Bevan, on the left, and the leadership of Hugh Gaitskell, but they stayed inside Labour. Left-wing Conservatives similarly remained comfortable in the Tory party. The approach of the 1955 general election caused dissenters in all parties to unify for the coming battle.

In October 1955 the Group voted narrowly to move back into the Liberal Party, considering it was the most likely vehicle to bring success to its aims and objectives. Thereafter it continued as a social liberal ginger group, supportive of Grimond's electoral strategy of realignment.

Together with the defection of leading economic liberals connected with the Institute of Economic Affairs (q.v.), the return of the Radical Reform Group helped to set the progressive tone of Liberal politics during the years of Grimond's leadership, when the party tended on the whole to choose the social liberal and Keynesian (q.v.) economic approach. The Liberal *News Chronicle* summed this position up in welcoming the return of the Group to the Liberal fold in their leader of 23 February 1956, entitled 'Left or Limbo':

> Social reform without socialism; order without tyranny; these are the first principles which the radical reformers preach, and as texts for our times they are very apposite ... Within the Liberal Party the Radical Reform Group would find its place somewhere left of centre, and that is where all Liberals ought to be.

Key works
In addition to the preamble to its unpublished constitution (1952), the key works of the Radical Reform Group (all privately published by the Group itself) are:
* *Radical Approach: A Statement of Aims by the Radical Reform Group* (1953)

- *Radical Aims, Social Reform without Socialism* (undated, probably 1953 or 1954)
- *Radical Challenge* (1960)

Further reading

There has been no major study of the Radical Reform Group, but see:

- Vernon Bogdanor, *Liberal Party Politics* (Oxford University Press, 1983), chs. 3, 9
- Alan Watkins, *The Liberal Dilemma* (MacGibbon & Key, 1966), ch. 4

Graham Lippiatt

Radicalism

Radicalism refers to a British political movement of the late eighteenth and nineteenth centuries. Although 'radical' activists and organisations can appear diverse in their politics and aims, they were unified in their pursuit of rights and justice for ordinary people. They drew upon a range of political ideas that were committed to this end, which developed into a distinctive and influential critique of the social and political status quo.

In the British political context, 'radical' refers to a body of specific political traditions and worldviews, rather than just positions that are perceived to be extreme. Early radicals did not employ the term 'radicalism', so historians have to be wary of anachronism when conceptualising it as a unified phenomenon with a coherent identity and ideology.

The movement developed in the last third of the eighteenth century, a time when few people could vote and when government was perceived to be aristocratic, remote and corrupt. Radicals were activists drawn from all classes who sought political, social and legal justice for those who were denied them. Their campaigns concerned civil liberties such as freedom of speech, of association and of religious conscience, and later radicals were also concerned with the social and economic plight of working people. The most important goal of the radical movement, however, was the extension of the franchise. This was partly because of its symbolism and value as a rallying point, but also because the radical critique was fundamentally political. Radicals believed that if ordinary people had the vote then Parliament would legislate for the general good; although some radicals believed that social and economic change required direct action, most had faith that this could be accomplished within the legislative sphere.

By and large, radicals therefore sought to work within the existing political system. The constitutionalist idiom of mainstream radicals emphasised that the national political tradition guaranteed them historic rights which they were being denied, a rhetorical tactic that underlined the legitimacy of their claims and campaigning methods. British radicalism, however, always drew strength from new intellectual currents. In the period of the Enlightenment, Thomas Paine (q.v.) rejected historic constitutionalism and espoused a republicanism that was founded upon the inherent rights of men; whereas the later tradition of philosophic radicalism explored the implications of Benthamite utilitarianism (q.v.). Over the course of its history, British radicalism also engaged with traditions as diverse as Tory paternalism, utopian socialism and Marxism, serving to emphasise its ideological vitality and heterogeneity. Radical politics, however, should be viewed as ideas in action, so it is necessary to sketch its history.

Although radical ideas have a long heritage, the movement was inaugurated in the political conflicts of the 1760s, when politicians began to pursue libertarian (q.v.)

causes by appealing to the extra-parliamentary nation. Much of the credit for this conventionally goes to John Wilkes (1727–97), the notorious rake and social climber, who was adept at elevating his personal disputes with government into popular causes of press, legal and electoral liberty. Revolutions in America and France both stimulated and hindered British radicalism. Radicals corresponded with fellow travellers abroad, a dialogue that radicalised their critiques and inspired campaigns for parliamentary reform at home. At the same time, governmental fears of disorder meant that even moderate radicals were tarred with the revolutionary brush, leading to the suspension of civil liberties and mass arrests. It also made it more difficult to assert a patriotic constitutionalist position, which some radicals disowned altogether in favour of internationalist republicanism. During the 1790s, a working-class radicalism developed with its underground culture of meetings, societies and illicit printing.

Radicalism revived in the later years of the Napoleonic Wars and the period of economic hardship that followed. In the Midlands and the north, skilled textile workers known as Luddites targeted the new technology that contributed to unemployment in a wave of machine-breaking. This suggests that radicalism was developing an economic critique of industrial capitalism, but mainstream radicals in this period continued to prioritise political methods and aims. The 'mass platform' employed the tactic of monster outdoor meetings of working people. They asserted both their physical numbers and their political responsibility through peaceable behaviour, a claim underlined by the presence of 'gentleman leaders' such as Henry Hunt (1773–1835). Their primary goal was manhood suffrage: although women participated in the movement, the vote was usually sought for men in their capacity as breadwinners and household heads. Many radicals were therefore disappointed by the Reform Act of 1832, which largely enfranchised the propertied middle classes to the exclusion of the many working-class men who had campaigned for the measure.

Radicalism subsequently diverged in class terms, as working-class radicals rallied around Chartism. The significance of this movement has been hotly debated. Given its working-class character, historians have often regarded Chartism as a 'social' movement, but the Charter itself was exclusively focused upon parliamentary reform, consistent with the old radical faith in the ability of representative politics to achieve social and economic change. Middle-class radicals, on the other hand, developed a radicalised Victorian Liberalism of free trade (q.v.), individual liberty and moral respectability. The Anti-Corn Law League (q.v.), founded by the manufacturer Richard Cobden (q.v.), sought to end the agricultural protectionism that enriched land-owners at the expense of industrialists and poor families alike. The politics of the League were recognisably radical in their pursuit of social justice (q.v.) and individual independence, in opposition to the traditional monopolies enjoyed by the privileged. The moral basis to this struggle is discernable in the passionate Christian rhetoric of Cobden's colleague John Bright (1811–89), who was subsequently a leading spokesman in the long campaign that led up to the Second Reform Act of 1867.

In later-Victorian Britain, radical causes were commonly pursued under the broad umbrella of Gladstone's (q.v.) Liberal Party. The colourful politician Charles Bradlaugh (q.v.), for example, conducted a wide range of radical campaigns in the 1880s as Liberal MP for Northampton; these causes included republicanism, birth control, compulsory education and – as an atheist – the right of MPs to affirm rather than take the oath. Radicalism, however, retained its distinctiveness. New currents such as socialism, anti-landlordism and collectivism were mediated through the indigenous radical tradition, in terms of what Belchem calls 'the triumphant crusade of the working people'.

By the end of the nineteenth century, many working-class activists had become frustrated with the Liberal Party and sought an independent representation in Parliament. The resultant Labour Party sought to get working men into Parliament, opposed protectionism and the landlords, and promoted trade unionism and interventionist social policies – a manifesto that suggests Labour politics in the twentieth century owed as much to radicalism as it did to Marxism.

Historians have conventionally conceptualised radical politics in terms of social class. 'Radicalism' is often regarded as the expression of a politically conscious working class, an ideology that reflected social conflicts and conditions. However, it is also productive to consider radical critiques, methods and cultures on their own terms. In this way, the striking continuities of the radical tradition are all the more apparent, as well as its close relationship with – and influence upon – the Liberal and Labour Parties. British radicalism in the late eighteenth and nineteenth centuries had many significant achievements and legacies; indeed, it should be central to our understanding of the development of left-wing and liberal politics in our own times.

Further reading

- John Belchem, *Popular Radicalism in Nineteenth-Century Britain* (Macmillan, 1996)
- J. R. Dinwiddy, *Radicalism and Reform in Britain 1780–1850* (Hambledon, 1992)
- Gareth Stedman Jones, *Languages of Class: Studies in English Working Class History, 1832–1982* (Cambridge University Press, 1983)
- E. P. Thompson, *The Making of the English Working Class* (Victor Gollancz, 1963)

Matthew McCormack

Rationality

Liberalism envisages a fundamental role for rationality, in the sense of conscious thought and planning, in the construction of political institutions. Liberals have not always coped well with irrational forces in politics, but liberalism's response to the uncovering of the dark side of human nature has been to emphasise the importance of openness and discussion in politics, so that these motivations can be brought to the surface.

Given the multiple meanings of both 'liberalism' and 'rationality', a full treatment of the relationship between the two would require several books. Even a historical account would be controversial. Some writers place the beginnings of liberalism at the point at which humans first started to live in cities, and so needed social and political doctrines that allowed for acceptance of other forms of life. At the other extreme, some see liberalism as a child of the Enlightenment, and thus a creature of a certain type of political rationalism. As for rationality, at one extreme it pertains merely to formal features of thought (very roughly the property of consistency) – features to which all forms of political thought would lay claim, apart from perhaps the wilder forms of romantic nationalism and Dadaist situationism. At the other extreme, rationality can be seen as the core method of ethical and political doctrines that claim to overcome the fact–value distinction by establishing the truth of particular values by force of argument.

This entry concentrates on one very small, but significant, part of the picture. It takes liberalism in its political form, which sees the prime task of politics as the construction of a state that respects and protects political freedom, and it takes rationality primarily to refer to conscious thought and mental effort rather than to any particular features of that thought.

There can be little doubt that liberalism envisages a fundamental role for rationality, in the sense of conscious thought and planning, in the construction of political institutions. Liberals are the original constitutionalists, in the sense that they advocate a conscious reconstruction of the state so that it is built around specific procedures, institutions and rights. They reject political authority that is built on custom, religious belief or personality. In Max Weber's (q.v.) famous threefold typology of authority, liberals reject traditional and charismatic authority and accept only legal-rational authority. Liberals do not deny the existence or effectiveness of non-rational forms of authority, but from a liberal point of view, such forms constitute problems to be managed.

In contrast, for conservatives, traditional authority is 'real' authority, to which legal-rational and charismatic forms of authority constitute threats, while socialists can fall into either camp. Some socialists celebrate sub-rational forms of authority, especially class solidarity, but others look to a rational reconstruction of the whole of society, not just of the state, and thus to a much broader rationalism than that of liberals, who tend to be highly suspicious of attempts rationally to reconstruct social relationships.

Another way of putting the same point is that liberalism prefers law to history, whereas conservatism prefers history to law. Law allows us to attempt to make new social structures out of rules. Conservatives, such as Oakeshott, distrust such attempts. They point out that they can have unintended negative effects and that they assume that legislators know more about the world than they possibly can. Liberals, on the other hand, point out that muddling through usually leads to muddle and that it is very difficult to change the world without a specific conception of how it could be different. Liberals characteristically exaggerate the importance of legal instruments, such as written constitutions, but conservatives characteristically under-estimate their importance, because they fail to understand the constructive, constitutive role of law. Institutions develop well beyond their legal form, but law allows us to create new ones.

One point of tension in liberalism is the extent to which it should accept the tendency of social democracy (q.v.) to advocate the legal-rational reconstruction of economic relationships. Indeed, Oakeshottian criticism of liberal rationalism is perhaps better seen as an attack on social-democratic technocracy than on political liberalism's commitment to universal human rights.

Another standard intellectual attack on liberalism, and one which contributed to its temporary eclipse in the mid-twentieth century, is the claim that its commitment to a politics of conscious thought fails to appreciate what we know about human beings' unconscious desires and drives. In the last century that meant the challenge of the will to power and of sex – Nietzsche and Freud. In this century it means coping with the insights of evolutionary psychology.

Liberalism certainly runs into difficulty if it sees itself as offering an explanation of human behaviour at the same level as psychology, whether Freudian or evolutionary. Any theory of human behaviour that relies solely on conscious motivation and thought will fail as a comprehensive explanation. But liberalism is not a theoretical explanation of human behaviour. It is a set of ideas about what to do about politics. It is not a theory about how we behave, but rather about how we ought to behave. Liberalism's response to the uncovering of the dark side of human nature has been to emphasise the importance of openness and discussion in politics, as in the idea of deliberative democracy, so that these motivations can be brought to the surface, or as near to the surface as it is possible to go. In an odd sort of way, liberalism has adopted a Freudian approach; it proposes a kind of 'talking cure' for political problems.

L. T. Hobhouse (q.v.) made the point in another way. He remarked in *Liberalism* (1911) that liberty rests in the end on our duty to treat other people as rational beings. Whether other people are in fact rational is a different and not particularly relevant point. Liberalism requires us to honour the rational, thinking part of people and to build political institutions in ways that protect and encourage that part. The way we build has to take into account human beings' real motives, for otherwise our constructions will be swept away. As the American liberal theorist Bruce Ackerman puts it, there is an economy of virtue. Virtue exists but it is scarce. Our task is to use the virtue that exists to best effect. But that does not change what we are building and why.

There is another attack on the link between liberalism and rationality, namely the link made by some critical theorists of the Frankfurt School between rationality and Nazism. To simplify only a little, the accusation is that fascism is a consequence of, and a deformation of, liberalism.

Liberalism promotes rationality, but rationality, far from being a liberation, leads to an age of the ruthless pursuit of efficiency for its own sake, an age in which human values are crushed. That in turn makes fascism possible. The end point of this development is death, on an industrial scale, in the camps. This view of liberalism became part of the standard mental equipment of the intellectual left, and explains some of the residual hostility to liberalism found in such circles even today, when it plays a part in post-modernism's rejection of the Enlightenment.

Indeed, post-modernism combines both the lines of attack against liberalism and rationality we have discussed. It develops the anti-Enlightenment tendency of the Frankfurt School, although it removes any residual element of Marxian optimism. It rejects all 'grand narratives', not only Marxian theories of history but also concepts, such as 'human rights', which imply any form of universalism. Post-modernism sees all reason as local and temporary. Although it uses a very different rhetorical style from that of Oakeshott, post-modernism arrives at a similar political position, that we should distrust reason and analysis and conduct politics only in the short term and at the surface of things.

Liberalism's response to the first part of the post-modern attacks is so obvious that it hardly requires exposition. Nazism was not the apotheosis of rationality but its opposite. It was a celebration of irrationality, of the very dark forces in human beings – violence, domination, cruelty – that liberal politics seeks to manage and to suppress. The industrial organisation of death was not a consequence of rationality and liberalism but a consequence of their political defeat. The only element of truth in this part of the post-modern attack is that liberalism fundamentally weakens itself if it allows itself to forget that it is a normative political doctrine with values that it must defend. But post-modernist relativism leaves us much more vulnerable to the irrational politics of faith and nation than liberal universalism.

The second part of the attack, however, has more substance. Exaggerating the power of human reason, and, especially, translating that over-confidence into political action, is a real danger in some forms of liberalism, especially in liberal imperialism and its latest descendant, liberal interventionism. But an appreciation of the limits of human reason and of the dangers of over-confidence in the ability of politics to control events is not inconsistent with liberalism, and it does not imply abandoning rationality in politics. As Herbert Simon said, human beings are rational, but boundedly so. They think their way to solutions, but imperfectly. Liberalism can be committed to a similar view of politics. The fact that we build institutions imperfectly is a reason to build them so that we can alter them if we need to. It is not a reason to refuse to build them at all.

Further reading
- F. Adorno and M. Horkheimer, *The Dialectic of Enlightenment* (English translation, Verso, 1979)
- B. Ackerman, *We, the People:* vol. 1, *Foundations* (Belknap Press, 1991)
- L. T. Hobhouse, *Liberalism* (in James Meadowcroft (ed.), *Hobhouse: Liberalism and Other Writings* (Cambridge University Press, 1994)
- J-F. Lyotard, *The Postmodern Condition* (English translation, Manchester University Press, 1984)
- M. Oakeshott, *Rationalism in Politics and Other Essays* (Methuen, 1962)
- H. Simon, *Models of Man* (John Wiley & Sons, 1957)
- M. Weber, *Economy and Society* (English translation, University of California Press, 1979)

David Howarth

John Rawls   1921–2002

Rawls's great achievement was to revive liberal political philosophy, and indeed all political philosophy, in the Anglo-American world. Before Rawls liberals appeared to have given up on finding a normative base for their political beliefs and practice and to have fallen back on a mixture of utilitarianism, relativism and political compromise. After Rawls, although still controversial and contested, liberal political thought returned to its position as the tradition in political thought against which all others must expect to be measured.

Key ideas
- *Justice as fairness*: Rawls reinvigorated the contractarian tradition in political philosophy, using the thought experiment of an 'original position' in which we ask ourselves what we would accept as fair if we were unaware of our position in society.
- *Equal basic liberty*: Rawls argued that no society could count as fair unless it established a system of political liberties available to all. Establishing a scheme of equal liberty takes precedence over all other forms of fairness, but Rawls recognised that it was important for people to be able to exercise their liberties in practice (the *fair value of liberty*).
- *Difference principle*: Rawls argued that, having satisfied the requirements of equal liberty, and having established rules against discrimination, material inequality could be justified, but only to the extent that it maximised the welfare of the least advantaged.

- *Political liberalism and overlapping consensus:* Rawls distinguished between liberalism as a *comprehensive* and as a *political* doctrine. He advocated *political liberalism* as the foundation for the conduct of the state. In doing so he appealed to the notion of *public reason* and to common interests and he sought to make persuasive his belief in an *overlapping* – politically liberal – *consensus*.
- *Law of Peoples*: Rawls developed a framework of ideas that were intended to serve as a guide to both liberal and non-liberal states in regulating international relations.

Biography

John Borden Rawls was born in Baltimore on 21 February 1921; his father was a lawyer specialising in tax law and his mother a political activist. He graduated from Princeton in 1943 and joined the US Army as an infantryman, serving in the Pacific and in Japan as a private soldier.

In 1946 he returned to Princeton to study for a doctorate in moral philosophy, which he completed in 1950, the year after his marriage to Margaret Fox. After teaching briefly at Princeton, in 1952, Rawls went to Oxford, where he was influenced by Isaiah Berlin (q.v.) and H. L. A. Hart. He returned to the US to teach philosophy at Cornell, after which he moved to MIT. In 1964 he accepted a job at Harvard, where he taught for almost forty years. His influence as a teacher, especially of graduate students, has been almost as great as his influence as a writer. He died on 24 November 2002.

Ideas

John Rawls is best known for his writings on justice; most notably, justice as fairness and the associated ideas of the 'veil of ignorance' and the 'original position'.

For Rawls the first virtue of political institutions was justice. The question is how to discover what justice demands. Rawls' main technique, which he derived from Kant (q.v.), was to ask whether political arrangements would strike us as fair if we were not aware of our own position within those arrangements. This 'veil of ignorance' procedure is a way of abstracting from our own particular interests to arrive at a position that we can justify by reference to principles, such as that of reciprocity, to which we are rationally committed. Since 'behind the veil of ignorance', we would not know our own particular talents and defects, reasoning effectively takes place in a context of fundamental equality between persons, in a situation Rawls, echoing social contract theory, called 'the original position'. It should be stressed, however, that Rawls did not envisage any sort of real meeting or process of contracting. He proposed a fair technique that we can all use to arrive at what we consider to be just. His main goal was to move discussion beyond the utilitarian (q.v.) world of what we and others want to a world in which we have a common starting point for discussing what we ought to want.

Rawls's theory of justice relied upon an intellectual process he called 'reflective equilibrium'. It helps us to refine what we take to be just by comparing the various positions that we might take as a result of abstracting from our particular interests and removing the contradictions between them by abandoning or modifying those positions to which we are less committed. The process was intended to result in a set of positions that were both just and consistent.

Rawls believed that if we did not know our position in society we would agree that the first principle of political organisation should be that each person should have an 'equal right to the most extensive basic liberty compatible with a similar liberty for others'. Later this became the principle that each person has an equal claim to a fully adequate scheme of basic rights and liberties – the same basic scheme for all. He believed that a liberal state, based upon these principles, would guarantee political liberty, including, crucially, the right to effective political participation. Political liberty was, for Rawls, 'lexically prior' to any other aspects of political organisation, especially to broader ideas of social justice (q.v.). For countries in which everyone's most basic material needs were capable of being satisfied, the state would never be justified in sacrificing political liberty for the sake of economic prosperity. Political liberties might sometimes need to be sacrificed for the sake of other political liberties, but that is an entirely different matter.

Especially in his later works, Rawls emphasised that when he gave priority to political freedom he was not talking about merely formal or legal rights. People would opt for a system that gave them rights that could be used effectively – or the 'fair value' of their rights. To achieve the 'fair value' of their right freely to participate in politics, people could reasonably demand that a number of economic decisions should be made in specific ways – that it should not be possible to buy elections or to entrench political power using wealth, for example by building up a monopoly over the media. Guarantees of education might also be required to deliver the fair value of political rights. Indeed Rawls's fundamental idea became that all political decisions should be subjected to a test of the way they affect political liberty.

As long as the requirements of the fair value of political liberty are satisfied, the state could concern itself with distributional questions. Rawls's view was that if

we did not know about our own talents or lack of them, we would opt for a cautious view of the degree to which society would tolerate inequality. From this perspective social and economic inequalities should satisfy two rules: (1) different rewards should only be attached to positions and offices open to all under conditions of fair equality of opportunity; and (2) inequalities should be to the greatest benefit of the least advantaged members of society. The second rule, dubbed the 'difference principle', proved controversial both in its interpretation (note the notion of the *greatest* benefit, not just any benefit) and in its justification: does fairness really commit us to such a risk-averse view, or would we rather opt for a safety-net approach in which, apart from guaranteeing that failure should not lead to abject poverty or starvation, we would favour allowing any inequality that raised average incomes per head?

One criticism of Rawls's first major statement of his views, in *A Theory of Justice* (1971), was that he was calling for all people to adopt liberalism as the basis of their own lives, an impossible and indeed illiberal demand. Rawls's response was that he meant only to put forward liberalism as a 'political' doctrine – the basis for the conduct of the state – and not as a 'comprehensive' doctrine – the basis for all human conduct. He further claimed that the stability of liberal regimes came not from a general adoption by the population of liberalism as a comprehensive doctrine but rather as a common core of beliefs about politics itself around which people of otherwise differing beliefs could unite. This is the idea of the 'overlapping consensus'.

Rawls's concern with the separation of the political and the personal also drew him into a debate about what kind of arguments are proper for public use in a liberal polity. His view was that there are kinds of reasoning ('public reason') that promote an overlapping consensus and thus help to maintain political liberty and kinds that do not. In particular, Rawls was concerned about the use in politics of references to holy texts and religious reasons that not all participants in the debate would recognise as authoritative. He wanted political actors to confine themselves to reasons that could count as reasons for all the participants in the debate.

While Rawls did not transfer his ideas directly to international politics he hoped that his ideas had an international resonance. He did not believe that the purpose of foreign policy was to impose liberal regimes on other countries. He did believe that there was a duty to assist poorer countries, to bring them to a point (though no further) at which they could determine their own political future. This meant, in his view, that as long as a regime was 'decent' (for example by not violating human rights) it was no affair of other countries whether it was fully democratic. He did, however, recognise a category of 'outlaw' states in which intervention was permissible.

Rawls is widely accepted as the most important liberal political thinker of the twentieth century. Liberals have every reason to read and to discuss his ideas in order to sharpen their own understanding of social justice, political liberalism and the role of reason in political debate.

Key works
- *A Theory of Justice* (1971; revised edition 1999)
- *Political Liberalism* (1993, 1996 (paperback edition, slightly revised), 2005 (much expanded))
- *The Law of Peoples* (1999)
- *Lectures on the History of Moral Philosophy* (2000)
- *Justice as Fairness: A Restatement* (2001)

Further reading
- Samuel Freeman (ed.), *The Cambridge Companion to Rawls* (Cambridge University Press, 2003)
- Robert A. Talisse, *On Rawls* (Wadsworth/Thomson Learning, 2001)

David Howarth

Joseph Raz   1939–

One of a small number of contemporary jurisprudentialists who have made significant and influential contributions to liberal political theory, stressing the continuing importance of personal autonomy and value-pluralism.

Key Ideas
- Legal positivism.
- Liberal perfectionism.
- Personal autonomy.
- Value-pluralism.

Biography
Joseph Raz was born in Israel in 1939 and educated at the Hebrew University in Jerusalem and Oxford University. Raz has held academic positions at the Hebrew University, the University of Oxford and Columbia University. He is currently a fellow of Balliol College and Professor of the Philosophy of Law at Oxford University, and Professor of Law at Columbia University, New York.

Ideas
Raz was a pupil of H. L. A. Hart and has been a high-profile advocate of legal positivism ever since. This means that, like Hart, Raz believes that there is no necessary link between the *authority* of a law and whether or not that law is *moral*. Unlike natural law theorists, for example, legal positivists believe that it is possible to argue that 'unjust' laws have authority as long as they were created via due process etc.,

irrespective of whether or not they can be said to be *moral* or *just* in nature. The authority of a law is afforded by the way in which that law was made. Whether or not the law is a moral or just one is a separate question, and one which does not necessarily bear upon the first.

Raz's most important contribution to liberal political theory remains *The Morality of Freedom*, published in 1986, which represents a broad and thorough statement of what Raz believes to be the aims and core principles of contemporary liberalism. *The Morality of Freedom* emerged at a time when liberal political theory was generally characterised as an impartialist, contractualist doctrine. Reinterpreting the work of the founding fathers of liberalism like John Locke (q.v.), Thomas Hobbes (q.v.) and Immanuel Kant (q.v.), contemporary thinkers like John Rawls (q.v.) and others conceptualised liberal principles as those which would be chosen by individuals in an appropriately modelled agreement situation; Rawls famously called this the 'original position'. Such thought experiments helped to show how liberal principles of toleration, state neutrality, equality (q.v.) and freedom (q.v.) could be justified to all rational people, and hence represented a way of making a case for the universal validity of these principles while respecting the crucial liberal claim that liberalism should not be rooted in any particular substantive way of life or set of beliefs. What makes a life valuable is not that it is rooted in a particular set of beliefs which are 'true' or valuable for all, liberals tend to argue, but that it is lived in pursuit of goals which the individual has him or herself decided to be valuable given their wider commitments and ideals.

Raz eschewed the impartialist approach, and instead sought to build his conception of liberalism from the ground up. Raz's liberalism is often thought to differ from the mainstream of liberal political theory in that it is 'perfectionist' rather than 'impartialist' – that is, it proposes that certain ways of life are better than others and claims that it is the job of social and political institutions to encourage and defend these ways of life at the expense of less valuable ones. Raz's perfectionism is based upon a complex theory of the importance of human well-being – an approach which itself differs from many liberals who speak less about 'well-being' as such and more about core principles like freedom and equality. Raz believes that these principles are an important component of 'valuable' lives, but he believes that it is not enough for liberal states to encourage these principles and then take an impartial view as to the *content* of people's lives; rather, he believes that states should work to establish social and political norms which make it possible for individuals to *choose* what kind of lives they want to live among an array of valuable, worthwhile options.

Consequently, Raz believes that liberalism is rooted in the twin ideas of individual autonomy and value-pluralism: all members of a liberal society should be able to live a life in pursuit of goals that they themselves have chosen and endorsed as worthwhile from a range of options which are valuable and rewarding. Autonomy is therefore important to personal well-being in the traditional liberal sense that the goals, relationships and commitments that individuals possess should not be imposed by external authorities or powerful groups but rather should be endorsed and accepted by individuals themselves. However, personal autonomy is not the end of the story: individuals need to use their autonomy to choose ways of life which contribute to their well-being, and not all ways of life do this. Indeed, there is a sense in which people who choose to pursue empty or worthless goals are not being autonomous at all. Raz therefore subscribes to a positive account of freedom, which requires liberal states to encourage in all individuals the 'inner capacities' necessary for them to work out what is valuable in life and what is not, among those options provided by society.

Raz's theory is complex and controversial. His claim that people should be encouraged to live valuable lives, where the value in a life comes partly but not wholly from the fact that they chose it autonomously, raises significant questions as to who should judge what is a valuable life and what is a worthless one. And his conception of individual autonomy as linked to membership in recognisable social forms and communities is an important one which can be seen to have influenced other liberal theorists (like Will Kymlicka (q.v.)). However, his trenchant defence of personal autonomy and the need for liberal institutions to encourage 'valuable lives' sets him against many liberals who seek a more tolerant, impartialist approach to cultural, religious and moral diversity. His account of liberal society as a moral community founded upon a thoroughgoing account of individual freedom raises questions as to how in his mind liberal states should treat non-liberal communities which may exist in their midst. Raz is more forceful in his attitude toward these groups than many liberals, arguing that for groups which seek to deny education or opportunities to their members to flourish outside the community, 'assimilationist policies may well be the only human course, even if implemented by force of law'.

In saying as much, Raz is confronting head-on a debate which rages at the core of liberal political theory, and offers a methodical defence of the principle of autonomy against those liberals and non-liberals who are more sceptical of liberalism's ability to require autonomy-supporting norms not only from its state, but from those social, political, and cultural groups which exist in society. Raz has gone on to develop these arguments in his later works which, together with the *Morality of Freedom*, represent a major statement of perfectionist liberal political philosophy which has influenced many within the discipline.

Key works
- *The Authority of Law* (1979)
- *The Morality of Freedom* (1986)
- *Ethics in the Public Domain* (revised edn., 1995)
- *Practical Reason and Norms* (2nd edn., 1999)
- *Engaging Reason* (2000)

Phil Parvin

David Ricardo   1772–1823

One of the most important liberal economists, Ricardo developed the theory of comparative advantage that stands at the centre of the classical liberal case for free trade.

Key ideas
- The theory of comparative advantage.
- Proposed independent central banking.
- Defended the quantity theory of money.

Biography
David Ricardo was born on 19 April 1772 at Broad Street Buildings, in the City of London, into an orthodox Jewish family. His father, Abraham Ricardo, had come to Britain from Holland, to where an earlier generation of the family had emigrated to escape the Inquisition.

Ricardo started work in his father's stockbroking business at the age of fourteen, but left it at the age of twenty-one, when his marriage to Priscilla Wilkinson, a Quaker, estranged him from his parents, though he and his father were subsequently reconciled after the death of his mother. On leaving his father's business he set up as a stock jobber on his own account and in the turbulent years of the Napoleonic Wars – turbulent financially as well as in other ways – made a vast fortune, and gradually started to retire from business from 1815 onwards.

In 1819, Ricardo became member of Parliament for the pocket Irish borough of Portarlington, and was re-elected in 1820. Although an independent, he tended to support the Radicals, using his position to oppose religious persecution, and his appointment to a select committee to advocate reform of the Corn Laws. He died, still an MP, on 11 September 1823, at his country estate, Gatcomb Park in Gloucestershire.

Ideas

Ricardo was a financier whose success outstripped even that of his very successful father, but that in itself would have made him no more than a minor figure in the history of war finance. He is remembered because he was a very great economist.

Ricardo first encountered economics when he came across Adam Smith's (q.v.) *Wealth of Nations* while visiting Bath, for his wife's health, in 1799. His interest remained focused on the natural sciences, however, and he did not return to economics until 1809, when he entered the bullion controversy with an anonymous letter in the *Morning Chronicle*. Convertibility of sterling into gold had been suspended in 1797, and this had been followed by a fall in the value of paper currency. Ricardo maintained, in that letter and then in his pamphlets *The High Price of Bullion* and *Reply to Mr. Bosanquet* (both 1811), that this was the result of over-issue of paper currency by the Bank of England, and was only capable of being corrected by a restriction of the note issue. He defended the quantity theory of money.

Next came his *Essay on the Influence of the Price of Corn on the Profits of Stock* (1815), which opposed a proposal for an increased tariff on corn. Ricardo argued that if corn imports were restricted there would have to be either more intensive or more extensive cultivation, either of which would raise rents on land and thus squeeze the earnings of capital and, through the consequent reduction in demand for labour, also those of labour. Hence, Ricardo concluded, 'the interest of the landlord is always opposed to the interest of every class in the community'. This, it has to be observed, was a very disinterested conclusion; Ricardo was himself now a landlord, but was led by intellectual integrity to oppose his own interest.

James Mill (q.v.) had been urging Ricardo to publish his ideas in a treatise rather than in occasional pamphlets, and he did so in 1817, when his *Principles of Political Economy and Taxation* first appeared. There is much in this book that has endured, either as the basis for development by others or as a cause of controversy and regular reinterpretation. But one section above all has dominated subsequent work on its subject, and has produced consensus among all who can claim to be serious economists. This is Ricardo's theory of comparative advantage. This shows the paradoxical, but important and universally valid, fact that a country can gain from international trade even though it is at a cost disadvantage in the production of every traded good as compared to the rest of the world, so long as the degree of disadvantage varies so that there are relatively smaller disadvantages in some activities than in others. Although Britain did not become a free-trading nation until the 1840s, the writings of pamphleteers and the speeches of parliamentarians in the cause of free trade (q.v.) show frequent reference to Ricardo's demonstration. It is a result not only important in economic theory, but also in advancing the well-being of nations. Free trade has been and always will be an engine of prosperity, and it is to David Ricardo that we owe the design of that engine.

In 1816 Ricardo published his *Proposal for an Economical and Secure Currency*. He criticised the profits the Bank of England had made through its dealings with the government, again urged a return to convertibility into gold bullion rather than minted coin, and advocated the establishment of a central bank independent of government. This last proposal, adopted increasingly widely in the twentieth and twenty-first centuries, was developed more fully in the posthumously published *Plan for the Establishment of a National Bank* of 1824. With a lag even longer than that with which he had affected tariff policy in Britain, Ricardo influenced central bank constitutions world-wide.

Ricardian equivalence, the notion that when the government borrows the private sector saves more in anticipation of future taxes, was also developed by Ricardo. He regarded it as a theoretical curiosity. He may have thought differently had he been writing in circumstances such as the present, when government borrowing is both high relative to national income, and regular. But whatever one thinks on that is purely conjecture. Nowadays one can and should turn to the evidence.

Ricardo has also proved influential on the method of economic analysis. He was continually striving to make economics like a natural science, and to that end abstracted from all irrelevances in reaching his conclusions. His work is almost bare of institutional detail – an approach which, unique to him at the time and for many years subsequently – is one of the modern methods of economics. Some economists may now carry it too far. One very great economist – Joseph Schumpeter – has maintained that even Ricardo did: 'He then piled one simplifying assumption upon another until he was left with only a few aggregative variables ... so that the desired results emerged almost as tautologies. The habit of applying results of this character to the solution of practical problems we shall call the Ricardian Vice.' But few economists have even a vice named after them.

Among his contemporaries, Ricardo was esteemed highly both by those who agreed with him (James Mill, John Stuart Mill (q.v.), Nassau Senior, Ramsay McCulloch) and those who did not – most notably Thomas Malthus (q.v.), between whom and Ricardo there was, despite deep disagreement, a long correspondence. In short, Ricardo was a sufficiently great economist to be esteemed both by those who knew him and by those who, a century and more after his death, knew only the works. He was important, and, on many major issues, he was right.

Key works
- *The High Price of Bullion* (1811)
- *Reply to Mr. Bosanquet* (1811)
- *Essay on the Influence of the Price of Corn on the Profits of Stock* (1815)
- *Proposal for an Economical and Secure Currency* (1816)
- *Principles of Political Economy and Taxation* (1817)
- *Plan for the Establishment of a National Bank* (1824)

Further reading
- Mark Blaug, *Economic Theory in Retrospect* (Cambridge University Press, 1997)
- Samuel Hollander, *The Economics of David Ricardo* (Heinemann, 1979)

- Samuel Hollander, *Ricardo: The New View* (Routledge, 1995)
- Joseph A. Schumpeter, *History of Economic Analysis* (Allen and Unwin, 1954)

Geoffrey Wood

D. G. Ritchie   1853–1903

Academic and idealist philosopher, Ritchie examined the implications for politics of new ideas of evolution. His arguments for extending state action for the general good of society made him an important intellectual support of the New Liberalism.

Key ideas

- Darwinism applied to politics implies not less but more state action.
- Utilitarianism must be revised on idealist lines.

Biography

David George Ritchie was born at Jedburgh on 26 October 1853. His father was a minister in the Church of Scotland, Moderator of its General Assembly in 1870, and the family had strong academic connections.

After a brilliant career at Edinburgh University (1869–74), Ritchie entered Balliol College, Oxford, where his tutors included Benjamin Jowett and T. H. Green (q.v.). Green he described as 'the philosophical teacher from whom I have learnt most', and from him Ritchie derived the foundations of his own philosophy and political thinking. He gained first-class honours in both Moderations and, in 1878, the Final School of Greats; in the same year he won a fellowship at Jesus College, becoming tutor in 1881.

Ritchie was a popular and effective teacher; he also published widely, including two short books addressed to a general audience, *Darwinism and Politics* (1889)

and *The Principles of State Interference* (1891). These were reprinted several times and established him as a lively, clear-headed, accessible and progressive writer on political philosophy and contemporary political controversies.

From 1894 Ritchie was Professor of Logic and Metaphysics at St Andrews University until his death in St Andrews on 3 February 1903. He married Flora Lindsay MacDonell in 1882; she died in 1888. The following year he married Ellen Haycraft. He had a daughter from the first marriage and a son from the second.

Ritchie held advanced liberal views throughout his life. Generally he was not a political activist, apart from occasional lectures, though in 1887–88 he did publicly support Gladstone (q.v.) in the controversy over home rule for Ireland. He had some contact with the Fabians, but broke with them when in 1893 they declared war on the Liberal Party. He favoured an increased role for government, and is often regarded as providing intellectual foundations for the New Liberalism (q.v.).

Ideas

Ritchie tackled a major question of the day – what light did the new and epoch-making biological conceptions of Darwinism throw upon social and political problems? He was sharply critical of those, above all Herbert Spencer (q.v.), who argued that it was foolish and dangerous to interfere with natural selection, and that state activity should be minimised so that individuals were left to compete and the fittest individuals survived while others perished.

In *Darwinism and Politics* Ritchie showed how, in the case of human evolution, the struggle was not between individuals but between social units, and that the crucial level of selection was not of individuals but of institutions and ideas.

The permanent task of the reformer was criticism of the customs, laws and institutions of society, checking that they were continually revised to be the best fitted to promote the well-being of the whole community. Everyone should be ensured a fair start in life, releasing them from the necessity of perpetual struggle for the mere conditions of life, so that they had the freedom to work according to their capacity and develop their potential. (Ritchie was particularly concerned with improving the position of women.) Thus the reformer reflected on what conduced to the well-being of society and pre-empted natural selection by deliberate state action, thereby avoiding much waste and suffering for individuals. In other words, the idea of evolution through natural selection and the survival of the fittest, far from supporting the political dogma of laissez-faire (q.v.), drove one to endorse a policy of increased state action.

These general principles could not predict a priori when and how the state should intervene. In applying them, Ritchie advocated taking the utilitarian (q.v.) approach for practical political purposes. One should ask whether a proposed measure was expedient in the particular case: was the object aimed at good, and would the proposed means attain it at reasonable expense? For instance, compulsory education was justified. Ritchie accepted the legitimacy of some socialist proposals, though he was no doctrinaire socialist and was wary of over-regulation because of the cost in individual freedom (q.v.). Ritchie's utilitarianism, however, had been fundamentally revised in the light of idealist (q.v.) philosophy. Ritchie rejected traditional utilitarianism's hedonism and individualism in favour of idealism's ethics. The individual could realise the best life only in an organised society, so the moral end was the well-being of society as a whole (ultimately, the well-being of mankind). What was understood as 'the best life' and 'well-being' constantly developed or evolved as man progressed; hence Ritchie referred to 'evolutionist utilitarianism'.

At the end of the 1880s, Ritchie judged (with good reason) that the efforts of English Liberals were shifting from the negative work of removing mischievous laws made by an elite in its own interest to the more positive task of employing the power of a government which had become more or less the representative of the general will, for the well-being of the community. His own writings assisted this shift significantly. He used idealist principles to capture evolution and to revise utilitarianism, and then set them to work for a progressive and constructive liberalism.

Key works
- *Darwinism and Politics* (1889, enlarged edition 1891)
- *The Principles of State Interference: Four Essays on the Political Philosophy of Mr. Herbert Spencer, J. S. Mill, and T. H. Green* (1891)
- *Darwin and Hegel with Other Philosophical Studies* (1893)
- *Natural Rights: A Criticism of Some Political and Ethical Conceptions* (1894)

Further reading
- David Boucher and Andrew Vincent, *British Idealism and Political Theory* (Edinburgh University Press, 2000), ch. 4
- Robert Latta, 'Memoir: Biographical and Philosophical', in David G. Ritchie, *Philosophical Studies: Edited, with a Memoir, by Robert Latta* (Macmillan, 1905)
- Sandra M. den Otter, *British Idealism and Social Explanation: A Study in Late Victorian Thought* (Clarendon Press, 1996)

Peter Nicholson

J. M. Robertson   1856–1933

A polymath and a prolific writer who made original contributions in political ideas, free thought, sociology, economics, philosophy and literary criticism. A leader of the secularist movement and a prominent Liberal politician, Robertson is a key figure of the radical rationalist tradition in liberal thought.

Key ideas

- Militant atheist rationalism.
- New Liberalism based on the utilitarian ethical principle of reciprocity.
- The advance of understanding and reason as the cause of progress.
- Anti-militarism.
- Free trade as an ethical as well as an economic imperative.
- Excessive saving leads to under-consumption in an economy.

Biography

John Mackinnon Robertson was born on 14 November 1856 on the Isle of Arran and left school at the age of thirteen to become a clerk and later a journalist.

In 1878 he joined Charles Bradlaugh's (q.v.) secularist movement in Edinburgh and later London where, as a protégé of Annie Besant, he mixed in literary and scientific circles and competed with George Bernard Shaw for Besant's attention. Many of Robertson's ideas first appeared in Besant's magazine, *Our Corner*, and in Bradlaugh's weekly political review, the *National Reformer*, which he edited 1891–93. By the mid-1880s, Robertson was seen as Bradlaugh's natural heir, but he broke with the movement in 1893 after G. W. Foote succeeded Bradlaugh as president.

Robertson was a lecturer for many years at the freethinking South Place Ethical Society; he was feared as a relentless and combative debater and polemicist. Though close to Besant and Shaw, he never became active in the Fabian Society, rejecting the Fabians' 'unquestioning certainty of superiority of judgment'. He was more involved with the Rainbow Circle of New Liberals (q.v.) and socialists.

In 1903 he lost a libel case against the *Leeds and Yorkshire Mercury*, which had attacked him for writing on 'matters unmentionable in polite society' (a reference to his advocacy of birth control). This aggravated his chronic, life-long financial difficulties.

He stood for Parliament, unsuccessfully, for Bradlaugh's old seat of Northampton, as an independent Radical Liberal in 1895. He was Liberal MP for Tyneside from 1906–18 and candidate for Hendon in 1923. He was Parliamentary Secretary to the Board of Trade 1911–15, and a Privy Councillor. Not a natural party politician, Robertson was nevertheless regarded as a devastatingly forensic debater. He was chairman of the Liberal Publications Department from 1915 to 1927, president of the National Liberal Federation in 1920 and 1921–23 and vice-president of the Liberal Council in 1927.

He married Maud Mosler, an American, in 1893, and was the father of two children. He died on 5 January 1933.

Ideas

Many of Robertson's ideas were typical of the advanced progressive of his day. He favoured birth control, female suffrage and educational equality, and opposed censorship, jingoism and imperialism, the Boer War and armaments expenditure. He advocated an alliance of progressive forces around an ethically-based liberal programme with a marked egalitarian flavour, including direct taxation, public works and the gradual increase of state ownership of transport, power and land. Such ideas are set out in his *The Meaning of Liberalism* (1912), which derives a New Liberal programme based on the strictly utilitarian (q.v.) 'universal moral law of reciprocity' ('doing as you would be done by'). For Robertson:

> The permanent vindication of Liberalism as against Conservatism must lie in the profession of general standards and ideals which are founded on an inclusive as against an exclusive bias, or rooted in a general sympathy and not in antipathy, in aspiration and not in ill-will. Liberal movement or impulse starts in a simple desire for 'better life' for those who lack it.

Robertson shared many ideas on social welfare and the economic inefficiency of competitive capitalism with his socialist contemporaries, and sometimes described himself as a socialist. He argued that 'the justification of laissez-faire (q.v.) disappears before a system of State interference, which is democratically motivated and scientifically planned with an eye not to the enrichment of classes but to the well-being of the entire community.' But he opposed state monopoly and revolution. Socialists under-estimated the resistance to change in society and the need for painstaking reform in order to approach what Robertson regarded as a distant socialist utopia. His approach was gradualist, pluralist and voluntarist. He rejected class antagonism as 'an insane conception of social progress' and dismissed 'the Marx-Engels doctrine [as] both philosophically and politically unintelligent', because of its 'failure to understand that history is a process of choices, of reciprocal adjustments'.

Robertson's ideas on international relations were Cobdenite (q.v.). He supported arbitration of disputes according to international law and campaigned for these ideas as president of the Rationalist Peace Society (1910–21). Despite his generally anti-militarist views, he supported the First World War as essential to combat German militarism. He advocated a cautious and steady devolution of power within the British Empire to self-governing dominions.

In *The Fallacy of Saving* (1892) he attacked the orthodoxy that saving is always beneficial, arguing that it could depress demand in an economy. He advocated old age pensions as a means to boost consumption. His book anticipated Keynes (q.v.) by four decades, and pre-dated the similar and better-known work of J. A. Hobson (q.v.).

In the 1920s Robertson was a fierce critic of Lloyd George (q.v.), partly because of the latter's wavering on free trade (q.v.), which for Robertson was an article of faith as the expression of the principle of reciprocity in international economic relations. His *Decadence* (1929) is a futuristic portrait of Britain's decline as a result of its abandonment of free trade and liberalism.

Robertson was a historian-sociologist in the tradition of Enlightenment thinkers such as Hume (q.v.), Adam Smith (q.v.) and Turgot who traced the conditions causing progress or regression. He rejected Spencer's (q.v.) view that progress was evolutionary and the inevitable result of laissez-faire, as well as Marx's focus on economic relations as the motive force. He was strongly influenced by Henry Buckle's *Introduction to the History of Civilisation in England* (1857–61), setting out his analysis mainly in *Buckle and His Critics* (1895) and *The Evolution of States* (1912). Robertson saw the causes of progress as intellectual, that economic and ethical advances were a consequence of improved knowledge and reason, with social class and power-political factors helping or hindering development trends. Some consider Robertson's sociology and theory of progress as comparable to that of Max Weber (q.v.) and other pioneers.

Robertson wrote over a hundred books, including at least thirty substantial and original works in many fields. His encyclopaedic histories of free thought remain unsurpassed. He was the foremost advocate in his day of the view that the Jesus of the Gospels never existed, presenting his arguments in several books. He was also wrote extensively on Shakespeare, Walt Whitman and other literary figures.

Key works

- *The Fallacy of Saving* (1892)
- *Buckle and His Critics: A Study in Sociology* (1895)
- *Christianity and Mythology* (1900)
- *Pagan Christs* (1903)
- *The Meaning of Liberalism* (1912; 2nd edn. 1925)
- *The Evolution of States* (1912)
- *History of Freethought, Ancient and Modern* (2 vols, 1915; definitive 4th edn.1936)
- *Mr Lloyd George and Liberalism* (1923)
- *The Decadence: An Excerpt from 'A History of the Triumph and the Decay of England'* (dateable 1949, as 'L. Macauley', 1929)

Further reading

- Odin Dekkers, *J. M. Robertson: Rationalist and Literary Critic* (Ashgate, 1998)
- G. A. Wells, *J. M. Robertson (1856–1933): Liberal, Rationalist, and Scholar* (Pemberton, 1987)

Jaime Reynolds

Rowntree Trust see Joseph Rowntree Reform Trust Limited

Rule of Law

The rule of law is a key principle of a liberal political order, protecting individuals and minorities from oppression in the name of democracy. Nevertheless, its meaning and interpretation have changed significantly over time.

In England, the legal and political roots of the aspect of the rule of law that requires that government action be justified by law go back to Magna Carta (1215), with its promise that no man should be punished except by the judgement of his peers or the law of the land and that to none should justice be denied. The intellectual roots of a broader concept of the rule of law lie in liberal political philosophy at it was expounded in the late seventeenth and the eighteenth centuries, with its emphasis on the rights of individuals, as opposed to communities, and on the principle of equality (q.v.). Both rights and equality were to be protected by law, including an independent judiciary, rather than by political processes. The rule of law has become a key principle in a liberal political order, protecting individuals and minorities from oppression in the name of democracy.

It is, however, difficult to be precise about the meaning of the phrase 'the rule of law': the theory has developed substantially since the classical liberal (q.v.) or Whig (q.v.) exposition of the rule of law by A. V. Dicey (q.v.) in his *Introduction to the Study of the Law of the Constitution* (1885). According to Dicey the twin pillars of the British constitution were the principle of the legislative sovereignty of Parliament, and the rule of law. The latter consisted of three elements: an absence of wide discretion or arbitrary power in the hands of persons in authority; the equal subjection of all, including public officials, before the law; and that the British constitution was the result of decisions taken by the ordinary courts, in effect of the common law rather than of a constitutional code or Acts of Parliament. There was a fundamental contradiction in Dicey's acceptance of the sovereignty of Parliament alongside the rule of law, since Parliament itself has wide discretion and arbitrary power, and yet Dicey made no criticism of it for that.

Robson in *Justice and Administrative Law* (1928) criticised Dicey's exposition for overlooking the fact that many public officials had special statutory coercive powers, for the abuse of which no court could give a remedy. Jennings in *The Law and the Constitution* (1933) drew attention to the fact that Dicey's hostility to discretionary power amounted to a preference for a minimalist state as against a socialist state. Dicey's was a liberal, in the sense of laissez-faire (q.v.), and an anti-socialist position. A state that takes on responsibilities for matters such as town and country planning and the provision of welfare and public services requires discretion. It would be impossible and undesirable to reduce decisions on such matters to the application of rules that do not include elements of discretion. Rule-of-law theory has developed in response to criticisms of this kind so as to acknowledge that official discretionary power may be desirable but that it needs to be appropriately controlled.

Dicey's theories of the rule of law coupled with the legislative supremacy of Parliament were subject to further criticism in the second half of the twentieth century and the aftermath of the Second World War for being highly formal and positivist, not concerned with the content or quality of the law, and mutually contradictory. Seen from this post-war perspective, Dicey's theory was not essentially liberal. The point illustrates the ambiguity of the term 'liberal' when applied to the rule of law. It would appear to be entirely consistent with Dicey's theory of parliamentary sovereignty for a Parliament to require by statute that all Jews or black people be imprisoned or discriminated against by officials for their race or their colour. Since it was passed by Parliament such a provision would be the

supreme and therefore valid law; it would allow for no official discretion; and there need be no right of access to a court to complain of the fairness, as opposed to the validity, of the law. To that extent it would be consistent with Dicey's rule-of-law theory and parliamentary sovereignty.

Liberal thinking about the rule of law in academic and judicial legal circles in England then moved on in stages to its current more social liberal (q.v.), substantive and human-rights-based approach. These features began to emerge in case law as the English courts developed the common law of judicial review in the post-war period, and particularly from the 1960s. The case law required that, for instance, discretionary powers that affected the interests of individuals or companies should be exercised by those in authority in a procedurally fair way, for the purposes for which they were assumed to have been granted by Parliament and not for ulterior purposes, in good faith, and not irrationally. These grounds were summarised as principles of procedural propriety, legality, and rationality (q.v.) in the leading case of *Council of Civil Service Unions v. Minister for the Civil Service* [1985] AC 374.

These elements of the grounds for judicial review reflected liberal traditions of respect for individuals and suspicion of state power – in which respect the British constitutional tradition differs radically from the French tradition, where the state is revered and there are relatively clear understandings of its role.

Since about the 1990s the courts and some judges (in extra-judicial lectures) have become active in developing rule-of-law theory, previously the special interest of academic lawyers. Theories about the rule of law have moved on to embrace the idea – essentially again a liberal idea, though not necessarily involving a laissez-faire approach to commercial activity – that the rule of law entails respect for the rights of individuals. This shift was influenced by the development of international human rights protections, such as the International Covenant on Civil and Political Rights and the European Convention on Human Rights, which were accepted by the British government. To that extent there is an internationalist influence in theorising about the rule of law. The principal provisions of the European Convention were incorporated into UK law by the Human Rights Act 1998. Importantly, that Act preserved the sovereignty of Parliament: courts may not refuse to give effect to a statutory provision that is incompatible with a Convention right.

The courts have further developed judicial review and the rule of law so as to enumerate what they call common-law constitutional or fundamental principles or rights of a broadly liberal kind, many of them mirroring rights in the European Convention on Human Rights. In doing so the courts have explicitly tied them to theories of democracy, human rights and the rule of law. Law Lord Lord Steyn has stated, for instance, that the UK Parliament 'does not legislate in a vacuum ... Parliament legislates for a European liberal democracy based upon the principles and traditions of the common law ... unless there is the clearest provision to the contrary, Parliament must be presumed not to legislate contrary to the rule of law'. Hence principles of statutory interpretation have been developed by the courts to protect the rule of law. In 2005 the Appellate Committee of the House of Lords based a decision that evidence derived from torture should not be admissible in court on principles of the common law that were developed as long ago as the early fifteenth century. Thus adjectival law – the law of evidence – may

also be called in aid in support of the rule of law. The courts regard freedom of speech as fundamental in a democracy, as part of the rule of law, and the rule of law embraces the idea that miscarriages of justice should be rooted out, if necessary by facilitating the activities of investigative journalists.

In a case in 2002 on whether goods could be sold in (English) imperial measures rather than in (European) metric measures, as required by European law, Lord Justice Laws started to bridge the inconsistency gap between Dicey's principle of parliamentary sovereignty and the rule of law. He expounded a distinction between constitutional statutes and other statutes, holding that the European Communities Act 1972 (which incorporated European law into British domestic law) was a constitutional statute. Contrary to the orthodox view of parliamentary sovereignty, that a later statute impliedly repeals provisions in an earlier one to the extent that they are incompatible, a constitutional statute could only be repealed by express provision making clear that it was Parliament's intention to repeal it. Thus the ease with which a majority in Parliament may change the law in ways that undermine constitutional principles is being reduced. A liberal approach prevails over a majoritarian or 'democratic' one here. Importantly the judge held that this position was required by the common law (i.e. not by European law) thus claiming an English pedigree for the rule and the imposition of conditions on the exercise of legislative power by Parliament where important constitutional principles are at stake.

The Constitutional Reform Act 2005 (which abolishes the role of the Lord Chancellor as head of the judiciary, establishes a new Supreme Court and provides for a Judicial Appointments Commission) purports not to 'adversely affect ... the existing constitutional principle of the rule of law' and preserves the Lord Chancellor's 'existing constitutional role in relation to that principle'. This is probably the only mention of the rule of law on the British statute book, but it does not elaborate on the meaning of the concept. The Act also requires the Lord Chancellor and ministers to uphold the continued independence of the judiciary, independence being an essential feature of the rule of law. However, there is no legal mechanism for enforcement of these provisions, which will have their effect, if any, mainly in the political sphere. These provisions were inserted by agreement with the Lord Chief Justice for England and Wales, and reflect concerns among the judiciary that the central constitutional importance of the rule of law and the independence of the judiciary might not be recognised in Cabinet in the absence of a high-status champion such as, by convention and tradition, the Lord Chancellor had been.

In summary, theories of the rule of law have developed substantially in England since Dicey's seminal exposition in 1885. Developments have been expounded by academic lawyers and, increasingly, by judges. They reflect the establishment of and changes in the welfare state and the workings of the economy. They reflect in many ways changing political, social and economic liberal (q.v.) theory and the pressures to which it has been subjected. The rule of law as understood in England has not, however, been an internationalist theory.

Further reading
- Lord Bingham, 'The Rule of Law' (Sir David Williams Lecture, 2006, to be published in the *Cambridge Law Journal*, 2007)
- P. P. Craig, 'Formal and Substantive Conceptions of the Rule of Law: An Analytical Framework', *Public Law* 467 (1997)

- A. V. Dicey, *Introduction to the Study of the Law of the Constitution, 1885* (10th edn., ed. E. C. S. Wade, Macmillan, 1961)
- J. L. Jowell, 'The Rule of Law Today', in J. Jowell and D. Oliver (eds.), *The Changing Constitution*, (6th edn., Oxford University Press, 2007)
- T. R. S. Allan Law, *Liberty and Justice: The Legal Foundations of British Constitutionalism* (Clarendon Press, 1993)
- B. Z. Tamanaha, *On the Rule of Law: History, Politics and Theory* (Cambridge University Press, 2004)

Dawn Oliver

Conrad Russell   1937–2004

Academic and Liberal Democrat peer who helped to define and assert the Liberal Democrats' philosophical and historical roots after the merger of the Liberal Party and SDP.

Key ideas
- Liberalism as a philosophy is primarily concerned with the use and dispersal of power.
- Defence of rights of the individual, particularly those who do not fit neatly into government-prescribed categories.

Biography
Conrad Sebastian Robert Russell was born on 15 April 1937, the son of the philosopher Bertrand Russell and the great-grandson of the Liberal Prime Minister Lord John Russell (q.v.). Educated at Eton and Oxford, he pursued an academic career of some distinction at three colleges of London University (Bedford, University and King's), interspersed with five years at Yale; from 1990 to 2003 he was Professor of History at King's. He wrote particularly on the struggle between Parliament and the monarchy in the sixteenth and seventeenth centuries, his

most influential work being *The Fall of the British Monarchies 1637–1642* (1991). A leading revisionist on the English Civil War, he aimed to refute the conventional view that the clash was the outcome of long-term constitutional conflicts between King and Parliament, arguing instead that it had more to do with immediate causes, mainly the English attitude to Charles I's attempt to enforce observance of the Prayer Book in Scotland and the ensuing revolt.

In 1987, he became the fifth Earl Russell, succeeding his half-brother, and began his unlikely progress towards the status of radical hero to his own party. The mixture of freedom fighter, modern politician and traditionally schooled intellectual was unusual and potent. He had a careful, precise way of speaking, using humour and soundbite to great effect to help him deliver immensely popular speeches, at party conference and in the House of Lords alike. He fully exploited his persona of eccentric academic, and used the past as a window on the present and the future, peppering his speeches with historical allegories, many drawn from the seventeenth century.

Russell took up a wide range of causes, including, most notably, constitutional affairs, education, social security, refugees and asylum. He consistently attacked government's assumption that it knows best what is good for the citizen – as he put it, the belief 'that the state's judgment takes priority over that of the people concerned'. He was particularly critical of official attitudes towards those who did not fit easily into the stereotypes promulgated by government bureaucracies. He was also active in drawing attention to seemingly unimportant secondary legislation; his efforts led directly to the establishment of the House of Lords Delegated Powers Scrutiny Committee and the Merits of Statutory Instruments Committee.

It was no surprise that when the Labour government abolished the rights of hereditary peers to vote in 1999 he was elected as one of the ninety-two who survived the cull. He played an active part in Liberal Democrat policy-making, was a frequent speaker in conference debates and fringe meetings, and wrote a popular column for the party newspaper. He enjoyed associating himself with the more radical and anti-establishment elements of the party.

In 1962, he married Elizabeth Sanders, one of his students, and they had two sons. His life-long addiction to cigarettes finally caught up with him, and he died of complications from emphysema on 14 October 2004.

Ideas

Russell's political speeches and writings were informed by a deep and scholarly understanding of British politics. His main political work, *An Intelligent Person's Guide to Liberalism,* is a typical Russell product, a concise and beautifully written text. In it he argued that modern liberalism was the inheritor of a long and continuous tradition, concerned primarily with the use of power. He traced this back to seventeenth-century conflicts over church power, and to Whig opposition to Stuart absolutism and to the exercise of hereditary power in the absence of consent. The Glorious Revolution of 1688 committed the Whigs (q.v.) to the 'ascending theory' of power, in which power came up from the people, who conferred it – or not, as the case may be – on government. Liberal achievements in curbing executive power and patronage, including the steady widening of the franchise throughout the nineteenth century, stemmed from this basic approach. The Gladstonian (q.v.) commitment to retrenchment, superficially so different to the following century's New Liberal (q.v.) belief in public spending for social ends, derived in practice from the desire to limit expenditure on the armed forces, police and the diplomatic service, then the main areas of state spending, which primarily benefited the upper classes; it was another means of constraining executive power.

Along with the control of power went its dispersal, which Russell linked to the promotion of diversity – religious, social, geographical and cultural – to form pluralism. Again there were strong historical roots: the Whig rejection of the Tory view of church and state as coterminous, Gladstone's acceptance of the United Kingdom as a country of several nations, and the long-held belief in the autonomy of local government. The liberal commitment to equality (q.v.) derived from this belief in a diverse and tolerant society. Such a society could not exist where individuals were treated differently by the law and by government institutions because of their nature. 'Equality before the law' was one of the great rallying cries of liberalism from the earliest days of the Whigs; 'equal justice', 'non-discrimination' and 'concern for the underdog' were just as valid ways of expressing it.

This concern over the use and dispersal of power provided the principles on which all areas of liberal policy were based. This included international issues, where liberals sought the creation of a strong framework of international law, wherein every country, no matter how small and weak, could enjoy the same rights to equal treatment as its larger and more powerful neighbours. And it applied to economic policy, though since liberalism had such deep roots, going back before the state could exert any significant control over the levers of economic activity, Russell argued that the party did not have an economic philosophy. Economics was important principally because it affected the distribution of power in society and could thereby enlarge, or diminish, the life chances of individuals. Liberals opposed concentrations of economic power as they did of political power, and for the same reasons.

Russell was not a particularly original political thinker, but his writings and speeches were important in helping to assert the Liberal Democrats' historical and philosophical roots in the period after merger. He helped to make the party feel good about itself.

Key works
- *The Crisis of Parliaments: English History 1509–1660* (1971)
- *The Causes of the English Civil War* (1990)
- *The Fall of the British Monarchies 1637–1642* (1991)
- *An Intelligent Person's Guide to Liberalism* (1999)

Further reading
- 'Liberalism and Liberty from Gladstone to Ashdown: Continuous Thread or Winding Stair?' (*Journal of Liberal Democrat History* 20, Autumn 1998)

Duncan Brack

Lord John Russell   1792–1878

The leading Liberal politician from the mid-1830s to the mid-1850s, Russell was twice Prime Minister; he was associated particularly with the issues of parliamentary, educational and Irish reform. He expressed his coherent set of political and religious ideas in a number of works of history and biography as well as in many major speeches.

Key ideas
- Reform of the English constitution so as to maintain the country's libertarian and representative traditions.

- State support for a broad moral and religious education for spiritual and social reasons.
- Religious integration in Britain and Ireland through constitutional pluralism and avoidance of dogmatic narrowness.
- A strong British presence in the world on behalf of liberty.
- Great emphasis on the responsibility of politicians to promote all the above.

Biography

Lord John Russell was born in London into one of the leading Whig (q.v.) families; his father became 6th Duke of Bedford in 1802. Born prematurely, he remained puny through life, and ill-health as a child meant that he was educated mostly by private tutors, including Edmund Cartwright, inventor of the power-loom. He studied at Edinburgh University from 1809 to 1812, and attended lectures by Dugald Stewart and other Enlightenment intellects. He travelled to Spain three times during the national and liberal struggle against Napoleon, which fired his imagination. After the war ended in 1815, he also visited France and Italy frequently, developing a strong interest in European culture.

He became an MP in 1813, initially for the family borough of Tavistock. The Whigs remained in opposition for the next seventeen years, and authorship was his main activity in this period. He wrote a biography of his ancestor Lord William Russell, a novel, a play, an essay on the English constitution and a number of historical surveys. All these breathed the spirit of Foxite Whiggism; Russell kept a statue of Charles James Fox (q.v.) by his writing desk. In Parliament, his mentor was Lord Holland, Fox's nephew and political heir, and Russell quickly became a prominent member of the Foxite wing of the opposition. His most important cause during these years was that of parliamentary reform, and when the Whigs came to power in 1830 he was selected as a member of the Committee of Four to prepare their Reform Bill, and introduced it. He was promoted to Cabinet during the Reform Bill struggles in 1831.

Russell's initiative of 1834 in favour of the principle of state appropriation of the surplus revenues of the Anglican Church of Ireland was one of the factors precipitating the political crisis of 1834–35. This saw the Whigs briefly thrown out of office, only to return in 1835 with Lord Melbourne as Prime Minister and Lord John as Leader of the House of Commons. He held this post for the next six years, with great distinction, and became the leading figure in the party. As Home Secretary he supervised key reforms of the criminal law, policing and prisons, and was responsible for the educational legislation of 1839. Then as Colonial Secretary between 1839 and 1841 he helped to settle Canada after the 1837 rebellion.

When the Whigs returned to power after the Corn Law crisis of 1846, he was the obvious choice as Prime Minister. His government extended state support for education and passed important public health and factory reform measures. But it soon became politically beleaguered, because of its lack of a majority, the fragmentation of the two-party system, and the severe tensions thrown up by the Irish famine and then by the economic and social turbulence of 1847–49 at home and abroad. After 1848, Russell always struggled to assert his authority, and was damaged particularly by his alienation of Irish MPs after his criticism of the Pope in 1850, and by his unpopular dismissal of the buccaneering Palmerston from the Foreign Office in late 1851. After his government fell in 1852, Russell had to play second fiddle to Palmerston in Liberal politics until the latter's death in 1865, when he returned as Prime Minister. During those years he was associated, like Palmerston, with an assertively liberal foreign policy (over the Eastern and then the Italian questions) and, unlike him, with the cause of parliamentary reform. His first major act as Prime Minister was to propose a substantial Reform Bill in 1866, but this was defeated by Liberal dissidents, and Russell resigned, never to hold office again.

Having sat for the City of London since 1841, he accepted a peerage as Earl Russell in 1861. He died on 28 May 1878.

Ideas

As a professional politician, Russell had to express opinions on a vast range of issues, during a career that spanned almost sixty years. A short article can only indicate the flavour of some of his most distinctive and significant attitudes. Essentially he was a Foxite Whig who updated Fox's attitudes to make them more relevant to the second quarter of the nineteenth century, and added to them a strong sense of Christian responsibility.

On the constitution, Russell was an unwavering admirer of the men of the seventeenth century, including his ancestors, who had fought successfully to secure civil liberties from the potential oppression of an over-mighty crown. On the one hand, therefore, he continued to believe that there was a greater threat to liberty from the abuse of power than from mass uprisings, since he tended to think that if men of property remained active, visible and public-spirited political leaders they would generally command popular loyalty. His main fear was of executive misgovernment and of decadent, selfish, irresponsible aristocrats – whom he blamed for the French Revolution. Like all Whigs, he was suspicious of George III and Pitt's apparent revival of royal power in the late eighteenth century. On the other hand, he was a great patriot, confident that

since 1688 the British political system had been much purer and more libertarian (q.v.) than that of the continental powers and that relatively minor changes to the constitution would be enough to maintain the legitimacy of the regime.

In fact by the late 1820s there seemed less danger from government abuse of power than from its weakness in the face of rapid social change. Like many Whigs of his generation, Russell saw the need for a bold and systematic social policy to tackle the problems of population growth and urbanisation, and argued that one great merit of parliamentary reform would be to bolster public confidence in government's legitimate authority. He believed that the 1832 Reform Act would force ministers and local leaders to be more active and accountable, and would facilitate a more legislative style of party politics, in tune with his strand of Whiggism. Similarly, his main reason for advocating further reform in the 1850s and 1860s was to revitalise a sluggish House of Commons, particularly on Irish and educational questions, and to revive party spirit on the Liberal benches – again to the benefit of politicians like himself, rather than his rival Palmerston.

Russell's long-term commitment to education legislation was the best example of his active approach to social issues. Deeply affected by the French Revolution, he rejected a merely utilitarian (q.v.) idea of the state, asserting instead that government was a divinely ordained agency for the promotion of a common humanity; it had a duty to build a nation of people deriving their strength, conduct and loyalty from enlightened religious and moral principles. His anxiety that the state should promote, subsidise and regulate schooling in order to attack vice and sensuality, which bore fruit in the legislation of 1839 and 1847 and further initiatives in the 1850s and 1860s, was originally encouraged by his anxiety about Chartism and his hostility to the attempt by High Church Anglicans to dominate education through the National Society.

As the last point suggests, one of Russell's strongest antagonisms was to narrow clericalism. He had a simple faith himself, based on the precepts of full-hearted love of God and the human race. He distrusted religious dogmas, which he saw as man-made inventions which created division and conflict for the benefit of sectarian institutions and power-hungry egos. He was committed to a pluralist politics in which Dissenters, Catholics and Jews had full political rights, and in which the state exerted itself to check assertions of ecclesiastical power which threatened to endanger stability and mutual tolerance.

These approaches dictated his approach to the Irish problem. He supported the Union because he believed that only the British state could be sufficiently powerful, progressive and disinterested to impose a fair and workable settlement of the denominational and class tensions in Ireland. He wanted to clip the wings of the Protestant ascendancy landlords, by a more equitable distribution of political patronage than the Tories had delivered, and by land reform. Not only would Catholic emancipation and high-profile appointments to political and judicial office signal a new partnership between the state and lay Catholics, but Russell also wanted a government compact with the leading Catholic, as well as Protestant, clergy. This would involve financial support for each sect ('concurrent endowment'), replacing the existing Anglican Church Establishment. He hoped that, between them, these lay and clerical strategies would convince leading Catholics of the benefits of Union and would check the influence of political agitators and partisan local priests. The first was pursued

successfully in 1835–41, but the second failed, along with Russell's land reform hopes, in the chaotic social and political circumstances of the late 1840s. His criticism of papal interference in Britain in 1850 reflected his frustration at the failure of his plans for an ecclesiastical partnership of this sort, and the growth of Ultramontane attitudes among the Catholic bishops instead.

Russell's pride in British liberal constitutional traditions and his ancestral Whiggism convinced him that political leaders had a duty to promote Britain's libertarian values abroad. This, he felt, was the way to uphold national and personal honour, which were both important concepts for him. So foreign slights to Britain's global standing could not be tolerated. When Russia seemed to ignore British attempts to settle the Eastern question in the summer of 1853, he declaimed that 'if peace cannot be maintained with honour, it is no longer peace'. The difficulty for Whig foreign policy was how to square Fox's principle of 'the cause of civil and religious liberty all over the world' with the maintenance of peace and low taxes. Most Whigs had been uneasy about the wars against America and Revolutionary France, because they had involved much bloodshed and, by expanding bureaucracy and jobbery, had strengthened Tory power and massively increased the national debt, impoverishing taxpayers. The cry of military non-interference in the domestic affairs of other countries therefore became a staple of progressive politics after 1815. However, in parts of the world where Britain could support the cause of liberty and self-government against foreign oppression, a strong case for action could be made. Hence Russell's youthful enthusiasm for the Spanish insurgency against Napoleon, and his later passionate support for Italian constitutionalism. He was also vigorously committed to the maintenance

of a more or less self-governing white settler empire, seeing it as a symbol of Britain's
global power and political liberalism.

The common threads in Russell's
political philosophy were his Whiggish
constitutionalism and his sense of Christian responsibility. In 1850 he defended the
expense of a naval squadron stationed off
the African coast to try to stop the slave
trade, on the grounds that its abolition
would betray Britain's 'high ... moral, and
... Christian character', forfeiting any right
she might have to expect the continuation
of the divine blessing that had allowed her
to escape revolution in 1848. His religious
principles explain much of his pressure for
a more active role for the state in social and
Irish affairs; his was not a laissez-faire (q.v.)
liberalism. Though he supported low taxes
on grounds of constitutional accountability,
he was not a keen political economist. Often
earnest and aloof, sometimes dogmatic and
naïve, Russell made many political mistakes;
but his lineage, principles and moralism
nonetheless ensured that most of the more
zealous Liberal MPs of the day never ceased
to regard him as their natural leader.

Key works
- *Essay on the History of the English Government and Constitution* (1821)
- *Selections from Speeches, 1817–1841* (2 vols,
  1870)
- *Essays on the Rise and Progress of the Christian Religion* (1873)
- *Recollections and Suggestions, 1813–1873*
  (1875)

Further reading
- Richard Brent, *Liberal Anglican Politics:
  Whiggery, Religion and Reform 1830–1841*
  (Oxford University Press, 1987)
- Jonathan Parry, 'Past and Future in the
  Later Career of Lord John Russell', in
  T. C. W. Blanning & D. Cannadine

(eds.), *History and Biography: Essays in
Honour of Derek Beales* (Cambridge University Press, 1996)
- Jonathan Parry, 'Lord John Russell and
  the Irish Catholics, 1829–1852', *Journal
  of Liberal Democrat History* 33 (Winter
  2001–02)
- Jonathan Parry, *The Politics of Patriotism:
  English Liberalism, National Identity and
  Europe, 1830–1886* (Cambridge University Press, 2006)
- John Prest, *Lord John Russell* (Macmillan,
  1972)

Jonathan Parry

Herbert Samuel   1870–1963

One of the most prominent Liberal politicians of the twentieth century, Samuel's long
political career spanned both the high and
low points of the Liberal Party's electoral fortunes. During the late Victorian and Edwardian period, he sought to reinterpret liberalism
in a way that advocated a greater role for the
state in eradicating poverty through measures
of social reform.

Key ideas
- Duty of the state to use its powers to
  ensure all citizens have 'the fullest
  opportunity to lead the best life'.
- Liberal reform as superior to utopian
  socialism in achieving progressive social
  objectives.
- Economic regeneration of rural areas in
  the face of increased urbanisation.
- Civilising role of empire and its capacity
  to generate wealth for domestic social
  reform.

Biography
Herbert Samuel Samuel was born on 6
November 1870 into a wealthy Jewish
banking family. His father's death when

he was six years old provided him with an inheritance that freed him of the need to earn a living for the rest of his life. He was educated at University College School, London, and Balliol College, Oxford, where he took a first in modern history.

His experience of campaigning for his brother Stuart in the 1889 London County Council elections made a great impact on him and led to a concern to tackle urban poverty and squalor. He stood unsuccessfully for Parliament in 1895 and 1900 as Liberal candidate for South Oxfordshire, which gave him a particular interest in the problems of rural depopulation and economic stagnation. He was a member of the Fabian Society, and was influenced by Sidney and Beatrice Webb, who were at this time seeking to encourage the left wing of the Liberal Party in a collectivist direction, and an active participant in the Rainbow Circle, a group of social reformers who included the economist J. A. Hobson (q.v.) and Ramsay MacDonald. In 1902 he entered Parliament for the northern industrial constituency of Cleveland at a by-election.

Samuel held ministerial office under both Campbell-Bannerman and Asquith. As junior minister at the Home Office he was responsible for the 1908 Children Act, which formed the basis for much future child protection legislation. He achieved Cabinet rank in 1910 as Postmaster-General, and served as Home Secretary for a few months during the Great War; he left office when the Asquith coalition fell in December 1916. He had become a supporter of Zionism during the war and in 1920 he was appointed High Commissioner of British-mandated Palestine, the first Jewish ruler of the territory since biblical times. In his five years in office he helped lay the foundations of the Jewish national home.

Samuel returned to the House of Commons in 1929, serving as de facto deputy to Lloyd George (q.v.), the Liberal leader. In 1931 he became leader of the party, and held office again as Home Secretary in Ramsay MacDonald's National Government. When the government introduced protectionist measures in 1932 he attempted to keep the Liberal Party in the government, despite its commitment to free trade (q.v.), through an 'agreement to differ', which relaxed Cabinet collective responsibility. However, his position became untenable and he and his Liberal colleagues resigned in September. This formalised a split in the party, as some Liberal ministers remained within the government as 'Liberal Nationals' (q.v.).

As leader Samuel presided over a decline in party fortunes, and he lost his seat at the 1935 general election. He continued to be active in Liberal politics, was ennobled, as Viscount Samuel, in 1937, and served as party leader in the House of Lords from 1944 to 1955. In 1951 he became the first politician to deliver a televised party political broadcast. He died on 5 February 1963, living just long enough to see Eric Lubbock, victor of the Orpington by-election, take his seat in the House of Commons.

Ideas

Samuel's most significant contribution to Liberal political thought was his 1902 book, *Liberalism: An Attempt to State the Principles and Proposals of Contemporary Liberalism in England*. Rather than a philosophical tract or personal manifesto, the book is a summary of the reforms that might be expected from a future Liberal government. Writing at a time when there was considerable division within the party, Samuel tried to avoid offending the rival factions. As a result, while *Liberalism* is an effective summary of Liberal thinking on the policy issues of the day, its key weakness is that it puts party unity above a clear statement of the author's own views. Nonetheless, it is one of the key texts of New Liberal (q.v.) thought, outlining the way the party was revising its view of the state in society.

To Samuel, liberty meant not only that the state should not impose restrictive laws, but also that it should actively intervene in order to ensure that freedom (q.v.) was a practical reality for all citizens. This meant that apparently coercive legislation, particularly concerning industry and employment, which appeared to restrict liberty, in fact enhanced it. He argued that poverty was not simply the result of idleness, but of wider economic conditions. He advocated a number of measures to alleviate unemployment, including state-sponsored forestry schemes and public improvements carried out by local authorities. However, Samuel was enough of a traditional liberal to oppose the abolition of the Poor Law and to continue to support the punitive workhouse regime for those who were genuinely unwilling to work. He was also sceptical about continental-style schemes of compulsory unemployment insurance.

In order to promote the regeneration of rural areas, Samuel advocated state-sponsored growth in the system of smallholdings and reform of tenancy laws to give tenants compensation for improvements they carried out. He rejected socialist ideas of land nationalisation, on the grounds that it would mean unjust confiscation and would be unlikely to produce economic advantages for the rural poor.

In his treatment of empire, an issue that had led to serious divisions among Liberals, Samuel tried to please both sides. His own views, as outlined in papers to the Rainbow Circle, were in favour of empire, both as part of an international civilising mission and as a way of generating wealth to fund measures of social reform at home. In *Liberalism*, he balanced a chapter stating the arguments for empire with another that set out the arguments against. Likewise he appeared ambivalent in his attitude towards Irish home rule.

Liberalism received a mixed reception from reviewers and did not sell particularly well. It was praised by the mainstream Liberal press but was attacked by left-wing Liberals and socialists, in particular for its imperial enthusiasm. It remains a useful survey of the issues that would confront the Liberal governments of 1905–15 and the way in which the party should approach them.

Samuel wrote relatively little during his years as an active politician. However, after 1935 he published several works of philosophy. Although he was not taken particularly seriously by professional and academic philosophers, his *Belief and Action* (1937), an attempt to introduce philosophy to a popular audience, sold nearly 100,000 copies. Other works included a utopian novel, *An Unknown Land* (1952), and *An Essay in Physics* (1951), which included a postscript by Albert Einstein. He took an empiricist approach to knowledge and attempted in his work to produce a synthesis between politics, philosophy and religion.

Key works

- *Liberalism: An Attempt to State the Principles and Proposals of Contemporary Liberalism in England* (G. Richards, 1902)
- *Memoirs* (The Cresset Press, 1945)

Further reading

- Bernard Wasserstein, *Herbert Samuel: A Political Life* (Oxford University Press, 1992)

Iain Sharpe

E. F. Schumacher 1911–77

An internationally renowned economist who worked as chief economic adviser to the

UK's National Coal Board from 1950 to 1970. Although not associated with the Liberal Party, his classic text *Small Is Beautiful* has had a profound impact on liberal ideas on environmental sustainability.

Key ideas

- Environmental sustainability.
- Intermediate technology.

Biography

Born on 16 August 1911 in Bonn, Ernst Friedrich Schumacher studied at Bonn, Berlin, Oxford and Columbia University. Opposed to Nazism, he settled in the UK prior to the Second World War. Although interned as an 'enemy alien' during part of the war, and forced to work on a farm, he continued to write on economics and impressed J. M. Keynes (q.v.), who had him released so that he could help the British war effort.

After the war, Schumacher worked on the reconstruction of Germany as an economic adviser to the British Control Commission, before becoming the chief economic adviser to the British National Coal Board in 1950, a post he held until 1970. During this time he carried out much other work. He wrote regularly in *The Times*, being was one of its main editorial writers, and advised the governments of India, Zambia and Burma. While in Burma, he developed the theory of 'Buddhist economics' which said that individuals needed to be engaged in 'good work' if there was to be proper human development. Working with developing countries more generally in the 1960s, Schumacher developed the idea of intermediate technology and founded the Intermediate Technology Group (now known as Practical Action) in 1966.

In the 1970s, Schumacher's two key works were published: *Small Is Beautiful* (1973) and *A Guide for the Perplexed* (1977). Both made him a key thinker in the growing environmental movement, but further work was cut short when he died on 4 September 1977 while on a lecture tour in Switzerland.

Ideas

Soon before he died, Schumacher told his daughter that *A Guide for the Perplexed* (1977) was 'what my life has been leading to'. This book, influenced by his conversion to Roman Catholicism, was an analysis of the nature of human knowledge and attacked what he called 'materialistic scientism'. In its place, he advanced the idea of there being four levels of being: mineral, plant, animal and human; he was critical of orthodox scientific methods which did not accept these differences. He was particularly critical of the idea of scientific 'truth'.

Yet it is other work by Schumacher that has had the greatest impact on political thinking. Schumacher had a major practical impact on the developing world through his development of the idea of intermediate technology, which would improve the lives of its users while at the same time minimising ecological damage and social disruption. By definition, it would advance developing economies, but not necessarily along the same path as the industrialised world. Intermediate technology recognised that developing societies had different needs and contexts to those of the industrialised world; and it also recognised that development along the route industrialised countries had followed might lead to social and environmental destruction.

Originating in his work in the 1960s, this idea was placed in a broader context in Schumacher's classic collection of essays, *Small Is Beautiful: A Study of Economics as if People Mattered*, in 1973. Published in the aftermath of the first international oil crisis, the book struck a chord with a public increasingly concerned over environmental issues of resource shortages and pollution; in 1995 the *Times Literary Supplement* included it in their list of the hundred most influential books published since the war. Schumacher challenged the approach of orthodox economists who elevated output and technology to primacy. Within that, the principle of sustainability was crucial; natural resources should be considered as capital, in that they are frequently not renewable and will eventually run out. For this reason, he argued that government should prioritise sustainable development and reduce the emphasis on consumption. He said that because 'consumption is merely a means to human well-being, the aim should be to obtain the maximum of well-being with the minimum of consumption'. In securing this, as the title of *Small Is Beautiful* suggests, Schumacher believed that small-scale organisations would be most successful because they would be most in tune with human needs. Although not always acknowledged as coming from Schumacher, these ideas have underpinned liberal approaches to sustainability (see environmentalism) since the 1970s.

Key works
- *Small Is Beautiful: A Study of Economics as if People Mattered* (1973)

Further reading
- Barbara Wood, *E. F. Schumacher: His Life and Thought* (Harper & Row, 1984)

Richard S. Grayson

J. R. Seeley   1834–95

A leading late-Victorian public intellectual, known best for his writings on religion and empire, Seeley was also an important figure in the development of the academic study of history in the United Kingdom.

Key ideas
- Emphasised the value of the Empire, and offered support for imperial federation.
- Stressed the importance of historical understanding in addressing humanity's greatest problems.
- Critical of religious dogma and political partisanship.

Biography
John Robert Seeley was born in London on 10 September 1834 to Robert Benton Seeley, a distinguished evangelical publisher, and Mary Anne Seeley, another keen evangelical. He was educated at the City of London School and Christ's College, Cambridge, where he was elected a fellow after his graduation in 1857. In 1859 he returned to the City of London School as a Latin teacher, before moving to University College London as Professor of Latin in 1863. At UCL he was influenced by the positivism of Auguste Comte, Christian socialism, and in particular the religious thought of the Broad Church movement, which traced its intellectual roots back to Samuel Taylor Coleridge. In 1869, at the request of W. E. Gladstone (q.v.), Seeley took up the Regius Professorship of Modern History at Cambridge, a position he retained until his death.

Seeley first came to wide public attention with the publication (initially anonymous) of his highly controversial *Ecce Homo: A Survey of the Life and Work of Jesus Christ*, in 1865. Over the following two decades he published a variety of other works, the most substantial of which was a three-volume historical study, *The Life and Times of Stein, or Germany and Prussia in the Napoleonic Age* (1878), although none had the same impact. He played a significant role in university administration, helping to establish history as a separate tripos, and pushing for the admission of women to the ancient universities.

His political vision darkened over the course of the 1870s and 1880s, although he always remained a liberal (albeit a Unionist). During the early 1880s he turned his attention to the past, present and future of the British Empire, seeing in its 'vast expanses' part of the solution to many of the problems he identified in domestic politics. Increasingly concerned with the dangers heralded by democracy, disgusted by party-political squabble, and fearful about the rise of international competition, he sought the moral rejuvenation of British society in order to equip it to face an uncertain future. In 1883 he published his lectures on *The Expansion of England*. The book was an instant success, and it helped set the terms for the imperial debates of the late-Victorian and Edwardian years. Seeley was knighted at the instigation of the Liberal Prime Minister Lord Rosebery in 1894, and died on 13 January 1895.

Ideas

Like many of his contemporaries, Seeley wrote on a wide range of topics, spanning literature, history, classics, religion and politics. But it was his religious writings and his views on empire that attracted most attention. *Ecce Homo* sought to apply the methods of critical historical investigation to Christ's 'commonwealth', aiming to explore the meaning and consequences of his role as legislator and judge. The answer lay in a form of ethical universalism, and a general 'enthusiasm for humanity', all underpinned by a positivistic belief in the power of science to dispel superstition and bring the light of reason to bear on the world. The book was not especially radical, but it infuriated many orthodox believers;

Lord Shaftesbury famously proclaimed that it must have been 'vomited from the jaws of hell'. Seeley later reiterated a number of these themes in *Natural Religion* (1882), although he focused more on elaborating a non-dogmatic approach to scripture and stressing the inseparability of religion and the nation-state. This volume comprised his quite distinctive contribution to political theology, developing a Broad Church conception of religion as a form of positive political morality, emphasising the centrality of the state and the necessity of a virtuous national community, and challenging the corrupting influence of egoistic materialism and unencumbered individualism. Seeley's views on the importance of the state in history, and also the role of history in formulating a 'science of politics' and a guide to practical statesmanship, can also be discerned in his posthumously published *Introduction to Political Science* (1896), edited by his friend the philosopher Henry Sidgwick (q.v.).

The Expansion of England, today best known for its sarcastic exclamation about the Empire being created in 'a fit of absence of mind', was a sustained, though frequently ambivalent, analysis of the importance of the Empire in both British historical development and in securing the greatness of Britain. It can be read as applying many of the political-theological insights of *Natural Religion* to the plane of global politics. Moving beyond what he saw as the Whiggish (q.v.) parochialism of his fellow historians, he sought to demonstrate the centrality of imperial expansion in modern British history, highlighting in particular the importance of the eighteenth century; he characterised this period, with its long line of conflicts against France, as a 'second hundred years' war'. But the book had a political purpose also. Reacting against what he (and many others) saw as 'indifference' about the

Empire, he argued that in an age of increasing international competition, the settler colonies of 'Greater Britain' (primarily in Australasia, Canada and South Africa) were vital for British power. Whilst he also argued that the British had a duty to remain in India, it was these colonies that held the key to the future. This argument, not itself original, resonated widely, and secured Seeley a place as the leading intellectual light of the movement for 'imperial federation'. His work remained an inspiration to imperialists over the coming decades, and *The Expansion of England* stayed in print until 1956, the year of Suez.

Key works

- *Ecce Homo: A Survey of the Life and Work of Jesus Christ* (1866)
- *The Life and Times of Stein, or Germany and Prussia in the Napoleonic Age* (1878)
- *Natural Religion* (1882)
- *The Expansion of England: A Course of Lectures* (1883)
- *Introduction to Political Science: Two Series of Lectures*, ed. Henry Sidgwick (1896)

Further reading

- Duncan Bell, *The Idea of Greater Britain: Empire and the Future of Global Order, 1860–1900* (Princeton University Press, 2007)
- John Burrow, Stefan Collini, and Donald Winch, *That Noble Science of Politics: A Study in Nineteenth-Century Intellectual History* (Cambridge University Press, 1983)
- Richard Shannon, 'Sir John Seeley and the Idea of a National Church', in Robert Robson (ed.), *Ideas and Institutions of Victorian Britain* (Bell, 1967)
- Deborah Wormell, *Sir John Seeley and the Uses of History* (Cambridge University Press, 1980)

Duncan Bell

Arthur Seldon   1916–2005

In his role as founder editorial director of the Institute of Economic Affairs, Seldon was probably one of the most influential liberal thinkers and publicists in Britain in the period from the 1950s to the 1970s, although his influence was greater on the Conservative Party than the Liberal Party.

Key ideas

- Application of micro-economic principles to the supply of goods and services by the public sector.
- Importance of establishing and deepening property rights, for example in education and health care.
- Critique of corporatism as the inevitable consequence of government provision of goods and services.

Biography

Arthur Seldon was born Abraham Margolis on 29 May 1916. Both his parents died in the Spanish flu epidemic of 1918 and he was raised by foster-parents, adopting an Anglicised version of their surname. After his foster-father's death in 1927 his foster-mother set up 'shop' in the front room of their East End home selling lisle stockings in order to pay the rent. The family were kept afloat by a £100 payment from a friendly society, paid for by his late foster-father's weekly contributions of two shillings.

After winning a free place at an east London grammar school Seldon went to the London School of Economics and graduated with first-class honours in economics in 1937. At the LSE he studied under many liberal, and Liberal, academics including F. A. Hayek (q.v.), Lionel Robbins, Frank Paish, Arthur Plant and George Schwartz, and on graduation he was appointed research assistant to Plant. It was via Plant's recommendation that Seldon was to work on two important Liberal Party publications, *Ownership for All*, adopted by the 1938 party assembly, and *The Drift to the Corporate State*, published in 1941. These two publications established themes that would run throughout Seldon's work.

Seldon served in the army in north Africa and Italy from 1941 to 1945. After the war he worked as an economist in industry. He and his wife Marjorie (they married in 1948) were active in the Orpington Liberal Association in the 1950s and he seems to have regarded himself as a Liberal throughout the Grimond (q.v.) era. In 1957, he was appointed Editorial director of the fledgling Institute of Economic Affairs (q.v.) on the recommendation of Arthur Plant, a function he held until his retirement in 1981, and then again between 1986 and his second and final retirement in 1988. In his time at the IEA Seldon was commissioning editor of more than 350 monographs and author of twenty-eight books and monographs and 230 articles. His long stint at the IEA gave him ample opportunity to develop the ideas he had first set out in his Liberal Party publications.

He died on 11 October 2005, a few days after receiving the seventh and final volume of his collected works published by Liberty Fund of Indianapolis.

Ideas

Central to Seldon's approach was the application of micro-economic principles to government action. The importance of scarce resources and of establishing relative values of different goods, services and factors of production could not be assumed away simply because a good happened to be provided by government. Rather, Seldon saw economic analysis as essential to ensuring that scarce resources were allocated efficiently. In the absence of market prices, Seldon contended, such an efficient allocation was almost impossible to achieve.

To establish genuine market prices implied the existence of private property rights in goods and services. The creation of private property rights that extended throughout society had been a theme of Seldon's earliest paper for the Liberal Party. *Ownership for All,* the report of a Liberal Party inquiry chaired by Elliott Dodds (q.v.) but drafted by Seldon, attacked the maldistribution of wealth and property in inter-war Britain. The causes of the maldistribution of property were traced to faulty laws and policies, particularly inheritance law, lack of educational opportunity for the poor, encouragement of monopolistic industrial concentration, divorce of ownership from control of companies, and indirect taxation on wage-earners in the form of tariffs, quotas and subsidies. The report rejected statist solutions, such as planning and public ownership, and instead argued for market solutions, greater competition and the extension and permeation of property ownership throughout society.

A similar approach was taken in Seldon's writings on the provision of education and health care. Seldon argued that efficient allocation of resources in these sectors could only come about if private property rights were established that empowered consumers to choose the education and health care they wanted, rather than having politicians choose for them. In education, Seldon proposed vouchers as a means of achieving such property rights; parents would have the right to spend their vouchers at the school of their choice and schools would be forced to compete for customers in the same way as private-sector providers of food or clothing.

A third important theme of Seldon's work was his critique of democratic corporatism. Seldon's 1941 Liberal Party pamphlet, *The Drift to the Corporate State*, had linked wartime economy measures, especially those encouraging monopoly, to the creation of a corporate state in Britain. While conceding the need for some industrial concentration and planning in time of national emergency, Seldon was blunt about the potential dangers it posed: 'It is the corporative system of industrial organisation, which is incompatible with parliamentary democracy; it is the British variant of what in Italy is called Fascism.' Where monopoly was unavoidable ('natural monopolies') he argued that 'public regulation may ... be more suitable ... than public ownership ... [and] there would appear to be no good reason for exclusive public ownership in the public utility field, where a mixed regime of private, public, and semi-public monopolies, all equally subject to regulation by Parliament or a delegated authority, would be superior'. He called for 'State action to "cleanse" industry of its avoidable monopoly; and this will involve a more active State, a State more conscious of the conditions and consequences of monopoly'.

Twenty years later, in a publication for the IEA, Seldon echoed his original critique of corporatism:

> Representative government ... at its worst ... impoverishes and enfeebles the community by capitulation to articulate and persistent sections at the expense of the long-term general interest. Much so-called 'economic policy' can be understood only in terms of pressure from organised producers – in trade associations, trade unions or other groups.

For Seldon, the tyranny of the majority that had so concerned classical liberals (q.v.) like John Stuart Mill (q.v.) and Alexis de Tocqueville (q.v.) had been realised in the ability of organised *minorities* to extract privileges from government at the expense of the unorganised majority. The result of the ability of such groups to capture the political process for their own advantage was not only the unfair transfer of resources via political means (rent-seeking), but distortions of the price system that impoverished society as a whole because it led producers to misallocate capital in response to distorted price signals.

The influence of Arthur Seldon and the IEA was most profound within the Conservative Party, probably because David Steel decided to position the Liberal Party on the Keynesian (q.v.) centre-left following his election to the leadership in 1976, at a time when the Conservatives under Margaret Thatcher were rejecting the postwar consensus and seeking an alternative economic approach – opening them to the IEA's classical liberal prescription. Yet it can nevertheless be argued that Seldon applied classical liberal principles to the political problems of post-war Britain more effectively than any other thinker.

Key works

*   *The Collected Works of Arthur Seldon in Seven Volumes* (Liberty Fund, 2004–05)
    John Meadowcroft and Jaime Reynolds

Jean-Jacques Servan-Schreiber
1924–2006

A leading French liberal politician, journalist and writer, 'JJSS' championed decolonisation, supported feminism and was excited about the possibilities offered by new technologies. While it is today commonplace to warn of the dangers of US-led globalisation and the dominance of American culture, JJSS wrote about these challenges as early as the 1960s. In his heyday, he had the reputation of being a French JFK.

Key ideas

*   Decolonisation.
*   An early appreciation of US, and later Japanese, economic global dominance.

- European union as a response to these trends.
- Decentralisation of political power within France.

Biography

Jean-Jacques Servan-Schreiber, generally known as JJSS, was born in Paris on 13 February 1924, the son of a prosperous publisher. He studied to be an engineer but in 1943, at the age of nineteen, he joined de Gaulle's Free French forces and went to America to train as a pilot. He later served in the French army of occupation in Germany.

After the war he became a foreign affairs correspondent for *Le Monde*, specialising in America and the Cold War. His journalistic support for decolonisation in the French Empire led to political connections and he became a strong adherent of Pierre Mendès-France, leader of the liberal-leaning Parti Radical, who became Prime Minister in 1954–55. In 1953, he co-founded the magazine *L'Express* with his lover, the radical feminist journalist Françoise Giroud (1916–2003) who herself went on to be a government minister. The pair filled its pages with contributions from the leading intellectuals of the 1950s and '60s, such as Camus, Malraux and Sartre.

In 1956, JJSS was conscripted and sent to Algeria. On his return, he published his first book, *Lieutenant en Algérie*, a memoir containing allegations of torture and brutality by the French authorities. In 1958, he unsuccessfully campaigned against the return of de Gaulle to the French presidency but over the next few years his relationship with Mendès-France worsened and he experienced difficulties in his journalistic and personal life. However by 1964 he had married again and had turned *L'Express* into a successful weekly publication modelled on *Time* magazine.

In 1967, JJSS published the book that established his reputation as an original and radical thinker. *Le Défi américain* (*The American Challenge*) argued that the US was not just a rival free-world economy, temporarily outpacing Europe industrially and commercially. JJSS believed that America was engaged in a struggle with Europe that would turn Europe into an American economic colony. The book was a commercial and critical success, and JJSS used his wealth to become more directly involved in politics. In 1969 he became secretary-general of the Parti Radical, helping to modernise the party and its policies. Two years later he was elected party president. He was elected to the National Assembly and served briefly as Minister of Reform in 1974. The Parti Radical moved to the left under his leadership but not far enough to enter a formal arrangement with President Mitterrand's coalition of socialists and communists. In 1972, the party split with the left becoming the Parti Radical de Gauche and the remainder joining the centre-right coalition that eventually evolved into the Union pour un Mouvement Populaire, currently led by President Chirac. By this time, to the French left, JJSS had acquired the reputation as something of a political gadfly.

In 1980, JJSS expanded the thesis of *Le Défi américain* in his book *Le Défi mondial* (*The Global Challenge*), which focused on the rise of Japanese economic power based on technological superiority. He remained close to the heart of French political life, serving as a counsellor to both Presidents Mitterrand and Giscard d'Estaing. In the mid-1980s he lived in the US and was director of international relations at Carnegie Mellon University in Pittsburgh. He died in France on 7 November 2006.

Ideas

Through his journalism, his books and his politics, JJSS consistently advanced and promoted radical and left-wing causes and ideas, even when these were unpopular outside liberal-leaning elites. He supported decolonisation and exposed the brutal realities of colonial rule in Algeria, opening himself to charges of demoralising the French army. He opposed de Gaulle becoming President in 1958, when the latter was widely seen as the wartime hero responding to the call of a grateful nation to guarantee political stability.

His thesis on American economic superiority and the ability of America to outstrip Europe at all levels, industrially and commercially, laid the basis for many future warnings about American economic power; his writings have been seen as paving the way for the later articulation of fears about American cultural dominance. His thinking also signposted a way forward for Europe which would be based on international political cooperation and, given JJSS's later writings about the challenge posed by Japanese superiority in developing technology, increased European investment in scientific and technological research.

In his role as a politician, JJSS promoted ideas on European cooperation to counter-balance American power, including the possibility of a common European currency, decentralisation of power and regionalism, as well as opposing nuclear energy, favouring women's liberation and the development of new technologies.

Key works
- *Lieutenant en Algérie* (1957; English translation, *Lieutenant in Algeria*, 1958)
- *Rencontres* (*Meetings*) (1959)
- *Le Défi américain* (1967; English translation, *The American Challenge*, 1968)
- *Ciel et terre: Manifeste radical* (jointly with Michel Albert, 1970; English translation, *Radical Alternative*, 1970)
- *Le Défi mondial* (1980; English version, *The World Challenge*, 1981)

Further reading
- Jean Bothorel, *Celui qui voulait tout changer: Les Années JJSS* (R. Laffont, 2005) ('The man who wanted to change everything: The life and times of JJSS', no English version yet published)
- Jean Lacouture, *Pierre Mendès-France* (Editions du Seuil, 1981; English translation, Holmes and Meier, 1984)
- Francis de Tarr, *The French Radical Party from Herriot to Mendès-France* (Oxford University Press, 1961)

Graham Lippiatt

Henry Sidgwick   1838–1900

A Victorian philosopher, ethicist, political and legal theorist, economist, parapsychologist, and educational reformer, Sidgwick's classic work, *The Methods of Ethics*, marked the culmination of the classical utilitarian tradition of Jeremy Bentham and John Stuart Mill, and the beginnings of the Cambridge School of economics.

Key ideas
- The utilitarianism of Bentham and Mill lacked solid philosophical foundations and needed to be grounded on rational intuitionism.
- Utilitarianism could largely account for common-sense morality, but stood in conflict with rational egoism, thus producing a dualism of practical reason.
- The classical doctrine of laissez-faire failed to recognise the many cases of market failure.
- Educational opportunities must be widened and opened up to women.
- Machiavellianism in international politics was as objectionable as it was in domestic politics.

Biography

Henry Sidgwick was born on 31 May 1838 in Skipton, Yorkshire, and he was educated at Rugby and Cambridge, where he excelled at both mathematics and classics. The secret Cambridge discussion society known as the 'Apostles', along with the works of Jeremy Bentham (q.v.) and John Stuart Mill (q.v.), profoundly shaped his outlook. He would stay at Cambridge his entire life, first as a fellow of Trinity and lecturer in classics, and then, from 1883, as Knightbridge Professor of Moral Philosophy. He resigned his fellowship in 1869, when he could no longer sincerely subscribe to the Thirty-Nine Articles of the Church of England, but he continued as a lecturer and regained his fellowship when subscription was no longer required.

Sidgwick's scrupulous conscientiousness was very widely admired, and he moved in many influential circles. He corresponded with Mill, was friendly with Gladstone (q.v.), and was very close to J. A. Symonds, one of the pioneers of gay studies. He married Eleanor Mildred Balfour in 1876, thus making his former student, the future Prime Minister Arthur Balfour, his brother-in-law. The Archbishop of Canterbury, Edward White Benson, was another brother-in-law.

Politically, Sidgwick was sympathetic to a broadly Millian position, but over his life he moved from calling for a Millian liberal party to supporting Gladstone to supporting Liberal Unionism (q.v.) (opposing Irish independence) to an eclectic, occasionally Tory stance, mixed with many of the elements of liberal imperialism (q.v.). To all of these positions he brought a comprehensive philosophical, political and economic outlook. Best known as a moral philosopher, he was also a first-rate economist and one of the founding figures of the Cambridge School. He was active in charity organisation societies, and, with Eleanor, was a founder of both the Society for Psychical Research and Newnham College, Cambridge, one of England's first women's colleges.

Sidgwick published widely, but his major works were *The Methods of Ethics* (1874–1907), *The Principles of Political Economy* (1883–1901) and *The Elements of Politics* (1891–1919). These works continue to be influential, particularly the *Methods*, which has often been hailed as a classic.

Ideas

Sidgwick's *Methods* sought 'to put aside temporarily the urgent need which we all feel of finding and adopting the true method of determining what we ought to do'. Instead, Sidgwick tried 'to consider simply what conclusions will be rationally reached if we start with certain ethical premises, and with what degree of certainty and precision'. The result was an exhaustive comparison of the methods of ethics known as intuitional or common-sense morality, rational egoism and utilitarianism (q.v.), which concluded that, although common-sense moral rules (e.g. 'don't lie') could be largely subsumed under utilitarianism, there was a 'dualism of the practical reason' when it came to egoism and utilitarianism, each of which was as well grounded in rational (cognitive) intuition as the other.

Sidgwick himself favored the utilitarian view, holding that the normative bottom line ought to be producing the greatest happiness for the greatest number, with happiness construed in hedonistic fashion as pleasurable or desirable consciousness. But his position was quite eclectic, incorporating elements from Aristotle, Butler, Kant and Whewell. And he was haunted by his inability to demonstrate that one ought ultimately to maximise the general happiness rather than one's own. The effort to harmonise the individual and general happiness led him to pursue parapsychology, as a possible defense of theism, and greater educational and cultural opportunities that might move humanity in the direction of greater altruism and compassion.

In his normative political and economic work, Sidgwick simply assumed the utilitarian position. Both the *Principles* and the *Elements* took laissez-faire (q.v.) individualism – that 'what one sane adult is legally compelled to render to others should be merely the negative service of non-interference, except so far as he has voluntarily undertaken to render positive services' – only as a starting point from which to highlight a long list of limitations and failures of the market: monopoly, public works and goods (lighthouses, pure research, environmental protections, defence), education, child care, poor relief, disease control, collective bargaining and others. Sidgwick argued that the 'humane treatment of lunatics, and the prevention of cruelty to the inferior animals' are especially illustrative of the limitations of the principle of individualism, since restrictions concerning these do not aim at securing the freedom of lunatics and animals, but are 'a one-sided restraint of the freedom of action of men with a view to the greatest happiness of the aggregate of sentient beings'.

Arguably, it was Sidgwick, rather than Alfred Marshall (q.v.), who developed the crucial framework for the welfare economics of A. C. Pigou. He clearly demonstrated the conflicts between private and social interest, and how 'there is no general reason' to think that 'the individual can always obtain through free exchange adequate remuneration for the services he is capable of rendering to society', since, for example, 'there are some utilities which, from their nature, are practically incapable of being appropriated by those who produce them

or who would otherwise be willing to purchase them'. For Sidgwick, the notion of 'wealth' was not exhausted by the exchange values of goods produced.

Although Sidgwick was cautious in the extreme about calling for socialist measures, because he worried about their effects on incentives, his work was quite subversive of classical political economy – 'the absolute right of the individual to unlimited industrial freedom is now only maintained by a scanty and dwindling handful of doctrinaires, whom the progress of economic science has left stranded on the crude generalisations of an earlier period'. But he favored 'ethical socialism' – the idea that humanity could develop more altruistic motivations to work. He lamented narrowly self-interested, materialistic tendencies in both domestic and international politics, and sought to advance international law and morality.

Elitist in the fashion of Mill, albeit with more regard for the benefits of religion, he was too complacent about the imperialistic aspirations of liberalism and their racist underpinnings. He allowed that 'the nations most advanced in civilization have a tendency – the legitimacy of which cannot be broadly and entirely disputed – to absorb semicivilised states in their neighbourhood, as in the expansion of England and Russia in Asia, and of France in Africa'. His opposition to realist or Machiavellian international politics could be laudably cosmopolitan, but it too often relied on a Eurocentric faith in the high-mindedness of the so-called 'civilised' nations.

Key works
- *The Methods of Ethics* (1874–1907)
- *The Principles of Political Economy* (1883–1901)
- *The Elements of Politics* (1891–1919)
- *The Development of European Polity* (1903)

- *Miscellaneous Essays and Addresses* (1904)

Further reading
- J. B. Schneewind, *Sidgwick's Ethics and Victorian Moral Philosophy* (Oxford University Press, 1977)
- Bart Schultz, *Henry Sidgwick, Eye of the Universe* (Cambridge University Press, 2004)

Bart Schultz

Ernest Simon   1879–1960

A city councillor and MP, Simon was a significant figure in the Liberal Party of the inter-war years. In 1946, he defected to Labour. His later life was marked in particular by his work as chairman of the BBC, but his contribution to political thought came from his earlier Liberal career, when he wrote on citizenship and on slum clearance.

Key ideas
- In a democracy, 'the state exists to enable every individual to develop to the utmost his own personality as a member of the community'.
- 'Economic equality (at least of opportunity) is probably the acid test as to whether the Liberal Party still represents a Liberal spirit.'

Biography
Ernest Darwin Simon was born on 9 October 1879 in Didsbury, Manchester, to immigrant parents from eastern Europe. His education was at Rugby and Cambridge, before he succeeded his father in his industrial businesses.

In 1912, he was elected city councillor for Didsbury ward, and a decade later, was Lord Mayor of Manchester. He was first elected to the House of Commons for Manchester Withington in 1923, lost the seat the following year but, despite his dislike of parliamentary life, stood again and returned to Parliament in 1929. He stood down from Manchester City Council but became a figure of importance in the national Liberal Party, being vice-chairman of the committee that produced the 'Yellow Book' in 1928.

He joined Ramsay MacDonald's National Government as Parliamentary Secretary to the Ministry of Health in 1931, only to be defeated in that year's general election. He was knighted in 1932. After the war, he changed his party allegiance and, when given a peerage in 1947, took the Labour whip in the House of Lords; at that time, he commented: 'The two-party system is the best and only way of working our democracy successfully.'

In the post-war years, he was best known for his time as chairman of the BBC, though he showed an active interest in a range of matters from family planning to the development of university education; he was, for a long time, chairman of the Council of Manchester University. He died on 3 October 1960. Despite his later activities, his main practical contribution to politics was undoubtedly during his early years on Manchester City Council where, among his fellow councillors, was his wife Shena Simon, née Potter.

Ideas
On Manchester City Council, there was a division of labour between Shena and Ernest Simon: while she concentrated her energies on issues of education and female emancipation, he focused his attention on housing. His major concern was to rid his city of slums and over-crowded housing. In pressing for this during his time as the chair of the Housing Committee, he came to enunciate a position which differentiated Liberals from both Conservatives and Labour.

Simon was an avowed supporter of municipal intervention in housing, in contrast to a previous tradition, characterised by reformers like Octavia Hill, who wished to avoid large-scale council developments. The Liberal Simon in Manchester saw before him a reactionary Conservative Party which 'strongly objected to municipal competition with the speculative builder'. On the other side, he found Labour councillors who, while in principle supportive of council housing projects, were often more concerned with the interests of the building workers than the future inhabitants. Simon differentiated the Liberal position from both the other parties, adopting as his slogan: 'equality of opportunity for every child'.

The emphasis on children was at the heart of Simon's work to abolish the slums. For him, it was a campaign for the next generation. This might seem a counsel of despair, failing to recognise what local government can do to help adults, but Simon's hope was twofold, that those who had endured the slums could be encouraged to regain pride in themselves and that their children would enjoy better standards and a better life than their parents had suffered.

Meanwhile, Simon's emphasis on equality (q.v.) marked him out from many of his colleagues in the Liberal Summer Schools (q.v.) in which he was an active participant. He defined himself as a Radical Liberal, prepared to support 'any steps, however drastic … to fight inequality', claiming 'it is necessary not only to make the poor richer, but to make the rich – especially the very rich – poorer'. This declaration placed him on the left of the party, but certainly within a Liberal ambit.

Simon described the sometimes arcane workings of Manchester City Council and his own experience as a councillor in his *A City Council from Within* (1926). The book appeared with a preface by the New Liberal (q.v.) thinker Graham Wallas (q.v.), with whom Simon shared an interest in the Athenian *polis* as an ideal of civic spirit and community engagement. This thread in his thinking became all the more manifest in the 1930s.

With the rise of the European dictatorships, Simon turned his interests to the defence of democracy. In 1934, he founded, with his wife and Eva Hubback, the Association for Education in Citizenship. The Association was keen to promote a consensus across the political parties on the value of democracy. While Association chairman, Simon penned an essay on 'The Faith of a Democrat' to define the difference between the democrat and the totalitarian. The latter 'holds that the individual exists for the sake of the power and glory of the state, and fulfils himself in service to the dictator', while for the democrat the state exists to enable individuals to achieve their full potential.

This was, however, democracy in which engagement, if not required, was forcefully encouraged. As Simon put it:

> We cannot, even in the best democracy, expect *everybody* to take an active interest in public affairs. But unless the great majority do so, and unless the tasks of citizenship are generally held to be among the highest duties of man, we can never hope to succeed in the most difficult task before mankind: the building of a just and efficient social order.

Civic involvement was part of that very Aristotelian concept, the good life.

Aristotle's influence was also apparent in another of Simon's works of this period, on the need for education for citizenship. In this pamphlet, written with Eva Hubback, the authors argued that men and women, however intelligent or well educated, had to be trained for the special task of being citizens.

It was in these same years that Simon's wife left the Liberals and joined the Labour Party. His own defection followed after the Second World War, but he had already made his mark in Liberal politics and Liberal political thinking. It was, indeed, in his own combination of thought and action that he demonstrated how the Liberal good life could be lived.

Key works

- *A City Council from Within* (1926)
- *How to Abolish the Slums* (1929)
- *Training for Citizenship* (1935)
- 'The Faith of a Democrat', in E. Simon et al., *Constructive Democracy* (1938)

Further reading

- Mary Stocks, *Ernest Simon of Manchester* (Manchester University Press, 1963)

David Rundle

Adam Smith   1723–90

The foremost economic thinker of the liberal tradition, Smith's book *The Wealth of Nations*, is the most famous and influential treatise on the benefits of economic liberty, free trade and the division of labour. While Smith's reputation as the founding father of liberal economics has long obscured his political and moral writings, recent scholarship has helped to rediscover the rich body of political liberalism that can be found in his writings. In contrast to the popular image of Smith as a laissez-faire doctrinaire, his work seeks to demonstrate that a liberal polity can enjoy the benefits of individual liberty and free markets, but need not – and ought not – to neglect social cohesion and basic human needs.

Key ideas

- Praises liberty in economic and political life.
- Human self-interest is tamed by 'sympathy', an innate sense of fellow feeling.
- Argued against mercantilism and for a liberal economy based on enterprise and free trade.
- The 'invisible hand' of the market directs the pursuit of individual interest to produce a decent society.
- The role of government is limited, but includes education, public infrastructure, justice and national defence.

Biography

Adam Smith was born in Kirkcaldy, near Edinburgh, most probably in 1723 (he was baptised on 5 June 1723). Earlier that year his father, a customs officer, had died and Smith was raised by his mother, Margaret Douglas, and guardians appointed in his father's will. At the age of fourteen, he matriculated at Glasgow University where he was educated in logic, physics and philosophy. Smith proved himself a talented student and was rewarded with a prestigious scholarship enabling Glasgow University graduates to pursue a further course of study at Oxford University. Having been nominated a Snell Exhibitioner in 1740, he went to Balliol College where he read widely in classics, philosophy, jurisprudence and literature.

On returning to Scotland in 1746, Smith's academic studies soon bore fruit. He began to deliver public lectures in rhetoric, philosophy and jurisprudence in Edinburgh and, in 1751, was appointed Professor of Logic at Glasgow University. Only a year later he became Professor of Moral Philosophy, teaching theology, moral philosophy and jurisprudence for the next twelve years. It was the last of these subjects which allowed him to include in his teaching aspects of politics and economics and, alongside his philosophical studies, to develop a life-long interest in political economy. His academic reputation, however, was initially to be built on the basis of his philosophical work. Smith's first book, *The Theory of Moral Sentiments*, was published in 1759. The treatise critically examined the moral thinking of the time and set out Smith's own theory of moral behaviour and judgement, based on an innate human desire to sympathise with others and arrive at impartial moral judgements. According to Smith, conscience arises from social relationships.

In 1764 Smith decided to leave Glasgow University for good and take up an invitation to travel abroad with the third Duke of Buccleuch. The position as travelling tutor offered Smith not only a higher annual income, including a life-long pension, but also an opportunity to find more time for his economic writings and to meet leading French thinkers of the Enlightenment. In Geneva, Smith was introduced to Voltaire (q.v.), whose literary and political achievements he greatly admired. During his stay in Paris in 1766, Smith participated in the discussions of a group of liberal economists, the Physiocrats.

While Smith used his stay in France to broaden his economic understanding, he had already worked out the basic principles of his liberal economic doctrine before embarking on the journey. After his return to Scotland at the end of 1766, he began work on his second book, which, eventually, was to gain him world-wide fame as one of the most eminent liberal thinkers of all time. In 1776, *An Inquiry into the Nature and Causes of the Wealth of Nations* was published to great success and world-wide acclaim.

As a result of the success of this economic theory and his reputation as a university administrator, Smith was offered the position of Commissioner of Customs in Edinburgh, which he took up in 1777. During his years in public office, he continued his economic, political and philosophical studies and worked on further editions of his two books. In addition, he embarked on two new projects, to write a history of philosophy and a theory of law and politics; these efforts, however, remained unfinished, and at Smith's request, most of his handwritten notes on these subjects were posthumously destroyed.

Apart from his two published works, only a small number of philosophical essays, lectures on rhetoric and literature as well as student notes from his lectures on jurisprudence survived. Adam Smith died on 17 July 1790, in Edinburgh.

Ideas

Adam Smith's writings on the economy are a synthesis of various strands of eighteenth-century economic thought. They presented the first systematic critique of the then prevailing orthodoxy of mercantilism, which dominated economic thought and policy throughout the seventeenth and eighteenth centuries. Mercantilism assumed that national wealth rested on the possession of bullion, and that the global quantity of gold and silver was largely fixed. Economics was thus a zero-sum game in which different societies competed with each other and sought to increase gold and silver reserves by creating a favourable trade balance. Mercantilists therefore prescribed large-scale state intervention in the domestic economy and international trade. In developing his critique of mercantilism, Smith elaborated several key ideas and concepts that remain central to liberal economic theory and practice today, including, among the most important, the role of self-interest, the 'invisible hand' of the market, division of labour, free trade (q.v.) and the limited role of government.

As befits any liberal thinker, Smith's starting point is the individual, and individual liberty. Humans are driven by *self-interest*, which is the key source of change in society and the economy. In line with Scotland's eighteenth-century Enlightenment tradition, he sees humans as innately social, with an instinct 'to truck and barter'. Unlike some moralists of his time, however, Smith believes that self-interest and the interests of society need not clash with each other. Indeed, a well-ordered and decent society can coexist with a system of free economic exchange, for the human desire for economic betterment does not derive from narrow selfishness but from individuals' search for recognition in society.

Smith posits an underlying harmony of interests in society, which becomes a reality through the '*invisible hand*' of the market mechanism. Individuals may not have the larger benefit of society in sight when they pursue their own interest, but the market produces socially beneficial outcomes as unintended consequences of individuals' self-interested behaviour. In Smith's own famous words:

> It is not from the benevolence of the butcher, the brewer, or the baker, that we expect our dinner, but from their regard to their own interest. We address ourselves, not to their humanity but to their self-love, and never talk to them of our own necessities but of their advantages.

While the concept of the 'invisible hand' does not feature prominently in Smith's work – in fact, it appears only once each in *The Theory of Moral Sentiments* and *The Wealth of Nations* – it encapsulates Smith's key insight into the beneficial nature of the market and the spontaneous order that arises from free economic exchange. Mercantilists had argued that in order to maximise a nation's wealth, the state had to direct domestic economic activity and manipulate foreign trade so as to achieve a positive trade balance. Smith rejects this by showing that governmental restrictions on the free operation of the market only serve to reduce society's wealth and stunt economic growth, by misdirecting investment and reducing the ability of individuals fully to make use of their talents.

The opening section of *The Wealth of Nations* introduces the concept of the *division of labour*, which Smith sees as the engine of economic growth. The division of labour operates at every level of the economy, from a single factory to global markets. Just as manufactured goods can be made more cheaply if the production process is broken down into its constituent parts and workers perform specialised tasks, so can whole societies gain economically if they choose to specialise in those economic sectors where they possess an advantage. The division of labour promotes technological innovation and thus increases human productivity and universal wealth.

It follows from this that *free trade* should become a key component of Smithian political economy and of all subsequent liberal economic doctrines. Once the benefits of the division of labour are recognised, free trade becomes essential to promoting specialisation and increasing productivity. Opening up markets creates ever more incentives to deepen the division of labour and allows societies to allocate capital and labour in the most efficient manner. Rather than seeing international trade as a kind of 'zero-sum game' in which nations competed for a bigger slice of a fixed amount of economic wealth, as the mercantilists did, Smith argued that free trade would help unlock the growth potential of all societies and thus increase 'universal opulence'. Smith's arguments in favour of free trade formed the basis for later, economically more sophisticated, theories of trade. They also provided a powerful economic rationale for arguments against colonial expansion and preferential trading systems.

One of the most frequently misunderstood aspects of Smith's political economy is his advocacy of a *limited role of government*. Against the background of mercantilist politics in eighteenth-century Europe, the *Wealth of Nations* did indeed call for a reduced role for the state in economic affairs. But the anti-statist turn in later liberal economic thinking, particularly in the era of nineteenth-century Manchester School liberalism (q.v.), provides a distorted lens through which Smith is wrongly viewed as the forerunner of the laissez-faire tradition (q.v.). Besides wishing to limit market-distorting state interventions, Smith defined three positive roles of the state: national defence; the provision of a system of justice; and investment in public infrastructure. Smith reasoned that, as none of these so-called 'public goods' are produced by the market, the state has to step in to overcome the dilemmas of 'market failure'. We cannot know what Smith would have made of the rise of the welfare state in the twentieth century, but even in its contemporary context, this list of governmental functions, which included the provision of transport networks and universal education, was by no means a plea for a minimal state.

Adam Smith's influence on posterity can hardly be over-stated. While initial reactions to the publication of the *The Wealth of Nations* were positive but not enthusiastic, it became clear from the early nineteenth century onwards that this would become one of the canonical texts in liberal economic thinking. Many of Smith's ideas, from the concept of the invisible hand to his advocacy of free trade, have permeated modern political and economic discourse, to the extent that not only liberals but also conservatives now claim Smith as one of 'theirs'. In the twentieth century, his ideas came to be associated as readily with Thatcherism and Reaganite economics as with more liberal movements.

The popularity of Smith's ideas has, therefore, come at a cost, and nineteenth- and twentieth-century caricatures of his work as a laissez-faire doctrine have prevented a more balanced view of Smith's moral, political and economic ideas. *The Wealth of Nations* needs to be read in conjunction with *The Theory of Moral Sentiments* in order fully to appreciate that Smith viewed the economy as part of society, and society to be based on moral principles shared by free citizens. Smith's intellectual challenge – to show how a free and prosperous economy can be combined with the ideals of a decent society – remains as important today as ever before.

Key works

- *The Theory of Moral Sentiments* (1759)
- *An Inquiry into the Nature and Causes of the Wealth of Nations* (1776)

Further reading

- Knud Haakonssen (ed.), *The Cambridge Companion to Adam Smith* (Cambridge University Press, 2006)
- Gavin Kennedy, *Adam Smith's Lost Legacy* (Palgrave Macmillan, 2005)
- Ian Simpson Ross, *The Life of Adam Smith* (Clarendon Press, 1995)
- Emma Rothschild, *Economic Sentiments: Adam Smith, Condorcet and the Enlightenment* (Harvard University Press, 2001)
- Donald Winch, *Riches and Poverty* (Cambridge University Press, 1996)

Robert Falkner

Sydney Smith   1771–1845

A writer, wit, preacher and reformer, Smith founded the *Edinburgh Review* (the first successful literary review, which also served as a vehicle for propagating Whig ideas). Although a Church of England clergyman, his writings did more than most to promote Catholic emancipation.

Key ideas
- Promoted religious toleration for Catholics through satirising the fears of Anglicans.
- Encouraged social reform by highlighting best practice in mental health care, encouraging education for girls and attacking the game laws.
- Campaigned for the Great Reform Bill of 1832.

Biography
Sydney Smith was born on 3 June 1771 at Woodford in Essex, the second son of a merchant, Robert Smith, who lost most of his wealth in the American War of Independence. Robert's frequent trips abroad to rebuild his fortune meant that Sydney and his siblings were left largely to the care of their mother, Margaret (née Olier), who was of Huguenot descent. Smith was educated at Winchester and New College, Oxford, where his unhappiness with a curriculum that was heavily reliant on the classics did not prevent steady progress towards his degree in 1792 and his MA in 1796. Discouraged by his father from a career in the law, Smith obtained a curacy at Netheravon and took holy orders in 1796.

While at Netheravon, the local squire engaged Smith to tutor his son on a continental tour. War with France prevented the planned tour and Smith took Michael Hicks-Beach to Edinburgh in 1798 instead. Here Smith studied medicine, chemistry and philosophy under Dugald Stewart. He formed friendships with Henry Brougham, Francis Jeffrey and Francis Horner, young Whigs (q.v.), who, at Smith's suggestion, founded the *Edinburgh Review* in 1801.

Funded by the bookseller Archibald Constable, the first issue was published in October 1802.

Sydney married Catharine Pybus in 1800, and moved to London in 1803, where he won celebrity as a preacher at fashionable London chapels and as a lecturer at the Royal Institution. When his brother Bobus married into Lord Holland's family, Sydney became a regular visitor to Holland House, welcomed for his vivacious and witty conversation. This acquaintance with senior Whigs secured Sydney the living of Foston-Le-Clay in Yorkshire during the 'Ministry of All the Talents' in 1806. The subsequent Tory ministry passed an Act requiring Anglican clergymen to carry out their duties in person, forcing Smith to move to Yorkshire in 1809, where he lived for the next twenty years.

In 1828 he was promoted to prebendary at Bristol Cathedral and, in 1829, swapped his living at Foston-Le-Clay for Combe Florey in Somerset. Although Smith stopped writing for the *Edinburgh Review* at this time, he was disappointed that Grey's 1832 Whig ministry did not reward his loyalty, and his campaigning for electoral reform, with a bishopric; he regarded his appointment as a canon at St Paul's, one of the Church's best-paid positions, as poor compensation. Smith became more conservative over the life of the Melbourne government. In *Three Letters to Archdeacon Singleton*, he opposed Whig plans for limiting clergy patronage, seeing them as attacks on his personal position, and in *The Ballot* he opposed secret voting. Despite his advancing years, Smith's pen remained spasmodically active and, in 1842, he attacked the practice of locking railway carriage doors on safety grounds and, in 1843, attacked Pennsylvania for defaulting on bond payments. Since he always indulged his love of good food and drink, it is perhaps no surprise that he suffered a major heart attack in the autumn of 1844. He died in London on 22 February 1845.

Sydney and Catharine Smith had three sons and two daughters. His eldest son died in 1829 and a daughter in infancy. His other daughter, Saba, married Henry Holland, a doctor to Queen Victoria, and published a memoir of her father.

Ideas

Smith's experience as a parish priest both at Netheravon and in Yorkshire, where he also sat as a magistrate, made him acutely aware of the condition of the poor. As part of his ministry he established schools and administered health care. This practical understanding informed his views on social issues while his Anglican ministry and educational background equipped him to comment on the religious issues that were at the forefront of politics during his lifetime.

Established during a period of wartime Tory repression, when criticism of government was dangerous, from the beginning the *Edinburgh Review* was a vehicle for Whig politics and social reform as well as literary endeavour. Although the articles were published anonymously to minimise the risk of prosecution, Smith appears to have contributed as many articles to the early editions as any of his co-founders, and he remained a contributor for over twenty-five years. His strengths lay in the identification of social problems and in undermining Tory policies with wit and satire.

He was particularly concerned with the young, campaigning against the treatment of young chimney-sweeps and advocating education for girls as well as boys. Typical of his approach was his attack on the game laws which outlawed shooting, even on the owner's land, unless rents amounted to more than £100 p.a., but tolerated the use of spring guns and man-traps to catch poachers. His solution to the extensive spread and harsh punishment of poaching was the creation of an open, legitimate game market. However, in common with most Whigs, he generally relied on the local hierarchy taking appropriate steps in individual cases rather than grand legislative solutions. One area where his thinking was well in advance of his time was in the treatment of the mentally ill. Smith used the *Review* to back an asylum run by the Quakers in which patients were given occupational therapy rather than incarcerated and punished.

Smith's most extensive campaign was for religious toleration, particularly in the series of ten pamphlets, *Peter Plymley's Letters*, published in 1807, only a few years after the Act of Union with Ireland and during the Napoleonic wars. Under the guise of sympathising with Protestant extremists in their disgust at Roman Catholic practices, he argued for the abandonment of the civic disabilities that prevented Catholics pursuing military and other careers. Harassing them for their beliefs, he believed, could drive Catholics to rebellion. When every man was needed to serve in the navy and the army against Bonaparte, why should religious tests for employment deprive the country of the services of so many of its Irish and English citizens? The pamphlets owe much of their effectiveness to Smith's wit and his sideswipes at the hypocrisy of prominent Tory ministers. His case was strengthened by arguing, not the viewpoint of the victims of discrimination, but the disadvantages of intolerance to the oppressors, a Protestant Britain depriving itself of military strength and magnifying its enemies within by the unfair treatment of a minority of its citizens.

Key works
• *Peter Plymley's Letters* (1808)

- *A Letter to the Electors upon the Catholic Question* (1826)
- *Three Letters to Archdeacon Singleton* (1837–39)
- *The Ballot* (1839)
- *Letters on American Debts* (1844)

Further reading
- Alan Bell, *Sydney Smith, A Biography* (Oxford University Press, 1980)
- Saba (Lady) Holland, *A Memoir of the Reverend Sydney Smith* (2 vols., Longman Brown Green & Longmans, 1855)
- Nowell Smith, *The Letters of Sydney Smith,* (2 vols., Clarenden Press, 1953)
- Sydney Smith, *Works* (3 vols., Longman Brown Green & Longmans, 1845)
- Peter Virgin, *Sydney Smith* (Harper Collins, 1994)

Tony Little

Social Democracy

The term 'social democracy' is descriptively imprecise, and its usage has varied according to historical circumstance. In British politics it came to be associated, first, with the revisionist socialism of Crosland and his colleagues in the Labour Party of the 1950s and '60s, and later, the breakaway Social Democratic Party of the 1980s. After 1994, New Labour's ideological approach under Tony Blair's leadership purported to be that of a modernised social democracy.

Before 1914 the term 'social democracy' usually denoted organised Marxism. It was thus the title designating most Marxist socialist parties between 1880 and 1914 – particularly the German and Russian Social Democratic Parties. After the 1917 Russian Revolution, however, the term came to mean organised, non-Marxist reformist socialism.

Social democracy in the latter sense is, as S. Padgett and W. E. Paterson have observed, 'a hybrid political tradition [which] is inspired by socialist ideals but is heavily conditioned by its political environment, and it incorporates liberal values'. The social-democratic approach may thus be defined as 'the attempt to reconcile socialism with liberal politics and capitalist society'.

After 1945 social democracy came to mean not just non-Marxist, evolutionary or democratic socialism but also, in M. B. Hamilton's definition, 'a non-transformative type of socialism or social reformism' – for its primary goal has been 'amelioration of injustice and the promotion of common welfare and a measure of equality rather than transformation of the economic and social structure'. In practice, this non-transformative approach has entailed the pursuit of its reformist aims within the context of a mixed economy rather than upon the basis of the public ownership of the means of production. Social democracy has thus sought to modify and manage capitalism, rather than to transform it.

In Britain, social democracy gradually evolved in the twentieth century as an ideological synthesis of Fabian collectivism, Edwardian New Liberalism (q.v.) and Keynesian economic theory (q.v.). In the 1930s Keynes's (q.v.) case for indirect control of the economy by means of demand management was directed against both free-market Conservative and fundamentalist socialist views. Keynes's arguments were embraced by young Fabian intellectuals such as Hugh Gaitskell (1906–63), Douglas Jay (1907–96) and Evan Durbin (1906–48), who were eager to introduce into the Labour Party Keynesian ideas on macroeconomic intervention. Their advocacy thus helped to strengthen what was in effect a developing social-democratic position distinct from both economic liberal (q.v.) and traditional socialist viewpoints.

In the post-1945 period social democracy in Britain became synonymous with the revisionist tendency within the Labour Party during the 1950s and early 1960s. The terms themselves, 'social democracy' and 'social-democratic', were not, however, to be widely used in British political discourse until the early 1970s.

As it was developed throughout the 1950s, Labour revisionism steadily acquired its distinctiveness as a body of theory and as a set of policies. Its central ideas and arguments were most thoroughly and coherently expressed in Anthony Crosland's (q.v.) major work, *The Future of Socialism* (1956). The period from 1956 onwards, following Gaitskell's accession to the party leadership, witnessed its increasing prominence as a major ideological influence within the Labour Party. During those years revisionist ideas – on public ownership and economic strategy in particular – were developed and promoted by Gaitskell and his supporters, notably Crosland, Jay and Roy Jenkins (q.v.), and incorporated into party policy statements.

Revisionist socialism involved two major, highly controversial deviations from accepted Labour orthodoxies. First, it repudiated the traditional view that socialism could be defined as, or at least identified with, the public ownership of the means of production. It thereby questioned the established Labour commitment to extensive public ownership as a precondition of achieving all major reformist objectives.

Second, revisionist socialism diverged from orthodox Labour thinking by presenting a distinctive ethical interpretation of socialism in terms of values and ideals such as personal liberty, social welfare and, in particular, social equality (q.v.). Labour revisionists thus viewed socialism as a collection of ideals, not as a form of economic organisation. The traditional doctrine of public ownership – enshrined in Clause IV of the party constitution as the symbol of Labour's socialist identity – was therefore regarded as merely one useful means among several others for fulfilling those socialist values and ideals, which were to be pursued, moreover, within a mixed economy.

The intellectual foundation of the first part of the revisionist project – its repudiation of the orthodox identification of socialism with public ownership – was provided by Crosland in *The Future of Socialism*. In his analysis of changes within post-war capitalism, Crosland argued that a transfer of economic power away from the pre-1939 capitalist class had occurred in three directions: towards the state, towards the trade unions, and towards salaried directors and managers within private industry. As a result of this shift of economic power, the nature of capitalism, in Crosland's view, had been radically altered. In addition, he argued, Keynesian techniques of economic management had resolved many of the deep-seated problems inherent in capaitalism, for full or near-full employment had been attained and governments appeared to have the policy instruments for achieving sustained economic growth.

Central, therefore, to revisionist socialism as formulated by Crosland was the belief that a democratic government had the ability to control, by Keynesian methods, private economic power and thereby pursue desirable social objectives within a mixed economy. Keynesianism thus provided the economic cornerstone of revisionist socialism since it offered both the means by which governments would seek to achieve economic growth and full employment, and the economic surplus, derived from sustained growth and hence buoyant tax revenues, which could be redirected into higher social expenditure.

The main features, then, of what later became identified as the social-democratic approach, which substantially influenced Labour thinking and policy from 1956 until the 1970s, were: a rejection of the traditional association of socialism with large-scale public ownership; an ethical reformulation of socialist aims; the acceptance of a state-regulated yet market-oriented mixed economy; the promotion of a welfare state, financed by economic growth and redistributive taxation; and an underlying commitment to full employment and sustained economic growth by means of Keynesian techniques of demand management.

These amounted to the distinguishing features of what David Marquand (q.v.) subsequently described as Keynesian social democracy. In his view, it was also the governing philosophy of the post-war collectivist consensus. The term provided a 'shorthand for a set of commitments, assumptions and expectations, transcending party conflicts and shared by the great majority of the country's political and economic leaders, which provided the framework within which policy decisions were made'. On a deeper ideological level, that set of dominant ideas and policy commitments comprised 'a philosophy of the middle way' since its various adherents were agreed in 'repudiating the dichotomies of market versus state; capital versus labour; private enterprise versus public ownership; personal freedom versus social justice'. Instead, they believed that elements of both capitalism and socialism could be combined 'in a synthesis more benign than either'.

However, in the face of the harsh inflationary pressures of the 1970s, Keynesian social democracy appeared to lose its political and intellectual appeal. Its confident assumptions were undermined by the economic stagnation, financial crises and bitter industrial strife of those years, and consequently by the strains of office exerted on the Wilson and Callaghan governments between 1974–79. All these factors challenged the central beliefs of Keynesian social democracy – namely, that rapid and sustained economic growth could be achieved; that governments had the capacity to achieve such growth; and that the egalitarian and welfarist objectives of social democracy could be fulfilled through the political and administrative machinery of the British state.

In the face, too, of the growing ideological polarisation of British politics, social democracy seemed an increasingly marginalised force by the late 1970s. On its left flank, it found itself challenged within the Labour Party by the revived fundamentalist socialism of Tony Benn and his supporters. On its right flank, meanwhile, it was confronted by the revived economic liberal doctrines of a resurgent Conservative Party under Margaret Thatcher's leadership.

Social-democratic decline within the Labour Party became even more evident after Roy Jenkins's departure from British politics in 1976 to become President of the European Commission and with the deaths of Crosland in 1977 and John Mackintosh, another iconoclastic political thinker, in 1978. Moreover, the Labour left's major constitutional and policy victories of 1979–81 precluded any significant recovery of the social-democratic position. Its fading intellectual influence had been symbolised, too, by the demise in December 1978 of *Socialist Commentary*, once the leading revisionist socialist journal.

Nevertheless, some social-democratic politicians and thinkers, notably Mackintosh, David Marquand, and Evan Luard (1926–91), had begun to develop a critique of the centralist and corporatist tendencies inherent in state socialism. Both Mackintosh and Marquand had stressed the need to revise Croslandite social democracy in the harsher economic and political climate of the 1970s, and thereby to work out what Marquand called the purposes of 'a new-model libertarian, decentralist social democracy' – for, as he later observed, Crosland's version of social democracy had in time degenerated into 'state-directed social engineering'.

Little systematic progress was made in the direction of this new revisionism. But both Marquand, by implication, and Roy Jenkins, more explicitly, indicated that a new political vehicle might be needed for a revised social-democratic philosophy and strategy. In his 1979 Dimbleby Lecture, *Home Thoughts from Abroad,* Jenkins thus welcomed the possibility of a new party of the 'radical centre' which would support state intervention and market forces in equal measure, and which would be committed to a programme of social and constitutional reform.

When that new Social Democratic Party emerged in March 1981, its launch statement, *Twelve Tasks for Social Democrats,* together with books by three of its founder leaders, David Owen (q.v.), Bill Rodgers and Shirley Williams, sought to provide it with a clear political identity. This consisted of a developed critique of the bureaucratic centralism and statism of established Labour policy, together with a commitment to the principle of political and economic decentralisation previously affirmed by Marquand, Mackintosh and Luard in the late 1970s, and shared with their Liberal allies, the first British political party to value and emphasise that principle.

This decentralist emphasis was thus a crucial part of the developing social-democratic critique of an over-centralised and

bureacratic state, associated both with traditional socialism and with the post-war collectivist consensus in general. This critique was reinforced by an eagerness to embrace a market-oriented mixed economy, which Marquand regarded as one of the most distinctive and important principles of social democracy. In his view, the mixed economy was 'neither a staging post on the road to full socialism nor a regrettable compromise between economic sin and economic virtue, but an entity in its own right, positively desirable in and for itself'.

David Owen, however, SDP leader from 1983 to 1987, gradually came to discard the term 'mixed economy', regarding it as too broad and imprecise. In its place, he favoured the idea of a 'social market economy' (q.v.) as a means of defining the SDP's ideological position. The phrase signified, he argued, a desirable combination of market realism and social concern, of competitiveness and compassion.

Although it became a central part of SDP strategy from 1984 onwards, the idea of a 'social market economy' exerted little influence on the SDP/Liberal Alliance programme in the run-up to the 1987 general election. It was nonetheless one of the few distinctive ideas to emerge from SDP thinking between 1983 and 1987. In other respects, the SDP's doctrinal and strategic platform was built upon ideas and attitudes long espoused by its Liberal allies – political and economic decentralisation, constitutional reform, selective state intervention within a market economy. Such positions thus helped to strengthen the Alliance after 1981, marking out a broad common ground of principle and policy.

What remained, however, of the SDP's original social-democratic legacy was perhaps more a political style and approach – pragmatic, flexible, favouring cautious reformism with the aid of active government and an enabling state. But what had given British social democracy its distinctive character in the period from the mid-1950s to the mid-1970s – namely, its central strategy of egalitarian redistribution by means of both fiscal and social policy and on the basis of Keynesian economics – had by the late 1980s largely declined as a major political influence.

Such a strategy, John Gray (q.v.) argued in 1996, had been undermined by 'voter resistance and the global mobility of capital', and in reality embodied 'assumptions and modes of thought that belong to an historical context that has vanished beyond recovery'. Against that view, it can be argued that as a political ideology social democracy has prospered in the past through its flexibility and pragmatism. Historically, as Marquand and others have pointed out, it has always in an important sense been a revisionist creed, adapting its ideas to take account of both mutations in capitalism and fluctuations in electoral opinion. From that perspective the guiding principles of New Labour's ideology after 1994 could be depicted by Tony Blair and his supporters as those of a modernised social democracy.

Further reading

- C. A. R Crosland, *The Future of Socialism* (Cape, 1956, rev. edn., 1964)
- G. Foote, *The Labour Party's Political Thought* (Croom Helm, 1997)
- J. Gray, *After Social Democracy* (Demos, 1996)
- M. B. Hamilton, *Democratic Socialism in Britain and Socialism* (Macmillian, 1989)
- T. Jones, *Remaking the Labour Party: From Gaitskell to Blair* (Routledge, 1996)
- D. Marquand, *The Unprincipled Society* (Cape, 1988)
- D. Marquand, *The New Reckoning* (Polity 1997)

- S. Padgett and W. E. Paterson, *A History of Social Democracy in Post-war Europe* (Longman, 1991)
- D. Sassoon, *A Hundred Years of Socialism: The West European Left in the Twentieth Century* (Tauris, 1996)

Tudor Jones

Social Justice

A critical and much-disputed concept in political philosophy generally and in liberal political thought in particular, the notion of social justice is concerned with the ways in which members of a political community determine the extent of their obligations to one another. There are a number of competing liberal ideas about social justice which give rise to strikingly different recommendations about the claims that members of a political community have upon one another.

Social justice is a particularly difficult concept for liberals. Liberalism in all its many forms embraces the beliefs that every citizen should stand equal before the law, that citizens should have the right to associate freely, to express themselves as they choose and to participate in free and fair elections, and that citizens should enjoy full civil rights, including the right to own property and to enter into contractual agreements of their own choosing. Many liberals, however, struggle with the proposition that respect for the rights of others requires them to support public policies that go well beyond the defence of individual liberties and basic political equality (q.v.).

The term 'social justice' is widely employed as a label for sets of ideas and intuitions commonly found in both theology and political theory about the obligations that flow from being children of a divine creator and/or quintessentially social creatures. Ideas about what is socially just are meant to guide communities and individuals when they decide how to share the burdens and benefits of a common existence. Perhaps the best-known precept in the Judeo-Christian tradition, which can also be described as a principle of social justice, is that 'you should do as you would be done by'.

The most notable contributor to the twentieth-century discussion of social justice, John Rawls (q.v.), is a representative of a school of philosophical thought often known as contractarianism, most strongly linked with the work of the philosopher Immanuel Kant (q.v.). The publication of his *Theory of Justice* in 1971 generated great interest in the idea that a liberal society could and should be based upon principles of justice that invited each and every member of society to do much more than simply respect other people's basic liberties. Rawls fashioned a political argument – what he called a theory of justice – that urged people to give their active support to political institutions specially engineered to distribute assets and opportunities as fairly as possible. Rawls described this as *justice as fairness*. Almost all of us recognise or are capable of recognising, he implied, that if we really want to reach a secure agreement about what it takes to create political institutions for a just society, it will be necessary to fashion the institutions, so far as possible, in a way that does not give or appear to give undue weight or influence to any particular interest.

According each citizen equal respect, a basic liberal value, requires that the interests of each and every person should be seen to carry an equal weight. Rawls noted that the liberal and utilitarian (q.v.) philosopher Jeremy Bentham (q.v.) had proposed that the surest way for any government to do exactly that was to use a calculus of benefit

and harm that made the greatest good and the good of the greatest number the fulcrums of public policy. Rawls rejected such an approach for fashioning the institutions and policies of a just society. Utilitarianism (q.v.) was fatally flawed; it permitted, for example, the interests of minorities to be disregarded, and could in theory sanction slavery, as long as the majority benefited as a result.

If individuals mattered, if each person was entitled to equal respect, and utilitarianism was rejected because it could not entrench equal respect, how could liberals set about formulating principles of social justice that were fair, robust and capable of protecting personal liberty? Rawls's answer was a philosophical method that would enable people to devise an agreement about fair principles of justice in a way that was itself both transparent and fair.

Rawls's theory is in effect a thought experiment dedicated to the search for general principles capable of commanding the support of reasonable people. Rawls was convinced that a debate about the principles needed to underpin a just society – a debate that he imagined taking place behind a 'veil of ignorance' depriving individuals of any knowledge of their individual interests and personal circumstances – would lead to agreement that the just society would give priority to fundamental or basic liberties which every member would enjoy. Such an agreement became the foundation for his first principle of justice.

Rawls was confident, however, that his debaters would go further and agree, subject to first securing basic liberties, that everything possible should be done to protect the weakest and most disadvantaged members of society. This commitment to a liberal egalitarianism was, above all else, a consequence of strong beliefs about the origins of material differences in human societies. Rawls considered that the most significant differences in life chances, and as a consequence in personal wealth and income, were undeserved, that the most telling material differences in life arose from initial endowments of ability and opportunity that were arbitrary from the moral point of view. When we think about our own circumstances and the distribution of life chances in general, Rawls was convinced that we would come to the conclusion that luck played an enormous – almost certainly the decisive – part in personal fortunes. We do not choose our parents, the time or place of our birth, our ethnicity or our gender. Rawls's judgement, therefore, about the outcome of a fair and informed debate concerning the principles for a just society was that the participants would agree a constitution in which inequalities of wealth and income would only be sanctioned and justified if they served the interests of the most disadvantaged members of society. He referred to this, his second principle of justice, as the 'maximin rule'.

Rawls's formulation of what appeared to be a wide-ranging and radically egalitarian liberal principle of social justice attracted considerable criticism from other liberals, most notably his Harvard colleague and fellow political philosopher Robert Nozick (q.v.), the author of *Anarchy, State, and Utopia* (1974). Nozick criticised Rawls for propounding a notion of justice that justified never-ending and liberty-destroying interference by public authorities in the lives of individuals who had, quite justly and fairly, acquired all that they possessed.

Citizens who respected the basic liberties of others were entitled to their holdings: their property and income. They should not be dragooned into supporting a social purpose that they had not freely chosen, so taxation to fund social programmes designed to modify life chances and redistribute income was therefore unjust and illiberal. A government that took income and property from individuals in order to secure the defence of the realm could, with difficulty, be justified but governments that imposed taxes in order to achieve some grand social design would be behaving unjustly. A just society was one that respected the results of trades and agreements between free citizens, and justice would only be served by ensuring that the most basic rights, the rights that underpinned individual freedoms and title to the fruits of one's own labours, were respected. In Nozick's opinion, Rawls's liberal egalitarianism – as expressed in his maximin rule – could not be reconciled with the most elemental liberal ideas about justice.

Another liberal, Friedrich Hayek (q.v.), was equally scathing in his criticism of Rawlsian justice and similar notions. The notion of social justice, Hayek declared, should be dismissed as nonsense, because there was no certain way of judging any particular distribution of wealth or income superior to any other in terms of justice. In the absence of an archimedian point from which to judge the relative justice of an array of different distributions, how was it possible to tell which of many possible distributions was the fairest? While Hayek could agree with Rawls that market distributions were arbitrary from the moral point of view, and he accepted that what many regarded as virtue or hard work often went unrewarded, it would, in his opinion, be illogical and illiberal to call for an alternative distribution because it could be said to be fairer. Furthermore, although market distributions were frequently shaped by chance factors they had a great advantage, in facilitating the most efficient allocation of scarce resources amongst competing ends. Hayek argued that attempts to modify market distributions were not only likely to reduce the allocative efficiency of market exchange but were also likely to extend the powers of government at the expense of the individual.

Hayek's rejection of the term 'social justice' has itself attracted criticism. Judith Shklar argued that the concept of social justice need be neither arbitrary nor indeterminate, but was simply a recognition of the fact that human beings are capable of formulating, agreeing and implementing social and economic plans, reflecing the popular will, aimed at modifying some of the economic and social consequences of unfettered markets. Hayek might well be justified in warning those who favoured actions that entailed constant interference in markets of the dangers of unintended and damaging consequences – but the spontaneous order of the market place, which had such virtue in his eyes, was not necessarily superior to the social and economic order that followed from the choices of an active and informed political community. Hayek, in Shklar's view, had been unable to sustain his general objection to public policies aimed at promoting social justice.

Objections to Nozick's criticisms of Rawls's liberal egalitarianism go deeper still. Other liberals, such as Ronald Dworkin (q.v.), have objected to Nozick's insistence on the overriding importance of rights of acquisition, describing them as unreasonable and arbitrary. Surely in a political community, Dworkin argued, we are entitled to express concern for others? Indifference to the fate of one's fellows or reliance upon the unpredictable and charitable impulses of neighbours cannot be accepted as an adequate basis for the shared existence of a community. Nozick's philosophy is, in Dworkin's terms, based upon an all-or-nothing conception of individual

rights, whereas it may be more reasonable to start with the proposition that the right to property is only one amongst many – competing, for example, with a right or entitlement to assistance from others in an emergency. Similarly, if rights to private property are absolute and unchallengeable, does that mean that the whole of humanity must accept, for all time, that the children of those who first laid claim to the ownership of the earth's natural resources should inherit an unbreakable title to whatever their forebears acquired? If rights or entitlements need to be balanced against one another then the attractions of a political philosophy that regards one right or value as overriding all others are greatly diminished.

Nozick and Hayek are far from being Rawls's only critics, however. Communitarians attacked Rawls's restrained and highly conditional egalitarianism because it gave, in their view, a wholly unjustified weight to individual preferences and led to a serious neglect of the myriad ways in which the beliefs and behaviour of individual human beings are shaped by their membership of particular human communities with distinctive ideas about what is good and just. The dispute between liberals and communitarians has been a striking feature of political and philosophical argument over social justice for more than thirty years, reflecting to a certain extent a tension between different interpretations of liberalism: those that are self-regarding and individualistic and others that are other-regarding and more socially aware.

Whatever may be said about the obscurities of academic debate over the notion of social justice, discussion of what it means to be just and what it takes to be fair is unmistakeably alive and kicking. Liberals and their political rivals continue to engage in fierce arguments about how far the state can reasonably be expected to go in accepting responsibility for the distribution of income and opportunity. Information about how well or badly public institutions, such as schools or hospitals, work, and ideas about what they can or should do to make society fairer have a special significance at the cutting edge of contemporary politics. It is especially important therefore, for the quality of political debate and the impact that liberal arguments can have, that those who regard themselves as liberals are aware of the origins and understand the controversies that now surround a key – if much disputed – concept in liberal political thought: social justice.

Further reading

- Ronald Dworkin, 'Philosophy and Politics: Dialogue between Bryan Magee and Ronald Dworkin', in Bryan Magee (ed.), *Talking Philosophy* (Oxford University Press, 1982)
- F. A. Hayek, *Law, Legislation and Liberty,* Vol. ii: *A New Statement of the Liberal Principles of Justice and Political Economy: The Mirage of Social Justice* (Routledge, 1976)
- Will Kymlicka, *Contemporary Political Philosophy: An Introduction* (Oxford University Press, 2nd edn., 2002), ch. 3: 'Liberal Equality'
- Stephen Mulhall and Adam Swift, *Liberals and Communitarians* (Blackwell, 2nd edn., 1996)
- Robert Nozick, *Anarchy, State, and Utopia* (Basil Blackwell, 1974)
- John Rawls, *A Theory of Justice* (Oxford University Press, revised edn., 1999)
- Judith N. Shklar, *The Faces of Injustice* (Yale University Press, 1990)
- Michael Walzer, *Politics and Passion: Towards a More Egalitarian Liberalism* (Yale University Press, 2005)

Ed Randall

Social Liberalism

Social liberals believe in individual freedom as a central objective – like all liberals. Unlike economic or classical liberals, however, they believe that poverty, unemployment, ill-health, disability and lack of education are serious enough constraints on freedom that state action is justified to redress them. The British Liberal Democrats are generally considered a social liberal party, as are a number of other European liberal parties.

The development of social liberalism can be seen as a response to the problems of industrialisation in the mid- to late nineteenth century. Although free trade (q.v.), the opening up of global markets and the transformation of European economies from agriculture to manufacturing delivered prosperity for many, they were also accompanied by a rising incidence of poverty amongst the new urban working classes.

In Britain the New Liberalism (q.v.) of T. H. Green (q.v.), L. T. Hobhouse (q.v.) and J. A. Hobson (q.v.), among many others, was the response. They argued that laissez-faire economic policies (q.v.) and the unrestrained pursuit of profit had given rise to new forms of poverty and injustice; the economic liberty of the few had blighted the life chances of the many. Negative liberty, the removal of constraints on the individual – the central aim of classical liberalism (q.v.) – would not necessarily lead to freedom of choice for all, as not everyone enjoyed access to the same opportunities; freedom of choice was therefore heavily constrained. Green proposed the idea of *positive freedom* (not to be confused with Isaiah Berlin's (q.v.) notion of positive liberty): the ability of the individual to develop and attain individuality through personal self-development and self-realisation. Since much of the population was prevented from such self-realisation by the impediments of poverty, sickness, unemployment and ignorance, government was justified in taking action to tackle all those conditions. This was not a threat to liberty, but the necessary guarantee of it. As David Lloyd George (q.v.) put it in 1908, 'British Liberalism is not going to repeat the errors of Continental Liberalism ... Let Liberalism proceed with its glorious work of building up the temple of liberty in this country, but let it also bear in mind that the worshippers at the shrine have to live.'

The social reforms of the 1906–15 Liberal government, including the introduction of old-age pensions, national insurance and progressive taxation, can be seen as the realisation of the New Liberal social programme in action, though it drew its inspiration from many sources, including the experience of the active municipal liberalism of Joseph Chamberlain (q.v.) and other Liberals in local government. Later in the century, the economic genius of J. M. Keynes (q.v.), the imaginativeness of Lloyd George's 'Yellow Book', *Britain's Industrial Future*, and the welfare reforms of William Beveridge (q.v.) seemed to cement the triumph of social liberalism.

The distinction between social and economic (or classical) liberals, therefore, revolves around attitudes to the balance between the free market (see Economic Concepts: Markets and Prosperity) and state intervention. Social liberals do not, in general, question the value of market-based economies, but accept a significant role for state action in adjusting or supplementing market outcomes, for example through generous welfare provision (see Economic Concepts: Welfare State), socialised medical care, state education and so on. This usually implies a higher level of taxation than economic liberals would desire, and also a greater role for the use of redistributive fiscal policy. In recent years, social liberals

have also tended to accept a growing role for the state in regulating economic activity to tackle environmental degradation.

The growth in the size of the state throughout the twentieth century, however, has led to new problems, including the increased power of bureaucracies, and the infringement on civil liberties that may entail, the tendency for elites to capture elements of state power (leading to market distortions such as subsidies), the growth of corporatism, a rising burden of taxation and so on. In response, in many European countries since the war, economic liberals have made something of a comeback, drawing intellectual strength from writers such as Friedrich von Hayek (q.v.) and, more recently, Robert Nozick (q.v.).

Despite this resurgence of economic liberal thinking, however, in Britain the Liberal Party/Liberal Democrats has remained a social liberal party. In the early 1950s a determined attempt was made by the 'radical individualists' to return the party to its traditional commitments to free trade, minimum government and individual liberty. This was not a success, partly because the party leadership was too cautious about moving away from the prevailing Butskellite consensus, and partly because of the activities of the Radical Reform Group (q.v.) in countering the rightward trend. The accession of the Radical Reform Group supporter Jo Grimond (q.v.) to the leadership in 1955 signalled the defeat of the economic liberals; some of them drifted into the Conservative Party and others to pro-market fringe groups, while Arthur Seldon (q.v.) helped to set up the Institute for Economic Affairs (q.v.), which became an important source of economic liberal thinking and propaganda.

The breakdown of the post-war economic consensus in the 1970s could perhaps have pushed the Liberal Party back in an economic liberal direction, but in fact the IEA found a much readier welcome for its proposals in the Conservative Party under Margaret Thatcher. The resulting association between economic liberalism (q.v.) and other aspects of the Thatcher style, authoritarian, nationalistic and socially reactionary, helped to keep the Liberal Party firmly in the social liberal camp. This was reinforced by the Alliance with the Social Democratic Party in the 1980s, and also by the growing influence of local councillors within the party, comfortable with using the power of the state at local level to improve their constituents' lives.

From the 1990s, although the economic policies of the Liberal Democrats – along with other political parties – have shifted back in a more pro-market direction, in its approach to an activist role for the state, particularly over public services and environmental issues, and in its taxation policy, it has remained a social liberal party. There are inevitably some disagreements over the precise role of the state in particular sectors, but these do not signal any fundamental division within the party.

Although they accept the need for state intervention, social liberals have also responded to the dangers of the growth in state power highlighted by Hayek and others. The social liberal answer, though, is not, in general, to seek the withdrawal of the state from areas of activity, but to make it more accountable and responsive to its citizens, for instance through decentralisation of power, the creation of federal systems of government and electoral reform, and to constrain it through mechanisms such as written constitutions. In this way social liberals can be distinguished from social democrats (q.v.), who tend to be much less suspicious of state power, although they may share similar approaches to the mixed economy.

In most of Europe in the early twentieth century, many liberal parties stayed true to their classical liberal belief in free markets and a limited state. Since they also in general fared badly electorally in the competition between socialist, or social democratic, and anti-socialist parties that characterised most of the century, their influence on government was accordingly limited. Most European governments did not adopt the Thatcherite economic liberal approach and, as a result, liberal parties have often been able to remain in command of this particular political niche. Nevertheless, some European liberal parties, chiefly though not exclusively in northern Europe, are avowedly social-liberal in character. Some countries, including Denmark, Lithuania and the Netherlands, possess two liberal parties, one economic liberal and one social liberal.

It should be clear, however, that there is no firm divide between social liberalism and economic liberalism; rather, there is a spectrum of views and positions, depending strongly on the economic and social circumstances in a given country at a given time. Even before the New Liberalism, some of the icons of economic liberalism, including Adam Smith (q.v.) and Richard Cobden (q.v.), were never as purely laissez-faire as is sometimes supposed; both of them supported, for example, state intervention in education.

What unites liberal parties of both tendencies – a commitment to civil liberties, human rights, open and tolerant societies, and a just international order – has usually proven stronger than what may divide them. Indeed, as Conrad Russell (q.v.) has argued, since the roots of liberalism stretch back well before the state could exert any significant control over the levers of economic activity, arguably liberalism is not a philosophy that can be described in terms of economics – unlike, for example, socialism. Economics is important simply as a means to an end, because it affects the distribution of power in society and can thereby enlarge, or diminish, the life chances of individuals. Social and economic liberals may differ over economic means, but they do not disagree over their ends.

Further reading

- Ronald Dworkin, *Sovereign Virtue: The Theory and Practice of Equality* (Harvard University Press, 2000)
- Will Kymlicka, *Contemporary Political Philosophy: An Introduction* (Oxford University Press, 2nd edn., 2002), ch. 3, 'Liberal Equality'
- Martin Pugh, *The Making of Modern British Politics 1867–1945* (Blackwell, 3rd edn., 2002), ch. 6, 'Edwardian Progressivism'
- Amartya Sen, *Development as Freedom* (Oxford University Press, 1999)

Duncan Brack

Social Market

The use of the term 'social market' in British politics is most strongly associated with Dr David Owen, the second leader of the Social Democratic Party. Owen used it more as a political slogan than as a precise term, first to signal his split from the Labour Party, and then to mark his increasing attachment to market, rather than government-interventionist, policy solutions.

The phrase 'social market' was first coined in Germany in 1946, by Alfred Müller-Armack, an adherent of the Freiburg School of 'ordo-liberal' economists. Writing in the wreckage of Nazi totalitarianism, the Freiburg School was searching for an economic system that would keep the state from interfering in individuals' lives:

a perfect, undistorted, liberating market, in which the only role of government would be to ensure that market forces worked freely, through breaking up concentrations of economic power.

The theory was turned into practical politics by the German Christian Democrats in their 1949 Dusseldorf Programme. For them, the social market represented a third way, between socialism and monopoly capitalism: the Programme included minimum state control of industry, powerful anti-trust laws and cooperation between trade unions and companies. 'Outlaw monopoly,' wrote Ludwig Erhard, the Minister for Economic Affairs, 'turn the people and the money loose and they will make the economy strong.' One factor that was *not* noticeably present, however, was social justice (q.v.); Erhard was implacably opposed to universal welfare provision and redistributive fiscal policy. True competition would by itself produce prosperity and higher living standards for all.

The term was first introduced to British politics by Sir Keith Joseph, and his creation, the Centre for Policy Studies, whose first publication, in 1975, was called *Why Britain Needs a Social Market Economy*. In his foreword to the booklet, Joseph explained how he founded the CPS, 'to survey the scope for replacing increasingly interventionist government by social market policies'. For Joseph and the booklet's authors, the meaning of the term 'social market' was the same as it had been for Müller-Armack and Erhard: 'a socially responsible market economy, for a market economy is perfectly compatible with the promotion of a more compassionate society … Industry alone creates the wealth which pays for social welfare'. Government intervention was justified only where it was designed to limit market distortions such as the abuse of monopoly power or restrictive practices.

The 'social' aspect derived entirely from the surplus produced by an efficient and competitive economy: higher profits, higher wages and higher employment all resulted in a higher tax yield, which could be used to 'alleviate distress and advance education'.

Despite Joseph's support, however, the term never featured in the slogans of Thatcherism, and so David Owen (q.v.) was able to appropriate it, initially in May 1981, just two months after the formation of the SDP, in a lecture to Strathclyde University; he used it more frequently after he became SDP leader in 1983. As Owen argued, the source of Britain's economic decline was poor productivity, caused by a failure to develop a commercially oriented social climate within industry, far too weak an emphasis on winning markets, and insufficient priority given to exports. His solutions included the creation of a Ministry of Competition to break up cartels and monopolies and to promote competition and fair trading, denationalisation in the public sector – an innovation in the early 1980s, before the large-scale Conservative privatisation programme – and labour market reform, including greater trade-union democracy and disaggregation of wage bargaining structures.

Although there were strong similarities here with the original ordo-liberal conception of the social market, there were also marked differences: an incomes policy to control inflation, an industrial strategy to assist firms to develop and adjust to changing patterns of demand, and central planning. Social partnership took its place beside industrial partnership to create 'the background of understanding and shared interests that is inherent in the social market'. This theme was developed further by other SDP thinkers such as Nick Bosanquet, who argued explicitly that government had

to intervene to create the political climate necessary to allow the market to operate – not only by redistributing the surpluses of 'market gainers' but also by investing in human capital and through electoral reform and political decentralisation.

As Owen steadily moved the SDP to the right, however, and particularly after he founded the 'continuing SDP' in 1988, his commitment to market solutions, and his contempt for interventionism, grew much stronger. He advocated much more extensive privatisation, argued again for labour market reform to hold down real wages and increase international competitiveness, and supported selectivity in social security, while at the same time dropping the proposal for an incomes policy and relegating the commitment to redistribution. Thus he worked his way back to something which Müller-Armack and Erhard would probably have recognised.

Despite some interest in the concept of the social market amongst commentators after the 1987 election, the term never really took off outside the SDP. Partly this is because Owen never defined precisely what he meant by it; the SDP only finally published a policy paper on the social market after he had left it, in January 1988. Mainly, however, it is because his main use of the term was as a way of distancing himself from whoever he saw as his immediate political enemies. Initially this was his former colleagues in the Labour Party, but increasingly it became his internal opponents, the Jenkinsites in the SDP and his Liberal partners in the Alliance. As early as 1984, David Marquand (q.v.) warned the SDP against adopting a 'junior Thatcherite' approach, and Roy Jenkins (q.v.) pondered why the Social Democrats should put so much effort into promoting the market when it was the public sector that was going under.

So inevitably the term tended to change emphasis depending on who it was used against – and because in the end Owen failed, it did not appear particularly attractive to anyone else. The term has not featured in Liberal Democrat policy statements, and although the Social Market Foundation think-tank was set up by Owenites in 1988, it seems to display few links with Owen's thinking. Perhaps the most that can be said of Owen's use of the term 'social market' is that it formed one element of the general trend in British politics away from the corporatism and interventionism of the 1960s and '70s towards a greater acceptance of the role of the market in the 1980s and '90s.

Possibly the real inheritors of Owen's social market economy are New Labour; as Peter Mandelson put it in June 2005, 'New Labour's blueprint is quite distinct from any US model. It is far closer to Ludwig Erhard's post-war social market economy.'

Further reading

- Leighton Andrews, *Liberals versus the Social Market Economy* (Hebden Royd, 1985)
- Nick Bosanquet, 'The 'Social Market Economy': Principles behind the Policies?', *Political Quarterly,* vol. 55:3, July–September 1984
- Duncan Brack, *The Myth of the Social Market: A Critique of Owenite Economics* (LINk Publications, 1989); a summarised and updated version is in 'David Owen and the Social Market Economy', *Journal of Liberal History* 47 (summer 2005)
- Centre for Policy Studies, *Why Britain Needs a Social Market Economy* (CPS, 1975)
- Alex de Mont, *A Theory of the Social Market* (Tawney Society, 1984)

Duncan Brack

Herbert Spencer 1820–1903

An important pioneer of the disciplines of sociology and psychology, Spencer located moral and political ideas and individual conduct in a general 'evolutionary' context. He outlined an alternative vision of individual and collective advance to those proposed by idealists, Fabian socialists and New Liberals.

Key ideas

- General theory of directional evolution, including psychological and social evolution.
- Individual liberty essential for progress, subject to equal freedom for all and with individuals adapting through receiving the consequences of their conduct.
- Early advocacy of a form of 'welfare pluralism'.
- Sustained criticism of socialism and parliamentary Liberalism, especially the trend to New Liberalism.

Biography

Herbert Spencer was born in Derby on 27 April 1820. His father was a teacher and honorary secretary of the Derby Philosophical Society, an important strand in the town's radical and scientific outlook. Nonconformism in religion was shared by his parents but in other respects there was little common ground, and his mother had less impact on his childhood development than the passion for unearthing the causes of things and questioning of authority characterising his father.

From 1833 Spencer's education rested with his uncle Thomas, Cambridge graduate and perpetual curate of Hinton Charterhouse, south of Bath. Coupled to unorthodox schooling came assisting with his uncle's production of pamphlets on religious belief and the application of political economics to Poor Law reform, of immense political and popular concern with the publication of the Report of the Royal Commission on the Poor Law of 1834. In his parish, and as chairman of the Bath Board of Guardians, Thomas pursued the policy prescribed, curtailing outdoor relief to the able-bodied in the interests of rewarding virtue and punishing vice. Here was a novel fusion of political economics and natural theology yielding insights into human motivation and pathways to material and moral advance for individuals. Spencer's own first publication, on the Poor Law, appeared in the *Bath and West of England Magazine* of 1836.

Formal education at an end (he did not go to university), Spencer embarked on two overlapping careers, assisted by family connections. He became an early participant in the construction and promotion of railways, employed in London and the Midlands on civil engineering tasks and securing parliamentary approval for lines. He also wrote on radical politics, notably in association with the Complete Suffrage Union. A series of 'letters' to the *Nonconformist*, which he described as 'very good remedies for Tyranny and Toryism', were reissued in 1843 as *The Proper Sphere of Government*.

A letter from Thomas secured appointment in 1848 as a sub-editor with *The Economist* in London. Residence in the capital meant his contacts and cultural horizons expanded rapidly; G. H. Lewes, Marian Evans (later George Eliot), T. H. Huxley and J. S. Mill (q.v.) were new and influential friends. Thomas's death in 1853 brought him money, permitting resignation from *The Economist* and more time to write. The next decade or so was his intellectually most productive. Prospects of marriage, though, receded; he found Evans, clearly keen on him, insufficiently attractive physically for marriage, and he remained a bachelor. Essays appeared in the main periodicals exploring the implications of adaptation

and the passing on of acquired characteristics through inheritance as the explanation of progressive development in society and other contexts. Work on his *Principles of Psychology* (1855), however, brought on a mental collapse that, he felt, never fully righted itself.

Nevertheless, by 1857 he had formulated his general theory of evolution; *First Principles* (1862) and subsequent volumes on biology, psychology (reworking the earlier study), sociology and ethics elaborated the theory. This ten-volume *System of Synthetic Philosophy* was finished in 1896. Separate was *The Man versus the State* (1884), polemical and influential.

By the 1870s Spencer was well known and widely translated. A visit to America in 1882 cemented his reputation there, and in 1884 he declined an approach to be put forward as a Liberal parliamentary candidate for Leicester. He died on 8 December 1903.

Ideas

The central theme of *The Proper Sphere of Government* is that governments should not do more than protect persons and property, and prevent the aggressions of the rich on the weak; in other words, administer 'justice'. Provided 'justice' is in place the self-adjusting 'laws of society' will keep elements in equilibrium. Legislation to regulate actions in general achieves effects the opposite of those desired: the old Poor Law and proposals for national education and public health were targets. Moreover, as government commits these sins it omits to ensure the prompt, easy and free administration of 'justice' for citizens, its sole responsibility.

Social Statics, dated 1851, strengthened the analysis of *The Proper Sphere* by highlighting the Lamarckian mechanism of adaptation to circumstances together with the inheritance of acquired characteristics as the key to *all* change, and by arguing that that mechanism ensured change was progressive in direction. 'Justice' is now: 'Every man has freedom to do all that he wills, provided he infringes not the equal freedom of any other man.' Within this framework, 'justice' requires that individuals shall take the consequences of their conduct. Otherwise adaptation is punished and non-adaptation rewarded. Spencer attacks private property as contrary to the necessary 'co-heirship' of all men to the soil (a position later diluted), and asserts equal rights to freedom for women.

His *Principles of Psychology* (1855) presented a dynamic version of associationism in which physical and psychical phenomena developed in parallel throughout all life up to human life in its most social forms. He rejected freedom of the will, attracting the charge of materialism, which he denied. No logical space remains for moral exhortation to elicit a direct change of heart in an agent; exhortations form part of an 'environment' to which gradual adaptations of physical and psychical brain states will arise.

In the volumes of the *System of Synthetic Philosophy*, Spencer laid out an all-embracing theory of (directional) evolution, a movement from homogeneity to heterogeneity, powered by physical principles and, in organic life, by the inheritance of acquired characteristics producing functional specialisation. This was intended to give a scientific underpinning to liberalism, and succoured those who objected to authority, religious and secular, exercised against 'justice'. Spencer opposed 'militancy': in 1881/82 he promoted the Anti-Aggression League. He sided against Governor Eyre over brutalism in Jamaica, and against the Boer War.

However, in 1859 Darwin had argued in favour of natural selection as a major factor in biological selection, whereby out of (genetic) variations only some were 'selected' to survive in an inevitable struggle for existence. Spencer incorporated this mechanism into his theory, calling it the 'survival of the fittest' (in 1864), but retained his Lamarckianism. Spencer's position, and his concern with direction, led to misunderstandings in the 'Social Darwinist' literature that developed over how Darwin's own distinctive theory might relate to social life. By the 1890s, though, experimental evidence told against the Lamarckian theory of the inheritance of acquired characteristics.

Other factors too led to a decline in Spencer's reputation as the century ended. The moral interdependence of individuals in society was being stressed in idealist social thought, for example by Bernard Bosanquet (q.v.). Spencer's advocacy of altruism, the free administration of 'justice', 'beneficence' (or informal care) between family members and others and across generations, and small-scale, non-bureaucratic charities was an early pluralistic vision of 'social welfare', but his depiction of social legislation as interfering with 'nature' was arbitrary, and contrary to the increasingly common conceptualisation of the state as enabling people to be free to achieve aims, rather than merely freeing them from constraints. Spencer, critical of Gladstone's (q.v.) liberalism, viewed these developments as illiberal, though they became the core of the New Liberalism (q.v.) and the Fabianism of Beatrice Webb, whom Spencer had long known well as one of his friend Richard Potter's daughters.

Central was a split over the conception of 'society': idealists (and Tönnies and Durkheim in their approaches to sociology) took the 'social organism' to be a moral or spiritual whole which a wise state, tapping into the 'general will', advanced. Spencer judged this dangerous rhetoric, ignoring the sociological reality of his version of the organic analogy, construing individuals as fundamentally autonomous, though altruistic, in no need of 'moral governance' save to enforce 'justice' and prevent external aggression. Although partially eclipsed, Spencer's political thought still appealed to liberals such as John Morley (q.v.) and Auberon Herbert (q.v.), and to the Liberty and Property Defence League.

Since the 1970s there has been a revival of critical interest in Spencer's social, political and moral thought. He provided an enduringly powerful critique of the fallibility of government action in the pursuit of 'positive freedom' and the panoply of associated paternalistic professionals, audit mechanisms and regulatory bureaucracy.

Key works
- *The Proper Sphere of Government* (1843)
- *Social Statics* (1851)
- *The Man versus the State* (1884)
- *The Principles of Ethics* (2 vols., 1892–93)
- *The Principles of Sociology* (3 vols., 1876, 1882, 1896)

Further reading
- John Offer (ed.), *Herbert Spencer: Political Writings* (Cambridge University Press, 1994)
- John Offer (ed.), *Herbert Spencer: Critical Assessments* (4 vols., Routledge, 2000)
- J. D. Y. Peel, *Herbert Spencer: The Evolution of a Sociologist* (Heinemann, 1971)
- M. W. Taylor, *Men Versus the State: Herbert Spencer and Late Victorian Individualism* (Clarendon Press, 1992)

John Offer

Tawney Society

A policy think-tank associated with the SDP, the Tawney Society proved effective in stimulating discussion and debate within the party, but did not long survive the SDP's merger with the Liberal Party.

The Tawney Society was founded in early 1982 by the innovative sociologist Lord Young of Dartington, as a think-tank for the Social Democratic Party. It was designed to be a forum for the discussion and debate of ideas among Social Democrats, whilst remaining independent of the official policy-making machinery of the SDP. It thus aimed to provide a testing ground for new ideas and for fresh and serious thinking without formally committing the party itself to open espousal of such ideas.

The Tawney Society's first general secretary was Tony Flower, serving in that role for six years until the merger of the SDP with the Liberal Party in 1988. The Society's name, honouring the eminent economic historian and democratic socialist thinker R. H. Tawney, was, as Flower later acknowledged, 'deliberately and brilliantly mischievous'. Certainly it aroused the indignation of many British socialists at the time; the historian Raphael Samuel, in particular, recorded at length his political and ideological objections to what he considered the SDP's misappropriation of Tawney's socialist legacy.

Nonetheless, the Tawney Society soon drew significant support from the leadership of the SDP as well as from its rank-and-file activists. The original founders of the SDP were all involved in the Tawney Society from its inception: David Owen (q.v.) opened its first conference, Roy Jenkins (q.v.) delivered the first annual Tawney Lecture, and both Bill Rodgers and Shirley Williams spoke from Tawney platforms.

The Society sought to promote the development of ideas through publications, regular meetings, summer schools, the annual Tawney Lecture, study groups, local branches and fringe meetings at SDP conferences. Among its publications were pamphlets, occasional papers and the quarterly *Tawney Journal*, edited by Tony Flower. The Tawney pamphlets' authors included distinguished academics such as Professors Ralf Dahrendorf (q.v.), Ronald Dore, Dorothy Emmet, Peter Hall, Alec Nove and W. G. Runciman.

The acrimonious merger of the SDP with the Liberal Party in 1988 split the Tawney Society, as it did, of course, the Alliance. On the merger question itself the Society took a stance of principled neutrality. Tony Flower resigned as general secretary towards the end of 1988, handing over to Tim Rycroft as his successor.

Eventually, following the merger and the subsequent launch of the Liberal Democrats, the Tawney Society ceased to exist as an active think-tank. In 1992, however, the New Tawney Society was launched under the supervision of Mike Reynolds and Margaret Sharp, both Liberal Democrat parliamentary candidates. Its interim committee included Richard Holme, David Marquand (q.v.), Bill Rodgers and Nancy Seear. But in spite of these promising beginnings, this reincarnate body did not endure long into the early life of the new party.

The historians of the SDP, Ivor Crewe and Anthony King, later concluded that the original Tawney Society was 'too small and too new to exert any substantial influence outside the party's ranks'. However, within the SDP the Society for six years proved effective both in stimulating discussion and debate, significantly, for example, over David Owen's advocacy of a 'social market economy' (q.v.), and in promoting carefully developed ideas designed as the bases for social-democratic policies.

Further reading
- The Society's archives are located in the Albert Sloman Library at the University of Essex.

Tudor Jones

Temperance Movement

A popular social movement, strongest in the latter half of the nineteenth century, the temperance movement provided the Liberal Party with militant grassroots electoral activists, but its fissiparous nature, the uncompromising stance of its leaders and the doubtful electoral popularity of its policies all posed major problems for the Liberal leadership.

The British temperance movement emerged in the 1830s as a teetotal movement favouring total abstinence. The foundation of the prohibitionist United Kingdom Alliance in 1853 marked its emergence into political significance; this body was the strongest of the numerous organisations, peaking in membership and political influence in the 1890s. The Church of England Temperance Society appealed to more moderate opinion and to reforming Conservatives. After 1906 the UK Alliance was challenged by the Temperance Legislation League, which argued for experiments in 'disinterested management' of the drink trade and other restrictionist controls.

The early twentieth century marked the decline of the temperance movement, although its influence remained, but stronger at the elite than the popular level. It retained a not insignificant parliamentary lobby until the 1970s, active on issues such as hours of opening and regulations concerning the advertising of alcohol.

The temperance societies attracted people from all parts of the UK and all social classes. They provided an avenue for women to participate in social and political affairs. However, their core support came from the respectable middle classes and artisans, particularly Nonconformists, in the north of England, Scotland and Wales. Both leadership and financial support were also provided from wealthy manufacturers and industrialists, as well as Quaker cocoa families. Throughout the latter Victorian period the parliamentary leader of the UK Alliance was Sir Wilfrid Lawson (1829–1906), a Cumberland baronet and a classic backbencher, who espoused a raft of radical causes. By the end of the century Lawson's leadership was being challenged by Sir T. P. Whittaker (1850–1919), who served as a temperance member of a Royal Commission on licensing and who became the foremost advocate of disinterested management. In the early twentieth century a leading figure was the Wesleyan minister Reverend Henry Carter (1854–1951), who served as a member of the wartime Central Control Board.

Prohibition was an authoritarian policy which was incompatible with classic liberal political ideas, as expounded by J. S. Mill (q.v.). However, in 1864 the UK Alliance adopted the device of the 'local veto', whereby the ratepayers of a locality would be given the option of voting for their parish to go dry. This could be justified in terms of local self-government and political education and hence appealed to broader shades of progressive opinion.

After 1870 temperance or liquor licensing reform became increasingly polarised in party political terms. With the rise of Nonconformity (q.v.) as a force in the radical wing of the Liberal Party, temperance reform became a key plank in the 'advanced' wing of the party, featuring, for example, in the National Liberal Federation's Newcastle Programme of 1891. During this period, both liberal intellectuals

and Liberal politicians became more sympathetic to action by the state; T. H. Green (q.v.), for example, saw restrictive temperance legislation as a means of enhancing the true potential and freedom (q.v.) of the individual. Moreover, excess drinking was increasingly seen as a contributory cause of social evils, such as poverty, poor housing and prostitution.

However, the growing support of temperance reformers for Liberalism was a two-edged weapon. On the one hand, the temperance societies provided some of the most zealous and committed electoral workers for the party after the extension of the franchise in 1885. On the other hand, the prohibitionists dogmatically refused to sanction any scheme for a wider licensing reform and continued to adopt a model of political progress based on the example of the Anti-Corn Law League (q.v.), which eschewed political parties and saw political progress stemming from the force of public opinion 'from below'. The result was that the Liberal leadership was continually frustrated in its attempts to rally prohibitionist support for reforming legislation or broad compromise programmes for licensing reform. Another problem was that temperance reform was of doubtful general electoral popularity and the more the 'Trade' became driven into the arms of the Conservatives the greater the electoral dangers. By the 1890s the temperance reformers began to be regarded as 'faddists' who had alienated many of the working-class voters the party was seeking to rally. After the electoral defeat of 1895 the party leadership sought to distance itself from more militant prohibitionists; but the Unionist Licensing Act of 1904 and the Asquith's government ill-fated Licensing Bill of 1908, thrown out by the House of Lords, ensured that the issue remained of central importance in Edwardian politics.

A further complication for the Liberal leadership was that after 1895 the temperance movement became bitterly divided between the orthodox prohibitionists, wanting local veto, and advocates of Swedish-style 'disinterested management' whereby the licensee had no direct interest in the sale and the drink trade became a local monopoly under the control of a municipality or trust. This schism lasted until the 1930s. During the First World War the drink issue became redefined in terms of 'national efficiency' and far-reaching controls were imposed on hours of sale for the duration under the auspices of a Central Control Board. Alcohol control ceased to be of interest solely to the temperance societies and after 1914 its party-political salience faded away. Lobbyists on both sides concentrated their efforts as much upon influencing Whitehall departments as political parties.

Further reading

- A. E. Dingle, *The Campaign for Prohibition in Victorian England: The United Kingdom Alliance 1872–1895* (Croom Helm, 1980)
- David M. Fahey, 'The Politics of Drink: Pressure Groups and the British Liberal Party, 1883–1908', *Social Science*, 1979, 54:2
- John Greenaway, *Drink and British Politics since 1830: A Study in Policy-Making* (Palgrave Macmillan, 2003)
- David W. Gutzke, *Protecting the Pub: Brewers and Publicans against Temperance* (Boydell Press, 1989)
- D. A. Hamer, *The Politics of Electoral Pressure: A Study in the History of Victorian Reform Agitations* (Harvester, 1994)
- Brian Harrison, *Drink and the Victorians: The Temperance Question in England 1815–1872* (Keele University Press, 2nd edn., 1994)

John Greenaway

Henry David Thoreau   1817–62

American writer, naturalist and philosopher, best known for *Walden*, a reflection on simple living amongst nature, and *Civil Disobedience*, an argument for moral resistance to unjust laws.

Key ideas

- The supremacy of individual conscience over statutory law and social conformity.
- The justification – and obligation – of civil disobedience in response to gross injustice.
- The value of personal development and enriched experience, centred on the pursuit of knowledge of self and nature rather than the accumulation of wealth.
- The importance of untamed nature.

Biography

Henry David Thoreau was born in Concord, Massachusetts, on 12 July 1817; except for brief periods he lived there all his life. He was one of four children born to John Thoreau, a pencil-maker, and Cynthia Dunbar Thoreau, who was active in the Concord Anti-Slavery Society. He attended Harvard College (1833–37), receiving a bachelor's degree. Afterwards he became a grammar school teacher, worked as a land surveyor and helped run his father's pencil and graphite factory. All these jobs were secondary to his career as a writer and to his exploration of the woods, fields, lakes and streams of his beloved Concord countryside.

Thoreau never married, living with his family for most of his adult life. He died on 6 May 1862 of tuberculosis aggravated by bronchitis he had developed counting tree rings during a winter storm.

Ideas

Thoreau's main intellectual influence came from his close friendship with Ralph

Waldo Emerson (1803–82), America's most important nineteenth-century public thinker, and his neighbour in Concord. In his great work, *Nature*, Emerson urged his fellow seekers to find themselves through the study of nature. Thoreau dedicated himself to living this idea, exploring nature in every way possible: fishing and picking huckleberries, writing poetry and nature essays, counting tree rings and studying forest succession. In the process, he found his own voice; few writers are so thoroughly identified with their local landscape.

Thoreau is best known for two pieces of writing begun in 1845. In that year, he was arrested and sent to jail for refusing to pay his poll tax, in protest against state support for slavery and the Mexican–American War. In the essay *Civil Disobedience* (originally published as *Resistance to Civil Government*), Thoreau makes the case that citizens should not allow government to overrule individual conscience; we have a moral duty to oppose such terrible injustices as slavery and imperialism. He goes on to argue the superiority of moral law over statutory law and the priority of moral conscience over personal comfort and social conformity. 'Disobedience is the true foundation of liberty. The obedient must be slaves.' Thoreau's positions have been hotly contested, but it should be noted that he explicitly states that civil disobedience should not be undertaken for trivial reasons, but rather as a response to gross, systemic injustices.

Also in 1845, Thoreau began a two-year experiment in simple living, at Walden Pond, on the outskirts of Concord village. There this 'self-appointed inspector of snow storms and rain storms' built a sturdy one-room cabin, cleared a few acres of forest to grow potatoes and beans, walked, fished, watched the seasons come and go, and began to write an account of his stay. Over nine years and eight revisions, this work became *Walden*, one of the most important and enduring books written in America during the nineteenth century.

Walden describes a life devoted to personal development and enriched experience, centred on the pursuit of knowledge of self and nature. It advocates ethical, intellectual and creative striving; as Thoreau explains:

> I went to the woods because I wished to live deliberately, to front only the essential facts of life, and see if I could not learn what it had to teach, and not, when I came to die, discover that I had not lived ... I wanted to live deep and suck out all the marrow of life ... to know it by experience, and be able to give a true account of it in my next excursion.

Much more than a literal account of Thoreau's two years in the woods, *Walden* is a social critique of contemporary American and Western civilisation, with each chapter focused on some aspect of our humanity that needed to be either developed or reformed, starting with 'economy'. Part of *Walden*'s success lies in its seamless blending of seemingly disparate aims and elements. It combines personal honesty and outrageous tall tales; ethical idealism and direct, affectionate engagement with the material world; accurate natural history and poetic descriptions of nature; no-nonsense techniques for dealing with life's minutiae and soaring, transcendental flights into the ether.

While *Walden*'s literary brilliance has ensured it a place in the American canon, it has also become a bible to many environmentalists. One of Thoreau's aims was to demonstrate that a life 'simple in (material) means' can be 'rich in (cultural and spiritual) ends'. He makes a strong case that lives dedicated to exploring and enjoying nature are better than lives devoted to piling up wealth or to gross material consumption. A major challenge to the view that the natural world is there to be exploited, this perhaps has a stronger resonance in the modern day, when resource depletion, over-consumption and the conjunction of material wealth with moral sickness are all increasingly recognised as urgent challenges.

The other half of Thoreau's environmental philosophy centres on his appreciation and advocacy for the wild. His writings are filled with detailed descriptions of the local flora and fauna. He explored his native landscape with the intelligent curiosity of a scientist and the creativity and heart of a poet. As he wrote in *Walden*, 'We can never have enough of Nature.' This love for nature and appreciation for what it contributes to human life were reinforced in later writings, drawn from the detailed observations of natural history he kept over a period of twenty-four years. Thoreau argued that every village should preserve wild forests, river walks and other places of natural beauty, for public enjoyment and education. His realisation that many wild species retreated as human settlement advanced led to one of the first proposals for a system of national parks or 'national preserves', to protect the full complement of native species and keep some lands unmanaged and unmodified by human beings.

Thoreau's writing has been influential in many schools of thought, including anarchism (q.v.) and environmentalism (q.v.). Leo Tolstoy, Mahatma Gandhi and Martin Luther King Jr., among many others, all cited *Civil Disobedience* as an inspiration. In his championing of the individual conscience and self-realisation, Thoreau can also be claimed for liberalism: 'If a man does not keep pace with his companions, perhaps it is because he hears a different drummer. Let him step to the music which he hears, however measured or far away.'

Key works
- *On the Duty of Civil Disobedience* (1849)
- *A Week on the Concord and Merrimack Rivers* (1849)
- *Walden* (1854)
- *Walking* (1862)
- *Life without Principle* (1863)

Further reading
- P. J. Cafaro, *Thoreau's Living Ethics:* Walden *and the Pursuit of Virtue* (University of Georgia Press, 2004)
- L. N. Neufeldt, *The Economist: Henry Thoreau and Enterprise* (Oxford University Press, 1989)
- R. D. Richardson, Jr., *Henry Thoreau: A Life of the Mind* (University of California Press, 1986)
- L. D. Walls, *Seeing New Worlds: Henry David Thoreau and Nineteenth-Century Natural Science* (University of Wisconsin Press, 1995)

Philip Cafaro

Alexis de Tocqueville   1805–59

The greatest figure of the second generation of French liberals, Tocqueville was active in politics, but died too young, and was in other ways too unlucky, to win effective power. Nevertheless, his influence as a thinker was pervasive in nineteenth-century liberal Europe and, after fading, revived during the era of the Cold War, especially in the United States.

Key ideas
- The age of aristocracy and traditional monarchy is over; the age of equality, or democracy, has arrived.
- Democracy does not have to be revolutionary, and should not be anti-religious; as the example of the United States shows, it can be perfectly compatible with just and efficient government.

- But equality, unless wedded to liberty and the rule of law, may breed a modern version of despotism: the autocratic rule of one man, a demagogue or a military dictator, ruling arbitrarily in the name of the people.
- Liberty is the greatest of all political values, for only through liberty can individuals and societies perfect themselves.

Biography

Alexis de Tocqueville was born in the wake of the great Revolution, on 29 July 1805, to one of the most distinguished families of the French nobility. His father's ancestors had for centuries cherished their lands in Normandy and served the King as army officers. His mother's family, the Le Peletiers, was among the greatest of the legal clans which, in the ancient *parlements*, shared the government of the country with the King, enforced the laws, and protested against royal acts of tyranny. The Le Peletiers suffered grievously in the Revolution; in 1794 six of Tocqueville's nearest relations were guillotined, his parents escaping the same fate only because of the fall of Robespierre.

The family tradition was therefore strongly royalist and anti-revolutionary. Experience of Napoleon's rule also made them anti-dictatorial, though few of them held this point of view as staunchly as Alexis was to do. When the Bourbon dynasty was restored in 1814 Tocqueville's father immediately entered the royal service as a provincial prefect, and served the Bourbons in one way and another until their final fall in the July revolution of 1830.

Alexis de Tocqueville was then twenty-five. He had been trained as a lawyer, and his acute intelligence had despaired of the Bourbon regime long before it fell, but his career prospects under the new monarchy of Louis Philippe were poor, and anyway his talents and tastes were those of a political writer. Wishing to understand the actuality of democratic government, which was clearly a rising force, Tocqueville travelled for ten months in the United States, the only modern republic, and after his return to France published the first part of *Democracy in America* (1835), which made him famous overnight.

A few years later he was elected to the Chamber of Deputies by a Norman constituency. He was active in the politics of the July Monarchy (1830–48) and the Second Republic (1848–51), and served briefly as Foreign Minister in 1849. He steadily opposed the dictatorial ambitions of Louis Napoleon, and after the Bonapartist coup d'état of 1851, which opened the way to the Second Empire (and during which he was briefly imprisoned) he retired from public life and wrote his second masterpiece, *The Ancien Régime and the French Revolution* (1856), in which all his main ideas were re-examined, historically rather than theoretically. He died of tuberculosis, however, on 16 April 1859, before he could get very far with a planned sequel.

In 1835 Tocqueville married Mary Mottley, an Englishwoman. They had no children.

Ideas

Tocqueville was in love with great ideas – liberty chief among them – but he was a moralist rather than a philosopher, and the value of his writings lies not so much in his doctrines as in his very concrete sense of how ideas operate in society. The first part of *Democracy in America* was his greatest achievement.

Tocqueville's abounding energy, and his even greater capacity for acquiring and analysing information, meant that he was able to write the first treatise to do justice to the government and society of the United States; and his third great merit, his supremely lucid and charming style, meant that his treatise was uniquely readable. He may even be said to have invented modern political science by his example – an achievement that he looked forward to when, in the introduction, he demanded a new political science for a wholly new world. His emphasis throughout the 1835 *Democracy* was on the fact that the American political and social system, though profoundly and inescapably egalitarian, worked, and worked well. He was not blind to America's deficiencies, slavery and racism above all, but in the monarchical and reactionary Europe of the 1830s his demonstration of the viability of democratic government was revolutionary, much though he disliked the word. After reading Tocqueville it could no longer be argued seriously that republicanism was bound to be utopian, bloodthirsty and incompetent.

The second part of the *Democracy*, published in 1840, was in part a further discussion of some of the risks and weaknesses of democracy which had been raised in part one, and partly a speculative exploration of the impact of egalitarianism on manners and customs, for example on family life. It demonstrated another peculiarity of Tocqueville's mind: though he could not always, or indeed very often, supply the right answers, he was amazingly fertile in asking the right questions. To read Tocqueville attentively, above all in the 1840 *Democracy*, is to be compelled to reflect on topics which have never since ceased to preoccupy liberals and democrats. They may be summed up as the great question of what are the duties and rights of the individual citizen in a free society.

Liberty, Tocqueville's most cherished political value, was under siege in France from the revolution of 1848 until long after his death. His last book, *The Ancien Régime*, was an admirably scholarly attempt to discover why France, the progenitor of liberty in Europe, had plunged so often into revolution, submitted to dictatorship, and embraced the most vulgar forms of egalitarianism. Tocqueville's conclusions were somewhat weakened by his inability to get beyond the dogmas of classical economics and to envisage a state committed, in the name of justice, to reducing the fearful gap between rich and poor (he hated all forms of socialism). But his depiction of the processes of history, of the opportunities, dangers and constraints, of the inescapable continuities and discontinuities which confront all statesmen and citizens as they try to shape the nation's course in the modern era, is quite as thought-provoking as *Democracy in America*.

Tocqueville was a liberal who refused both foolish optimism and facile pessimism. At great cost to himself (some of which he recounted in his *Recollections*, which dealt with the revolution of 1848) he rejected the extremes of both right and left, and showed that although the centre is often a difficult and unsatisfactory place to occupy, it has the merit of being reasonable and fair-minded.

Tocqueville pleased the Americans of his own and later times by his intelligent praise of their institutions. His reputation as a historian was always high in France, where his standing as a political scientist has recently revived. Yet it was an Englishman, John Stuart Mill (q.v.), who in his lifetime read Tocqueville's works most intelligently and, by incorporating Tocqueville's insights into his own writings, made sure they were retained in the mainstream of European liberal thought.

Key works

- *De la démocratie en Amérique* (*Democracy in America*) (2 vols., 1835, 1840)

- *L'Ancien Régime et la Révolution* (1856; translated into English many times, and various titles)
- *Souvenirs* (1942; translated into English as *Recollections* in 1970)

Further reading

- Hugh Brogan, *Alexis de Tocqueville: Prophet of Democracy in the Age of Revolution* (Profile, 2006)
- Seymour Drescher, *Dilemmas of Democracy: Tocqueville and Modernisation* (University of Pittsburgh Press, 1968)
- André Jardin, *Tocqueville: A Biography* (1984; English translation, Halban, 1988)
- Jack Lively, *The Social and Political Thought of Alexis de Tocqueville* (Clarendon Press, 1962)
- G. W. Pierson, *Tocqueville and Beaumont in America* (Oxford University Press, 1938)

Hugh Brogan

John Trenchard   1662–1723

One of the leading Whig polemicists of the late seventeenth and earlier eighteenth centuries, Trenchard produced some of the most influential political essays of the day.

Key ideas

- A standing (professional) army is a dangerous support of arbitrary government and liberty is best defended with a citizen militia.
- Tyranny is illegitimate and can always be resisted.
- Men possess the natural rights to life, liberty and property, and civil government should be established by contract and on the basis of consent.
- Liberty of conscience is a fundamental right: government should not interfere in matters of religious belief and practice.
- The clergy should be denied civil or temporal power.

Biography

John Trenchard was born in 1662. His father, William, who possessed landed estates in Wiltshire and Somerset, was Whig MP for Westbury in the exclusion parliaments of 1679–81 and his distant relative, Sir John Trenchard, was also an MP and government minister.

Trenchard read law at Trinity College, Dublin, and was called to the bar in 1689; he soon abandoned law, however, for a career as a polemical Whig (q.v.) pamphleteer and journalist. He was aided by marriage to a woman of substance (possibly a daughter of Thomas Scawen) and by an inheritance from his uncle, Sir George Norton. In 1697 and 1698 he played a major role in the successful press campaign against William III maintaining a standing army in peacetime; perhaps because his family were staunch Whigs, the King declined to have him arrested. In 1699 Trenchard was one of seven commissioners appointed to look into what had been done with the estates forfeited by Jacobites in Ireland since 1689. The report was strongly critical of how these estates had been granted mainly to foreign favourites of William III, and an Act of Resumption was passed shortly afterwards, despite the wishes of the King and his Whig ministers, a great triumph for the opposition. Trenchard served as a trustee to manage the forfeited estates (1700–04).

Trenchard became increasingly interested in natural religion. In 1709 he produced *The Natural History of Superstition*, an attack on superstition, witchcraft and the mysterious in religion, and he probably drafted his essay on miracles at this time (it was published posthumously in 1755, along with several other short essays on moral and political issues). In 1718 his wife committed suicide and a year later, Trenchard married Anne, daughter of the wealthy Sir William Blackett.

Trenchard's career as a political polemicist burst back into life in 1719, when he met Thomas Gordon, a young Scot. The two men soon began to collaborate on some of the greatest political essays of the age. Alarmed by the activities and propaganda of Jacobites and High Churchmen, and deeply concerned at the corruption that the Whig ministers appeared to be tolerating, Trenchard and Gordon produced a stream of individual pamphlets and two series of essays, *The Independent Whig* and *Cato's Letters*. They attracted enormous attention and were reprinted in collected editions in both England and the American colonies over the next thirty or so years.

In 1722 Trenchard was elected MP for Taunton, and became a critic of Robert Walpole's administration. He died on 16 December 1723. His rich widow married Thomas Gordon, his great collaborator.

Ideas

Trenchard's first pamphlet, *An Argument, shewing, that a Standing Army is inconsistent with a Free Government, and absolutely destructive to the Constitution of the English Monarchy* (1697), written with Walter Moyle, sparked a lively debate over William III's efforts to maintain a large army in peacetime. The following year he produced *A Short History of Standing Armies in England*; it was deeply resented by the King and his ministers as it implied that William could not really be trusted with a peacetime standing army.

Trenchard's writings have been located by historians of ideas within two different political discourses. Some regard him as belonging to the Country or Classical Republican tradition, stressing that civil liberty depended on the minority of citizens possessing sufficient landed property to make them economically independent, developing civic virtue and participating actively in the political life of their community. Trenchard can be associated with this tradition because of his social background, his urging of landed men to resist corruption by the court, his attacks on a standing army as a threat to the liberty of the subject and the independence of the legislature, his vitriolic report on William III's grant of Irish forfeited estates to his court favourites, and his bitter criticisms of the South Sea Bubble scandal, in which corrupt politicians sought to increase their influence through an alliance with the rising financial interest.

Other historians, more persuasively, locate Trenchard in a different paradigm, the Radical Whig tradition of Algernon Sidney and John Locke (q.v.). Trenchard supported both the notion of an ancient English constitution promoted by Sidney and the idea that all men possessed natural rights, as advanced by Locke. On the constitution, Trenchard wrote of a past in which freeborn Englishmen had struggled for centuries to limit the power of the crown and to promote the rights of Parliament: the balance of King, Lords and Commons. Trenchard also adopted Locke's ideas, denying the legitimacy of absolute, arbitrary government; stressing the natural rights of all men to life, liberty and property; maintaining that civil government should be the creation of a social contract and based on consent; and insisting that all men had the right to oppose tyranny by force if necessary.

In *Cato's Letters* (1720–23), Trenchard did not confer political authority on landed men alone and he showed no hostility to the world of commerce per se, but to its corruption by ill-designing court politicians. He attacked the corrupt Whig ministers of the day, but did so as a committed supporter of the Revolution Settlement and the Hanoverian Succession. He was bitterly anti-Jacobite and feared that corrupt Whigs were endangering what honest Radical Whigs had been promoting since the Glorious Revolution. It is also difficult to describe the essays in *The Independent Whig* (1720–21) as anything other than Radical Whig. They are virulently anti-Catholic, markedly anti-clerical and strongly opposed to the privileges of the Church of England. They stress that religion is a private matter and that the form of worship adopted by men should be a voluntary act. The state has no right to examine the consciences of its citizens, but should allow them free will and free expression in religious matters. Reason is the only guide given to men in the state of nature and men should be allowed to use it as their guide in civil society.

Key works

- *An Argument, shewing that a Standing Army is inconsistent with a Free Government, and absolutely destructive to the Constitution of the English Monarchy* (1697)
- *A Short History of Standing Armies in England* (1698)
- *The Independent Whig* (with Thomas Gordon, 1720–21)
- *Cato's Letters* (with Thomas Gordon, 1720–23)
- *Essays on Important Subjects, by the late John Trenchard Esq., never before published* (1755)

Further reading

- Ronald Hamowy, 'Cato's Letters, John Locke, and the Republican Paradigm', *The History of Political Thought*, 11 (1990)
- Marie P. McMahon, *The Radical Whigs, John Trenchard and Thomas Gordon: Libertarian Loyalists to the New House of Hanover* (University Press of America, 1990)

- Caroline Robbins, *The Eighteenth Century Commonwealthman* (Harvard University Press, 1959)
- J. A. R. Séguin, *A Bibliography of John Trenchard (1662–1723)* (Ross Paxton, 1965)

H. T. Dickinson

Pierre Trudeau   1919–2000

A liberal democrat intellectual, lawyer and journalist, a charismatic personality, a leader of the 'Quiet Revolution' in Québec and, as Prime Minister of Canada, a vigorous proponent of enhanced democratic rights and responsibilities for all. Trudeau's lasting gifts to Canada were official bilingualism and the patriation of the constitution from Westminster with an entrenched Charter of Human Rights and Freedoms.

Key ideas

- Constant critique through democratic means of established institutions, through 'reason over passion'.
- Fundamental need for individual freedoms to be entrenched in constitutions with interpretation by the courts.
- The inclusiveness of federations including Québec in Canada.
- Advocacy of Canadian internationalism.
- Peace and negotiated settlements of international disputes.

Biography

A lawyer, writer and political activist before he succeeded Lester Pearson as leader of the Liberal Party of Canada in 1968 and as Canada's fifteenth Prime Minister, Pierre Trudeau led the Liberal Party in five elections, winning all but one. A man of great style and outspoken intellectual convictions, he was the subject of both a devoted and enthusiastic following and of deep dislike by traditionalists on the left and right.

Joseph Philippe Pierre Yves Elliott Trudeau was born on 18 October 1919 to a prosperous family in Montréal. He received a classical education at Collège Jean de Brébeuf and went on to study at the University of Montréal (law), Harvard (master in political economy), l'Ecole des Sciences Politiques in Paris and the London School of Economics. He travelled internationally, but also in the Canadian north; his annual canoe trips into the wilderness were an important part of his understanding of himself and Canada. However, nothing was as important as the intellectual and political struggle that shaped his life in the years leading to the end of the Duplessis government in Québec. He became a supporter of workers involved in the asbestos strike of 1949, expressing his ideas in progressive journals and newspapers, and later directed an analytical study of the dispute. From 1949–51 he worked in the Privy Council office in Ottawa and later taught constitutional law at Montréal University.

In the 1965 federal election, Trudeau joined the Liberal Party and ran for Parliament. He became Parliamentary Secretary to Prime Minister Pearson and then a reforming Minister of Justice. Becoming leader of the Liberal Party in April 1968 and then Prime Minister in June, he set out to make institutional changes to enhance democracy in Canada and to bring Québec into a full role in Confederation. He enhanced the role of backbenchers in Parliament by providing them with the resources to be effective legislative participants and critics.

After two successful terms, he was defeated in 1979 by Joe Clark's Conservatives. Clark's minority government fell a few months later and by February 1980, Trudeau was back with a majority government. This time he faced a referendum on separation in Québec led by his former colleague, now separatist, René Lévesque. Winning the referendum, Trudeau set out on his grandest mission of all, to patriate from Westminster the British North America Act of 1867 and to entrench the Charter of Human Rights and Freedoms. Queen Elizabeth II signed this into law on Parliament Hill in Ottawa in April 1982.

'Reason over Passion', the Joyce Weiland quilt that hung on his wall on Parliament Hill, captured Trudeau's approach to challenges. He loved debate and struggled with provincialists, separatists, single-issue movements and isolationists. Not a party devotee, he worked with all who shared his convictions and negotiated with those who did not at home and internationally. He visited Cuba several times; Fidel Castro attended Trudeau's funeral in 2000. With the exception of Carter and Ford, his relations with US Presidents, as with de Gaulle and Thatcher, were edgy. His understanding of China and relationships formed through his travels led to Canada's recognition of the country in 1969, before the US, upsetting President Nixon. At the same time, in counterbalance, he established diplomatic relations with the Vatican.

On retirement in early 1984, Trudeau joined a law firm in Montréal. With the exception of some devastating speeches in the Senate opposing the provincialist constitutional proposals of the Conservative government of Brian Mulroney, he remained a private person. Devastated by the death of his youngest son Michel in a skiing avalanche in 1998, his health deteriorated. His death on 28 September 2000 led to an extraordinary public outpouring of grief across Canada as even his adversaries acknowledged his great spirit and impact on his country and the world.

He married Margaret Sinclair in 1971 but they separated in 1977 and divorced in 1984; they had three children.

Ideas

Trudeau's life-long struggle with provincialism, nationalism, corporatism and clericism emerged from his childhood and young adulthood in the province of Québec, then a closed society led by a corrupt paternalistic government. The same dominant Catholic Church that fuelled his outrage at narrow thinking provided an excellent education, so that public debate, deep reading and enlightenment ideas informed his life's work. He made a clear separation not only between church and state but also between the state and the individual. His reforms as Minister of Justice, in the 1960s, to divorce laws, birth control and abortion and the rights of homosexuals were consistent with his greatest achievement, the Charter of Human Rights and Freedoms that was eventually entrenched in the Canadian constitution.

Ideas of social justice (q.v.) were also expressed in his work on behalf of the 1949 asbestos strikers and the 'Just Society' campaigns to improve social programmes, youth employment, support for children and families and income support in the 1970s and 1980s. The Canada Health Act (1984) was an expression of his desire to see social equality (q.v.) through access to good health care.

His most important ideas concerned the potential for Québecers to celebrate their historical role in North America and maintain their language and culture within the Canadian nation. Official bilingualism across the country was one success. The patriation of the constitution and the Charter of Human Rights and Freedoms was another. Although compromised domestically by the failure of Québec to ratify the constitution, the Charter has influenced constitutional and human-rights thinking and reforms throughout the world. The constant struggle against the separatist movements in Québec through speeches, programmes and, in response to kidnapping and murder, armed intervention, showed his conviction that the rule of law (q.v.) was necessary for democracy. He embraced the pluralist society in all aspects of rights and responsibilities. Equally, he believed in internationalism, an independent foreign policy for Canada and the role of Canada in supporting developing countries.

Key works

- *Federalism and the French Canadians* (1968)
- *Approaches to Politics* (1970)
- *Conversations with Canadians* (1972)
- *Against the Current: Selected Writings 1939–1996* (1996)

Further reading

- Thomas Axworthy and Pierre Trudeau (eds.), *Towards a Just Society* (Viking, 1990)
- John English, *Citizen of the World: The Life of Pierre Elliott Trudeau, Vol. 1: 1919–1968* (Knopf Canada, 2006)
- Ivan Head and Pierre Trudeau, *The Canadian Way: Shaping Canada's Foreign Policy 1968–84*, (M&S, 1995)
- Jacques Hébert and Pierre Trudeau, *Two Innocents in Red China* (Oxford University Press, 1968)
- Donald Johnston (ed.), *With a Bang, Not a Whimper, Pierre Trudeau Speaks Out* (Stoddart, 1988)

Lorna R. Marsden

United Nations Association *see* League of Nations Union

Unservile State Group

Founded in 1953 and wound up in 1990, the Unservile State Group provided a platform for the dissemination of ideas that were distinctly liberal. It left a legacy that reflected the rich nuances and applications of liberalism, rather than any specific school of thought.

The appearance in 1928 of the 'Yellow Book' (*Britain's Industrial Future*) was followed by a long silence in the publication of any comparable collection of liberal writings. To make good this deficit, the Unservile State Group was formed, its first meeting taking place in Oxford in 1953. Thereafter meetings were held at irregular intervals – first in Oxford and later at the London School of Economics, occasionally in Cambridge. At these meetings papers were read and discussed, many of them in draft form prior to publication as Unservile State Papers.

If there was a moving spirit it was Elliott Dodds (q.v.), who for many years remained the group's chairman. He was succeeded as chair by Heather Harvey, then by Nancy Seear. There was no formal membership, though there was a treasurer, a secretary and a nucleus of regulars who attended meetings, supplemented by guests. Among the regulars was Cambridge don George Watson, who edited both the full-length volume *The Unservile State* (1957) and the entire output of Unservile State Papers (thirty-six in all), published by the group between 1961 and 1990. By 1990 it was agreed that the Group had run its course and it was duly wound up.

The Unservile State Group had no formal party connection. It sought to promote no specific brand of liberalism; nor was there a 'mission' to establish any new variety of the creed or to strike out on a particular path. Despite its name, it owed nothing to Hilaire Belloc's (q.v.) 1912 polemic *The Servile State* – a reaction to modernism and the New Liberalism (q.v.). Rather, it embraced ideas about free markets and the welfare state.

The Unservile State Group provided a platform for the dissemination of ideas that were distinctly liberal – initially at a time when the Liberal Party was at a low ebb and when liberalism, if very much extant, seemed in danger of being appropriated and emasculated by other political forces. Ironically, the first Unservile State Paper (*Has Parliament a Future?*) was written by former Conservative MP Christopher Hollis and published in 1961, a decade before he joined the Liberal Party. It was commissioned as well as edited by George Watson. Sometimes authors were leading lights within the Liberal Party – Jo Grimond (q.v.), David Steel, Conrad Russell (q.v.) and Donald Wade (q.v.) among them. Others, like Hollis, bore wider allegiance – such as David Marquand (q.v.), Aubrey Jones and Samuel Brittan (q.v.). Intellectuals made a significant contribution since, above all, the Group traded in ideas. Thus while some papers engaged with ephemeral matters of the day, others emphasised the philosophical bearings of liberalism – for example Elliott Dodds's and Erna Reis's *The Logic of Liberty* (1966), Maurice Cranston's paper *The Right to Privacy* (1975) and Ralf Dahrendorf's (q.v.) *After Social Democracy* (1980).

It is difficult to assess the impact of the Unservile State Group. Through publications based upon the broad-church approach, it left a legacy that reflected the rich nuances and applications of liberalism, rather than any specific school of liberal thought or 'tidemark' of new thinking. It kept the lamp of liberalism burning when it might otherwise have been extinguished, providing inspiration for those who sought a touchstone which, while broad, was nevertheless distinctly liberal.

Further reading
- George Watson (ed.), *The Unservile State: Essays in Liberty and Welfare* (George Allen & Unwin, 1957)

Peter Barberis

Utilitarianism

Utilitarianism is an ethical doctrine which states that the right action is that which maximises welfare. An action is evaluated (1) according to its consequences and (2) according to the amount of welfare which it produces. The term 'welfare' is used generically in order to embrace different conceptions of 'the good', for instance, pleasure, knowledge, wealth or the satisfaction of preferences.

The doctrine of utilitarianism emerged in eighteenth-century England amongst a group of writers who have become known as the Theological Utilitarians. The most prominent was William Paley (1743–1805), whose *Principles of Moral and Political Philosophy* (1785) dominated the subject for many years at the universities of Oxford and Cambridge. Paley stated that the will of God formed the criterion of right and wrong, and that God willed the happiness of his creatures. It was, therefore, right to promote happiness. Happiness consisted in a balance of pleasure over pain. Moral duty was enforced by an expectation that the righteous person would, in an afterlife, enjoy the pleasures of heaven, while evil-doers would suffer the pains of hell.

The doctrine was secularised, and given its classical form, by Jeremy Bentham (q.v.). Bentham began with an empirical observation concerning psychology: every sentient creature was motivated by a desire for pleasure and an aversion to pain. Pleasures and pains could be measured and compared by reference to their intensity, duration, certainty and propinquity. The individual would choose to perform that action which would bring the greatest amount of pleasure (or avoid the greatest amount of pain). From here Bentham constructed a standard of morality, which stated that an action was right insofar as it maximised the pleasure and minimised the pain of all persons

affected by it. The pleasures and pains of each and every individual had to be given equal consideration. Pleasure was the only good, and pain the only evil, and happiness consisted in a balance of pleasure over pain. Hence, the right action was that which promoted 'the greatest happiness of the greatest number'.

The utilitarian doctrine was used by Bentham to criticise existing laws, institutions and practices, and led him to advocate the introduction of representative democracy and a codified system of law. His doctrines were promoted by a group of theorists and politicians who became known as the Philosophical Radicals, and included Edwin Chadwick, the sanitary and poor-law reformer, James Mill (q.v.), the philosopher, and his son John Stuart Mill (q.v.). The younger Mill, while accepting the essential elements of Bentham's utilitarianism, attempted to incorporate within it what he considered to be a more wide-ranging conception of human nature. His main theoretical innovation, of dubious value, was to distinguish between higher and lower pleasures, the former associated with intellectual pursuits and the latter with bodily functions. Mill claimed that those who had experienced both would sacrifice a large amount of lower pleasure in order to enjoy even a minuscule amount of higher pleasure. The most influential product of the younger Mill's utilitarianism was *On Liberty* (1859), the defining text of liberalism. He argued that the individual should enjoy a sphere of freedom (q.v.) in which he would be protected from coercion on the part of the state and the more insidious pressure of public opinion.

Utilitarianism has developed into a number of variant types, often in response to objections levelled against it. These variants are generally described by reference to the following dichotomies: mental state v.

preference utilitarianism; act (or direct) v. rule (or indirect) utilitarianism; and aggregate v. average utilitarianism.

The classical utilitarianism of Bentham and Mill belongs to the category of mental state utilitarianism, in that the good which they wished to see maximised was the mental experience of pleasure. It is objected that this is to base an ethical standard upon a fact about the physical world (the existence of feelings of pleasure), and hence to commit the 'naturalistic fallacy'. Whether the naturalistic fallacy is a fallacy is itself a topic of some controversy, but many moral philosophers accept that it is so. A further objection is that hedonistic psychology is flawed in that individuals are not always motivated by a desire for pleasure. Preference utilitarianism is a response to these objections. According to preference utilitarianism, the good which should be maximised is the satisfaction of people's preferences. An elaborate methodology (cost–benefit analysis) is used to measure the relative strength of different people's preferences. The difficulty with preference satisfaction is that it gives moral value to repugnant desires, for instance, desires to discriminate against persons exhibiting a particular racial characteristic.

Act utilitarianism states that each and every action should be evaluated by direct reference to the principle of utility (hence the alternative term, direct utilitarianism). Act utilitarianism is criticised for not ruling out a priori actions which are considered to be plainly wrong, and for not providing absolute guarantees for human rights, for instance, a right against torture or a right not to be punished if innocent. The point is that circumstances may arise in which utility dictates the torture of a suspect or the punishment of an innocent person. Act utilitarians respond that the threshold for permitting such actions

remains high, and, more aggressively, that the whole thrust of utilitarianism is not to confirm our intuitions (or prejudices), but to provide a critical standard by which to challenge them.

A different response has been the development of rule utilitarianism, where actions are judged not by a direct appeal to the principle of utility, but by appeal to utility-maximising rules. Hence, if it would maximise utility overall to have a rule which prohibited torture under any circumstances, then such a rule would form the appropriate standard by which individuals would decide how to act. It is unclear, however, whether rule utilitarianism is, in the end, distinct from act utilitarianism. For instance, would the rule utilitarian not accept the appropriateness of torturing a terrorist if it was known that they had planted a device which would kill thousands of people, but it was not known where the device was planted? If so, might there not be more and more exceptions to the rule forbidding torture? If so, rule utilitarianism collapses into act utilitarianism. Rule utilitarianism has been taken even further. It might be that greater utility is produced not by linking decision-making to those rules which are utility-maximising, but to rules which are non-utilitarian. It remains unclear whether versions of the theory which incorporate a non-utilitarian decision procedure (known as indirect utilitarianism) are properly described as utilitarian.

Aggregate and average utilitarianism give different answers to questions concerning the size of population and the amount of welfare in possible future states of affairs. Aggregate utilitarianism demands the maximisation of the total quantity of welfare which will exist, while average welfare demands the maximisation of the quantity of welfare enjoyed by each individual. The former endorses an unappealing future state in which there exists a massive population, with each individual enjoying a minimally pleasurable life (e.g. 100 billion people each enjoying two units of welfare is better than a population of 10 billion people each enjoying 19 units of welfare). The latter endorses what appears to be a more appealing future state in which there exists a small population, with each individual enjoying a maximally pleasurable life (e.g. 1 billion people each enjoying 150 units of welfare is better than 10 billion people each enjoying 100 units of welfare). But this is to deny existence to many individuals who would have enjoyed fulfilling lives. Moreover, it appears that the average utilitarian is committed to exterminating any relatively less happy people who exist, in that this will raise the aggregate welfare of the community as a whole. To resolve the dilemma, a principle needs to be found which guarantees the provision of a certain level of welfare which will result in each individual enjoying something more than a minimally pleasurable life.

Although it has been somewhat overshadowed in recent decades by the emphasis placed on human rights, utilitarianism remains a vigorous moral and political philosophy within the liberal tradition.

Further reading
- Roger Crisp, *Mill on Utilitarianism* (Routledge, 1997)
- Jonathan Glover (ed.), *Utilitarianism and its Critics* (Macmillan, 1990)
- Brad Hooker, *Ideal Code, Real World: A Rule-Consequentialist Theory of Morality* (Clarendon Press, 2000)
- I. M. D. Little, *Ethics, Economics, and Politics: Principles of Public Policy* (Oxford University Press, 2002)
- Frederick Rosen, *Classical Utilitarianism from Hume to Mill* (Routledge, 2003)

- J. J. C. Smart and Bernard Williams, *Utilitarianism For and Against* (Cambridge University Press, 1973)
- The journal *Utilitas* (established 1989), published by Cambridge University Press, is devoted to all aspects of utilitarian studies

Philip Schofield

Voltaire   1694–1778

The quintessential Enlightenment figure, Voltaire achieved great renown in pre-Revolutionary France as a dramatist, essayist and polemicist. He spent much of his exceptionally long life challenging and evading censorship. Voltaire's wit and style made him one of France's greatest writers at a time when French culture was dominant in Europe.

Key ideas
- The vital importance of promoting and defending human rights and civil liberties.
- The need for religious toleration, and recognition of the part played by toleration in building a humane and prosperous society.
- The belief that freedom of expression is a vital requirement for realising the good society.
- The importance of establishing an open society so that reason can flourish.
- The necessity of an independent legal system, able to guarantee fair trials.

Biography
François Marie Arouet (always now known by his pseudonym, Voltaire) was born on 21 November 1694 in Paris. His father wanted his son to follow him into the law, but Voltaire had literary ambitions, a knack for making money and – above all – a sense of fun. He also had an irresistible desire to cock a

snook at authority, a characteristic which led in 1717 to his imprisonment in the Bastille and, a decade later, to exile in England.

Exile, however, enabled him to learn English and he became familiar with the works of leading English thinkers, including John Locke (q.v.). Voltaire admired England's constitutional form of government, its philosophical rationalism and prowess in the natural sciences, and when he returned to Paris he wrote about the superiority of English science, political culture and government. This admiration for a foreign culture rekindled the hostility of parts of the Paris establishment and again attracting attention as a critic of both church and state – and despite his growing success as a playwright – Voltaire was forced to leave Paris. He had managed to assemble a substantial fortune before departing, which helped secure his independence and sustained him as a very public intellectual and critic of *l'infâme* (clerical superstition).

Voltaire's literary successes, determined opposition to censorship, advocacy of rational thought and passion for scientific inquiry were combined with an international reputation for witty and irreverent conversation. They attracted lovers and monarchs and won him popular acclaim. He was the renowned author of over fifty plays, of which the most notable were *Oedipe* and *Zaïre*; they fiercely attacked religious orthodoxy and prejudice and issued a passionate plea for toleration. *Candide*, his best-known work, has been described as 'a pot-pourri of autobiography, [pacifism] and anticlerical satire … gloriously humane [and full of] good humour and good sense'. In common with a great deal of his literary work its polemical purpose did not divert him from his mission to amuse and entertain.

Banished from Paris Voltaire spent the better part of a decade with Mme du Châtelet, his intellectual equal and lover, despite her marriage to M. du Châtelet. They pursued a mutual interest in the natural sciences and Voltaire maintained his considerable literary output. Their relationship faltered, however, when Voltaire appeared about to gain readmission to Parisian society.

Following Mme du Châtelet's death in 1749, Voltaire left France and travelled to Potsdam, at the invitation of Frederick the Great of Prussia. He lived under the Prussian King's protection from 1749 to 1753, although he found himself increasingly at odds with his protector. In 1759, searching for a secure base beyond the easy reach of the French authorities, he acquired an estate, Ferney, close to the Swiss–French border. He lived there with his niece, Mme Denis, many years his junior; their relationship lasted until his death on 30 May 1778.

Despite the years of exile Voltaire died in Paris, where he was lionised as one of France's greatest writers. The Catholic authorities denied him burial in consecrated ground, however, but in 1791 his remains were returned there, to the Pantheon. They did not remain undisturbed; in the 1860s it was discovered that Voltaire's corpse had disappeared.

Voltaire's defiant spirit and liberal outlook are well illustrated in his best-known and most accessible work, *Candide* (1759). It is a searing satire of corrupt and hypocritical religious leaders written to encourage readers to reject metaphysical notions and rely, instead, on their own capacity to make the most of life, while respecting, whenever possible, the ability of others to do the same. There can be little doubt that Voltaire would have taken immense pleasure from the knowledge that even though his body would be stolen away his literary legacy would remain to attract praise and admiration.

411

Ideas

Voltaire was above all a critic of fanaticism. The French society he knew so well struck him as unreasoning and intolerant. He believed its intolerance was largely built upon religious prejudice and superstition, and these were the principal targets for his plays and his historical and philosophical works. French society exemplified a form of Christianity that had little to do with Christ: 'if you would resemble Jesus Christ, you must be martyrs ... not executioners'. The richest and most powerful members of French society belonged to a religious and social order that ruled by fear and depended, above all else, on the perpetuation of ignorance. The persecution of the Huguenots illustrated, in Voltaire's view, the cruelty, stupidity and wastefulness of a society driven by superstition.

Those who rejected superstition and believed in reason had an obligation to open the eyes of their fellow citizens; to challenge hypocrisy with intelligence and humour. Voltaire's plays, his account of life in England, his histories, *Dictionnaire Philosophique* (1764) and campaigns against individual acts of injustice, were all designed to ridicule superstition, expose corruption and focus attention on hypocrisy. He was appalled by the shortcomings of the French legal system and the injustices it perpetrated.

Although Voltaire was not the author of the famous line 'I disapprove of what you say, but I will defend to the death your right to say it', it has come to symbolise his opposition to censorship. He was an adept opponent of censorship and went to great lengths to have his work disseminated. Better than any man of his time, he understood that the printing press and rise of adult literacy had ushered in a new age, affording new opportunities to shape and harness public opinion. Free expression and toleration, powered by rational thought, offered the best chance, as he put it in *Candide*, to 'cultivate our garden'.

Voltaire was a man of his times. It would be misleading to suggest that he did not share the aristocratic beliefs that reflected the Parisian society in which he grew up; it was, after all, the same society that he wanted to admire his prodigious literary talents. His suspicion of democracy reflected a lack of confidence in the abilities of a majority of his fellow citizens to make good decisions unguided. After all, he wrote: 'If God did not exist, it would be necessary to invent him.' Nevertheless he is rightly honoured, in France and beyond, as a literary genius who campaigned with extraordinary vigour for civil rights, fair trials, freedom of religion, free speech and reform of the *ancien régime*.

Key works

- *Oedipe* (1718)
- *Zaïre* (1732)
- *Letters on the English* (1778)
- *Le Mondain* (1736)
- *Discourses in Verse on Man* (1738)
- *Zadig* (1747)
- *Micromégas* (1752)
- *Candide* (1759)
- *Philosophical Dictionary* (1764)
- *Letter to the Author of The Three Impostors* (1770)

Further reading

- Ian Davidson, *Voltaire in Exile – The Last Years, 1753–1778* (Atlantic, 2005)
- Roger Pearson, *Voltaire Almighty: A Life in Pursuit of Freedom* (Bloomsbury, 2005)
- David Williams (ed.), *Voltaire: Political Writings* (Cambridge University Press, 1994)

Ed Randall

Donald Wade   1904–88

A leading Liberal politician in the years after the Second World War when the party faced the challenge of survival, Wade's reputation as a thinker rests on his efforts to ensure that the party had a thorough understanding of the philosophy of liberalism and could draw clear distinctions with its opponents. He also particularly campaigned for a Bill of Rights.

Key ideas

- Primacy of the individual and their personal liberty.
- Protection of the individual against the arbitrary use of the power of the state through the development of truly democratic institutions.
- The creation of a society whose citizens are informed and well educated and who participate.
- Acceptance of a positive role for the state in the establishment and maintenance of a welfare society and in the overall management of the economy.

Biography

Donald William Wade was born at Ilkley in Yorkshire on 16 June 1904. He was educated at Mill Hill and attended Trinity Hall, Cambridge before training for the law and becoming a solicitor in 1929.

In the general election of 1950, Wade gained the seat of Huddersfield West from Labour and held it until 1964. This was thanks to an arrangement with local Tories who did not oppose Wade in return for the Liberals giving them a straight fight against Labour in Huddersfield East. Although there was never a formal, signed pact between the parties, the deal did include a joint Liberal/Conservative statement binding the candidates to oppose further nationalisation. The arrangement inspired Liberals and Conservatives in Bolton to strike a similar deal there, leading to the election of Arthur Holt as Liberal MP for Bolton West from 1951–64. Wade was Chief Whip 1956–62 and deputy chairman of Liberal MPs 1962–64.

The decision of the Liberal Party to contest Bolton East in a by-election in 1960 led to the collapse of the Bolton and then the Huddersfield pacts and Wade, opposed by the Tories, lost his seat to Labour by 1,200 votes at the 1964 election. He went to the House of Lords later that year, on four occasions introducing and piloting a Bill of Rights (incorporating the European Convention on Human Rights into English law) through all of its stages in the Lords. He was deputy whip of the Liberal peers from 1965–67, and president of the Liberal Party in 1967. He died on 6 November 1988, in Harrogate.

Ideas

Wade's first important work was *Liberalism, Its Task in the Twentieth Century* (1944), written against the background of the Second World War, the fight against Nazism and fascism, and the decline of the Liberal Party in Britain since 1918. It was written in anticipation of the end of the war, the coming of a general election and a return to ordinary politics; its purpose was to state that Liberalism was as strong, valid and relevant as ever. Its main audience was likely to have been committed Liberals, potential parliamentary candidates and supporters, but the fact that it was produced as a twenty-page sixpenny pamphlet suggest that Wade hoped to reach a wider readership, and that he wanted it to persuade and influence electors in the coming general election, as a complement to the official manifesto. In it, Wade examined themes which were to surface again in later publications, sought to connect the policies and programmes of the current Liberal Party with the legislation enacted by past Liberal governments and to root all this in basic, unchanging Liberal values:

> The aim of Liberalism is always liberty – more liberty and liberty for more persons. This constant Liberal aim ... springs naturally from something fundamental in the Liberal philosophy – that is from the belief in the value of the individual personality.

Many of these themes were reworked in Wade's 1961 pamphlet, *Our Aim and Purpose*; indeed some of the text is borrowed from the 1944 book. But the 1961 publication made good use of diagrams to explain the distinctions and similarities between different ideologies, a useful method at a time when two-party politics still dominated and politics was seen as a simple 'left–right' model. Wade's analysis demonstrated how much more sophisticated politics really was and showed how Liberals could open up political and electoral space for the party. This was valuable ideological underpinning at a time when the Liberals were beginning to revive under Jo Grimond's (q.v.) leadership.

Wade's other main contribution was his chairmanship of a party commission on Liberal philosophy; it was set up in 1968 with the aim of ensuring that the party had a clear and consistent philosophy to steer it, and to inform policy-making and communication with the electorate. The creation of the commission came against a background of internal party criticism of the leadership of Jeremy Thorpe, who many at this time felt did not have the intellectual force and sense of direction of his predecessor. It was born through discussion on the Liberal Party Council led by Young and Student Liberals; an interim report was debated at the Liberal assembly in Edinburgh in 1968. The final 24,000-word report, *Liberals Look Ahead*, was debated section by section and received in near-unanimity by the 1969 Liberal assembly at Brighton. Many from the youth, student and activist wing of the party contributed to the report's conclusions and the debates at Edinburgh and Brighton. Perhaps this ferment of ideological discussion and thinking informed the development of the community politics (q.v.) approach to Liberalism which was agreed at Eastbourne just a year later.

In 1977, Wade published jointly with Lord (Desmond) Banks the booklet *The Political Insight of Elliott Dodds*. Wade and Banks admired Dodds (q.v.) and shared his passion for exploring the meaning of liberty and the need for a radical alternative to socialism – themes reflected in Wade's writings and politics and which had informed Banks's role in setting up the Radical Reform Group (q.v.) twenty-five years earlier.

Key works

- *Liberalism, Its Task in the Twentieth Century* (1944)
- *Our Aim and Purpose* (1961)
- *Liberals Look Ahead* (1969)
- *The Political Insight of Elliott Dodds* (jointly with Desmond Banks, 1977)

Further reading

- Richard Wainwright, 'Address at Memorial Service for Donald Wade', in reprint of *Our Aim and Purpose* (Liberal Movement Publication, 1989)

Graham Lippiatt

Graham Wallas   1858–1932

A political theorist, educationalist and social psychologist, Wallas is remembered for his contribution to the development of 'behavioural' political science. His liberalism was dedicated to what he saw as the 'real' nature of human beings. He agued that 'rationality' was a baseless notion in the study of politics, and sought to explore ways in which this could be overcome in order to create a 'good society'.

Key ideas
- The fallacy of the 'intellectualist assumption' that political actions should be seen as the result of 'rational' calculation.
- The danger of an impersonal industrial environment to the creation of the 'great society'.
- The importance of 'social scale' to the individual and to society as a whole.

Biography
Graham Wallas was born on 31 May 1858, in Monkwearmouth, Sunderland, the fifth of nine children of Gilbert Innes Wallas and Frances Talbot (née Peacock). His father was an Evangelical curate in the Church of England in Barnstaple, Devon, where the family grew up.

Wallas went to Shrewsbury School (1871–77) and then to Corpus Christi College, Oxford (1877–81) on a classical scholarship; he read Greats and obtained a second-class degree in Literae Humaniores. It was at Oxford that he met Sydney Olivier, who became a life-long friend and fellow Fabian. It was also at Oxford that Wallas first sought to reconcile scientific and idealist thinking.

On leaving Oxford Wallas became a classics master at Highgate School in London, but his resistant attitude towards religion led to his dismissal within a year. He taught at various schools over the next few years while focusing on the development of socialism. He joined the Fabian Society in 1885 and quickly became a leading light, with Sidney Webb (who he met through Olivier) and George Bernard Shaw. He felt that socialism was the fulfilment of liberalism and so remained a Liberal though a supporter of 'permeation'.

In 1895 Webb asked Wallas to be the first director of the London School of Economics – the result of a bequest – but Wallas declined. By this time, he was an Extension lecturer but he also taught at the new LSE. He became its first Professor of Political Science in 1914, and remained until his retirement in 1923, becoming Professor Emeritus.

The years 1897 and 1898 were important to Wallas. Politically he became chair of the School Management Committee of the London School Board, and a working member of the London County Council's Technical Education Board. Academically, he completed *The Life of Francis Place*, an analysis of the early nineteenth-century radical. On the personal front, he married Ada (Audrey) Radford (1859–1934), a teacher, writer and Liberal. Soon after they were married they had their daughter, May.

Wallas's work in education led to problems with the Fabians, as his ideas on liberty, and particularly his opposition to religious education, gradually put him in direct opposition to Webb. The final break came in 1904 when Shaw attempted to associate the Fabians with Joseph Chamberlain's (q.v.) campaign for protectionism.

In 1904 Wallas was elected to London County Council, serving until the Progressives' defeat in 1907; he continued to serve on the Council's Education Committee for another three years as a coopted member. Freed from other commitments, Wallas developed his thinking with the New Liberals (q.v.), particularly his friends J. A. Hobson (q.v.) and L. T. Hobhouse (q.v.), and published his most famous works. He also spent time in the United States, as Lowell Lecturer in Boston (1914) and as Dodge Lecturer at Yale (1919), where he made a significant impact on American sociology.

He died in London on 9 August 1932.

Ideas

Wallas sought to relate social problems to individual psychology. He observed a discrepancy between democratic theory and the way in which people actually behaved. Thus, he argued for a 'realistic' view which took into account individuals' motivation and 'nature' as well as their 'rational' position. *Human Nature in Politics* (1908) was arguably his best statement of this approach. Doubtful about 'contemporary democracy', he identified the need to look beyond the 'intellectualist fallacy'. He felt that 'irrational' forces such as prejudice, custom and accident were more likely to affect politics than calculation alone. He attempted to develop democratic theory given his knowledge of practical politics and understanding of psychology.

The Great Society (1914) was an attempt to go beyond his Fabian past to examine the problems of a loss of 'social scale'. As its sub-title, 'A Psychological Analysis', suggests, he used his previous book to develop his analysis. Recognising the fundamental changes in social intercourse, he sought to examine the impact on 'basic' human issues such as instinct, intelligence, habit, fear, pleasure-pain and happiness. Using the ideas of Aristotle and Bentham (q.v.), he concluded that there was still a role for collectivism and rational process but that, as a 'practical collectivist', he could not ignore the psychological dislocation 'pure' collectivism and state mechanisms created.

He continued this investigation in *Our Social Heritage* (1921), where he argued that principles such as liberty and natural rights had been treated as ends in themselves. He suggested that humans possessed something he called 'social heritage', passed from one generation to the next; though much of that heritage was being rendered irrelevant by change. The

Art of Thought (1926) was a departure, in which Wallas attempted to create a structure for the development of thought while using an overtly psychological framework; although not without interest, it was not particularly successful.

For the rest of Wallas's life he worked on *Social Judgment*, a broad work that attempted to move his analysis from thought to 'judgment', which, in his view, transcended thought. He did not complete the book, but his daughter, May, revised and published it after his death.

Wallas was both a liberal and a socialist, a theorist and a practical politician. His classical training led him to a view of the good life that sought an integrated society in which all members could relate to each other in all spheres. He was a social reformer and committed internationalist, as his work in education and politics, and his influence in the United States, attests. His focus on wider intellectual frameworks led to a body of work that provided a far-sighted critique, though not a blueprint for the democratic institutions he sought to reform. He is remembered as a thinker who clearly saw the impact of modernisation and not only offered a prescient analysis of that change but also influenced the way in which the generation that followed him would frame the same questions.

Key works
- 'Property under Socialism', in G. B. Shaw and H. G. Wilshire (eds.), *Fabian Essays in Socialism* (1889)
- *The Life of Francis Place* (1898)
- *Human Nature in Politics* (1908)
- *The Great Society: A Psychological Analysis* (1914)
- *Our Social Heritage* (1921)
- *The Art of Thought* (1926)
- *Social Judgment* (ed. May Wallas, 1934)
- *Men and Ideas* (ed. May Wallas, 1940)

Further reading

- Terence Qualter, *Graham Wallas and the Great Society* (Macmillan, 1980)
- Martin Wiener, *Between Two Worlds: The Political Thought of Graham Wallas* (Clarendon Press, 1971)

Alison Holmes

Max Weber   1864–1920

One of the last of the great polymaths, Weber's writings include studies in politics, religion, organisation, law and economic life; he was also a political writer and activist. His was a paradoxical liberalism, heavily influenced by an intense realism about the forces that have shaped and continue to shape modern society. He combined calls for democracy with a form of elitism, and nationalism with opposition to racism of all kinds.

Key ideas

- 'Rationalisation' of modern society proceeds through processes of secularisation and bureaucratisation.
- 'Rationalisation' undermines ideas of natural law and natural rights, but personal freedom and individualism remain important.
- The distinction between fact and value is vital to the social sciences and the social sciences must strive to distinguish between factual and evaluative questions.
- Politics requires acceptance of a special ethic: political actors should take responsibility for the consequences of their acts rather than rely on an ethic of pure intention that might suffice in private life.
- Politics oriented solely towards power is empty and worthless, though a politics of responsibility based on strongly held values is increasingly rare in societies dominated by professional politicians and organised parties.
- Political systems should encourage charismatic leaders who can push through reform against the bureaucratic state. Such leaders need to have their own mandate from the people ('charismatic plebiscitary leadership').
- Parliamentary democracy is valuable as a counterbalance to bureaucratic rule. Parliament's main role should not be to govern, but to provide for the peaceful transfer of power from one leader to another.

Biography

Maximilian Carl Emil Weber was born on 21 April 1864, in Erfurt in Germany, the eldest of seven children of Max Weber Sr., a National Liberal parliamentarian and civil servant. From 1882 to 1891 he was educated in law, economics, philosophy and history at the Universities of Heidelberg, Berlin and Göttingen.

In 1894 he started teaching economics at Berlin and in 1897 at Heidelberg. In 1893 he married Marianne Schnitger, and in the same year he joined the Pan-German Union, a nationalist association. From 1897 to 1903 he suffered from mental illness, almost certainly depression, and in 1903 he resigned from his teaching position at Heidelberg. In 1904 he took over the editorship of *Archiv für Sozialwissenschaften und Sozialpolitik* (*Archives for Social Science and Social Politics*). In 1909 he co-founded the Deutsche Gesellschaft für Soziologie (German Society for Sociology) and started to identify himself as a sociologist; in 1911 he started work on his sociological masterwork, *Wirtschaft und Gesellschaft* (*Economy and Society*).

During the First World War he was a reserve officer in the German Army, managing several military hospitals. He opposed the German policy of annexation and the escalation of the U-boat campaign against

Allied shipping, and at the end of war he called for the abdication of the Kaiser, but at the same time opposed revolution. In 1918 he joined the workers' and soldiers' council of Heidelberg and co-founded the German Democratic Party, a social liberal (q.v.) party.

Weber was appointed to the Chair of Economics at Munich University in 1919, and headed the first German university institute of sociology. His academic achievements are recognised across the social sciences but he is best known in academic communities for his contributions to the discipline of sociology. His most famous work is probably his essay *The Protestant Ethic and the Spirit of Capitalism* (1904–05), which stressed the importance of particular characteristics of Protestantism which led to the development of capitalism, bureaucracy and rational-legal states.

Weber died in Munich on 14 June 1920, of pneumonia.

Ideas

Weber's political views are difficult to categorise. He was at once a liberal and a believer in strong leadership, a democrat and an elitist, an anti-racist and a German nationalist. His commitment to speaking 'inconvenient truths' led him to offend almost everyone. He told liberals that developments in Western society made direct democracy impossible and parliamentary democracy vulnerable to capture by party bureaucracies dominated by professional politicians; the best one could hope for was a system in which elites competed for popular (and often irrational) support. He told socialists that their dreams of liberation through the state were bound to fail, since bureaucratisation was common to all economic development, whether capitalist or socialist. And he taught nationalists that nations had no biological foundation and

that they should incorporate, rather than exclude, minorities.

In a sense Weber stands in the republican tradition of Machiavelli, for whom patriotism meant being prepared to sacrifice even one's soul for the sake of the freedom of one's country. He rejected Marxism and hoped for an alliance of non-revolutionary social democrats and social liberals but he was never optimistic about the capacity of such a political alliance to shape politics in the face of party competition and the impersonal and bureaucratic processes of modern government and public administration.

Some revisionists and detractors, including the liberal historian Wolfgang Mommsen, have accused Weber of moral and political relativism and of 'decisionism': the belief that rival values and political interests are ultimately irreconcilable, so that politics reduces to power and the will to decide what to do. Detractors have also pointed to Weber's embrace of 'charismatic plebiscitary leadership' as further evidence of decisionism.

The Weberian scholar Mark Warren has pointed out that Weber was essentially a neo-Kantian. Like other neo-Kantians, he moved away from Kant's (q.v.) fully impersonal and universal ethics to a position that recognised the importance of historical and cultural conditions, a move that also explains Weber's own move away from the ethic of pure intention and his espousal of an ethic of responsibility. Warren also suggests that Weber accepted that different spheres of human life (spiritual, economic, cultural, erotic) were non-commensurable so that there is no single perfectly good life. However, that does not amount to and should not be read as an acceptance of relativism. Weber believed that there were good and bad ways to act within each different sphere of life and within the constraints imposed by the times in which one lived. His view of ethics and politics thus anticipated Isaiah Berlin's (q.v.) 'tragic' liberalism or pluralism: there are many fundamental values and the fact that we have, on occasion, to choose between them should not lead us to regard any of them as ultimately more important or fundamental than other core values with which they come into conflict.

Key works

- *Economy and Society* (1922)
- *The Protestant Ethic and the Spirit of Capitalism* (1904–05)
- *Political Writings* (ed. Peter Lassman and Ronald Speirs, Cambridge University Press, 1994)
- *The Vocation Lectures: 'Science As a Vocation', 'Politics As a Vocation'* (ed. David Owen and Tracy B. Strong, Hackett, 2004)

Further reading

- Reinhard Bendix, *Max Weber: An Intellectual Portrait* (Routledge, 1998)
- Sung Ho Kim, *Max Weber's Politics of Civil Society* (Cambridge University Press, 2006)
- Wolfgang Mommsen, *Max Weber and German Politics* (University of Chicago Press, 1984)
- Stephen Turner (ed.), *The Cambridge Companion to Weber* (Cambridge University Press, 2000)
- Mark Warren, 'Max Weber's Liberalism for a Nietzschean World', *American Political Science Review* (1988) 82:1

    David Howarth and Horst Wolfgang Boger

Whiggism

Whiggism emerged in the late seventeenth century as an ideology of resistance to the threat of royal absolutism, and it underpinned the subsequent evolution of a system of parliamentary government within which 'constitutional' monarchs were obliged to act. It continued, into the nineteenth century, to assert the role of the territorial aristocracy as the natural champions of popular liberties, and as the leaders of movements for political and religious reform.

Although the principles associated with Whiggism had their intellectual roots in the civil war of the 1640s, and even earlier, it was during the Exclusion Crisis of 1679–81 that 'Whig' was first used as a political label. It denoted those, such as Lord Shaftesbury (1621–83), who tried unsuccessfully to remove James, Duke of York (later James II) from the royal succession. The Whigs feared that, as a convert to Catholicism, James would inevitably subvert the Protestant Church of England and establish a despotic government on the continental, Catholic model, using the army to subordinate Parliament.

Intellectual validation for the Whig position was found in the argument, derived from 'natural law', that kings exercised their authority only by the consent of the people. A 'contract' had originally been entered into, when the people entrusted some of their powers to the King, and this was only binding for as long as royal authority was exercised for the common good. If the King betrayed his trust, the people were no longer obliged to obey him and had the right of resistance. In these circumstances, Parliament, representing the people, could determine the royal succession. This happened (so it was claimed) during the 'Glorious Revolution' of 1688–89, when James was driven from the country and his crown offered to William of Orange and his wife Mary (James's daughter). In 1701, the Act of Settlement fixed the succession on the Protestant Hanoverians.

The duty of governments was to protect the people in their lives, liberties and estates, and the Whigs attached particular importance to the defence of property rights. It was through ownership of land that a man was believed to attain true liberty and independence (by being financially independent and so able to resist corruption and influence-peddling). Property secured the means to resist an over-mighty government. 'Liberty and Property' (a popular and enduring political slogan) went hand in hand, and it was the large stake they held in the country's soil that enabled the Whigs to claim for themselves the responsibility to act as guardians of the rights of the people.

John Locke (q.v.) was the first and perhaps the greatest of the Whig writers. A friend and protégé of Shaftesbury's, in 1689 he published *Two Treatises of Government*, in which he attacked the Tory, 'patriarchical' concept of kingship, and expounded the 'contractarian' theory described above. In the same year, his *Letter Concerning Toleration* advocated religious toleration for Protestant Dissenters.

Religious liberty played a central part in Whig thinking. Like Locke, the first Whigs found valuable political allies in the Protestant Dissenters, whose right to worship without state interference was acknowledged. Late-eighteenth-century Whig latitudinarianism moved further, towards a policy of religious *equality*, by advocating repeal of the Test and Corporation Acts, which (symbolically) barred Dissenters from holding public office. Early Whiggism was virulently anti-Catholic in character, and toleration of 'Papists' was unthinkable. By the early nineteenth century, however, with British Catholicism no longer perceived as a threat to the established church, and the practical problem of reconciling the Catholic majority in Ireland to the Union with Britain, the Whigs favoured the removal of discriminatory legislation against their old enemies.

In the late eighteenth century, Edmund Burke (q.v.), an MP and protégé of the Whig leader, Lord Rockingham (1730–82), provided intellectual justification for the parliamentary opposition to George III's governments in his pamphlet *Thoughts on the Cause of the Present Discontents* (1770). Burke's definition of 'party', as an honourable body of men joined together in the pursuit of common principles, helped to legitimise the Whig strategy of *systematically* opposing the King's chosen ministers, in order to force him to replace them *en bloc* with members of the Whig party. The Whigs' growing determination to assert the primacy of Parliament, by using party connection to restrict monarchical freedom in the appointment of ministers, pointed towards modern constitutional practice.

The Whigs were bitterly divided by the French Revolution. Some, most notably Charles James Fox (q.v.), Charles Grey and Richard Brinsley, expressed their sympathy for French radicalism; others, most notably Burke, became fierce opponents of the revolution in France. Burke left the Whigs and joined the Tories; when others followed in the 1790s the Whig cause and its parliamentary strength were, for a time, considerably reduced. Whig differences over Britain's relations with France and the dramatic changes in French society had their counterpart in a general political caution about reform in Britain.

If Whiggism sought to impose limits on monarchical government, it was equally clear about the dangers of conferring unlimited power on the people, insisting that an aristocracy was needed to act as mediators between these two essential, but potentially destructive forces. Society was conceived of in hierarchical terms, and, while the early-nineteenth-century Whigs recognised the changes being wrought by the processes of urbanisation and industrialisation, they looked to promote what they termed 'rational liberty'. By carrying the Great Reform Act of 1832, which cleansed the electoral system of its most corrupt features and extended the franchise to the industrious, respectable 'middle classes', the Whigs aimed to restore confidence in Britain's existing political institutions. A virtuous, aristocratic ruling elite would command 'legitimate deference' from the people.

The Whig belief in gradual progress was most famously decribed by the Whig politician and historian Thomas Babington Macaulay (q.v.). In his four-volume *History of England* (1848–55), Macaulay celebrated what he saw as the uninterrupted 'physical ... moral and ... intellectual improvement' of the nation since the Glorious Revolution. He believed that measures such as the Great Reform Act demonstrated the capacity of the political system to adapt gradually to changing circumstances, without the need for violent revolution. Macaulay's work formed the basis of what became known as the 'Whig interpretation of history'.

Whiggism was always more of a practical, working political creed than an abstract philosophy. Its legacy was to Victorian liberalism, within which the Whig tradition occupied a proud position. Leading Whigs of the 1820s and 1830s, Earl Grey and Lord John Russell (q.v.) especially prominent amongst them, championed electoral reform and secured a place in British Liberal politics for Whiggism, alongside growing middle-class and radical parliamentary representation; the Whigs won and retained influence in a reform-minded party collaboration that was able to operate successfully in a deeply class-conscious society. Indeed the aristocracy provided an administrative cadre for Liberal governments until the late nineteenth century, and Whiggism was seen as exercising a guiding and moderating influence over the Liberal Party. It ultimately inspired a centrist style of politics that has never disappeared.

Further reading
* Richard Ashcraft, *Revolutionary Politics and Locke's 'Two Treatises of Government'* (Princeton University Press, 1986)
* H. T. Dickinson, *Liberty and Property: Political Ideology in Eighteenth-Century Britain* (Weidenfeld & Nicolson, 1977)
* Abraham Kriegal, 'Liberty and Whiggery in Early-Nineteenth Century England', *Journal of Modern History* LII (1980)

Terry Jenkins

Woodrow Wilson   1856–1924

The twenty-eighth President of the United States, Wilson became a hero to many liberals during the First World War for his advocacy of 'peace without victory', national self-determination and a league of nations to provide collective security. His earlier work as an academic had focused particularly on the structural requirements for successful democratic government.

Key ideas
* The need to end great-power wars, and belief in a league of nations as the means to achieve this.
* The principle of government by consent – entailing opposition to imperialism and support of the right of national self-determination.
* The need in a representative political system for publicly identifiable and accountable leadership.
* That successful leadership in a democracy requires an ability to interpret public opinion as well as skill in persuasion.

Biography

Thomas Woodrow Wilson was born in a manse in Staunton, Virginia, on 28 December 1856, the eldest son of the Reverend Dr. Joseph Ruggles Wilson and Jessie Woodrow Wilson (who was the daughter and sister, as well as the husband, of a Presbyterian minister). Although the family left Staunton soon after Wilson was born, his upbringing remained entirely in the South until he went to Princeton as an undergraduate. From his father, whose parents had been Scotch-Irish immigrants from Ulster, Wilson derived a fascination with oratory as well as a love of English literature and poetry. As an adolescent, he dreamed of being a political leader; Gladstone (q.v.) was his hero.

After graduation, Wilson qualified as a lawyer because he saw this as a route into politics, but he quickly became disenchanted with the practice of law and entered Johns Hopkins University as a graduate student in history and political science. Here, much influenced by Walter Bagehot's (q.v.) work *The English Constitution*, he wrote a critical analysis of the way the American political system had come to work in practice; in 1885 this was published as *Congressional Government*. The book attracted national attention and launched Wilson on an academic career, during which he published extensively on American history as well as political science.

After holding posts at Bryn Mawr College and Wesleyan University, he returned to Princeton in 1890 and was elected president of the university in 1902. As an energetic and imaginative reformer, Wilson did much to raise Princeton's standing, but a rather high-handed attempt to replace the established eating clubs with residential quadrangles evoked a strongly negative reaction from alumni. In public speeches, Wilson presented the issue as one of democracy against privilege and the power of money, thus aligning himself with the progressive movement that was the prevailing force in American politics at the time. This provided a basis for Wilson's entry into the political arena; in 1910 he became Governor of New Jersey, and two years later only the second Democrat to be elected President since the Civil War. He was re-elected in 1916.

During his first eighteen months in office, Wilson secured the passage through Congress of four major reform measures, a legislative achievement matched only by Franklin Roosevelt and Lyndon Johnson among his twentieth-century successors. But it was in shaping America's response to the First World War that he became a figure of international significance in the history of liberalism. As the head of a neutral power seeking an early end to the war, in 1916–17 he committed the United States to participation in a post-war league of nations, and called for 'a peace without victory'. After the United States had itself entered the war in response to Germany's unrestricted submarine campaign, Wilson set out, notably in his 'Fourteen Points' speech of January 1918, a programme for a peace settlement based upon 'impartial justice', the self-determination of peoples as far as practicable, an end to discriminatory trade barriers, and a league of nations that would protect the 'political independence and territorial integrity' of all states.

Enthusiastic crowds greeted Wilson's arrival in Europe for the Peace Conference but many liberals, like Keynes (q.v.), criticised Wilson bitterly when the Treaty of Versailles failed to fulfil the hopes he had aroused. Further disillusionment followed the US Senate's refusal to approve the Treaty, which kept the United States out of the League of Nations. After making a nationwide speaking tour to develop public support for the Treaty and the League,

Wilson was disabled by a major stroke in October 1919, although he remained in office until the end of his presidential term in 1921. He died on 3 February 1924.

Ideas

Although Wilson expressed opinions about many issues in his voluminous writings, he devoted particular attention to the role of leaders in modern democracies, and this has been seen as his distinctive contribution to political theory. The central argument of *Congressional Government* was that both efficiency and democratic accountability suffered from the lack of clearly identifiable and adequately empowered leadership, such as was provided by the Cabinet in Britain. In later writings, he explored the relationship of successful leaders with public opinion, concluding that it was essentially interpretative as well as persuasive. He was influenced by Edmund Burke (q.v.), whose view that political structures and processes were organic in nature accorded with ideas Wilson had imbibed at Johns Hopkins. Accordingly, he conceived of the League of Nations not as a contractual arrangement so much as 'a living thing' which would develop in strength as nations came to rely on it for their security.

Key works and speeches
* *Congressional Government: A Study in American Politics* (1885)
* *The State: Elements of Historical and Practical Politics* (1889)
* *Division and Reunion, 1829–1889* (1893)
* *Constitutional Government in the United States* (1908)
* Address to the Senate, 22 January 1917
* 'Fourteen Points' Address to Congress, 8 January 1918
* Address presenting the League of Nations Covenant to the Peace Conference, 14 February 1919

Further reading
* John Milton Cooper, *The Warrior and the Priest: Woodrow Wilson and Theodore Roosevelt* (Harvard University Press, 1983)
* Thomas J. Knock, *To End All Wars: Woodrow Wilson and the Quest for a New World Order* (Oxford University Press, 1992)
* Arthur S. Link and others (eds.), *The Papers of Woodrow Wilson* (69 vols., Princeton University Press, 1966–94)
* John A. Thompson, *Woodrow Wilson* (Longman, 2002)
* Niels Aage Thorsen, *The Political Thought of Woodrow Wilson 1875–1910* (Princeton University Press, 1988)

John A. Thompson

Mary Wollstonecraft 1759–97

An English radical, whose advocacy of equal rights for women and men attracted considerable attention in her lifetime, Wollstonecraft has subsequently acquired a reputation as the pre-eminent feminist polemicist of her age. The range and quality of her literary work helps to explain much of the contemporary interest in her life and thought.

Key ideas
* The ability to reason should be accepted as the foundation of human political community.
* Women and men cannot be distinguished in terms of their inborn capacity to reason.
* Women and men should, therefore, be treated as equals.
* All need to learn how to employ reason in their own and one another's best interests.
* Equality of educational opportunity is, therefore, an essential requirement for a fair and a decent society.

- Men – as well as women – will be the beneficiaries if women are no longer subjugated and degraded by men.

Biography

Mary Wollstonecraft was born in London on 27 April 1759. Her childhood was, by her own account, despoiled by her father's bullying, drinking and dissolute behaviour. Her brother Edward was the only one of the seven Wollstonecraft children to receive an extended formal schooling; Mary went to school only briefly, in Yorkshire, where she learnt to read and write. She was a truly exceptional autodidact with a great appetite for literature and languages. She worked as a teacher, governess and ladies' companion before attempting (and failing) to make a success of a girls' school in London in the mid-1780s.

In 1787 Joseph Johnson published her *Thoughts on the Education of Daughters* and then employed her to write for his literary publication, the *Analytical Review*; she had acquired a sponsor and supporter with whom she was able to work closely for the rest of her life. It was a mutually advantageous relationship: he published her work and it contributed greatly to his success as a publisher. It was Johnson's patronage and encouragement that led to the publication of *A Vindication of the Rights of Men* (1790) and *A Vindication of the Rights of Woman* (1792).

Wollstonecraft's personal and emotional life was tempestuous; she attempted suicide at least twice and became entangled in disastrous personal relationships. One of those, with the American Gilbert Imlay, began in Paris, and despite his rejection of her she subsequently travelled to Norway to help him resolve a commercial dispute. Her happiest relationship was with the political philosopher William Godwin. In August 1797 she gave birth to their daughter but, eleven days later, on 10 September, died from puerperal fever. Although Godwin had initially been opposed to marriage he and Wollstonecraft were married six months before the birth of their daughter, who became best known as Mary Shelley, the author of *Frankenstein*.

Ideas

Mary Wollstonecraft's career was tragically short: if the work that first acquainted large numbers of readers with her opinions can be said to mark its beginning, it lasted just seven years. Those opinions strongly reflected the radicalism (q.v.) of her times. Her reputation, as a political writer, was built upon her highly combative response to Edmund Burke's (q.v.) *Reflections on the Revolution in France* (1790). The first edition of Wollstonecraft's reply, *A Vindication of the Rights of Men*, was rushed into print in a bid to be the first of a torrent of radical responses. It was soon joined by others, most notably Thomas Paine's (q.v.) *The Rights of Man*, but Wollstonecraft gained considerable prestige from being first.

All Burke's opponents were scathing in their criticisms of his defence of hierarchy and the *ancien régime*, but what Wollstonecraft did was to apply the kernel of the radicalism that had informed her response to all of humankind. She dealt with a male blind spot, applying liberal principles to women as well as to men. Her approach rested on the equal value of all human beings, and the critical role of reason in human affairs. If it was possession of reason that distinguished human beings from other creatures, surely every human being, women as well as men, should be entitled to equal respect and to self-determination. Reason itself should be developed and encouraged by coeducational schooling. Respect for the mental abilities that women and men shared should, as Wollstonecraft put it, make it possible for men and women to enjoy 'rational fellowship' and bring an end to 'slavish obedience'. Men who helped to snap the chains that degraded and subjugated women would benefit too – 'they would find us more observant daughters, more affectionate sisters, more faithful wives, more reasonable mothers – in a word, better citizens'.

However, in *Vindication of the Rights of Woman*, Wollstonecraft sounded what must, to the ears of her twenty-first-century sisters, appear a surprising note. She urges women to pursue those 'talents and virtues' that will enable them to become 'more masculine'; it was the use of reason, which 'ennoble[d] the human character', that she had in mind. Social conditioning and social structure meant that men were much more likely to benefit from opportunities to develop the mind. She believes that both men and women were culturally conditioned, but that women were the more likely to be damaged and diminished by it. Elsewhere, in *Vindication of the Rights of Woman*, Wollstonecraft criticises women who are 'proud of their weakness'; she makes it plain that she sees women's reluctance to strive for independence throughout their lives as a source of vulnerability. She even warns other women that they should not expect to be valued 'when their beauty fades'. Wollstonecraft feared for women who 'will not listen to a truth that experience has brought home to many an agitated bosom'.

Wollstonecraft's fierce and didactic criticism of her own sex should be contrasted with the worldly wise and tolerant viewpoint found in her later fiction. In *The Wrongs of Woman*, the novel she was writing at the time of her death, she describes a friendship between two women, an heiress confined to an asylum by a husband who covets her fortune, and an asylum attendant who had earlier earned her living as a washerwoman, thief and prostitute. The solidarity between them, which Wollstonecraft commends, was meant to challenge social distinctions, recognise economic injustices and suggest to readers that they should consider economic injustice, not only the oppression that women experience at the hands of men.

In her account of the French Revolution, published in 1794, Wollstonecraft made it clear that even though she continued to believe that 'a new spirit ha[d] gone forth, to organise the body politic [and] … Reason ha[d], at last, shown her captivating face …' she was much less sanguine about finding a clear path to a better society. Wollstonecraft's partnership with William Godwin might, if she had lived, have helped them both to develop and express their political ideas. Unfortunately, she was denied the opportunity to fulfil her great promise as a thinker and writer during a period of extraordinary change brought about by rapid urbanisation and industrialisation, and the political upheaval that accompanied it.

Key works
- *A Vindication of the Rights of Men* (1790)
- *A Vindication of the Rights of Woman* (1792)
- *An Historical and Moral View of the French Revolution* (1794)
- *Maria, or The Wrongs of Women* (1798)

Further reading
- Lyndall Gordon, *Vindication: A Life of Mary Wollstonecraft* (Virago Press, 2006)
- Janet Todd, *Introduction to Mary Wollstonecraft's* A Vindication of the Rights of Woman, A Vindication of the Rights of Men, *and* An Historical and Moral View of the French Revolution (Oxford University Press, 1993)

- Ralph M. Wardle, *Collected Letters of Mary Wollstonecraft* (Cornell University Press, 1979)

  Ed Randall

Young Liberals *see* National League of Young Liberals

INDEX TO CONTRIBUTORS

R. T. Allen (*Polanyi*)

obtained a PhD from the University of London with a thesis on *Transcendence and Immanence in the Philosophy of Michael Polanyi and Christian Theism* (Edwin Mellon Press, 1992). He edited *Society, Economics and Politics: Selected Articles by Michael Polanyi* (Transaction Pub. 1987), wrote *Beyond Liberalism: The Political Thought of F. A. Hayek and Michael Polanyi* (Transaction Pub., 1998) and co-edited *Emotion, Reason and Tradition: Essays on the Social Political and Economic Thought of Michael Polanyi* (Ashgate, 2005).

Ralf M. Bader (*Hayek*)

read philosophy, politics and economics at the University of Oxford (St Edmund Hall), gaining a first class degree. Whilst at Oxford, he refounded the Oxford Hayek Society. He is currently working on his PhD in philosophy at the University of St Andrews.

Peter Barberis (*Grimond, Unservile State Group*)

is Professor of Politics at Manchester Metropolitan University. He is the author of *The Elite of the Elite: Permanent Secretaries in the British Higher Civil Service*, and the editor and co-author of *Encyclopaedia of British and Irish Political Organisations: Parties, Groups and Movements of the Twentieth Century*. His most recent book is *Liberal Lion: Jo Grimond, a Political Life*.

Norman Barry (*Brittan*)

is Professor of Social and Political Theory at the independent University of Buckingham, with research interests in political philosophy, political economy and business ethics. He has written extensively on market economics and the theory of capitalism; his books include *Hayek's Social and Economic Philosophy, An Introduction to Modern Political Theory, On Classical Liberalism and Libertarianism, The New Right, Welfare* and *Business Ethics*.

Duncan Bell (*Seeley*)

is a university lecturer in international relations at the University of Cambridge, and a fellow of Christ's College. He is the author of *The Idea of Greater Britain: Empire and the Future of World Order, 1860–1900* (Princeton University Press, 2007), and the editor of *Victorian Visions of Global Order: Empire and International Relations in Nineteenth-Century British Political Thought* (Cambridge University Press, 2007).

Jonathan Bell (*New Deal*)

is a lecturer in United States history at the University of Reading. He was educated at the Universities of Oxford and Cambridge. He is the author of *The Liberal State on Trial: The Cold War and American Politics in the Truman Years* (Columbia University Press, 2004) and several scholarly articles on American political history.

Adrian Blau (*Hobbes*)

is Hallsworth Junior Research Fellow (Government) at the University of Manchester. His research interests include democratic theory and elections.

Dr Horst Wolfgang Boger (*Montesquieu, Weber*)

studied psychology, social sciences and philosophy at the Universities of Mannheim and Cologne and has been a lecturer in psychology, social sciences and political theory at the Universities of Bonn, Constance and Mannheim. Currently he is an adviser at the Liberal Institute of the Friedrich Naumann Foundation in Potsdam.

Hardy Bouillon (*Kant*)

is a lecturer at Trier University, Germany, and has been at times guest professor in Prague, Salzburg and Zagreb. He is also head of academic affairs for CNE, a think-tank in Brussels. A member of the Mont Pelerin Society and many other (inter)national academic societies, he has published fifteen books and some eighty articles.

Richard Bourke (*Burke*)

is Senior Lecturer in History at Queen Mary, University of London. He specialises in the history of political thought, and has written on Romanticism, the Enlightenment and on the political history of Northern Ireland. His most recent book is *Peace in Ireland: The War of Ideas* (Pimlico, 2003). He is currently completing a study of Burke's career, *The Political Life of Edmund Burke*.

Allen D. Boyer (*Coke*)

is a lawyer in New York City. He is the author of *Sir Edward Coke and the Elizabethan Age* and a member of the advisory board for the Yale Center for Parliamentary History.

David Boyle (*Belloc, Distributism*)

is the author of a series of books about history, social change and the future, including *Authenticity: Brands, Fakes, Spin and the Lust for Real Life* (Flamingo, 2003) and *Blondel's Song: The Imprisonment and Ransom of Richard the Lionheart* (Viking Penguin, 2005). He is an associate of the New Economics Foundation, edits the journal *Radical Economics*, and sits on the Liberal Democrats' Federal Policy Committee.

Duncan Brack (*Economic Liberalism, Environmentalism, Equality, Free Trade, New Liberalism, Conrad Russell, Social Liberalism, Social Market*)

is a freelance researcher, mainly on international environmental issues. A former director of policy for the Liberal Democrats, he is the editor of the *Journal of Liberal History* and has also co-edited the *Dictionary of Liberal Biography*, *Dictionary of Liberal Quotations* and *Great Liberal Speeches*.

Ian Bradley (*Milton*)

is Reader in Practical Theology and Church History at the University of St Andrews, a university chaplain and associate minister of the town church. A former Liberal parliamentary candidate and speech-writer for Liberal Party leaders, he is the author of *The Optimists: Themes and Personalities in Victorian Liberalism* and *The Strange Rebirth of Liberal Britain* among many other books.

Hugh Brogan (*Tocqueville*)

is a research professor of history at the University of Essex, where he has taught since 1974. Before that he was a fellow of St John's College, Cambridge. He is the author of the *Longman History of the United States of America*, the *Life of Arthur Ransome*, and, most recently, *Alexis de Tocqueville: Prophet of Democracy in the Age of Revolution*.

Dr Robin Bunce (*Locke*)

gained a PhD in the history of political thought from Downing College, Cambridge, in 2004. He is a regular contributor to the *Modern History Review* and *Talking Politics* magazine.

Tony Butcher (*Bagehot*)

is a former senior lecturer in the Department of Politics at Goldsmith's, University of London. He has written widely on the civil service and public sector reform. He is the author of *Delivering Welfare* (Open University, 2nd ed., 2002) and, with Gavin Drewry, of *The Civil Service Today* (Blackwell, 2nd ed., 1991).

Philip Cafaro (*Thoreau*)

is Associate Professor of Philosophy at Colorado State University in Fort Collins, Colorado. A former ranger with the US National Park Service, his main academic interests are environmental ethics, ethical theory and wild lands preservation. He is the author of *Thoreau's Living Ethics: Walden and the Pursuit of Virtue* and co-editor of the recent anthology *Environmental Virtue Ethics*. He is active in local politics, helping elect progressive candidates and protect natural areas in northern Colorado.

Jonathan Calder (*Popper*)

writes for *Liberal Democrat News*, *Liberator* and other publications, including *The Guardian*. He studied philosophy at the University of York and Victorian studies at Leicester. He has been a district councillor and a member of the Liberal Democrats' Federal Policy Committee.

Patricia Clark (*Anarchism*)

is the Co-ordinating Lecturer in Philosophy at the Cardiff Centre for Lifelong Learning at Cardiff University. She has written about anarchism, ethics and health care issues.

Richard A. Cosgrove (*Dicey*)

is University Distinguished Professor Emeritus of History at the University of Arizona. He has published *The Rule of Law* (1980), *Our Lady the Common Law* (1987), and *Scholars of the Law* (1996).

George Crowder (*Berlin*)
is Associate Professor in the School of Political and International Studies, Flinders University, Adelaide, Australia. He is the author of *Classical Anarchism* (1991), *Liberalism and Value Pluralism* (2002) and *Isaiah Berlin: Liberty and Pluralism* (2004). He is currently co-editing (with Henry Hardy) a collection of essays by several contributors on the work of Isaiah Berlin.

Dr. A. J. Crozier (*Federal Union*)
was educated at the School of Oriental and African Studies and the London School of Economics. He was lecturer in modern European history at the University College of North Wales, 1969–89. Since then he has on several occasions been visiting professor at Chulalongkorn University, Bangkok. He has published widely on Anglo-German relations and the origins of the Second World War.

Lord (Ralf) Dahrendorf (*Freedom*)
is a social scientist, author and cross-bench member of the House of Lords. He is Research Professor at the Social Science Centre, Berlin, and is a former director of the London School of Economics (1974–84), Warden of St Antony's College, Oxford (1987–97) and pro-vice-chancellor of the University of Oxford (1991–97). He was a junior minister in Willy Brandt's government, 1969–70, and a member of the European Commission 1970–74. *(Also see Dahrendorf entry.)*

Marco de Waard (*Morley*)
holds MA degrees from the University of Amsterdam and the University of Sheffield. He is currently completing a doctoral thesis entitled *John Morley and the Liberal Imagination: The Uses of History in English Liberal Culture*, while teaching at Utrecht University in the Netherlands.

H. T. Dickinson (*Trenchard*)
spent forty years teaching at the University of Edinburgh, where he was Richard Lodge Professor of British History 1980–2006. He is the author of many books on eighteenth-century Britain. A former president of the Historical Association and vice-president of the Royal Historical Society, he is still a Concurrent Professor of History at Nanjing University in China.

Detmar Doering (*Bastiat, Blackstone, Bodichon, Classical Liberalism, Federalists, Humboldt, Jefferson, Manchester School*)
is director of the Liberales Institut (Liberty Institute) of the Friedrich Naumann Foundation in Potsdam, Germany. He has written several books, including (in English) *Readings in Liberalism* (Adam Smith Institute, 1992). He has also published numerous articles in German and international academic journals and daily newspapers on economic, political and historical subjects.

Dr Ian Donnachie (*Robert Owen*)
is Reader in History at the Open University. He has published widely in social and economic history, including a biography of Robert Owen, and numerous related works on Owenism. He is currently researching international dimensions of Owenism and connections to other reformers in Europe and the United States during the early nineteenth century.

David Dutton (*Liberal Nationals*)
is Professor of Modern History at the University of Liverpool, where he teaches and researches twentieth-century British political history with an emphasis on the Conservative and Liberal parties. His *History of the Liberal Party in the Twentieth Century* was published by Palgrave Macmillan in 2004.

Ella Dzelzainis (*Martineau*)
lectures in the School of English and Humanities at Birkbeck College, University of London. Recent publications include work on Charlotte Elizabeth Tonna and the Ten Hours campaign, and gender politics in Ernest Jones's fiction. She is writing a book on women and political economy in English industrial fiction.

Robert Falkner (*Laissez-faire, Liberal Internationalism, Adam Smith*)
is lecturer in international relations at the London School of Economics. After reading politics and economics at Munich University, he

received his doctorate in international relations from Oxford University (Nuffield College). He is an associate fellow of Chatham House and associate editor of the *European Journal of International Relations*.

Victor Feske (*Churchill, Hammonds*)
has taught at Connecticut College, Wellesley College and Yale University and currently teaches European history at the Louisiana School for Math, Science, and the Arts. He is the author of *From Belloc to Churchill: Private Scholars, Public Culture, and the Crisis of British Liberalism, 1900–1939*.

Roger Fox (*Friedman, Malthus*)
is a visiting fellow at the University of Buckingham. He was educated at Ruskin College, Oxford, after gaining a TUC Scholarship, and the University of Warwick where he gained a BA (Hons) in economics. He was head of economics at the University of Greenwich.

Ruth Fox (*National League of Young Liberals*)
completed an MA on the history of the Young Liberals 1970–79 and subsequently a PhD on 'The Liberal Party 1970–1983: Its Philosophy and Political Strategy' at Leeds University. She is currently a political adviser to Bill Rammell, the member of Parliament for Harlow and Minister of State at the Department for Education and Skills.

Sharif Gemie (*Anarchism*)
is a Reader in History at the University of Glamorgan and editor of *Anarchist Studies*. He has written on French political history, Breton identity politics and the history of Galicia (in north-west Spain).

Dr Richard S. Grayson (*Crosland, Equality, Layton, League of Nations Union / United Nations Association, Muir, Pacifism and Pacificism, Peace Society, Schumacher*)
is lecturer in British politics at Goldsmiths College, University of London. He has written two books on inter-war British history, and several articles on twentieth-century British politics. He was director of policy of the Liberal

Democrats in 1999–2004 and Charles Kennedy's principal speech-writer in 1999–2001.

Dr John Greenaway (*Temperance Movement*)
is a senior lecturer in politics at the University of East Anglia. He has research interests in modern British political history and policy-making. His publications include *Drink and British Politics since 1830: A Study in Policy-making* (Palgrave 2003).

Clive E. Hill (*Masterman*)
teaches historical political theory and modern British history at Royal Holloway, University of London. He is the editor of the well-known collection of academic essays *Intellectuals, Identities and Popular Movements* (Middlesex University Press, 2000) and of a number of scholarly articles.

Roland Hill (*Acton*)
is a retired journalist. He began his career writing for the *Tablet*, a British Catholic weekly, and later worked as a staff correspondent of German and Austrian newspapers in London. He was friends with members of Lord Acton's family and has written extensively about Acton since the 1950s.

Alison Holmes (*Wallas*)
is a postdoctoral fellow at the Rothermere American Institute of Oxford University. Prior to receiving her PhD from the LSE in 2005, she held a variety of senior positions in communications, politics and business, including ten years spent working for the Liberal Democrats.

Karen Horn (*Constant*)
has been an economic policy editor for *Frankfurter Allgemeine Zeitung* since 1995. She has been awarded a couple of prizes for economic journalism, and has published a book on *Morals and Markets* and another one on the French philosopher Benjamin Constant. She has translated Wilhelm von Humboldt's *Limits of State Action* into French, and the *Reader's Digest* version of Friedrich August von Hayek's *Road to Serfdom* into German.

John Horton (*Gray*)
is Professor of Political Philosophy and head of the School of Politics, International Relations

and Philosophy at Keele University. He has published extensively in the field of contemporary political philosophy, and is the author of *Political Obligation* and numerous articles on topics such as toleration, justice, multiculturalism and political authority.

David Howarth (*Economic Concepts: Markets and Prosperity, Economic Concepts: Welfare State, Hobhouse, Rationality, Rawls, Weber*)
is the Liberal Democrat member of Parliament for Cambridge. He taught law and economics at the University of Cambridge from 1985 to 2005; his published work includes a textbook and a casebook on the law of tort and articles on that subject and on legal philosophy, comparative law, environmental law and labour law. His political experience includes spells as a shadow local government spokesperson, shadow energy minister and leader of a local authority.

Pertti Hyttinen (*Chydenius*)
is a researcher at the Chydenius Institute – Kokkola University Consortium, affiliated to the University of Jyväskylä. He is engaged in studying the life and work of Anders Chydenius and, for the period 2006–10, in editing his collected writings.

Robert Ingham (*Community Politics, Dodds, National League of Young Liberals, Radical Action*)
is a historical writer and biographies editor of and a regular contributor to the *Journal of Liberal History*.

Dr. T. A. Jenkins (*Macaulay, Whiggism*)
was a postgraduate student and British Academy post-doctoral fellow at Cambridge University. He has lectured at several universities and is now a senior research officer at the History of Parliament in London. His books include *The Liberal Ascendancy, 1830–1886* (1994), and *Britain: A Short History* (2001).

Dr J. Graham Jones (*Davies, Lloyd George*)
is senior archivist and head of the Welsh Political Archive at the National Library of Wales,

Aberystwyth. He has published a large number of articles on twentieth-century political history in academic journals and volumes, and is a regular contributor to the *Journal of Liberal History*.

Dr Tudor Jones (*Marquand, David Owen, Social Democracy, Tawney Society*)
is research fellow in politics at Coventry University. His publications include *Remaking the Labour Party: From Gaitskell to Blair* (1996) and *Modern Political Thinkers and Ideas: An Historical Introduction* (2002); his forthcoming book, *The Revival of British Liberalism: From Grimond to Campbell* will be published in 2007. He fought seats for the SDP/Liberal Alliance in 1987 and the Liberal Democrats in 1992.

Richard Laming (*Lothian*)
is director of Federal Union and a member of the Council of the Federal Trust.

Michael Levin (*Bentham, Harriet Taylor Mill, James Mill, John Stuart Mill*)
was a reader in political theory at Goldsmiths College, University of London. He has also taught at the Universities of Leicester, Leeds and Wales, and been a visiting professor at San Diego State University. His most recent book is *J. S. Mill on Civilisation and Barbarism* (Routledge, 2004).

Graham Lippiatt (*Acton, Radical Reform Group, Servan-Schreiber, Wade*)
is a former civil servant who now writes and researches on aspects of Liberal history. He holds master's degrees in international history and race and ethnic relations from London University. He was a Liberal councillor in Harrow and is currently secretary of the Liberal Democrat History Group.

Tony Little (*Gladstone, Liberation Society, Miall, Sydney Smith*)
is chair of the Liberal Democrat History Group. He jointly edited *Great Liberal Speeches* with Duncan Brack, and was a contributor to the *Dictionary of Liberal Biography*, the *Dictionary of Liberal Quotations* and *President Gore … and Other Things that Never Happened*. Between 1982 and 1990, he led the Liberal-SDP Alliance (later

Liberal Democrat) group on the London Borough of Hillingdon.

Neil McArthur (*Hume*)

is Assistant Professor of Philosophy at the University of Manitoba. He holds a PhD from the University of Southern California. He has served as an adviser to the Social Policy Directorate and to the Privy Council Office of the Government of Canada.

Matthew McCormack (*Radicalism*)

is senior lecturer in history at the University of Northampton. His publications include a number of essays on British politics in the eighteenth and nineteenth centuries, and his book, *The Independent Man: Citizenship and Gender Politics in Georgian England* (Manchester University Press, 2005).

Martin McIvor (*Hegel*)

is a postdoctoral research fellow at the University of Edinburgh. His PhD on the relation of Marx's thought to German idealism was completed at the LSE, where he also taught courses in the history of political thought.

Lorna R. Marsden, CM, PhD (*Trudeau*)

is president and vice-chancellor of York University, Toronto. She served on the National Executive of the Liberal Party of Canada from 1975 until appointed to the Senate of Canada by Prime Minister Trudeau in 1984. She resigned from the Senate in September 1992 to return to academic life.

Peter Marsh (*Chamberlain*)

is Emeritus Professor of History and Professor of International Relations at Syracuse University, New York, and Honorary Professor at Birmingham University School of History. He has written widely on nineteenth-century history, including *Joseph Chamberlain, Entrepreneur in Politics* (1994). He was senior editor and adviser for the microfilm publication of the Chamberlain Papers.

Dr John Meadowcroft (*Austrian School, Buchanan, Friedman, Institute of Economic*

Affairs, Libertarianism, Mont Pelerin Society, Neo-liberalism, Nozick, Seldon)

is lecturer in public policy at King's College London. He is the author of *The Ethics of the Market* (Palgrave, 2005), co-editor of *The Road to Economic Freedom* (Edward Elgar, 2006) and deputy editor and book review editor of the journal *Economic Affairs*.

Michael Meadowcroft (*Angell*)

joined the Liberal Party in 1958. He was the party's local government officer before serving as a Leeds city councillor, as a West Yorkshire metropolitan county councillor and as Liberal MP for Leeds West. He has written numerous pamphlets on Liberal philosophy and policy. Since 1991 he has worked as consultant with new and emerging democracies. *(Also see Meadowcroft entry.)*

Christian Moon (*Idealism*)

is deputy head of policy and research for the Liberal Democrats. Educated at Brasenose College, Oxford, his previous career includes working as a civil servant in the Department of Trade and Industry, as a constituency worker for Graham Watson MEP and as head of office for David Heath MP.

Ann Moore (*Liberal Summer School*)

is a legal correspondent specialising in maritime and insurance law, currently with *Fairplay International Shipping Weekly*. Her mother, Sydney Brown, was organising secretary of the Liberal Summer Schools 1921–39 and the immediate post-war years, and Ann was chair of the Liberal Summer School Committee 1989–2001. She has also been a Liberal / Liberal Democrat county and district councillor. She is a Deputy Lieutenant for East Sussex.

Dr Simon J. Morgan (*Anti-Corn Law League, Cobden*)

is lecturer in modern British cultural and social history at the University of Leicester. He has published several articles on Richard Cobden and the Anti-Corn Law League, and is currently working with Professor Anthony Howe of the University of East Anglia on an edition of Cobden's letters.

Dr Paul Mulvey (*George, Henry George Foundation*)
teaches international history at the London School of Economics and is currently completing a biography of the radical politician Josiah C. Wedgwood (1872–1943).

David Nicholls (*Dilke*)
is Professor of History at Manchester Metropolitan University. He is currently campaigning to get history reinstated in the post-14 national curriculum and has produced a film for the Historical Association, distributed free to secondary schools, entitled *Choosing History at 14*.

Peter Nicholson (*Ritchie*)
was Reader in the Department of Politics, University of York. He retired in 2001. He is the author of *The Political Philosophy of the British Idealists* (Cambridge, 1990).

John Offer (*Bosanquets, Herbert, Spencer*)
is Professor of Social Theory and Policy in the School of Policy Studies at the University of Ulster, Coleraine, Northern Ireland. His most recent book is *An Intellectual History of British Social Policy* (Policy Press, 2006) and he has also edited *Herbert Spencer: Political Writings* (Cambridge University Press, 1994) and *Herbert Spencer: Critical Assessments* (4 vols., Routledge, 2000).

Dr Dawn Oliver (*Rule of Law*)
has been Professor of Constitutional Law at University College London since 1993. Author of *Government in the United Kingdom: The Search for Accountability, Effectiveness and Citizenship* (1991) and *Constitutional Reform in the UK* (2003). Co-editor, with Professor Jeffrey Jowell, of *The Changing Constitution* (6th edn., 2007).

Dr Mark Pack (*Fox, Halifax*)
is a regular contributor to the publications of the Liberal Democrat History Group and completed a history PhD at the University of York on nineteenth-century English elections, with special reference to Yorkshire. He works in the Liberal

Democrats Campaigns Department, where he specialises in legal and internet matters.

Ian Packer (*Haldane*)
is senior lecturer in the Faculty of Media and Humanities at the University of Lincoln. He is the author of a number of books and articles on Edwardian Liberalism, including *Lloyd George, Liberalism and the Land* (2001) and *Liberal Government and Politics, 1905–15* (2006).

Dr Jonathan Parry (*Lord John Russell*)
is Reader in Modern British History at the University of Cambridge and a fellow of Pembroke College. He is the author of three books on nineteenth-century Liberalism, including *The Rise and Fall of Liberal Government in Victorian Britain* (1993) and *The Politics of Patriotism: English Liberalism, National Identity and Europe, 1830–1886* (2006).

Phil Parvin (*Kymlicka, Raz*)
teaches political philosophy at the University of Cambridge. He has held teaching posts at the London School of Economics, Queen Mary University of London, and the University of Oxford. His research interests are in liberal political theory, international political theory and contemporary debates about justice. He is currently writing a book on the political thought of Karl Popper.

Ed Randall (*Beveridge, Condorcet, Galbraith, Hobhouse, Hobson, Keynes, Keynesianism, Liberal Democracy, Liberalism – Pre-Enlightenment and non-Western, Marshall, Social Justice, Voltaire, Wollstonecraft*)
is a lecturer in politics and social policy at University of London Goldsmiths College. Prior to becoming a university teacher he trained and registered as a nurse at St Thomas' Hospital, London. He served as an elected member of a London borough council from 1982 to 1998. He is the author of *The European Union and Health Policy* (2000), *The Plan for a European Food Authority and the Politics of Risk in the Union* (2001) and *A Union for Health* (2002). He is currently working on a book for Manchester University Press entitled *Politics, Risk and Food*.

Dr Jaime Reynolds (*Free Trade Union/ Cobden Club, Hirst, Lippmann, Robertson, Seldon*)
studied at LSE and has written extensively on British and east European political history.

Keith Robbins (*Bryce, Nonconformity*)
has written biographies of Sir Edward Grey, John Bright and Winston Churchill, edited *The Blackwell Biographical Dictionary of Modern British Political Life* and also produced many other books, the most recent being *Britain and Europe, 1789–2005* (2005). He has edited *History* and been president of the Historical Association. He is Vice-Chancellor Emeritus of the University of Wales, Lampeter.

Edward Royle (*Bradlaugh, Paine*)
is Emeritus Professor of History at the University of York. His work over many years on popular irreligion and radicalism in the nineteenth century has resulted in several publications, including *Victorian Infidels* (1974), *Radicals, Secularists and Republicans* (1980), *Robert Owen and the Commencement of the Millennium* (1998) and *Revolutionary Britannia? Reflections on the Threat of Revolution in Britain 1789–1848* (2000).

David Rundle (*Micklem, Simon*)
is a member of the History Faculty, University of Oxford. His main interests are Renaissance history and the history of political thought. He is also author of *Henley and the Unfinished Management Education Revolution*. Since 2002, he has served on Oxford City Council.

Andrew Russell (*Association of Liberal Democrat Councillors*)
is senior lecturer in politics at the University of Manchester. He researches elections and parties in Britain. He is co-author (with Ed Fieldhouse) of *Neither Left Nor Right? The Liberal Democrats and the Electorate* (Manchester University Press, 2005).

Philip Schofield (*Utilitarianism*)
is Professor of the History of Legal and Political Thought in the Faculty of Laws, University College London. He is director of the Bentham

Project and general editor of the new authoritative edition of *The Collected Works of Jeremy Bentham*, which is being published by Oxford University Press.

Bart Schultz (*Sidgwick*)
is a fellow and lecturer in the Humanities and Humanities Collegiate Division at the University of Chicago. He has published widely in philosophy and political theory, and his most recent book, *Henry Sidgwick: Eye of the Universe*, won the Jacques Barzun Prize from the American Philosophical Society.

Daniel Scroop (*Lippmann*)
is a historian of the New Deal and of twentieth-century US liberalism more generally. Educated at St Anne's College, Oxford, his first book, *Mr. Democrat: Jim Farley, the New Deal, and the Making of Modern American Politics*, was published by Michigan University Press in 2006. He is currently a lecturer in American history at Liverpool University.

Iain Sharpe (*Liberal Imperialists, Liberal Unionists, Samuel*)
has studied history at Leicester and London Universities and is currently conducting research towards a doctorate on Liberal Party organisation in Edwardian Britain. He has been a Liberal Democrat member of Watford Borough Council since 1991 and is currently majority group leader.

Dr Julie Smith (*Dahrendorf, Liberal International*)
is deputy director of the Centre of International Studies, Cambridge University, and a fellow of Robinson College. She was head of the European Programme at Chatham House (Royal Institute of International Affairs) from 1999 until 2003. She has published widely on European politics.

Professor Trevor Smith (*Joseph Rowntree Reform Trust Ltd.*)
was a director of the Joseph Rowntree Reform Trust Ltd. from 1975 to 2006 (chair 1987–99). He is an honorary professor at the University of

Ulster where he was vice-chancellor 1991–99. A past president of the Political Studies Association, he was knighted in 1996 and appointed a life peer in 1997 (Liberal Democrat).

Mark Smulian (*Meadowcroft*)

has been a member of the Liberal Party and Liberal Democrats since 1970. Since the mid-1980s, he has been involved with the production of *Liberator* magazine and with writing for Liberal Revue's satirical shows at conferences. He is a journalist and lives in London.

Julia Stapleton (*Barker*)

is senior lecturer in politics at the University of Durham. She is the author of books and articles on British intellectual history during the twentieth century; her most recent book is *Sir Arthur Bryant and National History in Twentieth-Century Britain* (Lexington Books, 2005).

Michael Steed (*Fisher*)

is honorary lecturer in politics at the University of Kent. He was president of the Liberal Party in 1978–79 and was elected to the Liberal Democrat Interim Peers Panel in 2006. He contributed 'The Liberal Tradition' to D. N. MacIver (ed.), *The Liberal Democrats* (Prentice Hall Harvester Wheatsheaf, 1996).

Zofia Stemplowska (*Dworkin*)

is a lecturer in political philosophy at the University of Manchester. She is currently researching contemporary theories of justice, particularly the relationship between equality and responsibility.

Neil Stockley (*Acland, Jenkins*)

is a director of a leading public affairs consultancy. He is a former Liberal Democrat policy director and still takes an active role in developing the party's election platforms. He is a frequent contributor to the *Journal of Liberal History*.

John A. Thompson (*Wilson*)

is a reader in American history in the University of Cambridge and a fellow of St Catharine's College, Cambridge. His publications include *Reformers and War* (Cambridge, 1987), and

Woodrow Wilson (Longman, 2002). His current project is an analysis of the dynamics of twentieth-century US foreign policy.

Colin Tyler (*Caird, Green, Mazzini*)

is a senior lecturer in political theory, and joint director of the Centre for Democratic Governance, at the University of Hull. He has written widely on nineteenth-century political thought, as well as editing various scholarly editions, including a two-volume collection of previously unpublished manuscripts by the British idealists. His most recent book is *Idealist Political Philosophy: Pluralism and Conflict in Absolute Idealist Thought* (Thoemmes Continuum, 2006).

Randolph Vigne (*Paton*)

joined the Liberal Party of South Africa at its inception in 1953 and served as national deputy chairman from 1960 until he was banned from all political and social activity in 1963. The following year he escaped to Britain from where he continued to campaign for democracy in South Africa and Namibia.

William Wallace (*CentreForum*)

was appointed to the Lords (by Paddy Ashdown) in 1995. He has fought five parliamentary elections, and chaired the party's manifesto working group for the 1979 and 1997 general elections. His PhD thesis (Cornell, 1968) was on 'The Liberal Revival: the Liberal Party, 1955–1966'; he has taught at Manchester and Oxford Universities, and at the London School of Economics. He is honorary president of the Liberal Democrat History Group.

Peter Wilson (*Murray*)

is a senior lecturer in international relations at the LSE. He is co-editor of *Thinkers of the Twenty Years' Crisis* (1995); co-author of *The Economic Factor in International Relations* (2001); and author of *The International Theory of Leonard Woolf* (2003).

Geoffrey Wood (*Ricardo*)

is Professor of Economics at Cass Business School in London, and Professor of Monetary Economics at the University of Buckingham.

He has for many years served as an adviser at the Bank of England, and has advised among other organisations the New Zealand government and the Bank of Finland. He has also worked in the Federal Reserve System. Currently he is on the board of Hansa Trust and economic adviser to PI Capital.